Systematic Quality Management

Practical Laboratory Management Series

Other Volumes in the Practical Laboratory Management Series

Volume I: Developing Performance Standards for Hospital Personnel by Lucia Berte

Volume II: The Customer-Oriented Laboratory by William Umiker

Volume III: Implementing Quality Assurance by Paul Bozzo

Systematic Quality Management

Gary B. Clark, M.D., M.P.A.

ASCP Press
American Society of Clinical Pathologists
Chicago

Printed in the United States of America.

95 1

Dedicated to
Nancy H. Campbell,
Harold N. Harrison, MD, and
Maria-Magdeline Tomaszewski, MD,
who provided the committed leadership;
and to
the entire laboratory staff of the
Department of Pathology and Area Laboratory Services
at Walter Reed Army Medical Center
who demonstrated that team work can improve the quality
of employee welfare
and patient health care

Contents

Author's Foreword

This book integrates the managerial and leadership experiences of a 23 year military medical career. Particularly, it summarizes lessons hard-learned as Chief of the Department of Pathology, Walter Reed Army Medical Center, and as a masters degree student at The George Washington University. In a sense, it is my final "after action report" for those years.

As a compilation of theoretical, historical, and practical information, this text presents a synthesis of a unified managerial system. It proposes certain hypotheses along with supportive justification for the adoption of a systematic approach to total quality management (TQM) and continuous quality improvement (CQI). Considering chaos theory, there is really no absolute, "unified" formula to laboratory management. However, at the very least, we can attempt to be appropriately systematic, customer satisfaction–oriented, and wary of organizational needs and management resources.

As proposed in this text, there is a three-program approach to TQM and a combined philosophy-process approach to CQI. Such systematic laboratory management relies on an effective interface between quality control (ie, the prospective evaluation of quality *before* a test result is released for patient care utilization) and quality assessment and improvement (ie, the retrospective evaluation of quality *after* a test result is released for patient care utilization).[1]

I have developed, used, and tested these managerial hypotheses and models against the reality of day–to–day, practical medical laboratory operations over the span of more than a decade. In addition, I have passed these problem solving concepts before the professional scrutiny of more than a thousand laboratorians attending my American Society of Clinical Pathologists (ASCP) workshops. The work has also withstood the critical gaze of literary peer review in the form of journal articles.

Writing *Systematic Quality Management* has been especially challenging since I have had to compose these chapters in an environment of increasing expectations by the healthcare industry. Especially over the past six years, I have had to contend with the "continuous improvement" of the rules of the game at both the federal and state levels—eg, Clinical Laboratory Improvement Amendments of 1988 (CLIA '88)—and the national peer level—eg, Joint Comission on Accreditation of Healthcare Organizations (JCAHO).

One unique tool presented in this book is quality profiling. First published in 1992, the quality profiles presented here exemplify the selection and prioritization of quality indicators of the performance of the most important laboratory operational processes.[2] These sample profiles provide model templates of the full scope of laboratory operational processes, including all aspects of the laboratory path of work flow. However, these profiles do not serve as any written-in-stone, ideal listings of quality indicators for any particular laboratory. Rather, each laboratory must ascertain its own customer needs, path of work flow, and important aspects of care—creating its own indicators of quality and balancing those indicators against its own quality management assets.

The quality profile approach to laboratory management, as illustrated in this text, nicely complements the grid-type *Quality Program* of the American Association of Blood Banks (AABB), as well as emerging quality surveillance matrices of the other organizations such as the ASCP and JCAHO. Generally speaking, the key management areas (KMAs), indicator groupings, and specific indicators of this text correspond to the critical control points (CCPs), key elements (KEs), and system checks (SCs) of the developing AABB system.[3] Such a spreadsheet-like management system also facilitates following the standards and certification/accreditation requirements of the ISO 9000 program and its clones, Food and Drug Administration, Occupational Safety and Health Administration, CLIA '88, JCAHO, and College of American Pathologists (CAP).[a] However, the quality profile approach of *Systematic Quality Management* balances the total path of work flow against the decision making steps of the quality improvement cycle more clearly than other, currently proposed quality management grid systems.

For the sake of consistency from one chapter to the next, the quality profile incorporates the Joint Commission's ten-step process (TSP) as a quality improvement cycle of general example—but not a process of absolute choice. The TSP is worth consideration for many quality improvement

[a]The ISO 9000 series of standards is produced by the International Organization for Standardization. ISO is not an acronym but is a prefix derived from the greek word *iso*, meaning equal.

purposes; however, it is not the only process available. First, there are several other formalized quality improvement approaches. Second, there are many more approaches that can be devised or tailored specifically to fit any given laboratory setting. Most important, each laboratory must choose an improvement process that matches its special needs and management resources.

In addition, there are portions of this book that address workload recording and productivity quotients. With the recent demise of the College of American Pathologists' *Workload Recording Program*, productivity measurement based on time-weighted unit values has been eclipsed by the College's *Laboratory Management Index Program* (or LMIP). As a result, nontime-weighted indicators of productivity (based largely on billable tests) have gained ascendency. However, there is still credence for knowing time-weighted workload recording concepts as a basis for understanding productivity measurement; thus, I have included information on the use of both systems to assist in the transition.

As always, the laboratorian must take advantage of the managerial data that are at hand. Therefore, do not collect numbers and file them without applying those data to some productive use; otherwise, the beans are not worth counting. In other words, "profile" only the data that deserve the expending of corresponding laboratory management resources.

I sincerely hope that this text will be of some use to the healthcare laboratory industry as we are poised on the brink of such a promising, exciting new century. I welcome any suggestion for improvement of this material from my readers at any time.

Gary B. Clark, MD, MPA
5 November 1995

1. Lind AC, Bewtra C, Healy JC, Sims, KL. Prospective peer review in surgical pathology. Am J Clin Path, 1995;104:560–566
2. Clark GB. Quality assurance, an administrative means to a managerial end. Part IV. Choosing quality improvement indicators in a TQM and CQI environment. Clin Lab Man Rev. 1992;6:426-40.
3. Berte, LM. A quality system for transfusion medicine...and beyond. Med Lab Observer, 1995;27:61–64.

Acknowledgments

Many individuals have assisted in producing this text. They have shared valuable time for proof reading and have contributed their expertise through corrections, amendments, references, and administrative support. Each bit of assistance has been of significant value—definitely improving my tortuous prose and compulsive systems approach.

Where I have been incomplete, they have added.
Where inaccurate, they have corrected.
Where antiquated, they have updated.
Where loquacious, they have pruned.
Where too authoritarian, they have mellowed.
Where too simplified, they have expanded.
And where I have been too obtuse and hypothetical,
they have brought me back to the real laboratory.

For their truly unselfish efforts and friendship, I thank Marie A. Bass, MT(ASCP), Patricia A. Bergbauer, Nancy H. Campbell, F. Patrick Carr, Martin A. Davidson, MD, Robert A. Dietrich, MD, JD, LuAnn M. Eley, Ann R. Gaines, PhD, Robert W. Guokas, Chi Ho, MD, Barbara Parham Hughey, Jennifer Labunetz, Nels N. Niemi, MBA, Louis A. Parker, EdD, Pearl Quermbach, Kate Rasmussen, Maria Eugenia Rueda-Pedraza, MD, Cherylnn R. Sherman, Patricia A. Taylor, Jennifer L. Thomas, Joshua R. Weikersheimer, David S. Wilkinson, MD, PhD, Jack A. Wilson–and Marlyn, my wife, for her unfailing support.

1. The History Of Healthcare Quality Management

QUALITY IS THE hallmark of healthcare excellence. It is the linchpin of all functional elements of structure, process, and outcome. However, there are always problems in delivering consistently high-quality care. As a result, there has been burgeoning national concern about the management of healthcare quality, including the quality of laboratory services. Society and the healthcare profession have realized the need for an administrative program to systematically evaluate, assess, and improve the effectiveness of healthcare quality control measures. In the 1980s, healthcare management concentrated on establishing quality assurance (QA). In the 1990s, attention has turned to the broader issues of total quality management (TQM) and continuous quality improvement (CQI).

Quality management theory and application methods have become increasingly important in all healthcare managerial and administrative circles. Federal law and Joint Commission for the Accreditation of Healthcare Organizations (JCAHO) standards have formed the regulatory basis for the quality management of hospitals and other healthcare organizations. These rules have rapidly driven implementation of quality management—especially at the laboratory level. In addition, the College of American Pathologists (CAP) has assumed an increasingly prominent role in overseeing laboratory accreditation and quality management.

Because the government, the JCAHO, and the CAP are emphasizing quality management so much, demonstration of an effective program that includes quality improvement has become crucial for successful hospital and laboratory accreditation, certification, and licensing. In 1992, the transition from QA to quality assessment and improvement (QI) began. By 1994, a full-fledged TQM system of quality management programs and CQI process should be under way in all JCAHO-accredited laboratories.

The challenge for all hospital and laboratory managers is to meet accreditation standards, to upgrade the quality—including the medical appropriateness—of laboratory support, to improve patient care, and to accomplish all of this while saving healthcare dollars. Ironically, although improving medical quality is of paramount concern to the accreditating agencies, implementing quality management programs and process is demanding more and more of our limited healthcare resources. The question everyone asks is: can quality truly be free as is often promised?[1] Quality cannot be totally free, but, in the long run, quality management will contribute significant savings. These savings will be in real dollars, as well as in other favorable socioeconomic externalities. However, certain sunken costs must be expected in the form of initial dollars, time, and other valuable organizational assets. These resources must be invested before quality management activities will result in operational cost savings, an improved end product, and increased customer satisfaction.

Healthcare quality management has been developing in the United States since the first practitioner arrived on the continent. However, the healthcare industry has only recently begun to accrue significant expertise in systematic assurance. In formulating quality management concepts, healthcare providers have borrowed heavily from the lessons learned by the nonhealthcare manufacturing sector.[2] In addition, quality management has been tempered by unique professional (peer), medicolegal (nonpeer), and socioeconomic forces.

It is helpful to explore the development of quality management in both the nonhealthcare and healthcare industries. This historical review leads to a better understanding of the development of federal and professional quality management efforts and the emphasis placed on the laboratory.

QUALITY MANAGEMENT IN THE EARLY NONHEALTHCARE INDUSTRY

Industrial process control began taking shape at the beginning of the Industrial Age in the 18th century; it became fully developed by the beginning of the Age of Information in the 20th century. The American industrial revolution began with the cottage industry. In that early manufacturing milieu, private industrialists lived amidst their own enterprises and generated their products by skilled handcraftsmanship.

The individual personally manufactured an item and guaranteed that product's quality.

There was no systematic use of quality control (QC). The craftsperson satisfied the consumer's needs in a customized fashion as befitted the professional, social, legal, and industrial expectations of that time. The quality of craftsmanship was not predetermined; it depended on the craftsman's proficiency, training, experience, judgment, and manual dexterity. Consequently, uniform quality was continually at risk throughout the manufacturing process.

In the late 18th century, innovations such as the water wheel and the spinning jenny began to improve manufacturing productivity. Inventors began producing more sophisticated machines that facilitated the development of automation and mass production. Eli Whitney, inventor of the cotton gin, was one such inventive industrialist. By the early 1800s, he became particularly important in the American defense industry when he contracted with the government to mass produce matchlock rifles. Initially, he was successful in meeting his manufacturing objectives of volume and speed of production–but not in achieving interchangeability of parts. After devising better methods for basic process control, his rifle parts became more uniformly interchangeable, and customer satisfaction was greatly improved.

Whitney had difficulty consistently attaining the *quality of conformance to design specifications*—until he instituted a form of manufacturing *process control.* Still, he and his pioneering contemporaries had much to learn about the control of quality during the specific manufacturing process and the assurance of quality throughout the entire industrial life cycle of the product.

The Beginning of Statistical Process Control And Quality Assurance in the United States

As industrialization expanded, business management theory focused on organizational function and productivity—instead of focusing on process. Theories of organizational control evolved parallel to early technical and industrial advances. Pioneering authorities, such as Adam Smith (18th century), Max Weber (19th-20th century), and Frederick Taylor (20th century), emerged as leading theorists in the School of Scientific Management. They developed such principles as organizational hierarchy, span of control, line and staff organization, foreman or middle management level supervision, specialization, time motion studies, flow line production, and worker incentive.[3]

Scientific management emphasized improving organizational efficiency and productivity by controlling the *quantity* of the manufactured product—rather than by controlling the *quality* of the manufacturing process. As a result, industrial QC became sporadic, lacking any detailed, systematic approach. It consisted of intermittent, on-line inspections, haphazard sorting, and discarding of "defective" items. It was more of a visual, qualitative examination than a precise, quantitative measurement, and tolerance limits were poorly defined. Consequently, products of unacceptable quality were often missed and sold—resulting in repeated customer dissatisfaction. At the same time, the rejected items included a significant number of non-defective products that would have been found acceptable by better QC methods and would have resulted in customer satisfaction. It did not take long before the ability to produce volume outstripped the ability to adequately inspect for quality.[4]

These inefficient inspections occurred because of the inability to accurately measure the quality of products during the manufacturing process. The lack of effective process control resulted in wasted material, labor, and time; increased production costs; endproducts of inconsistent quality; excessive waste products; potentially hazardous or polluting waste; dissatisfied customers; and all of the subsequent undesirable outcomes (complications) and socioeconomic externalities. What was needed was a more systematic form of process control.

In the early 20th century, process QC emerged as a new aspect of scientific management. The new methods focused on the systematic control of the manufacturing process and resulted in an end product of consistently reproducible high quality. For example, as early as 1900, Moline began to apply the probability theory and statistics to on-line sampling and inspection. In the early 1920s while working for Bell Telephone Laboratories, W. A. Shewhart first published his theories on applying statistics to process QC. In 1929, Dodge and Romig presented their theory of applying small batch sampling to process control management.[4]

In 1931, Shewhart published his classic contribution, *Economic Control of Quality of Manufactured Product*, in which he defined concepts of *statistical* quality control (SQC).[5] Shewhart and others of his era demonstrated how to apply several tools for QC analysis, including frequency distribution curves and measurement of central tendency and variance; the use of check sheets, histograms, scatter diagrams, correlation coefficients and ratios; the use of regression analysis, analysis of levels, trends, and patterns (or cycles), and probability analysis; the establishment of control limits; and the use of control charts. Over the years, Shewhart's approach has been improved by additional analytical and problem solving tools, including flow charts (work step sequences, input-process-output modeling), Pareto charts, cause-and-effect diagrams, run charts, and stratification charts.[6,7,8]

Shewhart's SQC approach was an improved means of assessing conformance to production design specifications. As a result of meeting specifications more often, manufacturers markedly reduced the volume of rejected products and improved general product reliability. Shewhart's SQC offered a preventive processing approach: promote the best quality of effort along the entire assembly line by *preventing* error. Although zero defects was not really expected, Shewhart's statistical approach still aimed at doing the job right the first time, as often as possible. Compared to the earlier days when the handcraftsman practiced workmanship of inconsistent quality, modern production workers can claim workmanship of controlled quality. Because of his pioneering work, the nonhealthcare manufacturing industry recognizes Shewhart as a founder of the School of Process Control Management.

With the onset of World War II, private industry mobilized in response to the nation's defense needs. The federal War Production Board soon recognized the importance of quality management to a successful war effort. Consequently, the Board established SQC training programs throughout the defense industry. Simultaneously, industry organized the American Society for Quality Control (ASQC) to encourage the application and continued development of SQC.

Unique and extensive QC problems permeated the newly formed defense industry. These problems were unmasked by the very lethality and enormity of the war effort. For starters, many war products were inherently unsafe, requiring special handling specifications. In addition, many products had extremely demanding climatic and storage requirements. Thus, for safety and logistical reasons, war materials demanded diverse, yet exact tolerance levels. Also, a high-level interest in total life cycle reliability of defense products created additional demands for conformance to design specifications.

As a result of these complex quality management requirements, the defense industry added a new level of extensive life cycle inspections to ensure the effectiveness of the SQC program. This secondary level of quality management scrutinized the efficiency and the effectiveness of defense manufacturing from the initial design concept to the final product use. The combination of SQC management and systematic, administrative-level, life cycle inspections resulted in one of the earliest examples of manufacturing quality assurance on a nation-wide scale in American industrial history.

Following World War II from 1946 to 1950, the practice of quality management in domestic and defense industries began to grow apart. At one end of the spectrum, the domestic industry—subordinate to emergency war requirements for so many years—elected to ignore the wartime emphasis on systematic QA. The emergency war measures rapidly became *passé*. As a result, the life cycle quality of domestic products diminished as the domestic industry began sacrificing quality for increased *volume productivity* and profit. At the same time, the government practiced its usual peacetime, *laissez faire* attitude toward the free market and private enterprise and did not actively support ASQC advocacy of effective quality management in the domestic industrial sector.

Meanwhile, from 1946 through the 1970s, the government continued to develop an increasingly formidable quality management system for the defense industry. Ironically, the federal emphasis on *quality productivity* was opposite to the private sector's post-war direction toward *enhanced volume.*

The driving force for the continued emphasis on defense industrial quality was ongoing large-scale military conflicts—and a very "hot," strategic cold war. These military efforts were carried on with increasing technological complexity and cost of military equipment. Therefore, as the Korean and Vietnam conflicts were being supplied, the defense industry continued to fine-tune its QC and QA programs.

During the post-World War II phase of its growth and development, United States defense quality management grew remarkably effective. However, there have been a few embarassing design and purchasing mishaps. Perhaps some of the most dramatic have been the problems of the National Aeronautics and Space Administration (NASA), whose quality management policies are directly descended from the defense quality management program. NASA has had its share of quality-related mishaps, some of which have been quite costly in American lives, national resources, and exploration delays—Apollo I, the Challenger, and the Hubble telescope being memorable examples. These mishaps are dramatic testimony that the efficiency of quality management is continually threatened by organizational size, complexity, and planning. This should be a lesson for everyone—including today's proponents for burgeoning national healthcare quality management—that TQM and CQI demand a pragmatic and systematic approach.

The Transfer of Process Control And Quality Assurance to Japan

Following World War II, while the United States domestic industry was reducing systematic SQC and QA, a Japanese industrial renaissance occurred. That small nation set out to gain industrially what it had not won militarily. Product innovation fed the post-victory glut in the United States while process innovation filled the post-defeat void in Japan. The result was a high-stakes race for cornering world markets with modern technology. The United States played the hare; Japan was the tortoise.

Immediately following the armistice in 1946, members of General MacArthur's staff introduced Shewhart's SQC and various tools for quality management to the surviving remnants of Emperor Hirohito's domestic industry. In doing so, the American consultants taught the Japanese the same quality management system that had helped to seal that small island's military defeat. During the immediate post-war period of 1946 to 1950, Japanese industry began to respond, showing signs of revitalization. In an important early move, they formed a Union of Japanese Scientists and Engineers (UJSE)—an organization similar to the ASQC in the United States. However, in contrast to the ASQC, the UJSE enjoyed substantial government support. During this time, the Japanese concentrated on perfecting statistical process control—the first chapter of their post-war revival.[9]

Beginning in the early 1950s, the Japanese began approaching quality management from the behavioral aspect–thus writing the second chapter in their extremely innovative industrial history. J.M. Juran, an American consultant, introduced "company-wide" QC to the Japanese industrialists. He taught that SQC should be an integral element of quality management throughout a firm and that quality should be evaluated through the entire life cycle of a product. Of key importance, he emphasized that quality management should be taught to all middle managers, not just to key individuals.

Japanese industry graduated from QC to QA partially because of a cultural twist in their interpretation of Juran's advice. The Japanese carried out his suggestion to teach SQC to all middle managers by instructing *all* factory personnel—right down to the assembly line worker. Upon assuming such an unprecedented, expansive scale of communication, Juran's company-wide SQC program evolved into a form of company-wide QA. Today, the fruits of Juran's concepts (among those of other individuals) are known as total quality management, which incorporates organization-wide team building, planning, and quality surveillance.[10]

An important adjunct to Juran's total approach to quality management are the principles developed by W. Edwards Deming (among others). Also a consultant to the Japanese in the early 1950s, Deming taught the importance of organizational commitment to continuous quality improvement as evidenced by customer satisfaction. His fourteen points have become a cornerstone of the American quality management movement.[7]

Both Juran and Deming have been recognized by the Japanese for contributing extraordinary influence on Japan's development of a winning industrial system. Through their teachings, the integration of TQM *and* CQI has come to symbolize the melding of scientific process management and the behavioral management sciences. TQM has become recognized as the managerial means and CQI as the managerial end.

In the course of applying the principles of TQM and CQI, the Japanese also began to develop the use of quality control circles—more commonly known today as "quality circles." A form of team building, this culturally natural, intuitive quality management approach stimulated maximum employee participation and helped to solidify the second chapter of modern Japanese industrial history.

The success of quality circles stems from the use of small groups of employees for planning and problem-solving. The technique encourages voluntary employee involvement from all levels of management and production—throughout the traditional organizational hierarchy from the highest to the lowest level. Quality circles provide enhanced opportunities for company-wide employee participation in both QC and QA, resulting in greatly improved organizational communication and employee motivation.[9]

During a speech to the Japanese in 1950, Deming accurately predicted that the trademark "Made in Japan"—then a synonym for poor quality in the Western world—would soon become an international hallmark of quality.[11] Today, "Made in Japan" is unquestionably a symbol for high-quality products, and the Japanese are leaders in world-wide manufacturing and trade. Over the last three decades, many major economic markets, once cornered by the United States and other Western nations, have fallen under Japan's industrial influence.

In 1985, at 80 years of age, Juran was asked the question, "Has Japan's industrial advance been due chiefly to a cultural difference?" He answered, "No." To understand how they got their results, study the deeds they've done, not their culture."[12] On the other hand, it is prudent to understand the Japanese style of quality management. Simply put, Japanese management listens to what its work force says about how to make better quality products. Japanese workers send the same message that the American work force has always sent to American management—but American management has not been listening.

Juran was correct: we don't have to learn the mysteries of Japanese culture; all we need to do is listen to our workers tell us what it is like "closest to the work." And, we need to listen while the workers are on the job, not while they are giving their exit interview. In addition, we must give workers enough time to do the job right. Rather than increase productivity and profit by increasing production volume, we need to pursue quality workmanship. Increased profit will follow improved quality and increased customer satisfaction.[13,14]

The Return of Quality Management to the United States

American leaders such as Shewhart, Juran, and Deming conceived and developed the basic theories and methods of SQC, TQM, and CQI. The Japanese assimilated and nurtured these quality management lessons, developing them into an enhanced managerial art and science. Two decades after the transfer of World War II-style control management theory to Japan, the evolution of QC and QA in the United States finally began to turn full circle. After a lapse of emphasis on quality, American domestic industry began refocusing its attention on quality management.

In the 1970s, the emphasis on quality management quietly returned to the United States as Japanese-style total or company-wide QC and QA. In 1973, Lockheed Aircraft was one of the first manufacturers to embrace the combination of United States-style SQC and Japanese-style quality circles. Since then, many United States industrial giants have followed suit—by 1984, at least half of the Fortune 500 companies had begun some form of SQC and systematic monitoring, assessing, and improving of manufacturing quality.[11,15]

Today, Shewhart's SQC is still highly regarded—although modern industry refers to it as statistical *process* control.[16] Just as his tools of quality management are commonly used at the industrial bench, they also are becoming commonly referenced in healthcare publications and conferences. Juran's and Deming's precepts of TQM and CQI also are being increasingly used throughout industrial management in both the private and public sectors, including the healthcare industry. These revolutionary teachings continue to sweep the nation—along with the messages of other popular proponents of modern quality management. The government also has instituted more active incentives for quality management such as the Malcolm Baldridge Award for excellence in quality improvement.[17]

What about the quality management of health care? The evolution of quality improvement in the American healthcare industry is discussed in detail next.

QUALITY MANAGEMENT OF HEALTH CARE IN THE UNITED STATES

Over the past century, at the same time as the private industrial sector experienced the growth of quality management, the American healthcare industry has developed its own management capabilities. For many reasons, the approach to healthcare quality has progressed slowly and conservatively. For example, a pervasive attitude among pathologists of the early 1900s was that the practice of pathology *was* quality assurance. Similar attitudes still exist today, but they do not prevail.

In recent years, most healthcare professionals—including those in pathology and laboratory medicine—have begun to view systematic QC, QA, QI, TQM, and CQI as important tools in managing high-quality patient care. Quality management has become particularly important as a continually expanding requirement for accreditation. As a result, considerable effort has gone into developing and improving healthcare quality management methods.

During the development of quality management, the definition of healthcare quality has derived meaning from a multitude of disciplines and influential forces. Just as beauty, quality has also been philosophically defined as something that can be appreciated only through "the eye of the beholder"—be it in the eye of the patient, the physician, a federal bureaucrat, or a congressional staffer.

It is true that there are many variables that have to be considered. There are normal variations in the quality of care that depend on the type of medical or surgical practice, the type of patient support services available, the general geographic location, the setting—urban or rural, the socioeconomic status of the patient, and the personal characteristics of the physician. In fact, part of the art of medicine has always been making a diagnostic or therapeutic decision under conditions of natural uncertainty.

For whatever reason, it has become increasingly evident that healthcare providers need a system of programs to formalize the management of quality of patient diagnosis and treatment. The *laissez faire* approach has proven too dangerous to human life and limb and too costly for the public economy. The many reasons cited for the growing necessity for quality management include ethical, academic, professional, legal, social, and economic forces.

Healthcare Ethics

The leading professional standard for health care, *primum non nocere*, is incorporated in the Hippocratic Oath (*circa* 400 BC): "Above all, do no harm." This historic admonition against nonmaleficence is the foundation for all professional healthcare standards and strongly implies the need for quality management—everything necessary should be done to ensure that care is provided the right way and for the right reasons.

A footnote to the Hippocratic ethic was penned during the post-World War II trials at Neurnberg. Those hearings uncovered many atrocities that were performed in the name of health science. Subsequently, special ethical scrutiny has focused on any form of experimental medicine and surgery, and stringent restrictions have been applied to the ethical quality of clinical investigation.

Healthcare Academic Standards

American history supports evidence of significant disparity between the art and science of academic medicine versus the reality of medical practice. Abraham Flexner's 1910 report, *Medical Education in the United States*, has become one of the most publicized and influential studies in the history of American education.[18] This landmark survey showed early 20th century medical education to be suboptimal because of the lack of uniformity and national standards. The report resulted in reorganization of the American Medical Association, standardization of medical education, and a surge of professional concern for improvement of healthcare quality in the United States.[19,20]

Healthcare Peer Studies

Disquieting reports of poor control and assurance of health care exist throughout American medical literature. The reports cited below are but a few examples; many more have appeared during the 20th century.

As early as 1913, Ernest A. Codman was emphasizing the importance of patient-care outcome as the main product of healthcare. An originator of outcome studies, Codman surveyed the incidence of poor healthcare in Boston; in 1925, he publicized his findings of negligence and malpractice. Because of his writing and speaking on his findings, he was considered professionally eccentric and dangerous, resulting in the revocation of his privileges at Massachusetts General Hospital. Afterwards, he established his own hospital where he continued to practice outcome studies to assess results of patient care. He is now considered to be a founder of medical quality management and peer review.[21]

Many more revelations of suboptimal health care have been published. In 1956, P. A. Lembcke published equally revealing studies based on hospital clinical record auditing.[22] In 1957, R. E. Trussell published process and outcome studies on the healthcare of teamster union members in New York City; he showed that at least 20% had received poor health care.[23] In 1973, D. M. Kessner and C. E. Kalk published a study of a pediatric population that showed significant levels of ineffective or inappropriate treatment.[24] In 1976, R. H. Brooke and F. A. Apfel reported a five method study of urinary tract infections, hypertension, and peptic ulcer disease; they showed that 25% of the outcomes should have been better.[25] In 1981, K. Steel reported an outcome study of 815 patients in a Boston community hospital; 36% of those patients showed evidence of iatrogenic illness—9% of these incidents were life threatening and 2% contributed to death.[26] In conclusion, there has been ample evidence from peer review that the efficiency and effectiveness of clinical care can be greatly improved.[19]

Legal Mandates

Society has mandated improved quality of health care through its own form of outcome monitoring in the courtroom, where certain standards of practice have become forged by the rules of law. Many of these judgments have been reinforced by federal and state statutory directives. Tort law has always been an extremely important form of societal QA, a form of non-peer review that has filled the void when healthcare QC and QA have been inadequate.

The definition of liability for negligent medical conduct has become increasingly refined in the Western world over the last five centuries. The general, objective standard of practice is "what a reasonable physician, possessed of the same degree of skill and learning, would have done under the same or similar circumstances." Some examples of standard rules of negligence that prevail through the United States are paraphrased as follows[27]:

- In diagnosing, treating, or operating on a patient, a physician (eg, pathologist, internist, or surgeon) must possess and, using best judgment, apply with reasonable care the degree of skill and learning ordinarily possessed and used by other members of the profession in good standing, engaged in the same type of practice or specialty in the same locality or in a similar locality. A failure to meet this standard is negligence.

- A person professing to practice surgery or the administration of medicine for compensation must bring to the exercise of the profession a reasonable degree of care and skill. Any injury resulting from a want of such care and skill shall be a tort for which a recovery may be had.

- A physician shall use such reasonable care, diligence, and skill as physicians, surgeons, or other specific specialists in the same general line of neighborhood and in the same general line of practice ordinarily have and exercise in a like case.

Surges in medical malpractice suits have occurred periodically in this country during the last two centuries. However, during the last two to three decades, the threat of litigation has been especially severe. The media has reported a steady stream of healthcare lawsuits in both the private and public sectors, and the courts have allowed increasingly high monetary awards. Negligent care, inadequate professional peer discipline, and a deterioration of the traditional doctor-patient relationship are some explanations for this increase of malpractice suits.

As medical tort law has evolved in this country, the courts have slowly and deliberately defined negligence. There are at least three levels of liability for negligence that have been recognized: institutional, employee, and individual provider. The finding of hospital institutional liability has been particularly important in the development of QA as a quality management instrument. Also, the influence of certain legal tenets has been instrumental in the development of medical case law, including charitable immunity and *respondeat superior*—"Let the master answer or be responsible."[28,29]

Before the 1890s, civil courts generally considered hospitals to be charitable institutions necessary for the shelter of the indigent sick. As such, hospitals were not held liable for malpractice; this special legal status was ascribed to the doctrine of <u>charitable immunity</u>. In other words, indigent patients were not offered the right of socially guaranteed healthcare—whatever care they received through charitable institutions was considered a privilege befitting their socioeconomic status. Because indigent healthcare was being donated, malpractice was not recognized under such circumstances. On the other hand, patients who were affluent enough to afford private healthcare had the privilege of guaranteed healthcare because their care was not donated—and they usually were able to afford legal recourse.

In these earlier days, physicians rarely admitted their private patients to hospitals. Instead, private patients were treated in the physician's office or the patient's home. This included the performance of major surgery. Liability for malpractice was tried largely on the basis of a patient's complaint of an individual physician's practice. This case-by-case approach was never very effective as a societal means of improving the overall proficiency of the profession.

By the turn of the century, hospitals began to charge for their services and to improve their facilities. As the quality of institutional services improved, physicians began to admit their private patients to the hospitals. Then the question of legal liability began to center on hospital health care. The court began defining healthcare provider and institutional responsibility. If responsibility rested with the hospital, the court had to decide whether the hospital was to be considered a charitable institution and immune from legal liability, or if it was a business and liable for suit.

Until recently, the courts paid significant attention to individual practitioner liability on a case-by-case basis. However, the question of institutional liability has become more fundamental to the overall development of healthcare quality management. What follows are a few representative cases that demonstrate the general progression of medicolegal events in the late 19th and early 20th centuries. For a comprehensive description of such cases, excellent reference texts are available.[19,29]

- In 1872 (*MacDonald v. Massachusetts General Hospital*), a patient sued because of unsatisfactory treatment of a fractured leg by an attending staff physician at a charity hospital. The court held that neither the hospital nor its staff was liable for negligence because the hospital was a charitable institution. The doctrine of charitable immunity prevailed.[30]

- In 1879 (*Glavin v. Rhode Island Hospital*), a patient sued because of unsatisfactory treatment of a traumatized hand. An intern in the charity hospital did not follow the institutional rules–resulting in the inappropriate use of a tourniquet and eventual amputation of the arm. The court rejected the hospital's defense of charitable immunity and found the hospital liable for an employee's administrative negligence under the doctrine of *respondeat superior*. In other words, the institution was responsible for the intern's neglect. This judgement was also considered a matter of interpretation of privity of contract. Nevertheless, for more than three quarters of a century (until 1957), the doctrine of charitable immunity continued to prevail in many court cases.[31]

- In 1957 (*Bing v. Thunig*), the doctrine of charitable immunity was finally dismantled. A patient sued after suffering burns during surgery brought on by negligence of the nursing staff. The hospital defense was based on the doctrine of charitable immunity and separation of administrative responsibility from professional negligence. Pleas for both charitable immunity and the dichotomy of professional and administrative responsibility were soundly denied. The court imposed the doctrine of *respondeat superior* and found the hospital liable for the professional negligence of its nursing employees.[32]

- In 1965 (*Darling v. Charleston Community Memorial Hospital*), a patient sued after a cast was applied to a broken leg with inadequate padding or space to allow for swelling—essentially, another tourniquet problem. The patient's leg eventually had to be amputated because of lack of adequate physician supervision. The court found the hospital liable for inattention to the enforcement of requirements written as law and assumed by the hospital through its acceptance of accreditation standards of practice included in its own bylaws. The physician settled his responsibilities through a separate court case.[33]

The above cases demonstrate that the targets for legal accountability have run the gamut from the hospital administrative staff to the healthcare provider staff. The next three cases illustrate that, after 1965, the courts began to direct their attention to institutional control and assurance of healthcare quality. The courts addressed institutional accountability for its employees and employee and staff peer accountability for each other.

- In 1967 (*Fiorentino v. Wenger*), a patient sued because a surgeon did not obtain an appropriate informed consent. The court held that the hospital was not responsible for ensuring that a surgeon obtain an informed consent. However, the court did record by dictum that it is the duty of a hospital to monitor the quality of care practiced within the institution and that the hospital could be held liable for an act of negligence by an attending or staff physician if the hospital has some reason to know that the negligent act would occur.[34]

- In 1971 (*Joiner v. Mitchell Community Hospital Authority*), the court held that a hospital is not only responsible for its physician staff's negligence but should also stimulate the staff to review the professional qualifications and performance of each individual physician member.[35]

- In 1975 (*Corleto v. Shore Memorial Hospital*), a suit was brought against the hospital, its administrator, its board of directors, and its physician staff. The plaintiff alleged that all the defendants allowed a surgeon to operate, even though they knew that the surgeon was incompetent. The court held that it is the hospital's duty to monitor the quality of care provided by a staff physician. The staff, although unincorporated, was also held liable for failing to perform its own peer review.[36]

By 1965, the nation's court system recognized employee or staff accountability—an early form of medicolegal QA. By 1975, the courts mandated the necessity for institutional peer review of health care, accompanied by action and follow-up. By then, the courts were finally imposing a reasonably effective type of medicolegal quality surveillance on the healthcare system.

More recently, a 1988 Missouri case, *Harrel v. Total Health Care*, focused on the issue of the selection of physicians by a managed care plan. In this case, the corporate negligence doctrine was extended to a health maintenance organization (HMO).[37] This case is easily applicable to the responsibilities of *locom tenens* agencies in their selecting pathologists and other laboratory healthcare providers for temporary employment.

Court cases have also focused on liability resulting from injuries due to negligent acts associated with laboratory patient-care support. Technicians, technologists, pathologists, other staff members, and even the hospital, can be held accountable. Liability has been connected to specimen mishandling, loss of specimen integrity, misdiagnosis of a specimen, use of improper techniques or reagents, improperly performed tests, and improper autopsy technique.[29]

Another recent turn of events has been the passage of "shield laws," which provide legal immunity for hospital peer review committees, hospital staffs, and witnesses.[38] For example, the Health Care Quality Improvement Act of 1986 (HCQIA '86) provides limited immunity to medical peer review activities from federal and state lawsuit.

HCQIA '86 is intended 1) to provide incentives and protection for physicians to engage in effective professional peer review and 2) to restrict incompetent and unprofessional physicians from moving from state to state without disclosure or discovery of previous incompetent or unprofessional activity. Such laws protect the peer review system from retaliatory lawsuits filed by physicians who are subjects of disciplinary action. Quality management documentation has also been found to be nondiscoverable by the patient plaintiff. The intent of these laws is to minimize institutional risk as it goes about its business of peer review. The pendulum of medicolegal immunity seems to have come full swing from charitable hospital immunity to hospital peer review immunity.

In summary, the courts have clearly determined the responsibilities for the quality of health care and have created clear-cut legal mandates for the development of quality management programs by all concerned parties. At the same time, these quality management programs are receiving reasonable legal protection to operate without fear of reprisal.

Technological Advances

Technological research and development have immensely influenced the quality, including the ethics, of health care. The effects are multifaceted, including increased complexity of medical practice, changes in the physician-patient relationship, overutilization of finite technical resources, and increasing national healthcare costs.

With increased complexity of medical practice, all biomedical disciplines have experienced a technological explosion of tremendous dimensions. These rapid and extensive advances have caused a staggering increase in the sheer mass of knowledge. The integration of modern technical advances with clinical care requires constant updating by the physician. As this complexity continues to unfold, more adverse events can potentially befall the patient simply by chance or by negligence through misdiagnosis or maltreatment. Additionally, there is a constant drive toward increased regulatory control.

Also, an increased dependence on technical resources—including laboratory testing—has developed. Advanced technology and the heightened threat of litigation are linked to an increased practice of defensive medicine. Some physicians excessively use diagnostic laboratories for fear of being accused of negligence. Overutilization because of "defensive medicine," besides any excessive use contrived for extra profit, tends to foster decreased reliance on traditional physical findings and drives the healthcare dollar upward.

Changes in the Physician-Patient Relationship

Increased technological complexity, as well as managed care, has eroded the traditional one-on-one, doctor-patient relationship to which the American culture was once accustomed. Particularly for patients in the urban centers, health care is commonly perceived as "high-tech/high-volume/low-touch." In spite of its advantages, a major, adverse impact of modern technology on medical care has been the loss of the humanistic, personable approach of the physician to the patient.[39]

As the modern physician becomes increasingly reliant on space-age laboratory instrumentation for diagnosis and treatment, there is a temptation to shorten the traditional interchange between physician and patient—resulting in less personal attention paid to the patient's complaints, history, and physical findings. In exchange for the advantages of modern medical science, the physician's art of communication and observation have suffered. Patients have come to regard doctors more as technicians than as skillful diagnosticians. High-volume patient loads, managed healthcare organizations such as health maintenance organizations, and the use of physician surrogates have also added to the doctor-patient communication gap.[40,41]

Diminished communication between the patient and the doctor results in reduced quality of care. Ineffective exchange of information breeds patient anxiety, patient distrust of the physician, and physician mistakes. These seeds of discontent breed litigation. In turn, malpractice suits contribute significantly to the escalation of healthcare costs.

Societal Expectations

Another aspect of the changing physician-patient relationship is social in nature. The citizens of the United States expect adequate access to proficient healthcare, and they often complain through the courts when they experience less. Since 1900, this great expectation has emerged as an unwritten bill of health rights for the unwell. Since the 1965 Medicare law, society has realized that health is a necessity of life—no longer controlled by its practitioners. Health care has become more of a *right* that is guaranteed—instead of a *privilege* that is earned. Health is certainly important to "life and the pursuit of happiness." This social philosophy continues to evolve and to increasingly affect the use of national healthcare resources.

Economic Realities

The combination of increased litigation, high technology, increased complexity, defensive medicine, increased public demand, changing demographics, and diminished resources is causing national healthcare costs to spiral out of control.[42] Approximately 12% of US citizens are older than 65 years and that figure is steadily rising. By 1990, healthcare was absorbing 11% (about 800 billion dollars) of the gross national product, and this trend is expected to continue to increase geometrically, reaching 12% (about one trillion dollars) by 1995.[43]

Now, quality management is becoming recognized as a valuable administrative tool for monitoring and improving the cost-effectiveness of health care. However, the expanded use of QC, QI, TQM, and CQI in modern medicine invokes Shewhart's warning: "The better the quality, the higher the manufacturer's cost of quality control."[5] The irony is that the costs of injudicious team building, planning, control, and assessment efforts must be balanced against the costs of wasteful, negligent healthcare practice. Quality management must be practiced pragmatically to be cost-effective.

Authors, such as Crosby, point out that significant long range savings are possible if quality management is effectively employed over an adequate period of time.[1] On the other hand, it has been suggested that, to date, more people might have profited from quality management as consultants than have benefited from it medically as patients.[44]

INSTITUTIONALIZATION OF HEALTHCARE QUALITY MANAGEMENT

Over the years there has been a significant transfer of management theory and experience from the manufacturing industry to the healthcare industry. In the process of learning from the non-healthcare manufacturing industry, many physicians have tried—both individually and through organizations—to move the healthcare industry toward an increased awareness of quality management. However, because of professional parochialism, scientific and academic conservatism, socioeconomic complexities, and the deliberate speed of medical tort law, the success of healthcare quality management has lagged behind societal expectations. As one consequence, the definitions and methods of quality management have remained in a state of flux, moving from one stage of development to the next. The evolution of healthcare quality management is described more fully in the following sections.

Formation of the Joint Commission on Accreditation of Healthcare Organizations

As recommended by the Flexner Report, the 1912 Third Clinical Congress of North America called for the development of a standardized program of medical education. In 1913, the American College of Surgeons (ACS) was founded, and it embraced the "standardization of hospital equipment and hospital work" to enhance the quality of institutional patient treatment across the United States.[45] ACS interest was spurred on by concern about the state of the American hospital system and the competence of the practicing physician. In its first three years, the ACS rejected 60% of its applicants for institutional membership because of insufficient proof that the applicants' clinical competence met ACS standards.[46]

In 1917, the ACS established the Hospital Standardization Program (HSP) for hospital survey. In 1918, it published its first "Standard on Efficiency." In 1919, field trials of that standard revealed a pass rate of only 89 out of 692 hospitals of 100 beds or larger. As a result, in late 1919, the ACS adopted five new requirements that were referred to as "The Minimum Standard." These guidelines were aimed at improving hospital staff competence, including the laboratory and radiology staff. The Minimum Standard was the first national requirement for regular review and evaluation of the quality of care provided to hospitalized patients. This standard was the beginning of institutionalized quality management in American medicine.

Essentially, the HSP inaugurated hospital accreditation in the United States. Hospitals entered the program voluntarily. It was a peer survey program in which qualified surgeons, representing the ACS, inspected the participating hospitals. By 1951, the ACS had approved more than 3,000 U.S. hospitals—more than 50% of American hospitals at that time—using progressively expanded and more stringent standards.[47]

As successful as it may have been, the HSP also became increasingly demanding of ACS resources as the number of inspectors, the amount of administrative support, and the operational expense mounted. A singular fact regarding the 1951 survey was that it cost the ACS more than $2 million. That year, because the expanding charter and resource burdens were outstripping the capabilities of the ACS, a partnership of major North American healthcare organizations formed the Joint Commission on Accreditation of Hospitals (JCAH).[a] Initially, the JCAHO included representatives from the American Medical Association, the American College Physicians, the ACS, the American Hospital Association, and the Canadian Medical Association (CMA); the CMA later dropped out to form its own joint committee and the American Dental Association has been added. The member organizations agreed to share professional responsibility and to broaden the resource base for the survey program.[46]

In 1953, the JCAHO published its first standards and inspection criteria and offered accreditation to hospitals on a voluntary basis. Per its corporate charter, the JCAHO has continued to establish professional care and safety standards for healthcare organizations. The development of specific standards for clinical practice remains the responsibility of the individual medical societies.

Federal Regulations and JCAHO Standards for Accreditation and Quality Management

In 1965, a milestone event occurred when Congress passed Public Law 89-97, which amended the Social Security Act—this was the Medicare Act. After many attempts, including the Wagner-Murray-Dingell bills, the Forand bill, and the Kerr-Mills bill, the United States finally had federally financed health care under the Social Security Act.[48]

The law outlined how hospitals could participate in the Medicare and Medicaid healthcare payment programs. Hospitals could choose to be inspected for accreditation by the JCAHO or by the state. Hospitals certified for JCAHO accreditation were *deemed* to be in compliance with most of the Medicare conditions of participation for hospitals and, therefore, met the eligibility requirements for participation in the

[a] In 1987 the JCAH became known as the Joint Commission on Accreditation of Healthcare Organizations (JCAHO). The latter name and abbreviation will be used through the remainder of the text.

Medicare and Medicaid programs.[46] Because the majority of the nation's hospitals were meeting the current standards and because of the pressure of federal regulation, the JCAHO completely revised their standards in 1966 to reflect an *optimal achievable* level of care—not ideal but the best that could be achieved–rather than a *minimal essential* level of care, as was formerly prescribed. Most important, the 1965 law allowed the JCAHO, a peer organization, to be responsible for surveying and enforcing a federal requirement, rather than having a federal agency directly involved.

In 1967, Congress passed the Clinical Laboratory Improvement Act (CLIA '67). For the first time, healthcare laboratories earning Medicare/ Medicaid funds were brought under the specific scrutiny of federal regulation. Subsequent amendments to this regulation are discussed later.

In 1970, the Citizens for Better Care filed a suit in California, claiming that federal recognition of the Joint Commission's accreditation program was an unconstitutional delegation of federal powers. Responding to the findings of that suit, the Senate Finance Committee amended the Social Security Act in 1972 through Public Law 92-603. The law included[49]:

- *A requirement for federal validation and complaint surveys of accredited hospitals.* This stipulation confirmed ultimate federal authority over Medicare hospital programs.

- *The repeal of the portion of the original legislation that stipulated that the Department of Health and Human Services (DHHS) could set no standards for hospitals that would be more demanding than those set by the Joint Commission.* This action strengthened DHHS authority by emphasizing that federal power was being delegated, rather than abrogated, to the JCAHO.

- *Requirement for DHHS to submit an annual report to Congress describing the results of the validation and complaint surveys.* This report includes a review of JCAHO accreditation findings, ensuring federal oversight of Joint Commission activities.

In 1978, the DHHS determined that the Joint Commission's professional standards for laboratory operations, including quality management, were not equivalent to the newly established Medicare requirements. In addition, the DHHS claimed that the Joint Commission's survey process did not adequately evaluate hospital laboratory operations. In response, the Joint Commission rewrote its laboratory standards and reorganized its survey methods. This included hiring laboratory technologists as surveyors. Since these modifications, the laboratory component of the Joint Commission hospital accreditation has been recognized by the DHHS as supportive of the Medicare/Medicaid programs.

In 1988, Congress enacted Public Law 100-578—the Clinical Laboratory Improvement Amendments (CLIA '88)—revising CLIA '67. This law addresses laboratory quality management through several new surveillance initiatives as directed by the Health Care Financing Administration (HCFA), the executive agency.[50] CLIA '88 is intended to upgrade the performance of all healthcare laboratory testing. This new level of regulatory control is based on the complexity of the testing in question.

- As of January 1990, *all* laboratories desiring eligibility for Medicare and Medicaid reimbursement must be certified every two years. This regulatory requirement includes physician office laboratories. To obtain certification, the laboratory must formally apply to an accrediting agency approved by the HCFA (eg, JCAHO or CAP) as having deemed status. Inspection and certification procedures will then follow.

- Laboratory tests will be categorized in three levels: levels I and II (the more stringent) and waivered. Those tests granted a waiver will not be subject to inspection for certification. Certification waivers can be obtained for laboratory tests that are listed by HCFA as being very limited, simple procedures that offer insignificant risk to patient care if a result is erroneous.

- To be certified, a laboratory must show evidence of effective quality management programs. The HCFA will ultimately establish standards for these activities.

- The HCFA will establish standards for various proficiency programs. Laboratories will be tested tri-quarterly for each examination and procedure within the categories that they are certified. HCFA will establish national standards for acceptable performance of all analytes. The results of the proficiency tests will be available to the public. Specific attention will be paid to cytology laboratories.

In 1989, the Omnibus Budget Reconciliation Act (OBRA '89) was enacted and was implemented on January 1, 1991. One of its stipulations is the establishment of the Agency for Health Care Policy and Research (AHCPR). The AHCPR is responsible for:

- Outcomes research

- Practice guideline development

- Data base development

- Education and dissemination.

As an adjunct to this program, an Office of Forum for Quality and Effectiveness in Healthcare is developing, periodically reviewing, and updating clinical practice guidelines, standards of quality performance measures, and healthcare review criteria.[51] With all the laws and regulations that have been passed or loom on the horizon, it is obvious that the federal government intends to significantly influence the quality of clinical and laboratory management.

College of American Pathologists Standards for Healthcare Laboratory Accreditation and Quality Management

Throughout the development of healthcare quality management, there has been a clear realization that credible, effective peer review must start from within the healthcare industry itself. Otherwise, governmental forces will force federal (non-peer), regulatory control on healthcare institutions, including laboratories, because of the socioeconomic importance of healthcare to the nation.

In keeping with this philosophy, peer management of quality in laboratory medicine has developed parallel to the rest of the healthcare industry. Perhaps it has even developed a little faster than in other healthcare disciplines—the laboratorian has enjoyed some advantage of quality management expertise, particularly in the analytical laboratory where QC is built on statistical process control.

Nationally, the CAP has been the peer organization for laboratory quality management since its founding in 1947. The development of the role of the CAP has paralleled the natural evolution of QC, QA, and QI throughout the nation's healthcare laboratories.

As a general rule, the federal government and the JCAHO establish the broad policies, guidelines, and format for high quality, appropriate care in the general hospital and laboratory environment. The CAP contributes the specialized standards, professional expertise, and up-to-date direction that are required for implementing healthcare laboratory operations.

The CAP adopted its first systematic standards for anatomic and clinical laboratory quality in 1961.[52] In 1973, the CAP formed the Council on Laboratory Improvement, including the Standards Committee. In 1976, the latter council was reformed as the Council on Quality Assurance (CQA), one of six ongoing councils within the college. From 1976 to 1990, the CQA grew with several structural changes in scientific resource committees–but still maintaining the basic elements of the 1976 council. In 1990, the CAP formed a new Council on Scientific Affairs, absorbing the former CQA but including a newly formed Commission on Quality Assurance (a new "CQA"). Also, there have been several separate executive-level committees acting as liaison with important public and private sector quality management organizations, including the JCAHO. It is under the new CQA that the CAP Standards Committee now resides.[53]

Using the above-described organizational structure to keep in step with changing JCAHO focus, the CAP standards have undergone most recent revision in two key areas: personnel requirements (Standard I) and QA (Standard III). Through *Standard I*, the College has clarified requirements for the laboratory director and personnel. The importance of the laboratory medical director as a physician-manager is explicit. As the leading manager in the laboratory, the director has clear-cut responsibilities for laboratory QA, safety, and resource management programs.[54]

Since the inception of the CAP laboratory inspection and accreditation program, the College's inspection checklist has addressed an ever expanding scope of QC and QA issues. The checklist requirements emphasize the surveillance of intralaboratory resources and process. Increasing attention is being paid to extralaboratory resources and processes, such as ancillary testing. As of yet, little CAP attention is being directed to the effect of laboratory support on laboratory test selection, utilization, and patient-care outcome, except in specific areas such as Transfusion Medicine.

In 1987, the CAP introduced *Standard III*, which is aimed specifically at quality assurance. The CAP still refers to the JCAHO's "quality assessment and improvement" as "quality assurance." This standard addresses quality management requirements for "the pathology service" in very broad terms. It states: "Quality assurance applies equally to anatomic pathology, surgical pathology, autopsy pathology, and cytopathology." However, the standard does not include any direct reference to clinical pathology laboratory activities.

The CAP does define QA as "the process of assuring that all key pathology services involved in the delivery of patient care have been accomplished in a manner appropriate to maintain excellence in medical care."[54] With their own definitions of QA as a reminder, the emphasis placed on anatomic pathology in CAP Standard III will hopefully be replaced with a more balanced reference to clinical pathology in future versions.

Concurrent with the establishement of its standards, institutional surveillance of healthcare laboratory quality formally began in 1961 when the CAP introduced its hospital Laboratory Accreditation Program (LAP).[52] Subsequently, CLIA '67 recognized the LAP as an equivalent program for interstate licensure requirements. Therefore, hospital laboratories accredited through the LAP were deemed as meeting interstate licensure requirements and could apply to the DHHS for a letter of exemption.

In 1979, the JCAHO began to exempt hospitals with CAP laboratory accreditation from the on-site visit by the laboratory technologist surveyor.[49] The JCAHO continues to review CAP inspection and accreditation findings and to include these findings in its accreditation report to the DHHS. The Joint Commission still includes the hospital laboratory in their regular hospital survey. However, if the laboratory is CAP accredited, the JCAHO surveyors usually limit themselves to focusing on the laboratory quality assessment and improvement program. Hospitals certified for laboratory accreditation by CAP inspection are considered to be subdeemed in compliance with Medicare requirements. The term "subdeemed" is used by the CAP in referring to its having "subdeemed status" as granted by JCAHO and "deemed status" as granted by the CLIA '88.[55]

This incorporation of the CAP by the JCAHO in support of the Medicare program was based on the merits of the LAP. The role of the College is also consistent with the precedent set by the federal recognition of CAP accreditation for interstate laboratory licensure as granted by CLIA '67. About 50% of the states that have licensure laws accept CAP accreditation for state licensure.

The LAP now consists of a well-organized, well-trained cadre of inspectors armed with a comprehensive, up-to-date, checklist of requirements. The participating laboratory also has the opportunity to conduct its own in-house accreditation self-inspection in the interim period between CAP on-site visits.

The Fall 1988 edition of the CAP Inspection Checklist included the CAP's first specific inquiry into a laboratory's practice of quality surveillance. Up to the 1992 edition, the checklist stipulated only that an accredited laboratory must demonstrate an ongoing surveillance program. The 1992 CAP checklist specified six phase II requirements whereby the resolution of any phase II deficiency is required for accreditation. Those requirements were that:[56,57]

- There be a planned and systematic QA program for the entire laboratory service/department led by a physician director
- The QA program be in effect at the sectional level
- There be documentation of monitoring and evaluation of QA indicators in each section during all shifts
- Monitoring and evaluation efforts are documented and reported with appropriate actions
- There be an annual internal appraisal of the QA program that assesses the overall effectiveness of all elements of the QA program

- The laboratory director and professional staff actively participate in department and hospital-wide QA activities.

It is natural that the CAP checklist is always catching up with the continually evolving JCAHO standards and requirements. Currently, the most obvious difference in parlance is the CAP's continued use of the phrase "quality assurance" versus the JCAHO's revised use of "quality assessment and improvement"—and, now, "improving organizational performance (PI)."[58]

Other CAP Quality Improvement Programs

In addition to the accreditation standards and LAP on-site and interim surveys, the CAP continues to improve its support of laboratory compliance with federal and JCAHO quality management requirements through a continually expanding laboratory improvement program. It has developed many industry-wide, voluntary programs for interlaboratory peer oversight. The CAP programs include several proficiency testing survey programs in anatomic and clinical pathology and a workload management program.

In 1945, that Belk and Sunderman first sampled the adequacy of laboratory testing in Philadelphia. That survey was followed by a second in 1947, encompassing all of Pennsylvania by distributing unknown samples to 59 laboratories and compiling the aggregate results for interlaboratory analysis.[59,60] This study demonstrated not only the need but also the feasibility of laboratory comparison on a large scale. Initial results showed serious proficiency problems. Consequently, in 1949, the same two investigators initiated a national proficiency testing survey program sponsored by the CAP.[61,62] The first published CAP survey consisted of 515 laboratories reporting on 10 chemistry analyses. By 1988, 14,500 subscribers tested more than 1.5 million survey analytes producing millions of data elements.[60]

Since 1972, the proficiency survey program has been a part of the CAP Quality Assurance Service (QAS), as a daily external quality control/assurance program. This survey process has facilitated significant improvement of participating laboratories throughout the country and has created an immense database covering all clinical laboratory disciplines.[60]

In 1950, laboratory QC methods were revolutionized when Levey and Jennings reported on the management of a frozen plasma pool using control charts to document QC data. Their QC charting method was an early laboratory adaptation of the manufacturing industry's statistical QC techniques. This technique has become a milestone contribution to laboratory quality management.[63] The Levey-Jennings method is a direct application of Shewhart's SQC approach, using a control chart to graphically illustrate the trends of process control by plotting control levels against standard deviation and time.

Many superb methods of laboratory QC have been devised since Levey and Jennings. New methods reflect changing resources and technology. An outstanding example is Westgard's multi-rules. Aimed at process control for today's highly accurate and precise analyzers, these modern instrumental tolerance levels have helped to establish a foundation for effective analytical quality management at the laboratory bench—the multi-rules resembling the threshold levels of the JCAHO ten-step process.[64]

In 1969, the concept of "total quality control" began to appear in the laboratory management literature. Based on the teachings of Feigenbaum and Juran, Eilers emphasized that every aspect of laboratory operations must be systematically surveyed, including the mission statement and all functional administrative and operative activities. Westgard and others have further expanded the concepts of TQM in the laboratory.[65,66,67]

The CAP proficiency testing program for clinical pathology, begun by Belk and Sunderman, continues to provide an excellent interlaboratory comparison of the quality of specimen analysis for all sections of the laboratory. The CAP proficiency testing program for anatomic pathology provides external quality assessment of surgical pathology, cervicovaginal cytopathology, autopsy pathology, immunohistochemistry, forensic pathology, and flow cytometry. For example, the Performance Improvement Program (PIP) in surgical pathology was developed in the 1970s as an external QA and educational program. The participant receives glass slides with patient histories and is required to select the appropriate diagnosis from a master list and to answer supplemental multiple choice questions.

Although relatively new, the external survey program, *Q-Probes*, has proven to be extremely valuable as a means of providing a structured QI program at the national level. Begun as a pilot project in 1988 and started as a full program in 1989, *Q-Probes* provides ready-to-use, short-term indicator studies to help assess the quality of laboratory services affecting patient care. Indicators are being generated for both anatomic and clinical pathology. Each *Q-Probes* indicator includes an objective, definitions of terms, recommended data collection methods, worksheets, and data input forms. The participating laboratories then share their surveillance data, which are collated and published for interlaboratory comparison by the CAP. At the same time, an immense database is being gathered for future reference.

The CAP Laboratory Management Index Program (LMIP) was begun in 1991, supplanting their Workload Recording Program. The program provides valuable assistance in resource management by collecting, calculating, and publishing fiscal, workload and productivity statistics for subscribing laboratories, again affording nation-wide interlaboratory comparison. The LMIP provides pathologists and other laboratory managers with a comprehensive and systematic program for assessing laboratory operating performance, covering productivity, utilization, cost-effectiveness, and revenue.[61]

ASCP Laboratory Quality Improvement Programs

The American Society of Clinical Pathologists (ASCP), the American Association of Blood Banks (AABB), the Clinical Laboratory Management Association (CLMA), and other national organizations also have responded aggressively to the industry-wide drive toward improved healthcare quality. Founded in 1922, the ASCP is a leading provider of up-to-date continuing medical education for pathologists, laboratory nurses, technologists, technicians, laboratory managers, and other laboratorians. In addition, the ASCP has pioneered in developing external proficiency testing and educational programs tailored to meet the needs of its many constituents. These quality management programs include *Check Sample*, *cognitive examinations*, *Tech Sample*, *challenge examinations*, *CheckPath*, and *Cytoscreen*.[68]

- *Check Sample* started in 1958 as a healthcare laboratory self-study and proficiency testing program. The program covers all major areas of anatomic and clinical pathology. Each *Check Sample* consists of two parts: a clinical problem, usually including a specimen to be tested or diagnosed by the participant and an educational component covering the subject in detail, providing the solution to the problem or the correct diagnoses and key recent references.

- *Cognitive examinations* began in the early 1970s. These collections of multiple choice examination questions are used for evaluation of pathologists and other laboratory personnel.

- *Tech Sample* started in 1979 as a comprehensive, self-study, continuing education program for all laboratorians but targeted particularly at technicians and technologists. *Tech Sample* provides timely, relevant, cost-effective exercises in major areas of anatomic and clinical pathology as well as management and education.

- *Challenge examinations* in surgical pathology, hematopathology, and cytopathology began in 1988. These examinations test the ability of a pathologist to diagnose lesions commonly encountered in practice. All examinations use microscopic slides that have been peer reviewed by a group of nationally-known experts.

- *CheckPath* started in 1988 as an external QA exercise designed to test the managerial, diagnostic, and technical competence of pathologists and technologists. The program covers surgical pathology, hematopathology, cytopathology, and clinical pathology. Each case consists of a brief case history, some with either a glass slide or color transparency, and a list of differential diagnoses and interpretations from which the single best response is to be selected. The *CheckPath* program is designed to assist subscribers in assessing and improving their laboratory skills.

- The *Cytoscreen* video disk program started in 1990 to simulate screening of Pap smears of the female genital tract and to evaluate proficiency of screening interpretation. The interpretive exercises presented by the *Cytoscreen* disks are designed for use by the individual examinee, working under controlled, closed-book examination conditions.

National-level committees, workshops, seminars, and publications have been vigorously raising awareness and understanding of the QA process at all levels of laboratory management. In addition, the CLMA has added institutional incentive by creating an annual quality management award, modeled after the National Institute of Standards and Technology's (formerly the National Bureau of Standards) Malcolm Baldridge Award. Throughout this course of developing hospital and laboratory quality management programs, there has been a clear realization by all concerned that credible and effective healthcare peer review must start from within the healthcare industry itself. Otherwise, external, governmental forces will continue to force federal, non-peer regulatory control and inspections on the healthcare industry. As it is, federal agencies have already become significantly involved in hospital and laboratory inspections and certification.

REFERENCES

1. Crosby PB. Quality is Free. New York: McGraw-Hill Book Co., 1979.
2. Hungate RW. Quality assurance: lessons from ndustry. Phys Exec, 1989;15:13-16.
3. Massie JL. Essentials of Management. Englewood Cliffs, NJ: Prentice-Hall, 1987.
4. Sasaki N, Hutchins D. The Japanese Approach to Quality Control. New York: Pergamon Press, 1984.
5. Shewhart WA. Economic Control of Quality of Manufactured Product. New York: Van Nostrand, 1931.
6. Scholtes PR. The Team Handbook: How to Use Teams to Improve Quality. Madison, WI: Joiner Assoc, Inc, 1989.

7. Walton M. The Deming Management Method. New York: Putnam Pub Group, 1986.
8. The Memory Jogger: A Pocket Guide of Tools for Continuous Improvement. Methuen, MA: GOAL/QPC, 1988.
9. Crocker D, Chaney OL, Chiu JSL. Quality Circles: A Guide to Participation and Productivity. New York: New American Library, 1984.
10. Juran JW. Juran on Leadership for Quality: An Executive Handbook. New York: The Free Press, 1989.
11. Ross JE, Ross WC. Japanese Quality Circles and Productivity. Reston, VA: Reston Publishers, 1982.
12. Hillkirk J. A quality master's advice: USA managers need dedication to defeat quality crisis. USA Today, 26 July 1985.
13. Hummel RP. Behind quality management: what workers and a few philosophers have always known and how it adds up to excellence in production. Organizational Dynamics, Summer 1987:71-78.
14. Umiker WO. You can learn a lot from your new employees. Med Lab Obs, 1991;23:45,48.
15. Ouchi WG. Theory Z. Addison-Wesley Publishing Company, Inc, 1981.
16. Oakland JS. Statistical Process Control. New York: John Wiley and Sons, 1986.
17. Garvin, DA. How the Baldridge Award really works. Harv Bus Rev, 1991;69:80-93.
18. Flexner A. Medical Education in the United States and Canada. New York: Carnegie Foundation for the Advancement of Teaching, 1910.
19. Pena JJ, Haffney AN, Rosen B, Light DW. Hospital Quality Assurance. Rockville, MD: Aspen Press, 1988.
20. Raffel MW. The U.S. Health System Origins and Functions. New York: John Wiley and Sons, 1980.
21. McClendon WW. Ernest A. Codman, MD (1869-1940), the end-result idea, and *The Product of a Hospital*: the challenge of a man ahead of his time and perhaps ours. Arch Path Lab Med, 1990; 114:1101-1104.
22. Lembcke PA. Measuring the quality of medical care through vital statistics based upon hospital service areas. Am J Pub Health, 1952; 42:276-280.
23. Trussell RE. The Quantity, Quality, and Cost of Medical and Hospital Care Secured by a Sample of Teamster Families in the New York Area. New York: Columbia University School of Public Health and Administrative Medicine, 1962.
24. Kessner DM, Kalk CE. Contrasts in Health Status: a Strategy for Evaluating Health Services. Washington, DC: Institute of Medicine, 1973.

25. Brooke RH, Appel FA. Quality of care assessment: choosing a method for peer review. NEJM, 1973;288:1323-1329.

26. Steel K. Iatrogenic illness on a general medical service at a university hospital. NEJM, 1981;304:638-642.

27. Hargis DM. The health care provider: liability implications. In: Howanitz PJ, ed. Conference Proceedings on Quality Qssurance in Physician Office, Bedside, and Home Testing. 2-4 April 1986, Atlanta, GA. Skokie, IL: College Am Path, 1986.

28. Berman HJ, Greiner WR. The Nature and Functions of Law. Mineola, NY: Foundation Press, 1980.

29. Miller RD. Problems in Hospital Law. Rockville, MD: Aspen Systems, 1983.

30. *McDonald v. Massachusetts General Hospital*, 120 Mass. 432 (1872).

31. *Glavin v Rhode Island Hospital*, 12 R.I. 411 (1879).

32. *Bing v Thunig*, 2 N.Y.2d 656, 143 N.E.2d 3, 163 N.Y.S.2d 3 (1957).

33. *Darling v. Charleston Community Memorial Hospital*, 33 Ill.2d 326, 211 N.E.2d 253 (1965), aff g 50 Ill. App.2d 253, 200 N.E.2d 149 (1964).

34. *Fiorentino v. Wenger*, 19 26 N.Y.2d 407, 227 N.E.2d 296, 280 N.Y.S.2d 373 (1967).

35. *Joiner v. Mitchell County Hospital Authority*, 125 Ga.App. 1, 12, 186, S.E.2d 307, 308 (1971) aff'd, 229 Ga. 140, 142, 189 S.E.2d 412, 414 (1972).

36. *Corleto v. Shore Memorial Hospital*, 138 N.J. Super. 302, 311 350 A.2d 534, 538 (1975).

37. Managed care involvement increases liability expenses. Hospitals, 1990;64:40-41,44.

38. Curran WJ. Medical peer review of physician competence and performance: legal immunity and the antitrust laws. NEJM, 1987; 316: 597-598.

39. Johnson GT. Restoring trust between patient and doctor. NEJM, 1990; 322:195-197.

40. Almy TP. The role of the primary physician in the health-care "industry." NEJM, 1981;304:225-228.

41. Radovsky SS. U.S. medical practice before Medicare and nowdifferences and consequences. NEJM, 1990;322:263-267.

42. McGregor M. Technology and the allocation of resources. NEJM, 1989;320:118-120.

43. Coile, RC. Technology and ethics: three scenarios for the 1990. Qual Rev Bull, 1990;16:202-208.

44. Batsakis J. Quality Assurance Programs in Pathology. Conference on Quality Assurance in Pathology and Laboratory Medicine: Perspectives for the 1990s. Washington, DC: College of American Pathologists, April 30, 1990.

45. Davis L. Fellowship of Surgeons: A History of the American College of Surgeons. Chicago, IL: American College of Surgeons, 1973.

46. Roberts JS, Coale JG, Redman RR. A history of the Joint Commission on Accreditation of Hospitals. JAMA, 1987;258:936-940.

47. Stephenson GW. The college's role in hospital standardization. Bull Am Coll Surg, 1981;66:17-29.

48. Coleman FC. The legislative history of Medicare. Skokie, IL: College of American Pathologists. Pathologist, 1981;35:156-158.

49. Mullen P. Joint Commission on Accreditation of Healthcare Organizations. Personal communication, February 23, 1990.

50. Washington report. Lab groups assess implementation of CLIA. Med Labs Obs, 1989;21:17-18.

51. Combined Washington staffs of the American Society of Clinical Pathologists and College of American Pathologists. Summary of Pertinent Provisions of the Omnibus Budget Reconciliation Act of 1989 (OBRA '89). Chicago and Northfield, IL: American Society of Clinical Pathologists and College of American Pathologists, 1990.

52. Laboratory Inspectors Manual. Skokie, IL: College of American Pathologists, 1989.

53. VanBremen, L. Chicago, IL: College of American Pathologists. Personnel communication, July 12, 1991.

54. Standards for Laboratory Accreditation. Chicago, IL: College of American Pathologists, 1988.

55. Mullen, PE. Chicago: Joint Commission on Accreditation of Healthcare Organizations, Personnel communication, April 29, 1991.

56. Laboratory Accreditation Program General Checklist. Skokie, IL: College of American Pathologists, Fall 1988.

57. Laboratory Accreditation Program General Checklist. Skokie, IL: College of American Pathologists, 1992.

58. The Joint Commission 1990 Accreditation Manual for Hospitals. Chicago, IL: Joint Commission on Accreditation of Healthcare Organizations, 1989.

59. Belk WP, Sunderman FW. A survey of the accuracy of chemical analyses in clinical laboratories. Am J Clin Pathol, 1947;17:853-861.

60. Dorsey DB. Evolving concepts of quality in laboratory practice. Arch Pathol Lab Med, 1989;113:1329-1334.

61. Skendzel LP, Hayson DJ, Civin WH. The 1949 College of American Pathologists survey revisited. Am J Clin Path, 1970;54:493-495.

62. Langdell, RD. College of American Pathologists laboratory improvement programs. Arch Pathol Lab Med, 1984;108:947-948.
63. Levey S, Jennings ER. The use of control charts in the clinical laboratory. Am J Clin Path, 1950;14:1059-1066.
64. Westgard JO, Barry LB, Hunt MR, Groth T. A multi-rule Shewhart chart for quality control in clinical chemistry. Clin Chem, 1981;27:493-501.
65. Feigenbaum AV. Total Quality Control. New York, NY: McGraw Hill International Book Co: 1951.
66. Eilers RJ. Total quality control for the medical laboratory. Southern Medical Journal, 1969;62:1362-1365.
67. Westgard JO, Barry PL. Total quality control: evolution of quality management systems. Lab Med, 1989;20:377-384.
68. National Office Staff. Chicago, IL: American Society of Clinical Pathologists, April 29, 1991.

2. Basic Definitions and Concepts of Laboratory Quality Management

DEFINITIONS AND CONCEPTS are at the heart of any discussion of laboratory quality management. The professional literature attests to the enormous effort that has gone into developing the language and methods of this growing organizational discipline.

It is revealing to note the changes in the language of laboratory quality management over the last decade. In 1981, the focus was on size, stability, reputation, leadership, knowledge, service, and quality control.[1] By 1986, interest had moved to quality assurance, a process which seemed very ambiguous at that time.[2] Then, the focus shifted to the principles of total quality management and continuous quality improvement—with shaky understanding and enthusiasm.[3] The latest new terms are quality assessment and improvement and improving organizational performance.[4,5] A chief purpose of this text is to clarify the definitions, programs, and processes of QC, QA, QI, TQM, and CQI and to demonstrate how to make practical application of these valuable concepts to the management of modern laboratory quality.

Although significant progress has been made over the past few years, the methods of assessing quality are still hampered by a lack of consensus on terminology among the rank and file of the medical laboratory industry. An agreement on the basic terminology of quality management requires modifying a significant segment of professional managerial opinion—and definite obstacles stand in the way of such consensus. Unfortunately, quality management concepts and definitions are subject to many interpretations because of the diverse personalities, multiple laboratory disciplines, differing managerial styles, constrained resources, and inherent complexity of medical laboratory operations that are involved in forming a consensus—that is a general or majority opinion.[6]

First and foremost, professional conservatism and natural subjective resistance pose significant obstacles to change. Second, laboratorians represent divergent disciplines of anatomic, clinical, and research pathology. These varying disciplines attract different personality types with their own decision making and managerial styles. Third, the financial and personnel resources needed to effect change in quality management are not forthcoming.

Finally, effective integration of modern quality management into the sheer complexity of the modern medical laboratory is theoretically very difficult. A truly comprehensive representation of the quality of any laboratory product would require a multifactorial equation solved simultaneously for several variables, including the entire range of severity of a given illness and all the different patient populations at risk—a complexity that is inherently repelling to even the most ener-getic manager.[7]

Because of so many barriers, there is less than a nationwide consensus. Without a consensus, quality management literature and conference dialogue is often imprecise and confusing. Because of unclear language, there is an industry-wide lack of understanding of quality management methods and a reticence among medical directors and laboratory managers to buy into the programs.[8]

As Richard Diamond pointed out in 1986, the ambiguity of quality management terminology is continually heightened by the proliferation of federal regulations and implementation of accreditation standards.[2] Recently, Diamond's observations have been corroborated by the inconsistent requirements of the Clinical Laboratory Improvement Amendments of 1988 (CLIA '88) and the rapidly progressive changes in the language of the Joint Commission for the Accreditation of Healthcare Organizations (JCAHO).[4,5] Regulatory directives and accreditation guidelines are focusing more and more directly on medical laboratories. This special emphasis includes the targeting of cytology laboratories, physician office laboratories, and ancillary (point-of-care) testing; direct access testing promises to become a future target. As they continually strive to improve medical quality, the regulating and accreditating agencies must provide uniform and precise concepts and definitions of quality in a coordinated manner. Because laboratorians are obliged to implement any new requirements, they must continually strive for clarification of new quality management concepts and terminology.

To contend with a quality-driven regulatory environment and customer-oriented market, laboratorians must be able to solve the operational problems at hand and to identify and take advantage of opportunities for quality improvement. To better understand these methods, a review of the basic definitions and concepts of laboratory quality management is provided in this chapter. The review also offers a general frame of reference for the development of models in later discussion. The information that follows is largely derived from JCAHO and CAP publications and is refined by gleanings from general managerial theory and practice.

GENERAL QUALITY MANAGEMENT DEFINITIONS AND MODELS

Healthcare industry refers to the entire medical-industrial complex of healthcare professionals, facilities, manufacturers, and suppliers—in both the private and public sectors—that provide health care in the United States. This large complex includes laboratories.

Healthcare laboratory refers to any anatomic pathology, clinical pathology, or clinical research laboratory activity that supports patient care. It can be hospital-based, physician office-based, or independent. Most often, it is simply referred to as "laboratory" in this text.

Anatomic pathology (AP) refers to the laboratory discipline that is dedicated primarily to the study and interpretive diagnosis of disease by gross and microscopic examination of tissues. This includes cytopathology, surgical, autopsy pathology, their subspecialties, and support services. For the sake of convenience, hematopathology (HP) is included under the category of AP in this text. Even though HP is traditionally located in the clinical pathology service, it is practiced as a diagnostic, interpretive procedure.

Clinical pathology (CP) refers to the laboratory discipline that is dedicated primarily to the study and diagnosis of disease by the gross, microscopic, and qualitative/quantitative analysis of body fluids and waste products. This includes chemistry, hematology, urinalysis, transfusion medicine, microbiology, immunology, their subspecialties, and support services. The phrase "clinical pathology" is also used as a more generic reference to the practice of all pathology and laboratory medicine as applied to clinical patients (eg, the American Society of Clinical Pathologists).

Clinical research laboratory (CRL) refers to either an AP- or CP-related laboratory activity that is engaged in medical scientific investigation. Such a laboratory may produce laboratory products that support patient care and that are used for diagnostic or therapeutic decisions. In this text, CRL activities should be assumed to be included in any mention of an AP or CP function. In any laboratory where there is a mixture of patient care (AP or CP) and CRL activities, the control and assurance of patient care activities take precedence for patient outcome and laboratory employee safety reasons.

Laboratory product or *service* refers to any contribution to patient care by a healthcare laboratory, including:

- An analytical test result, usually performed by the CP service
- An interpretive diagnosis, usually performed by the AP service and hematopathology in the CP service
- A therapeutic component or service, usually performed by the blood bank
- A patient/donor procedure such as phlebotomy or apheresis, usually performed by the phlebotomy section or blood bank
- A clerical product such as a written laboratory report or other laboratory record, usually performed by clerical support staff.

Laboratory function refers to any activity accomplished at any of the three primary operational levels of Donabedian[9]:

- Structure—The establishment and maintenance of operative and organizational resources
- Process—The application of interpretive, analytical, clerical, or other operative and organizational resources
- Outcome—The operational activities centered on managing the use of the interim laboratory end product or result, the resultant patient care, and the ultimate outcome of customer satisfaction.

In this text, the term "operational" is used as a global reference to all organizational- and operative-level laboratory activities.

- *Organizational* activities include all the administrative, infrastructural programs for team decision making, strategic planning, and assessing and improving quality that serve to maintain cultural strengths, prognosticate forseeable customer expectations, and achieve quality improvement.
- *Operative* activities include all the technical, interpretive, clerical, and support procedures directly related to the hands-onproduction of a laboratory end product. These procedures include quality control.

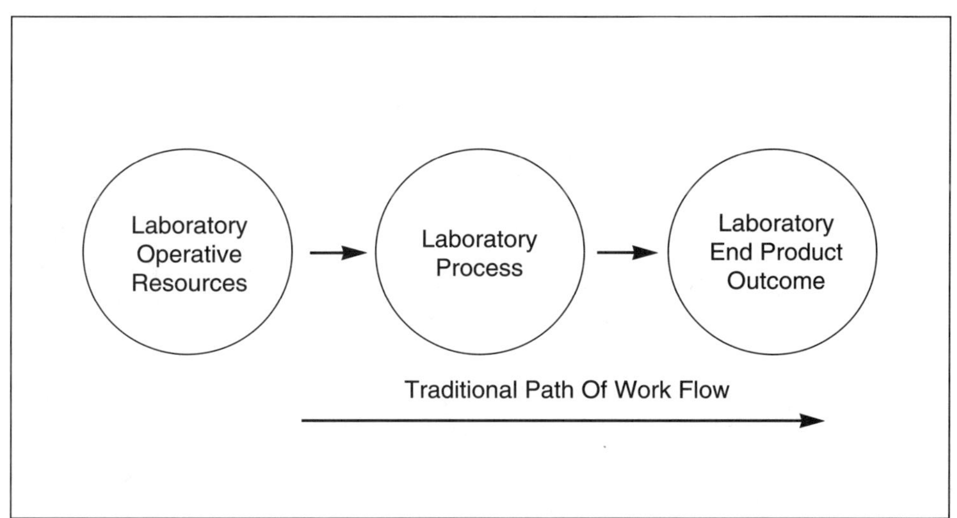

Figure 2.1 Flow model of traditional laboratory functions

Ideally, the three functional levels—structure, process, and outcome—should form a continuum of work flow and organizational communication, melding infrastructural administrative and "bench-level" operative activities. Each organization and its subunits carry on organizational and operative activities within each resource, process, and outcome operational level. These relationships should exist within the largest organizational unit down to the smallest subunit—unchanging in scope although diminishing from macroscopic to microscopic economies of scale. At the same time that there is so much internal exchange of information, there should also be an exchange of information with multiple external activities in the surrounding healthcare environment.

A traditional concept of laboratory function is illustrated in Figure 2.1. In laboratories prior to the 1980s, there tended to be a one-way flow of managerial information from the operative resource input level, to the process level, and on to the end product output level. Traditionally, technical-diagnostic skill was paramount and emphasis was placed on the quality of procedural performance as evidenced by accuracy, precision, sensitivity, and specificity based on statistical QC.[10] Additionally, the overall concept of structure was often restricted to operative resources, with very little attention directed to organizational resources.

Figure 2.1 also depicts the traditional path of work flow as progressing from the beginning of laboratory process to the final laboratory endproduct outcome. This flow usually was considered to begin from the time that a specimen and test request was received by the laboratory to the time that a laboratory end product was completed and sent to the patient chart. The dashed line indicates that operative resource

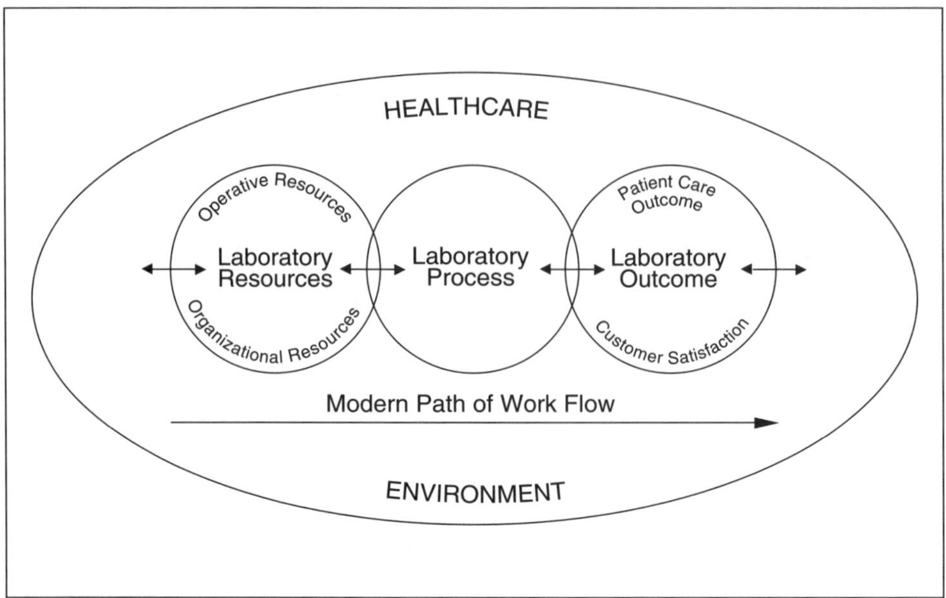

Figure 2.2 Flow model of modern laboratory functions

management was only occasionally included in the scheme; organizational resource management was almost always ignored as part of the path.

A modern laboratory design has emerged in today's healthcare industry. Figure 2.2 illustrates a Venn model of the ideal modern laboratory, where emphasis is placed not only on laboratory procedural and end product quality but also on the quality of all resources (organizational and operative), endproduct utilization, patient care outcome, and customer satisfaction. We must guage postlaboratory quality through joint laboratorian-clinician assessment of the needs and satisfaction of the patient, as well as other laboratory customers.

As indicated by the model in Figure 2.2, for this organization-wide approach to be successful, there must be:

- Bi-directional communication
- Internal integration of the three basic laboratory functions, as well as external integration with the clinical environment
- Total quality control and coordination of all resource, process, and outcome management activities.

Such enhanced communication and control can be accomplished only through bidirectional flow of information as depicted in Figure 2.2. As also indicated, the path of work flow moves from the initiation of the very

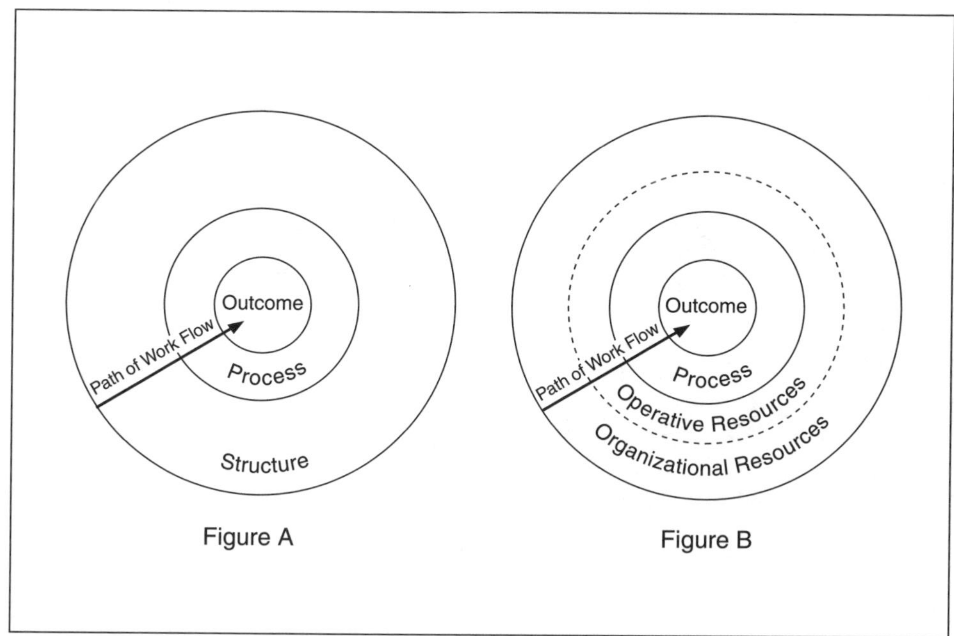

Figure 2.3 Venn model of the three basic operational functions for any size laboratory organization

earliest resource management activities to the final patient care and customer satisfaction outcomes.

Figure 2.3A illustrates a Venn model of all laboratory functions. The outer circle represents structure (resource) functions. The middle circle represents process (technical or diagnostic) activities. The innermost circle, the center, represents the ultimate objective of outcome (customer satisfaction). The outermost circle represents the earliest occurring function. Each successive function is represented by a circle located closer to the center. Thus, all three major laboratory functions or activities are represented in their sequential order of occurrence.

The structure and process circles are represented as larger and thicker than the outcome circle. The thickness of an individual circle reflects relative volume or complexity of procedures: the thicker the circle, the more numerous or complex the managerial and technical procedures that are involved.

As already implied, the radius of this circular paradigm represents the dimension of procedural sequence. This path of work flow begins with the outermost circle and then proceeds toward the center. Diagramatically, work flows centripetally from the outer circle representing resource management, moving through process management, until the work flow reaches the final circle and the common center, representing outcome management and work flow completion. Figure 2.3B expands the circle

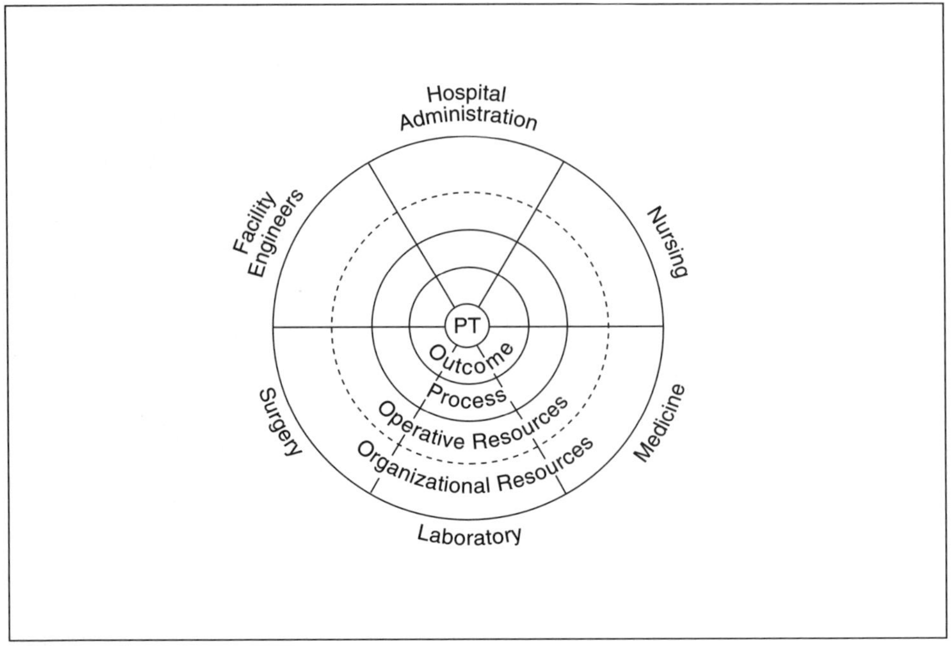

Figure 2.4 Venn model of the three operational functions distributed hospital-wide

representing structure into the two component parts of operative and organizational resources.

Figure 2.4 divides the basic, circular Venn model into several sections or wedges that represent various multidisciplinary divisions, departments, or services that comprise a typical hospital organization. The hospital units depicted in this example are the laboratory, internal medicine, surgery, nursing, facility engineers, and the hospital administration. The model illustrates that the function of any hospital unit—regardless of its size or position in the organizational hierarchy—consists of the same three elements of structure, process, and outcome. This is true regardless if the unit is at the same departmental level as the laboratory, is at a lower service level, or is at a higher, administrative echelon. This cellular organizational model resembles an organic structure, as opposed to the traditional rank and file mechanical structural approach. This sociobiological perspective becomes important when the discussion turns to TQM and CQI. The patient (PT)—or any other external or internal customer of importance—resides in the very center of this organic model.

Figure 2.5A is a modification of the previous Venn diagram. A hierarchical pyramid can be formed by removing the pie-shaped wedge from the Venn circles and flattening the wedge at the base. Again, the

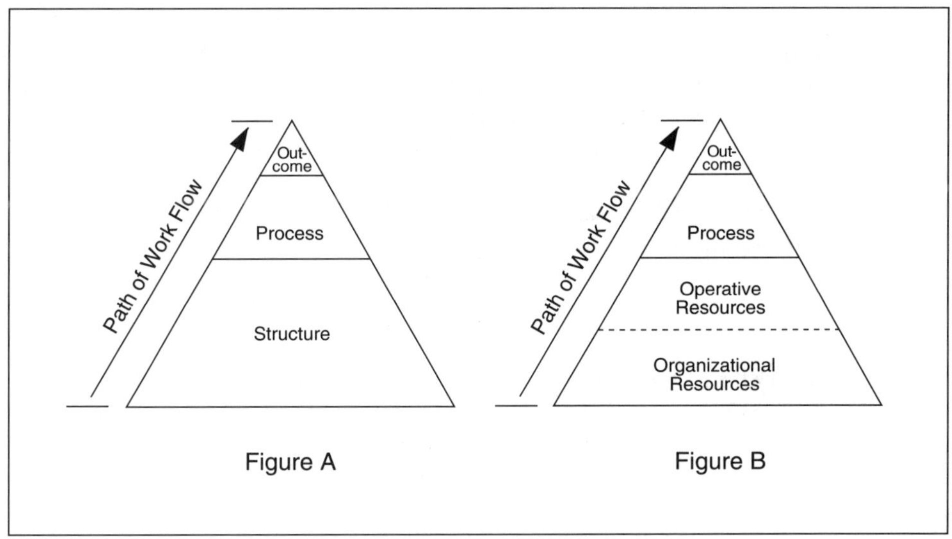

Figure 2.5 Model of the three basic laboratory functions based on a hierarchical design

thickness of a hierarchical level reflects procedural volume and the position of a level reflects a relationship to the path of work flow—reminiscent of Maslow's pyramidal hierarchy of needs.

The most basic organizational functional requirements are symbolized at the base of the pyramid, the most fundamental being realization of employee behavioral needs. The most refined organizational outcomes are symbolized at the peak of the pyramid, the most ideal being actualization of continuous improvement of the organization's product as evidenced by customer satisfaction.

A side of this pyramidal model is diagramatically the same as the radius of the circular model of Figures 2.3 and 2.4. As with the radius of the Venn diagrams, one pyramidal side conceptually equates with the laboratory path of work flow. The base of the model can be used to represent the organization as an entire unit or the base can be divided to represent parts of the organization, including services, sections, teams, or individual laboratory products. Figure 2.5B expands on the first pyramidal model, separating structure into its two component parts.

Laboratory path of work flow, or product life cycle, refers to the entire span of organizational and operative procedural events that occur in support of the selection, preparation, and utilization of a laboratory product. The total path of work flow includes all organizational and operative activities, defined as follows:

- Organizational resource work flow activities incorporate all organizational effectiveness, planning, and quality surveillance path of work flow segments—beginning with the former.

- Operative resource work flow activitiesincorporate all operative resource, process, and outcome management path of work flow segments. In laboratory literature, process is divided into periods that are referred to as pre, intra, and postlaboratory and as pre-, intra-, and postanalytical. This text divides process into pre, intra, and post*determinative* periods, in order to encompass both the analytical functions of clinical pathology and the diagnostic functions of anatomic pathology.

GENERAL QUALITY MANAGEMENT CONCEPTS AND DEFINITIONS

Healthcare laboratory management is a complex topic and a potential controversy begins with its nomenclature. The word management is derived from the Latin word, *manus*, meaning "hand," and is defined as "the judicious use of means to accomplish an end."[6] Used as such, the word denotes the broadest concept of general organizational control. In actual practice, there are two levels of management in the majority of laboratories—operative management and administrative management.

Understanding the relationship between the two general terms, management and administration, helps to clarify the more specific intricacies of quality management. A typical obstacle to understanding the relationship between the two general terms is their dictionary definitions; at first glance, management and administration seem confusingly synonymous. Another obstacle to clarity is colloquial misrepresentation: middle managers are traditionally identified as "the management" while top level managers are considered "the administration." This common usage reflects an unfortunate polarization of two areas of organizational activity that are actually very closely related and should work in unison. As a result, even though the modern organizational goal is to bring management and administration together to form a cohesive, decision-making entity, the actual relationship is too often an adversarial "us" versus "them" situation.

Because of some confusion associated with the two terms, the following definitions are purposefully presented *de rigueur*—using precise descriptions of the two echelons of laboratory quality management. Exceptions to the rule are also given.

Webster clearly distinguishes between the subcategories of operative management and administrative management.[6] Whereas the single term, management, is used as an all-encompassing designation for decision making and action taking at all organizational levels, the subcategories of operative management and administrative management are more specialized indicators of control and assessment activities, respectively.[11,12]

Operative management. In its simplest form, operative management consists of methods by which the manager "directly" controls the performance of a group of employees or other operative-level resources. This group comprises a management center. A laboratory management center can be characterized in terms of the three levels of laboratory functional activities—structure, process, and outcome.

- Regarding structure, a laboratory operative management center usually:

  1. is of sectional size or smaller (eg, chemistry, histology, or secretarial pool)
  2. specializes in a specific interpretive, technical, or support discipline (eg, chemical analysis, histopathologic diagnosis, or typing)
  3. ensures the best quality of operative resource management.

- Regarding process, a laboratory operative management center:

  1. applies operative resources to achieve specific procedures
  2. accomplishes certain related professional interpretive, technical, or support procedures that are focused on some specific type of patient-care support (eg, blood gas analysis, tumor diagnosis, or report production)
  3. is responsible for maintaining the integrity of the process from the receipt of a laboratory product request and specimen to distribution of the final laboratory product, as long as the specimen or product remains within the immediate working area
  4. operates on the basis of authority and direction of technically-focused plans that are narrow in scope and procedural in intent (eg, laboratory procedure manual, or standing operating procedure)[a]
  5. ensures the best quality of specific laboratory methods, techniques, and results over a comparatively short period of time.

- Regarding *outcome*, a laboratory operative management center is expected to produce laboratory products of the best possible

[a] Contrary to popular opinion—even in the military—the phrase SOP refers to "standing" operating procedure not "standard" operating procedure. This phrase is borrowed from the military penchant for titles, abbreviations, and acronyms. Army Regulation 310-50, the official glossary for Army military words and phrases, lists SOP as referring to "standing operating procedure," which implies that the given written procedure is in effect but is always open to revision.

quality, including end products that meet predetermined specifications for appropriate clinical laboratory product utilization.

In this text, QC is considered an operative managerial activity that does not stand alone. QC must be an integral part of every operative procedure that is practiced at every level of resource, process, and outcome management.

In reality, operative managerial activities are seldom practiced as purely as described above—the descriptions serve only as a working model. In fact, operative management can be practiced at any organizational level in which a laboratory management center requires direct control. Such focused managerial activity even extends to the top administrative management level where the administrator directly controls the operative (hands-on) activities of the primary administrative staff.

Administrative management. The word administration is derived from the Latin word, *administrare*, meaning "to serve," (ie, as a public servant). Administration is defined as "the phase of business management that plans, organizes, and controls the activities of an organization for the accomplishment of its objectives in the long run."[6]

In its simplest form, administrative management consists of methods by which the corporate leader "indirectly" controls the performance of several management centers and controls organizational-level resources. Several management centers comprise a *management system*. A laboratory management system can also be characterized in terms of structure, process, and outcome.

- Regarding *structure*, a laboratory administrative management system:

    1. consists of several, combined operative management centers that represent differing but interrelated medically-oriented scientific and support disciplines
    2. is usually a service or department-sized activity, such as an anatomical or clinical pathology service or a department of pathology
    3. is broad-based in its specialized technical orientation
    4. ensures the best quality of organizational resources to support quality assessment, strategic planning, and organizational effectiveness programs.

- Regarding *process*, a laboratory administrative management system:

    1. accomplishes a matrix of interrelated medical, technical, and

support programs that are directed at managing a wide range of operational activities at the organizational infrastructural level
2. operates on the basis of authority and direction of regulations, guidelines, and written policy that are technical in nature but very broad in scope and regulatory in intent
3. ensures the best quality of process throughout the entire life cycle of the laboratory product, including clinical selection of laboratory products over a long range period of time.

- Regarding *outcome*, a laboratory administrative management system:

1. assures the quality of all laboratory end products
2. monitors and assesses the quality of clinical utilization in concert with the clinical staff as evidenced by patient outcome and overall customer satisfaction.

In this text, QA (or QI) is considered an administrative program, along with other programs of the TQM system. This process of indirect monitoring and evaluating quality would be integrated into every operative activity and organizational program.

The administrator's quality management responsibilities are on a grander scale than those of the operative manager. Although amounting to indirect control, the responsibilities include design, coordination, evaluation, and improvement of quality. One leading objective of administration is to optimize the yield of the entire laboratory organization's resources. At this managerial level, the administrator should focus on laboratory-wide effectiveness; this requires attention to resources, processes, markets, and customers—all potential targets for quality management surveillance.

Administrative activities are not practiced exclusively at the top management level of the organization. Just as operative management activities can be carried on at the top management level, some administrative functions are routinely exercised at any sectional (or lower) organizational level. Examples of such administrative functions include gathering, evaluating, acting on, assessing, and reporting quality management data at the section level for department-wide administrative surveillance requirements. However, with even the broadest delegation or empowerment of administrative duties, the ultimate responsibility for these top management functions still rests on the shoulders of the chief director or administrator at the highest organizational level.

As implied above, the manager's ultimate responsibility is to control, either directly (operatively) or indirectly (administratively). In the current era of TQM and enhanced organizational behavior, some

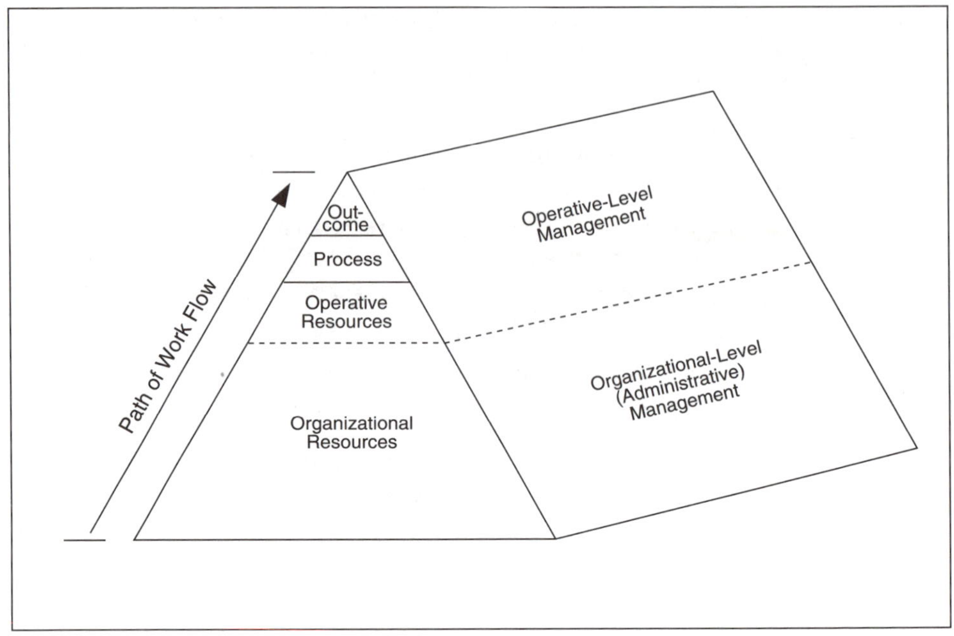

Figure 2.6 Hierarchical model of the three basic laboratory functions as related to the two fundamental levels of laboratory management

individuals have difficulty accepting the word "control" when applied to a managerial setting. Other words or phrases, such as to influence, to contribute direction, to orchestrate, to conduct, to facilitate, or to enlist cooperation are often considered more desirable. Such understanding, benevolent management styles are very important and reasonable, but remember one rule: there must be a leader. Someone, over all, has to be in charge of coordination and communication to see that the organizational values, mission, goals, and objectives are achieved. Using one analogy, the experienced jockey must "control" his mount, no matter how "soft" his handling (ie, *manus*) might be.[13]

Ultimately, some degree of direct, unmodified control must be exerted when difficult decisions concerning laboratory product quality arise—as when a tie vote has to be broken. The manager must be ready to assume absolute, direct control when necessary.

Figure 2.6 expands the triangular model of Figure 2.5 to depict the two major levels of laboratory management. The scope and volume of organizational procedures can be much greater than that of operative management—operative management can be just the tip of the proverbial laboratory management iceberg. Based on the above development of operative and administrative managerial concepts, there are the following quality management terms.

Laboratory quality management is any managerial activity aimed at ensuring the control and improvement of the quality of any laboratory product. The term refers to all aspects of QC, QI, TQM, and CQI.

The *quality* of a laboratory product or service is a fundamental characteristic of an analytical test, a consultative diagnosis, a component preparation, a patient/donor procedure, a clerical procedure—or any other laboratory support procedure—that is monitored at some phase of the life cycle (path of work flow). Such a characteristic must ultimately satisfy the needs of the customer—any customer. The customer is any internal (eg, employee) or external recipient of a laboratory resource.

If the basic problem is that a quality of the resource, process, or outcome can vary, to what measurable degree can that quality vary? Traditionally, laboratorians have concentrated on the variable quality of the laboratory end product, paying most attention to its related technical process. Likewise, clinicians have been concerned with the variability of the laboratory end product as it affects the process of patient care and patient-care outcome. In reality, equal attention must be paid to the quality of the laboratory product from both laboratory and clinical perspectives at all three functional levels (ie, structure, process, or outcome).

Quality control (QC) is an operative managerial method for controlling the quality of any laboratory product at any specific phase of the laboratory process of any of the three functional levels. If the basic problem is that quality varies, then how much can it be allowed to vary while still being maintained or controlled within acceptable limits? QC is performed on-site, at the bench level, and at the time the procedural activity occurs or very shortly afterward. This control is accomplished by monitoring and evaluating the degree of conformance of any procedure to its design specifications.

Usually control in CP is accomplished by monitoring the performance of standardized analytes and by statistically evaluating the performance. Control in AP is usually performed by peer review. Initially focused on process control in CP and outcome control in AP, QC is now being applied more universally to all three functional levels of laboratory operations in all laboratory areas.

Peer control, a form of QC, is a peer review process that provides a means of controlling the quality of cognitive, interpretive diagnosis at the operative management level. Peer control consists of the examination of an initial pathologist's diagnostic interpretation—along with relevant case materials (eg, tissue preparations and medical records)—by a second pathologist. If the review is accomplished by a panel of peers, the process becomes more "quality diagnosis by consensus" than controlled diagnosis quality.

Peer control can also be used for surveying the interpretive results of nonpathologists by members of their peer group (eg, technologists, cytotechnologists). Again, such a review assesses the results of cognitive, interpretive laboratory procedures.

Total quality management (TQM) is a system of anticipatory or preventive quality management programs that emphasizes the use of systematic team building, planning and assessment throughout all organizational and operative levels of function. Based on the early statistical quality management theories of the 1930s and the behavioral management theories of the 1950s, TQM was pioneered by James W. Juran (among other individuals) in post-World War II Japan, where it was first known as "company-wide" control. This omnibus approach to quality management is the centerpiece for the JCAHO *Agenda for Change* and is being adopted by increasing segments of the healthcare industry. The three interrelated, component programs of TQM are:

- quality actualization—abbreviated in this text as QAc
- quality anticipation—abbreviated in this text as QAn
- quality surveillance—abbreviated in this text as QI, unless QA is referred to historically.

Quality actualization is an administrative program designed to systematically create and sustain an organizational culture committed to maximum effectiveness in decision making and quality improvement—to ensure maximum organizational effectiveness in striving for CQI. The program should create optimal conditions for organization-wide decision making. It includes education, training, maintenance, and improvement of skills in individual (self) and organizational (interpersonal) awareness, communication, cooperation, negotiation, decision making, participative management, and team building.

Quality anticipation is an administrative program designed to systematically formulate and manage organizational research, development, and strategic planning projects for quality improvement—to ensure that there are short-, medium-, and long-range plans for all laboratory operations aimed at CQI. This program should include activities for researching and developing new missions and strategies based on customer need. It also includes managing an agenda of established short-, medium-, and long-range goals, objectives, taskings and milestones.

Quality surveillance is an administrative program designed to systematically monitor, evaluate, act on, and assess quality improvement at all organizational and operative levels on an ongoing schedule—to ensure systematic monitoring and evaluating of indicators of quality for any laboratory product or service in any phase of its life cycle. Known in the 1980s as quality assurance and, in the 1990s, as quality assessment and improvement, this program is easily institutionalized by using an analytical approach of which there are several successful examples (eg, the JCAHO ten-step process).

- Quality assurance (QA) was the quality surveillance program of the 1980s. During the 1980s, the JCAHO introduced QA and the ten-step process to institutionalize the principles of systematic quality surveillance and TQM. It was the archetype of surveillance programs and the direct predecessor of QI and PI. If a basic problem is that quality varies, requiring a need for quality control, then how successful is the administrative management of the control procedures? QA answers that question. Unfortunately, QA became known as a remedy of problems and was practiced in an incremental fashion.

  There are several complex control processes to keep under surveillance. For example, laboratory quality involves selecting (requesting) the appropriate laboratory procedure for the given clinical situation, then correctly performing the required laboratory procedures, and then appropriately and correctly utilizing (clinically applying) the laboratory end product for the given clinical situation.

  To achieve a surveillance of such a complicated system, the QA program monitors and evaluates the caliber of patient-care support, comparing measurable indicator data against laboratory and clinical criteria, standards, and thresholds. A complete QA program assesses the quality of all aspects of laboratory operations, including resources, processes, and outcomes.

  The QA process of monitoring and evaluating quality should be integrated into every organizational resource, operative resource, process, and outcome management activity. The program should be considered an essential aspect of an organization's nervous system, facilitating multichannel communication and homeostatic feedback.

  Peer assurance, a form of QA, is a peer review process that provides a means of surveillance of the operative control of interpretive diagnosis at the administrative management level. Peer assurance consists of the examination of the peer control findings by a review panel or QA committee. Peer assurance can also be used for surveying the interpretive results of nonpathologists by their peer groups. Again, such a review is usually by committee and assesses the findings of peer control of cognitive, interpretive laboratory procedures.

- Quality assessment and improvement (QI) has become the quality surveillance process of choice. Since 1987, the JCAHO goal has been to complete the transition from QA to the more proactive concept of QI. This is a change of JCAHO emphasis from incremental problem solving to the broader scope of continuous improvement of nonproblematic processes that are still worthy of being performed better.

Founded on the QA tenets of monitoring and evaluating quality problems, the QI approach is aimed more specifically at assessing and improving the quality of processes. The JCAHO introduced QI in the 1992 *Accreditation Manual for Hospitals (AMH)* and plans that it be fully institutionalized by 1994 in the form of "improving organizational performance"(PI). PI will remain the centerpiece of JCAHO transition over the next several years.

Two other programs, Utilization Review and Risk Management, are also considered as TQM components. They are discussed only briefly in this text.

Utilization review (UR) is an ancillary quality management program designed for hospital-wide monitoring and evaluating of the utilization of healthcare resources. UR is usually a hospital committee function into which resource utilization data is fed for evaluation and action. Medical appropriateness of utilization is a quality of key importance.

Risk management (RM) is another ancillary quality management program of "clinical and administrative activities designed to identify, evaluate, and reduce the risk of patient injury associated with care. The full scope of risk management functions encompass activities in healthcare organizations that are intended to conserve financial resources from loss."[8] The major goal of RM is to identify adverse events, limit malpractice liability payments, and preclude any increase of malpractice liability insurance premiums.

QI and RM are interrelated in that both seek to reduce patient risk. Quality surveillance is aimed at risk prevention through anticipatory evaluation of the adequacy of quality management measures. RM is devoted largely to liability limitation or "damage control" through retrospective surveillance for adverse incidents in which a patient, an employee, or some other customer experiences injury or damage. The JCAHO emphasizes the importance of the managerial linkage between surveillance and RM.

Continuous Quality Improvement (CQI), a concept largely attributed to W. Edwards Deming when he served as a consultant in post-World War II Japan, is an important adjunct to TQM. CQI is a managerial process based on the principles of organizational commitment to continuous improvement. The prime goal of CQI is continuous quality improvement as evidenced by customer satisfaction. This process should energize an organizational drive toward total laboratory operational excellence.

CQI can be implemented by use of the QAn, QAc, and QI programs of the TQM system of administrative-level managerial programs. Coupled with TQM, the goal of CQI should be an organization-wide commitment to improvement that marshalls all the strengths and assets of organizational and operative resource, process, and outcome management. TQM becomes the means; CQI becomes the ultimate end—a never-ending quest for organizational excellence.

REFERENCES

1. Reece RL. What to look for in a quality laboratory. The Pathologist, 1981;35:203-207.
2. Diamond I. Quality assurance and/or quality control. Arch Path Lab Med, 1986;110:875-876.
3. Conference on Quality Assurance in Pathology and Laboratory Medicine: Perspectives for the 1990s. Washington, DC: College of American Pathologists; April 29 - May 2, 1990.
4. 1992 Joint Commission Accreditation Manual for Hospitals. Oakbrook Terrace, IL: Joint Commission on Accreditation of healthcare Organizations, 1991.
5. 1994 Joint Commission Accreditation Manual for Hospitals. Oakbrook Terrace, IL: Joint Commission on Accreditation of healthcare Organizations, 1993.
6. Webster's Third International Dictionary of the English Language. Springfield, MA: Merriam Webster, Inc, 1984.
7. Klint RB and Long HW. Toward a definition of quality. Phys Exec, 1989;15:7-11.
8. Hungate RW. Lessons from industry. Phys Exec, Jan-Feb 1989:13.
9. Donabedian A. Evaluating the quality of medical care. Milbank Memorial Fund Quarterly, 1966;44:166-203.
10. Barr JT. Clinical laboratory utilization. In Davis BGH, Bishop ML, Mass D, eds. Clinical Laboratory Science: Strategies for Practice. Philadelphia, Pa: JB Lippincott, 1989.
11. Drucker PE. Management: Tasks, Responsibilities, Practices. New York, NY: Harper and Row, 1973.
12. Brown DS. Management Concepts and Policies. Washington, DC: National Defense Univ, 1989.
13. Brown DS. Personal communication. July 20, 1990.

3. Healthcare Laboratory Operations and Quality Management Programs

CHAPTER TWO ADDRESSED the basic definitions and concepts of healthcare quality management in an introductory nature, covering only selected topics with a very broad, generic approach. This third chapter further examines the descriptions and modeling of all major quality management activities in much more expanded and integrated detail.

QUALITY OF HEALTHCARE LABORATORY OPERATIONS

Quality is derived from the Latin *qualitas or qualis*, meaning "of what kind" or "how constituted."[1] The quality of any entity is a characteristic of inherent value of structure, function, or utility—an element of goodness or excellence that is often appreciated only through the eyes of the beholder. Consequently, the definition of laboratory quality can be vague and elusive. The following statement has been heard at many professional medical meetings: "It is difficult to get a general agreement on what constitutes quality in medicine."[2] The assessment of quality often depends on who is making the judgment and against whose standards that quality is being measured—be it in the eyes or standards of the pathologist, the primary care provider, the government, the court, the public, the employer, the payor, or the patient.

Dictionaries define quality as "a characteristic, property, or peculiar and essential character; a degree of excellence" or as "an essential character; a degree of conformance to a standard."[1,3] So defined, quality can be equally objective and subjective and is, very often, multifactorial.[4] To measure quality in the laboratory, we must be able to identify quality more succinctly.

The quality of health care has been discussed in professional literature as long ago as the Code of Hammurabi of 1800 B.C. Babylonia.[5] The quality of patient care still remains the common denominator for all healthcare quality management concepts—including laboratory support—but neither *Stedman's Medical Dictionary* nor *Dorland's Illustrated Medical Dictionary* defines quality.[6,7] In 1986, the American Medical Association (AMA) published a statement that quality health care should:[8]

- Be based on accepted principles of medical science and proficient use of appropriate technological and professional resources
- Be sensitive to the stress and anxiety generated by illness and be concerned for the patient's overall welfare
- Be provided in a timely manner—without undue delay, inappropriate curtailment, or unnecessary prolongation
- Achieve the informed cooperation and participation of the patient during the healthcare process, including decisions regarding that process
- Efficiently use the available technological resources to achieve the desired treatment
- Promote good health, prevent disease or disability, and detect and treat illness as early as possible
- Produce maximum possible improvement in the patient's physiological function, emotional and intellectual performance, and physical comfort at the earliest possible time
- Be sufficiently documented in the patient's medical record to enable continuity of care and peer evaluation.

The JCAHO states that the quality of patient care is:[9]

> the degree to which patient-care services increase the probability of desired patient outcomes and reduce the probability of undesired outcomes, given the current state of knowledge. Potential components of quality include the following: accessibility of care, appropriateness of care, continuity of care, effectiveness of care, efficacy of care, patent perspective issues, safety of the care environment, and timeliness of care.

Citing the 1990 *Consolidated Standards Manual* of the JCAHO, the CAP defines medical laboratory quality as:[10]

> the degree of adherence to generally recognized contemporary standards of practice and achievement of anticipated outcomes for a particular service, procedure, diagnosis, or clinical problem.

The definition of quality used in this text expands on the AMA, JCAHO, and CAP definitions and borrows from the theory and practice of quality management in the nonhealthcare industry, as follows:[9,10,11]

- *Laboratory product or service quality* is a fundamental characteristic of an analytical test, consultative diagnosis, product preparation, patient/donor procedure, clerical procedure, or any other operational procedure that can be monitored at some phase of its path of work flow (life cycle).

- Such a characteristic *must ultimately satisfy the need of the customer*. Defining the customer and the customer's needs is the challenge. Is the customer the patient, the attending physician, or the laboratory employee? They are all customers. Of the three, who is the most important? The answer depends on the issue at hand. When it comes to patient care, the patient is most important. If the subject is standards of practice, the pathologist and the attending clinical physician are most important. If it is an issue of laboratory safety, the employee is the most important customer. Then, there are potentially other customers, including ancillary support, higher level administrative support, commercial supply and manufacturing, and community activities.

Until the publication of the JCAHO 1992 *Accreditation Manual for Hospitals (AMH)*, the JCAHO was characterizing the overall caliber of any aspect of patient care in terms of two essential subcategories: quality and medical appropriateness.[12,13] This JCAHO parlance contributed an unfortunate overlap of terms since the term "quality" was used as both an overall concept of constituted value and a subcategory of patient-care assessment; this semantic problem has been resolved by the 1992 revisions of the JCAHO accreditation standards.

First, the JCAHO has considered the quality of patient care as meaning performing a procedure correctly. In this regard, laboratory quality denotes accuracy, efficiency, and other measurable characteristics of resource procurement; process performance; and the ultimate provision of a laboratory product for clinical utilization. If these three facets of product production were managed well, the product would be of the highest inherent technical quality and would result in optimum support of patient-care outcome.

These precepts are still true today. For example, the laboratory product must be accurate, precise, specific, sensitive, safe, and timely for the patient—whether it is a chemical profile, a surgical diagnosis, a unit of O-positive packed red cells, or a clerical record.

Second, the JCAHO has stressed that medical appropriateness means performing the correct procedure. In the laboratory setting, it means selecting and utilizing the correct laboratory procedure in support of a diagnostic and therapeutic patient care procedure. The dictionary definition of appropriate is "specifically adapted to a special purpose [patient care] or condition [state of health]."[3] Thus, medical appropriateness refers to the effectiveness of professional judgement leading to a desirable patient-care outcome. If professional judgement or interpretation is performed correctly, patient-care outcome will be optimum under the given clinical circumstances. Then, the correct patient-care support will have been provided.

Although not emphasized as strongly as in previous editions of the *AMH*, the usefulness of medical appropriateness as a quality indicator of patient care provider proficiency is still valid today. For example, every laboratory product must be selected and utilized by the clinician based on appropriate medical indications and contraindications. Likewise, any pathologist's professional, diagnostic interpretation must be appropriate to the medical situation based on clinical indications and contraindications. Other areas of laboratory product preparation that warrant the consideration of medical appropriateness will be discussed later.

Medical appropriateness is characterized by the efficacy of the patient care provided and the professional effectiveness of the laboratory care provider. Judging the degree of appropriateness requires that a model exist for each medical condition. Such a model should describe the problem, the patient's characteristics, the diagnostic options, the recommended treatment options, the possible outcomes, and all associated risks and contraindications.[14] In other words, patient care should be provided to the correct patient for the correct clinical indications—without significant, overriding contraindications that threaten life, limb, or disfigurement—and with the best possibility of remission, rehabilitation, recovery, and return to a productive, desirable life.

Assessing The Quality of Laboratory Function

Avedis Donabedian, a modern theorist in the practice of medical quality management, helped point the way toward quality assessment for medical laboratorians. In 1966, he defined three key elements for assessing the quality of medical activities—structure, process, and outcome—the same three elements that have been used earlier in this text to characterize laboratory functional activities.[15,16,17] Since the JCAHO has adopted Donabedian's approach for quality assessment, the component elements warrant further definition and translation into laboratory quality management terms.[18,19] Characteristics of these three elements areas follows:

Structure is input—the physical resources and organizational setting used to provide laboratory patient-care support for diagnosis or therapy. Donabedian divided structure into the two subcategories of organizational resources and operative resources.

Organizational resources are all the administrative-level programs and activities that promote intra- and extraorganizational quality assessment, planning, decision making, and communication. Examples of these resources include the following programs:

- Quality surveillance: monitoring and assessing indicators for quality improvement—described by JCAHO in 1992 as "quality assessment and improvement" (QI) and in 1994 as "improving organizational performance" (PI)
- Quality anticipation (QAn): formulating values, mission, vision, strategies, goals, objectives, and taskings for short-, medium-, and long-range quality improvement
- Quality actualization (QAc): team decision making focused on customer satisfaction and quality improvement.

Organizational resources comprise the laboratory's administrative infrastructure. The quality of these administrative resources can be assessed in terms of the following measurable characteristics:

- Quality surveillance through choice of quality indicators, assessment of indicators, communication, and use of lessons learned from quality surveillance, or any other aspect of the improvement process
- Quality anticipation through research, development, and implementation of quality improvement projects
- Quality actualization through bolstering personnel morale and commitment to quality improvement, personnel training in quality management skills, personnel actions, awards, and other incentives, and participative decision making to resolve opportunities for improvement.

Operative resources include all physical components that are directly applied to perform operative-level processes. Examples of these resources are:

- Organizational structure—including staff position relationships and responsibilities, work flow elements, and information flow elements
- Workload

- Technical, clerical, and managerial plans and procedures—based on clinically-derived diagnostic and therapeutic protocols
- Staff—including personnel, training, and methods of performance evaluation
- Technical, clerical, and other managerial supplies
- Information management methods and devices—including computers and other means of electronic and mechanical handling of data
- Equipment
- Facility
- Budget.

The quality of these operative resources can be assessed in terms of the following measurable characteristics:

- Organizational structure
    1. alignment of staff positions and responsibilities
    2. sequence of work flow elements
    3. sequence of information flow elements.
- Workload
    1. volume in raw or weighted units
    2. nature of specimen, request, and laboratory end
    3. product delivery and handling.
- Personnel
    1. type of staffing positions
    2. staff position responsibilities
    3. number of filled positions
    4. productivity
    5. availability.
- Plans and procedures
    1. state-of-the-art methods
    2. compliance with workload requirements and clinical protocols

3. up-to-date review
4. safety.

- Supplies
    1. delivery time
    2. condition on delivery
    3. inventory
    4. storage
    5. safety.

- Information management
    1. computer hardware and software support
    2. archival capacity
    3. degree of integration
    4. other means of information handling.

- Equipment
    1. instrument function
    2. machinery function
    3. safety.

- Facility
    1. space
    2. environmental control
    3. safety.

- Budget and funding
    1. compliance with expenditure limits
    2. cost-effectiveness.

Process is action—the application of operative laboratory resources to procedural plans, resulting in a laboratory end product. Process activities include all aspects of interpretive, technical, clerical, or other operative or administrative procedures that affect the efficiency and effectiveness of patient care. For assessment purposes, process can be expressed in terms of the following measurable characteristics:

- Medical appropriateness of selection of laboratory product

- Specimen integrity
- Precision
- Accuracy
- Specificity
- Sensitivity
- Turnaround time (TAT).

Outcome is result—the laboratory end product and the ultimate effect of the medical laboratory product on the patient and other customers. For assessment purposes, outcome can be expressed in terms of the following measurable characteristics:

- Laboratory end product outcome
    1. quality of function (eg, blood component efficacy)
    2. medical appropriateness of utilization
- Clinical procedure outcome (eg, patient-care outcome)
- Nonclinical procedure outcome (eg, employee safety)
- Customer satisfaction outcome
    1. internal customer satisfaction (eg, laboratory employee)
    2. external customer satisfaction
        a. patient
        b. attending physician
        c. other clinical staff
        d. other hospital departments
        e. merchandise supplier
        f. hospital administrator
        g. funding body
        h. governing body
        i. community.

Examples of two general categories of customer satisfaction outcome are patient-care outcome and laboratory employee safety.

- Patient-care outcome includes all aspects of patient recovery—remission of signs and symptoms, restoration of the patient's physical or mental health status, and resumption of a productive life of optimal quality.

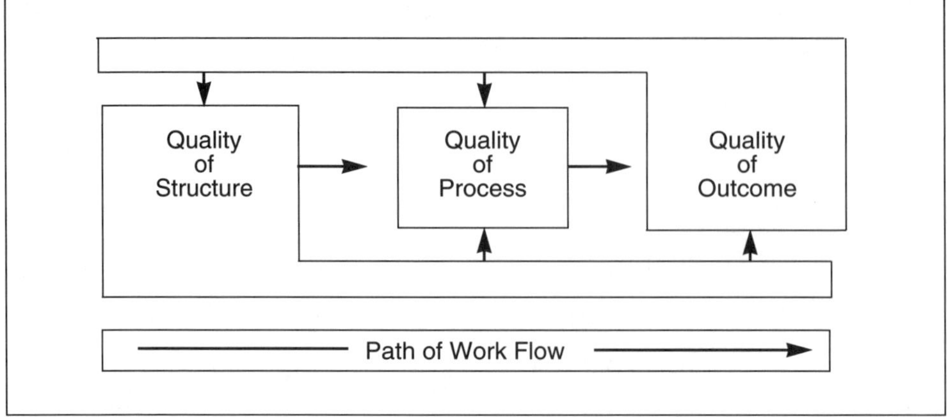

Figure 3.1 Flow model showing the basic relationship of the three elements of quality assessment

Patient safety is a special characteristic of the quality of patient-care outcome. As is seen later, safety is an important factor throughout the life cycle of the laboratory product—from ensuring that bed rails are in place following a phlebotomy procedure to ensuring that a unit of packed red cells is free of hepatitis virus before a transfusion.

- Laboratory employee safety outcome focuses on a work environment that is safe from any threat to any employee's health or general welfare. This includes any laboratory employee in any staffing position, as well as any other hospital employee or other individual who enters the laboratory environment.

There are many potential customers and many outcomes, and their relative importance assumes varying degrees of precedence as preplanned criteria dictate. Ultimately, however, the most important healthcare customer is the patient.

The quality of the three basic laboratory functions must be assessed in context with one another as they are all linked by 1) direct cause-and-effect and 2) feedback. Figure 3.1 illustrates that the qualities of structure (total resources) influence the quality process; likewise, the quality of process influences the quality of outcome as a direct, one-by-one linkage. Also, resources and processes can act in an additive, one-on-one fashion to influence the ultimate outcome. At the same time, process and, especially, outcome generate feedback information that can modify earlier functions, causing a synergistic, push-pull coordination of multi-level activities. Note that the path of total operational work flow progresses from far left of the figure (from the earliest structural

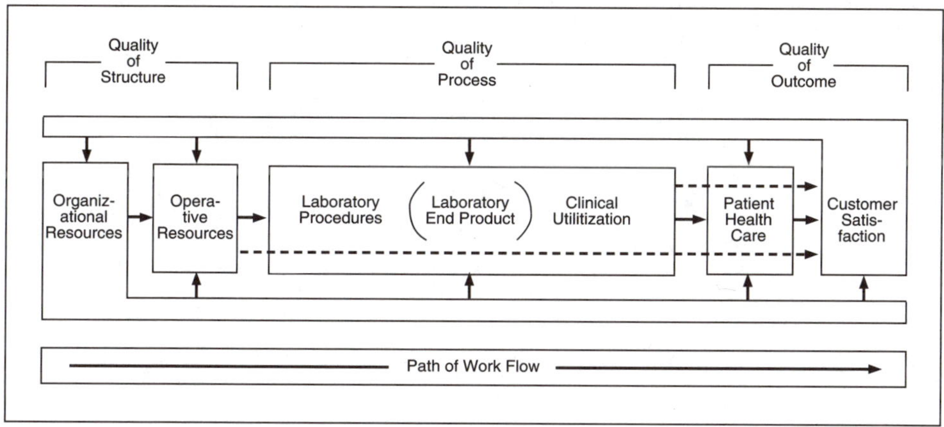

Figure 3.2 Flow model showing the complexity of the three elements of quality assessment

activities) to far right (to the ultimate outcome activities).

Figure 3.2 reveals the inherent complexity of structure, process, and outcome as functional activities and quality assessment elements. Beginning at the far left of the figure, structure consists of two separate functional levels that have significant bearing on overall work flow. First, the nontraditional organizational resources exert direct effect on the quality of operative resources. Bypassing the direct linkage of the chain of laboratory events, organizational resources also can influence each of the other elements, extending along the entire operational span. As a result, the effect of the quality of the organizational resource programs is pervasive throughout the laboratory system, impinging on all other functional activities—often very subtly.

Continuing with the more traditional portions of the chain of cause-and-effect, operative resource input is the direct precursor of all process components: the quality of operative resources is predictive of the quality of process. Again, there is the additive, indirect effect of the quality of operative resources on all the elements of outcome—as well as on organizational resource activities in a retroactive, feedback fashion.

Process, the next step in the chain, consists of a particularly complicated series of compound functional events. As shown in Figure 3.2, process does not simply consist of applying operative resources to laboratory procedures resulting in the laboratory end product as the major outcome—as in the traditional operational model. Rather, the laboratory end product is most often only an interim product—the end product of laboratory process, yes, but not an end result of patient care. The laboratory product usually must be transported or transmitted to a point of care where it is used in the clinical setting, influencing patient health status and causing an ultimate effect on customer satisfaction. Consequently, the

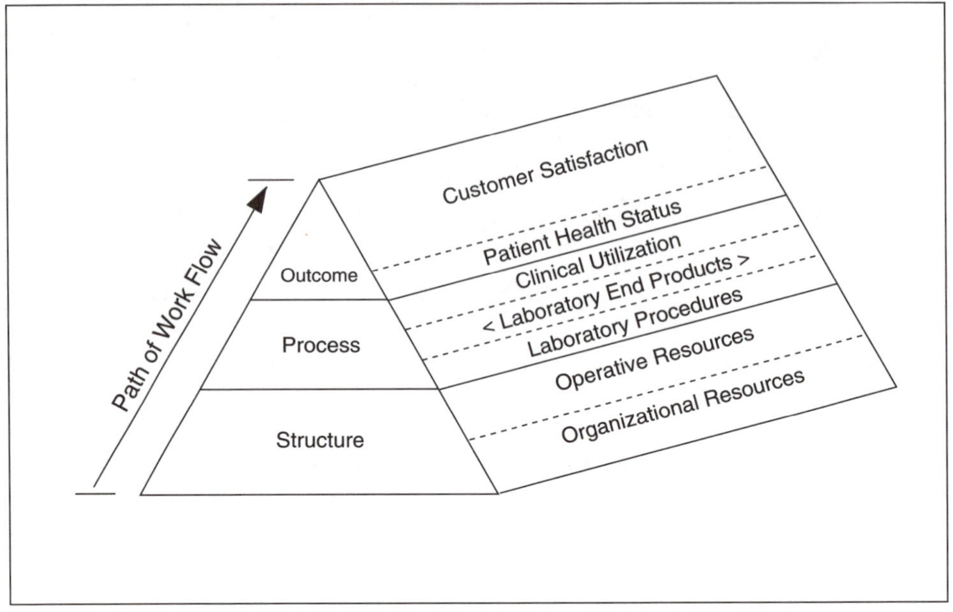

Figure 3.3 Hierarchical model of the three elements of quality assessment

modern concept of laboratory operations must include the postlaboratory application of the laboratory end product to clinical patient care—the interim laboratory end product becomes a clinical operative resource at this point.[a] The process function also can exert retroactive, feedback effect on operative and organizational resources.

Outcome, the third basic functional activity and quality assessment element, is also a complex of related activities and effects, all of which can be managed. Multiple outcomes can stem from a single process activity. The first outcome component is the customer's primary status. If the customer is a patient, the initial outcome is the effect on health status; if it is an employee, it is the effect on safety (eg, health status, or morale, or earning power) or other employee welfare—and the examples of customer types can go on and on. Since the patient is the primary customer, it is only after clinical utilization of the laboratory product—still a part of overall process—that the final results of all the work flow are reflected in the potentially complex outcome of patient health status.

The second major component of the outcome complex is customer satisfaction. The ultimate outcome of customer satisfaction depends on

[a] Only in a relatively few examples—such as in therapeutic phlebotomy—is the laboratory service/product both a laboratory and a clinical end product, simultaneously. As in the example cited, the service is also an actual clinical treatment for which the pathologist takes clinical responsibility.

several interrelated factors, stemming from all component portions of the path of work flow. Communication can be one of the most crucial items.

The two events, resultant customer end status and satisfaction, are not necessarily directly related or proportional to one another. They are neither mutually inclusive or exclusive. They can be positively or negatively related. These two events provide a good example of Juran's issue over "conformance to specifications" versus "fitness of use," which is further addressed below.

As implied in the figure, outcome also has a modifying feedback effect, just as organizational and operative resources and process. Based on feedback amplification of lessons learned, all preceding elements of the functional cause-and-effect chain are modulated by outcome—in the ideal, modern managerial system, that is.

Note that the path of operational work flow is also shown in Figure 3.2. It progresses from the beginning of organizational resource management to the final outcome. As suggested by this complex flow model, the path can be divided into periods and phases following the sequence of the operational functions. These divisions of the path of work flow are shown in greater detail later in the text.

The chief lesson of this model is that laboratory "work" does not begin with the selection of a laboratory test on the ward or clinic or receipt of a specimen at the accessioning window. Rather, all laboratory work begins when two or more people decide to come together and establish the initial organizational infrastructure on which is based all other administrative- and operative-level resource, process, and outcome management activities.

Figure 3.3 is a hierarchical model that translates the latter flow model into the pyramidal relationships of the three quality assessment elements, (which are also the three levels of laboratory managerial activity) and the total path of work flow. This model applies to any-sized organizational unit.

As the pyramidal model suggests, comprehensive surveillance of the quality of laboratory structure, process, and outcome easily seem too complicated and expensive. As a result, priorities are often set in an incremental fashion. For example, assessing the quality of the laboratory process usually receives the most attention, followed by limited aspects of operative resource input. Organizational resource input receives least notice.

Assessing outcome receives minimal attention, although some precedent has been set in blood utilization studies—a combined surveillance of end product utilization, patient care outcome, and customer satisfaction. Tissue and tumor boards have also set precedents in clinical peer review of tissue diagnosis (an interim laboratory end product), clinical utilization, and clinical outcome. In contrast, directing more balanced, systematic attention to the quality of all three aspects of laboratory function would result in greatly improved laboratory support of patient care.

Table I
Comparison of Elements of Laboratory Quality Assessment and Management

Elements of Quality Assessment	Elements of Quality Management
■ Outcome quality	■ Outcome management
■ Process quality	■ Process management
■ Structure quality	■ Structure management
1. Operative resource quality	1. Operative resource management
2. Organizational resource quality	2. Organizational resource management
a. Surveillance quality	a. Quality improvement (QI)
b. Planning quality	b. Quality anticipation (QAn)
c. Team quality	c. Quality actualization (QAc)

Comparison of Laboratory Quality Management and Quality Assessment

As discussed in the previous chapter and implied through much of the latter discussion, laboratory quality management can be considered at two fundamental levels—operative and organizational (administrative). Also based on what we know from Donabedian's model for assessing healthcare quality, assessment activities include structural (organizational and operative) resources, process, and outcome. Table I demonstrates the pairing of these twin concepts, the components of quality management and quality assessment mirroring one another.

Conformance to Design Specifications

Another important aspect of the definition of laboratory quality is conformance to design specifications. It is described as:[11]

> the degree by which the performance of a laboratory procedure corresponds to the original specifications as written in the laboratory procedural manual. An example of such

specifications could be the degree of accuracy, precision, sensitivity, and specificity required for a specific pregnancy test method that would cause the test to identify a reasonable portion of the pregnant patient population with minimal false positives and false negatives.

Essentially, all laboratory quality control (QC) control levels and most QI indicators focus on procedural conformance to design specifications, whether it be a procedure in resource management, a technical procedure at the bench, or a clinical procedure at the bedside utilizing a laboratory product. A design specification is an expectation of whatever quality characteristics are desired.

Juran further distinguishes between "conformance to design specifications" and "fitness for use." Whereas, any product (service) can conform to its design specifications, it can still be "unfit for use." For example, the laboratory interim end product might be absolutely within QC and QI tolerance limits for accuracy and precision, but the product will not be fit for use if it is not timely delivered or appropriately utilized in the clinical setting. Another example of this bimodel quandary is the variable (sometimes unpredictable) relationship between resultant customer status and customer satisfaction.[20]

LABORATORY QUALITY CONTROL

QC is an internal assessment of the essential characteristics of laboratory procedural performance. QC has been defined as "the monitoring of a procedure to ensure that specific operational goals are realized."[21] QC is formulated by laboratory management, translated into a written procedure, and occurs at the bench (or bedside) wherever analytical, diagnostic, or component preparation procedures; patient/donor procedures; or clerical procedures are performed.

Although the JCAHO has not published a definition of QC in their glossary, the CAP has defined it as:[10]

> an integral component of quality assurance and ... the aggregate of processes and techniques so derived to detect, reduce, and correct deficiencies in the analytical process.
>
> Quality control is a surveillance process by which the actions of people and materials are observed in some systematic, periodic way [that] provides a record of consistency of performance and action taken when performance does not conform to standards [that] have been established in the laboratory.

This CAP definition of QC singles out the analytical laboratory, emphasizing CP over AP (eg, "deficiencies in the analytical process") and excluding the broader aspects of laboratory function as established in the earlier-mentioned CAP definition of quality. The definition also overlaps their definition of quality assurance (QA) (eg, "surveillance process ... observed in some systematic, periodic way ... a record of consistency of performance and action").

The definition used in this text expands on the CAP statements and definitions and also borrows from the theory and practice of quality management in the nonhealthcare industries, as follows:[9,10,22]

- *Laboratory quality control* is an operative managerial method for directly controlling the quality of any laboratory product or service in any phase of the laboratory path of work flow (life cycle). This control is accomplished by monitoring, evaluating, and maintaining the prescribed degree of conformance to design specifications of any analytical test, consultative diagnosis, component preparation, patient/donor procedure, or clerical activity that results in the laboratory product. Such control can be applied at any level of operative resource input, process, or outcome management (eg, monitoring the performance of a blood warming device).

- *Monitoring* is usually based on calibrating instruments against standard analytes, observing the performance of control analytes during actual procedural testing, and observing instrumental/equipment/environmental characteristics such as temperature. Such surveillance should be integrated into all laboratory procedures or activities at all three operative levels of laboratory function.

- *Managerial adjustment* of a given laboratory procedure should result from control monitoring. Adjustments can take three forms: upgrading, stabilizing, or downgrading the conformance of the laboratory procedure to its design specifications to meet specific management objectives—based on the organization's team decisions (through the QAc program) and strategic plan (through the QAn program):

  1. upgrading enhances some on-site service(s)—such as increasing accuracy, reducing TAT, or increasing volume of production.
  2. stabilizing maintains all management parameters at the current level.
  3. downgrading curtails some on-site service(s)—such as decreasing accuracy, increasing TAT, decreasing the volume of production, or stopping the service entirely and sending specimens to a reference laboratory.

- *Operative management objectives* for QC are tailored for each respective management center (usually at the laboratory section level). Examples of such objectives include judicious resource utilization, technical efficiency, professional competence, laboratory employee safety, and patient satisfaction.

The Quality Control Process

The effectiveness of direct managerial control of laboratory quality can be determined for any of the three elements of quality assessment; again, these elements include *organizational and operative resource QC*, *process QC*, and *outcome QC*. Physiologically speaking, the QC process is analogous to the humoral feedback mechanisms of the endocrine system, providing the organization with a means of monitoring and responding to variances in performance that is operative center (eg, organ) and procedure (eg, function) specific.

Appropriate QC parameters can be measured against target levels and control limits. Ideally, meeting these standards and criteria should be an "all or nothing" proposition. In practice, however, multi-rules for evaluating compliance allow for an additional degree of random variation, especially with the more modern, extremely accurate, and precise instrumentation. Examples of QC parameters and their criteria are:

- Organizational resource control which includes ongoing continual follow-up of current:
    1. organizational needs assessment, team skills, training, and participative management projects (QAc program)
    2. organizational research, development, and implementation milestones (QAn program)
    3. quality improvement montoring and evaluation (QI program)
- Operative resource control which includes ongoing follow-up of current:
    1. personnel vacancy rates measured against current workload and productivity
    2. supply delivery measured against the expected delivery dates
- Process control which includes ongoing follow-up of current:
    1. test request completeness and specimen appropriateness measured against specific accessioning requirements
    2. accuracy, precision, specificity, and sensitivity of technical or clerical performance measured against procedural design specifications and management expectations

3. TAT and delivery time measured against joint laboratory-clinical standards

- Outcome control includes ongoing follow-up of current:
    1. medical appropriateness of current test utilization measured against joint laboratory-clinical indications and contraindications
    2. physician, patient, employee or other customer satisfaction.

Peer Control of Anatomic Pathology And Other Interpretive Procedures

Peer control is a specific form of quality management that consists of peer review at the operative managerial level. One pathologist (or a panel of pathologists) reviews the interpretive diagnoses of another pathologist, usually on a day-to-day basis. Peer control is routinely performed in AP for diagnostic activities such as intraoperative (frozen or cytologic), permanent surgical, cytopathologic, hematopathologic, and autopsy diagnoses.

Peer control compares the initial technical and final diagnostic performance against specific control criteria for quality, including medical appropriateness. The review is usually performed before finalizing the diagnostic report. In AP, peer control should provide ongoing, direct, professional managerial control at all functional levels, exemplified as follows:

- Organizational resource activities that directly affect the quality of:
    1. team decisions focused on diagnosis-related issues
    2. strategic plans focused on diagnosis-related issues
    3. quality surveillance of diagnosis-related quality indicators

- Operative resource activities that directly affect the quality of anatomic diagnosis-related procedures

- Prelaboratory process activities that directly affect the quality of the attending physician's test selection, specimen collection, and handling, including:
    1. the quality of the clinical information and specimen including the adequacy of:
        a. patient identification and supporting information
        b. the specimen, preservation, and timeliness of delivery
    2. the medical appropriateness of the requested examination and the submitted specimen as measured against clinical indications and contraindications as evidenced by the:

a. requested examination satisfying the clinical differential diagnoses
b. specimen satisfying the requirements of the examination
c. correlation between surgical and autopsy diagnoses and clinical diagnoses or therapeutic procedures

- Intralaboratory process activities that directly affect the prediagnostic technical quality of the:

  1. maintenance of specimen integrity
  2. adequacy of technical processing
  3. adequacy of clerical support

- Intralaboratory process activities that directly affect the quality of the pathologists' consultative diagnosis, including the:

  1. technical quality of the pathologist's diagnostic activity, including the:
     a. thoroughness of gross and microscopic evaluation
     b. timeliness of the diagnostic reporting process
  2. accuracy and medical appropriateness of the pathologist's consultative diagnosis, comments, and recommendations, all measured against clinical indications and contraindications as evidenced by the degree of correlation with:
     a. clinical history and supporting diagnostic information
     b. cytopathologic and permanent tissue histopathologic diagnoses
     c. intraoperative (frozen, touch preparation, smear) and permanent tissue histopathologic diagnoses
     d. previous and current tissue histopathologic diagnoses
     e. clinical outcome

- Postlaboratory process activities that directly affect the quality of diagnosis-related procedures

- Outcome activities that directly affect the quality of postdiagnostic clinical care (resultant customer status) and customer satisfaction.

Peer control can also be employed in CP when a clinical pathologist or other laboratorians render a professional diagnostic opinion (cognitive interpretation) on which medical or surgical diagnosis or treatment will be based. If used in CP, the peer control format of assessment can be modified as is described later in this text.

The immediate operative managerial objective of peer control is to upgrade, maintain, or downgrade the technical, clerical, or interpretive process—as is clinically appropriate—before the case has been completed and released to a patient's chart.

- Upgrading increases the overall quality of the ongoing diagnostic process immediately at hand by improving technical efficiency or pathologist effectiveness. These changes can be affected by on-the-spot corrections or improvements such as:
  1. reorienting tissue blocks
  2. obtaining deeper sectioning levels
  3. reducing TAT
  4. increasing volume of production
  5. increasing the statistical accuracy of the diagnoses by increasing the percentage of surgical cases that are reviewed
  6. obtaining a second consultative opinion
  7. providing timely feedback to the appropriate clinical staff if there is a QC problem that directly affects a patient's diagnosis or treatment.

- Stabilizing maintains the technical or diagnostic process.

- Downgrading decreases the overall quality of the diagnostic process by decreasing technical efficiency or pathologist effectiveness. Examples of curtailed services include:
  1. increasing TAT
  2. reducing the volume of production
  3. reducing the statistical accuracy of diagnosis by reducing the percentage of the surgical cases that are peer reviewed
  4. submitting part or all of the diagnostic work load to a reference laboratory.

  Any curtailment must be coordinated and accepted by the medical staff because any of these changes will result in less than optimum patient-care.

Because of personnel shortage and other current resource constraints, peer control of 100% of the cases is not usually feasible. Consequently, all cases should be ranked according to the urgency of patient need to determine the extent of review required. Cases not routinely reviewed must be surveyed periodically using a small but statistically significant sampling. Any disparity of opinion between the primary pathologist and the reviewer should be documented and submitted for QI review, along with all other scheduled QC data.

Nonpathologists are also subject to peer control review by their technologist supervisors or pathologists. This is only a slight

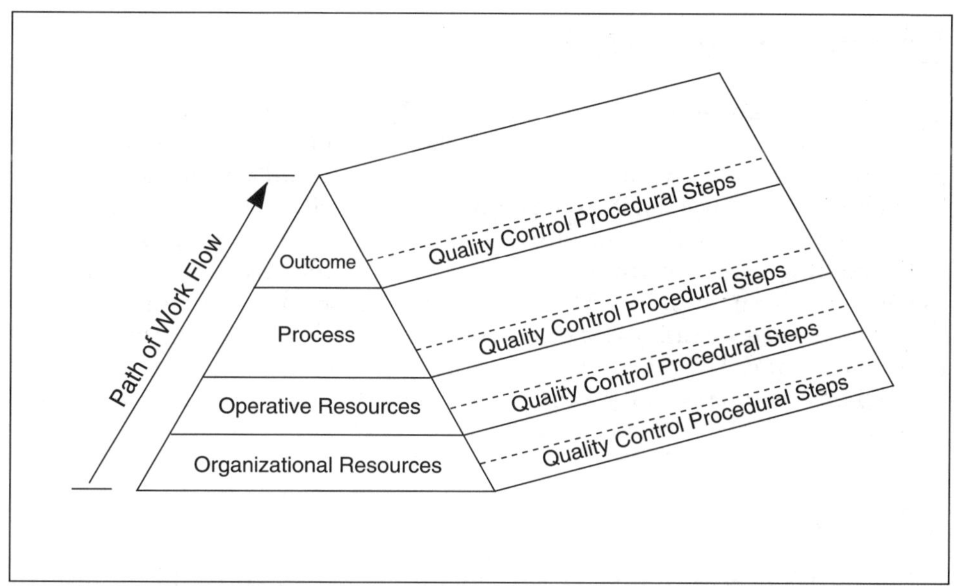

Figure 3.4 Hierarchical model of the three elements of quality assessment showing integration of quality control into all operational procedures

modification of the peer control used for pathologists in the AP service. Wheras the managerial objectives and methods are essentially the same, the control still focuses on the quality of the interpretive findings of nonpathologists—such as cytotechnologists and technologists in hematology, urinalysis, and microbiology—who routinely provide interpretive microscopic determinations used for diagnostic and therapeutic decision making.

Regardless of the mode of QC used in AP or CP, Figure 3.4 illustrates a model of those overall QC activities. Control activities are represented as a series of operative-level managerial steps that are integrated throughout each operational level of laboratory procedures. The model implies that QC is integral to each individual resource, process, and outcome procedure or event. As such, QC is a direct, "hands-on" operative-level activity—not an indirect administrative-level function.

This model raises an interesting management concept introduced in the previous chapter. If QC is a step required in the performance of all functional procedures, then QC is required not only at the operative level of process management but also at the operative and organizational (administrative or infrastructural) resource levels. Particularly, the performance of an administrative-level QI, QAn, or QAc program still requires direct operative-style QC procedural steps. Therefore, regardless of the operational level of management, QC is an operative management level activity—no matter at what operational level the QC step happens to be performed.

LABORATORY QUALITY SURVEILLANCE

Quality surveillance is exercised at the next lower level of the hierarchy of laboratory quality management and is the first of the three administrative programs that sustain total quality management and continuous quality improvement. Physiologically speaking, the quality surveillance program serves as the nervous system for all operational activities, providing the organization with an integrated "sensory" and "motor" function for detection, transmission of quality management information, and commensurate organizational-wide response. As compared to the endocrine model for QC, this neurophysiological model for quality surveillance connotes more subtle fine-tuning of organization-wide, multifunctional activities.

Quality Assurance

Laboratories practiced quality surveillance under the title of QA through the 1980s. One definition of QA is "the coordination of individual QC procedures and other QA activities on a wider basis than QC, so that resources are used to the best advantage, standards are set and maintained, and the end result should be the optimum of health care capable of being delivered to the patient."[22] The JCAHO *AMH* does not define QA specifically. The term QA is still used in the 1992 edition of the CAP inspection checklist and the CAP *Standards* defines QA as:[10]

> the process of assuring that all pathology services involved in the delivery of patient care have been accomplished in a manner appropriate to maintain excellence in medical care.

The definition for QA used in this text expands on the CAP definition and borrows from the theory and practice of quality management in the nonhealthcare industries:[9,10,23]

- *Laboratory quality assurance* is an administrative surveillance program for systematically monitoring the effectiveness of quality management for any laboratory product or service in any phase of its path of work flow (life cycle) and evaluating the performance of quality indicators in comparison to laboratory and clinical standards and thresholds.

- *Monitoring* is based on a regularly scheduled collection of measurable QA indicator data that reflect the quality of all laboratory operational levels of structural resource, process, and outcome activities. Since QC is an integral part of all operational functions, it is a key source of measurable indicators–especially in the laboratory.

- *Administrative adjustment* of department-wide laboratory operations should upgrade, stabilize, or downgrade elements of structure (both operative and organizational resources), process, or outcome to meet specific administrative goals.
    1. *Upgrading* is any administrative-level modification of resources or process that enhances procedural outcomes. Examples are decreasing TAT, increasing accuracy, or increasing scope of services.
    2. *Stabilizing* maintains all functions as they are.
    3. *Downgrading* is any administrative-level modification of resources or process that curtails procedural outcomes to maintain the overall balance of operational integrity in the face of some severe resource constraint or process limitation. Such a modification minimizes overall loss of quality to patient care. Examples are increasing intralaboratory TAT or sending a test to a reference laboratory.
- *Administrative goals* for QA are to capitalize on opportunities for improvement and to expeditiously resolve specific problems of quality. One goal is to assure the quality of specific operational resources, processes, and outcomes—including patient care and laboratory employee safety. Another goal is to target the quality of specific organizational programs—including strategic planning, organizational effectiveness, and the QA program, itself.

QA was intended to move laboratory management beyond the practice of retroactive, "problem-of-the-month," incremental crisis solving. The goal of QA always has been to move toward a concurrent—ie, while the patient is in the hospital—comprehensive, systematic assessment of patient-care quality and anticipation of needs. In practice, however, many laboratories have fallen into the trap of exercising QA more as a retrospective audit.

The Quality Assurance Process

The JCAHO has made a significant contribution of definitions, guidelines, formats, and models to assist with the understanding and implementation of QA. A key JCAHO innovation has been formalizing quality surveillance through their ten-step process (TSP). This process includes the selection of indicators of quality, determination of thresholds for evaluation, data collection, evaluation of opportunities for improvement, assessment of the effectiveness of the overall QA process, and communication of lessons learned.[b]

[b] Several quality surveillance (or quality improvement) processes are available as is explained in more detail later in this text. The TSP is the major example used in this test because of its proven effectiveness and the need for consistency.

The ten-step process can be expanded to monitor and evaluate all operational activities, including all three infrastructural programs. Subsequently, a complete QA program can be focused on several major areas of surveillance interest, including:

- Organizational effectiveness assurance
- Planning assurance
- Surveillance assurance
- Operative resource assurance
- Process assurance
- Outcome assurance.

At first glance, such an extensive surveillance program could appear unwieldy, impractical, and monetarily unfeasible to manage. However, a secret to a practical and successful QA program, especially on the grand scale of TQM, is capturing QA data that are *already available from other required documentation.* The data are already there, they just have to be found and used when justified.[24,25,26]

Indicators of quality, including medical appropriateness, can be determined and applied against all three quality assessment elements—*resource* (structural) QA, *process* QA, and *outcome* QA. Such a surveillance program, constitutes a key element of a total management system. Specific examples of QA indicators on a TQM scale of surveillance activity include the ongoing scrutiny of:

- Organizational resource activities such as:
    1. a QAc program that demonstrates steady progression of team skills assessment, training, incentive, and participative management activities that substantively contribute to enhanced team work, decision making, and organizational commitment to improved patient care and universal customer satisfaction.
    2. a QAn program that demonstrates steady progression of successful organizational research, development, and implementation projects aimed at improved patient care and customer satisfaction.
    3. a QA program that demonstrates steady improvement and effective communication of lessons learned based on effective monitoring, evaluation, and assessment of patient care and customer satisfaction.

- Operative resource activities such as:
  1. a personnel vacancy rate that is no greater than 10% of the authorized number of full time equivalents (FTE)
  2. a supply stock inventory that has been maintained with less than a 14 day average due-out status.

- Process activities such as:
  1. a test request and specimen invalidation rate that is no greater than 2% to 10%, depending on the functional type of laboratory section in question
  2. chemical analytical performance deviations that are no greater than plus or minus 2 standard deviations of the mean per Westgard's multi-rules for evaluation
  3. a TAT and delivery delay rate for routine chemistry profiles that is no greater than 10%.

- Outcome events such as:
  1. medical appropriateness of packed red blood cell utilization that precludes any incidence of a hemolytic transfusion reaction
  2. complete abscence of any threat of accidental contagion of any microbiology employee as evidenced by team satisfaction with the working environment.

Peer Assurance of Anatomic Pathology And Other Interpretive Procedures

Pathologist peer assurance is a specific form of peer review exercised at the administrative level—as opposed to peer control at the operative managerial level. Peer assurance occurs when one or more pathologists (or other physicians) examine the overall quality of an important aspect of professional medical care (usually an interpretive tissue diagnosis) provided by other pathologists over a month's time or longer. The review focuses on systemic professional diagnostic competency and on the entire laboratory system's ability to control and ensure a quality laboratory product during the review period. Peer assurance determines if there is adequate resource, procedural, and outcome quality, including medical appropriateness of the diagnosis and recommendations submitted by the pathologist staff.

Several hospital-wide activities—usually in the form of committees—have the potential to affect laboratory organization, staff, and operations. These external QA committee activities include credentials and privileges review; tissue review; morbidity and mortality review; utilization review, including blood utilization; and quality assurance review.

At the laboratory level, peer assurance is usually included in regularly scheduled departmental or service-level QA committee activities. Most often this peer review involves the AP service and focuses on the quality of consultative tissue and cytological diagnoses. The hematopathologist receives similar attention for bone marrow diagnoses in the CP service.

Peer assurance should examine 1) the overall quality of resource, process, and outcome management of technical and clerical procedures that affect selection, performance, and utilization of professional diagnoses and 2) the medical appropriateness of the staff pathologists' diagnostic interpretations and recommendations. The method of peer assurance should include a systematic monitoring of the indicators for technical, clerical, and pathologist proficiency and should use whatever additional pathology and clinical consultative follow-up is necessary.

Clinical criteria and thresholds must be determined and applied to all the specific cases. Any pathologist performance that exceeds the threshold must be reviewed. The necessity to enter any information into the National Practitioner Data Bank for Adverse Information on Physicians and Other Healthcare Practitioners must be considered by the appropriate due process as stipulated by Public Law 99-660, the Health Care Quality Improvement Act of 1986.

Administratively, the objective of peer assurance is to improve consultative diagnoses or to solve a problem by upgrading, stabilizing, or downgrading the interpretive or technical resources. Examples of options for action are similar to those given for the general definition of QA:

- *Upgrading* increases the systemic caliber of the technical or diagnostic resources or process. Examples include purchasing a more productive tissue processing machine, increasing continuing education and training, and increasing pathologist privileges

- *Stabilizing* makes no significant changes

- *Downgrading* decreases the systemic caliber of the technical or diagnostic resources or process. Examples include reallocating limited resources at the expense of technical or diagnostic efficiency or effectiveness but within bounds accepted by the medical staff and decreasing pathologist privileges.

Nonpathologists are also subject to peer assurance review by technologist supervisors or pathologists. As before, the review should focus on the administrative assurance of quality, including the medical appropriateness, of the interpretive findings of nonpathologists—such as

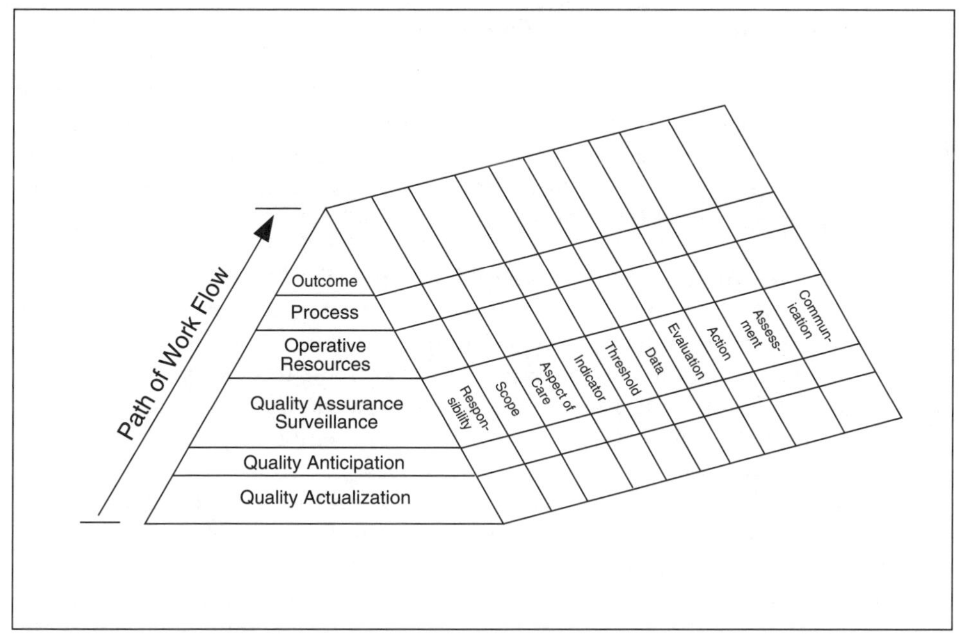

Figure 3.5 Hierarchical model of the quality assurance program showing its relationship to all other laboratory functions, including the ten-step process

cytotechnologists and technologists in hematology, urinalysis, and microbiology who routinely provide interpretive microscopic determinations used for diagnostic and therapeutic decision making. The administrative objectives and surveillance methods remain the same as for pathologist peer assurance.[27]

Figure 3.5 is a model of QA and its monitoring and evaluation process, as related to all operative and organizational activities. Adding the surveillance process contributes a third, temporal dimension to the model—a sequence of administrative managerial events that transect all other operational levels. The JCAHO ten-step process has been chosen for illustrative purposes, although several other choices are available.

Designed as such, the model demonstrates that the system of QC and other operational procedural steps (See Figure 3.4) and the quality surveillance process elements are oriented 180 degrees to each other. In other words, QA indicator monitoring is capable of sampling an immense surveillance data base at all operational levels.

Figure 3.5 portrays the QA program as an infrastructural, administrative-level activity for surveying the quality of all aspects of laboratory operations. This surveillance program occurs at the highest (ie, third in sequence) level in the hierarchy of infrastructural activities. The path of work flow is also incorporated into the model.

Quality Assessment and Improvement

All that has been said concerning QA applies as well to the quality surveillance approach of QI. The definition of QI is almost the same as that of QA—with an added emphasis on organizational commitment, identifying opportunities rather than problems, and assessing quality improvement. The JCAHO *AMH* defines QI as:[9]

> the ongoing activities designed to objectively and systematically evaluate the quality of patient care and services, pursue opportunities to improve patient care and services, and resolve identified problems. Standards are applied to evaluate the quality of a hospital's [*sic*, any healthcare organization's] performance in conducting quality assessment and improvement activities.

Actually, quality improvement is not a new laboratory theme. It has been a thread commonly woven through the fabric of even the earliest QA literature. The process is simply being emphasized in a new way.[28]

The definition for QI used in this text expands on JCAHO statements and borrows from the theory and practice of quality management in the nonhealthcare industries, as follows:[9,23]

- Laboratory quality assessment and improvement is an administrative surveillance program for systematically monitoring the effectiveness of quality management for any anatomic or clinical laboratory product or service throughout the path of work flow (life cycle) and evaluating the performance of quality indicators in comparison to laboratory and clinical standards and thresholds.
- Monitoring is that activity described for QA.
- Administrative adjustments are those described for QA.
- Administrative goals are those described for QA with the addition that there will be:
  1. total organizational commitment, starting with leadership support and involvement
  2. universal customer satisfaction
  3. continuous quality improvement.

The JCAHO 1992 *AMH* signaled a period of transition from one quality surveillance approach to another—from the concept of QA to that of QI. The transition constitutes a change from emphasizing the selecting and monitoring of indicators for incremental problem solving to emphasizing the proactive assessment of opportunities for continuous improvement.[9]

First, the surveillance process of "monitoring and evaluating *quality* and *medical appropriateness* of patient care" has been redefined as "monitoring and evaluating the quality of patient care." Thus, the JCAHO no longer makes special distinction between quality and medical appropriateness—solving a semantic problem of definition of the late 1980s. As listed in the JCAHO definition of patient care quality, appropriateness is now considered a subcategory of quality, just as accuracy, precision, sensitivity, specificity, efficiency, effectiveness and others are characteristics of overall quality. Medical appropriateness is still available for use as an indicator whenever practitioner quality is being scrutinized.

Second, the entire theme of quality surveillance has been changed from an established (stagnating) routine of QA to the never ending quest of QI. The 1992 *AMH* chapter that formerly was titled "Quality Assurance" was newly titled "Quality Assessment and Improvement" and the standards are referred to by the new acronym, QI. This new approach has been described as a quality management surveillance program focused on "assessing and improving patient care quality." Thus, the quality surveillance chapter and its standards have been completely rewritten with some semblance to the former QA chapter but with significant conceptual and mechanistic changes.

By virtue of these revisions, the 1992 *AMH* demonstrated a distinct consolidation of JCAHO strategic forecasting and currently in vogue semantics. Initially, the aim of healthcare quality management was to establish an administrative foundation of QA with a uniform ten-step monitoring and evaluation process—the goal for the 1980s. Focus has now shifted to establishing the administrative mechanisms that will foster TQM and CQI in healthcare management—the goal for the 1990s. As a result, JCAHO attention has subtly shifted from problem identifying to opportunity finding: there should be evidence of continuous improvement of the quality of laboratory activity performance, whether there is any adverse problem identified or not.

Third, beginning with the 1992 *AMH*, the ten-step process began receiving less emphasis. The process is no longer specifically listed as it was in the QA chapter of earlier editions of the *AMH*. It has not been abandoned—instead, it has been made an integral part of the quality monitoring, evaluating, and assessing process. A chief point made by the JCAHO is that there are means of obtaining quality management information and data other than the ten-step format. These other means include committee reports, task force studies, and surveys, as well as other formalized improvement processes. Consequently, the new chapter on QI no longer included the familiar preamble to the monitoring and evaluating standard itemizing the elements of the ten-step process. Instead, there was a general preamble for the entire chapter and the process was embedded within the matrix of the text of the QI standards and their required characteristics.

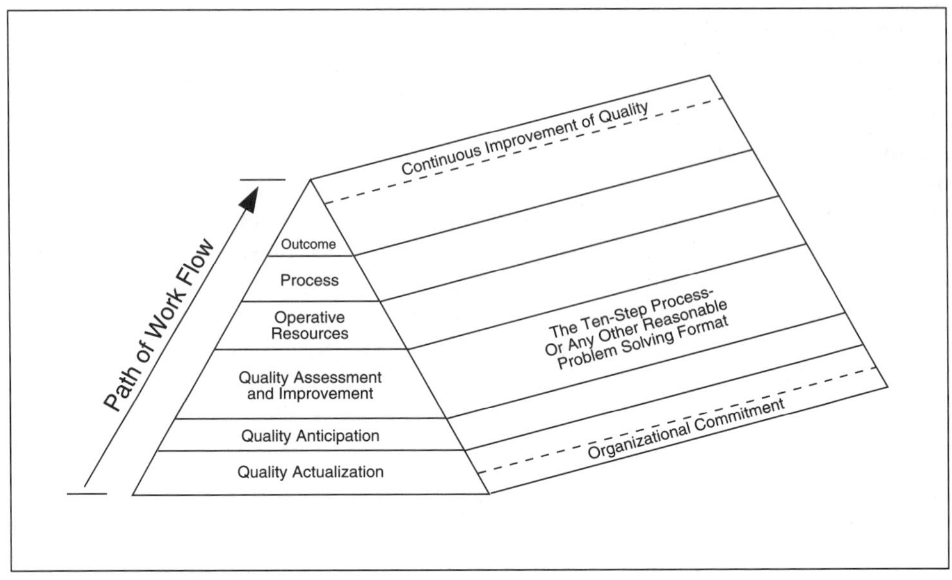

Figure 3.6 Hierarchical model of the quality assessment and improvement program

Explanation of the format and use of the ten-step process has been left intact in other JCAHO publications, such as the *Monitoring and Evaluation Series*, the *Primer on Clinical Indicator Development and Application*, and *The Transition from QA to CQI: An Introduction to Quality Improvement in Health Care.*[18,29,30] As focus on improvement is sharpened, the definition and use of certain elements of the TSP (such as threshold) will undoubtedly take on new form in future editions of the *AMH* and other publications. New indicator identifying and problem solving methods are being developed.

Further changes of accreditation standards should be assimilated as they evolve. For example, as is stated in the 1992 *AMH*, new quotas of specific ongoing indicators are being required for monitoring, evaluating, and assessing for improvement—revised requirements for blood usage review being a good laboratory example.

The one event that can be predicted in laboratory quality management is change, and changes in American medical quality management are surging again–as evidenced by the 1992 *AMH*. For the foreseeable future, what has been taught as QA will be transformed into QI and its successor programs (such as QI). Thus, it is easy to expect even further improvement of quality management nomenclature and clarification of semantics. Hopefully, the result will be continuous improvement of quality management concepts, methods, and resources—along with the improvement of patient care.

Figure 3.6 illustrates a model for QI which is very similar to that for QA—including notation of a reasonable assessment format. However, two major nuances are added to form the new panoply of QI surveillance targets: continuous improvement of quality and organizational (including leadership) commitment to the QI program: quality improvement as the quintessential organizational outcome goal and commitment as the most fundamental actualization goal. Both elements will be further discussed under the topic of CQI.

The extent to which the new JCAHO QI program includes so many aspects of the Deming approach to CQI reveals how far reaching this new program really is. Based on the presentation of their new surveillance program, the JCAHO promises to provide even further clarification and expansion of quality management processes. Therefore, we can plan on experiencing a continuation of rising expectations in laboratory quality management.

Improving Organizational Performance

In the 1994 AMH, the JCAHO changed the title for its quality surveillance program from QI to Improving Organizational Performance or PI. This was not so much a change in philosophy or process as it was a shift in emphasis to a structural, functional approach to evaluating and improving organizational performance. Although the abbreviation for the JCAHO program is PI, this text will address this particular quality surveillance process as QI to maintain consistency of style.

LABORATORY QUALITY ANTICIPATION

The quality anticipation program is exercised at the next lower level in the hierarchy of laboratory managerial functions and is the second of the three administrative programs that sustain TQM and CQI. Physiologically speaking, QAn serves as the skeletal support for all operational activities.

Incremental, crisis management must be absolutely minimized. Quality must be designed methodically into organizational function by careful planning. Quality must be determined by anticipatory management in an increasingly technocratic society: destiny should be by choice, not by chance. This is especially true in light of the federal and state demands that are being directed at the medical laboratory. Thus, planning is an important key to implementing, sustaining, and improving function organization-wide. Within larger operational units, it is often practical to plan for more specific, key operational areas (KOA). Such a KOA is smaller but discipline-specific in nature (eg, chemistry, immunology, equipment maintenance, supply). A suggested format for implementing a QAn program includes steps to:[31]

- Determine organizational values
- Determine the organizational mission
- Determine the organizational vision
- Identify all key management areas (KMAs) at each laboratory managerial level—ie, departmental, service, and section
- Identify and prioritize all customers (and suppliers) and their needs for each KMA
- Design short-, medium-, and long-range strategies for each important customer need
- Phase organizational research, development, and implementation projects for each strategy
- Develop the following planning elements for each strategy:
    1. goals
    2. objectives
    3. specific taskings with milestone dates, action teams, and action "officers."

As the first team effort, identify organizational values. These fundamental socioeconomic precepts should mirror the more general personal values or work ethics of the members of the organization, as well as the more focused, operationally-oriented values regarding specific customer-supplier relationships.

Second, the organization should determine its single, most important mission. A general mission statement is a summation of what the organization can attain today. The universal mission is to satisfy all customers' needs.[32] So each organization should determine what its unique mission is for its own general customer public. The laboratory should ensure that its mission statement is known by all employees, external customers, and suppliers.

Third, the organization should establish a vision statement—a summation of what the organization wants to attain tomorrow. This requires anticipating what changes are likely to occur in the general customer population and what new products and services generally are going to be available.

Fourth, each organizational level of operations (department, service, section, and smaller unit) consists of KMAs—and they should be identified at each operational level. The same KMAs exist at every hierarchical level of function and for every operational subunit.

Examples of important KMAs include:

- Quality actualization—organizational effectiveness program
- Quality anticipation—organizational research, development, and implementation program
- Quality assessment and improvement—organizational surveillance program
- Control and communication
- Budget management
- Safety management
- Reports and records management
- Training and education
- Methods and procedures (including emergency contingency preparedness); these amount to standing plans for all operative-level procedures, including all quality control steps
- Logistics (supply and equipment) management
- Facility management
- Personnel management
- Operative-level process management
- Outcome management.

Fifth, identify *all* current customers (formerly referred to as "key stakeholders") for each KMA; also, identify and prioritize their most important needs. A customer is any individual or group that derives some benefit—or experiences an adverse effect—from any organizational function. That should include all customers internal or external to the organization. Internally, the operative employee is a customer of the laboratory management, just as the organization's administrative and operative managers are customers of a higher administrative echelon. All lateral departments and services—clinical and non-clinical—are external customers. The list of customers (and suppliers) is potentially endless.

There is a reciprocal relationship between the customer and supplier status: at one moment, an individual (or group) enjoys the customer status; at another time and in another setting, the same the individual can provide a service as a supplier.

In addition, laboratory operations can create remote, "downstream" events, known as *externalities*. Individuals affected by such externalities also are customers. Although a more indirect type, they can become adversarial in nature unless treated as customers in a preventive fashion.

Sixth, consider short-, medium-, and long-range strategies to meet each important customer need. Determination of the strategic timeline can be on the basis of the so-called "SWOT" market analysis of internal strengths and weaknesses and external opportunities and threats.

Short-range strategies are usually chosen for more focal, operative-level activities, usually requiring less than a year for completion. Often short- to medium-range plans are interim measures that must be taken before ultimately realizing full improvement. Long-range strategies consist of more global, administrative-level projects that require one or more years for fruition—a five-year strategic plan is common. Being so far-reaching in this fast moving world of science and technology, such a mixture of short-to-long range timelines must be up-dated every year.

Seventh, establish phasing plans for meeting the organizational mission and customer need for each strategy. Each phasing should define the approach to resolve each customer-related problem or "opportunity for improvement." Thus, a QAn strategy can consist of three phases: research, development, and/or implementation.

The *organizational research* phase should produce new, fresh approaches to accomplishing the mission in the face of internal and external changes—taking advantage of current and anticipated internal strengths and external opportunities and overcoming internal weaknesses and external barriers.[c] Such research requires ongoing, active organizational assessment of these internal and external changes through recognized team approaches (eg, brainstorming) and analytical methods (eg, surveys). This research should target the improving of all levels of laboratory function, not just the laboratory technical process, alone.

Most research projects should stem directly from the lessons learned through the quality surveillance (eg, QI) process. Other means for idea generation, analysis, and decision making are described in greater detail later in this text.

The *development phase* should include follow-up on the ideas generated through organizational research. Although some developmental projects might begin de novo at the development stage, teams or task force groups are fitted to pilot projects. These projects are tested to

[c] A distinction is made here between organizational research and basic research. Some laboratorians tend to interpret the term "research" as technical research—as we so well know from our basic science and technological orientation. Rather, organizational research is the search for new operational management procedures and processes, organization-wide, along the entire path of work flow.

ascertain whether or not the proposed innovation is worthy of full-fledged implementation in the final strategic planning process.

The research and development phases are essential to maintaining a continual quest for improvement of all aspects of organizational and operative activities and the laboratory product. Unfortunately, these two aspects of QAn that are often not done very well are research and development. It requires a consistently systematic and inquiring attitude to discover new approaches to improving organizational operations.

The *implementation phase* consists of the plans for the full-fledged institutionalizing and sustaining of improvements at all organizational- and operative-level activities. This phase might be very quickly accomplished or might require step-wise, carefully timed staging. In some situations, customer need may require all three phases—from research through implementation. In other situations, the implementation phase might be all that is required to satisfy a customer need. Regardless of what phasing might be required, formulate strategic phasing plans based on lessons learned from earlier planning projects and current QI surveillance.

Next, select general *goals* for each strategy-phase project. The solution for each goal can be reduced to more specific *objectives* that can be met by one or more very specific *actions* or *taskings*. For each tasking, there should be a *milestone* date of expected completion and a designated *action team* and *officer* that are specifically responsible. The action team also might be known as a committee, a task force, or by some other unique designation. There can be any number of strategies, any number of phases per strategy, any number of goals per phase, any number of objectives per goal, and so on.

The final step in the QAn program is evaluation. This step is the key to monitoring the success of the entire planning process. Each planning project in each phase can be periodically evaluated through the ongoing QI program. At the very least, the entire QAn program warrants a systematic review on an annual basis.

A QAn program might or might not use all of the above elements or components—there are several schools of thought on the subject. In many ways, it depends on whether the organization wants to behave as right- or left-brained or as a "splitter" or a "lumper". Whatever the choice, it is most important that there is consistency of usage and practice.[33,34]

The monitoring and evaluation of the QAn program should be carried out at both the operative QC and administrative QI levels. At the operative section team level, the action officer can exercise direct managerial QC over each tasking and milestone on a regularly scheduled basis. Review of the efficacy of the overall plan at the service or departmental level constitutes administrative-level QI surveillance.

Figure 3.7 depicts an algorithmic model of a QAn program. Although linear in appearance, the model is actually cyclical. The evaluation step brings the model around full circle.

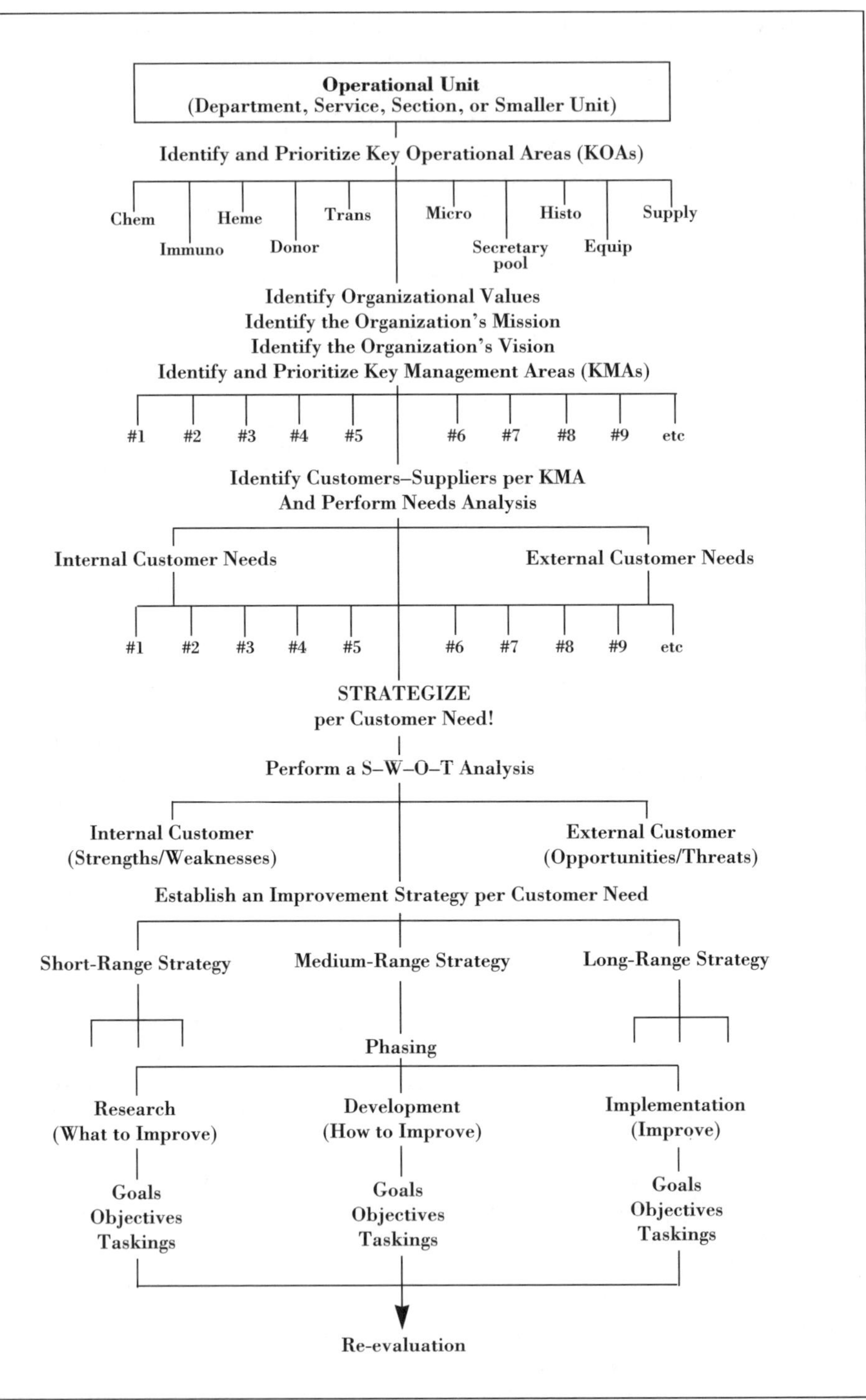

Figure 3.7 Algorithmic model of a quality anticipation program

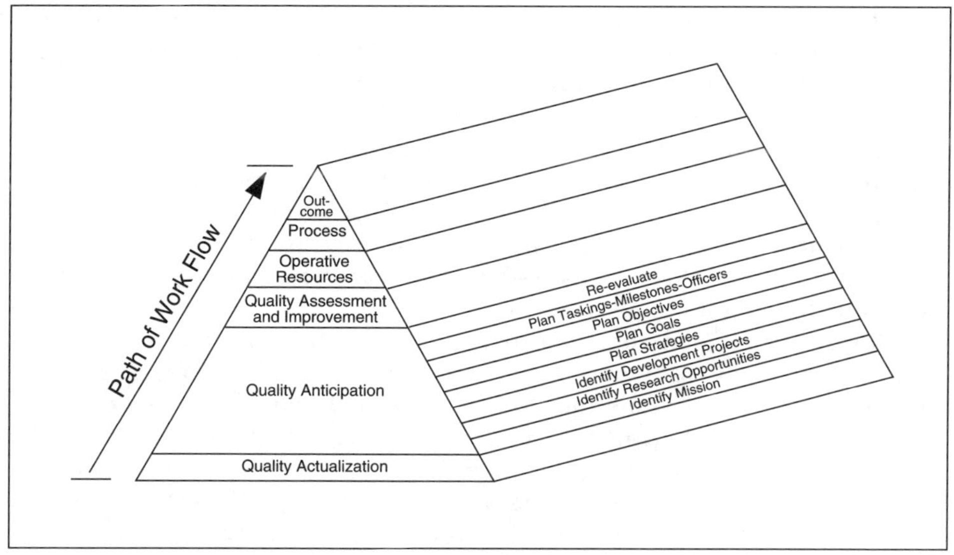

Figure 3.8 Hierarchical model of a quality anticipation program

Figure 3.8 illustrates a hierarchical model of a QAn program. The model demonstrates the levels of importance (and normal sequence of progression) of the chief components of the program. Whereas values are the most basic, repeat evaluation with appropriate readjustment of the anticipatory process is the final step before the cyclical chain of events are repeated.

QC procedural steps are a part of each procedural level of the QAn program—as is true for every managerial program and every operational level of laboratory function. This model integrates the QAn program with all other aspects of laboratory operations, including the path of work flow.

LABORATORY QUALITY ACTUALIZATION

The quality actualization program is exercised at the most basic level in the hierarchy of laboratory managerial functions. It is the most fundamental of the three administrative programs that sustain TQM and CQI. Physiologically speaking, QAc serves as the organizational intellect and conscience.

TQM and CQI require an organizational commitment to improvement that can be realized only if there is an appropriate "cultural" understanding and behavior at all organizational levels of responsibility. Both are essential elements of organizational effectiveness. Neither, however, occurs spontaneously; each must be taught and steadily nurtured with purposeful intention.

Thus, it is purposeful that the title for this program is quality "actualization." This is a direct reference to Maslow's theory of hierarchy of needs, which models stages of individual behavioral requirements; self-actualization is the ultimate need (and achievement). In an organizational sense, the epitome of behavioral success or excellence is reaching continuous quality improvement as evidenced by customer satisfaction. Organizational-actualization of this most important achievement must be founded on a specific program designed to make it happen. Thus, QAc serves as the fountainhead of organizational "passion" for quality improvement.[35, 36]

Culture is defined sociologically as "the sum total of ways of living built up by a group of human beings and transmitted from one generation to another."[3] As a summation of organizational behavior, this definition applies easily to the healthcare laboratory: organizational culture is the sum total of ways of working together that are developed by any group of employees and customers or customer-suppliers. All members of the organization have a role to play in that development, including those that are internal and external to the laboratory organization. The effectiveness of transmission of cultural principles, programs, and procedures is a measure of its operational integrity—a true strength of the organization.[37]

The most effective laboratory organization enjoys a group cohesiveness demonstrated by the ability of all personnel to work together, communicate, and participate in managerial decision making. Only by cultivating these specific organizational strengths can group commitment to quality improvement be fully actualized, achieving an organizational equivalent of Maslow's self-actualization—but, in this case, it is organizational-actualization. Total organizational commitment to quality improvement is a prime characteristic of organizational-actualization.

Figure 3.9 provides a model for QAc, integrating organizational effectiveness activities with the QAn program, the QI program, and all operative laboratory activities. Again, the model depicts the path of work flow.

The model demonstrates the level of importance (and the normal sequence of progression) of the chief components of the QAc program. Again, determining organizational values is the most fundamental step to actualization of organizational plans, while realizing "company-wide" organizational commitment to quality improvement is an ultimate goal of the program. Such commitment cannot be achieved until all members (including all leaders) have been trained and allowed to "buy in" to the program.

Who teaches QAc concepts and skills? The teacher-facilitator must be proficient in teaching quality actualization skills and inspiring or motivating individual and organization-wide commitment. It is often preferable that the facilitator be from outside the organizational unit that is being trained—at least, from another section of the laboratory. The team members usually perceive an "outsider" as being disinterested or

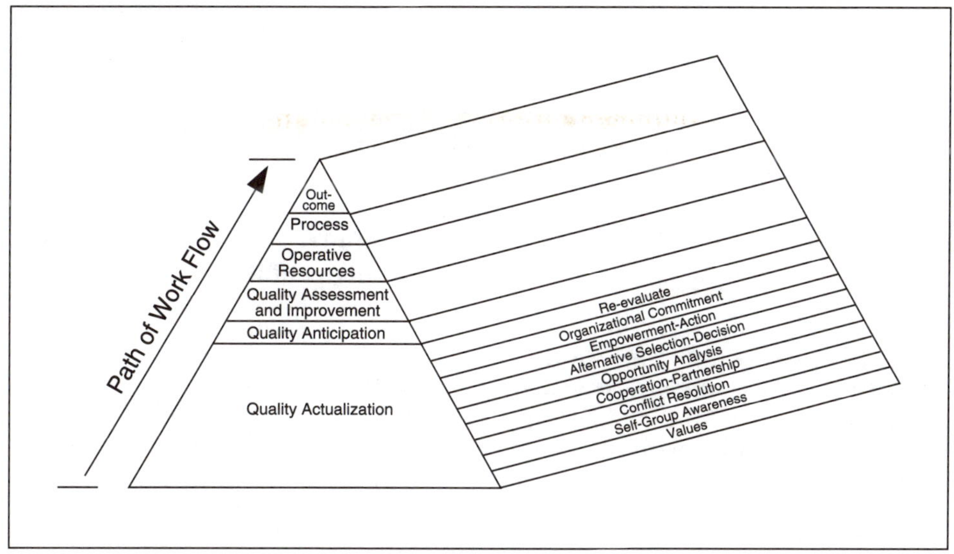

Figure 3.9 Hierarchical model of a quality actualization program

unbiased and, as such, the facilitator can elicit more cooperation and voluntary participation from the trainees. Because the training includes the possibility for rather frank discussions that can cause trainees to feel vulnerable, trainees are often less threatened by an outside facilitator. Thus, there is minimal potential for interpersonal repercussions after the training is completed.

Table II outlines a suggested curriculum for organizational development through QAc team skills training. Creating cultural strengths requires significant education and training of all personnel in specific organizational skills. A QAc program for organizational effectiveness should be based on the realization that every laboratory organization is comprised of people of various and diverse personalities, backgrounds, values, education, training, experience, and responsibilities.[38] All of these personnel should become committed to meeting the organization's mission to serve all customers. Ultimately, a collection of inherently disparate individuals should meld into a cohesive group with a growing mutual understanding, acknowledging common organizational values, mission, goals, and objectives.

First, as in formulating the QAn program, the entire organization must agree on the fundamental values that can be applied to the work place, particularly those values that concern interpersonal working relationships. Discussing individual and organizational values is very important; it can become a cement for interpersonal, group cohesion.

Societal values are a form of quality that individuals and organizations expect in personal and group behavior, including the work

Table II
Outline of a Basic Curriculum for Organizational Development

Individual and group values:	getting to what is fundamentally important
Personality profiling and behavioral traits; Jungian theory, and the Myers-Briggs personality type indicator—all promoting awareness of individual behavior:	getting to who we are
Modes of interpersonal reaction; Freudian theory and transactional analysis—all promoting awareness of interpersonal behavior:	getting to how we send and receive signals to one another
Conflict resolution skills:	getting to "let's be professional and not take this personally"
Communication skills:	getting to interact and follow-up
Cooperation skills:	getting to partnership
Negotiation skills:	getting to "yes" and consensus
Empowerment skills:	getting to participative management
Opportunity identification and analysis skills:	getting to strengths, weaknesses, opportunities, and threats
Alternative finding and decision making skills:	getting to the best option
Action skills:	getting to closure and achievement of objectives
Evaluation skills:	getting to quality improvement and total commitment

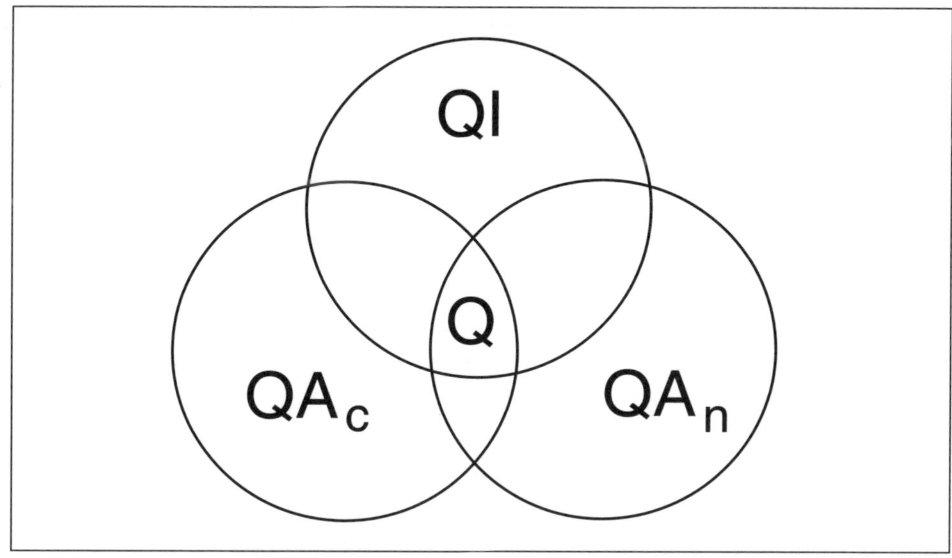

Figure 3.10 Venn diagram (mandala) of a total quality management system

ethic. All personnel need to realize that even though there may be a perception of external differences in individual values, there are basic values that are almost always the same for all individuals in this society. Variations in individual work styles and habits are bound to exist because of wide differences in personalities and backgrounds; but fundamental professional work ethics are usually very similar.

Certain values cannot be taken for granted. After some discussion, many seemingly problematic disparities will become unimportant. Interpersonal problems can also surface and move toward resolution.

Second, there should be a fundamental understanding among all personnel of the existence of personality types and individual behavior.[39,40] One example of a popular personality survey instrument is the Myers-Briggs Type Indicator (MBTI), based on Jungian theory of personality development. No matter what the method of approach (and there are several good survey instruments available), it is of importance to develop self and group awareness of the wide range of constitutional differences that affect individual personality and behavior. Consequently, much behavior can be anticipated, understood, accepted, and even modified—but not managed or engineered.

Individuals can gain an increased sense of self-identification and self-worth after learning how to characterize their own personality profile. It is not surprising that such self-awareness can lead to voluntary behavior modification after a person recognizes certain strengths and weaknesses in his or her information processing skills.

Third, all organizational members should gain a general understanding of group or interpersonal dynamics. Transactional analysis (TA), based on

Freudian theory, is one of several approaches. A well known reference source on TA is Eric Berne's popular book, *Games People Play.*[41]

A central QAc objective in team building is to facilitate and improve group decision making. To develop this organizational ability, teach specific organizational skills aimed at[42]:

- Conflict prevention and resolution
- Communication
- Cooperation
- Negotiation
- Empowerment
- Problem or opportunity identification and analysis
- Alternative finding and decision making
- Action
- Evaluation.

This text cannot go into these various skills in any great detail; each is a subject for an entire text in itself. However, each skill is critically important, and collectively these skills result in the building of a functional team.

One particularly crucial organizational hurdle worthy of note is empowerment. The evidence of power sharing is in 1) delegation of responsibilities, 2) participative management, and 3) quality circle style decision making. Company-wide managerial participation bolsters group commitment to TQM and CQI—everyone should be entitled to "a piece of the action."

Once team building is institutionalized, then refresher training is required just as for any other technical, safety, or other aspect of professional expertise. New personnel have to be taught the basic skills and veteran personnel must receive refresher basic, intermediate, and advanced training. These phases of training should include leadership exercises of increasing complexity. Organizational education and training must never stop.

LABORATORY TOTAL QUALITY MANAGEMENT

Incremental quality management can be defined as crisis management based on the principle of Murphy's Law and use of the quick fix. The credo of incrementalists is "If it ain't broke, don't fix it!"

TQM is a managerial counterforce to incrementalism. It can be defined as:

> a system of proactive quality management programs that fosters systematic quality performance throughout all organizational and operative levels of function to benefit all customers.

In this case, a system is understood to consist of two or more programs focused on a central theme. The credo of TQM is based on questioning:

> Is there any potential operational problem that is apt to affect the satisfaction of any customer? If so, what are all the significant systemic causes and effects of that problem that can be improved to prevent the problem from occuring?

A secret to success in the practice of TQM is remaining constantly aware of the entire system of laboratory activities, while—at the same time—focusing selectively on a specific activity when an opportunity for improvement is anticipated.

TQM is descendant from the "company-wide control" of J. W. Juran and the "total quality control" of Feigenbaum, Eilers, and others. It is achieved through the orchestration of the three administrative (organizational resource management) programs of QAc, QAn, and QI within the three levels of operative laboratory function (operative resource management, process management, and outcome management).

Figure 3.10 is an illustration of a Venn diagram of TQM. This figure is in the form of a mandala that represents the concept of TQM as a system of three interrelated programs (QAc, QAn, and QI) that determine the state of quality (Q)—if they all function together in concert. The integrated management of *all* operational activities should result in optimal:

- Quality organizational effectiveness
- Quality planning
- Quality surveillance
- Operative resource management
- Operative procedures
- Patient care and other customer status outcomes
- Universal customer satisfaction.

Although not explicitly mentioned in recent versions of the JCAHO *AMH*—in deference to its preferential focus on functional

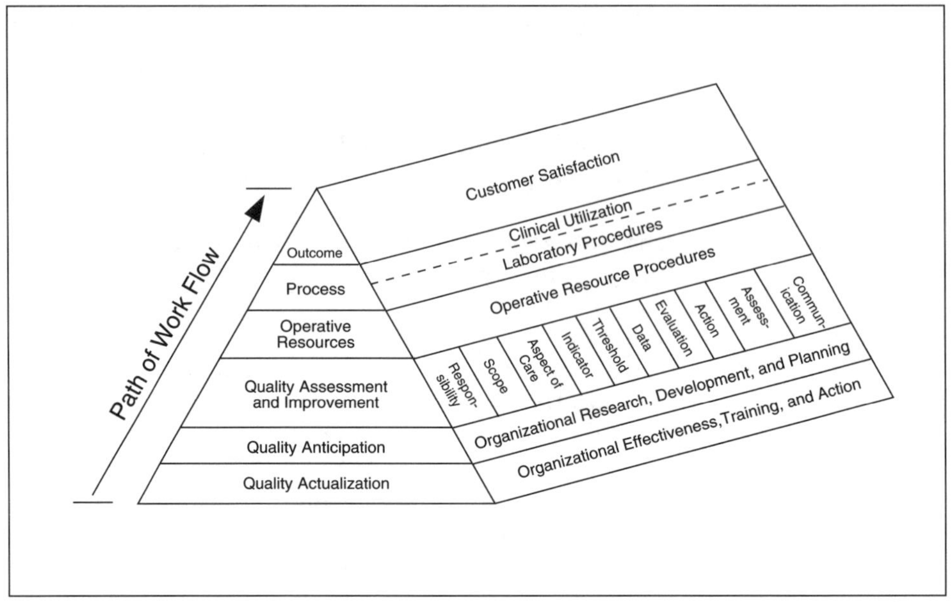

Figure 3.11 Hierarchical model of a total quality management system

organizational improvement—the *AMH* still reinforces the concepts of TQM by repeated emphasis on the importance of:

- Systematic, ongoing quality surveillance using an analytical process
- Strategic planning
- Organizational effectiveness.

These TQM principles are clearly woven into the matrix of the JCAHO accreditation guidelines, although they are not as explicitly designated as above.

The hierarchical model of TQM in Figure 3.11 emphasizes the importance of an analytical process of quality surveillance as a key to integrating all operational activity levels. The model includes the complete operational path of work flow as a major dimension.

This is a complex model, which befits the inherent complexity of TQM. All but one operational management level can be subdivided horizontally into their major program sequences. For example, QAc can be subdivided into a hierarchy of procedural events from determining organizational values and building individual and group awareness, to building organizational and analytical skills, to building personnel commitment, to realizing effective decision making; see Figure 3.9. At the next major operational level, the QAn program can be subdivided into its hierarchy of procedural events; see Figure 3.8.

The QI program can be subdivided into the steps of an analytical surveillance process, using the JCAHO ten-step format in this particular example. However, as the one exception in this model and as in all preceding models, the phases of the QI program are subdivided vertically. This vertical structure provides a temporal sequence of program development that transects all other programs and operational levels—as a surveillance program should.

The operative resource management level can be subdivided, again horizontally, into a hierarchy of important KMAs, providing a semblance of a pattern of cause and effect. The process management level can be subdivided horizontally into its three major phases (pre-, intra-, and postlaboratory), as well as the clinical utilization process; see Figure 3.3. Finally, the outcome management level can be subdivided horizontally into the general catagories of internal and external customer service outcome.

QC steps are expected to be included as a part of every procedure within every major program or management level. As such, all operational QC activities are symbolized as intersecting with the QI assessment and improvement function. This modeled portrayal of the interaction of the three administrative programs (QAc, QAn, and QI) with the operative-level activities is a conceptual fingerprint of the entire TQM system.

LABORATORY CONTINUOUS QUALITY IMPROVEMENT

Some say that TQM and CQI are synonymous terms: TQM being a quality management term used most often by the nonhealthcare manufacturing industries and CQI being a synonym used often by the healthcare industry. Such explanations of the relationship of TQM to CQI are semantic myths. Yes, there is a gray zone which obscures clearcut differentiaion between the two management approaches—both are linked to satisfying customer need. Still, the two terms are not synonymous and pioneering quality managers in the nonhealthcare industry generated both concepts long before health care adopted them.

Understanding and practicing the precepts of TQM are absolutely essential to successfully achieving the expectations of CQI. TQM is the managerial means, represented by the administrative resource management programs. CQI is the managerial end, represented by the desired operative resources, processes, and outcomes. TQM is the structural foundation on which an organization actualizes CQI.

TQM precepts emphasize building the culture by which the programs for organizational effectiveness, planning, and surveillance/communication can be successful. CQI philosophy emphasizes what direction an organizational culture should aim toward. The chief target should be meeting the customer's needs by continually seeking an improved total industrial operation in a changing social, economic, and technological environment.

On one hand, CQI is a managerial process that energizes organizational commitment to achieving continuous improvement of all operational functions as evidenced by a quest for zero defects and maximum customer satisfaction. On the other hand, it is a philosophy requiring total commitment including complete leadership support. The CQI credo is more than just. "Do it correctly the first time."[43] Rather, it is:

> Even with sustained quality that is continually acceptable to current standards of excellence, if there has been no sign of improvement over a reasonable period of time, it is quality management that must be broken and needs improvement.

In the quest for zero defects, should not 99.9% conformance to design specifications be acceptable? Only 0.1% error might sound "close enough." Testing this premise, it has been approximated that, if all air traffic control is performed correctly at O'Hare International Airport in Chicago 99.9% of the time, 0.1% error will result in 2 unsafe landings per day (assuming at least 2000 landings per day). Now, would that 0.1% error rate really be conscionably tolerable? In health care, zero defects might not always be attainable—or even desirable. The point is that CQI provides a force toward that elusive goal of zero defects—reminding us that we can always do better.[44]

In this age of ascending customer advocacy, increasing effort is being exerted to assure the quality of health care for the patient by reducing the incidence of adverse events and striving for excellence of patient care. Customers and their advocates have become increasingly influential over issues such as the quality of laboratory health care and safety, as exemplified by CLIA '88 and tightened OSHA requirements. Thus, the term "customer" is a broadening category that includes patients, clinical staff, laboratory employees, and many others: wherever there is a supplier there is a customer and vice versa.

CQI, descendant of the principles developed in post-war Japan by Deming, Crosby, and others, is a managerial approach that focuses on the customer as the ultimate arbiter of improved quality of health care—and the patient is the quintessential healthcare customer. An increasingly large segment of the healthcare industry is adopting this process as accreditation requirements tighten.

This omnibus approach to quality management is the centerpiece of the JCAHO *Agenda for Change* which establishes CQI as the chief approach for improvement of patient care quality and reduction of healthcare costs. However, the members of the JCAHO prefer to refer to "continuous quality improvement" in lower-case letters—they do not want CQI (or TQM) to become another professional management icon imprisoned in the hackneyed jargon of the day.

Tied closely to behavioral management theory, CQI is a comprehensive organizational process that poses a formidable challenge as it is being implemented in the laboratory. However, the theory is straightforward and implementation can be very practical. JCAHO guidelines and Deming's fourteen points can be translated into mutual terms of the laboratory CQI process as follows:[45,46]

- There must be *actualization* of:

  1. a committed leadership that actively promotes a process of continuous, never-ending quality improvement in an environment of constant change
  2. supervisors helping and inspiring employees, driving out feelings of fear, inadequacy, and lack of pride in the work place
  3. a constancy of organization-wide commitment to quality management
  4. teamwork and partnership as organizational approaches to making quality and productivity improvements; using cross-disciplinary teams; breaking down organizational barriers
  5. management of all quality work processes through an integrated systems approach.

- There must be *anticipation* of:

  1. who the customer is; the customer public is pluralistic; customers are internal as well as external to the laboratory
  2. what the customers' needs are; there must be plans to enhance customer-supplier dialogue whereby feedback information is available from both internal and external customers; managers must listen to suggestions from those who are closest to the work; enhance long-term customer-supplier relationships
  3. 100% conformance to expectations through plans for a work process that facilitates:

     a. performing the right procedure
     b. performing every procedure correctly the first time
  4. improved productivity through improvement of the quality of the laboratory product; personnel should strive for quality not for fulfillment of work standards
  5. modern education and training of the required quality management skills on the job.

- There must be *surveillance* ensuring that

  1. data is collected systematically
  2. variation is understood in the analysis of the data

3. analysis of data reveals opportunities for improvement, including underlying causes of problems
4. there is documented evidence of continuous quality improvement.

Notice that Deming's fourteen points can be structurally organized within the three programs of the TQM system.

The CQI process consists of both objective managerial and subjective cultural elements. It is a specific managerial process focused on a specific outcome of continuous quality improvement and customer satisfaction. CQI is also an organizational process, a cultural attitude, a subjective state of mind, a philosophical template for organizational expectations—- a way of doing routine business.

The JCAHO has adopted certain principles of continuous quality improvement that are applicable to any healthcare organizational plan. They are summarized as follows[47]:

- Mission statement: the chief organizational mission is to guarantee *continuous quality improvement* to its customers.

- Scope: CQI is an *organization-wide process* involving

  1. All people–all leaders, all workers, and all customers
  2. All activities that impact on the quality of outcome, process and resources.

- Responsibility: CQI requires total organizational commitment, including that of the leadership.

- Objectives:

  1. Anticipate and identify opportunities to improve, instead of just identifying and reacting to acute problems.
  2. Focus on improving the whole system of processes and functions—instead of individual people.
  3. Select measurable indicators of quality.
  4. Improve information management; improve the data.
  5. Strive for *improved communication* (feedback) from all customers (internal and external).
  6. Create an *organizational culture* that welcomes improvement— even though improvement means change.

Similarly, the leader's role in a CQI setting is to:

- Learn: Become personally knowledgeable about CQI concepts and methods.

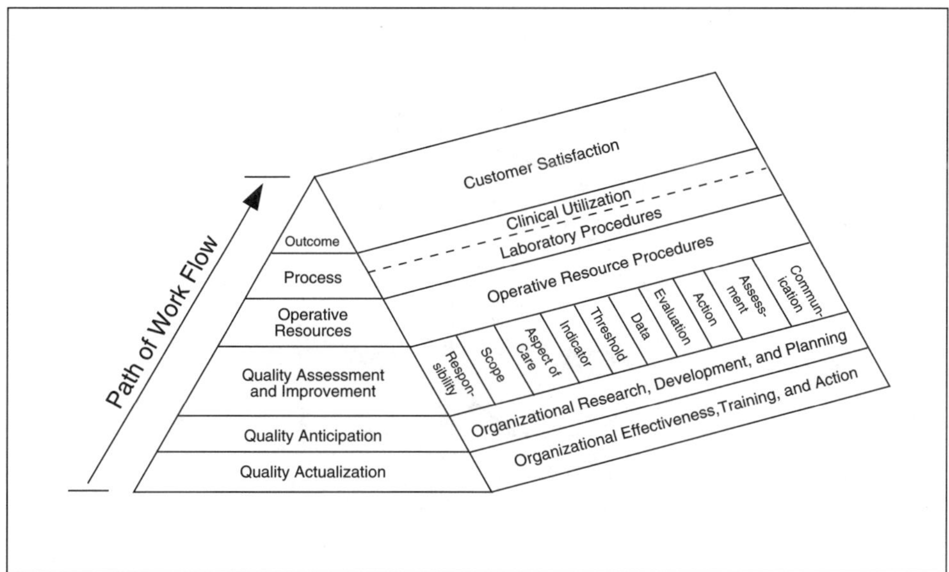

Figure 3.12 Hierarchical model of the continuous quality improvement process integrated with the total quality management system

- Use: Explicitly consider CQI in all decision making.
- Encourage: Promote CQI throughout the organization.
- Facilitate: Work with other leaders to evaluate and improve quality.
- Support: Provide the resources, including time, to assess and improve quality.
- Focus: Seek and use customer feedback and performance data to assess quality.
- Self evaluate: Periodically evaluate their own effectiveness in improving quality.

A model of the CQI process (integrated with the TQM system) is symbolized in Figure 3.12. The model depicts the three major elements of CQI, beginning with the paramount goal of *continuous improvement* of satisfying the customer's needs through total *organizational commitment*. The success of the model is dependent on the organization's bidirectional flow of communication with both internal and external customers. Objective managerial procedures must be linked to subjective organization-wide commitment for there to be continual improvement of

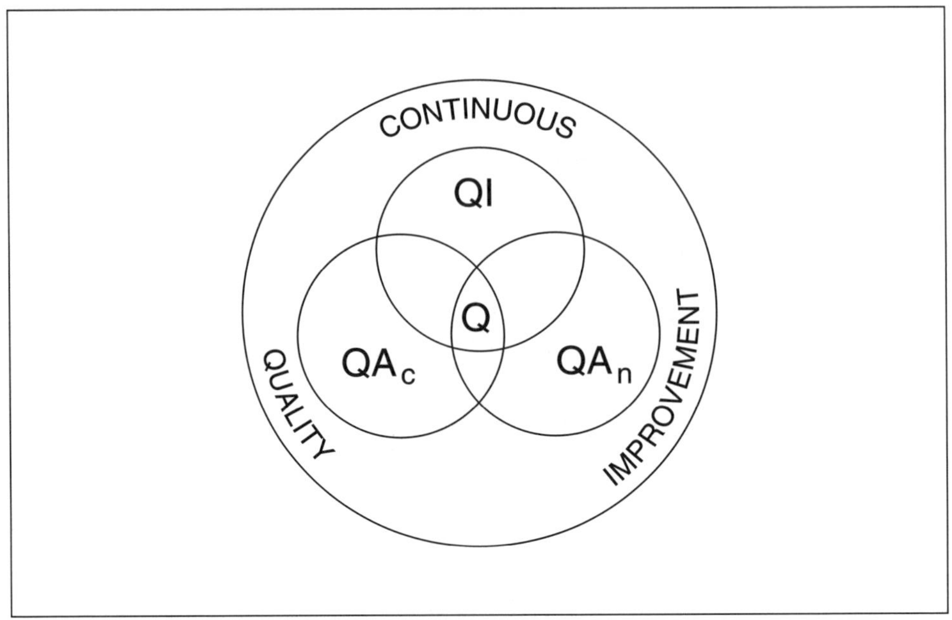

Figure 3.13 Mandala for total quality management and continuous quality improvement

all important (prioritized) operational activities. The means by which the laboratory can achieve these three chief elements of CQI are the TQM programs for team building (commitment), quality planning (prioritizing needs), and quality surveillance (improvement). Figure 3.12 highlights the chief elements of the CQI process with a hint of the QI surveillance process always operating in the background. The model also includes the complete path of work flow as a major dimension.

Figure 3.13 represents an expansion of the mandala of Figure 3.10. The initial figure for TQM is enhanced by a fourth circular component representing the concept of the CQI philosophy and process that embraces the programs of TQM and provides guidance toward the ultimate goal of continuous improvement of quality and laboratory excellence. This outer circle represents the CQI environment in which TQM activities should function.

Figure 3.14 further illustrates application of the philosophy of continuous improvement. Previous QC and QA practices have focused on the establishment of averaged criteria for QC standards and QA indicators. The traditional symbol for excellence has been the bell-shaped curve bracketing a central mean. The mean value for a given procedural result has represented the QC "normal" standard. The control limits for QC purposes have classically been expressed as ± 2 SD about the average or mean. Both the mean and the control limits have been used to characterize the definition for a traditionally QC-based QA indicator.

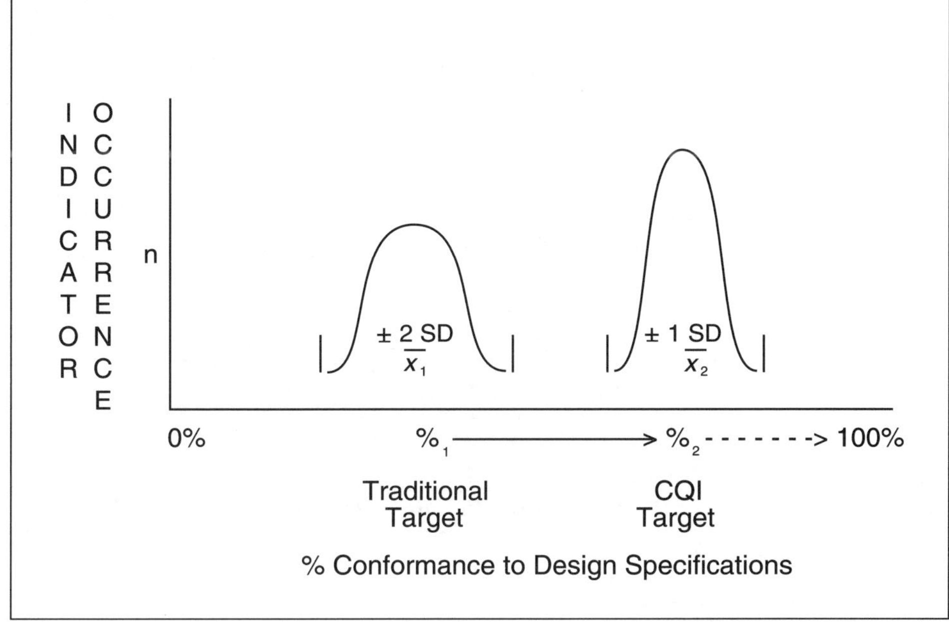

Figure 3.14 The target for indicator quality in a traditional versus a CQI laboratory

A typical quality surveillance threshold would be reached when the indicator event exceeded the ± 2 SD control limit for more than a given percentage of the total number of indicator occurrences. The traditional emphasis has been on maintaining statistically minimal variance from the mean value of a procedure's design specifications.

Practicing TQM in the CQI environment, the objective is threefold. First is to move the initial percentage of conformance ($\%_1$) continually nearer to 100% conformance ($\%_2$)—a TQM-CQI corollary would be reducing a QI indicator's threshold. Second is to reduce the range of the control limits; for example, improving the QC control limit from ± 2 SD to ± 1 SD—analogous to tightening a QI indicator's criterion. Third is to reduce the absolute indicator occurance rate. Such improvement objectives require maximum organizational efficiency and effectiveness: an organization performing an appropriate procedure correctly the first time. Such organizational overall efficacy requires organizational effectiveness, methodical planning, and prioritized surveillance.

Ironically, the frequently made comment that modern quality management is a "shift to a new paradigm" is historically inaccurate. In his 1932 classic text, Shewhart described a quality improvement cycle and philosophy that presaged the modern CQI process and TQM system. His model, a version of which is illustrated in Figure 3.15, is cited often in the quality management literature and is the basis for practically every modern assessment and improvement process.[48,49]

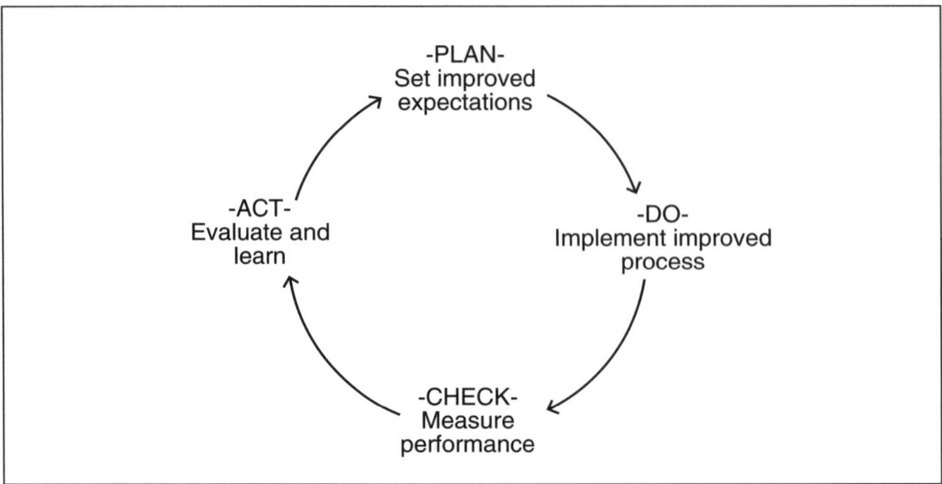

Figure 3.15 Model of the Shewart quality improvement cycle

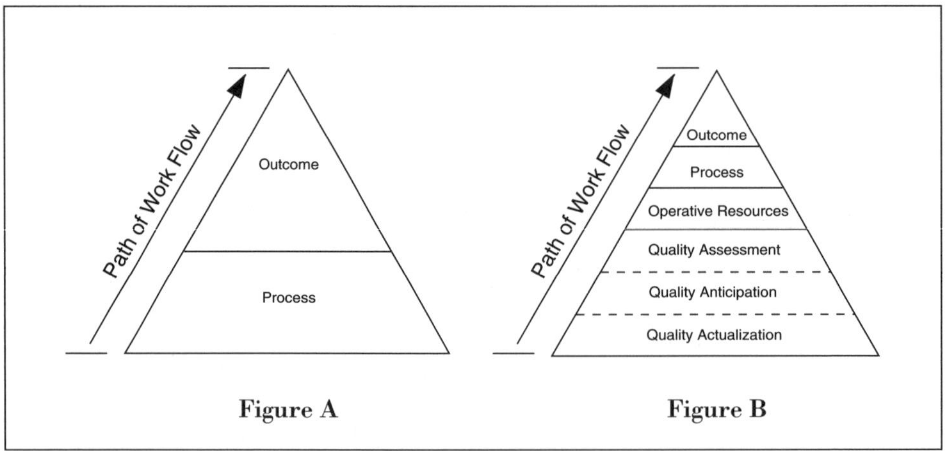

Figure 3.16A Model of the traditional, operative path of work flow
Figure 3.16B Model of the modern, total operational path of work flow

INCORPORATING TQM AND CQI INTO THE COMPLETE OPERATIONAL PATH OF WORK FLOW

As illustrated in Figure 3.16A, the traditional path of laboratory work flow is represented by operative process and outcome: beginning with laboratory product selection (test need) and ending with customer satisfaction (patient outcome). Considering all of the nontechnical laboratory activities that are really involved in support of laboratory technical operations and outcome management, the modern, total operational path of work flow is much more extensive in scope and complexity, as is schematically shown in Figure 3.16B.

Table III
Sources of Indicators for Monitoring Laboratory TQM and CQI

- Quality Actualization Program
  - Team building indicators
    - Team morale
    - Team skills
  - Team maintenance indicators
  - Team effectiveness indicators
    - Decision making
    - Leadership

- Quality Anticipation Program
  - Key management area indicators
  - Research indicators
  - Development indicators
  - Long-, medium-, and short-range goals, objectives, taskings, and milestone indicators

- Quality Surveillance Program
  - Aspects of care indicators
    - High-volume
    - High-risk
    - Problem-prone
  - Path of work flow quality—from QAc to continuous quality improvement of outcome and customer satisfaction

In its entirety, the operational path includes all infrastructural, organizational resource, administrative-level management elements of QAc, QAn, and QI—plus all the operative management elements of operational resources, process, and outcome. It begins with the actualization of personnel commitment and decision making and it ends with continuous quality improvement in answer to the needs of the customer. Thus, that which seems most apparent on a day-to-day basis—the technical process and customer outcome—is really just the tip of the proverbial iceberg when compared to all the organizational ingredients that affect the ultimate laboratory outcome.

Fully understanding the scope of the total path of laboratory work flow is essential to planning, implementing, and sustaining the TQM and CQI processes. Mapping the total path facilitates the selection of indicators for truly systematic quality surveillance.

Table IV
Schedule for the Integrated Implementation of TQM and CQI

Step	Actualization Phase	Anticipation Phase	Surveillance Phase
One	Select a leader and team to be responsible for coordination and follow-up	Select a leader and team to be responsible for coordination and follow-up	Select a leader and team to be responsible for coordination and follow-up
Two	Write the program plan including the training curriculum; identify the personnel to be taught	Write the program plan including the training curriculum; identify the personnel to be taught	Write the program plan including the training curriculum; identify the personnel to be taught
Three	Prioritize values	Prioritize values, mission and all customer needs for important KMAs	Prioritize important customer needs and related important aspects of care
Four	Study personality, self-awareness, group dynamics, and group awareness	Identify all strategies to meet important customer needs	Establish outcome surveillance indicators through joint lab/clinical collaboration
Five	Practice conflict resolution skills	Establish a research phase for each strategy	Establish initial process surveillance indicators
Six	Practice communication skills	Establish a development phase for each strategy	Establish operative resource surveillance indicators
Seven	Practice cooperation and negotiation skills	Establish an implementation phase for each strategy	Establish QI surveillance indicators
Eight	Practice empowerment skills	Establish goals and objectives for each strategic phase	Establish QAn surveillance indicators
Nine	Practice analysis, decision making, and action skills	Establish taskings with milestone dates and action officers for each strategic phase	Establish QAc surveillance indicators
Ten	Reappraise annually	Reappraise annually	Reappraise annually

Sources of TQM and CQI Quality Indicators

Since the QI process is integrated throughout all managerial aspects of TQM and CQI—including all three administrative programs for QI, QAn, and QAc—a wealth of potential indicators is available for monitoring and evaluating every conceivable technical, clerical, managerial, and administrative activity. If such a systematic approach is used, the requirement of the *Agenda for Change* to improve traditional clinical as well as behavioral management indicators can be easily met. Table III provides a general list of the indicator sources that can be applied to every laboratory-important aspect of care and to every KMA at every organizational level.

Implementing TQM and CQI

It would be ideal to methodically implement a TQM system and CQI process from the ground up. That is to say, plan and institute the actualization program first. Then, the organization-wide strategic planning program would follow. Next, establish the evaluation and monitoring program. Finally, build operative activities—operational resources, technical procedures, and outcome control—stepwise on top of the administrative infrastructure.

Of course, reality virtually never matches the ideal situation. Assumably, most laboratories already have established essential operations along with some form of quality surveillance and with some bits and pieces of planning and team building. How can TQM and CQI be implemented under such dynamic circumstances?[50,51]

Because of pragmatic necessity and the inherent hands-on nature of the laboratory profession, the initial approach begs to be incremental in nature. There has to be some starting point, so why not start with process surveillance? In fact, there is compelling urgency for an already-established laboratory to expeditiously begin with operative process surveillance. The attractiveness of this choice is based on the immediate criticalness of already-established technical processes to patient care, the laboratory's process control experience, and the already available QC database.

Selection of operative resource indicators often follows, again, incrementally. Selection of these indicators are also relatively easy since there is so much resource management data already available. Next, outcome surveillance indicators develop in the natural course of events because of the added time needed to establish effective communication between laboratorian and clinician. Finally, selection of indicators for the overall effectiveness of the surveillance program, as well as the QAn planning and QAc team building programs, follow in the same incremental fashion.

Now that the latter scenario has been described: beware that even though the initial selection of process QI indicators seems to be the logical first step toward attaining TQM and CQI—*the incremental approach is a mistake.* Instead, a combined, three-pronged campaign is needed with preferential emphasis on organizational actualization.

Table IV illustrates a balanced schedule for implementing all three administrative programs in synchronony and parallel to one another. First, select a leader for each of the three programs; that person is to follow-up all program activities—not to micromanage but to delegate (empower), facilitate, and coordinate. Additionally, select an appropriately multidisciplined team, representing all major functional sections of the laboratory and clinical activities that are involved.

Second, write a plan for each program, including the initial training curriculum and schedule, specifying which personnel are to be taught and in what sequence of phasing or grouping. Each program plan must dovetail with the other two—the training schedules, especially, must meld.

Table IV goes on to outline, the eight steps that follow. Steps three through nine, map out the procedural steps of "hands-on" implementation for each of the three programs. Note the emphasis on prioritization in step three and the emphasis on outcome over QC-rich process in step four. Step ten is reappraisal of each of the programs on, at least, an annual basis. Lessons learned from the appraisal must be documented, disseminated to all employees, and used as the main focus of follow-up training.

The scheduling and implementation of these three programs can be sequential, partially overlapped, or completely in tandem. However, if there is ever a necessity to rank the three programs in order of precedence, use the following formula: rank QAc first, QAn second, and QI third. To do otherwise is to stray from building and sustaining the necessary infrastructure—and falling prey, instead, to incrementalism.

REFERENCES

1. Webster's Third International Dictionary of the English Language. Springfield, MA: Merriam Webster, Inc, 1984.
2. Crandell DK. The Expanded Role of Quality Assurance. In: Howanitz PJ, ed. Conference Proceedings on Quality Assurance in Physician Office, Bedside, and Home Testing. April 2-4 1986, Atlanta, GA. Skokie, IL: College of American Pathologists; 1986.
3. The Random House College Dictionary. New York, NY: Random House, Inc, 1984.
4. Schenken JR. Medical care. Quality assessment and quality assurance. (editorial). Arch Path Lab Med, 1986;110:876-878.

5. Bowen OR. Shattuck lecture–what is quality care? NEJM, 1987;316:1578-1580.
6. Stedman's Medical Dictionary. Baltimore, MD: Williams and Wilkins Co, 1972.
7. Dorland's Medical Dictionary. Philadelphia, PA: W.B. Saunders Co, 1981.
8. Council Report: Council on Medical Service, American Medical Association. Quality of care. JAMA, 1986;256:1032-1034.
9. The 1992 Joint Commission Accreditation Manual for Hospitals. Oakbrook Terrace, IL: Joint Commission on Accreditation of Healthcare Organizations, 1991.
10. Standards for Laboratory Accreditation. Northfield, IL: College of American Pathologists, 1988.
11. Harris DH, Chaney FB. Human Factors in Quality Assurance. New York, NY: John Wiley and Sons, 1969.
12. Technical Briefing: The Joint Commission Quality Assurance Model. Chicago, IL: American Hospital Association, February 1989.
13. Schyve P. Moving toward quality improvement. Conference on Quality Assurance in Pathology and Laboratory Medicine: Perspectives for the 1990's. Washington, DC: College of American Pathologists, May 2, 1990.
14. Hungate RW. Lessons from industry. Phys Exec, 1989;15:13-16.
15. Donabedian A. The quality of care: how can it be assessed? JAMA, 1988;260:1743-1748.
16. Donabedian A. Evaluating the quality of care: Milbank Memorial Fund Quarterly, 1966;44:166-203.
17. Donabedian A. The Criteria and Standards of Quality. Ann Arbor, MI: Health Admin Press, 1980.
18. Frombert R (ed). Monitoring and Evaluation: Pathology and Medical Laboratory Services. Chicago, IL: Joint Commission on Accreditation of Healthcare Organizations, 1987.
19. Summary of the Second National Invitational Forum on Clinical Indicator Development. Chicago, IL: Joint Commission on Accreditation of Healthcare Organizations, Mar 31, 1989.
20. Total Quality Management in Healthcare Seminar (Module 1). Curtis Mathesin Scientific, Inc, 1990.
21. Bennett JS. Quality Assurance in the use of Monitoring Devices: The Canadian Experience. Howanitz, PJ, ed. Conference Proceedings on Quality Assurance in the Physician Office, Bedside, and Home Testing. April 2-4, 1986, Atlanta, GA. Skokie, IL: College of American Pathologists, 1986.
22. Peach P. Quality Control for Management. Englewood Cliffs, NJ: Prentice-Hall, 1964.

23. Nixon F. Managing To Achieve Quality and Reliability. London: McGraw Hill, 1971.

24. Best ML. A model QA program as a management tool. Med Lab Obs, 1990;22, 42-46.

25. Nosanchuk JS, Caverhill R. Quality assurance: a systematic approach. Chicago: American Society of Clinical Pathologists, Check Sample, Special Topics No. ST 89-1(ST-166), 1989;27(1):1-5.

26. Kinkus CA, McMann NW. A sweeping QA program for a large hospital lab. Med Lab Observer, 1990;22:31-35.

27. ASCP Board of Registry and Commission on Associated Members Activities. Monitoring performance of certified medical laboratory personnel through laboratory quality assurance programs. Lab Med, 1985; 16:349-351.

28. Beautyman W, Rawnsley HM. A proposal for a department of pathology improvement program. Pathologist, 1981;35:92-96.

29. Joint Commission Primer on Clinical Indicator Development and Application. Measuring Quality in Health Care. Oakbrook Terrace, IL: Joint Commission on Accreditation of Healthcare Organizations, 1990.

30. The Transition from QA to CQI: An Introduction To Quality Improvement In Health Care. Oakbrook Terrace, IL: Joint Commission on Accreditation of Healthcare Organizations, 1991.

31. Raslavicus PA, Kaufman HW. Use strategic planning to reshape your lab's future. Med Lab Obs, 1990;22:22-27.

32. Drucker PE. Management: Tasks, Responsibilities, Practices. New York, NY: Harper and Row, 1974.

33. Holmberg SR, Logue LJ. A clinical laboratory environmental assessment and its implications for strategic planning: Part I. Clin Lab Man Rev, 1991;4:16-23.

34. Holmberg SR, Logue LJ. Developing an environmental assessment for effective clinical laboratory strategic planning: Part II. Clin Lab Man Rev, 1991;4:99-104.

35. Maffetone MA. TQM: passion and process. Clin Lab Man Rev, 1991;5:476-478.

36. Rubin I, Inguagiato R. Behavioral quality assurance: a transforming process. Phys Exec, 1990;16:30-33.

37. Scheuing EE. Creating a quality culture in your organization. Clin Lab Man Rev. 1991;5:86,88-90,94-95.

38. Crocker OL, Charney S, Chiu JSL: Quality Circles: A Guide to Participation and Productivity. Agincourt, Canada: Methuen Publications, 1984.

39. Myers IB. Gifts Differing. Palo Alto, CA: Consulting Psychologists Press, Inc, 1989.

40. Lawrence G. People Types and Tiger Stripes. Gainesville, FL: Center for Applications of Psychological Type, Inc, 1987.
41. Berne E. Games People Play. New York, NY: Ballantine Books, 1964.
42. Fisher R, Ury W. Getting to Yes: Negotiating Agreement Without Giving In. New York, NY: Penguin Books, 1981.
43. Tomich N. TQM: "Doing it right the first time". U.S. Med, October 1989:1,8,13.
44. DeWar J. Quality consultant workshop, undated.
45. Develop internal standards to get ahead of advancing forces. Hospital Peer Review, 1989;14:41-43.
46. Walton M. The Deming Management Method. New York, NY: Putnam Publishing Group, 1986.
47. A Brief Overview of the Joint Commission "Agenda for Change." Oakbrook Terrace, IL: Joint Commission on Accreditation of Healthcare Organizations, 1989.
48. Shewhart WA. Economic Control of Quality of Manufactured Product. New York, NY: Van Nostrand, 1931.
49. Gottlieb LK, Margolis CZ, Schoenbaum SC. Clinical practice guidelines at an HMO: development and implementation in a quality improvement model. Qual Rev Bull, 1990;16:80-86.
50. Westgard JO, Barry PL, Tomer RH. Implementing quality management (TQM) in health-care laboratories: a how to approach. Clin Lab Man Rev, 1991;5:353-355, 358-359, 362-366.
51. Simpson KN, Kaluzny AD, McLaughlin CP. Total quality and the management of laboratories: implementation strategies and challenges. Clin Lab Man Rev, 1991;5:448-456.

4. JCAHO Quality Management Guidelines and the Ten-Step Process

ASSUMPTIONS ARE INFORMAL rules that are useful in initiating a laboratory quality management program—whether it be quality assessment and improvement (QI), quality anticipation (QAn), or quality actualization (QAc). Assess the facts that are immediately at hand and formulate straight-forward postulates that can serve as *ad hoc* mission and vision statements. Such assumptions help move early planning in the correct direction. For example, it normally should be accepted that a healthcare laboratory is:

- Patient-care oriented
- Technically sophisticated
- Environmentally inherently dangerous
- Resource intensive.

These observations hint of the organization's eventual mission statement of "what we are today."

Consequent to the above observations, it should be reasonable to assume that:

- Laboratory service to the patient *must* be of the highest medical quality.
- Laboratory procedures *must* be of the highest technical, state-of-the-art quality.
- Laboratory workers (and any others in the area) *must* be kept safe.
- Laboratory resources *must* be judiciously utilized.

The above assumptions reveal multiple customers of laboratory services with an agenda of many, diverse expectations for outcomes to be attained. These customers include the:

- Patient, aspiring to a satisfactory state-of-health
- Attending clinical physician, aspiring to a satisfactory state-of-the-art-and-science-of-healthcare
- Employee, aspiring to a satisfactory state-of-welfare—including safety
- Funding officer, aspiring to a satisfactory state-of-fiscal-balance
- And many others with their own aspirations to some state-of-satisfaction.

These assumptions and implications provide a basis for the organization's eventual vision statement of "what we want to be tomorrow."

National guidelines are formal rules, established by the federal government, the Joint Commission on Accreditation of Healthcare Organizations (JCAHO), the College of American Pathologists (CAP), and other organizations. The federal government and the Joint Commission are improving healthcare quality—including laboratory quality—by developing public law, federal regulations, professional standards, and implementation requirements. The CAP plays a partnership role by providing a laboratory-specific inspection and accreditation program that supports the federal and JCAHO standards. Several other national- and state-level organizations provide standards, inspection, and accreditation programs—all aimed at quality improvement; eg, the Food and Drug Administration (FDA), the American Association of Blood Banks (AABB), and state regulatory agencies.

A second set of rules, the JCAHO *Accreditation Manual for Hospitals,* (*AMH*) contains hospital-wide standards, emphasizing organization-wide functions rather than discipline-specific procedures. The manual's chapter on Improving Organizational Performance (PI) was formerly the chapter on Quality Assurance (QA). This revised chapter still incorporates elements of a formal, ten-step process (TSP) for uniformly monitoring, evaluating, and assessing opportunities for quality improvement, although the TSP is not spelled out as before.[1]

From 1984 until 1991, the JCAHO endorsed the ten-step model for quality surveillance. Most recently, however, the Joint Commission has begun to deemphasize the TSP and encourage consideration of all surveillance and analytical approaches. Still, the ten-step model is an effective means to organize the selecting, monitoring, and assessing of quality improvement indicators for all laboratory organizational and operative activities—it continues to be a very successful model for quality surveillance planning and minimal-cost screening purposes.

The JCAHO's *Agenda for Change* is a third set of rules—or rather a schedule for revising rules, at least through the next decade. Essentially, the *Agenda* is a strategic plan for institutionalizing the principles of total quality management (TQM) and continuous quality improvement (CQI) in all accredited healthcare organizations. In addition, it maps the modernization of the JCAHO hospital survey process.

The source of the following information is chiefly federal, JCAHO, and CAP documentation. However, some observations reflect personal managerial experience that is offered with the hope that they will be of practical assistance to the reader.

JCAHO LABORATORY ACCREDITATION GUIDELINES

JCAHO guidelines for quality management consist of policy statements, accreditation standards, and implementation requirements which undergo regular revision. Their most important publication is the *AMH*—the central source of accreditation policy and standards. In addition, the *Joint Commission Perspectives*, a bimonthly newsletter, reports changes in standards, survey policies, and procedures. Another publication, the *Agenda for Change Update*, has recently merged with *Perspectives*. The JCAHO also publishes a monthly *Quality Review Bulletin* (*QRB*) that provides valuable up-to-date information on JCAHO policies and advance notice of proposed revisions.

In addition, there are four helpful JCAHO manuals. *Monitoring and Evaluation for Pathology and Medical Laboratory Services* provides laboratory-specific instruction on establishing a quality management program based on the TSP.[2] The *Hospital Accreditation Program Scoring Guidelines for Pathology and Medical Laboratory Services Standards* (volume II of the *AMH*) provides information on interpretation of laboratory standards and the assessment of compliance.[3] A relatively new publication, the *Primer on Clinical Indicator Development and Application*, presents extensive information on the design and use of clinical indicators.[4] Another recent publication is The *Transition from QA to CQI: An Introduction to Quality Improvement in Health Care*.[5] Additional references continue to appear.

The *AMH* is a comprehensive collection of policies, standards, and definitions. The manual provides indispensable information for establishing and maintaining a successful quality management program and preparing for a satisfactory accreditation survey.

The *AMH* has also proven to be a very dynamic publication, steadily changing as the JCAHO develops its approach to quality management. A new edition is published every year and chapters will continue to change.

The *AMH* outlines universal goals and objectives for health care that must be met by a hospital and its central laboratory. On the other hand, the *AMH* does not specifically stipulate exactly how local institutional standards of practice should meet the JCAHO guidelines. Each healthcare organization is responsible for devising its own means of implementation and follow-up. The organization must determine its own scope of care, aspects of care, and procedures of quality care assessment by balancing local needs against local resources. Yet, once the hospital or laboratory establishes its own policies, programs, and procedures, the JCAHO and the CAP expect these rules to be followed as evidenced by sufficient documentation.

General Guidelines of Importance for Laboratory Services

The 1992 edition of the *AMH* was a bench mark issue.[6] Although future editions have continued to change substantivally in format and content, the 1992 edition served as an important, representative model, introducing major revisions. Both the 1992 and 1994 editions will serve as illustrations of those revisions in the following discussion.

The *AMH* includes introductory chapters that clearly explain the manual's intended use, recent standard revisions, and general administrative policies and procedures. The remaining chapters itemize specific accreditation standards and requirements by which the JCAHO measures the general operations of medical facilities for accreditation. These guidelines are presented in a convenient check list format that assists in self-assessment and final preparation for an on-site or interim survey. The 1994 *AMH* chapters are:[1]

- Patient Care Functions
    1. Rights of Patients and Organizational Ethics
    2. Assessment of Patients
    3. Entry to Setting or Service
    4. Nutritional Care
    5. Treatment of Patients
    6. Operative and Other Invasive Procedures
    7. Education of Patients and Family
    8. Coordination of Care.

- Organizational Functions
    1. Leadership
    2. Management of Information
    3. Management of Human Resources
    4. Management of the Environment of Care
    5. Surveillance, Prevention, and Control of Infection
    6. Improving Organizational Performance.

- Essential Structural Components
    1. Governing Body
    2. Management and Administration
    3. Medical Staff
    4. Nursing.

These *AMH* chapters contain general standards and specific requirements that apply directly to laboratory operations and accreditation, depending on the laboratory's size, scope, and workload distribution. Several chapters cover clinical and administrative activities and stipulate laboratory requirements that are necessary for high-quality patient care in those nonlaboratory disciplines. The laboratory director must be cognizant of those ancillary requirements even though they may not be under the direct control of a laboratorian; the laboratory director might still be responsible for the quality surveillance of these ancillary activities.

The *AMH* chapter covering "Pathology and Clinical Laboratory Services" (titled "Pathology and Medical Laboratory Services" in earlier editions) has become an entirely separate JCAHO *Accreditation Manual for Pathology and Clinical Laboratory Services* (*AMP*).[7] This manual includes revisions predicated on CLIA '88 requirements (ie, core standards) as well as intent statements and scoring guidelines.

Emphasis on Decentralized Laboratory Testing

The JCAHO has registered an abiding concern over decentralized medical laboratory services, referred to in this text as decentralized laboratory testing (DLT)—also known as ancillary or point-of-care testing. DLT includes any laboratory service performed outside the physical boundaries of the central laboratory department using noncentral laboratory personnel. The JCAHO began emphasizing DLT in the 1990 *AMH*, explicitly requiring coordinated monitoring by the central laboratory.[8] The 1990 *AMH* defined DLT as follows:

- Analytical testing performed at sites in the hospital but physically located outside the hospital's central laboratory. The testing sites are either under the jurisdiction of the organized pathology and medical laboratory or another department/service.
- Examples of such testing include bedside testing and in-unit testing such as occult blood testing, serological screens (for example mononucleosis or streptococcus), urine analysis, Gram stains, and glucometer testing.
- For the purposes of JCAHO standards, decentralized laboratory testing does not include testing in "satellite laboratories" under the jurisdiction of the organized pathology and medical laboratories that perform tests such as "stat" laboratory tests or off-site hemoglobins, hematocrits, or electrolytes. Other standards in the *AMH* (and, now the pathology and clinical laboratory services accreditation manual) apply to such satellite laboratories.
- Decentralized laboratory testing also does not include "special function laboratories" such as blood gas laboratories, most sites where intraoperative testing is performed, and cytogenetic laboratories.

- In addition, it does not include endocrinology laboratories that are not under the jurisdiction of the organized pathology and medical laboratory but that are sufficiently sophisticated to warrant evaluation using the standards in the *AMH* (and the pathology and clinical laboratory services manual).

The 1992 *AMH* incorporated all specific requirements for DLT under a new standard (PA.6.4). Although the JCAHO has emphasized "analytical" laboratories in the definition of DLT, there are some circumstances in which anatomical diagnostic laboratories also relate. The anatomical pathology service can refer certain tissue specimens to a clinical service for immunohistochemical or electron microscopic workup, with the final, written diagnosis being routed back through the anatomical pathology service to the patient record. For example, skin tissue specimens might be sent to the dermatology service for special histological and diagnostic workup. Under these conditions, the dermatopathology laboratory could meet the criteria of a DLT.

Many noncentral laboratories will have to stand the test of DLT criteria on a case-by-case basis. What might be considered a decentralized laboratory in one case could be considered a reference or totally separate laboratory service in another case—or, as is often the case in an academic medical center, it might be considered a clinical research laboratory. Each situation has to be dealt with individually, depending on laboratory location, directorship, operative versus administrative control, the quality of resources and procedures—and whether or not laboratory testing results are being used in any way to support clinical diagnosis or therapy.

All DLT must be considered in the quality management of hospital-wide patient care. They can be problematic if the:

- Patient specimen workload is high-volume.
- Tests done are of high-risk to the patient.
- Techniques used are inherently difficult to control (problem-prone).
- DLT technical personnel are inadequately trained in laboratory technique or in quality management.

The medical director of the DLT activity usually is responsible for the operative quality of whatever testing is being performed—a form of operative management responsibility at the quality control (QC) level. However, the responsibility for administrative-level quality management of these scattered laboratory activities often falls under the "jurisdictional cognizance" of the central laboratory director. Such a role is characterized by the laboratory director being responsible for coordinating, monitoring, and evaluating DLT quality without having direct, operative managerial authority over the actual laboratory procedures.

A well-established example of a rather unsophisticated form of decentralized testing is the semiquantitative dip-stick test employed in the home, in many clinics, and at the bedside. Reports are on record regarding the difficulty in assuring the control of accuracy of bedside glucose testing for diabetic patients.[9] In this case, the direct supervisory responsibility is usually that of the clinical and nursing services whose personnel are performing the tests.

More modern decentralized testing includes qualitative and quantitative analysis of body fluids and excretions using state-of-the-art electronics. Examples of such advanced DLT include bedside and intraoperative oximetry and glucose monitoring. These examples are just the beginning of testing capabilities that will continue to become more sophisticated with the development of ultrasensitive, noninvasive, biosensing devices and will become increasingly "user friendly." Thus, as DLT capabilities continue to expand, there promises to be an increase of control and surveillance requirements.

There are also the decentralized machines and instruments used to control and modify blood component transfusions—again, for bedside and intraoperative use. The use of blood warmers by the anesthesiology service is a classical area of laboratorian concern over sustaining quality during blood component utilization. Although blood bank personnel usually do not directly supervise or operate the warmers, the blood bank and the blood utilization committee are responsible for overseeing the quality of blood warming procedures.

JCAHO policy has generally excluded intraoperative testing as meeting the definition of a DLT. However, the quality management problems inherent in such testing are likely to make it an enlarging target for central laboratory oversight. Much of this decision depends on local circumstances and hospital leadership policy as the emphasis on DLT continues to develop.

In revising the standards for the 1994 *AMH*, the Joint Commission was obliged to recognize the impact of CLIA '88 on decentralized testing. Thus, there was modification of DLT standards that addressed waived testing. Standards addressing waived testing have been included in the *AMH* as well as in all other accreditation manuals for nonhospital-based, long term care, home care, and ambulatory health care organizations. As a result, the requirements for DLT are less explicit but are incorporated into the revised standards. For example, see standard requirement PA.1.2.6 of the 1994 *AMH*, which states:

> All laboratory testing done while an individual is under the care of the organization and of a member of the clinical staff is done in the organization's laboratories (including the central laboratory and any ancillary, near-patient-testing, and point-of-care-testing laboratories) or in approved reference laboratories;[1]

The CAP has adopted a similar position regarding DLT, referring to it as ancillary testing.

JCAHO Standards for Pathology and Clinical Laboratory Services

Describing JCAHO standards is fraught with one major challenge—every year they change. The following discussion addresses the standards published in the 1992 *AMH* as a foundation for consideration of the present and the future. From 1992 and onward, the JCAHO will continue to revise the standards for pathology and clinical laboratory services in the *AMP* or incorporate them under more general chapter headings in the *AMH*. How these changes will affect laboratory quality remains to be seen. However, it is predictable that the substance of the 1992 JCAHO standards—including the basic precepts of the ten-step model–will remain viable within the matrix of future Joint Commission accreditation guidelines for some time to come.

The 1992 *AMH* Chapter on Pathology and Clinical Laboratory Services described six JCAHO standards in detail. These were repeated in the 1993 edition of the *AMP*. They are as follows[6]:

Standard PA.1: *Pathology and clinical laboratory services and consultation are regularly and conveniently available to meet the needs of patients, as determined by the medical staff.*

> This standard covered requirements for the laboratory director, the pathologist staff, and the technical staff. To date, this is essentially unchanged in the *AMP*.

Standard PA.2: *There are sufficient space, equipment, and supplies within the pathology and clinical laboratory services to perform the required volume of work with optimal accuracy, precision, efficiency, timeliness, and safety.*

> This standard covered the resources required to support comprehensive testing and effective QC. To date, this is essentially unchanged in the *AMP*.

Standard PA.3: *Channels of communication within the pathology and clinical laboratory services, with other departments/services of the hospital and the medical staff, and with outside services and agencies are appropriate for the size and complexity of the hospital.*

> This standard covered requirements for adequate intra- and extralaboratory transfer of information, including electronic mail, satellite printers or terminals, written forms, and manual delivery capabilities sufficient to transmit test requests, specimens, and results. To date, this is essentially unchanged in the *AMP*.

Standard PA.4: *Required records and reports are maintained and, as appropriate, are filed in the patient's medical record and in the pathology and clinical laboratory services.*

This standard covered requirements for the adequacy of clerical services in providing and filing patient reports and records, as well as the timely distribution of laboratory reports to primary care providers. To date, this is essentially unchanged in the *AMP*.

Standard PA.5: *Quality control systems and measures of the pathology and clinical laboratory services are designed to assure the medical reliability of laboratory data.*

This standard covered requirements for appropriate licensing and certification of the laboratory and for adequate QC through proficiency testing, procedural plans, validation methods, test QC procedures, environmental control, reagent control, and equipment control. Special attention was paid to patient preparation, histocompatibility testing, and mixed lymphocyte culture techniques. To date, this is essentially unchanged in the *AMP*.

Standard PA.6: *Specific requirements are observed when anatomic pathology, blood transfusion, and clinical pathology services are offered.*

This standard included specific requirements for:

1. Anatomic pathology, including surgical pathology, autopsy and cytology services. These requirements address technical policies and procedures, facility adequacy, and staffing.
2. Blood transfusion service, including staffing, conforming with standards of the American Association of Blood Banks (AABB), and other specific technical policies and procedures
3. Clinical pathology, including staffing, proficiency testing, and specific technical policies and procedures for clinical chemistry, bacteriology, mycology, parasitology, virology, clinical microscopy, hematology, serology, radiobioassay, and any other intralaboratory disciplines
4. Decentralized laboratory testing.

To date, this is essentially unchanged in the *AMP*, except that waivered testing (viz, CLIA '88) supplants certain aspects of decentralized testing.

JCAHO QUALITY IMPROVEMENT STANDARDS AND THE TEN-STEP PROCESS

The JCAHO began requiring specifically delineated quality surveillance activities in 1979, referring to the process of "quality assurance". These indicator-focused standards were to eliminate retrospective audits and introduce the requirement for a systematic, hospital-wide quality surveillance program. In 1984, the JCAHO introduced a ten-step model for formalizing QA activities and for monitoring and evaluating patient care quality. In 1985, the *AMH* included a separate chapter on QA for the first time.

The 1985 QA chapter included four standards with their respective requirements. These standards were as follows[10]:

- QA.1 The requirement for an ongoing QA program
- QA.2 The required scope of a QA program
- QA.3 The requirements for QA monitoring and evaluating activity, including a preamble that specifically outlined the TSP. The process ensured that:

    1. *monitoring activities* will be ongoing, systematic, and comprehensive
    2. *data collection and evaluation activities* will be organized to identify problems and opportunities for quality improvement.
    3. *opportunity-finding and problem-solving activities* will be effective enough to show ongoing evidence of quality improvement.

- QA.4 The requirements for the administration and coordination of an overall hospital QA program.

In 1987, the JCAHO revised five elements of the ten-step model 1) to assist in indicator evaluation by introduction of the threshold element and 2) to emphasize the importance of communication of lessons learned. Table I lists the components of the process, highlighting the changes made in 1987 and indicating how the process facilitates monitoring, evaluating, and assessing continuous improvement. Since then, the JCAHO format has proven itself exceedingly valuable in meeting accreditation requirements for quality management.

Reminiscent of the scientific method and Shewhart's cycle, the JCAHO designed ten steps to counter the natural tendency for QA methods to vary from one organization to the next: various aspects of quality surveillance needed to be more uniform for easier survey and interorganizational comparison. The TSP also introduced certain principles of TQM into healthcare quality management—which has facilitated establishing the philosophy and process of CQI.

In the 1992 AMH, the quality management chapter and the TSP again took on an altered appearance[6]:

- The chapter title, Quality Assurance, changed to Quality Assessment and Improvement; since 1994 this title has been Improving Organizational Performance.
- The abbreviation, QA, remained as a reference label for the quality assessment and improvement standards, but that label eventually changed to QI for Quality Assessment and Improvement; the abbreviation QI is used in this text in reference to the quality

Table I7
The JCAHO Ten-step Process for Quality Indicator Monitoring and Evaluation

Original Format	1987 Revision
1. Assign responsibility.	1. Assign responsibility.(UNCHANGED)
2. Delineate scope of care.	2. Delineate scope of care. (UNCHANGED)
3. Identify important aspects of care.	3. Identify important aspects of care. (UNCHANGED)
4. Identify monitors by which the aspects of care may be evaluated.	4. Identify indicators of quality by which the important aspects of care can be evaluated. Establish an "indicator-specific information set" with measurable criteria for monitoring. (#4 and #5 MERGED)
5. Establish measurable criteria or standards by which the monitors may be evaluated.	5. Establish thresholds for evaluation of indicator data. Thresholds are control limits that should not be exceeded. If the threshold is exceeded, evaluation of its indicator and important aspect of care will be triggered. (NEW)
6. Monitor the important aspects of care and organize the data.	6. Monitor the important aspects of care and collect and organize the data. (UNCHANGED)
7. Reach a conclusion (interpretation) based on evaluation of the data.	7. Evaluate a quality indicator and its important aspect of care when a) the threshold level is exceeded or there are abnormal trends or patterns or b) there has not been any significant improvement over a reasonable period of time. Analyze the data and identify any opportunities for improvement. (REVISED)
8. Recommend action.	8. Recommend and take action to improve care. (#8 and #9 MERGED)
9. Determine the individual responsible for and take action.	9. Assess and document the effectiveness of the QI actions in terms of improvement of patient care. (RENAMED/RENUMBERED)
10. Evaluate the overall effectiveness of the QA monitoring results.	10. Communicate relevant information to the organization-wide QI program. (NEW)

assessment and improvement program. Since 1994, the JCAHO abbreviation is PI or (IOP) for the newest title.

- The phrase, monitoring and evaluating quality and medical appropriateness of patient care, changed to monitoring and evaluating quality of patient care, omitting medical appropriateness as the universal parameter that it had been.
- The emphasis on monitoring and evaluating problem indicators changed to evaluating and assessing improvement opportunities.
- The preamble to the previous Standard QA.3 disappeared. Thus, there was no itemized listing of the ten steps. Instead, most elements of the ten steps were integrated into the various standards and requirements of the QI chapter. Descriptions of the TSP continued to appear in other JCAHO publications—but further modifications of definition and emphasis could be anticipated.[2, 4, 5]

As of 1992, the JCAHO focus was no longer fixed on the process of selecting and monitoring indicators. Over the previous decade, the practice of QA and TQM was considered to have become bogged down in the first half of the TSP where indicator selection was the predominate exercise. The original intentions for QA had failed.

The quality management process can easily become mired in the natural morass of its own *problem-solving* philosophy—a problem of quality being restrictively defined as a lack of conformance to procedural design specifications. Such a quality management orientation quickly succumbs to the inherent tendency of drifting towards incrementalism—focusing on the first available problem which is the path of least resistance. Such a trend does not motivate the laboratorian to seek opportunities for improvement—*de novo*, nonproblematic opportunities, that is.

First, the problem-oriented approach can easily degenerate to a search for the proverbial bad apple, as decried by Berwick.[11] Gambino has pointed out that most laboratory errors are system dependent—not people dependent.[12] If poor personnel performance represents less than 1% of an organization's overall function, then emphasizing the correction of such relatively small error leaves more than 99% of the organization's potential unimproved. As a correlative, emphasis of improvement of organizational systems and processes is nonpunitive/nonpejorative and it unmasks much greater opportunity for important change.

Both Berwick and Gambino echo the teachings of McGregor's theories of X and Y.[11, 12, 13, 14] McGregor's Theory X tells us that:

- Members of an organization are unable to work out relations among their positions without thorough guidance and planning.
- Some members are aggressive and will trespass on the domain of others unless clear boundaries are drawn.

- Members are reluctant to assume responsibilities unless assigned a definite task.
- Members generally prefer the security of a definite task to the freedom of a vaguely defined one.
- Members are prone to interpersonal conflict.
- Justice is more certain if the enterprise is organized on an objective, impersonal basis.

McGregor's Theory Y reveals that:

- The expenditure of physical and mental effort in work is as natural as play and rest.
- People will exercise self-direction and self-control toward objectives to which they are committed.
- The average individual learns not only to accept but to seek responsibility.
- The human capacity of imagination, ingenuity, and creativity is widely distributed among individuals.
- In modern industrial life, the intellectual potentialities of the average human being are only partially utilized.

Unfortunately, many laboratory directors and managers are naturally attracted to the more conservative—quite pessimistic—Theory X. This is largely because it fits the classical, bureaucratic, incremental style of personnel management; also, something can be said, here, about the natural tendencies of introverted personality types working under operational stress. The mistake made is devoting too much energy to identifying and following indicators of blatant problems, instead of probing for nonproblematic opportunities to improve; thus, there has been too much emphasis on the first limb of the TSP. Quality managers such as Berwick and Gambino are saying, along with the JCAHO, that laboratorians need to devote more time to a more modern participative, system-oriented, management style; thus, concentrate on the second limb of the quality surveillance process where opportunity analysis and remedy dominate the exercise.

Second, when there are no identifiable problems, a stalemate—or program-lock—develops with no improvement gained. An old adage is, "If it ain't broke, don't fix it"—this is the motto of incremental quality management. In the modern environment of TQM combined with CQI, the managerial motto should be, "Even with sustained, acceptable quality, if there is no sign of continuous improvement, then quality management needs fixing." In fact, it could even be construed as, "If it ain't broke, break it!"

As a consequence of the JCAHO's initiative, the healthcare industry is moving into a new era of quality management, shifting from QA to QI in preparation for a full-fledged CQI approach. Mechanistically, this new management program emphasizes the second limb of the TSP and is based on the more preferable philosophy of *opportunity-seeking* with continuous improvement as the ultimate goal—whether there is an obvious problem of quality at hand or not.

It is important to understand that TQM and CQI are mutually related managerial concepts. Although there are historical and functional gray areas linking the two, they remain naturally sequential steps in the development of modern healthcare quality management:

> TQM is the system of administrative programs that are the *managerial means.*
>
> CQI is the philosophical process of creating organizational commitment to a goal of improvement that is the *managerial end.*

The JCAHO developed the concepts of their QA program as a logical first step toward introducing the precepts of TQM—using the TSP as a uniform template and pedagogic tool. Now, the QI program supplants QA as an introduction to the precepts of CQI into everyday practice—leaving the mechanistic TSP in place but diminishing its visibility by integrating it into the standards and readying it for further modification.

These changes in quality surveillance definitions and process accompany similar changes in the accreditation survey process. For one thing, survey input should become more broadened. Surveyors will continue to ask for evidence of quality indicator monitoring and *problem solving*, but they will also look for evidence of *opportunity finding* in the absence of specific, blatant problems. They will assess management of quality of care by means other than the former QA-style, indicator-based monitoring program. For example, they will review committee minutes, task force reports, staff reports, and customer satisfaction surveys as evidence of opportunity-finding and continuous improvement.

The JCAHO surveyors will even have to change their individual orientation and modify their personal approach. Some surveyors will probably not cope; therefore they will not survive—just as some medical laboratory directors and managers will not be able cope. The ongoing changes in laboratory quality management promise to produce brave new vistas in both philosophy and practice, requiring an open mind and an enthusiastic spirit.

It is helpful if every laboratorian understands the TSP, even though it reflects less JCAHO focus since the 1992 *AMH*. The JCAHO still requires that "there is a planned, systematic, and ongoing process for monitoring, evaluating, and improving the quality of care and of key governance, managerial, and support activities."[1] Although diminished in JCAHO emphasis, the TSP continues to fulfill a very pragmatic approach to quality management and facilitates uniform monitoring, evaluating, and opportunity finding. The JCAHO model process still works well as a broad brush stroke, general surveillance approach for laboratory activities of any size and at any hierarchical level—whether it be for a department, service, section, or smaller unit activity.

The TSP has also become a source of several important phrases and definitions that make up the special language of modern quality management. Table I highlights those contributions.

For the foreseeable future, the JCAHO probably intends to display the model as a viable framework for planning, implementing, and documenting quality management by healthcare organizations, including the laboratory—although some of the elements might yet change to fit the needs of CQI-style management. For instance, the definition and use of the *threshold* step is a questionable concept for some managers in the CQI environment and might undergo further modification, if not extinction in some—but, not necessarily all—management circles.

More specific, focused team and analytical processes are arguably better suited for use in various phases of problem solving and opportunity finding. Examination of QI information by these other approaches are worthy of further discussion.

ALTERNATIVE APPROACHES FOR ACHIEVING QUALITY ASSESSMENT AND IMPROVEMENT

Team Composition

The JCAHO describes a biphasic approach to team member selection. First, the team is a relatively small group of fully representative experts—the smaller, the better and the more expert, the better. Size is particularly important; cap the size of the team to a manageable number of individuals.[4, 5]

Second, team membership should reflect the nature of the improvement project at hand. Depending on the size of the parent organization, the team should include experts on team consensus methods and experts on subject content. There might easily be an overlap in these two areas of expertise. There should be enough expertise to optimize both perception and decision making.

Team membership also should be representative of the customers-suppliers affected by the project. Both internal and external customers (suppliers) deserve consideration. Internal customers would include laboratory employees whose health and welfare may be at stake. External customers might include patients, clinical staff, support staff, and administrative staff—all within the patient healthcare organization; outside that organization, external customers might include reference laboratories, other parent healthcare organizations or individual providers, peer review entities, potential patients (consumers), and various community organizations and agencies. Wherever there is a customer, there is almost always a reciprocal supplier relationship.

Selection of team members should involve consideration of all these potential candidates, based on the project at hand. The challenge is to optimize perception and decision making expertise, but minimize the number of individuals who need to reach a consensus. Choice of participative methods will facilitate this balancing act.

Team Analytical Processes

All *analytical processes* for QI data analysis, opportunity finding, and problem solving can be distilled to a primary form: Shewhart's cyclical Plan-Do-Check-Act (P-D-C-A) model, already described in Chapter Three. Deming and his associates modified PDCA to Plan-Do-Study-Act (PDSA). Table II compares Shewhart's P-D-C-A cycle to the other processes that are discussed here.

Whereas Shewhart's cycle is the simplest conceptual model, the JCAHO ten-step model represents one of the most broad-based approaches. In comparison, Juran's Journey is an equally generic approach which involves two phases with three steps each. The diagnostic phase steps are: 1) understand the symptom; 2) theorize the causes; and 3) test the theory. The remedial phase steps are: 1) formulate the remedy; 2) test the remedy under operating conditions; and 3) establish checks and controls to sustain the gain. Juran's Journey is a natural progression from his Trilogy, a system of three processes that include quality planning (Plan), quality control (Do), and quality improvement (Check and Act).[15]

There are more specialized, analytical models. These alternative processes are quite adaptable for more precise analysis ancillary to the basic, skeletal TSP. For example, the Joiner process consists of five steps. They are 1) *Understand* the process in question; 2) *Eliminate* errors in the process; 3) *Simplify* the process (remove unnecessary steps); 4) *Reduce* variation in the process by establishing statistical control; and 5) *Plan* for continuous improvement through use of the Shewhart cycle.[16]

Organizational Dynamics, Inc. (ODI), has published their FADE process. Based on a team effort, these four steps include 1) *Focus* by prioritizing a number of opportunities for improvement (OFI) to a single choice; 2) *Analyze* by collecting data and determining means for improvement; 3) *Develop* by planning a remedy for improvement; and 4) *Execute* by marshaling organizational commitment, putting the plan to action, and monitoring the effect.[5]

The Hospital Corporation of America (HCA) has developed its FOCUS–PDCA process. This organization's process is perhaps the most team-oriented. The steps in this process include 1) *Find* a process to improve; 2) *Organize* a team that understands the subject process; 3) *Clarify* what is known of the process; 4) *Understand* causes of process variation; and 5) *Select* a plan for improvement. Adapted to Shewhart's cycle, the FOCUS process interfaces with P-D-C-A at the third, fourth, and fifth steps.[5]

Table II
Comparison of the Ten-Step Process with Alternative Analytical Processes

Shewhart's Cycle	JCAHO's TSP	Juran's Journey
Plan	1-Responsibility 2-Scope 3-Important aspects of care 4-Indicators 5-Thresholds	Diagnostic Phase: 1-Understand the symptom
Do	6-Data collection	2-Theorize the cause
Check	7-Evaluate	3-Test the theory
Act	8-Action 9-Assessment 10-Communication	Remedial Phase: 1-Establish a remedy 2-Test the remedy 3-Establish controls

Note: ⟶ (P D C A) symbolizes merging with Shewart's cycle or any other alternative analytical process of choice

Table II demonstrates how all the described alternative processes overlap or dovetail in some way with the four components of Shewhart's cycle. Figure 4.1 also displays how the JCAHO TSP can interplay with P-D-C-A or any other, more focused approach. There are four general points at which more investigative, team specific processes can be used in concert with the TSP as the general background format. Those four points correspond with the four phases of Shewhart's cycle.

Figure 4.2 illustrates a more detailed view of the TSP planning stage. This first stage functions at two major managerial levels: organizational and operative. Thus, the first five steps progress from the most general, organizational level to the most specific, focused operative level of planning.

Team Participative Methods

Team methods vary in regard to the formality of process and freedom of individual contribution. The most rigorous approach is that of an established committee or panel operating under formal rules of order and a

Joiner's Process	ODI's FADE	HCA's FOCUS-PDCA
1-Understand the process	1-Focus	1-Find an opportunity 2-Organize a team
2-Eliminate errors 3-Simplify the process	2-Analyze	3-Clarify the process → P D C A
4-Establish control	3-Develop	4-Understand causes for variation → P D C A
5-Plan for continuous improvement → P D C A	4-Execute	5-Select a plan for improvement → P D C A

preplanned agenda. At the next level would be an *ad hoc* committee following the same rules, perhaps with less precision. In either case, majority rule often prevails.

The nominal group technique is a less formal approach aimed at reaching consensus. The nominal group ordinarily uses a less rigorous "agenda," consisting of a preselected chief issue and a collection of related, alternative factors for discussion. As an example of the nominal group process, the schedule of events would include 1) round robin additions to the preselected topics without in-depth discussion, 2) round robin discussions of each/all topics, 3) selective grouping, consolidation, and deletion of topics, and 4) confidential balloting by each participant to select the 3 to 5 most important factors on the list. Specific prioritization criteria might or might not be imposed on the group. The same group or a more specialized group can then proceed with further discussion, more in-depth analysis, and more precise decision making.

Using the nominal group approach, there does not have to be a preselected agenda of topics at the start—only a chief issue. A list of discussion topics then can be developed *de novo* by round robin contributions or brainstorming.

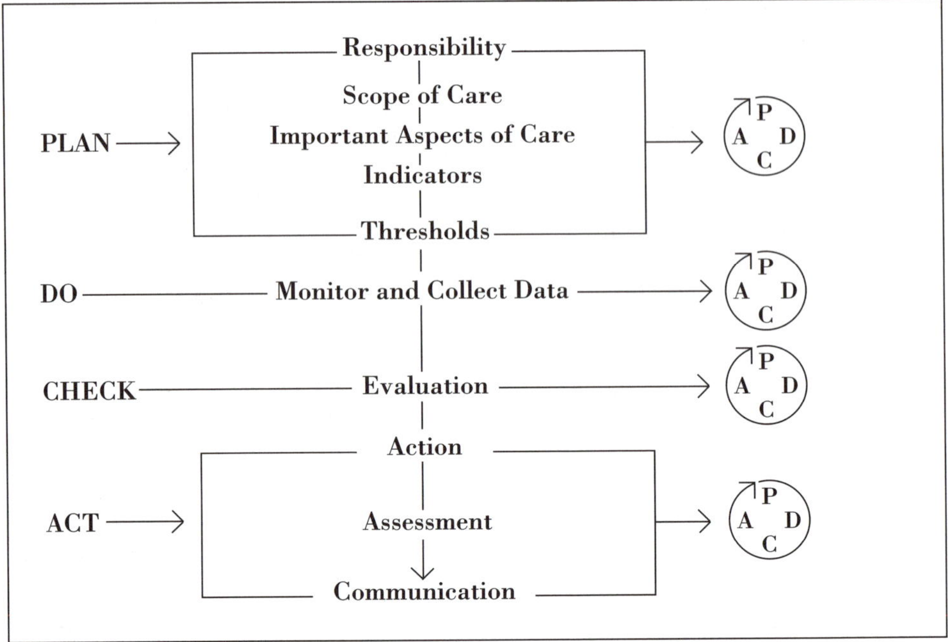

Figure 4.1 Interplay of the JCAHO ten-step process with P-D-C-A or other investigative processes

The Delphi group technique follows the example of the nominal group method with an additional element of total anonymity. All group "discussion" is carried on by mail or electronically, using written survey instruments and anonymous balloting. Each participant works alone, without any bias from any others working on the same project. Thus, such untoward events as Hawthorne effect, testing effect, and other transfer of individual bias are avoided.

Pure brainstorming is the least formal of all team techniques. Useful in any type of group session, the participants are invited to offer any idea that is remotely relevant to a chief topic or issue. This generation of ideas is usually orchestrated as a round robin progression of participant suggestions, proceeding around and around the meeting table until all ideas are exhausted. This technique encourages free association and flight of ideas with the intention of surfacing every possible suggestion for consideration as an answer to a specific question.

Team Analytical and Graphical Tools

Analytical and graphical tools include frequency distribution curves and measurement of central tendency and variance; the use of check sheets,

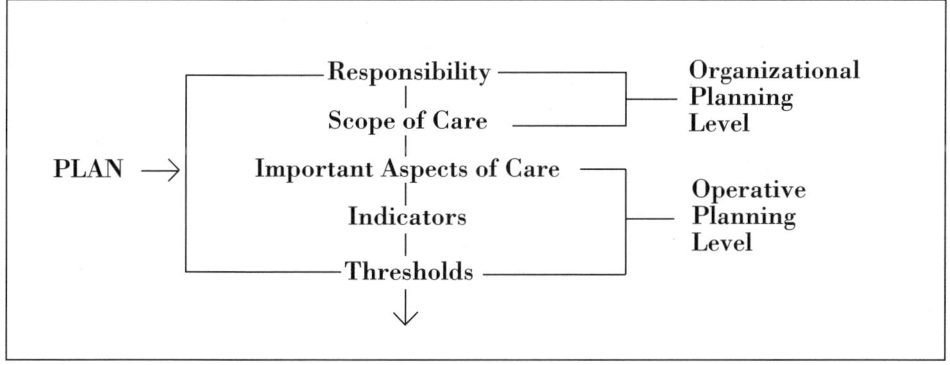

Figure 4.2 Two managerial levels of planning in the ten-step process

histograms, scatter diagrams, correlation coefficients and ratios; the use of regression analysis, analysis of levels, trends, and patterns (or cycles), and probability analysis; the establishment of control limits; and the use of control charts. Over the years, this approach has been improved by additional analytical and problem solving tools, including flow charts (work step sequences, input-process-output modeling), Pareto charts, cause-and-effect diagrams, run charts, and stratification charts. Seven commonly used tools for problem identification and evaluation are briefly described[16-18]:

Variable	Reporting Period			
	1	2	3	Total
A	II	III	II	7
B	I	I	I	3
C	~~IIII~~	II	~~IIII~~	12
Total	8	6	8	22

The *check sheet* is a form that is used to collect and tally data in a structured manner. The form organizes the variables to be measured for specific time periods.

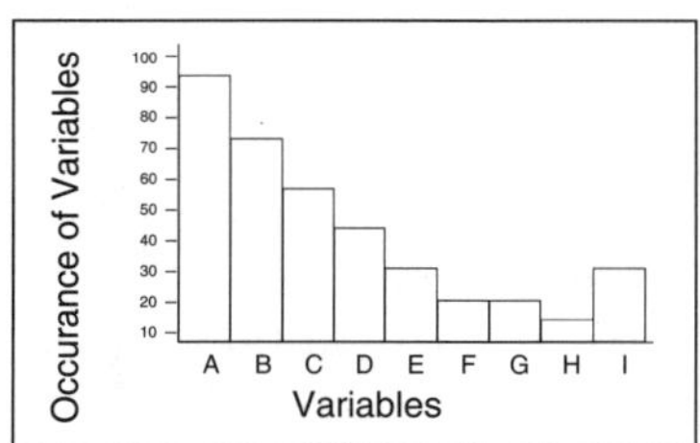

The *Pareto chart* is used in multifactorial analysis. A vertical bar graph, it is used to determine what problems to solve and in which order. The procedure is based on Pareto's Law, or the "80/20" rule: 80% of problems arise from 20% of the possible sources. Pareto analysis identifies the major potential problems, measures the actual incidence of these problems, ranks them, calculates cumulative distributions, draws frequency and distribution curves, and, finally, determines what few major problems are causing the most process ineffectiveness. The Pareto chart ranks characteristics of a product; it does not depict variance of measurements.

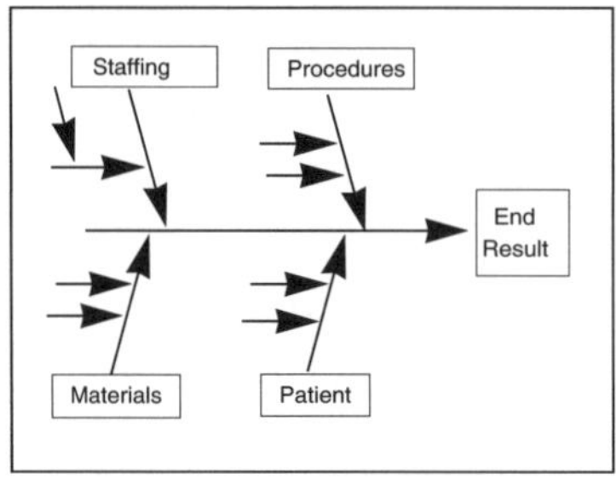

The *cause and effect diagram* determines contributing factors or causes of a given problem or effect. Also known as a fishbone or Ishikawa diagram, a cause and effect diagram looks like a fish skeleton—the problematic effect located at the head of the central spine and the multiple, sequential causes shown as converging ribs. This is an example of diagram analysis.

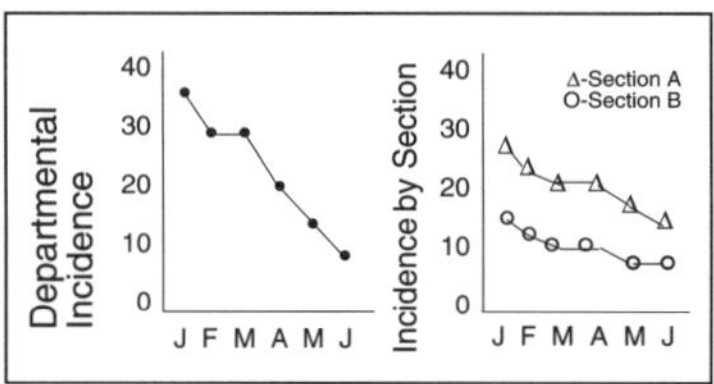

The *stratification chart* graphically subcategorizes or "stratifies" data to expose hidden patterns of events, and to localize causes of a problem or reveal improvement opportunities. Data can mask the real facts: stratification can expand single data points into meaningful categories or classifications that allows focus on corrective action. This analytical tool can be used in Pareto analysis before data collection, allowing evaluators to identify problematic events that should be monitored. It can also be used after data collection to determine actual causes of problematic events.

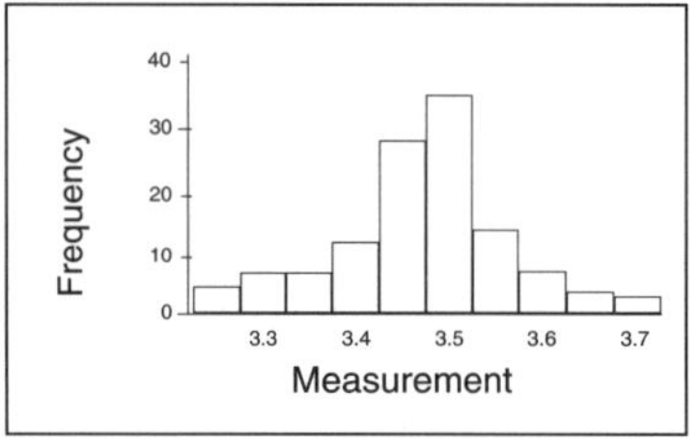

The *histogram* is a distribution graph that depicts the frequency of occurrence of control data. The area of each rectangle is proportional to the frequency of the observation. Histograms are very useful in Pareto analysis. Compared to a Pareto chart, the histogram depicts frequency distribution and variance of measurements; it does not rank problems.

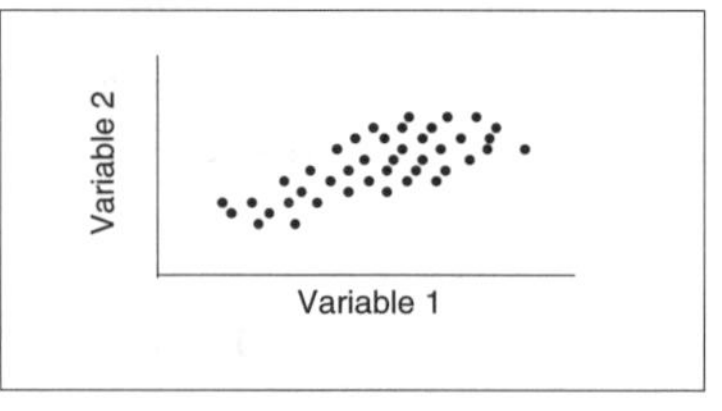

The *scatter diagram*, or correlation graph, graphically illustrates the relationship between two variable factors. Used to isolate the sources of a problem, these diagrams unmask cause and effect relationships between independent and dependent factors. The diagram cannot prove which variable actually causes the other, but it can clarify whether the relationship exists and indicates the strength of the relationship.

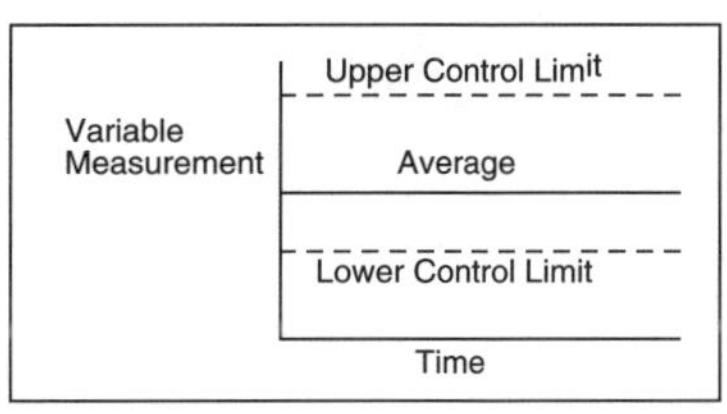

The *control chart*, originally attributed to Shewhart and later adapted by Levy and Jennings, presents tabulated data in a way that unmasks trends or patterns. A control chart is constructed as if a typical frequency distribution curve has been turned on it's side with standard deviation markers and control limits extending across the horizontal length of the chart. The matrix is completed by indicating passage of time, usually in days. It is useful in depicting the statistical behavior of control data and variability in a process due to random and non-random cause.

These tools have demonstrated great utility in problem identification and solving. Some are very useful for one or the other purpose—then, there is some overlapping application. Figure 4.3 shows an elegant summary of these relationships, after a model developed by Brassard at GOAL/QPC; it lists some additional techniques, as well.

THE INDIVIDUAL TEN STEPS

Because of its inherent merits, the TSP is used as a major theme throughout the remainder of this text to provide a uniform approach and a generally acceptable, skeletal format as a basis for discussion. A detailed description of each step of the JCAHO process follows. These vignettes convey the understanding that there has been a transition from the QA approach to a QI program. The most current Joint Commission interpretations of the TSP are taken from their publication on making the transition to QI (and, thus, PI).[5]

Although the chemistry section and blood bank are used frequently as examples to provide some consistency in the narrative, any anatomical or clinical laboratory activity would serve equally as well. Likewise, any reference to "customer and supplier" is used in the universal sense of the phrase—remembering that there are many customers and many suppliers both internal and external to the laboratory organization; there is usually a reciprocal customer-supplier relationship.

Step 1: Assign responsibility for all quality monitoring, assessment, and improvement activities.

This step should answer these questions:

- What are the key laboratory quality management *duties*?
- Who is specifically *responsible* for these leadership duties?

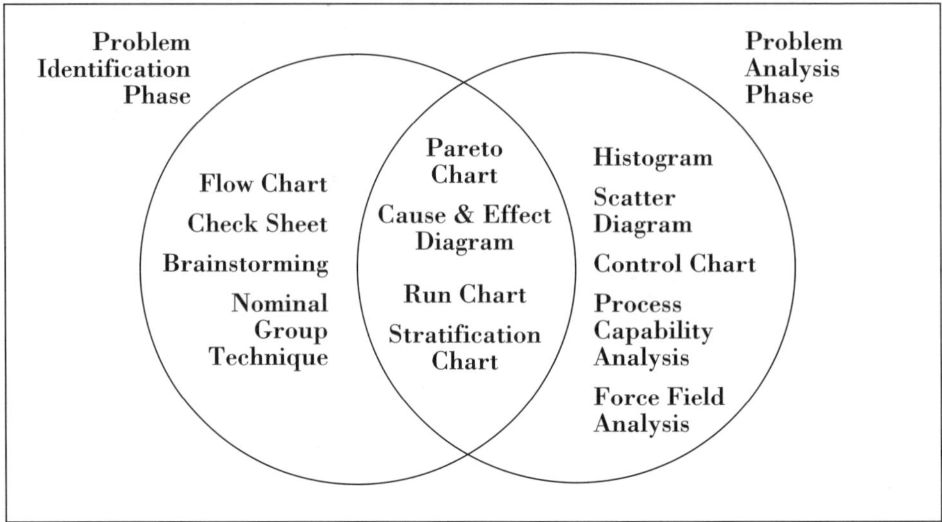

Figure 4.3 Relationships of analytical techniques to phases of problem solving (Reproduced by permission of GOAL/QPC, Inc.)

- Is the *structure* present by which the leaders and all others responsible for quality management activities can fulfill their duties?

Define and outline all quality management responsibilities in the QI plan. Accurately describe each responsibility with a specific title and assign each one to a specific organizational position, not by the current incumbent's name.

It is important that the laboratory medical director has overall responsibility for providing the direction and expert guidance for quality improvement in a medical laboratory. The director must also interact effectively as an advisor or consultant with the hospital medical staff and appropriate hospital committees on quality management issues. The written plan should specify the delegation (distribution) of authority and responsibility for all quality management activities, including:

- *Who* determines the important aspects of care, quality indicators, and other opportunities for improvement that will be monitored
- *When* QI data will be collected
- *What* QI data will be reported and to whom
- *Who* is responsible for follow-up activities
- *What* specific lines of communication exist within and between departments to facilitate QI
- *How* the QI plan is to be reviewed annually and by whom.

Quality management duties include providing organizational and operative (structural) resources, as well as the following:

- Directing
- Identifying problems
- Setting priorities
- Planning/designing
- Coordinating
- Selecting indicators
- Selecting thresholds
- Collecting data
- Evaluating
- Taking action
- Assessing
- Documenting
- Reporting
- Archiving
- Reviewing.

Individuals responsible for these activities might include the following:

- Medical director
- Laboratory manager
- QI coordinator
- Clinical and nonclinical, nonlaboratory personnel
- Section supervisor
- QC/QI technologist
- Bench technologist.

Determining Quality Improvement Responsibilities in the CQI Environment

The JCAHO describes responsibilities in the CQI environment as "The organization leaders oversee the design of and foster an approach to continuously improve quality that includes both intradepartmental and interdepartmental activities."[5] These leaders include members of the governing body, the chief executive officer, leaders of the medical staff and clinical departments, chief administrators, and leaders of the nursing staff.[1] Using this approach, these leaders are responsible for 1) overseeing the designing and fostering of an improvement program, 2) establishing responsibilities in the organization, and 3) setting priorities. In the CQI environment, this first step of the TSP includes identifying the quality management responsibilities of the laboratory staff and all key "customers and suppliers."

Determining interdepartmental responsibilities warrants the merging of the TSP with alternative specialized team and analytical approaches. This is especially true when this step is being implemented for the first time or whenever clinical decisions are involved.

Step 2: Delineate the scope of care and service provided by the organization.

This step should answer these questions:

- What *patient care activities* does the laboratory conduct?
- What other *customer-related* activities are performed?

Define, identify, and outline the scope of care in the QI plan or use the laboratory submission manual as the chief reference. In a healthcare laboratory, the scope of care is really the entire listing of all patient care support services—an inventory of all organizational (supporting) functions and operative activities that affect patient care. Use the laboratory submission manual as the chief reference.

The important *organizational functions* consist of the clinical, support, managerial, and governance processes that impart significant effect on the quality of laboratory contributions to patient care. These functions include all those listed as key management areas (KMAs) for strategic planning in Chapter Three under the QAn program. Suggested additions to those items already listed as KMAs include:[5]

- Leadership
- Patient rights
- Accessibility to laboratory service
- Patient evaluation
- Patient and family education.

Since 1994, the JCAHO has increasingly focused their standards and requirements on these important, nondiscipline-specific activities and functions. They have all become targets for quality improvement.[5]

The most important *operative activities* (ie, "procedures, treatments, and other activities") can be generally characterized as all the:[5]

- Types of patients served
- Clinical conditions, diagnoses, and treatments served, including all:
    1. patient care centers
    2. practitioners
- General and special laboratory services provided
- Specific analytical tests, diagnostic consultations, procedures, blood components, or clerical products that are provided as medical laboratory services
- Types of laboratory staff carrying out these activities
- Sites where services are provided
- Hours of routine and of special operation.

The scope of medical laboratory care and service also can be divided into three areas of operational importance for inventorying scope. These divisions will vary in size, complexity, and priority.[19] Examples include:

- Anatomic pathology services
  1. surgical diagnosis
  2. autopsy diagnosis
  3. cytopathology diagnosis
  4. histology, cytology, and immunohistochemistry laboratory
  5. electron microscopy.

- Clinical pathology services
  1. phlebotomy
  2. emergency (stat) analysis
  3. chemistry and toxicology
  4. hematology and coagulation
  5. immunohematology including donor, transfusion, and apheresis activities
  6. immunology
  7. microbiology
  8. urinalysis.

- Administrative pathology services
  1. personnel management
  2. education and training
  3. communication
  4. equipment and supply logistics
  5. computer support
  6. reports and records management
  7. quality management
  8. budget management.

Whatever the approach might be to determining the scope of care and services—by operative activity, supporting function, or operational division—this total inventory process should be a dynamic, ongoing activity. The listing should be continually updated as laboratory services are added, changed, or deleted on, at least, an annual basis.

Changes in the laboratory scope of care should be predicated on resource availability, state-of-the-art technology, physician selection preferences, patient needs, and all other customer needs. Therefore, all laboratory customers and suppliers should be given the opportunity to provide input into determining what the scope of care is today and what it should be tomorrow.

Determining the Scope of Care and Service in the CQI Environment

The JCAHO describes delineation of scope in the CQI environment as "The organization, as a whole or by department/service, delineates its scope of care and service."[5] The operative phrase is 'the organization, as a whole.'

Although most of a laboratory's operational scope remains very stable without change over a relatively lengthy period, some changes do occur because of evolving or new technology, shifts in customer preference, or variations of available resources. As a consequence, new laboratory products and services are added, others are deleted or curtailed in some way; and changes occur in patient accessibility and in patient population characteristics. Any major decisions regarding the overall laboratory scope made in response to such changes should be deliberated at a combined laboratory customer-supplier level—especially to guarantee clinical participation. Specific issues over significant changes will warrant a specialized team and statistical analysis approach.

Step 3: Identify the most important aspects of care provided by the organization.

This step should answer these questions:

- How can we reduce the scope of care and services to an inventory of laboratory procedures that are *most important* to the health, safety, or other welfare of our customers?
- How can we maintain that inventory at a *manageable level*?

Define, identify, and outline the most important aspects of patient care support in the QI plan. This step requires setting quality surveillance priorities for all analytical tests, consultative diagnoses, patient procedures, component products, clerical reports, and any other laboratory product or service. All customers and suppliers should be given the opportunity to provide input into this selection process.

The JCAHO describes important aspects of care and service (IACs) as high-priority functions, activities, processes, treatments, and other aspects of care that we monitor for quality improvement.[5] An essential characteristic of any important laboratory service is its effect on the outcome of the patient's medical care. A laboratory result, diagnosis, or other product identified as an IAC should satisfy *at least one* of the following questions[1]:

- Which laboratory results, diagnoses, or other products represent a *high-volume* of workload—affecting the largest number of patients at risk, as well as any other customers in need?

- Which laboratory products are so critical to the support of specific diagnoses or therapies—representing *high-risk* to patient care outcome or some other customer need?
- Which laboratory products are *problem-prone* for patient care, employee safety, or some other customer need—based on unusually demanding, potentially unstable laboratory procedural design specifications?

Examples of important aspects of care include:

- High-volume, such as routine, electrolyte test results, profile test results, or phlebotomies
- High-risk, such as sentinel activities like blood component transfusions, stat test results with a 1-hour turnaround time, priority test results with a 4-hour turnaround time, or critical test results identified by alarm values like therapeutic drug monitoring or anticoagulant monitoring
- Problem-prone, such as developmental, first-generation test results; potentially unsafe, dangerous procedures like infectious organism identification; or client satisfaction surveys, complaints, or incident reports.

Usually, the laboratory determines IACs in the course of designing the overall QI plan—along with scope of care. Occasionally, the quality of some laboratory service that is not listed as an IAC can suddenly change in some way, exceed operative control limits, and significantly influence patient care outcome. By definition, that aspect of care then becomes "important," should be added to the inventory, and warrants appropriate, ongoing surveillance treatment.

In the same vein, IACs can emerge as new methods develop in the course of technological advance or in the course of normal discovery through routine QI monitoring, evaluating, and assessing. The QI plan should cover such contingencies.

Identification of Important Aspects of Care in the CQI Environment

The JCAHO describes the determining of IACs in the CQI environment as "The organization, as a whole or by department/service, identifies high-priority important functions, processes, treatments, activities, and so forth, to be monitored"—again, it is the 'organization as a whole.'[5] Accepting the task of IAC management should be a "company-wide" activity, then selection and prioritization of laboratory IACs often warrant an interdepartmental, multidisciplinary team approach using statistical analytical tools, depending on the issues at hand. The team should be well-represented to facilitate the company-wide approach.

Because of the relevance of laboratory IACs to patient care, clinical physicians and other clinical staff must be involved in identifying laboratory products and services that are important to the clinical process. These nonlaboratory personnel provide invaluable assistance in designing the clinical questions that the medical laboratory process will be answering. Thus, incorporating clinical information ensures a high-quality laboratory service, as well as enhancement of clinical practice.

By JCAHO guidelines, once a laboratory product is identified as an important aspect of care, it must be periodically monitored and evaluated. In the CQI environment, however, if sufficient monitoring, evaluating, and assessing demonstrate that a particular aspect of care is consistently problem free *with no indication of quality improvement*, then the quality management process must become suspect and reevaluated.

For example, an activity or function that was formerly judged to be an IAC can eventually become unimportant enough to be deleted from the IAC inventory. Reasons for this action might include a decrease in 1) workload volume, 2) patient-risk, or 3) technical difficulty.

Step 4: Identify indicators and appropriate criteria for monitoring the quality of all important aspects of care.

This step should answer these questions:

- What laboratory activities demonstrate *problems* that diminish the quality of customer service?
- What laboratory activities offer nonproblematic *opportunities for improving* the quality of customer service?

Describe the definitions and selection methods for indicators of quality patient care services in the QI plan. The plan should define an indicator as a screening tool used to monitor, assess, and improve an important aspect of laboratory patient care support.

A QI indicator is not necessarily the immediate cause of a problem of quality delivery or an opportunity for quality improvement; an indicator is not usually a direct measure of fundamental quality. Most often, it is only a sign or symptom of an opportunity for improvement. However, it still provides a means for determining the real source of a problem or opportunity.

An indicator is a well-defined, quantifiable, but variable aspect of one of the three elements of infrastructural and operative laboratory functions—structural resource management, process management, and outcome management—that reflects a quality of laboratory support to patient care or to some other customer.[2] An indicator is a measure of the conformance to design specifications for any aspect of the path of work flow for any of the three functions.

Resource, process, and outcome management form an integrated system of mutually dependent activities. The definitions of these laboratory functions are reviewed as follows:

- Structural resources include:
  1. the *potential organizational capacity* to provide all planned laboratory patient care support
  2. all organizational and operative assets that constitute the input required by laboratory processes and outcomes
  3. indirect determinants of quality of the patient's clinical response or some other customer response
  4. indirect determinants of the satisfaction of a laboratory customer
  5. indirect determinants of improvement of a laboratory function.

Even though the JCAHO is deemphasizing the visible importance of structural resources, these resources cannot be dismissed. The quality of organizational and operative "structures" <u>can</u> be characterized by QI indicators and <u>should</u> be monitored by a schedule that balances the importance of structure, process, and outcome. Otherwise, we will not be able to fine tune the quality management of the crucially important organizational functions, such as effective organizational commitment to CQI. Such commitment includes the leadership involvement and support that are so critical to systematically achieving continuous, prioritized improvement.

- Processes include:
  1. the *application of organizational and operative resources* to operative procedures that results in all laboratory products and other customer services
  2. all laboratory techniques and procedures that support patient care services, staff safety, and other customer services
  3. the interim result of applying laboratory resources to some laboratory process; a technical or interpretive interim endproduct
  4. indirect determinants of quality of the patient's clinical response or some other customer response
  5. indirect determinants of the satisfaction of a laboratory customer
  6. indirect determinants of improvement of a laboratory function.

- Outcomes include:
    1. the *application of laboratory interim end products* (which become clinical resources) to clinical diagnostic or therapeutic processes by attending physicians or other clinical staff that results in diagnostic or therapeutic end results
    2. direct determinants of the quality of the patient's clinical status or some other customer status, such as the state of organizational solvency, or the condition of employee safety
    3. direct determinants of the satisfaction of a laboratory customer
    4. direct determinants of improvement of a laboratory function.

JCAHO urges all healthcare managers to concentrate on improving the performance of operational processes, as are outlined above. We are to avoid spending time on pursuing improvement of inadequate individual performance, unless all supporting processes have been proven satisfactory.

Very important, an indicator of quality must be *measurable*. As such, it can be most simply formulated as a "yes" or "no" statement (eg, present or absent, plus or minus, or one or zero) or it can be stated as a quantitative, numerical value. Indicators should also be:

- Customer-valid
- Relevant
- Objective
- Well-defined
- Comprehensive
- Manageable
- Specific
- Sensitive.

Indicator Characterization

Various components of an indicator have evolved significantly since the TSP was first introduced. For example, an indicator was formerly referred to as a "monitor." Now monitor is used as a verb meaning "to collect indicator data." Sometimes the distinction is forgotten and the term monitor is used incorrectly as a noun.

The JCAHO has defined the indicator very specifically by the *indicator information* set (IIS). The JCAHO recommended, at one time, that such an information set be systematically developed for each indicator. To formalize the characterization of indicators, the JCAHO has published a "Clinical Indicator Development Form." Although it represents a rather ponderous exercise, the IIS has merit, especially as an initial introduction to thorough characterization of an indicator. The set consists of seven elements:[4]

Element 1: Statement of the indicator. This statement includes the title and briefly describes the laboratory patient care occurrence being monitored.

Element 2: Definition of terms. This step clarifies the terminology used in the initial statement to ensure uniformity in the measurement of the indicator event. The definition can include appropriate laboratory or clinical criteria.

- An *indicator* can be defined in terms of any of the three prime areas of laboratory functions which mirror Donabedian's three elements of quality assessment.
- A *criterion* is a measurable design specification that is required to be met in order to attain the highest possible level of quality. A criterion should reflect an acceptable professional standard of laboratory technical practice or administrative managerial support. As the method for indicator selection is becoming more formalized, the criterion is taking on increased importance—especially in the form of clinical standards or parameters of practice.
- Examples of function-oriented indicators and their criteria for an important aspect of care such as a stat electrolyte analysis include:
    1. *resource indicators*, such as adequately maintenanced instrumentation, $\geq$ 5 personnel required on a particular shift to guarantee, or technical quality and turnaround time
    2. *process indicators*, such as $\leq \pm 2$ standard deviations for all stat electrolyte controls or $\leq$ 1-hour turnaround time for the stat electrolyte test result
    3. *outcome indicators*, such as normalization of the patient's serum electrolytes following appropriate parenteral electrolyte therapy based on appropriate utilization of the properly managed laboratory result or attending physician and patient satisfaction.

Element 3: Identification of the type of indicator. This step establishes a focus for indicator monitoring and interpretation. As amply illustrated, an indicator can be classified by its relationship to resource, process, and outcome. An indicator can also be classified as a rate-based indicator or a sentinel event indicator, depending on the required frequency of monitoring.

- Rate-based indicators. A rate-based—or comparative rate—indicator measures an operational event for which there is a known rate or level of occurrence. The observed incidence is compared to a normal incidence rate. Examples of rate-based indicators for any aspect of care include:

1. *resource indicators*, such as supply shelf-life or unscheduled computer down time
2. *process indicators*, such as specimen integrity, analytical control accuracy and precision, or average turnaround time
3. *outcome indicators*, such as patient's clinical response or customer satisfaction.

■ Sentinel event indicators. The JCAHO recognizes that all medical care activities demonstrate some inherent variability and that—usually—it is not practical or resource-effective to adhere to total conformance to design expectations. Yet, for certain important aspects of care, an indicator might have to be established with a 0% tolerance of variation. Such an event is referred to as a sentinel event indicator.

The JCAHO expects that a sentinel event will be identified especially whenever there is significant risk to patient-care outcome—thus, a "very high-risk" event. In fact, a sentinel event might just as likely arise if there is significant risk to employee health and welfare. It could even be a problem-prone or volume-related occurence. Occurrence of any such event warrants immediate investigation. Consequently, sentinel indicators should be monitored continuously during every monitoring period. Examples of sentinel events might include:

1. *resource indicators* such as any donor unit that tests positive for HIV antibody or any platelets stored in an ambient temperature that exceeds the range of 20°C to 24°C
2. *process indicators* such as any alarm value not reported to a patient's physician or any malfunction of a platelet pheresis machine
3. *outcome indicators*, such as any incorrect anatomic diagnosis that results in a patient undergoing unnecessary major surgery or any hemolytic blood transfusion reaction.

■ Other types of indicators. Administratively, some indicators are characterized in terms other than the three elements of operations or the frequency of occurrence. Thus, indicators also can be classified in terms of:

1. positive (desirable) versus negative (adverse) effects
2. specific hallmarks of quality such as accuracy, precision, timeliness, and medical appropriateness
3. patient orientation (a healthcare issue) versus provider orientation (a credentialing issue)—ie, customer type.

Element 4: Rationale. This element explains why the indicator is useful in evaluating the quality of the structure, process, or outcome of the important aspect of care. The rationale should explain the potential value of the indicator data for assessing quality improvement.

Patient-care outcome hinges on well-defined, clinically-based standards for the laboratory support of medical, surgical, and psychiatric care. Therefore, indicators should clearly measure the quality of technical, analytical, and diagnostic performance, as well as clinical staff selection and utilization of the laboratory end product. Accordingly, laboratory outcome indicators and their clinically-referenced criteria—especially—should be developed jointly by the laboratory director, pathology staff, clinical department or service chiefs, other appropriate clinical staff advisors, and the hospital chief of medical staff, whenever appropriate. These clinical parameters should reflect the philosophy and strategies of patient care unique to the hospital environment, types of patient care being provided, geographic location, and local medical practices.[20]

Consequently, monitoring laboratory indicators should unmask opportunities for more clinically effective laboratory products—be they consultations, interpretations, test results, blood components, patient treatment services, or clerical services. This enhanced effectiveness can be due to increased technical quality such as accuracy, precision, or turnaround time. Improved effectiveness can also be due to increased medical appropriateness of clinical selection, diagnostic interpretation, and clinical utilization. Otherwise, laboratory products can be clinically <u>ineffective</u> whenever they are:

- *Not* clinically utilized when clinically indicated
- *Not* clinically utilized correctly when clinically indicated.
- *Not* provided as a high-quality laboratory end product
- Inappropriately provided when *not* clinically indicated.

Because adverse patient events secondary to any type of laboratory service mishap are relatively rare and isolated, incident reports do not adequately account for the overall quality of patient care support activities. Such incident reports or complaints are of value when investigated individually—especially if it is a sentinel event—but they do not offer a systematic approach to quality monitoring. Thus, instead of primarily relying on random reports, a well-designed QI program addresses a balanced mixture of ongoing resource-, process-, and outcome-oriented indicators that monitor adherence to clinically-related standards, criteria, or protocols. The value of monitoring nonpreselected QI indicators is discussed under selection of indicators in the CQI environment.

Element 5: Description of the indicator population. This element defines the patient population being monitored by the indicator event. It is expressed as a ratio—a rate of occurrence of a particular event in a specific population. The description introduces patient risk assessment into the plan by incorporating patient population attributes into the indicator.

The ratio is expressed by a standard formula. For example, the numerator can represent the number of patients in a specific diagnostic group who are receiving a specific laboratory product and experiencing a specific clinical endpoint and who are monitored by the indicator during a specific period of time. The denominator can represent the total number of patients in the diagnostic category receiving the laboratory service or product, irrespective of the quality endpoint. An example of the formula follows, using hemolytic transfusion reactions as the end point :

$$\frac{\text{\# of hemolytic transfusion reactions}}{\text{total \# of patients receiving red blood cell transfusions}}$$

Element 6: Indicator logic. The indicator logic provides a format or matrix for collecting and sequencing data in preparation for efficient evaluation. All data elements and data sources should be itemized. A *data element* is a specific parameter used for indicator evaluation; it is translated from the indicator statement. A *data source* is a source document required for collecting a specific data-element.

Element 7: Delineation of potential underlying factors. This is an explanation of the possible sources of variance in the indicator data. These factors include:

- Patient factors
- Practitioner factors
- Systemic factors
    1. structural resource activities, such as organizational- (internal and external) or operative-level procedures
    2. process activities, such as prelaboratory procedures (eg, delivering an appropriate request and specimen to the laboratory); intralaboratory procedures (eg, producing a laboratory end product); or extralaboratory procedures (eg, delivering the laboratory end product to the point of patient care)
    3. outcome activities, such as clinical procedures (eg, utilization of the laboratory end product or ancillary clinical procedures).

The IIS is a detailed procedure to facilitate indicator characterization. It demands a significant amount of time and effort. Such formalization of the

TSP is helpful in terms of stimulating procedural thoroughness. But, it also causes quality management to be even more resource-intensive and, therefore, more costly. Thus, a break-even point must be found to keep laboratory quality management cost-efficacious—that is, both medically effective and efficient.

Unanticipated Indicators

Routine, ongoing monitoring of indicators is described in the QI plan and seperate schedules. In addition, the plan should include a method for identifying and evaluating unscheduled indicators. Such unanticipated quality indicators are often discovered in incident or spot reports and surveys; then, they have to be evaluated for further investigation. If appropriate, the new opportunity for improvement is incorporated into the quality management program as one or more new indicators.

Selection and Use of Indicators in the CQI Environment

The JCAHO describes the mode of identification of indicators in the CQI environment as, "Teams of experts, inter- or intradepartmental, identify indicators for the important aspects of care and service."[5] First, the operative word used here is 'team'. A team approach using statistical analytical tools is highly advised in performing this portion of the TSP (or any other improvement process). Second, the JCAHO intends that if any aspect of care is important enough to be so prioritized, than it is necessary to select and monitor appropriate indicators over a reasonable period for every IAC.

Quality indicators are so germane to total healthcare management that alternative, multidisciplinary, specialized team and statistical analysis approaches must be a part of the indicator selection process. This is a critical point in the TSP where alternative methods must meld.

During the practice of QA in the 1980s, indicators became very important as a part of the quality surveillance program for *problem solving*. As we engage with the QI (and, now, PI) approach of the 1990s, the character of indicators is changing. They must be more systematic, aimed at targets representing a wider scope of surveillance, such as organizational and operative resource management. They must be oriented more toward *opportunity finding*, rather than problem solving. With continuous improvement as the central goal, indicator criteria need to be periodically reevaluated and adjusted to produce a progressively higher quality result—even if the current criteria and thresholds are being met successfully.

There are two options for selecting laboratory quality indicators in the modern management setting. The least advisable method is on-the-spot selection of quality indicators of laboratory operations as they become

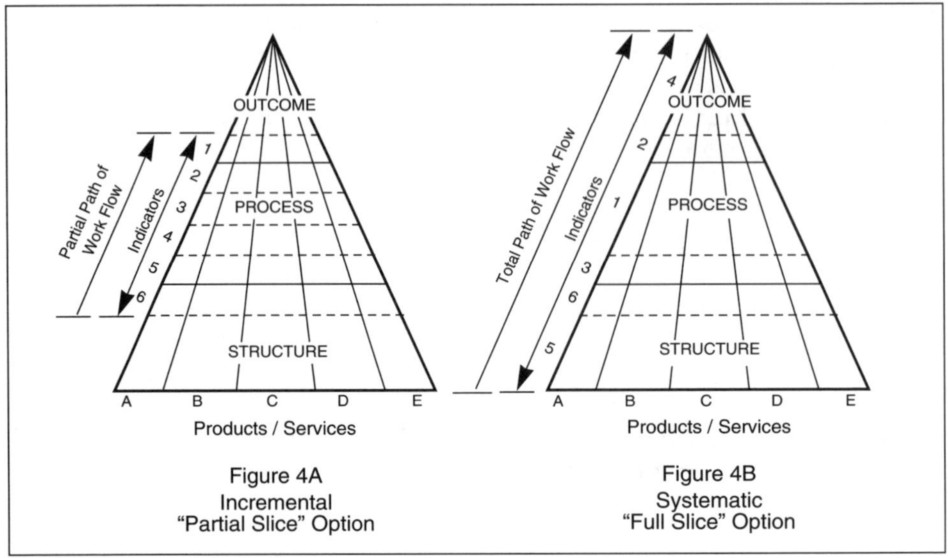

Figure 4.4 Two modes of indicator selection

problematic, one incremental issue at a time. The most desirable method is systematically and analytically preselecting *prioritized* indicators that are equally representative of all three major laboratory functions—structure, process, and outcome—which include the entire laboratory path of work flow.

Figures 4.4A and 4.4B compare the two modes of indicator selection for a number of laboratory products. The first model in Figure 4A demonstrates the incremental, "partial slice" option for indicator selection. Several indicators (nominally prioritized 1 through 6) have been selected for monitoring and evaluating five unplanned, nonprioritized laboratory products or aspects of care (identified as A through E). Three levels of operational function are also depicted, including outcome, process, and structural resource management.

Because time and other crisis-oriented resource constraints dictate this management approach, only the most *visibly* quality-affecting activities are targeted for monitoring and evaluating. Ordinarily, such indicators are often nonprioritized, and only one that "squeaks the loudest" gets first attention. But, for the sake of discussion, indicator number 1 in model 4A ranks highest in immediately visible priority and number 6 ranks as the lowest; also, the indicator numbers in model 4A apply to all products (A-E). However, the crisis-oriented ranking of these six indicators is not likely to represent true operational criticalness but, more likely, a time-weighted or politically-driven sense of urgency.

On one hand, figure 4.4A illustrates that poor planning and crisis management cause the placing of inordinate emphasis on process problems—Berwick's bad apples or 1% portion.[11] These problems are more frequently brought to the laboratorian's attention simply because they are more blatantly visible; consequently, resource problems especially, receive substantially less preventive scrutiny in an incremental program. Another aspect of this management style is that only a relatively small portion of the entire operational work volume is surveyed for opportunities of improvement—and virtually all opportunities surface as problems. In light of these weaknesses, an incremental quality management program becomes problem-oriented, poorly prioritized, and narrowly focused with very little attention paid to finding nonproblematic opportunities for improvement—the other 99% portion of the total work volume.

The model in Figure 4A illustrates that by using an unplanned, random approach, most quality management effort is exerted in response to "hot" problems that emerge from incident reports and complaints. This situation also arises if there is undue emphasis on outcome and process quality indicators with inadequate attention being paid to operative and organizational resource quality indicators.[a] When using these skewed modes of management, incremental crisis management prevails at its best.

The haphazardly stacked, horizontal appearance of the model is reminiscent of a manager's "in box" contents. As shown in the model, "quick fix" decision making usually results in a concentration of effort on process functions and the process segment of the path of work flow; there is minimal, nonsystematic attention to outcome and structural resources. Without appropriate planning, time and quality management resources are seldom available to address the remaining two operational functions or path of work flow elements in a truly systematic fashion. Consequently, only a portion of the true operational "slice" of functional activities is monitored and evaluated for any one laboratory product. Surveillance of organizational resources will be ostensibly ignored.

On the other hand, if the "full slice" approach to indicator selection is used, each of the five laboratory products is represented by a complete, three-level representation of all laboratory functions, as shown in Figure 4B. Using this option, both laboratory products (A-E) and indicators (1-6) are selected and prioritized according to a systematic plan so that all three functional activities and all path of work flow elements are monitored in a more balanced fashion.

This planned approach affords a variety of options for indicator preselection for each laboratory product based on analysis of structural

[a] The position taken in this text regarding the relevance of structure to quality management differs from that of the JCAHO which maintains that—in the transition from QA to CQI—"Indicators pertaining to structures of care are less important."[5] The latter statement reflects a recently differing stand compared to what the JCAHO has taken in the past; in fact, the JCAHO has published guidelines that vary on this issue, sometimes favoring the importance of structure in quality measurement, sometimes not. It is the author's opinion that the importance of structural quality must be recognized as indispensable and must be managed in reasonable balance with the quality of the other two operational functions—not deemphasized. It could be that clinical viewpoint is swaying opinion too far toward outcome and process and away from structure.

resources, process, and outcome. The balanced, orderly distribution of this model is more reminiscent of a good manager's sequentially-organized file drawer contents—that is, vertically organized as in a file cabinet in which each file is equally visible and accessible.

Also, as illustrated along the right hand border of model 4B—using the systematically planned, full slice approach, the indicator labeled number 1 for any of the five laboratory products does not necessarily rank at the highest operational functional level; the indicator numbers in model 4B apply only to product A. Depending on the circumstances at hand, the order of priority might even be totally reversed for any given product (or IAC). Ranking is determined by focusing on what is most important within the entire spectrum—the full slice—of operational work flow for each laboratory product according to its own priority.

With incremental problem solving being minimized, an organization-wide managerial surveillance system can be established. Such a system allows for more effective allocation of time and resources. This is not doing more with less, it is doing the best with what you have. Thus, laboratorians can improve whole processes rather than just solve incremental problems, by getting to the real root of those problems and preventing the problem from even happening.

In the CQI environment, there is another paramount change in the characterization of QI indicators: the multitude of sources that are available. As explained more fully under data collection, surveillance indicators are no longer relegated to typically preselected monitoring targets. They also can include surveillance issues that are reported by committee, survey, special studies, spot/incident, and other reports. These nonpreselected indicators do not always lend themselves to as precise a definition by criteria and threshold levels; as explained later—they are likely to be more subjective. Still, meaningful criteria and threshold parameters are possible. Likewise, nonpreselected indicator data can be easily consolidated with the more typical indicator data under the QI program umbrella.

Step 5: Establish thresholds for indicator levels, trends and patterns that will trigger evaluation of an important aspect of care–regardless of the source or form of the QI data.

This step should answer these questions:

- What indicator levels, trends, or patterns should *trigger an investigative evaluation* of a preselected characteristic of an important aspect of care?
- What form of threshold can be applied to *nonpreselected indicator QI data* to trigger investigative evaluation of an important aspect of care?

Describe the definition and the methods of choosing a threshold in the QI plan. The plan should also list specific thresholds for ongoing indicators, including sentinel events. Thresholds for unplanned (nonpreselected), developing indicator events can be determined *ad hoc* and recorded in documents such as feeder reports, summary profiles, and committee minutes.

The concept of threshold was first introduced in the 1987 revision of the ten-step process. A threshold is a quantifiable assurance limit or range of limits (rather than a control limit) against which an average level, trend, or pattern of indicator performance for a given monitoring period is measured to determine significant disparity. A threshold can be equated to the percent of conformance to design specifications above which indicator data can vary from the more ideal indicator criteria and still be acceptable without warranting investigative evaluation. If any operational indicator displays a level of performance that is below the predetermined percentage of conformance, investigative evaluation is mandated.

"Exceeding" the threshold limit or range triggers investigative evaluation of the subject indicator and the IAC that is under surveillance.[b] The threshold is a realistic managerial tool for dealing with natural variations of indicator data and for establishing a rational basis for triggering investigation—balanced against the availability of finite quality management resources.

In day-to-day monitoring, the indicator is expected to sporadically exceed the exact criteria or standards of practice to some degree. The level, trend, or pattern of variation is often not of sufficient consequence to warrant costly investigative evaluation. However, if the variation persists at an insignificant degree, the indicator criteria or the threshold should be reevaluated until the evaluation parameters are clinically and managerially reasonable. Using a threshold as a yardstick for evaluating laboratory QI indicator data at the administrative level is comparable to using Westgard's multi-rules for evaluating QC data at the operative level of the laboratory bench.

Threshold can be expressed in terms of levels, trends, or patterns. A common approach is to report the parameter as a percentage of variation or compliance, but other control parameters can be used, such as standard deviation indices (SDI), turnaround time limits, temperature ranges, productivity quotient ranges, or case backlog limits.

A threshold should be practical and feasible within staffing, budgetary, and other resource allowances. The actual numerical limits will depend on industry standards of laboratory practice and local expectations. Again, it is important that clinical input be obtained in determining threshold levels, especially for

[b] The semantics of threshold management can be a little complex. Indicator data might not actually "exceed" the threshold as an absolute quantifiable figure. Numerically, the indicator data can, in fact, be less than the absolute threshold limit and trigger an investigation. For example, the threshold for the average ambient temperature for stored platelets is a range of < 20°C to > 24°C. The threshold is obviously exceeded if the ambient temperature is 26°C (> 24°C). Also, the threshold would be "exceeded" if the temperature is 18°C (< 20°C).

critically high-volume, high-risk, or problem-prone laboratory services. Examples of thresholds include:

- Resource thresholds
    1. > 10% technologist vacancy rate
    2. > 24 hours computer unscheduled down time.

- Process thresholds
    1. percent test sensitivity or specificity
    2. any instrument exceeding Westgard's Rules and requiring a rerun of a specimen batch—ie, a sentinel event
    3. > 95% of all stat results being turned around in more than one hour.

- Outcome thresholds
    1. > 0% of stat electrolyte results exceeding the 1-hour turnaround time to the surgical intensive care unit—ie, a sentinel event
    2. > 98% of patients on laboratory-referenced parental electrolyte therapy normalizing their serum electrolytes following therapy.

In establishing the threshold value, the JCAHO recognizes that most medical care processes have some variability that is beyond complete control. Striving for 100% conformance to expectations may not be realistic, given available organizational and operative resources. Yet, setting a threshold at 0% variation is warranted for any sentinel event indicator, as shown in the examples above. Regarding sentinel cases, the threshold mirrors the criteria for the high-risk indicator.

Selection and Use of Thresholds in the CQI Environment

The JCAHO describes the use of thresholds in the CQI environment in the following excerpt. "Establish a means to trigger evaluation. Teams of experts establish the level or pattern in data for each indicator that will trigger intensive evaluation. Statistical methods are emphasized, as is the fact that performance levels of process and outcomes are not the only way evaluation is triggered."[5] In this case, the operative phrases are "teams of experts" and "statistical methods"—and the key word that is missing is "threshold!"

As with indicators and their criteria, in making the transition from QA to QI, thresholds are taking on a new status in the CQI environment. The fifth step of the TSP is becoming an element in the process of indicator characterization—as opposed to being a separate fifth step as threshold has been. In witness to this change, the term threshold is the one element of the TSP that did not appear in the quality assessment and improvement chapter of the 1992 *AMH*. A hallmark of this changing appreciation of threshold as a quality management tool is the JCAHO deemphasis of "threshold," as a management concept with new emphasis on "evaluation triggers" or "means to trigger evaluation."[1,5,6]

With increasing emphasis, JCAHO is pointing out that evaluation can be triggered not only by disparate QI data but also by "other ways," such as committee and team studies, customer surveys, and random reports. A main objection to the use of the threshold concept has been that it tends to direct focus on blatant problems instead of nonproblematic opportunities for improvement. How can thresholds expressed as percentages of conformance be universally applied to non-QI data such as committee findings? How can thresholds be assigned to indicator levels that will trigger improvement of the quality management process itself? Actually, the term threshold is being condemned by guilt of association—not by virtue of any true lack of merit.

Instead of continuing the use of the threshold concept, some consider it as a limited—if not limiting—convention and are moving to express the triggering concept in more generic, less exact terms. However, there is very little, if any, substantive difference between the terms "threshold" and "evaluation trigger" as they are defined in the literature. Still, some hope that this subtle change in language will semantically expand the potential sources of improvement opportunities. Usage and time will tell us in which direction the language will finally gravitate.

The quality management goal still is to continuously improve a function, activity, or process—always striving toward the illusive targets of 1) 100% conformance to design specifications and 2) fitness of use. When conformance and fitness targets are achieved, then the specifications for both parameters can be improved further through a never ending cycle of increasing expectations.

In a CQI environment, the concept of threshold can take on an expanded meaning—instead of its disappearing altogether. What if the threshold is being successfully met all the time, one reporting period after another? Then, it should be realized that the threshold—and all the other surveillance parameters for that particular IAC—need to be reevaluated and adjusted to create a constellation of new parameters that are adequately sensitive to detect opportunities for improvement. Even the IAC can be modified, or better specified, or even eliminated as being not so important after all. Any of these steps would be an improvement of the quality surveillance process itself.

Under appropriate circumstances, determination of threshold (or "evaluation trigger") definitely warrants transition from the routine, screening process to a specialized team approach using analytical tools. An alternative approach would definitely be advisable if the issue at hand directly concerns clinical decision making.

Step 6: Monitor the quality of an important aspect of care by collecting and organizing data for all related indicators on a regular, ongoing schedule.

This step should answer the questions:

- What is the *most meaningful information* that the indicator data-elements can provide for the reporting period?
- Is the monitoring of these indicators based on an appropriate scheduling?

Describe the method for collecting and organizing indicator data, including frequency and reporting format, in the QI plan. The methods should be:

- Team-oriented
- Comprehensive, integrating all laboratory activities and all relevant nonlaboratory agencies, divisions, departments, and services, including decentralized laboratory services
- Coordinated and systematic
- Complete, covering all quality management activities, including the surveillance of "other sources" such as patient and staff surveys and spontaneous comments.

The plan should define essential data-retrieval elements as carefully as essential indicator characteristics are described for the IIS. Major data retrieval elements are characterized as follows[4]:

- Data *sources* include:
    1. laboratory QC, QI, or other quality management documents
    2. incident reports and spontaneous "comments"
    3. customer satisfaction surveys
    4. utilization records
    5. medical charts
    6. autopsy reports
    7. computer listings
    8. committee minutes, other team studies, and random reports.

As this list illustrates, the QI program is not limited to surveillance of standard quality indicator data. All quality improvement information can be brought together under one administrative-level umbrella. This maximizes the ability to cross reference information from different sources, to collect and match data from supporting indicators, increase the program's overall effectiveness, and conserve management resources. As is discussed later under the topic of profiling, such a universal approach to QI data collection is very feasible.

- *Data collection methods* include the use of:

  1. trained personnel such as medical records staff
  2. *ad hoc* collection officers (clinician/pathologist, clerical, technical, and volunteer staff)
  3. specially tasked laboratory groups, hospital committees, or outside personnel.

- *Sampling technique and size* include:

  1. probability sampling—true random sampling, stratified sampling, or systematic sampling
  2. nonprobability sampling—convenience sampling, purposive sampling, or quota sampling.

- *Sampling frequency* is dependent on the number of data-elements, the sampling technique, and the clinical urgency of the patient care activity as determined by clinician-pathologist consensus.

- *Means of protecting confidentiality* include:

  1. limited, protected access to data at various user levels
  2. protected access to other archival files
  3. use of codes for physician and patient names in open minutes.

  Data security must be in place whether the system is computerized or manual. This is particularly important when handling peer review data regarding individual practitioners or patients.

- *Processes of organizing the accumulated data for evaluation* include the methods of tabulation, summation, and comparison of aggregate levels of performance with thresholds.

Collecting and organizing quality management data is one of the hardest steps to perform adequately—it seems as if one can never do enough. Accurate, concurrent, and effective collection of data is the heart of the monitoring process. Indicator data must be documented as thoroughly, yet as efficiently, as possible so that indicators requiring evaluation can be readily identified for rapid investigation and appropriate action.

Collection Format

If the monitoring process is adequately streamlined, most laboratory documentation can be made almost "invisible"—that is, minimally intrusive into the busy work schedule of supervisory and technical personnel. First, all quality surveillance forms should be a template of the QI plan, serving as a constant reminder of the plan's essential elements. Designing such a format facilitates the goal of maximum compliance to the plan and produces consistent, succinct records.

Second, multiple applicability should be planned into the use of all data forms and reports. By overlapping their designs, log sheets, worksheets, and data reports can be used for multiple purposes. Such aggregate data retrieval minimizes data entry and supports the "invisibility" of the paperwork.

The surveillance forms most commonly used are aimed at:

- Data collection
- Data evaluation
- Monitoring and evaluation tracking
- Summary profilings.

The form might incorporate any or all of these four uses. These types of forms offer the data either as single observations or as cumulative observations to show individual levels, patterns, and trends at their best advantage. Bar, pie, and line graphs are also helpful. Individual shifts and specific management targets can be highlighted for special study. As just one example, the JCAHO *Primer on Clinical Indicator Development and Application* is a good source for sample data collection formats.[4] Profiling is discussed in great detail further on in this text.

Collection Periodicity: Scheduling Indicators for Monitoring

Monitoring the quality of all laboratory services at the same time—including every structural, process, and outcome component—is physically impossible. Usually, the laboratorian must monitor a selected number of indicators. A monitoring agenda, calendar, or schedule will document the periodicity of indicator surveillance. A rotating schedule ensures that a maximum variety of indicators is addressed in a balanced, timely manner and that all IAC are monitored within a reasonable period.

There are three steps to indicator scheduling and sampling. They all involve some form of ranking for prioritization to reduce the quality management targets to a number that matches the management resources that are available.

- First, rank all IAC according to their degree of clinical or other customer type of urgency and schedule them for monitoring at appropriate intervals.
- Second, rank all indicators pertinent to each IAC according to the path of work flow and operational urgency; an indicator's relationship to the three elements of laboratory function is a most

important consideration for ranking purposes. The laboratory path of work flow is a very practical tool for mapping a balanced monitoring schedule at appropriate intervals.

- Third, monitor a statistically significant sampling of the indicator data and integrate them. One exception is that all sentinel indicators should be monitored during every scheduled period.

Document QI data by consistent, periodic feeder reports so that levels, trends, patterns, and important single events can be evaluated swiftly to determine the need for timely investigative evaluation. If the evaluation of trends is important, data should be on hand for at least the last three reporting periods. This accumulation of consecutive data points constitutes the basis for an "indicator profile." Numerical data are preferred; however, narrative notes might be necessary.

Periodicity or frequency of monitoring is a component of indicator logic and is important in practical indicator design. Ordinarily, total procedure volume, related patient risk, or inherent procedural risk determine periodicity. Additional factors include the availability of the technical, managerial, and administrative assets needed for monitoring. Reasonable choices of periodicity are *monthly*, *bimonthly*, *quarterly*, *semiannually*, or *annually*—all depending on the criticalness of the issue at hand.

The planning of periodicity requires that the laboratorian determine the urgency of the indicators on the laboratory's agenda. Priorities will depend on the clinical impact of the indicator, the extent to which it has been problem-free, and the resources available for surveillance.

Ongoing opportunities for improvement may remain unsolved for a long time. Sometimes it is prudent to table the monitoring of such indicator topics for several months to allow for coordination of opportunity resolution. This is particularly true when resolution requires a long-range plan with a need for an interim solution or a series of phased solutions. Such opportunities must still be reviewed, but with decreased frequency—depending on the severity of the clinical impact, the predicted rate of resolution, and the resources available for quality management.

Collection Automation

For a thorough, efficient, and responsive quality management system, the collection of qualitative and quantitative data should be automated as much as possible. A relational database management program with multilevel search capabilities provides the needed flexibility. Many computer programs are developed by the local laboratory; many good commercial packages are available as well. The JCAHO offers a reference guide to building a customized computer program.[21]

Monitoring Quality Management Data in the CQI Environment

The JCAHO describes quality monitoring as, "The data-collection methodology often includes a means by which feedback from sources other than ongoing monitoring is used to indicate areas for evaluation and improvement."[5] These "other sources" include surveys, comments, complaints, suggestions, and reports from any relevant individual, group, or team.

Much of the collection process involves facilitating the bidirectional flow of information between the laboratory and all customer-supplier groups. Additionally, alternative team and analytical approaches should be used whenever appropriate.

Step 7: Evaluate an important aspect of care when a threshold is reached and identify opportunities for quality improvement, including problems of quality.

This step should answer these questions:

- Has any indicator threshold been *exceeded*?
- If so, what *level*, *trend*, or *pattern* is demonstrated by the aggregate data-elements of that indicator?
- Does the level, trend, or pattern indicate that there is an *opportunity* for improvement or a systemic *problem?*
- Is the event significant enough to *warrant further investigation* or emergency recourse?

Describe the evaluation method, including the periodicity and reporting format, in the QI plan. The objective is to determine whether 1) anything can be improved or has gone wrong and 2) whether the opportunity or problem is significant enough to deserve further investigation and remedial action.

The first phase of evaluation, which actually occurs in the planning stage, is to determine the periodicity of evaluation: evaluation should be as timely as possible to identify any need for urgent action. Yet, the periodicity also should be as infrequent as possible, to allow time for other monitoring activity and to conserve quality management resources. Consequently, aggregate QI data must be tabulated, summarized, organized, and evaluated at regularly scheduled intervals. Evaluation is comparing the observed levels of performance to the predetermined thresholds and determining significance of variation.

Evaluation Processes, Team Methods, and Statistical Tools

The unmasking of an opportunity for improving a system or process should trigger investigative evaluation to characterize and maximize the opportunity and realize an improvement. Therefore, after initial screening evaluation identifies an opportunity for improvement, set priorities for investigative (intensive) evaluation.

Because a quality indicator seldom reflects the root of the opportunity or problem, further investigation is necessary to reveal the true, underlying basis for definitive action. Concern over improvement of individual performance should be minimized; systems and processes should be the chief target for continuous improvement.

At this point, processes, methods, and tools need to be considered. There are several texts available that describe the use of these approaches to assess quality and facilitate decision making.[16,17,18] The evaluation step is the most pivotal portion of the TSP at which to consider the use of team and analytical alternatives, melding those options into the overall TSP evaluation process.

Evaluation is the most appropriate step at which to link an alternative approach with the TSP, form a focused, expert team, and employ an analytical process of the team's choice. It is critical that expert individuals be able to exercise the most effective, informed decision making to determine precisely what laboratory product or service can be improved and how it can be improved. The end result should be a complete analysis or characterization of:

- The immediate opportunity (or problem)
- The causes or roots of the opportunity
- The underlying process that is to be improved
- Relevant "bench marks"—examples of similar QI events experienced successfully by other healthcare organizations, including laboratories
- The options for action or remedy.

At this juncture, we enter into a gray zone between the seventh and eighth TSP steps for evaluation and the action. It is almost impossible for a sentient human being (ie, a laboratorian) not to intuitively leap immediately from evaluation analysis to an action conclusion, once the facts are at hand. Thus, it is not uncommon for early action options to be formulated during and at the close of evaluation. Once causes or roots of an opportunity for improvement are revealed, it is almost a natural instinct to immediately recognize the "flip side" of the exercise which is the remedy to the opportunity—the solution to the puzzle. Consequently, it is naive to try to separate early action decisions from the evaluation analysis. Certainly, if any options come to mind, they should become a part of the evaluation report. Any evaluation options need to be documented and transmitted to the team responsible for the next step: action. The evaluation team might or might not be the same group that serves as the action team. However, avoid the major pitfall with the evaluation process: do not allow initial facts to lead to premature, false conclusions—instead, perform a thorough analysis and then design a thorough action plan.

Peer Review Evaluation

A departmental- or service-level peer review committee should be responsible for the evaluation of indicator data concerning individual laboratory physicians and nonphysicians, other nonlaboratory providers, and patients. This evaluation should be handled confidentially, allowing only limited access to the QI data and any other relevant archival information.

Documentation of Evaluation Findings

The evaluation can be reported as to the degree to which the indicator data "exceed" their respective thresholds. Rules for reporting data-threshold disparity include the following:

- When comparing the observed data to the predetermined threshold level or range, *data-threshold disparity* can be manifested by an inordinate excess or diminishment of indicator data levels.
- The *level* of any disparity can be graded as borderline, minimal, moderate, or severe, depending on local management philosophy.
- An inordinate data *trend* can be described as increasing, decreasing, plateaued, or continued—accompanied by some indication of severity.
- A *pattern* in the level or trend can be related to specific shifts, laboratory personnel, attending physicians, groups of patients, or a number of other operational variables. Even if thresholds are not actually exceeded, suspicious (subtle) or aggressive patterns should still be noted.
- A brief *narrative summary* can provide an interpretation or analysis of the event. The event should be documented as a new occurrence or a continuation of an earlier finding.
- The evaluation can be reported as "on target" or "disparity resolved" if there is 1) no *disparity* between the indicator data and the threshold, 2) no significant *adverse trend or pattern*, or 3) no need for an *initial baseline* profile.
- If six to nine months of active monitoring do not yield any improved quality of an aspect of care, then it can be reported that the QI process is broken and there is a need to *reevaluate the quality surveillance plan* for that IAC. This should include review of the threshold, indicator criteria, indicator topic, and aspect of care, including levels of prioritization of importance.

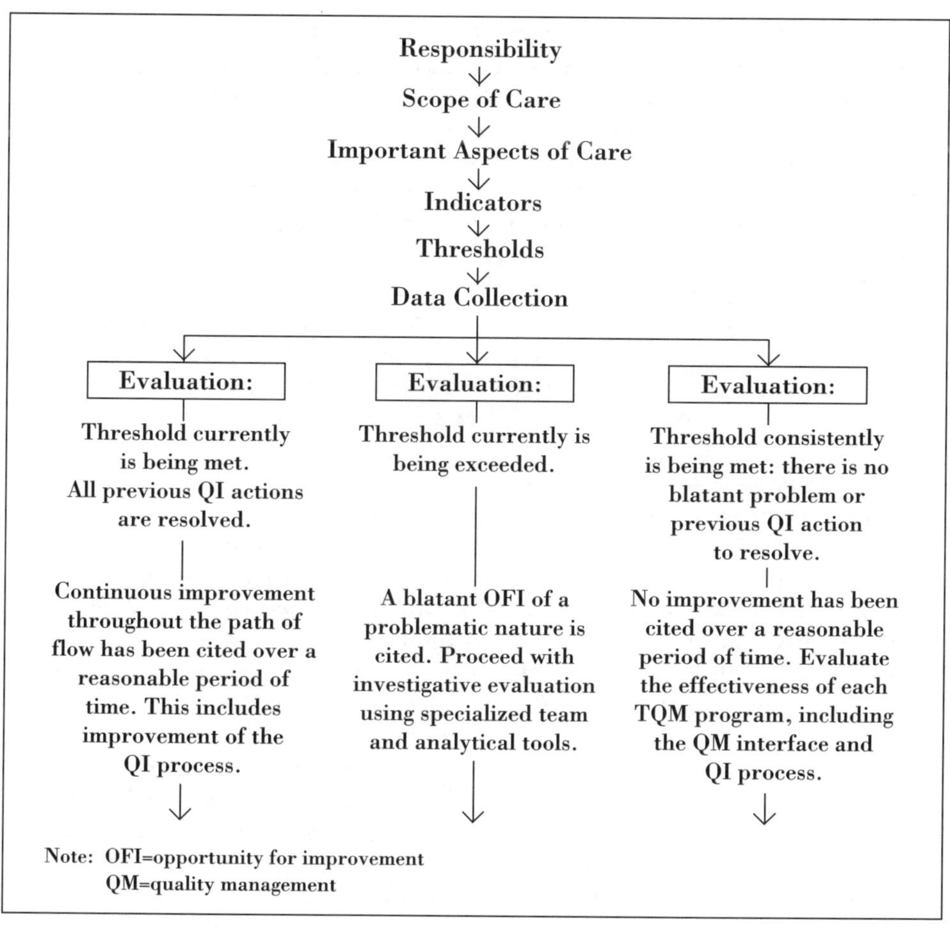

Figure 4.5 Three decision options at the evaluation step

Achieving Evaluation of Surveillance Data in the CQI Environment

The JCAHO describes evaluation in the CQI environment as "When the level or pattern in the data triggers evaluation, and also when other feedback (eg, patient reports, staff reports) identifies other opportunities for improvement, leaders set priorities for evaluation and establish teams, which evaluate the patient care or service function in question."[5] This summation emphasizes the importance of the leadership, alternative sources of QI data, and melding the use of specialized teams and statistical analysis with this pivotal segment of the TSP.

In the CQI environment, the possibility of *three decision options* develops during the evaluation step. Figure 4.5 introduces this decision tree in the seventh step of the TSP, the step of evaluation.

In the left-hand decision track, the threshold is currently being met. There are no previous QI actions that need attention. There is evidence of continuous improvement for that indicator and its IAC throughout the path of work flow over the past six to nine months. That improvement could have involved resolving an indicator-related problematic or nonproblematic opportunity for improvement. It also could have involved modification of the QI process or some other aspect of the TQM system.

In the central decision track, screening evaluation reveals that indicator data levels are exceeding their threshold. This signals a blatantly problematic opportunity for improvement and the need for further investigative evaluation. In the past, this was a predominant situation with the QA approach. Today, it is a common scenario in the practice of QI, but is intended to become less predominant as the practice of TQM and CQI progresses. An appropriate team needs to perform investigative evaluation using the necessary analytical tools.

In the right-hand decision track, the major target for consideration is a *nonproblematic opportunity*; the key to discovering a nonproblematic opportunity for improvement is illustrated here. In this case, QI data have been consistently "on target" in relation to the respective threshold. Consequently, there is no obvious problem, nor is there any previous QI action needing attention. However, a not-so-obvious problem is that there has been no significant improvement of any operational function or activity over the last six to nine months. There has been no evidence of any enhanced system, process, customer -related outcome, or customer satisfaction. In this situation, the laboratorian cannot say, "If it ain't broken don't fix it." In the CQI environment, one must say, "If there is no improvement over a reasonable period, the quality management process must be broken"—or, "Even though it may not seemingly be broke, break it!"

In regard to this third option, it is very common for the QI process to demonstrate many indicators that are consistently acceptable and do not trigger further investigation. Even though no problem or opportunity is identified after several repeated monitoring and evaluation cycles, surveillance of *all* IAC still must continue. Unbroken scrutiny ensures that the aspects of patient care remain at desired levels of quality and that opportunities and problems will eventually be identified when they do occur.

However, the "catch-22" is that the JCAHO expects the QI process to identify *at least some* opportunities for improvement or problems for remedy through the surveillance of even those seemingly "perfect," nonproblematic indicators. Thus, if there is no such discovery after six to nine months of routine monitoring, the laboratory should question the adequacy of its quality management program and should reevaluate these quiescent indicators, focusing on the first seven steps of the TSP, and improving the QI process itself.

One of the major points of contention in discussing the options in this decision tree is the amount of time that is reasonable for nonactivity, quiescence, or nonimprovement for any given indicator or IAC. In this

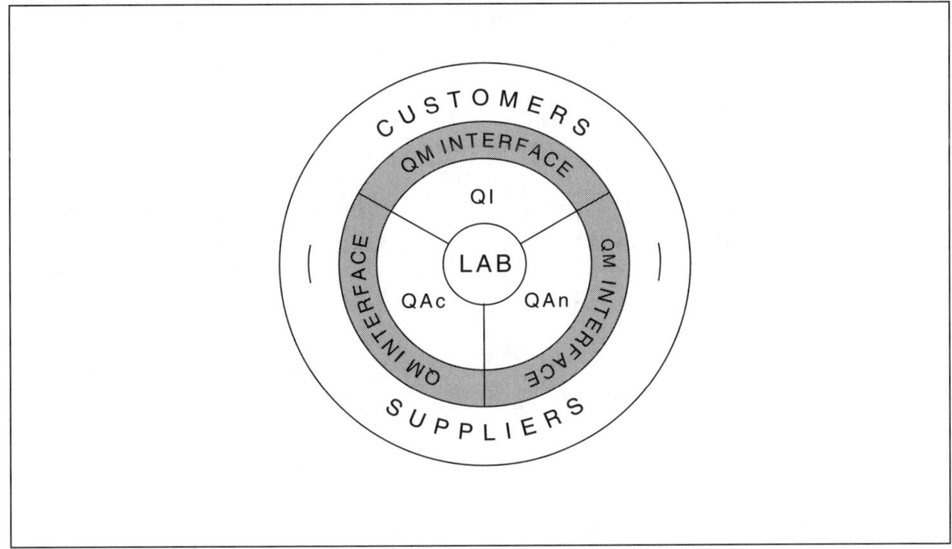

Figure 4.6 Vena model of quality management (QM) interface

text, a period of six to nine months per indicator is used as an arbitrary, empirical rule of thumb. In actuality, the duration of the period should vary from one indicator to the next and from one IAC to the next, depending on the priority and sense of clinical or operational urgency attributed to the given QI event. Thus, the actual criteria characterizing this waiting period are strictly up to each laboratory—but a choice needs to be made.

Therefore, if there is no improvement of a given important aspect of care over a reasonable, predetermined period, reevaluate the entire quality management process. The TSP must be reviewed and revised to realize its potential for improving the quality of laboratory support of patient care. The following questions need to be asked:

- Is there inadequate transfer of information or responsibility at the quality management (QM) interface?
- Should the monitoring continue as scheduled because there is an imminent possibility of discovering a significant opportunity of improvement?
- Does the monitoring schedule need to be increased in frequency to reach a better assessment?
- Does the threshold need to be more sensitive to variation?
- Is the indicator adequately defined? Are its criteria sensitive enough?
- Should the important aspect of care be redefined or subcategorized?

- Should the important aspect of care be moved to a lower rank of priority or should it be completely removed from the inventory?

Answering these questions constitutes an evaluation of the entire quality surveillance process. This review should be thorough, including the quality management interface, the first five planning steps, the data collection step, the two improvement steps, and the two follow-up steps. The quality management interface is the system of relationships that the laboratory develops with all of its internal and external customers—suppliers through its QAc, QAn, and QI programs. This interface is portrayed in Figure 4.6.

Again, an appropriate team needs to perform any investigative evaluation using the necessary analytical tools. This intensive analysis should focus on the lack of effectiveness of the entire TQM system, remembering all three programs, with an emphasis on the QI process and the QM interface. In the examples provided in this text, the QI process of choice is the TSP—but, other alternative surveillance processes are available, if desired, and easily merge with the TSP at this point.

Step 8: Take action to improve the quality of an important aspect of care, including the correction of identified problems.

This step should answer the questions:

- What is the most *appropriate* and *judicious action* needed to take maximum advantage of an opportunity for improvement or to achieve the most satisfactory remedy of a problem at hand?
- Who is *responsible* for the action?

Describe the method for establishing a plan of corrective action, including the format for transmitting assignments and recording the action taken, in the QI plan. Once investigative evaluation uncovers a problem or opportunity for improvement, the action process should identify:

- *What* improvement is expected to occur
- *What* action is appropriate in view of the nature of the opportunity's or problem's cause and scope; if there are interim phases to consider
- *Who* is responsible for implementing the action
- *When* the action is expected to occur; what the expected results are and when they should occur
- *Who* is responsible for follow-up of the action.

Developing and implementing a corrective action is one of the most difficult steps in the quality management process. Corrective action must be appropriate to the problem's cause and must be adequately documented. In 1988, the greatest number of JCAHO contingencies occurred in the functional area of medical staff QA monitoring; in 57% of the cases, corrective actions were not appropriate or were not adequately implemented, carried through, or documented.[22]

To identify and characterize the opportunity for improvement in the evaluation step is to lay the foundation for direct selection of major and interim remedial steps. The laboratory organization must identify, implement, and document definitive action for improvement or resolution of a problem. The evaluation step delineates the opportunities for improvement (problematic and nonproblematic) and the determinative causes for those opportunities; the action step delineates the remedy for realizing the improvement.

When the evaluation process mandates action, the definition of QI can be remembered as a model for action:

> *Laboratory quality assessment and improvement* is an administrative surveillance program for 1) systematically monitoring the effectiveness of quality management for any laboratory product or service in any phase of its life cycle and 2) evaluating the performance of quality indicators in comparison to laboratory and clinical standards and thresholds.
>
> Such a monitoring program can result in an adjustment of department-wide laboratory operations by upgrading, stabilizing, or downgrading elements of structure (including both operative and organizational resources), process, or outcome to maximally meet specific administrative goals.

Therefore, action must be in keeping with the nature of the opportunity at hand. Generally, opportunities for improvement are best accomplished by modifying operational processes at the organizational or operative managerial level. Examples of action responses include the following[4]:

- To enhance the organizational structure by improving:
    1. organizational expectations—eg, values, mission, vision, goals, and objectives
    2. organizational relationships at the QM interface—eg, hospital, departmental, service, section, and unit levels
    3. organizational resource programs—eg, quality surveillance (QI), quality planning (QAn), and quality team effectiveness (QAc)
    4. operative-level plans, policies, or operational procedures

5. operative resources—eg, personnel, budget, supplies, and equipment
6. intra- and interdepartmental communication—eg, manual or electronic.

- To enhance personnel knowledge by improving:
    1. organizational and individual expectations
    2. orientation procedures
    3. focused, remedial, or continuing education activities
    4. informational reference sources.
- To enhance personnel behavior or performance by improving:
    1. organizational and individual expectations
    2. informal or formal counseling
    3. team building—inspiring motivation, commitment, and decision making
    4. supervisory control
    5. clinical privileges
    6. duty assignments.
- *Only after* the above approaches do not result in systemic, process improvement, and it becomes evident that a problem exists that is truly caused by inadequate personnel performance, then the final recourse is individual disciplinary action, such as:
    1. a formal warning
    2. close supervision or consultation
    3. probation
    4. modification of staff privileges—eg, reduction, suspension, or revocation
    5. modification of staff appointment—eg, limiting, suspending, or revoking.

The above actions (originally formulated by the JCAHO) focus on two elements of quality laboratory functions—resources and process. There is always need to address outcome expectations, but that often amounts to an interim, not a definitive, realization of improvement. As demonstrated above, resources are a very important source of opportunities for improvement; this is particularly true of *organizational resources*.

If an opportunity for improvement is attainable, the definitive action can be to upgrade, stabilize, or downgrade a specific laboratory procedure, requiring a combination of administrative and managerial level actions. Upgrading or stabilizing actions are intuitively straightforward. However,

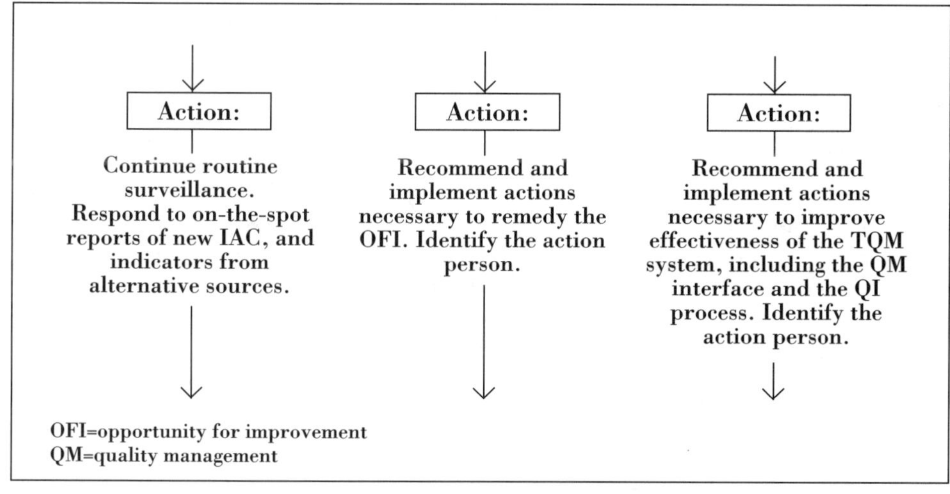

Figure 4.7 Three decision options at the action step

downgrading—or curtailing—laboratory operations runs against the natural grain of the laboratorian work ethic. Nevertheless, if the quality management process identifies an otherwise unsolvable problem, the decision to entirely curtail laboratory services in question might be necessary.

An example of downgrading is the rerouting of tuberculosis specimens to a reference laboratory because of an inoperable safety hood in the mycobacteriology laboratory section. Such a decision amounts to a conscionable decrease in conformance to testing specifications and indicator outcome criteria. For example, turnaround time will be prolonged and, thus, downgraded. The effect on patient care outcome will be a slightly increased but tolerable turnaround time as a trade-off for maintaining control of another outcome requirement—that of employee safety.

A definitive action might be implemented immediately, or it might be delayed, supplanted by an interim or time-phased solution. Whatever course of action is needed, it should be carefully planned and reported as such. If a previously identified problem or opportunity has been resolved, the action can be reported as such. If no problem has occurred during the reporting period, the action is reported simply as none needed.

Occasionally, the problem at hand will show no improvement by departmental efforts alone. Then the laboratory must seek assistance from other departments (laterally) or administrative echelons above the laboratory organizational level (vertically). In such an instance, review the problem, the cause, and any earlier action; revise the action; and schedule the next reassessment. If the problem is really too hard for laboratory solution, it will probably require specific assistance from higher administrative echelons and will have to be given to them for direct managerial control. In any case, coordinate and cooperate with other departments and the higher administration to achieve a reasonable resolution in a timely fashion.

Action Person

After the need for some specific action is determined, the QI report should identify an "action person" by job title. This individual is responsible for follow-up, which includes any intra- or extradepartmental coordination necessary for implementing and completing the action. The selection of a specific action person reflects the spirit of the first step of the JCAHO process. In addition, directed accountability makes managerial "horse sense."

Achieving Action in the CQI Environment

The JCAHO describes action in the CQI environment as "Greater emphasis is placed in focusing actions on processes, especially the hand offs between departments/services."[5] In the new management environment, three options for action present themselves during the action step. Figure 4.7 depicts this decision tree in the eighth step of the TSP.

In the left-hand track, the action is to continue routine surveillance as planned since there is no evidence of an opportunity for improvement. In this case, there has been documented improvement of the subject indicator and IAC over the past six to nine months; these time-related criteria are discussed under the evaluation topic.

In the central decision track, the response to the opportunity for improvement cited during evaluation is for the team to develop an action plan, including whatever number and type of actions that are necessary to resolve the problem at hand. Then, implement those actions and identify an action person for follow-up.

In the right-hand decision track, the action plan should include whatever changes have been deemed necessary to improve the effectiveness of any TQM program, including the QM interface and QI process. In all instances, where action is recommended or implemented, identify an action person responsible for follow-up.

The same alternative team and analytical approaches employed for evaluation can be used in the action step. A quality improvement team, task force, or *ad hoc* committee are all forms of action groups, that are empowered to formulate, implement, and follow-up actions.

If there is no improvement of a given important aspect of care over a reasonable period, the action is to reevaluate the entire quality management process. The following action decisions might be required:

- Continue the monitoring of the given indicator as scheduled.
- Increase the frequency of monitoring the given indicator to gain increased sensitivity to an opportunity for improvement.

- Modify the indicator's threshold to increase sensitivity to variation.
- Redefine or subcategorize the indicator and its criteria to increase their specificity.
- Redefine or subcategorize the related IAC.
- Move the IAC to a lower priority rank of importance.
- Remove the IAC from the inventory.

Step 9: Assess the effectiveness of action, document improvement in the quality of an important aspect of care, and assure improvement is maintained.

This step should answer these questions:

- What is the *overall effectiveness* of the quality management process in identifying the opportunity or resolving the problem at hand?
- Has there been any *improvement* of any important aspect of care?
- Is that improvement being actively *sustained*?

Describe the assessment method and the report format in the QI plan. The effectiveness of ongoing actions should be analyzed and documented after a reasonable period. The usual period of assessment is one to three months, which provides enough time for a planned action to be implemented and to have some effect. The effectiveness of the overall quality improvement plan, program, and process should be assessed annually, at a minimum.

The concept of assessment tends to be a little elusive, but it is really very straightforward. The first intention for this step is to assure that there is timely follow-up of any ongoing actions. The second intention is that there is general, ongoing, administrative-level scrutiny leveled at the overall QI process to ensure that the process has ample resources, sufficient operative procedures, and satisfactory outcomes. Follow-up assessment of QI actions commonly determines if:

- The nature and scope of the original opportunity or problem were correctly evaluated and analyzed, revealing accurate and precise causes or roots for the subject opportunity.
- The recommended actions were appropriate for a given opportunity's causes or roots.
- The recommended actions were reasonable, achievable, and adequately phased.
- The responsibility for implementing corrective actions were clearly specified, communicated, understood, and adequate in scope and authority.

- The corrective actions were implemented in a timely fashion.
- The result of the action was expected, desirable, and effective—or the converse.
- There are further recommendations for action that must be implemented.
- There is need for lateral or higher-level assistance when the opportunity at hand is too hard for the laboratory to handle alone.
- Ongoing monitoring needs to be maintained.
- Priorities for monitoring need reassessment.

The overall assessment of the management of an opportunity for improvement or a problem of quality can be reported in many ways. Examples of brief notations for reporting purposes include:

- Improved
- Minimally improved
- Marginally improved
- No improvement
- Desired quality maintained
- Borderline loss of desired quality
- Complete loss of desired quality
- Regaining desired quality
- Opportunity of improvement identified
- Opportunity of improvement partially attained
- Opportunity of improvement attained
- Beyond laboratory control—too difficult to be solved at laboratory level
- Follow-up is needed.

If the solution of a problem is unduly prolonged, a brief notation should describe the overall ineffectiveness of the quality management process, including the cause for delay. A prognosis for resolution should be delivered in the assessment. In determining a prognosis, there should be mention of the influence of any organizational or environmental internal strengths and weaknesses or external opportunities or threats (ie, SWOT analysis). It is particularly important to note extradepartmental obstacles. The overall assessment may be that the problem at hand is too difficult to be resolved at the laboratory level and must be dealt with by a higher managerial authority.

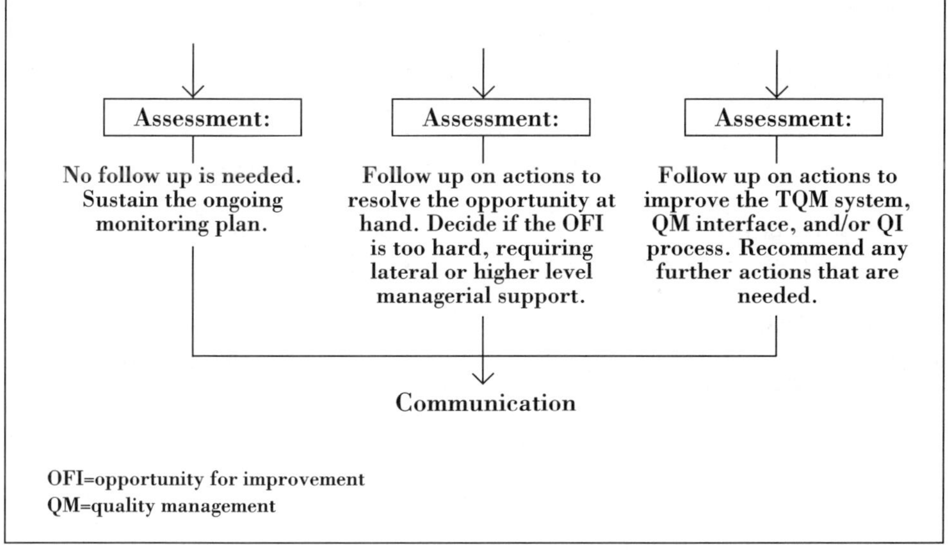

Figure 4.8 Three decision options at the assessment step

Achieving Assessment in the CQI Environment

The JCAHO describes assessment in the CQI environment as "A greater emphasis is placed on assuming that improvement is sustained over time through changes in process, as well as continued data collection."[5] In such an environment, three decision options present themselves during the assessment step. Figure 4.8 displays these options in the ninth step of the TSP.

In the left-hand decision track, the general assessment should be that there is evidence of continuous improvement of products and services over a reasonable period as evidenced by:

- Customer resultant status and satisfaction (ie, patients and others)
- An effective TQM system, QM interface, and QI process
- Effective monitoring priorities and scheduling.

Consequently, there is no need for any specific follow-up. Just sustain the established monitoring plan.

In the central decision track, the general assessment is based on there being blatant evidence of need for improvement of a given indicator and IAC. It usually takes a one to three month period for implementation of a recommended action to take effect. After a reasonable period, it is time to assess if the action has been effective. If not, why not and what further has to be done to close the issue at the laboratory or higher managerial level? Evaluate the effectiveness of the QM interface. Decide if the opportunity for improvement is too hard to be resolved at the laboratory level or if there is need for lateral or higher managerial assistance.

In the right-hand track, based on evidence of lack of continuous quality improvement over a reasonable period, the general assessment approach is to determine the effectiveness of the recommended actions to improve the quality management system. Do the TQM programs (surveillance, planning, and team building), the QM interface, or the QI process need further investigative appraisal? Recommend and implement any further actions deemed necessary to achieve CQI in this nonproblematic, nonimprovement scenario.

The sequences for the three decision tracks for evaluation, action, and assessment are consolidated in Figure 4.9. As demonstrated by this option model, the TSP links:

TQM (an organization-wide quality management system of administrative-level programs)
to
CQI (an organization-wide improvement process and philosophy).

There is no question that proper assessment often will require multi-disciplined, specialized teams and statistical analysis. The team can be the same used for the evaluation and action steps, or it can consist of a different composition.

Step 10: Communicate results of the monitoring and evaluation process to all individuals, departments, or services that have a need to know, including members of the organization-wide quality improvement program.

This step should answer the questions:

- What is the most effective means of communicating *relevant QI information* to *appropriate segments* of the healthcare organization, both inside and outside the laboratory?
- Do those that have a *need to know*—know?

Methods, formats, and schedules for disseminating quality management findings should be described in the QI plan. The JCAHO requires effective communication of these findings so that:

- The necessary action is transmitted to the those who need to know.
- The lessons learned from the QI process are shared, including bench mark examples.
- Quality management efforts are not duplicated.

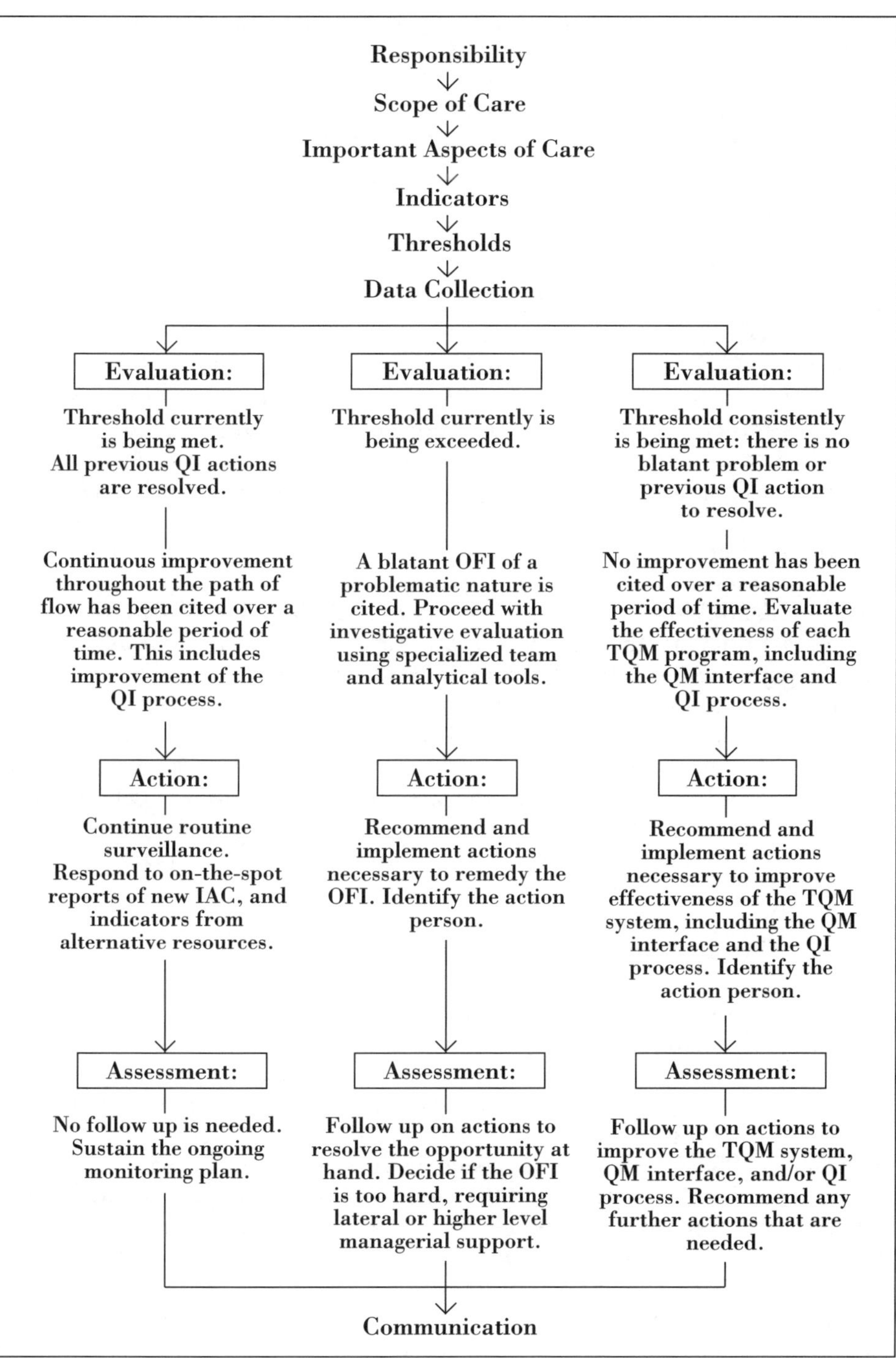

Figure 4.9 Integration of TQM and its QI process with CQI: three options for evaluation, action, and assessment

- Quality management findings are used in periodic reappraisal of clinical privileges.
- Quality management findings contribute to the detection of trends, patterns, and problems affecting more than one department.
- The quality of care is improved throughout the organization.

Brown has documented that one of the most fundamental sources of all organizational opportunities or problems is organizational communication.[23] In keeping with that theme, education should be an aspect of virtually every QI action plan in the communication step. Education is one of the most effective means of organizational communication.

Positive lessons learned from emerging trends in quality improvement are extremely valuable to all laboratory customers, not just the pathologists and quality management staff. For example, bench mark experiences should be included as "lessons learned." Relevant information should be circulated to all customers-suppliers, both inside and outside the laboratory boundaries.

Communication must be regular, timely, and effective. Quality management data should be summarized concisely, distributed, and reviewed by all appropriate parties throughout the laboratory and hospital administrative and support divisions. Regular committee meetings, minutes, and reports will facilitate this communication. Organizational integration of several quality-related activities can save time. Duplicative effort should be minimized. The types and frequency of reports depend on the organizational structure and the working relationships among the various quality management activities. Electronic mail, facsimile transmission, special in-service training, task forces, coordination meetings, and quality circles are also useful.

Effective Communication in the CQI Environment

The JCAHO describes communication in the CQI environment as "Findings of those performing monitoring and evaluation are forwarded to the leaders and to affected individuals and groups. Leaders also disseminate information, as necessary."[5] Lack of effective follow-up communication was a major contributing factor in the cases of survey deficiencies cited by the JCAHO in 1988.[22] The use of specialized teams and analytical tools are as relevant to the orchestration of the communication step as they are in any other segment of the TSP. Every possible effort must be made to ensure that there is most effective communication at the laboratory QM interface with both internal and external customers-suppliers—all who have a need to know the given facts. There is seldom "too much" communication in any organization—usually, there is "too little."

The communication step should ensure organization-wide dissemination of lessons learned, educational activity, action review, and archival documentation. Thus, the tenth step is absolutely crucial to all follow-up activities. It is particularly important in facilitating an improvement to be truly continuous rather than repetitive—a quality problem should not repeat itself, especially because of ineffective communication.

A SUMMATION OF THE TEN-STEP PROCESS

The JCAHO ten-step quality improvement format can be treated as a five-phased process that is continually recapitulating itself. The ten steps and five phases are illustrated in Figure 4.10. For comparison, an excellent five-phased approach for visualizing QI and the TSP has been described by Berte.[24]

- The first five steps (responsibility, scope, aspects, indicators, and thresholds) form the *planning phase*—Shewhart's *plan*.
- The sixth step (data collection) is the *monitoring phase*—Shewhart's *do*.
- The seventh and eighth steps (evaluation and action) are the *improvement phase*—Shewhart's *check*.
- The ninth and tenth steps (assessment and communication) are the *follow-up phase*.
- Following the tenth step, the entire process requires a *reevaluation phase* on a periodic basis along with the ninth and tenth steps—Shewhart's *act*.

QUALITY MANAGEMENT ACRONYMS: CRAE AND EVAAC

Until 1987, JCAHO literature energetically publicized the use of the acronym, "CRAE." This managerial "string around the finger" was a reminder of the last four elements of the original JCAHO ten-step format, before the 1987 revision:

- Conclusion
- Recommendation
- Action
- Evaluation.

These elements were very important for the QA program up to 1987, and CRAE was considered to be quite helpful. The JCAHO observed that if the last four steps of the process were not done well, the QA program was not being pursued to fruition—as evidenced by the report of 1988 JCAHO survey deficiencies cited above.[22]

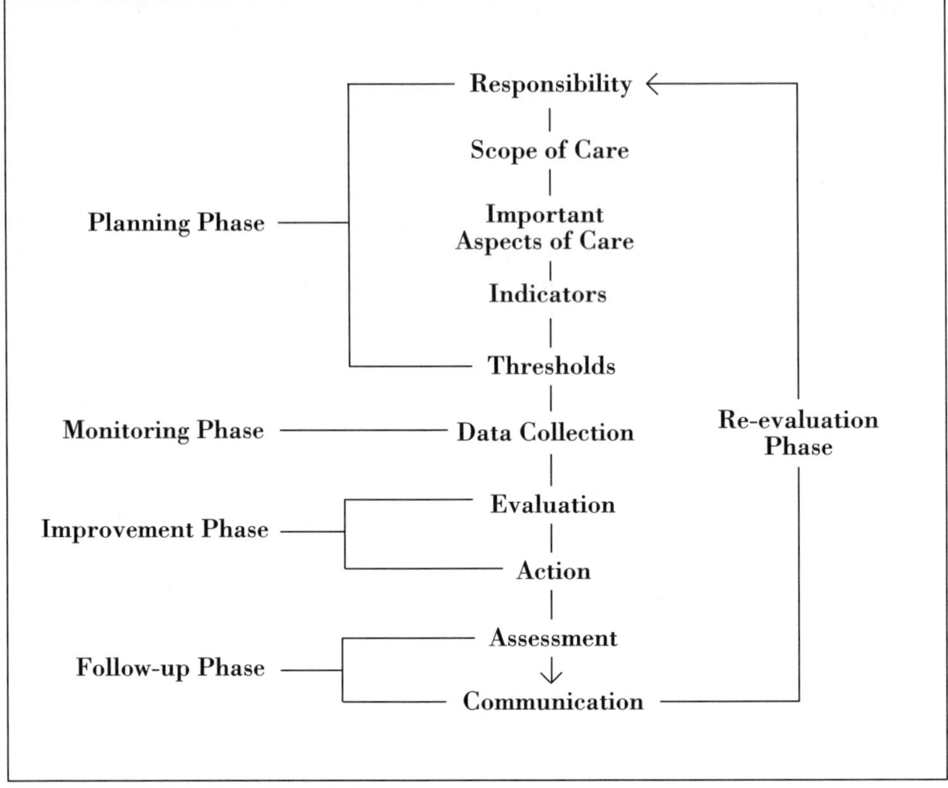

Figure 4.10 Five phases of the ten-step process

Subsequent to the 1987 modification of the ten-step format, the abbreviation, "CRAE," no longer applies. The last four steps have now become:

- Evaluation
- Action
- Assessment
- Communication.

Better defined than the earlier CRAE grouping, these four elements still are just as critical to the successful implementation of the JCAHO TSP. Also, the acronym, EvAAC, can be an equally helpful managerial reminder. In fact, the emerging importance of the second half or limb of the TSP in the CQI environment makes EvAAC even more relevant and useful today as a managerial abbreviation.

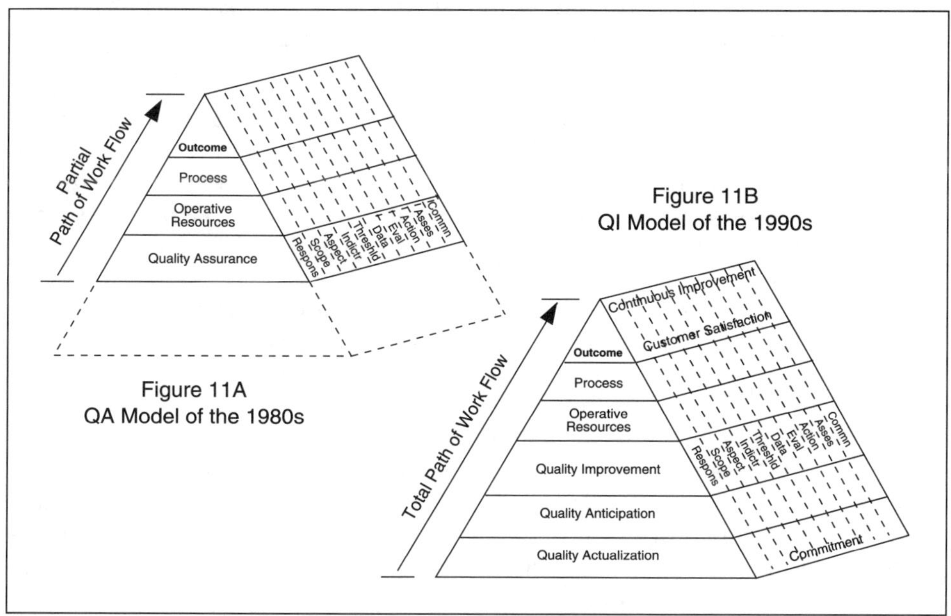

Figure 4.11 A quality surveillance model: the transition from quality assurance to quality improvement integrated with the ten-step process in a CQI environment

THE TEN-STEP PROCESS: A LINK BETWEEN QUALITY ASSURANCE AND QUALITY ASSESSMENT AND IMPROVEMENT

Modeling a quality management system is helpful in conceptualizing, planning, and implementing improvement management activities. Figure 4.11 illustrates models for both the QA and the QI (and PI) programs, showing them in transition in a CQI environment.

The JCAHO TSP is a key element of each model in this text—keeping in mind that there are other improvement processes or cycles available. The ten-step process receives so much emphasis here because it contributes a matrix that integrates the three levels of laboratory operation; the result is a surveillance program that is systematic and comprehensive. Consequently, administrative- and operative-level functions are all interlinked; thus, they are potentially most effective. At the same time, the quality management system is easily understood by JCAHO and CAP surveyors, based on their familiarity with QI documentation.

Figure 4.11A is a model of QA surveillance program of the 1980s. Most programs of that era ignored monitoring the quality of planning and team building. Nor were indicators for these activities stressed as accreditation requirements. Figure 4.12B offers a comparison of a modern QI (or PI) program in the TQM-CQI environment. The latter figure demonstrates the transition from QA to QI by the addition of two fundamental elements.

- Element One: Creating the force of a true cultural commitment to quality improvement throughout the organization. This amounts to the organization's achieving a cultural "Renaissance."
- Element Two: Systematically tailoring all three quality management programs for surveillance (QI), anticipation (QAn), and actualization (QAc) toward systematic continuous quality improvement as the ultimate outcome goal. This requires methodical planning at several organizational and operative levels.

A major lesson here is that we can develop indicators to assess and improve the quality of organizational commitment and continuous improvement. In many cases, these indicators will not resemble the "traditional" QA-type of indicator with analytically precise criteria and evaluation triggers. More likely, they will be of the type of indicators that are being promoted by the JCAHO as QI issues from sources "other than" the typical, ongoing indicator selection process. Instead of tightly controlled data sources, these organizational indicator data will stem from more subjective sources such as customer-supplier surveys, questionnaires, spontaneous suggestions, spot reports, and group (eg, committee, task force, quality improvement team) minutes, studies, and other reports.

Figure 4.11A suggests that the QA program of the 1980s was *intended* to promote development of the other two infrastructural programs (QAc and QAn). However, these two programs are depicted only in dashed outline at the base of the organizational pyramid, implying that many laboratories of that decade did not fully integrate the two programs with QA as a complete TQM system.

In studying the models of Figure 4.11, it should be remembered that the TSP is not the only process that could be useful. Any of the alternatives described in this chapter are also applicable. However, the JCAHO ten-step format is as generic and adaptable as any other approach. No matter what approach is chosen, the laboratorian must tailor its improvement program to local needs, laboratory complexity, and available resources.

REFERENCES

1. The Joint Commission 1994 Accreditation Manual for Hospitals Volume I. Oakbrook Terrace, IL: Joint Commission on Accreditation of Healthcare Organizations, 1993.
2. Frombert R (ed). Monitoring and Evaluation: Pathology and Medical Laboratory Services. Chicago, IL: Joint Commission on Accreditation of Healthcare Organizations, 1987.
3. The Joint Commission 1994 Accreditation Manual for Hospitals. Volume II. Oakbrook Terrace, IL: Joint Commission on Accreditation of Healthcare Organizations, 1993.

4. Joint Commission Primer on Clinical Indicator Development and Application: Measuring Quality in Health Care. Oakbrook Terrace, IL: Joint Commission on Accreditation of Healthcare Organizations, 1990.
5. The Transition from QA to CQI: An Introduction to Quality Improvement in Health Care. Oakbrook Terrace, IL: Joint Commission on Accreditation of Healthcare Organizations, 1991.
6. The Joint Commission 1992 Accreditation Manual for Hospitals. Oakbrook Terrace, IL: Joint Commission on Accreditation of Healthcare Organizations, 1991.
7. The Joint Commission Accreditation Manual for Pathology and Clinical Laboratory Services. Oakbrook Terrace, IL: Joint Commission on Accreditation of Healthcare Organizations, 1993.
8. The Joint Commission 1990 Accreditation Manual for Hospitals. Oakbrook Terrace, IL: Joint Commission on Accreditation of Healthcare Organizations, 1989.
9. Chu SY, Edney-Parker H. Evaluation of the reliability of bedside glucose testing. Lab Med, 1989;20:93-96.
10. The Joint Commission 1985 Accreditation Manual for Hospitals. Oakbrook Terrace, IL: Joint Commission on Accreditation of Healthcare Organizations, 1984.
11. Berwick DM. Continuous improvement as an ideal in health care. NEJM, 1989;320:53-56.
12. Gambino R. Most laboratory errors are system dependent--not people dependent. Lab Med, 1989;20:123.
13. McGregor D. The Human Side of Enterprise. New York, NY: McGraw-Hill Co, Inc, 1960.
14. Massie JL. Essentials of Management. Englewood Cliffs, NJ: Prentice-Hall, Inc, 1987.
15. Juran JM. Juran on Leadership for Quality. New York: The Free Press, 1989.
16. Scholtes PR. The Team Handbook: How To Use Teams To Improve Quality. Madison, WI: Joiner Associates, Inc., 1989.
17. Walton M. The Deming Management Method. Putnam Pub Group. New York,NY: 1986.
18. Brassard M. The Memory Jogger. Methuen, MA: GOAL/QPC, 1988.
19. Pennock, M. Quality assurance. Can J Med Tech, 1986;48:120-121.
20. Characteristics of clinical indicators. Qual Rev Bull, 1989;15:330-339.
21. Guide to Analyze Quality Assurance/Risk Management Needs. Oakbrook Terrace, IL: Joint Commission on Accreditation of Healthcare Organizations, 1988.

22. The Joint Commission quality assurance model. American Hospital Association Technical Briefing. American Hospital Association. Chicago: 1989.

23. Brown D. Criticisms of Large Organizations: Results of a Survey. Washington, D.C.: George Washington University, October 20, 1981.

24. Berte, LM. Growing into laboratory quality assurance. Med Lab Ob, 1990;22:24-29.

5. The Laboratory Path of Work Flow and Surveillance of Organizational-Level Quality Indicators

THE LABORATORY PATH OF WORK FLOW

The operational path of laboratory work flow is invaluable in establishing a thorough, systematic quality surveillance program. The quality assessment and improvement (QI) surveillance plan should incorporate the path as a guide to selecting indicators and organizing a monitoring schedule. Therefore, it is important to carefully analyze and understand the composition of the operational path.

The laboratory path of work flow should be mapped out for every important aspect of care (IAC). The resultant flow diagram should accurately reflect the sequence of all significant laboratory activities for each IAC–including all internal (intralaboratory) and external (pre- and postlaboratory) aspects.

Figure 5.1 demonstrates the overlapped timing of various internal and external operational events. This hierarchical model of the total laboratory path of work flow consists of four levels of management activities, assessment divisions, functional periods, and operational segments and phases. Whether the subject laboratory is designed for anatomic pathology, clinical pathology, decentralized (point-of-care or ancillary), or clinically-oriented medical research laboratory testing, the general nature of the path remains unchanged. Although complex at first glance, the path is very easy to apply as a quality management tool if it is properly analyzed and understood.[a]

[a] Both Figures 5.1 and 5.2 of this chapter are fraught with semantic and structural complexity. However, we have to start somewhere to reach a common ground of understanding.

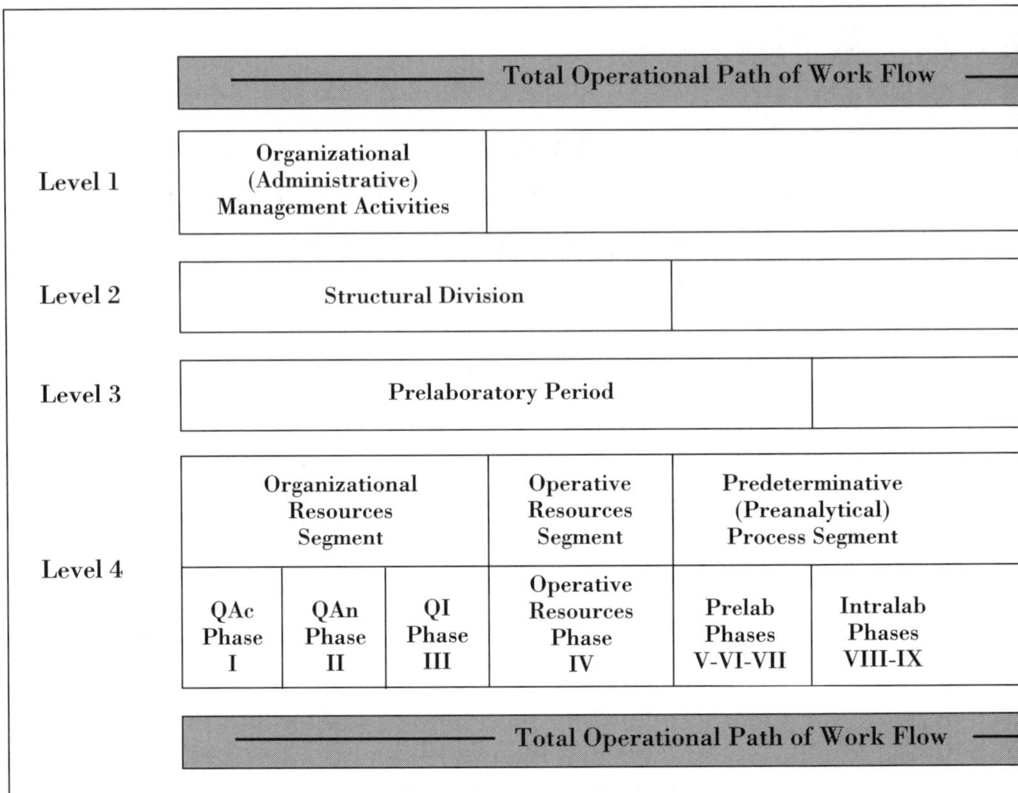

Figure 5.1 Levels, activities, divisions, periods, segments, and phases of the laboratory total operational path of work flow

At the first level of the flow diagram, organizational (administrative) and operative management activities comprise the most general, all-encompassing subdivisions of work flow. This is a reminder of the important distinction between organizational and operative management discussed earlier.

At the second level of the path diagram, work flow is divided into the three fundamental quality assessment divisions–structure, process, and outcome. These divisions are indispensable in the analysis of the flow operational activities.

The third level of the path complex focuses on the progression of prelaboratory, intralaboratory, and postlaboratory periods of work activity. These periods are determined by the functional timing and location of the laboratory-related work–whether it occurs inside or outside the physical boundaries of the central laboratory.

The fourth level highlights all specific operational segments and phases of laboratory work flow. Quality surveillance indicators are direct derivatives of these sequentially phased programs and processes of the path of work flow. Phases are assigned to all three organizational programs for

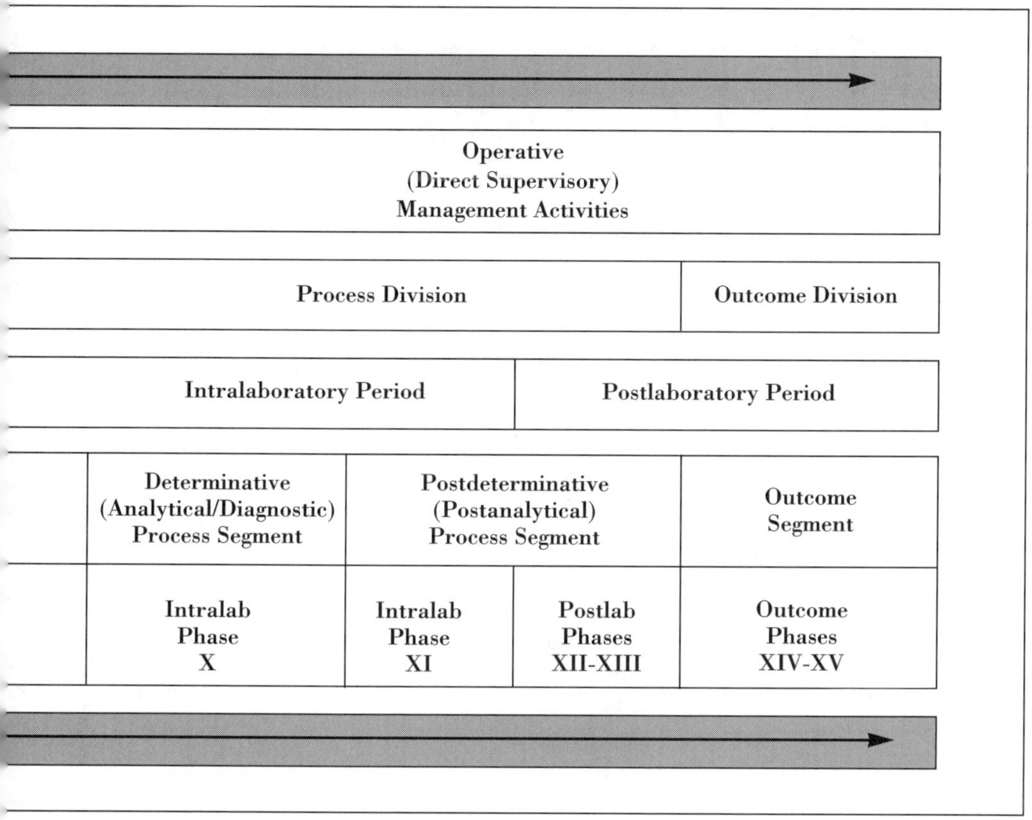

Operative
(Direct Supervisory)
Management Activities

Process Division	Outcome Division

Intralaboratory Period	Postlaboratory Period

Determinative (Analytical/Diagnostic) Process Segment	Postdeterminative (Postanalytical) Process Segment		Outcome Segment
Intralab Phase X	Intralab Phase XI	Postlab Phases XII-XIII	Outcome Phases XIV-XV

quality actualization (QAc), quality anticipation (QAn), and QI and to all major operative processes, including operative resource; predeterminative, determinative, and postdeterminative processes; and outcome management procedures.[1,2]

The numbered phases also are grouped into quality surveillance segments that cross relate with the major activities, divisions, and periods. The term "determinative" is preferred here in lieu of "analytical," since the path of work flow applies equally to clinical (ie, analytical) and anatomical (ie, diagnostic) laboratory operations.

In comparing the four levels of the path of work flow in Figure 5.1, three major aspects stand out: the chain of cause-and-effect, the timing sequence, and the overlap among the various segments, periods, divisions, and activities. These three characteristics drive the path's complexity. To simplify the path and cut through its complexity, one can use any one of the four levels of approach shown in the figure:

- Management level 1: emphasizing the overall importance of overall organizational and operative management activities

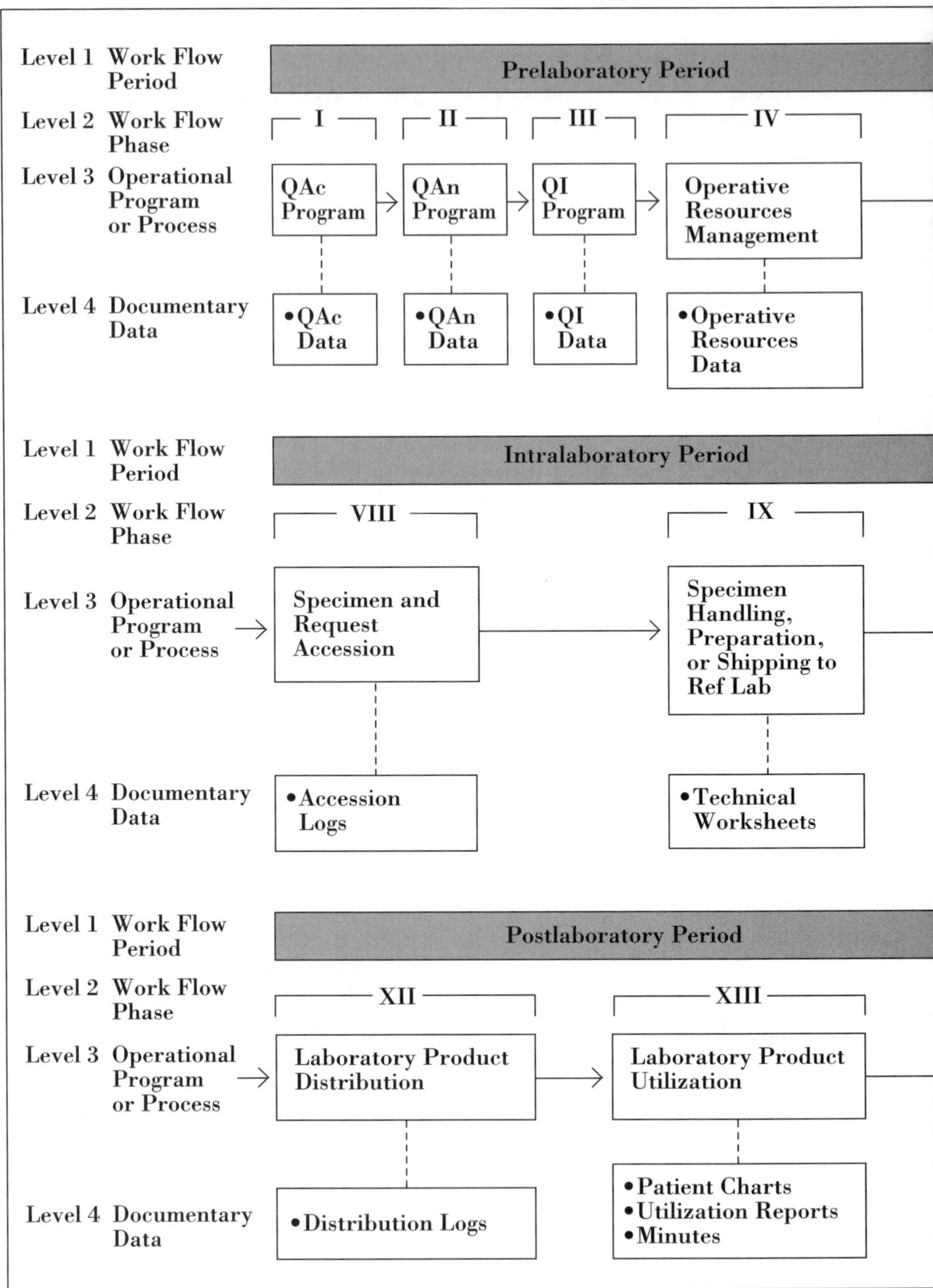

Figure 5.2 Laboratory total path of work flow for any important aspect of care

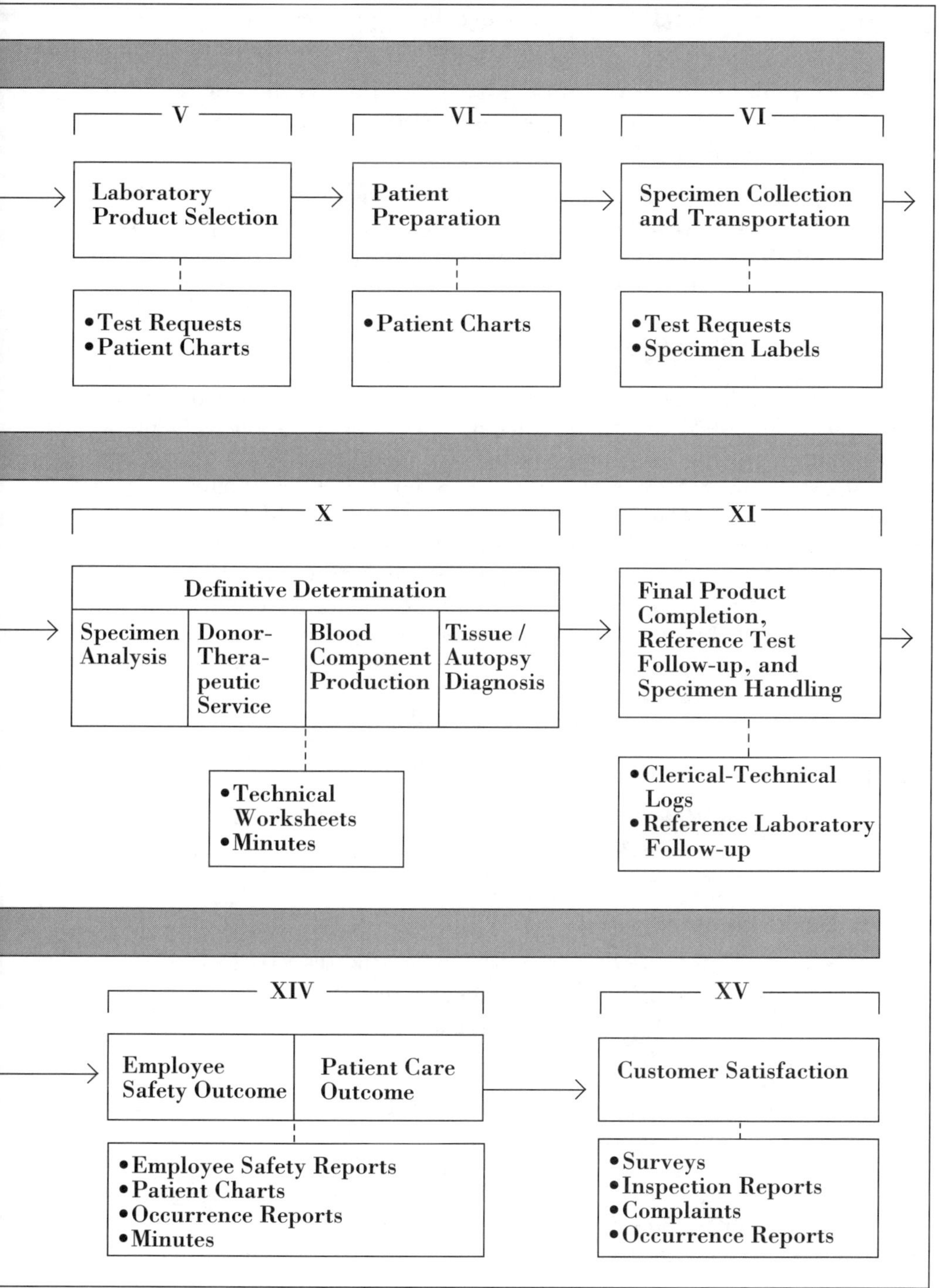
V
Laboratory Product Selection
• Test Requests
• Patient Charts
VI
Patient Preparation
• Patient Charts
VI
Specimen Collection and Transportation
• Test Requests
• Specimen Labels
X
Definitive Determination
Specimen Analysis
Donor-Thera-peutic Service
Blood Component Production
Tissue / Autopsy Diagnosis
• Technical Worksheets
• Minutes
XI
Final Product Completion, Reference Test Follow-up, and Specimen Handling
• Clerical-Technical Logs
• Reference Laboratory Follow-up
XIV
Employee Safety Outcome
Patient Care Outcome
• Employee Safety Reports
• Patient Charts
• Occurrence Reports
• Minutes
XV
Customer Satisfaction
• Surveys
• Inspection Reports
• Complaints
• Occurrence Reports

- Assessment level 2: emphasizing the importance of organizational assessment in terms of structural, process, and outcome divisions
- Functional level 3: emphasizing the importance of functional locations in terms of prelaboratory, intralaboratory, and postlaboratory periods
- Operational level 4: emphasizing the importance of the sequence of all specific organizational-level programs, such as QAc, QAn, QI, and operative-level procedures, such as operative resource, predeterminative, deter-minative, and postdeterminative process, and outcome laboratory operational activities in terms of work flow segments and phases.

In subsequent chapters, this text preferentially addresses work flow in combined terms of 1) functional periods and 2) operational segments and phases–although, the other approaches are mentioned when appropriate. The inherent value of functional work location (level 3 of Figure 5.1) as a major component of work flow is its focus on logistical resource and communication relationships. Consequently, work location serves as series of meaningful mileposts along the path of work flow, which are of very practical importance to the management applications of flow analysis.

The value of the operational approach (level 4 of Figure 5.1) is that it itemizes each key organizational- and operative-level step that must be taken to reach customer satisfaction. One can outline the functional, location-of-work periods and operational segments and phases as follows:

- Prelaboratory period
    1. Organizational structural resource segment (phases I-III)
    2. Operative structural resource segment (phase IV)
    3. Process segment (phases V-VII).
- Intralaboratory period
    1. Predeterminative process segment (phases VIII-IX)
    2. Determinative process segment (phase X)
    3. Postdeterminative process segment (phase XI).
- Postlaboratory period
    1. Process segment (phases XII-XIII)
    2. Outcome segment (phases XIV-XV).

It is important that whatever formal QI surveillance process is in use integrates with the path of work flow. For example, the Joint Commission on Accreditation of Healthcare Organizations (JCAHO) ten-step format easily melds with the path of work flow. The combination of the ten-step process (TSP) and work flow path generates a practical, yet comprehensive, matrix for the selecting and monitoring of a myriad and infinite variety of indicators of quality. Thus, the surveillance process should provide a template for a logical, analytical quality surveillance process; whereas, the path of work flow serves as a systemic map for the survey of all laboratory operational activities. Other analytical improvement processes can be used as the overall QI program template, but the TSP is very generic, universal, and practical.

USING THE PATH OF WORK FLOW TO IDENTIFY PRACTICAL QUALITY INDICATORS

A systematic approach to monitoring and evaluating laboratory quality is to select indicators that are related to the phases of laboratory work flow. However, as straightforward as that sounds, the path still remains inherently complex since it represents the entire, multilevel spectrum of laboratory-related events. These events span all organizational and operative functions from decision making, planning, and surveillance to operative resource, process, and outcome management. They also occur both inside and outside the physical confines of the laboratory. With such a complicated marriage of laboratory activities to evaluate, assess, and improve, is there really a practical way to identify quality indicators for all important laboratory activities? Yes.

The word "practical" usually connotes the implication of "easy." The dictionary definition for practical is "adapted or designed for actual use; useful."[3] What might be useful might not necessarily be easy. In the case of laboratory management (as it is for most medical endeavors), the practical answer to a complex, bioscientific question often begs to be simple, straightforward, and sensible–and is often wrong. A practical approach to laboratory management must still reckon with a complex system of interrelated multidisciplinary activities. So, an adequate selection of quality indicators is not necessarily easy–at least, not initially.

Figure 5.2 illustrates additional complexity of the path of work flow for any laboratory-important aspect of care. Three functional periods at level 1 and fifteen operational phases at level 2 typify a healthcare laboratory of any size or description. Levels 3 and 4 portray the relationships of specific operational activities and documentary data for specific work flow phases, segments, and periods. This model portrays the integrated management of all:

- Structural division components–including management of all organizational and operative resources (phases I-IV)
- Process division components–including management of all test selection, patient preparation, specimen handling, definitive determination, and data handling (phases V-XIII)
- Outcome division components–including management of all employee health and welfare, patient care outcome, and customer satisfaction (phases XIV-XV).

Traditionally, laboratory managers have mapped out only portions of the operative path of work flow for quality indicator selection. Process and outcome indicators have been developed most often, including markers for test selection, specimen preparation, specimen analysis, and laboratory product utilization–the traditional laboratory life cycle. Operative resource indicators have received minor attention, surveillance of workload statistics being one of a few examples. However, the JCAHO reform of quality surveillance mandates a more balanced monitoring of the management of prelaboratory organizational and operative resources; pre-, intra-, and postlaboratory processes; and postlaboratory patient care or any other customer satisfaction outcomes.

The usefulness of path of work flow analysis in quality management extends beyond the walls of the primary laboratory. For quality surveillance purposes, many laboratory activities outside the physical boundaries of the central laboratory still remain within the central laboratory's sphere of managerial responsibility or influence. For example, JCAHO standards stipulate that the central laboratory director is responsible for coordinating decentralized testing. Although the director's responsibility is clearly delineated by regulation and standards, a director's real institutional authority is frequently limited to the level of "jurisdictional cognizance:" which is explicit responsibility without direct authority. The effect of central laboratory management on decentralized activities can be immeasurably enhanced by planning appropriate QI indicators according to the path of work flow of the decentralized laboratory.

THE PERIODS, SEGMENTS, AND PHASES OF OPERATIONAL WORK FLOW

The *prelaboratory period* includes all organizational and operative activities that ordinarily occur outside the laboratory's central, operative "bench area." The typical prelaboratory period includes the following segments and phases:

- Organizational resources segment:
  - Phase I: Quality actualization phase
  - Phase II: Quality anticipation phase
  - Phase III: Quality surveillance(including internal and external) phase.
- Operative resource segment:
  - Phase IV: Operative resource management phase.
- Process segment:
  - Phase V: Laboratory product selection phase
  - Phase VI: Patient preparation phase
  - Phase VII: Specimen collection and transportation phase.

Blood and component donation, other phlebotomy procedures, blood and component production, and therapeutic procedures (eg, apheresis) are exceptions where phases V through VII of the predeterminative process segment all can occur within the laboratory operative area. Since these exceptions might not fit the typical laboratory path of work flow pattern, the paths of work flow for such procedures will need to be mapped out accordingly.

The *intralaboratory period* consists of specimen processing performed within the physical boundaries of the laboratory operative area, including the following segments and phases:

- Predeterminative process segment:
  - Phase VIII: Specimen and test request validation and accessioning phase
  - Phase IX: Specimen handling and preparation or shipping to a reference laboratory phase.
- Determinative process segment:
  - Phase X: Definitive specimen determination, including all clinical laboratory testing, blood component preparation, and anatomical tissue diagnosis phase.
- Postdeterminative process segment:
  - Phase XI: Product completion, reference laboratory result follow-up, verification, and final specimen handling phase.[b]

The *postlaboratory period* consists of the distribution and utilization of the laboratory product for patient care. These activities usually occur outside the laboratory. As previously mentioned, certain procedures as blood component donation typify exceptions in which all four phases of this period can occur within the laboratory. The postlaboratory period includes the following segments and phases:

- Process segment:
  - Phase XII: Product distribution and throughput phase
  - Phase XIII: Product utilization phase.
- Outcome segment:
  - Phase XIV: Specific employee safety and patient care outcome phase
  - Phase XV: Overall customer satisfaction: employee, patient, physician, and others phase.

[b] After sending specimens to an outside reference laboratory location for definitive determination in phase IX, any processing performed by the reference laboratory cannot be included in phase X. However, certain aspects of reference laboratory process management can still be followed later in phase XI.

PRELABORATORY PERIOD: SURVEILLANCE OF ORGANIZATIONAL-LEVEL RESOURCES

Phase I: *Quality actualization*

The first organizational resource is the quality actualization program or QAc. It is appropriate for the path of work flow to begin with the cultural administrative activities that are the fountainhead of organizational decision making and commitment to continuous improvement. Traditionally, however, this has not been the case. Instead, the classical path of work flow has begun at the phase of laboratory product selection–or at the accession phase even further beyond. The JCAHO *Agenda for Change* and subsequent revisions of the accreditation standards now mandate that quality surveillance includes QAc–the management of cultural activities–as a potential monitoring target.

Refer to the diagram for QAc in Figure 9 of Chapter Three. That model illustrates the progression of events that should ultimately result in organizational commitment. This hierarchy of steps leads to the actualization of good decision making with "company-wide" commitment to customer satisfaction through continuous improvement of the laboratory product and patient care outcome.

At each step toward actualization, specific resources, processes, and outcomes have to be managed. All of these organizational activities can be characterized by specific quality surveillance indicators. Thus, the QAc program should generate measurable results, such as the:

- Extent of the QAc program plan, including an ongoing education and training schedule and periodic reevaluation of the plan
- Extent of individual and organizational work-oriented values and ethics
- Extent of individual morale and overall opinion of the organization and its leadership
- Level of individual personality behavior awareness
- Level of group transactional behavior awareness
- Effectiveness of individual and organizational communication, cooperation, and negotiation tools and skills
- Effectiveness of conflict resolution tools and skills
- Effectiveness of employee empowerment tools and skills
- Degree of organizational commitment, including leader involvement and support
- Effectiveness of employee support, motivation, and incentive tools and skills

- Effectiveness of assessment tools and skills
- Effectiveness of opportunity analysis, alternative option selection, decision making, and action tools and skills.

Specific indicators of the quality of these activities are not standardized at the national level. The JCAHO did establish a task force to formulate national standards and indicators for organizational behavioral management. The task force published basic principles, but the standards and indicators have been tabled until further notice–process and outcome indicators currently being given priority. For the time being, QAc indicators must be generated locally, mostly on an empirical basis. Indicator criteria, thresholds, and data base lines must then be established accordingly.

Phase II: *Quality anticipation*

The second organizational resource is the quality anticipation program or QAn. As for any other major quality management program, the laboratory staff must first learn the basic tools and skills of organizational research, development, and implementation of strategic plans. An anticipatory process must be designed, implemented, sustained, and evaluated to support the principles of total quality management (TQM) and continuous quality improvement (CQI).

To accurately anticipate needs in this rapidly changing social, economic, political, and biomedical environment, serious attention must be directed to the research, development, and implementation of new or modified organizational plans, processes and procedures. Traditionally, the first two aspects of planning have been largely ignored in lieu of the quick fix of incremental management. However, based on JCAHO and other healthcare reform initiatives, none of the three aspects of organizational planning can be ignored any longer.

Quality indicators for a QAn program should reflect the effectiveness of all three aspects of planning. Referring to the model of QAn in Figure 8 of Chapter Three, a progression of three major phases results in a complete strategic planning program. Each phase must be addressed periodically at every organizational level for every key operational area (KOA) and key management area (KMA). As usual, for each step in the QAn process there are resources, processes, and outcomes that must be addressed, and these planning events can be characterized by quality surveillance indicators and monitored. The measurable attributes of a good planning program include the:

- Extent of the QAn program plan, including an ongoing schedule of research, development, and implementation projects for short, medium-, and long-range strategies, including periodic reevaluation of the plan

- Extent of the organizational values, mission, and vision statement
- Effectiveness of identification of key (high-usage, high-risk, problem-prone) customers
- Effectiveness of identification of KOAs and their KMAs based on customer need
- Effectiveness of customer needs analysis
- Effectiveness of market analysis of internal strengths and weaknesses and external opportunities and threats (eg, competition)
- Effectiveness of the analysis, selection, and scheduling of organizational research projects, goals, objectives, milestone dates, and action officers
- Effectiveness of analysis of the research projects and selection of development projects and programs
- Effectiveness of the scheduling of developmental projects, goals, objectives, milestone dates, and action officers
- Effectiveness of analysis of the developmental projects and selection of implementation projects and programs
- Effectiveness of the scheduling of short-, medium-, and long-range organizational implementation projects and programs, goals, objectives, milestone dates, and action officers
- Effectiveness of the analysis of the implementation phase based on consequent improvements.

Phase III: *Quality improvement*

The third organizational resource is the quality surveillance program, referred to in this text as quality assessment and improvement or QI; the JCAHO refers to it, now, as improving organizational performance or PI. This program is easily missed in the surveillance process as a source of quality indicators. This oversight is simply because we are asking to create quality indicators for the same program that is responsible for defining, creating, and monitoring indicators for all other operational facets of the laboratory. The QI program as a surveillance target is as plain as "the nose on our face"–and is just as easily overlooked.

However, the seventh step of the JCAHO ten-step format, ie, evaluation, routinely asks if the indicator data producing evidence of opportunities for improvement. If not, is the quality surveillance process, itself, functioning adequately? Or should the improvement process be evaluated for modification of thresholds, indicator criteria, indicator definitions, or even the importance of an aspect of care? The ninth step, ie, assessment, also asks if the overall quality surveillance process is effective as evidenced by ongoing quality improvement.

Thus, the surveillance process should be monitored by indicators that reflect its effectiveness in serving the principles and goals of TQM and CQI. Measurable attributes of a good program include the:

- Extent of the QI program plan
- Effectiveness of all elements of the chosen surveillance process. In the case of the TSP, this would include the measurable effectiveness of each of the ten components of that process, ie, from establishing responsibilities to communicating lessons learned.

The effectiveness of any one of the TSP components is measurable on an overall, program-wide scale.

REFERENCES

1. Bachner P. Quality assurance of the analytic process: pre- and postanalytical variation. Clin Lab Med, 1986;6:613-623.
2. Bachner P. Quality assurance: an accreditation perspective. Lab Med, 1989;20:159-162.
3. Webster's Third International Dictionary of the English Language. Springfield, MA: Merriam Webster, Inc, 1984.

6. The Laboratory Path of Work Flow and Surveillance of Operative-Level Quality Indicators

TOTAL SYSTEMATIC LABORATORY QUALITY management demands both control and assurance of all organizational and operative procedures. The work flow and quality indicators for organizational resource activities are discussed in Chapter Five. The present chapter continues the focus on phases of the path of flow and quality indicators for monitoring operative-level activities, resuming with the prelaboratory period. These include operative-level resource, process, and outcome quality management.

PRELABORATORY PERIOD—SURVEILLANCE OF OPERATIVE-LEVEL RESOURCES AND PROCESSES

Phase IV: *Operative resource management*

Introducing organizational resource management as the beginning of the path of flow is a somewhat revolutionary approach. Likewise, identifying operative resource management as phase IV (instead of phase I) also is unconventional, since it is at this point where many QI plans would traditionally begin—with exclusion of the three, earlier organizational phases.

Donabedian includes operative resources in the general category of structural functions. The JCAHO *Agenda for Change* also considers operative resources as part of the traditional aspects of healthcare management that must be targeted for routine quality surveillance when appropriate.

Operative resources are quite variable in scope and volume, depending on the size and function of the laboratory at hand. Even so, they are generally categorized in terms of:

- Workload
- Personnel
- Methods and procedures
- Computers—on-line data management and archival
- Equipment—instruments and machinery
- Supplies—reusable and expendable
- Facility—physical space, utilities, and environmental control
- Budget.

The availability and adequacy of operative resources have direct effect on intralaboratory process (ie, the application of resources), postlaboratory process (ie, the application of process end products), and outcome. Thus, operative-resource management activities should be targeted for quality surveillance on a regular basis, just as any other major segment of the path of work flow. Still, they must be prioritized and scheduled on basis of outcome—analyzed against customer needs and satisfaction.

Phase V: *Laboratory test, product, and service selection*

Twenty five to thirty five percent of all diagnostic and therapeutic procedures performed in the United States are alleged to be medically inappropriate.[1] The exact statistic might be arguable, but the fact still is irrefutable that a significant number of mistakes are being made in the selection of laboratory services—if nothing else, call it malutilization in the name of defensive medicine. Consequently, appropriateness of "test need" is attracting increased public, regulatory, and peer interest.

One common practice for controlling laboratory product selection of critical laboratory services has been requiring laboratory consultation on a case-by-case basis—the rationale for rationing laboratory services being the scarcity of operative resources. These carefully managed laboratory products are usually generated by "high-tech/low-resource" or high-tech/low-volume laboratory sections such as toxicology, coagulation, immunology, immunohematology, immunohistochemistry, and electron microscopy. Such personnel resource constraints are especially felt during the evening, night, weekend, and holiday shifts.

Now, the JCAHO expects more systematic surveillance of the appropriateness of selection of laboratory products and services by all healthcare providers. Joint Commission surveyors are beginning to ask for evidence of ongoing monitoring and evaluation of the medical appropriateness of laboratory service selection.[2,3] Thus surveillance of test selection should target IACs that meet resource-sensitive criteria. These important aspects of care can be characterized as:

- Procedurally high-volume, eg, electrolyte analysis, liver profile analysis
- Clinically high-risk, eg, stat electrolyte analysis, blood component preparation
- Procedurally problem-prone, eg, new, developmental analytical procedures, autopsy of an HIV-infected patient
- Procedurally high-tech/resource-intensive/low-volume, eg, therapeutic drug toxicology, flow cytometric tissue ploidy determination (a setup for proficiency or competence problems).

Indicators of appropriate laboratory product selection should be specifically defined by clinical practice guidelines—synonymous with clinical practice standards or criteria. One helpful definition of such guidelines is:[4]

> standardized specifications for care developed by a formal process that incorporates the best scientific evidence of effectiveness based on the clinical research literature and the collective judgments of expert physician opinion.

Clinical practice guidelines are necessary yardsticks for maintaining and appraising medical appropriateness and are usually presented in the form of clinical indications and contraindications. These criteria are based on:

- Patient complaint
- Patient history (symptoms)
- Physical examination (signs)
- Diagnostic laboratory and radiologic studies
- Clinical diagnoses
- Therapeutic course
- Postdiagnostic and post-therapeutic clinical and laboratory data.

There is a need for continued development of scientifically formulated clinical practice guidelines to evaluate the appropriateness of laboratory patient care support.[5] Ideally, they should be derived from large-scale case studies published in the professional literature.

Already, there have been extensive contributions to the control and assurance of laboratory test selection.[6,7,8] In many cases, these guidelines are being designed for diagnostic related groupings (DRGs) so as to fit the current model of prospective health care payments.

Specific testing strategies and algorithms have been devised for many laboratory procedures. For example, the CAP has published *Effective Laboratory Testing*, which lists test selection indications for 49 DRGs that account for approximately 66% of hospital admissions in the United States. This publication defines four levels of testing strategies for each DRG: basic, common, less common, and unlisted.[9] The Blue Cross/Blue Shield Association (BC/BS) has published a similar list of guidelines.[10] The CAP has pointed out strengths and weaknesses of the BC/BS listing.[11] Several other medical and surgical specialty associations are determining their own specific clinical practice guidelines.

Because the appropriateness of a physician's clinical decision is in question, assessment of laboratory product selection requires peer level review. Consequently, physician involvement—and involvement of any other relevant provider—is absolutely essential when considering IACs, indicator characterization, thresholds, evaluation, action, and assessment for laboratory requests. Both the laboratory pathologist and the ward or clinic physician must be directly involved in all of these deliberations.

Critical questions regarding the *appropriateness of laboratory product or service selection* include:

- Was the laboratory product or service <u>selected</u> when it *was* clinically indicated by patient complaint, history, symptom, sign, physical exam, clinical study, or clinical course? This would be appropriate selection in a disease state.

- Was the laboratory product or service <u>selected</u> when it *was not* clinically indicated? This would be inappropriate selection in a healthy state.

- Was the laboratory product or service <u>not</u> <u>selected</u> when it *was* clinically indicated? This would be inappropriate selection in a disease state.

- Was the laboratory product or service <u>not</u> <u>selected</u> when it *was not* clinically indicated? This would be appropriate selection in either a healthy or disease state and represents a corollary to the first option.

These questions concerning appropriateness are reexamined in the discussion of laboratory product utilization in phase XIII.

Correctness of request is another aspect of laboratory selection that needs consideration. Has the request for a laboratory product or service been submitted in the correct format? The format should include the following elements:

- Patient identification, eg, name, unique number, and location
- Requesting provider identification
- Date of request
- Priority of request
- Laboratory product or service requested
- Specimen type needed
- Special requirements for patient preparation.

Any of these items can serve as an indicator of the quality of correct test requesting. For some products or services, such as blood components, these items are important enough to be considered as sentinel events, requiring 100% conformance.

The emphasis on timely monitoring of test selection is generating a mounting incentive to upgrade hospital computer and laboratory information management systems. Concurrent—while the patient is under treatment—day-to-day surveillance of laboratory selection appropriateness requires a mastery of patient chart information and statistical treatment of related laboratory data through hospital-wide, interrelated computer networks and related, database software programs. Such data management systems should offer "real-time," on-the-spot coordination of specific laboratory product selection with individual patient diagnoses, cumulative medical laboratory and clinical status reports, specific primary care providers (the attending physician and other individuals), and entire clinical services or departments.

The JCAHO is enforcing the requirement to monitor test selection indicators regardless of the data management method used. If computerization is lacking, then hospitals must survey laboratory selection by retrospective chart audit. However, a nonautomated QI program is still expected to be comprehensive, systematic, and ongoing. Such a program requires more time consuming, labor intensive manual survey of clinical charts and laboratory records.

One key aspect of monitoring this work flow phase is that the laboratory often is considered responsible for the collection of selection (test need) data. Many laboratorians would prefer that the clinicians be required to monitor the quality of this aspect of patient-care decision making. However, the JCAHO is consistently placing the responsibility of product-selection monitoring on the shoulders of the laboratorians—with clinician input. Likely reasons for this decision are 1) as producers of the laboratory product, laboratorians should be the custodians or shepherds of their own work and 2) laboratorians usually have better control and faster access to the relevant laboratory data.

Phase VI: *Patient preparation*

Patient preparation is essential for a successful specimen collection procedure and an efficacious laboratory end product for patient care. The various steps of patient preparation are performed by the attending physician, nursing personnel, laboratory personnel—and even the patient. The laboratory has very little direct control over these events that have such a profound effect on the ultimate quality of the laboratory product or service.

Patient preparation consists of more than initially meets the eye. Complete preparation includes:

- *Explaining* to the patient the medical indications and contraindications of the laboratory procedure and the specimen collection method to be used

- *Obtaining* the patient's informed consent when medicolegally required

- *Instructing* the patient 1) how to prepare for the specimen collection procedure and 2) what precautions to take following specimen collection or other laboratory procedure

- *Preparing* the patient before performing specimen collection.

The adequacy of patient preparation can be monitored by selecting appropriate indicators for these four phases.

Perhaps the most important contribution to successful patient preparation is remembering that the patient is a customer who has a natural right to the best quality of health care. The patient cannot be considered "just another member of the laity," who is expected to blindly and dutifully comply with a physician's orders. Keeping in mind the patient's individuality and social and civil rights, expand the four steps of preparation as follows:

- *Explanation.* In this age of consumerism where activists and advocates work side-by-side, the patient should always be considered as having a "need to know." Therefore, the patient—or patient's legal custodian—should always be adequately informed about the diagnostic or therapeutic purposes of the laboratory procedure being considered by the primary care provider, as well as the specimen collection method. The extent of the explanation depends on the:

    1. complexity of the patient's clinical status
    2. complexity of the laboratory procedure that has been requested

3. prior experience of the patient with the procedure
4. patient-physician (or physician surrogate) relationship.

Clinical staff attendants, including the attending physician, are most often responsible for providing this explanation. However, laboratory personnel also might be responsible. It is of utmost importance to ascertain beyond a shadow of a doubt that the patient being instructed is identified as the correct patient.

- *Informed consent.* Informed consent must be obtained from the patient—or the patient's legal custodian—for any major invasive procedure such as hematopathologic aspiration, cytologic aspiration, surgical biopsy, autopsy, or a large volume phlebotomy or apheresis procedure. Depending on the collection procedure and the patient's circumstances, obtaining this consent can be either a clinical or laboratory responsibility. It is of utmost importance to ascertain beyond a shadow of a doubt that the patient whose consent is being obtained is the correct patient.

- *Preparation instructions.* Instructions to the patient--or the patient's legal custodian--are critical to the success of a number of laboratory procedures; fasting before blood glucose analysis is just one example. Although these instructions are often given verbally, they also can be supported by written directions, especially if the preparation is complex. Clinical attendants, including the primary care provider, are most often responsible for providing the instructions; laboratory personnel also can be responsible.

  Preparation instructions also must include any precautionary steps required after the specimen has been obtained or following whatever other laboratory procedure has been performed. As a classical example, blood donors need to be reminded to replenish fluids, maintain nutritional balance, and be prudent in their exercise immediately following their donation. It is of utmost importance to ascertain beyond a shadow of a doubt that the patient being instructed is the correct patient.

- *Preparation.* In many circumstances, the patient or custodian is directly responsible for complying with instructions. However, clinical attendants can assist patients or can even be fully responsible for the preparation of certain patients. Laboratory personnel can also assist or be fully responsible. It is of utmost importance to ascertain beyond a shadow of a doubt that the patient being prepared is the correct patient.

Effective indicators of patient preparation should measure the adequacy of the explanation of the laboratory procedure and ultimate service, the instruction for preparation, and the patient's compliance. Measure medical appropriateness, a special quality of patient preparation, with indicators of a medical-legal nature. These should reflect the effectiveness of ascertaining the correct identity of the patient and obtaining an informed consent—whenever the latter is necessary.

QI indicators for patient preparation should be specifically selected for the IACs for which patient preparation is most critical to the patient providing the specimen and to the procedure that is being performed. Not every phase for every IAC should be addressed—this is a very key, universal teaching point. Only the most critically important phases for any given IAC should be monitored based on appropriate criteria such as high-volume, high-risk, or problem-prone. The selective approach employed in this discussion of the patient preparation phase is absolutely true for the monitoring of any phase of the path of work flow for any IAC.

Examples of indicators and criteria for two different laboratory procedures are presented below. The examples include (1) a repeat ileal biopsy to rule out gluten hypersensitivity and (2) a fasting blood glucose analysis to rule out diabetes.

Step	Indicator
Explanation:	An itemized clinical note in the patient's medical chart should be present, documenting that adequate explanation was provided for 1) the repeat ileal biopsy and 2) the blood glucose analysis.
Informed consent:	A completed informed consent form should be in the patient's medical chart for the ileal biopsy procedure. Consent is not required for the blood glucose analysis. Since pretest phlebotomy is not usually considered an invasive procedure.
Preparation instructions:	An itemized clinical note in the patient's medical chart should document that adequate instruction was provided for 1) *several weeks to months of a gluten-free diet for the repeat biopsy and 2) a 12-hour fasting diet for the blood glucose procedure.*
Preparation:	A repeat ileal biopsy obtained from a patient with known nontropical sprue in remission should show normal ileal mucosa <u>if</u> the patient has complied with the prescribed therapeutic diet.

A blood specimen obtained from a patient for a fasting blood glucose analysis should not show evidence of a lipemic serum if the patient has complied with the prescribed fasting diet in preparation for the blood test; otherwise, an unexpected complication such as hereditary hyperlipemia should be evaluated.

Most often, monitoring patient preparation has been achieved after the fact, if it has been monitored at all. However, there are ways to *concurrently* monitor the thoroughness of patient preparation and determine its effectiveness. A direct question to the patient or attendant by the laboratorian before specimen collection is the simplest approach but is often neglected or is not documented.

Today, computer technology, including bar coding and computerized surveying, is rapidly improving the laboratory's capability to monitor patient preparation before the specimen is collected. Data automation facilitates concurrent surveillance and verification of all patient preparation in the ward, clinic, laboratory, and home. In fact, bar coding is becoming an increasingly important method of assuring a wide range of specimen work flow activities—both inside and outside the laboratory.

Phase VII: *Specimen collection, preservation, and transportation*

A potentially wide range of health care personnel are involved in specimen collection, preservation, and transportation—including the patient. As a result, the laboratory exercises questionable control over this phase of work flow. General quality surveillance indicators for monitoring phase VII include:

- *A complete test request form* generated by ward, clinic, or laboratory personnel for specific analytical procedures, diagnostic consultations, or laboratory preparations

- *An adequate patient specimen* collected by ward, clinic, laboratory personnel, or even the patient having used the correct procedure

- *Adequate preservation technique* as indicated for the laboratory procedure

- *A reasonable transportation mode and transit time* for delivery of specimens from any given ward or clinic to the appropriate laboratory destination.

The quality of these four aspects of prelaboratory request and specimen handling determines the initial integrity of the traditional laboratory patient-request-specimen-product-patient (patient-to-patient) chain of laboratory events. Examples of these quality indicators and their criteria are:

- *Laboratory procedure request information*—including correct patient demographics, laboratory procedure designation, specimen type, time of collection, special patient preparation requirements, and identification and location of the requesting healthcare provider

- *Patient identification*—including verification at the bedside or in the phlebotomy chair

- *Patient preparation*—including verification at the collection point or by medical chart review

- *Specimen sampling*—including correct specimen source or site of collection, adequate volume, appropriate size of needle, and correct performance of technically sensitive procedures, such as performing bleeding times without causing undue stasis or collecting venous samples without contamination by IV fluids

- *Specimen preservation*—including use of the correct preservative and container and storage in the proper environment (including temperature) at the time of collection

- *Specimen labeling*—including completion at the time of collection with label information corresponding to the procedure request form information (eg, patient name and identification number, and date/time of sampling, and collector's initials)

- *Specimen transportation*—including a means of delivery that has not subjected the specimen to harmful handling in terms of excessive temperatures or physical disturbance. Possible modes of delivery include a courier or mechanical, robotic devices. The measure of an acceptable transit time should be based on the degree of clinical urgency.

- *Additional specimen preservation, handling, and storage* procedures while in transit.

Again, computerization, bar coding, and robotics have great potential for revolutionizing the monitoring of almost all aspects of specimen collection, preservation, and transportation. Immediate, on-site validation of patient request and specimen is feasible using computerized bar coding of the patient wrist band, the laboratory service request form, and the specimen container label. Similar control can be attained as the specimen is routed, either automatically or manually, to appropriate laboratory destinations using bar coded addresses. Eventually, coding will improve the control of specimen integrity throughout all laboratory phases.[12,13]

Without adequate computerization and automation, prelaboratory collection and transportation are very difficult to control or assure *concurrently*. Consequently, the adequacy of collection and transportation often must be monitored *retrospectively* during phase VIII when the specimen is delivered to the laboratory for validation and accessioning.[a]

INTRALABORATORY PERIOD—SURVEILLANCE OF OPERATIVE-LEVEL PROCESSES

Phase VIII: *Specimen and test request validation and accessioning*

Traditionally intralaboratory quality surveillance of test request and specimen integrity usually begins in this phase when the laboratory accessions the patient material. At this point, the quality of the request form and specimen is inspected before the laboratory officially accepts the specimen for further processing. This process is often referred to as validation.[b]

The term "validation" refers to an inspection procedure which ensures that both the test request and specimen adequately fulfill essential submission criteria. Webster defines validation as:[14]

> to conform to essential conditions; to confirm that something is capable of measuring, predicting, or representing according to intentions or design.

Stedman subdivides validation into various categories. Most relevant to the laboratory is "content validity" which is described as "the extent to which the items of a test or procedure are in fact a representative sample of that which is to be measured."[15] The laboratory equivalent of content validity is when the specimen and test request information best reflects a patient's clinical condition, predicated on whatever patient preparation that was necessary.

[a] Some overlap is always likely between phases VII and VIII. With even the most sophisticated hospital/laboratory database management and robotics system, a certain number of specimens will still be manually delivered to the laboratory without having been monitored during the collection or transportation phase.

[b] The monitoring of specimen and test request integrity can begin earlier if there is concurrent surveillance of patient preparation in Phase VI and specimen collection, preservation, and transportation in Phase VII.

No matter how effectively the laboratory request and specimen are monitored in phases VI and VII, a significant number of specimens will always be delivered directly to the laboratory without having been checked concurrently. These specimens might be delivered to either a central accessioning point or more directly to a specific section, such as the blood bank.

Wherever the accessioning point is located, indicators and their criteria for validation should be standardized for each location. As a minimum, quality indicators should include those that have already been listed for patient preparation, specimen collection, and specimen transportation under phases VI and VII. Specialty sections such as the blood bank might expect very specific criteria for patient materials.

Funnelling specimens through the accession point creates problems that are inherent to employing a limited number of personnel with limited data collection resources handling a relatively large volume of requests and specimens. As a consequence, transcription errors are often the most common quality problem in this phase. As much as 25% of laboratory errors occur during specimen accessioning and process preparation.[16] These errors occur during the transfer of patient and test request data to the central laboratory database system. Transcription errors represent a loss of specimen integrity and are dangerous no matter whether the database system is computerized or manual. Accordingly, indicators of clerical accuracy also need to be identified and monitored.

Again, bar coding greatly facilitates the control and assurance of content validity. Specimen and request information can be coded and tracked from the time of patient preparation. Then, electronic surveillance can be repeated at the time of collection, followed by a confirmatory reading of the codes at the time of accessioning. Otherwise, validation must be accomplished by the usual visual and manual inspection of the specimen and the request form. For some sentinel indicators of quality (eg, hemolysis, clotting, and temperature upon receipt), it is possible that there will always be a need for some personal inspection.

Phase IX: *Predeterminative specimen handling, preparation, and shipping to a reference laboratory*

Special handling and preparation of specimens is monitored in this phase—before the performance of any definitive laboratory analytical or diagnostic procedure. This phase includes the shipment of specimens to reference laboratories. The quality management of specimen handling and preparation is universally similar for tissues, body fluids, or excretions, as is true in other operative phases of work flow.

A quality indicator for specimen handling and preparation in either anatomic or clinical pathology is:

> a measurable event in the handling and preparation of a specimen that reflects an opportunity for improvement, including the identification of

any adverse impact on patient care outcome that threatens the loss of life, the loss of limb, or any other significant state of customer health or welfare—or that of any other internal or external customer.

The quality of handling and preparing anatomic or clinical pathology specimens determines sustained integrity of the request, specimen, and technical preparedness for the determinative procedure. The surveillance approach is similar to that used for any phase of work flow where patient-request-specimen-product-patient integrity is at risk. Thus, phase IX can be monitored by indicators focused on:

- Preserving and storing the specimen
- Distributing the specimen or its aliquots, including distribution to a reference laboratory
- Preventing introduction of extraneous material
- Preventing loss of the specimen
- Preventing destruction of the specimen—the proverbial "lab accident"
- Preserving the specimen's identity with the correct patient during transcription of laboratory data to secondary labels or logs
- Preparing the specimen for definitive determination.

This phase warrants relatively little discussion. The need for surveillance and the characterization of appropriate indicators are straight-forward. Contrary to the brevity of the discussion, however, the gravity of phase IX to laboratory patient care support is significant. Aside from the threat of transcription error, predeterminative specimen handling is fraught with several, potentially disastrous events that must be prevented. Every possible effort must be directed toward improving the system of predeterminative processes, anticipating problems, and maximizing conformance to specifications—ie, seeking zero defects.

Phase X: *Definitive laboratory determination, including clinical analysis, blood component preparation, tissue diagnosis, and reference laboratory testing*

This phase incorporates two major modes of laboratory determination:

- Qualitative/quantitative analysis—including blood component preparation

- Tissue diagnosis—including cytopathology, surgical pathology, autopsy pathology, hematopathology, and, possibly, tissue receptor analysis and tissue flow cytometry.

The first mode of determination—laboratory analysis and blood component preparation—is traditionally performed by sections of the clinical pathology laboratory. Tissue diagnosis—the second mode—takes place primarily in the anatomic pathology laboratory, although some forms of tissue diagnosis do occur in CP.

A CP laboratory consists of several biomedical and functional disciplines and they can be organized in various organizational configurations. Using one scheme, analytical procedures include:

- Phlebotomy and specimen handling
- Clinical microscopy
  1. hematology, including hematopathology
  2. coagulation analysis
  3. urinalysis
  4. body fluid cytology
- Clinical chemistry
  1. routine chemistry
  2. special chemistry, eg, radioimmunoassay
  3. toxicology and therapeutic drug monitoring
  4. therapeutic and forensic drug analysis
- Microbiology
  1. bacteriology
  2. mycobacteriology
  3. mycology
  4. virology
  5. parasitology
- Transfusion medicine
  1. blood donor center
  2. blood bank and transfusion service
  3. immunohematologic testing
- Clinical immunology, including flow cytometry
- Clinical serology.

There is significant flexibility to CP configuration, all depending on local laboratory preference. In addition, more modern disciplines and techniques such as clinical molecular biology are beginning to be a part of CP organizations.

Quality indicators for definitive determination in CP fit into the same general categories as those listed for AP, although obvious distinctions can be made between the two basic modes of laboratory decision making. Whereas the two approaches to laboratory determination differ in procedural methods and reporting styles, it is important to understand that the same principles of quality improvement apply to both approaches. It is helpful to outline the distinctive differences between the two.

In the CP laboratory, including blood component preparation, general principles of quality management are:

- The *specimen* usually is a body fluid or excretion, although it can be parenchymal tissue.

- *Analysis* usually is achieved by instrumentation, is automated, and is highly objective. However, depending on the laboratory section involved, the procedure occasionally is visual, manual, and interpretive. Analysis usually produces a quantitative test result, but it also can be semiquantitative or qualitative.

- *QC* is usually achieved by statistical process control at the operative-level. This managerial tool is a concurrent measurement of the adequacy of analytic measurement based on parallel analysis of known control samples and standardized calibration references.

- *QI* is achieved by monitoring and evaluating indicators of resource, process, and outcome management that reflect the systemic quality of clinical laboratory results. This administrative level of surveillance is used to systematically scrutinize the overall quality of laboratory support to patient care. Attention can be focused on a specific clinical department or service, primary care provider, pathologist, patient, or disease process relatively soon after the fact.

Generally, quality indicators for CP determinative activities include any aspects of the technical determinative process that can unmask opportunities for technical improvement and lead to enhanced patient care outcome—or some other customer satisfaction. These include indicators of the quality of technical accuracy, precision, patient-to-patient integrity, and rate of turnaround time. Indicators of medical appropriateness in CP include adequacy of normal or reference ranges, critical values, test specificity, and test sensitivity.[c] Innumerable indicators are available that

[c]The term critical value also is known in various circles as an "alarm" and "panic" value. The first two terms—critical or alarm—are acceptable in their implication of the urgency inherent in particular laboratory value. However, the term "panic value" conveys an unnecessary, colloquial sense of lack of control that is unprofessional and unfortunate. It is unlikely to have been originally coined by a laboratorian, but, more likely, a nonlaboratorian inspector. The term panic value is not used in this text and should be avoided.

will reflect the quality of the resources, processes, and outcomes linked to a given determinative CP procedure.

On the other hand, tissue diagnosis is performed primarily in AP laboratories. An AP laboratory consists of several traditional disciplines and they are usually organized in a fairly typical configuration. These consultative diagnostic procedures generally include:

- Anatomic pathology
    1. cytological examination
    2. surgical tissue examination (frozen, needle aspiration, and permanent histological sections)
    3. autopsy examination.

- Hematopathology (often located in CP)
    1. bone marrow examination
    2. peripheral blood smear examination
    3. other body fluid cellular examination.

Ironically, more modern analytical disciplines such as flow cytometry and diagnostic molecular biology also are beginning to appear in AP organizations, requiring more CP-like quality management.

In the AP laboratory, principles of quality management can include:

- The *specimen* can vary. For surgical pathology, the specimen usually is some form of solid, parenchymal tissue; for cytology, the specimen is either a tissue aspirate, smear, or body fluid; for hematopathology, the specimen can be any of those four alternatives.

- *Diagnosis* is achieved by visual (noninstrumental) inspection and cognitive interpretation. The process usually consists of gross and microscopic inspection of a tissue specimen by a professionally trained individual who makes an interpretive judgment and provides a written diagnostic report in narrative form.

- *QC* is achieved by peer control at the operative level, a form of peer review in which a second pathologist reviews a primary pathologist's diagnosis. It is a form of concurrent professional process control that is performed before the final diagnosis is certified and released for distribution.

- *QI* is achieved by peer assurance, a form of monitoring and evaluating specific indicators of resource, process, and outcome management that systemically reflect the quality of anatomic diagnoses. Use this administrative-level of surveillance to systematically scrutinize the overall quality of diagnostic laboratory support. Attention can be focused on a specific clinical department or service, primary care provider, pathologist, patient, or disease process relatively soon after the fact.

Although analytical and diagnostic methods might differ procedurally, their paths of work flow are virtually the same. In the same vein, quality management of analysis versus diagnosis differs only to the extent that analytical exactness differs from diagnostic subjectivity. That is, each of the two determinative modes requires a slightly different style of QC and QI, but the basic principles of quality management remain exactly the same. The style of quality management in tissue diagnosis differs only in the subjectivity and confidentiality of peer review compared to the more objective, less confidential surveillance of CP.

General Peer Review

Until recently, the interpretive aspects of tissue diagnosis have absorbed the attention of many pathologists, causing them to shy away from quality management. Lately, however, pathologists have begun to realize that a high-quality tissue diagnosis is derived from a combination of technical procedures and professional interpretations that are best controlled at the pathologists' level of professional responsibility and expertise. They are beginning to understand that they must devote more time to operative control *and* administrative surveillance. This change means greater involvement in peer review.

One aspect of peer review that is particularly troublesome to some pathologists is the judgmental responsibility the reviewer must take in correcting or criticizing a diagnosis of a peer. Richard Diamond, a highly respected pathologist of our time, often spoke of the "policeman" role that a pathologist is often asked to assume in the line of duty. In the case of peer control, pathologists become a policeman within their own ranks—but, for the sake of internal control, it simply must be. Otherwise, if we do not do it ourselves, a nonlaboratorian will do it for us at the regulatory level.

Even more adamantly, Diamond warned against pathologists taking on the role of policeman outside their own ranks and overseeing the quality of clinical practice in the name of quality assurance, nowadays known as QI. His admonition against pathologists unilaterally policing clinicians is still quite valid. As he would say, pathologists practicing this unilateral style of policing would reduce their professional "half-lives" to a matter of days.

However, there is an increasing demand for external peer review. Instead of being unilateral, however, it must be administered under the auspices of joint laboratorian-clinician collaboration as a team effort. Still, external peer review must be. Otherwise, again, someone else will do it for us.[17]

In this regard, the words of another famous American pathologist should be remembered—the Quaker centenarian, James Earl Ash. When responding to comments on quality assurance of the 1980s, his alleged remark was, "Quality assurance? Why, in my time, pathology was quality assurance."[18] If we continue to practice pathology and laboratory medicine with an appropriate team style and analytical approach, the laboratory will continue to be a major source of healthcare quality assurance.

One of the major problems in developing an effective quality management philosophy in AP has been the limited technical and diagnostic standards available for quality surveillance of gross and microscopic diagnostic methods. This is mainly a matter of organizational experience. The overall quality of an anatomic diagnosis is determined by the effectiveness of the management of organizational structure, operative resources, process factors, product utilization, and outcome. This cause-and-effect chain of AP managerial events is exactly the same as in CP. Thus, with a little planning, reasonable QI indicators are easily available for monitoring AP on a systemic scope.

Overall quality in AP can be measured against typical professional standards of accuracy, precision, TAT, and medical appropriateness.[19] The quality of AP clerical activities requires greater consideration since there is so much dependence on the written, narrative-style report as the final product.

Quality management for AP includes both QC- and QI-level activities as components of peer review. At the operative managerial level, this text refers to diagnostic QC as *peer control.* At the administrative managerial level, this text refers to diagnostic QI as *peer assurance.*[d]

Peer Control

Quality management of tissue diagnosis begins at the operative managerial level with peer control, a concurrent peer review of both technical and interpretive quality. Peer control of technical and clerical quality consists of on-the-spot review and correction of technical histological and clerical deficiencies by the histotechnical and transcription supervisors and reviewed by the peer control pathologist—the primary diagnostician.

Peer control of interpretive quality requires "on-the-spot" review of the primary pathological and nonpathological tissue diagnoses by a second pathologist before manual verification or computer certification and release of the diagnoses for distribution. The extent of this review of medical appropriateness depends on the size, complexity, and resources of the facility. It should be based on a certain percentage of the case load, ranging from an acceptable minimum of 10% to a maximum of 100%.[20]

[d] Another general term for peer review would be peer surveillance. The more specific term peer assurance, is borrowed from the earlier concepts of quality assurance (QA). In the current era of quality assessment and improvement (QI), the term could just as well be peer assessment or peer improvement. However, peer assurance seems to be a commonly understandable, comfortable phrase at the time of this writing. As usual, these terms will all change as determined by usage.

Peer control of pathological diagnoses is often limited to the review of malignant diagnoses. Therefore, peer control of false-positive diagnoses is performed by correlating current:

- Peer control diagnosis with the previous primary pathologist's diagnosis
- Permanent section diagnosis with previous frozen section diagnosis
- Permanent section diagnosis with previous permanent section diagnoses
- Autopsy diagnosis with previous surgical diagnosis
- Permanent section diagnoses with previous cytological diagnoses
- Cytological diagnosis with previous cytological diagnosis
- Autopsy findings with previous clinical diagnoses.

In searching for false-negative diagnoses among cases diagnosed as nonpathological, peer control should consist of at least a 10% sampling review of bone marrow, cytology, surgical, and autopsy cases diagnosed as normal. Although a minimum 10% review rate has become a common standard of practice over the years, the rate is based mostly on empirical judgement—some studies have been reported that validate this 10% sampling rate. However, the review rate depends on several factors, the most significant being the size of the case population. Some case loads are so small that a 10% sampling is not statistically significant, giving reason to increase the sampling up to 100%, if necessary.

At the QC management level, any problems in technical quality or medical appropriateness should be individually resolved "on the spot." After documentation, significant occurrences are reported to the departmental quality surveillance system for administrative level peer review.

Peer Assurance[e]

Whereas peer control is direct, on-line, immediately corrective action of an aspect of technical, clerical, or interpretive quality, peer assurance is indirect, systemic correction of an aspect of quality management. This administrative level peer review can use the same QI surveillance process that is used for quality assessment of every other medical laboratory activity. The JCAHO TSP is one of several effective models available.

[e] In this instance, the word "assurance" becomes a necessity for lack of any better term. The author would welcome another phrase to differentiate between the two modes of peer review and not cause <u>any</u> confusion with the 1980s phrase, quality assurance. However, peer assurance is clearly defined in this text as the AP mode of QI-level quality management.

A general standard for peer assurance indicators of the quality of tissue diagnosis is that:

> there should be no inadequacy of technical or clerical processing or any diagnostic discrepancy between an initial pathologist's diagnosis and a peer control diagnosis that poses a threat to a patient's life or limb or any other significant aspect of a patient's health or welfare—or that of any other internal of external customer.

Defined as such, the occurrence of any significant technical, clerical, or interpretive deficiency should trigger an immediate QI evaluation to ensure the most expeditious identification and resolution of the opportunity or problem. The above standard spells out what can be considered as "significant." This standard reveals one other general quality management principle: in CP, the major source of QI data is generated by the QC process; in AP, the major source of peer assurance, (ie, QI) data is also generated by peer control (ie, QC).

Diagnostic criteria—or clinical standards of practice—and threshold levels should be based on local medical policy and whatever published standards are available at the local, state, or national level. These guidelines require the input of the attending clinical staff in support of the pathologist staff.

In daily practice, some degree of diagnostic discrepancies will almost always arise on peer assurance review. These findings can be wide-ranging in their individual significance, varying in the complexity of the clinical setting, the vagaries of histologic processing, and the scope of the diagnostic differential. Examples of technical and clerical process events that are potentially critical to patient care outcome and often warrant investigative evaluation include the adequacy of:

- Patient identification
- Accessioned specimen
- Clinical history
- Specimen technical processing, such as
    1. lost tissue specimens
    2. extraneous, foreign tissue in blocks
- Transcription of patient identity onto the final report
- Transcription of the diagnosis onto the final report
- Turnaround time.

Most aspects of technical or clerical quality are directly controlled by the on-line supervisor during tissue specimen accessioning and preparation, as well as during final product completion, eg, report transcription and typing. Ultimately, however, those same aspects of technical and clerical quality must be monitored by the primary pathologist. These include all indicators of the quality of available resources and technical-clerical processes that affect the pathologist's ability to render an appropriate diagnosis in support of a desirable clinical end result.

In comparison to the typical CP analytical process, the diagnostic "test result" in tissue pathology is a consultative opinion made at a different professional plane. The pathologist's cognitive consultation is interpretive and includes a deliberate balancing of differential diagnostic options, indications, and contraindications that will ultimately affect the clinical diagnosis and treatment provided by the attending physician. Consequently, peer assurance indicators for tissue diagnosis must reflect the medical appropriateness of the pathologist's consultative service in terms of acts of commission or omission as measured against clinical standards of medical practice.[4] Indicators of the appropriateness of a tissue diagnosis include adequacy of the:

- Clinical information provided with the consultation request by a clinician
- Diagnostician's gross and microscopic descriptions
- Diagnostician's correlations with supporting previous biopsy material
- Diagnostician's final interpretative opinion and consultative comments as related to the clinical history, clinical differential diagnoses, radiologic and other laboratory studies, resultant therapeutic (medical and surgical) decisions, therapeutic response, and resultant patient care outcome.

Aside from the formal, intramural QI program, peer surveillance is also attainable through intra- and extradepartmental consultations, as well as clinical teaching and patient management conferences. These are some of the "other" QI sources sought by the JCAHO in a well-rounded QI program. Inadequacies of original diagnoses can come to light during these intra- and extramural activities and should be referred to the departmental quality surveillance program for routine evaluation and follow-up.

Peer Review in CP

Certain activities in CP are noninstrumental, relying on visual inspection and cognitive interpretation and lending themselves to diagnostic-style QC and quality surveillance. Examples include white blood cell differential counting, microscopic urinalysis, and microscopic analysis of bronchoalveolar lavage for microorganisms. These functions are usually performed by trained medical technologists, and QC and QI are performed by peers such as senior medical technologists or supervisors. Therefore, whatever is said regarding peer control and peer assurance of pathologists' tissue diagnoses also can be translated to the quality management of medical technologists' interpretive activities in CP.

Reference Laboratory Testing

It should be remembered that in the general flow of events, reference laboratory testing also is occurring during phase X. It is obvious, however, that the primary laboratory has absolutely no direct control or power of assurance over the quality of the reference laboratory's operations being performed by an outside laboratory. Any managerial recourse must wait until susequent phases when follow-up procedures can be considered. On the other hand, if the primary laboratory is actually performing reference testing for other laboratories, all the above precepts of determinative management must be considered.

Phase XI: *Postdeterminative product completion, reference laboratory result follow-up, verification, and final specimen handling*

Postdeterminative finalization of the laboratory product includes all technical or clerical steps that must be taken to generate a finished analytical or diagnostic alphanumeric report or a laboratory product such as a blood component. Review of the end product at finalization also involves tracking reference laboratory results to ensure that they have been returned to the primary laboratory with evidence of proper control and are ready for distribution to the patient chart. There must be special attention paid to alerting clinical staff to <u>any</u> report values exceeding critical limits—including those values from reference laboratories.

Usually, the finalized laboratory report and other product documentation is legibly stamped, manually typed, or electronically printed. This is not necessarily so in the case of procedures such as intraoperative (frozen) biopsy consultations which are often initially handwritten and then are later typed as a part of the final diagnostic report. In any case, whatever is recorded must be legible.

The quality of the final laboratory product is *verified* at this juncture of the laboratory work flow. Webster defines verification as[14]:

> to confirm or substantiate by proof; to second the testimony of; to prove to be true; to establish the truth of; to check or test the accuracy of the exactness of by comparison with known data or recognized standards or authority; to confirm or establish

authenticity or existence of by examination, investigation, or competent evidence.

Therefore, verification is the last act of intralaboratory quality management before the official release of the laboratory product for distribution and clinical utilization.[f] Exceptions to this rule include laboratory services, such as apheresis, that begin and end in the laboratory; in these instances, verification is not the last act of intralaboratory quality management because the remaining phases of the work flow path are still performed in the laboratory setting.

Performance of the actual verification step is a QC procedure at the operative level of management. Monitoring and improving the quality (ie, the efficiency and effectiveness) of the verification step itself is a QI activity at the administrative-level of management. Examples of quality indicators for this purpose are technical-analytical, interpretive (diagnostic), or clerical and can include the:

- General appearance of the clerical product (eg, absence of white-outs or handwritten corrections)
- Accuracy of the clerical transcription (eg, correct patient identification, clinical, and laboratory information)
- Evidence of sustained QC and, thus, accurate technical results
- Presence of a pathologist's appropriate diagnosis, special comments, and dated signature; these aspects should be monitored by physicians during routine peer control
- Success rate of the verification process itself.

In most clinical laboratories, a technologist does the final verification of analytical results or component preparation. The technologist reviews QC data for appropriate control result levels and for trends and evidence of sustained specimen and request integrity, including clerical accuracy. These data are reviewed by a supervisor, but usually long after the laboratory product has been released for distribution. In the case of blood component preparation, the verification step includes a review of control sera, cell reactions, and patient identity documentation, and the physical appearance of the unit before release of the component for transfusion.

In the CP laboratory, verification can be documented manually by a technologist's signature or initials on the control sheets before the laboratory results are distributed to patient records and the attending clinical staff. Verification also can be documented electronically by a technologist entering

[f] Under various circumstances, the term verification also is referred to as confirmation or certification.

a dated, secured (confidential) code through a computer terminal. In this case, the term "certification" is often used instead of validation.

In the AP laboratory, verification of technical, clerical, and diagnostic quality is accomplished by the primary pathologist's inspection of the final diagnostic report. This review can be documented manually by the pathologist's dated signature or initials on a typed report or by a dated, secured certification code entered by the pathologist through a computer terminal. Verification of tissue diagnoses should be performed by the pathologist who is directly responsible for the primary diagnosis.

Report formatting is one other component of the finalization process and is becoming increasingly easy to modify with modern computerization, form generating programs, and desk top publishing programs. These reformatting tools provide enhanced ability to insert new elements into established forms and reports (such as standard international units or revised normal reference values). Consequently, laboratory documents are more current and the final report product is of a higher quality. In turn, enhanced formatting can facilitate the ease and effectiveness of verification and QI monitoring.

During this phase of the pathway, we must also monitor and evaluate the quality of postdeterminative specimen handling. At this point the specimen is either discarded or stored for future use. If discarded, specific saftey measures must be met and monitored. If the specimen is retained for future study or reference purposes, specimen integrity must be preserved and checked with QI indicators similar to those listed for phase IX.

POSTLABORATORY PERIOD—SURVEILLANCE OF OPERATIVE-LEVEL PROCESSES AND OUTCOMES

Phase XII: *Product distribution and throughput process*

There are several methods of distributing a laboratory report or product. These include direct (person-to-person) communication, hand delivery of hard copy, and electronic transmission via a computer network or telephone line that produces remote hard copy, facsimile copying, or a monitor screen message.

The effectiveness of distribution is measured in fairly absolute terms: did the laboratory product reach the designated point-of-care address? As a QI indicator, this is either a yes or no determination. As such, the effectiveness of distribution should be considered a sentinel event: whenever the product distribution process fails to deliver the product to the correct point-of-care address, investigative evaluation should ensue.

"Throughput" of the laboratory product is a modern managerial phrase couched in the telegraphic language of "technospeak," a direct descendent of "bureaucrateese" and government memos. However, the term has become an integral part of quality management language and useful as a key reference to the efficiency and effectiveness of laboratory work flow—from the time the laboratory service is selected (phase V) until the final report or product is distributed to its ultimate point-of-care destination (phase XII). Throughput is usually reported in terms of TAT, percent of workload accomplished, or workload backlog—incorporating the two dimensions of time or volume.

The quality of throughput is influenced by many resource or procedural (technical, clerical, or diagnostic) factors during any flow phase. Inadequate personnel or physical resources can especially affect TAT when the analytical or interpretive process is labor-intensive or when the final report must be manually typed or distributed.

Throughput can be directly scrutinized during a number of work flow segments. Four major TAT groupings of interest are:

- Collection TAT—from test request to accessioning; prelaboratory delays have been cited as a significant cause for prolonged overall TAT[21]
- Processing TAT—from accessioning to verification
- Distribution TAT—from verification and release from the laboratory to patient chart entry
- Overall TAT—from test request to patient chart entry.

The criteria for laboratory TAT can be stated in minutes, hours, days, or weeks—depending on the availability of operational resources, the complexity of laboratory methods, and the degree of clinical urgency. The TAT for a laboratory product can be categorized in terms of 1) critical or alarm, 2) emergency, rush, or "stat", 3) priority, and 4) routine. Examples of TAT criteria—measured at the delivery end point—are:

- Immediate (usually telephonic) notification of an above-therapeutic digoxin level for a one year-old pediatric ICU patient; this is a critical value.
- 1-hour delivery/notification for a stat chemistry analysis
- 4-hour delivery for a priority chemistry analysis
- 24-hour delivery for a rush surgical diagnosis
- 24-hour delivery for a routine chemistry analysis
- 48-hour delivery for a routine surgical diagnosis

- 7-working day delivery for a routine autopsy report

- 2 week delivery for a complicated autopsy report.

The TAT of reference laboratory determinations, intra- and extradepartmental consultations, special confirmatory studies, and other sources of addendum reports also can be monitored against predetermined indicator criteria and threshold targets.

Backlog is defined as workload volume yet to be accomplished and is a second QI measurement of throughput. Although backlog and TAT tend to be directly proportional to one another, backlog can provide information of different managerial value for identifying additional quality indicators, resetting priorities for action, and reallocating resources. Whereas TAT reveals how much time a customer currently has to wait to receive a laboratory service, backlog is helpful in calculating <u>how many</u> extra staff are needed to resolve a throughput problem and in projecting <u>when</u> a given sized staff can complete the backlog. Backlog also is valuable in balancing the personnel strengths of different shifts. Indicators of backlog are usually expressed in terms of case load.

Thresholds for TAT can be presented in two forms: 1) the maximum amount of TAT that is accepted or 2) the maximum percentage of workload or percentage of categories of workload that is expected to be completed in a given time frame. Backlog threshold can be expressed as the maximum number of patient cases or maximum volume of workload yet to be finished that is tolerable. Examples of throughput thresholds are:

- > 3 days TAT for immunoelectrophretic analysis; the interpretation can be 1) any cases that exceed 3 days TAT exceed the threshold or 2) an average TAT greater than 3 days exceeds the threshold.

- > 95% of all routine surgical reports distributed within 2 days; any less than 95% of all routine surgical reports distributed in 2 days "exceeds" the threshold.

- > 10 cytogenetic case backlog in a 30 day reporting period; more than 10 backlogged cases in 30 days exceed the threshold.[g]

Throughput thresholds also can be characterized in terms of clinical urgency. Examples include TAT thresholds for critical values and emergency or rush ("stat") requests that qualify as sentinel (zero defect) events. Thresholds for priority requests and routine laboratory request deliveries usually are rate dependent. TAT thresholds for reference laboratory determinations, intra- and extradepartmental consultations, special confirmatory studies, or other causes for addendum reports also are easily determined.

Robotics, electronic transmission, and bar coding are already facilitating high-volume, high-speed laboratory product delivery and will continue to provide improved control and assurance of TAT and distribution. For example, bar coding can match the final analytical result, product, or anatomic diagnosis to the appropriate ward or clinic patient chart address. At the same time, delivery to the patient chart can be readily confirmed, documented, and recorded for quality surveillance purposes.

Phase XIII: *Product utilization process*

Quality follow-up of the utilization of surgical biopsies has been common practice for many years. Surveying the appropriate utilization of blood components also has been a long standing JCAHO requirement. Now the JCAHO is urging the systematic surveillance of clinical utilization for *all* important aspects of laboratory services based on appropriate monitoring criteria (implying careful prioritization).

Utilization indicator criteria should be designed as clinical practice parameters—couched in the terms of indications and contraindications for healthcare use. As such, these indicators should echo the clinical surveillance parameters for laboratory test selection; the two parameters are closely linked. Thus, when establishing utilization indicators, ask these questions:

- Was the laboratory product or service used correctly when it *was* clinically indicated by patient complaint, history, symptom, sign, physical exam, clinical study, or clinical course? This would amount to appropriate usage in a disease state.

- Was the laboratory product or service used correctly when it *was not* clinically indicated? This event is likely to be a moot point since correct utilization of the laboratory product should have been preempted by the discovery of faulty selection in Phase V if concurrent surveillance is possible.

- Was the laboratory product or service used incorrectly when it *was* clinically indicated? This would amount to inappropriate usage in a disease state.

- Was the laboratory product or service used incorrectly when it *was not* clinically indicated? This event would be inappropriate in either a healthy or a disease state. This "double negative" scenario is least

[g] In expressing threshold levels, the interpretation of symbols for greater then (>) and less then (<) is confusing at times. This interpretive quandary is a right brain (subjective, intuitive) versus left brain (objective, sensing) phenomenon; ie, the cup is half full or half empty. Although interesting, the quandary is not so important as is deciding on a reporting format and using it with consistency.

likely to occur, but is still a possiblility. Again, this event would be theoretically moot since this inappropriate use should be preempted by discovery of inappropriate selection in phase V of surveillance.

Also, pay attention to the integrity of the complete patient-request-specimen-test-product-patient (patient-to-patient) axis when assessing effectiveness of laboratory product utilization. A flaw in this clinical-laboratory-clinical chain of events can lead to faulty utilization.

Utilization review, a form of peer assurance, requires the close cooperation of pathologists and attending physicians. When pathologists monitor clinical utilization of laboratory products or services, they often feel like policemen; pathologists balk at becoming watchdogs over clinical practitioners.[17] On the other hand, pathologists should be equally uncomfortable determining any IAC, or clinically-related indicators, criteria, standards, or thresholds for any phase of laboratory work flow without ward or clinic input. This is particularly true in designing the surveillance of laboratory utilization. It is absolutely essential to have coordinated clinical involvement when determining utilization surveillance parameters and plans for subsequent EvAAC activities.

There are already mechanisms in place to assist in this cooperative endeavor. Hospital utilization, blood use, and tissue committees are examples of joint laboratory and clinical staff forums established for general or specific laboratory utilization review. However, these committees are not always used to their best advantage for joint decision making because they are either too small and not representative enough—or too large and ponderous. Because of expanding JCAHO requirements, committee activities will have to become more productive; decentralization and empowerment of committee work through the formation of smaller, specialized, *ad hoc* task force groups is one answer.

Committee monitoring and other joint laboratory-clinical EvAAC activities need to be followed closely by the central laboratory's QI program. Such activities represent the "other" sources of QI data emphasized by the JCAHO in recent standards revisions. For example, decisions at the utilization committee level can dynamically affect the laboratory QI program by effecting changes in surveillance parameters and identification of new problems or opportunities for improvement. Thus, the laboratory QI program must respond by establishing appropriate internal indicators to monitor and evaluate external committee findings.

As when monitoring test selection, utilization data can be collected by a non-physician. However, a pathologist should represent the laboratory in EvAAC activities for utilization review. As usual, information regarding physician and patient identity should be confidential and nondiscoverable.

Anticipative, *concurrent* tracking of laboratory report or product utilization requires sophisticated computer support for data processing and statistical analysis if the monitoring is going to be cost-effective and timely. The computer can provide delta checking and related test data profiling to study laboratory utilization by clinical departments or individual clinicians or to focus on individual patients or specific diseases.

Many laboratories are obtaining this database management capability. However, if adequate computer support is not available, utilization review still must be accomplished by the more reactive, labor-intensive, retrospective method of manual collection, review, and evaluation of patient charts and laboratory data.

Phase XIV: *Patient care and other customer-related outcome*

Patient care outcome is what health care is all about; it is the quintessential result of all healthcare professional effort. All structural resource input and process activities are aimed at achieving the paramount result of a desired, efficacious change in a patient's health status.

Therefore, quality surveillance indicators of the quality of patient care outcome need monitoring. Although linked closely to the phases for clinical utilization and customer satisfaction, patient care outcome must be considered as a distinct element of the work flow path. The criteria for these laboratory indicators must be derived as clinical standards of practice at a joint level of decision making—the level of surveillance of this process is that of peer surveillance.

It is during this phase that statistical QC data for clinical relevance become important. Examples include the parameters of sensitivity, specificity, predictive value, and test efficiency.[6]

As already mentioned, there are other customer outcomes with which the laboratory must contend—aside from that resulting from patient care. As a primary example, laboratory safety is an equally paramount customer-related outcome. In this case, customer refers to all members of the laboratory organizational hierarchy.

Consequently, all customer-supplier relationships must be reviewed, and the expectations for related outcomes must be identified and prioritized. Judicious selection of appropriate indicators, criteria, and thresholds should follow, just as exercised for any other work flow phase.

Phase XV: *Customer satisfaction outcome: patient, clinician, employee, and others*

Peter Drucker, the champion of management by objectives, states that the fundamental purpose of any business is to create and sustain the customer.[22] In keeping with the theories and methods of TQM and CQI, customer satisfaction is a key outcome measure of laboratory service quality. In serving several types of customers, the laboratory is asked to satisfy their many desires, needs, and merits. The most effective way to discover those requirements is to communicate directly with the customer—ask and anticipate customer needs.

Unfortunately, we do not dedicate enough time to asking and anticipating. And, only rarely will the customer volunteer information without being asked. Spontaneous customer-laboratory communication is relatively rare and usually is limited to adverse complaint or incident reports. Then, the laboratory must react to a problem that has already occurred; a problem that might have been avoided. Concentrating on complaints is a good example of crisis management.

Since they are important in their individual right, all patient and hospital staff complaints still must be monitored and evaluated regularly. Even though they range from minimally problematic to life threatening, every complaint should be treated as a sentinel event. Unfortunately, complaint occurrence screening is the most passive mode of surveying customer satisfaction. In addition, because complaints are relatively rare and isolated, they are the least efficient gauge of what the general customer population really wants, requires, or deserves. Examples of common complaints are:

- A staff complaint via an incident report that a patient's test report has not reached the desired ward chart destination
- A patient complaint via the patient advocate's office that a phlebotomist was discourteous.

Customer satisfaction should be pursued energetically, rather than just by passively reacting to complaints. There should be an aggressive information gathering program rather than a reactive damage control, crisis management procedure. According to modern management theory, customer satisfaction is a telling characteristic of laboratory quality. The key question is, who is the customer? Or, as is often asked, who is the key stakeholder? Is it the patient? Or the primary care provider? Or the laboratory employee? Or the hospital chief administrator? Or the central source of operational funds? Or the regulating agencies and organizations? Is any customer more important than another?

The answers depend on what aspect of laboratory service is being addressed. The fact is that there are many more customers than can be listed, especially if one subscribes to the cyclical, heuristic theory of the customer-supplier relationship. For every customer, we have a supplier; in every supplier we have a customer—a perfectly reciprocal relationship. This bimodality is a major source of the ultimate outcome quandary: recognizing the difference between objective outcome and subjective customer satisfaction.

Customer opinion can be obtained from surveys, questionnaires, and customer advocacy meetings. The proverbial suggestion box is still a first option: a suggestion is more valuable than a complaint; a suggestion is apt to be more proactive than reactionary. Various rewards for suggestions can be offered. Such suggestion incentive programs can be very successful and are in keeping with TQM and CQI team building principles.

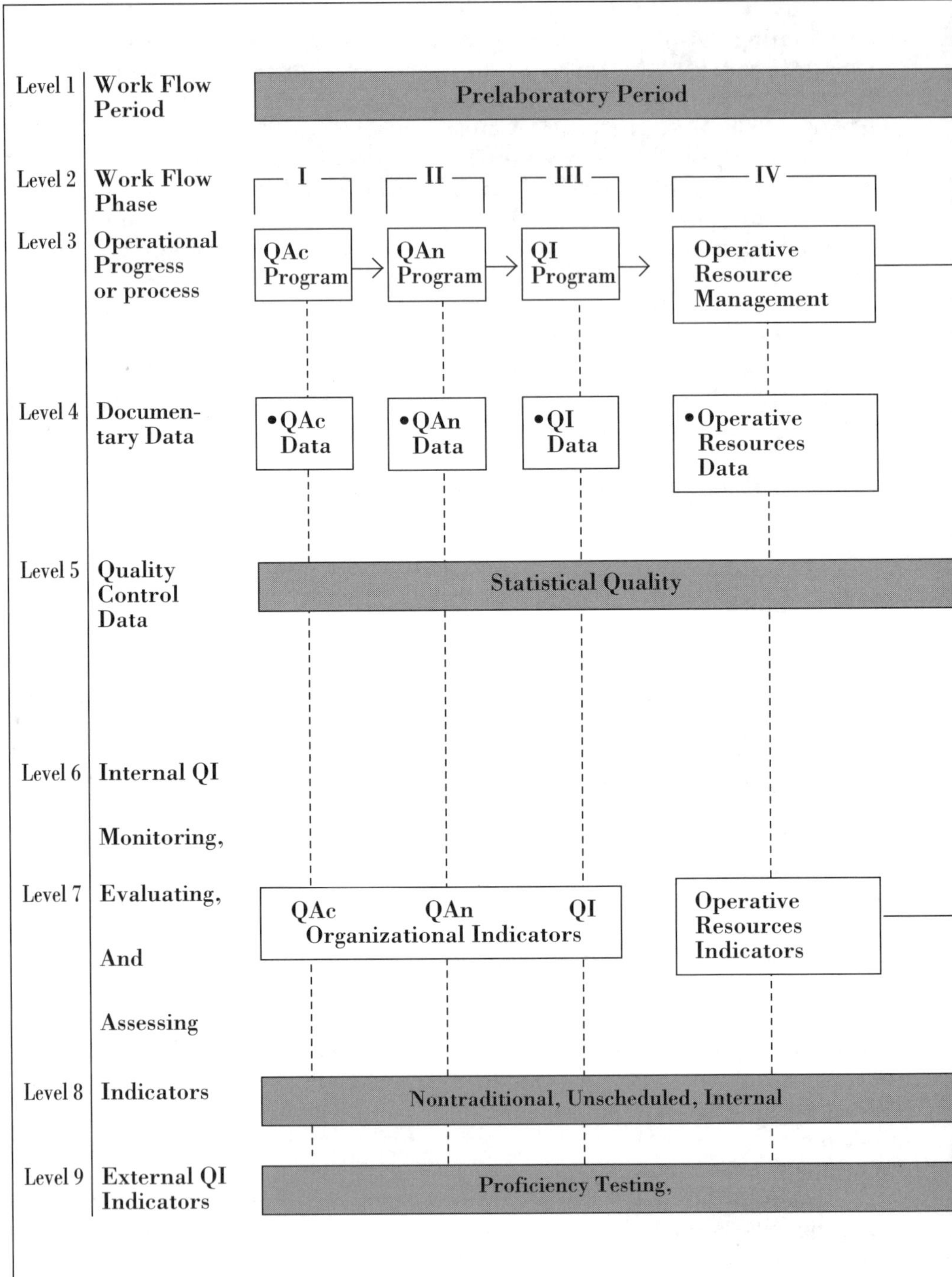

Figure 6.1A Prelaboratory period of total laboratory path of work flow for any important aspect of care

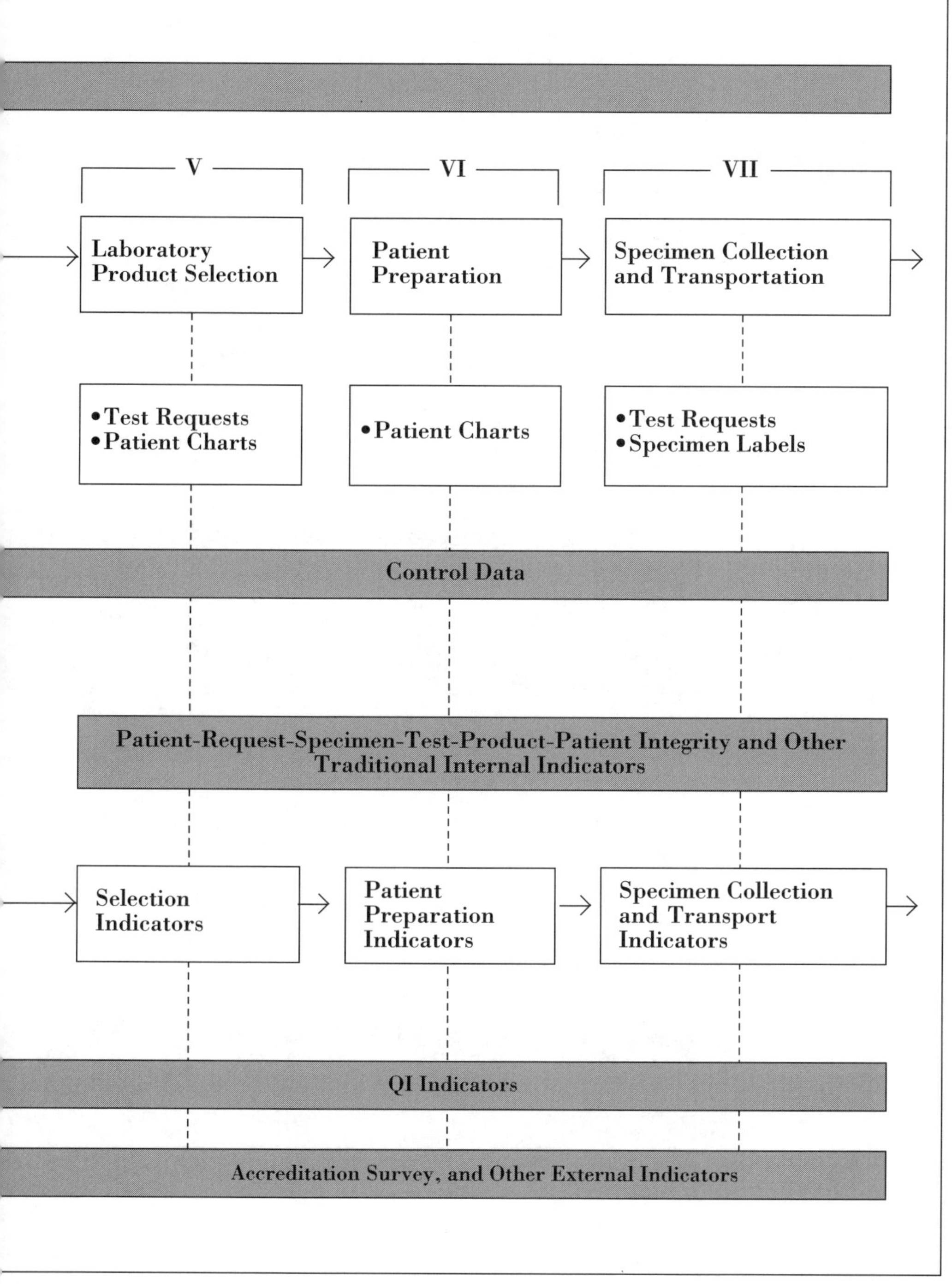
V
VI
VII
Laboratory Product Selection
Patient Preparation
Specimen Collection and Transportation
•Test Requests
•Patient Charts
•Patient Charts
•Test Requests
•Specimen Labels
Control Data
Patient-Request-Specimen-Test-Product-Patient Integrity and Other Traditional Internal Indicators
Selection Indicators
Patient Preparation Indicators
Specimen Collection and Transport Indicators
QI Indicators
Accreditation Survey, and Other External Indicators

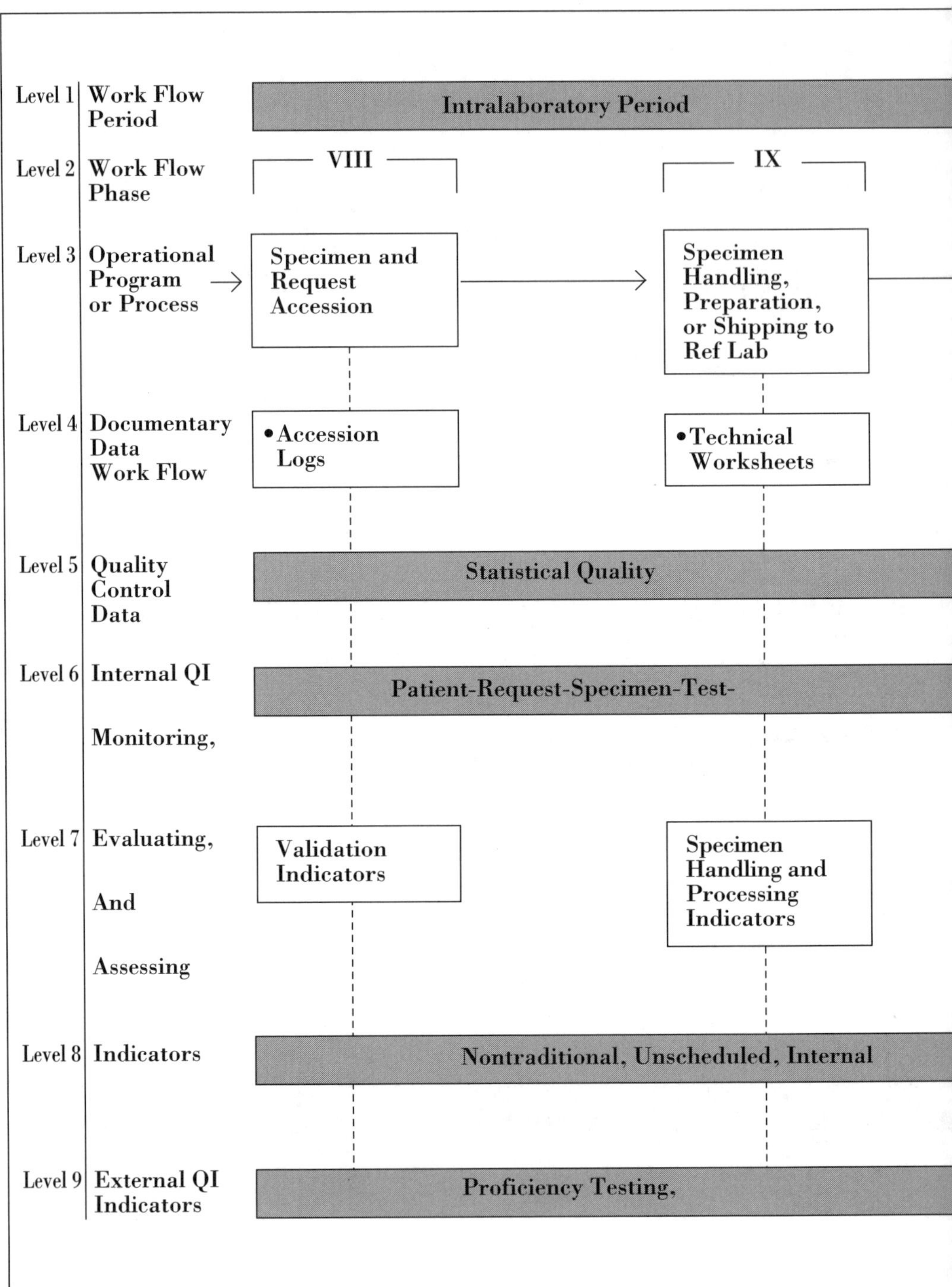

Figure 6.1 B Intralaboratory period of total laboratory path of work flow for any important aspect of care

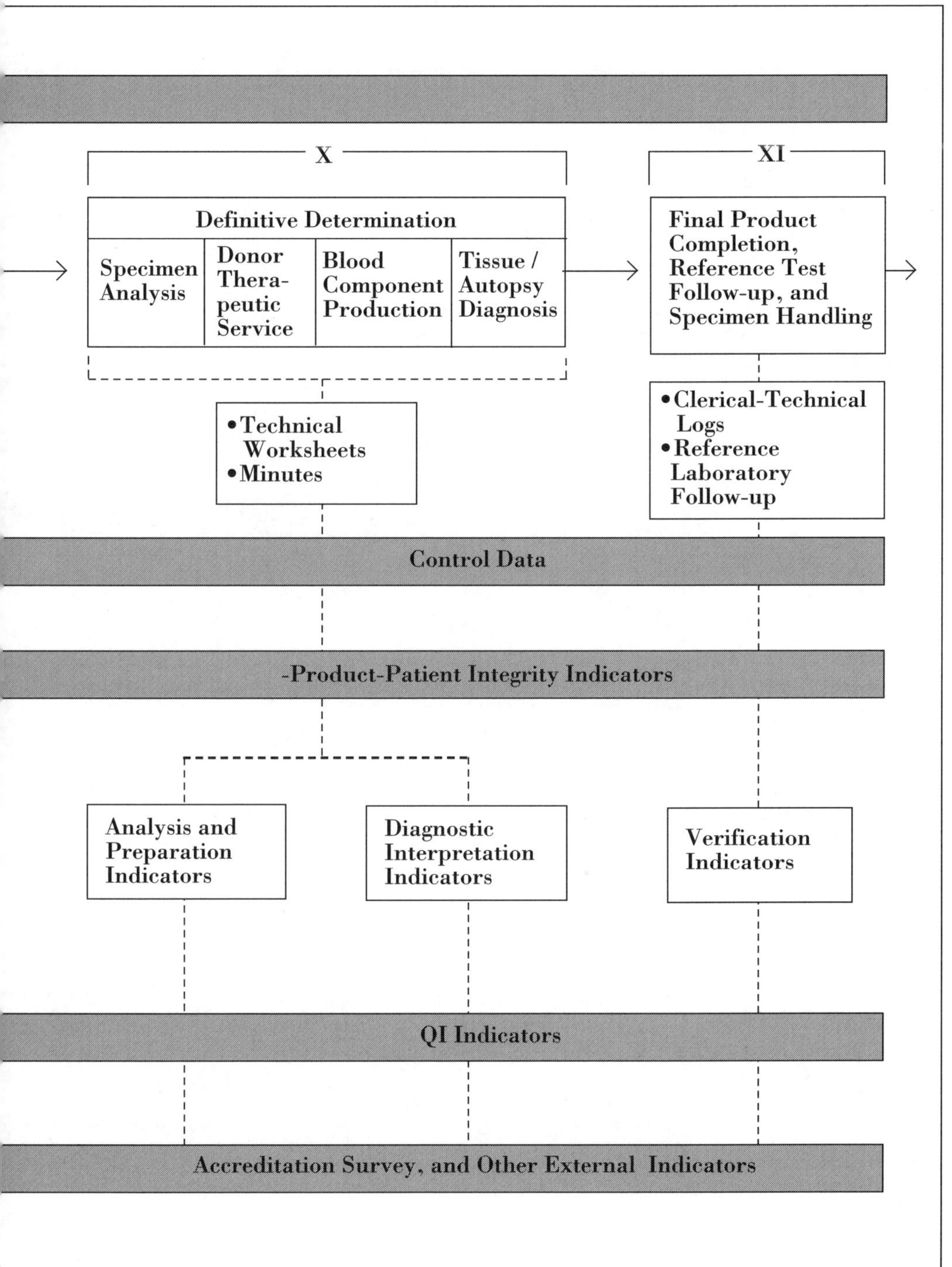
X
Definitive Determination
Specimen Analysis
Donor Therapeutic Service
Blood Component Production
Tissue / Autopsy Diagnosis
XI
Final Product Completion, Reference Test Follow-up, and Specimen Handling
•Technical Worksheets
•Minutes
•Clerical-Technical Logs
•Reference Laboratory Follow-up
Control Data
-Product-Patient Integrity Indicators
Analysis and Preparation Indicators
Diagnostic Interpretation Indicators
Verification Indicators
QI Indicators
Accreditation Survey, and Other External Indicators

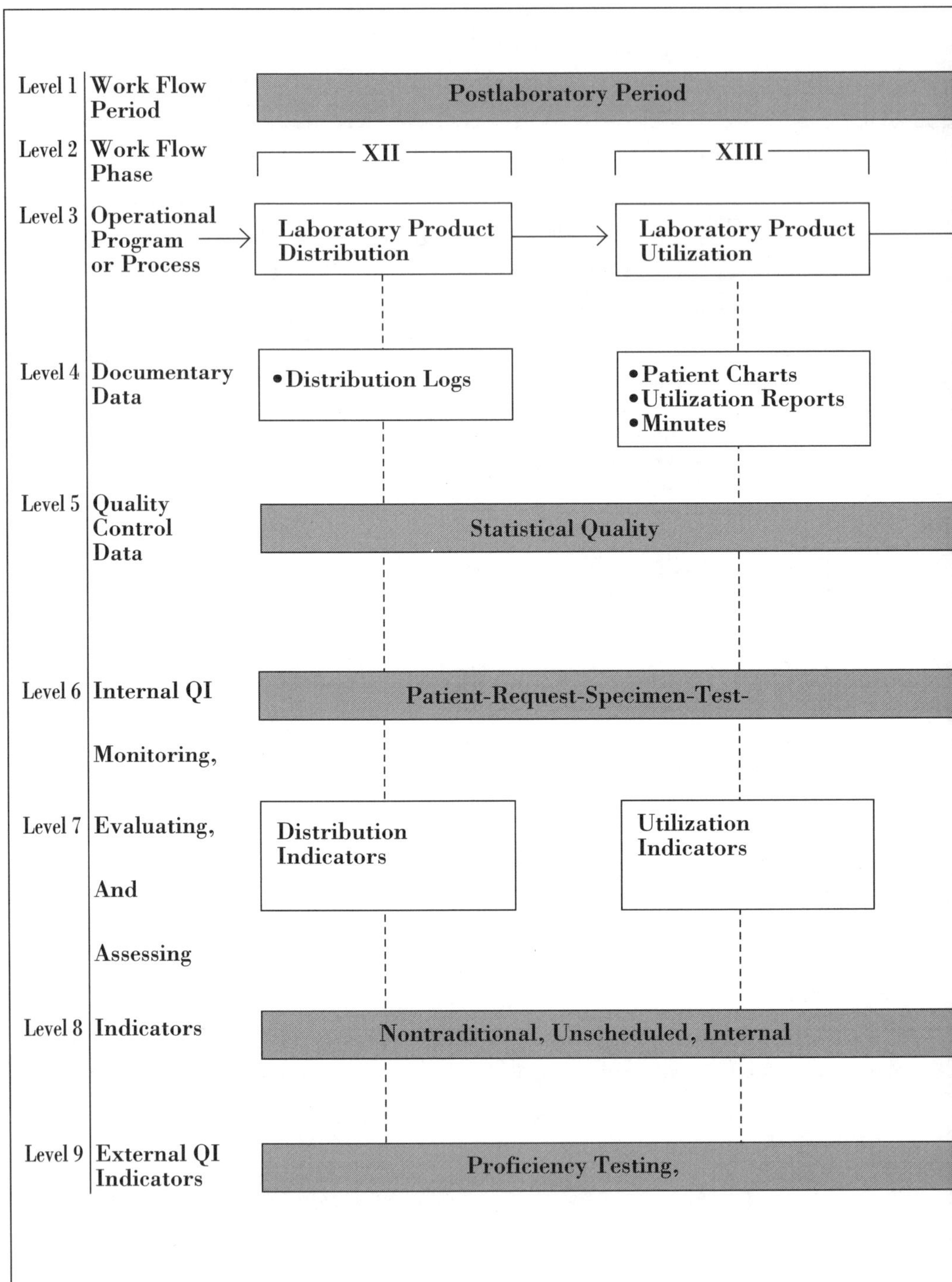

Figure 6.1C Postlaboratory period of total laboratory path of work flow for any important aspect of care

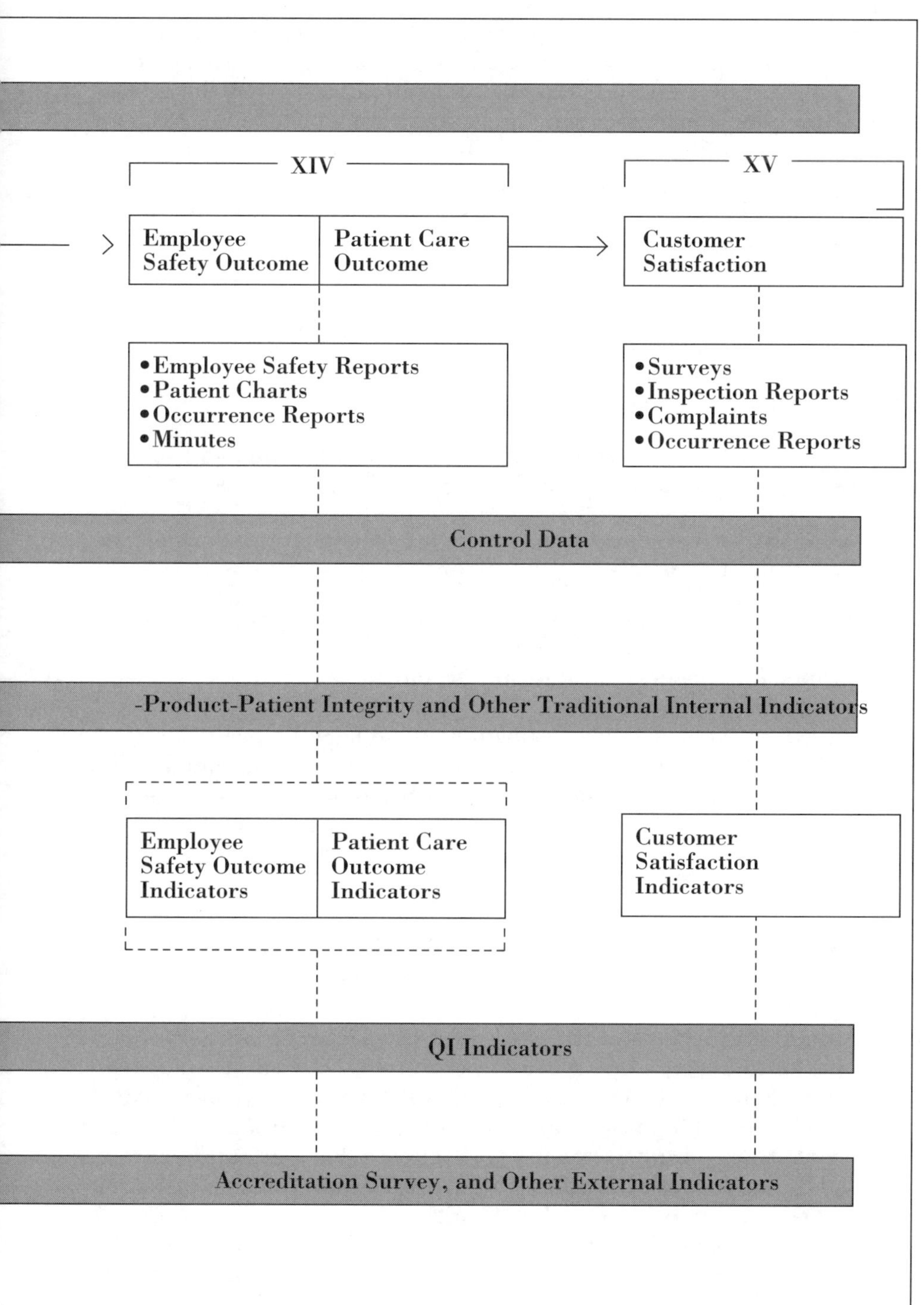

XIV
XV
Employee Safety Outcome
Patient Care Outcome
Customer Satisfaction
•Employee Safety Reports
•Patient Charts
•Occurrence Reports
•Minutes
•Surveys
•Inspection Reports
•Complaints
•Occurrence Reports
Control Data
-Product-Patient Integrity and Other Traditional Internal Indicators
Employee Safety Outcome Indicators
Patient Care Outcome Indicators
Customer Satisfaction Indicators
QI Indicators
Accreditation Survey, and Other External Indicators

More active surveillance of customer satisfaction by specific indicators is necessary. Surveys, questionnaires, interviews, and customer advocacy meetings can generate a myriad of quality indicators, along with the needed QI data. Examples of customer satisfaction indicators include following up on the effectiveness of:

- Patient care outcome from post-phlebotomy to post-diagnosis/therapy
- Laboratory personnel-customer relationships
- Primary laboratory end products
- Reference laboratory end products
- Suggestions of organizational research and development of new laboratory approaches, procedures, products, and services
- Laboratory service location—need for relocation, expansion, or decentralization of laboratory facilities
- QC and QI criteria for laboratory products and services
- Customer (supplier) education and training.

Aside from gathering customer information, these surveillance techniques also allow the customers more easy access to laboratory information. The resultant bidirectional flow of information can be additionally facilitated by advertisements, posters, brochures, meetings, and other communication techniques.

POTENTIAL QI DATA SOURCES AND QUALITY INDICATOR GROUPINGS

The preceding descriptions of the work flow phases serve as only a brief overture to the full symphonic score of potential QI indicators and their data sources. Figure 6.1 (A, B, and C) illustrates that there are several levels of indicator data sources and QI indicator groupings within the path of work flow for prelaboratory (Figure 6.1A), intralaboratory (Figure 6.1B), and postlaboratory (Figure 6.1C) periods. This work flow schematic was introduced as Figure 5.2.

The work flow periods and phases of levels 1 and 2 are carefully described in Chapters 5 and 6. Operational work flow is displayed at level 3 of the figure. Figures 6.1A, B, and C incorporate all major operational activities, including the three organizational-level programs and all operative-level functions.

Routine documentary data are portrayed at level 4 with all related quality control information at level 5. The documentary data work flow products consist of a massive pool of management information that involves every work flow phase. This large archival base is easily screened by focusing on the QC data which represent the most important source of organized QI data available. The documentary pool is always available for investigative evaluation when needed.

Of most importance in this discussion of the QI surveillance data base, levels 6 through 9 of the figure identify various QI indicator groupings that are directly related to the flow of operational activities. These groupings are divided into internal and external QI indicators and are symbolized by three levels. Level 6 is a reminder of the patient-to-patient chain of integrity as a key source of critical internal indicators that should be targeted. Level 7 includes the main collection of ongoing, traditional, scheduled internal indicators. Level 8 consists of the nontraditional, unscheduled targets that arise from the "other" sources emphasized by the JCAHO, comprising a third level of internal QI indicators. The latter indicators are mostly generated by committees and other types of quality teams.

Level 9 of the figure symbolizes the external QI indicator groupings. These indicators are derived from external surveillance programs such as proficiency testing, accreditation surveys (inspections), and external complaints. All of these data sources and indicator groupings are described further. To be sure, Figure 6.1 clearly illustrates that "practical" (ie, useful) quality management is not necessarily "easy;" rather, the fundamental basis of practical quality management can be quite complex.

Decentralized Laboratory Surveillance: An Ancillary Indicator Grouping

Level 3 of Figure 6.1 (A, B, and C) symbolizes all operational activities of a typical healthcare laboratory. This concept can be applied to a central laboratory or any ancillary laboratory activity. Because of the recent JCAHO emphasis on quality surveillance of decentralized laboratory testing (DLT) activities, a new source of quality indicators has become available to the central laboratory. DLT work flow is identical to that which has already been described for the central laboratory. No matter how small or complex the DLT activity might be, all work flow phases and operational levels remain the same. All QI sources and indicator groupings remain relevant.

Reference Laboratory Surveillance: A Unique Indicator Grouping

Also depicted at level 3 of Figure 6.1 (A, B, and C), quality surveillance of reference laboratory performance involves paying attention to the entire spectrum of specimen handling and processing, both inside and outside the primary laboratory. Consequently, reference laboratory activities provide a source of unique quality indicators.

The primary or central laboratory is directly responsible for the QC and QI of any specimen in its possession from phase VII through phase IX. When a specimen reaches the reference laboratory in phase IX, the primary laboratory still needs to monitor the handling of the specimen to the best of its ability. TAT is a common indicator of reference laboratory specimen handling. Indicators of specimen integrity can be tracked by providing surveys or questionnaires to the reference laboratory and end product customers and by requesting control data from the reference laboratory.

In addition, the primary laboratory should monitor the technical-interpretive performance of the reference laboratory; delta checks, if feasible, are one indirect approach. Proficiency surveys and accreditation inspections of the reference laboratory also can be reviewed. If the primary laboratory expects to be accredited by the CAP, all its reference laboratories also must be accredited by the CAP.

On return of the reference laboratory end product, the primary laboratory resumes responsibility for the control and assurance of the reference laboratory report or blood component and whatever specimen remains for further study. This responsibility includes maintaining the integrity axis and distributing the reference laboratory product or report to the correct patient care destination. In addition, reference laboratory proficiency problems can be discovered by follow-up of customer satisfaction indicators.

Operational Quality Control Surveillance: The Major QI Indicator Data Source

Unquestionably, the single, most valuable source of quality indicator data is QC. Level 5 of Figure 6.1 (A, B, and C) depicts QC activities as being pervasive through all phases of the path of work flow. Because QC is the key means of quality management at the operative, bench top level, every procedure in any phase of any work flow period should have some form of QC woven into its matrix. Potentially, every QC step should be able to produce at least one indicator that is useful for administrative-level quality surveillance.

The importance of QC as an indicator source rests in the fact that, since control steps or procedures exist throughout all laboratory operational levels, QC data is easily accessible for every imaginable indicator grouping. Consequently, quantitative surveillance data is readily available for organizational resource quality indicators as well as operative resource, process, and outcome QI indicators.

Patient-Request-Specimen-Product-Patient Integrity Surveillance: A Key Indicator Grouping

Level 6 of Figure 6.1 (A, B, and C) illustrates that QI surveillance of specimen integrity involves wide-ranging scrutiny of the integrity of the patient identification, laboratory request, patient preparation, patient specimen, laboratory product, and patient care support information throughout all pre-, intra-, and postlaboratory periods. For the purpose of systematic quality surveillance, the phrase "specimen integrity" must be considered as a very complex patient-to-patient axis or chain of events requiring unbroken linkage of related clinical and laboratory information.

As such, the "patient-to-patient" integrity axis is a global source of quality indicators related to all pre-, intra-, and postlaboratory chain of patient-related activities. It has been specifically mentioned in discussing several work flow phases, including:

- Phase V—laboratory product selection
- Phase VI—patient preparation
- Phase VII—collection and transportation
- Phase VIII—accessioning
- Phase IX—predeterminative specimen handling
- Phase X—definitive determination
- Phase XI—postdeterminative handling
- Phase XII—product distribution
- Phase XIII—product utilization
- Phase XIV—patient care outcome.

Therefore, vigilance over specimen integrity must be practiced in <u>all</u> phases of patient-related work flow—that is, throughout all production phases of the laboratory end product.

Committee, Task Force, and Specialized Quality Team Surveillance: The "Other" Indicator Source

Level 7 of Figure 6.1 (A, B, and C) illustrates the scope of the traditional, scheduled QI indicator groupings. They are discussed in great detail later in this text.

Level 8 of Figure 6.1 addresses nontraditional, unscheduled QI indicator groupings. Since the 1992 revisions of the JCAHO standards, these "other" QI indicator sources and targets have taken on increased precedence in the theory and practice of laboratory quality management.

The ascendance of the importance of these indicators is easily correlated with the TQM and CQI drive toward quality assessment and improvement using analytical tools for opportunity identification and decision making.

The forums available for this *ad hoc* approach to QI indicator targeting are manifold. These are most likely to be multidisciplinary teams within the laboratory or joint laboratory-clinical teams outside the laboratory. Candidate sources for this nontraditional QI approach include:

- Patient management conferences
- Teaching conferences
- Clinical-pathology correlation conferences
- Extradepartmental consultations
- Nursing-laboratory quality teams
- Customer advocacy committees
- Supplier advocacy committees.

External Quality Surveillance: A Mandated Indicator Grouping

There are both internal and external modes of QI activity. Each represents distinctly separate levels of administrative quality surveillance. Understanding the differing characteristics of these two levels is valuable in effectively planning indicators, criteria, and thresholds and in organizing follow-up EvAAC activities.

Internal QI is any form of quality surveillance performed by the primary laboratory using its own personnel within its own operational sphere. Internal surveillance includes monitoring of the traditional intralaboratory phases along with pre-and postlaboratory activities that occur outside the laboratory's physical boundary. Internal surveillance activities are depicted in levels 6 through 8 of Figure 6.1.

External QI is any quality surveillance activity performed by an organization outside the primary laboratory sphere and directed at the primary laboratory. Originating either inside or outside the hospital, external surveillance usually consists of four major activities: proficiency surveys, on-site inspections, interim self-inspections, and customer comments. The external QI indicator grouping is depicted at level 9 of Figure 6.1.

As one example, various national-level laboratory organizations offer proficiency surveys. These surveys are used for licensing, accreditation, interlaboratory comparison and self-assessment. Successful participation is required for CLIA licensing and CAP accreditation. There is no exemption, no matter at what academic level the laboratory may be considered. These surveys pinpoint analytical and diagnostic opportunities for quality improvement.

Some laboratorians consider proficiency testing to be a form of external QC rather than a form of QI; this difference of opinion has been voiced in journal articles on the subject. On one hand—and as outlined in the development of quality management theory and definitions in this text—QC should have an immediate, direct effect on real-time laboratory testing, product preparation, or other customer service at the operative management level. Proficiency testing does not meet any of those characteristics of QC.

On the other hand, QI activities should have a delayed, indirect, remedial effect on laboratory quality at the systemic, administrative management level. Proficiency testing meets the characteristics of QI; therefore, it is better considered a form of external QI.

Indicator criteria for a proficiency survey deficiency are easily stated in the same terms as the results are usually reported. Examples include:

- $> \pm 2$ SDI (standard deviation index)
- less than a "satisfactory" written rating.

Regarding thresholds for these external QI parameters, any deficiency usually qualifies as a sentinel event; thus, the threshold consists of a 0% occurrence rate.

A second external QI activity is the on-site inspection or survey. These are described as "voluntary" but, in fact, are required for licensure to operate within a state, for accreditation to participate in the Medicare payment program, or for certification to participate in such activities as interstate commerce. The proponent organizations are represented by a virtual legion of organizational abbreviations, including HCFA, FDA, OSHA, JCAHO, CAP, and AABB. These surveys pinpoint quality management problems in any phase of the laboratory work flow.

Of special note, the monitoring of decentralized, paralaboratory activities resides within the sphere of laboratory QI responsibility and is part of the primary laboratory's internal laboratory program. However, the DLT is also targeted by external on-site surveys.

Interim self-inspections are the third part of the external surveillance process. Although performed by primary laboratory personnel, self-inspections are a requirement for participation in the CAP accreditation program. CAP interim reviews are mandatory and expected to be performed every other year. This QI activity can be an extremely helpful part of the laboratory improvement process; unfortunately, the interim inspection is often neglected or performed in a superficial, perfunctory manner. These surveys have the potential to identify quality management problems in any phase of the laboratory work flow—but only if they are performed in earnest.

Any external quality inspection (whether on-site or self) generates findings or deficiencies that require 100% follow-up. An external QI deficiency usually signals a quality management problem that adversely effects laboratory support of patient care outcome or some other customer-related outcome. Consequently, any external deficiency is a sentinel event and should automatically become an indicator in the internal quality surveillance process. The participating laboratory must evaluate the external findings and act, assess, and communicate according to the usual internal, systematic QI approach. It follows that the threshold for an on-site CAP inspection deficiency would be the occurrence of any unresolved phase I or II inspection deficiency since any deficiency is a sentinel event.

A fourth external QI activity includes customer comments. These might reflect internal (employee) or external customer-supplier opinion. The comments might be that of customer satisfaction—but most often, they are complaints. The comments might be in the form of impromptu verbal or written communication, even as informal as contributions to a suggestion box. They might be in the more formal mode of incident reports. Regardless of the degree of formality, each customer opinion deserves acknowledgement and EvAAC-type follow up; each deserves treatment as a sentinel event.

A PRIORITY-PHASED AGENDA FOR MONITORING INDICATORS OF QUALITY

After systematically planning and selecting indicators for all important aspects of laboratory service throughout all phases of the work flow, it will be clear that 1) there are too many indicators to manage at the same time and 2) it is not obvious where to begin. Thus, efficient and effective data collection depends on the design of the quality surveillance plan. The JCAHO TSP and indicator information set (IIS) are examples of such a plan. Particularly, the IIS maps out a description of the indicator data elements, the data sources, and data collection intervals. Whatever format is used, it is important to include a calendar or schedule that specifies indicator monitoring dates. Such a schedule facilitates organizing and reviewing the indicator data and minimizes waste of time and effort.

All of this decision making should be done on a section-by-section basis, using a team approach with statistically-based analytical tools. First, the section ranks and prioritizes whatever IACs have been recognized. The section should then identify the best indicators that represent the most important aspects of laboratory service based on clinical and laboratory criteria. These indicators should reflect all important phases of the path of work flow for a given laboratory IAC (ie, test, product, or service). To make these choices, there must be coordinated input from both the laboratory and clinical physician staffs.

The highest ranked indicators will be those triggered by a sentinel event.

Table I
Priority-Phased Quality Indicator Monitoring Schedule for a Laboratory Section

Month	Indicator To Be Monitored	Phase I		Phase II		Phase III		Phase IV		Phase V	
		Mo	Qtr	Mo	Qtr	Mo	Qtr	Mo	Qtr	Mo	Qtr
Jan	A					A					
Feb	A B	B				A					
Mar	A B C	B				A				C	
Apr	B C D	B		D						C	
May	C D E X			D X				E		C	
Jun	A D E X			D X			A	E			
Jul	B E X		B	X				E			
Aug	C X			X							C
Sep	A D X			X	D		A				
Oct	B E		B						E		
Nov	C										C
Dec	A D X				D X		A				

Mo = Monthly Qtr = Quarterly

The next in priority will be the remaining high-volume, high-risk, and problem-prone indicators. Once a priority listing is made, an agenda matrix can be constructed as shown in Table I. The matrix is designed by matching priority-phased indicators against time.

The schedule exemplified in Table I is designed as if the laboratory section initiated implementation of quality surveillance in the month of January. The table illustrates that indicator A was chosen as the highest ranking IAC indicator, that it represents work flow phase III, and monitoring was begun in January.[h] Indicator A is monitored monthly as an ongoing indicator for three months (January through March) to establish a baseline. After the baseline has been established and as long as no opportunities for improvement arise, indicator A is monitored quarterly until an opportunity (or problem) is identified or it is deleted from the schedule.

Indicator B is the next priority IAC indicator representing phase I. Monitoring was started in February. This IAC could be entirely different from indicator A's aspect of care—it all depends on ranking and priority. Indicator C of phase V began in March, indicator D of phase II began in April, indicator E of phase IV began in May, and so on. It is realistic that the work flow phases represented are not being monitored in numerical sequence.

All indicators progress from a monthly to a quarterly monitoring schedule in a regular fashion once a data baseline has been established—and as long as they remain active with no opportunities being discovered. If an indicator is unrevealing over a reasonable amount of time (eg, six to nine months), the thresholds, criteria, definitions, and the aspect of care must be systematically reviewed to determine how an opportunity for improvement can be better detected. If an opportunity is discovered, investigative evaluation might follow.

Table 1 shows that, in June, a new opportunity for improvement—Indicator X—was identified outside the formal QI process. This unscheduled indicator could have surfaced through a number of means: for example, a customer's complaint or a committee's minutes. This indicator was inserted into the schedule in the month of its discovery. The opportunity or problem was resolved in June but the indicator remains on the monitoring schedule on an ongoing, monthly basis for an additional three months to establish a new data baseline. Afterwards, it converted to a quarterly schedule and rotated on a regular basis.

Table I provides only one example of all the possible approaches to ranking and scheduling planned and unplanned indicators. There is no limitation to the number of indicators being monitored in any phase. Approaches can vary from one laboratory section to another, depending on the laboratory process, the type of laboratory product, and the level of

[h] Table I shows only work flow phases I through V. It could demonstrate all phases through XV if need be. In the case of indicator A, phase III has been ranked and prioritized as most important for that particular indicator for that particular IAC.

clinical urgency encountered. In reality, longer baselines might be needed. In addition, clinical urgency and scarcity of resources might dictate the periodicity of indicator scheduling.

REFERENCES

1. Lundberg GD. Completing the laboratory test loop (editorial). Lab Med, 1990; 21:215.
2. Frombert R (ed). Monitoring And Evaluation: Pathology And Medical Laboratory Services. Chicago, IL: Joint Commission on Accreditation of Healthcare Organizations, 1987.
3. Schweighoefer H. Managing total quality: JCAHO compliance. Clinical Laboratory Management Association Hot Topic Seminar. Philadelphia, PA: Mar 1990.
4. Leape LL. Practice guidelines and standards: an overview. Qual Rev Bull, 1990;16:42-49.
5. O'Leary DS. The need for clinical standards of care. Qual Rev Bull, 1988;14:31-32.
6. Galen RS, Gambino SR. Beyond Normality: The Predictive Value and Efficiency of Medical Diagnosis. Toronto, Canada: John Wiley and Sons, 1975.
7. Lundborg GD (ed). Managing the Patient Focused Laboratory. Oradell, NJ: Medical Economics, 1977.
8. Lundborg GD. Using the Clinical Laboratory in Medical Decision Making. Chicago, IL: American Society of Clinical Pathologists, 1983.
9. Effective Laboratory Testing. Skokie, IL: College of American Pathologists, 1987.
10. Sox HC (ed). Common Diagnostic Tests: Use and Interpretation. Philadelphia, PA: American College of Physicians, 1987.
11. Guy GC (ed). Critique of BC/BS Association Guidelines. Skokie, IL: College of American Pathologists, 1988.
12. Maffetone MA, Watt SW, Whisler KE. Automated specimen handling: bar codes and robotics. Lab Med 1990;21:436-443.
13. Kasten B. Barcode barriers gone. CAP Today 1991;5:6,8.
14. Webster's Third New International Dictionary of the English Language. Springfield, MA: Merriam Webster, Inc, 1984.
15. Stedman's Medical Dictionary. Baltimore, MD: Williams and Wilkins Co, 1972.
16. Bachner P. College of American Pathologists Inspector Training Seminar. Radisson Cherry Hill Inn, Cherry Hill, NJ, April 27, 1990.

17. Diamond I. Quality assurance and/or quality control. Arch Path Lab Med, 1986;110:875-876.
18. McMeekin R. First Annual Ash Lecture. Washington, DC: Armed Forces Institute of Pathology, 1985.
19. Rickert RD. College of American Pathologists Inspector Training Seminar. Radisson Cherry Hill Inn, Cherry Hill, NJ: April 27, 1990.
20. Schmidt WA. Q and A. Peer Review Sampling. CAP Today 1990;4:59.
21. Valenstein PN. Preanalytic delays as a component of test turnaround time. Lab Med, 1990;21:448-451.
22. Drucker PF. Management: Tasks, Responsibilities, Policies. New York, NY: Harper and Row, 1985.

7. Using A Narrative Feeder Report at the Section Operative Management Level

REVIEW OF THE TEN-STEP PROCESS AND THE QC-QI INTERFACE

The Joint Commission on Accreditation of Healthcare Organizations' (JCAHO) ten-step improvement process is useful as an example here. There are several other improvement cycles to choose from, but all are based on the same precepts.

Planning activities—the "Plan" (P) step of the Shewhart P-D-C-A cycle—constitute the initial half of the JCAHO process. The second half of the process comprises the more action–oriented activities—the "Do-Check-Act" (D-C-A) steps of the Shewhart cycle. The last four steps of the ten-step process embody the Evaluation-Action-Assessment-Communication (EvAAC) "Check- Act" activities. The entire process represents the usual balance of planning and implementation steps—all of which rest on indicator strength.

If indicator data do not exceed the level or range of their respective thresholds or do not indicate an abnormal trend or predictive pattern over a reasonable period, then indicator performance is "on target." On the other hand, an opportunity for improvement is likely to be at hand if 1) a specific indicator data level exceeds its threshold level or range, 2) there is a significant trend of abnormally excessive data levels, or 3) there is a significant pattern of normal data levels below the threshold. Such events should trigger the EvAAC portion of the ten-step format—or the Check-Act steps of whatever surveillance format is being used—with appropriate investigative evaluation, action, assessment, and communication. The opportunity can be an operational problem to be resolved. More often, however, it should be a laboratory event or process that is operating in its normal range but still offers the possibility of improvement.

Not uncommonly, a significant period will pass when indicator data consistently remain below their threshold levels and there are no significant abnormal trends or normal patterns. This period of quiescence can extend from six to nine months, depending on the frequency of monitoring (eg, monthly versus quarterly) and the nature of the aspect of care being considered. After a reasonable amount of time has passed with no significant improvement of the subject indicator, the quality assessment and improvement (QI) process for surveillance of that indicator warrants evaluation and modification to increase its sensitivity to opportunities for improvement.

When exercising laboratory quality surveillance, remember that quality control (QC) is the major operative-level activity that feeds and drives administrative-level QI surveillance. This interaction is present at all three quality assessment levels of laboratory function—ie, structure, process, and outcome. An important distinction clearly is made in this text that QC refers not only to traditional process control but also to *resource* and *outcome* control.

In this context, QC consists of not just the traditional bench top comparing of reference analytes against industrial standards. It is a much more broadly-based quality management activity. It should include several other potential sources of control data such as on-the-spot reports, surveys or questionnaires, and team reports or minutes. In turn, QI provides a feedback mechanism that facilitates improvement of all facets of laboratory operations at all levels of resource input, operative process, and product outcome—including improvement of the QC activities themselves.

At the *QC-QI interface*, it is important to note that QC standards should mirror QI surveillance indicator criteria, just as QC control levels should recapitulate QI indicator thresholds or assurance levels. It is unusual, in fact, for a surveillance indicator "event" to reflect non-QC related data no matter what operational activity is under scrutiny, regardless of the source of the indicator.

The QC-QI interface and its feedback system are modeled in Figure 7.1. As depicted, the QI surveillance program acts similarly to an electronic operational amplifier. Such a surveillance amplifier samples indicator QC data and modifies the overall operational system by providing appropriate, corrective feedback. All quality management interfaces are appropriately depicted as being bidirectional, except for the laboratory path of work flow (resource to process to outcome).

In view of this bidirectional, operative-administrative interaction, the melding of QC and QI data collection methods can prevent duplication of quality management efforts. To bridge the QC-QI information gap and to facilitate participative decision making within the laboratory organization, planning, monitoring, and EvAAC activities should be delegated to the

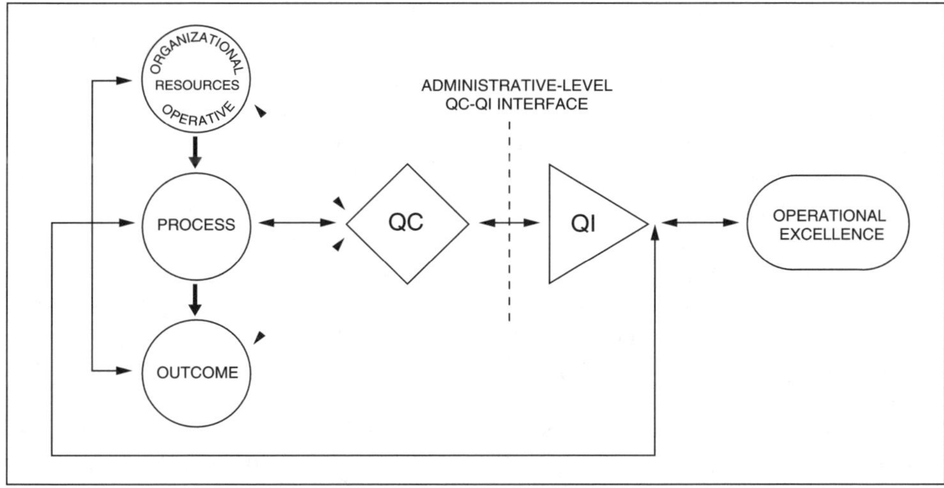

Figure 7.1 QC-QI interface model

lowest section managerial level. The technologists, clerks, and their supervisors who routinely perform operative-level procedures—including QC—should perform the first stages of QI surveillance every month. The rule of thumb is: those who perform the initial operative task should initiate QI surveillance of that same activity; they are closest to the work–and often are closest to the customer.

In the anatomical pathology (AP) laboratory, the individual, practicing pathologist exercises operative-level peer control (or QC)—which overlaps with the first stage of QI surveillance. This operative effort interfaces with peer assurance (or QI) at the administrative, committee level.

NARRATIVE-STYLE INDICATOR FEEDER REPORTS AT THE SECTION LEVEL

This chapter focuses on the initial planning portion of the quality surveillance process. The ensuing discussion of total operational quality management also flows in parallel with the presentation of a *narrative-style feeder report format*. This format facilitates initiating the QI process at the lowest operational level.

Using the model narrative report as a skeletal structure, this chapter explains how to approach QI planning activities at the operative-level within a section or even a smaller functional unit. Although the later monitoring and EvAAC—or Shewhart's "C-A"—activities are just as important at the operative level and are equally adaptable for use in the narrative-style format, these implementation steps are better illustrated by a departmental-level, profile type of reporting format in Chapter Eight.

Planning, collecting, organizing, and using quality indicator data can be more efficient and effective by using a standardized report format specifically adapted to an individual laboratory's needs. Either manually printed or computer generated reports can be designed for universal, department-wide use to target all fifteen phases of work flow at all three levels of quality assessment and laboratory function. There also are some unique laboratory activities for which special forms can be useful. The JCAHO *Primer on Clinical Indicator Development and Application* is a good source of examples of such general and specialty forms.[1]

There are two basic styles of reporting format: narrative and profile. The narrative report is vertical in style, structured as a series of consecutive paragraphs. These paragraphs can be in an outline form with space available for the insertion of numerical or narrative data of indeterminate length. In comparison, the profile report is horizontal in structure, as exemplified by a computerized spreadsheet or window approach. Numerical or narrative data are easily entered into a profile report; however, comments are limited to comparatively terse, telegraphic entries because of restricted space.

Each reporting style has its advantages and disadvantages. A vertically arranged series of narrative paragraphs provides relatively unlimited space for data and commentary. A horizontal spreadsheet provides a convenient snapshot view of several sequential surveillance steps at one glance, although the opportunity for narrative commentary is confined.

The narrative style is presented in this chapter as a model for section-level feeder reporting. A well-organized feeder report should help to ensure:

- An efficient and effective quality improvement program
- Use of a standardized quality improvement process down to the lowest functional laboratory unit level
- Documentation of a surveillance process with QI data that are easily reviewed during inspections, eg, JCAHO and College of American Pathologists (CAP)
- A flexible report structure that is readily modified to fit the laboratory's changing needs
- A means of presenting cumulative data portraying unusual indicator levels, trends, or patterns and facilitating recognition of opportunities for improvement
- A standardized format that facilitates organization-wide monitoring and EvAAC decision making for continuous quality improvement at the lowest possible organizational level
- A streamlined report mechanism that fosters bidirectional communication of QI information through all operative and administrative managerial channels.

Table I
Outline of QI Feeder Report Paragraphs

Block #	Type	Functional Level	Work Flow Phase	Subject
1	Info	–	–	Section (Scope) and reporting period identification
Postlaboratory Outcome Work Flow Segment				
2	Data	Outcome	XV	Customer satisfaction
3	Data	Outcome	XIV	Patient care outcome
4	Data	Outcome	XIV	Laboratory safety, environment, and security
Postlaboratory Process Work Flow Segment				
5	Data	Process	XIII	Laboratory product utilization
6	Data	Process	XII	Laboratory product turnaround time and backlog
7	Data	Process	XII	Laboratory report or other product distribution
Intralaboratory Process Work Flow Segment				
8	Data	Process	XI	Verification of postdeterminative product finalization, postdeterminative specimen handling, and integrity flow
9	Data	Process	XI	Reference laboratory studies
10	Data	Process	X	Analytical quality
11	Data	Process	X	Diagnostic quality and peer review
12	Data	Process	IX	Predeterminative specimen processing and integrity flow
Prelaboratory Process Work Flow Segment				
13	Data	Process	VIII	Validation of prelaboratory integrity flow
			VII	Specimen transportation, preservation, and collection
			VI	Patient preparation
14	Data	Process	V	Selection of laboratory test, product, or consultation
Operative Resource (Op Res) Work Flow Segment				
15	Data	Op Res	IV	Workload management
16	Data	Op Res	IV	Personnel strength
17	Data	Op Res	IV	Productivity measurement

Block # Type	Functional Level	Work Flow Phase	Subject
18 Data	Op Res	IV	Personnel utilization
19 Data	Op Res	IV	Continuing medical education, training, and expertise
20 Data	Op Res	IV	Procedural methods review
21 Data	Op Res	IV	Computer support
22 Data	Op Res	IV	Equipment procurement and maintenance
23 Data	Op Res	IV	Supply procurement and storage
24 Data	Op Res	IV	Facility, working environment maintenance, repair, renovation, and space utilization
25 Data	Op Res	IV	Budget management

Organizational Resource (Org Res) Work Flow Segment

Quality Improvement (QI) Work Flow Phase

26 Data	Org Res	III	Internal quality improvement
27 Data	Org Res	III	External quality surveillance: inspections
28 Data	Org Res	III	External quality surveillance: proficiency testing surveys
29 Data	Org Res	III	External quality surveillance: incidental reports, and complaints

Quality Anticipation (QAn) Work Flow Phase

30 Data	Org Res	II	Organizational research, development, and implementation

Quality Actualization (QAc) Work Flow Phase

31 Data	Org Res	I	Organizational effectiveness

Summary Information

32 Data	Org Res	–	Improvements made in structure, system, policy, process, method, and procedure
33 Data	–	–	Additional comments
34 Info	–	–	Quality management team signatures
35 Info	–	–	Feeder report routing list

Info = informational
Op Res = operative resource
Org Res = organizational resource

The narrative-style feeder report model consists of a number of information and data paragraph blocks. The example used in this text demonstrates three general information blocks and 32 specific data blocks. The composition of the overall report and each data block restates the JCAHO ten-steps.

The sequential order of the data blocks also retraces the fifteen phases of laboratory work flow. However, the report model is formatted in reverse order of the path of work flow, beginning with the "top line" of customer satisfaction rather than the proverbial "bottom line" of fiscal accountability. Further, the report is sequentially divided into the six work flow segments of postlaboratory, intralaboratory, and prelaboratory operative activities; quality surveillance (QI); quality anticipation (QAn); and quality actualization (QAc) organizational activities—the QAc program representing the real organizational bottom line.

The order of the data blocks also reiterates the outcome-process-structural resource sequence of general laboratory operations, including all structural elements of operative and organizational resource management. In actual practice—as the model illustrates—some work flow phases and segments overlap one another and are combined in the report to best reflect the point of data retrieval and to conserve document space. Data block 13 of the feeder report in the text below is a good example of such consolidation. The actual number of information and data blocks depends on the size and complexity of laboratory operations as well as the schedule for indicator monitoring. For example, not all work flow phases need be scheduled for the same reporting period.

An outline of the feeder report format is provided in Table I. The table shows the relationship of the report paragraph blocks to the three laboratory functional levels, the six work flow segments, and the fifteen work flow phases. This outline itemizes the subject topics for each paragraph; each of these topics is discussed at some length in this chapter.

The *information* blocks are straightforward and are explained within the text of this chapter. The *data* blocks are more complex. An example data module is illustrated as follows:

Data block #____. Indicator grouping title (work flow phase #____):

	Indicator (Step #4)	Threshold (Step #5)	Observation (Step #6)
a.	________	________	________
b.	________	________	________
c.	________	________	________
d.	________	________	________

Potential Shift Opportunity? Yes___ No___ If so, attach analysis per shift.
Evaluation:(Step #7)
Action/Action Person:(Step #8)
Assessment:(Step #9)

This is a typical data block used in the QI feeder report. Since the JCAHO ten steps are used as the primary example of an analytical format in this text, each block incorporates six elements of the improvement process: steps 4 through 9.

Indicator selection (TSP step #4), threshold determination (TSP step #5), and data collection and observation (TSP step #6) are all labeled in the sample data block. Regarding step #4, specific indicator criteria are not usually noted in any data block but should be found in the laboratory activity's QI plan or specific operating procedure. Four "surveillance" lines (a, b , c, and d) are presented in every sample data block; in reality, there could be more or less.

Several QI data blocks also include a reminder to identify opportunities for improvement during specific work periods or shifts. There could be a need to monitor and evaluate indicator data for a given work shift that are otherwise masked by the overall data. This would offer an opportunity to use stratification charting during EvAAC proceedings.

The space for evaluation of the observed data (TSP step #7) is for addressing interpretation of absolute levels, abnormal level trends, and abnormal level patterns of indicator data points.

- An absolute level refers to the magnitude of a single indicator data point, which is usually an averaged figure.
- An abnormal level trend is a steadily increasing or decreasing sequence of data points, all above or beyond the accepted threshold level or range.
- An abnormal level pattern is a repetitive, continuing sequence of data points that remains within the bounds of the respective threshold but suggests the possibility of an impending problem.

Any of these three data point characteristics can reveal an opportunity for improvement, whether it be problematic (with indicator levels exceeding threshold limits) or nonproblematic (with indicator levels remaining within threshold limits).

Action and action person (TSP step #8) and assessment (TSP step #9) also are labeled in the sample data block, needing no further explanation at this point. The remaining steps of the improvement cycle that have not been mentioned are addressed in other portions of the narrative report. For example, the signatures in the final information block verify the delineation of responsibilities (TSP step #1). The section identification in the first information block indicates scope of care (TSP step #2). The indicator grouping title and the individual indicator description identify the important aspect of care (TSP step #3) under consideration. Finally, the routing block at the end of the report witnesses the exercising of communication (TSP step #10) by using the report model to document and disseminate information.

Thus, all ten steps of the JCAHO process are addressed in this narrative report format.

As exemplified in this text, the feeder report data blocks provide limited space for written data or comments—in actuality, space is potentially unlimited. This paucity of space is intentional. Once one has become familiar with the format, surprisingly little room is necessary to write the most important information for effective documentation and communication purposes. However, since the report is constructed in vertical narrative paragraphs, spacing is very easily adjusted whenever more room for text is necessary. More detailed information on any quality management issue should be on file at the sectional or higher management level.

Quality indicator monitoring is usually scheduled on a monthly basis. The section quality management team reviews the indicator data that was gathered during the monitoring period—preparing a QI feeder report for submission to the service or departmental level quality management committee.

The sample feeder report presented in this chapter is abbreviated and segmented; Appendix A provides an unabridged, general version. Appendix B exemplifies a format for reporting anatomic pathology indicator data.

The following discussion is a detailed description of the design of the feeder report. More importantly, it stresses the application of indicators, criteria, and thresholds to the narrative-style report. Some comment is made concerning the use of the feeder report for data collection and documentation of evaluation, action, assessment, and communication. However, Chapter Eight provides a more detailed discussion of monitoring and EvAAC activities.

SCOPE OF CARE: IDENTIFYING SECTION AND REPORTING PERIOD

The heading paragraph for the report model is the first information block and addresses Step #2 of the JCAHO improvement process by indicating the general scope of laboratory patient care support. The laboratory section staff should initiate this reporting procedure at the operative level—that might be an analytical, diagnostic, or administrative support activity. The dates of report submission and the monitoring period are also recorded in this block.

Quality Improvement Feeder Report (General)
1.Section and reporting period identification Section / Service: _______________ Submitted: Month _________ Year ________ Reporting Period:______________________ thru ___________________________

POSTLABORATORY OUTCOME WORK FLOW SEGMENT

Customer Satisfaction Management

Outcome management has been a primary target for clinical quality surveillance, but not so common a target for laboratory QI programs. In view of the current JCAHO emphasis, as well as basic precepts of quality management, outcome surveillance deserves its fair share of laboratory attention. Thus, this report format begins with the postlaboratory outcome work flow segment as is appropriate for the routine pattern of analysis of the path of laboratory work flow.[2,3]

Paragraph 2, or data block 2, records quality management indicators at the outcome level of laboratory operations in the fifteenth and final phase of the work flow path: customer satisfaction. It documents the monitoring and EvAAC of any opportunities for improvement of laboratory quality as reflected by QI indicators of customer satisfaction. A customer code number is used to refer to a specific customer case file while still protecting the anonymity of the individual in this public document—if anonymity is appropriate.

2. Customer satisfaction (work flow phase XV):

Satisfaction Indicator: state customer code # if appropriate	Threshold	Observation
a. #____–__________	__________	________________
b. #____–__________	__________	________________
c. #____–__________	__________	________________
d. #____–__________	__________	________________

Evaluation:
Action/Action Person:
Assessment:

Indicators. This first indicator grouping represents the operational "top line" of quality management. The laboratory should systematically monitor customer satisfaction on an ongoing basis. Historically, however, monitoring of laboratory customer satisfaction has been sparse. If customer opinion has been tracked at all, the laboratory has focused on the patient or clinician. With the advent and continued growth of direct patient access to laboratory services, patient satisfaction is becoming an equally compelling indicator.[4]

Another key customer is the employee. Although patient care outcome and employee safety are covered in great detail under their specific report paragraphs, any significant aspect of any type of customer satisfaction, including the employee, should be addressed in this first data block. Additionally, many other internal and external customers-suppliers (eg, lateral or higher echelon hospital administrative support, commercial vendors, community contacts, or specific providers) can be identified and reported here as focused studies or via separate report paragraphs under postlaboratory outcome.

Simply waiting for comments or incident reports to be submitted is the most passive approach to surveillance of customer satisfaction with outcome; for example, the least desirable time to hear employee opinion is at the exit interview. A suggestion box is a slightly more active means of data collection, especially when supported by a suggestion award program. But even solicited suggestions represent a serendipitous windfall of information—based on a little more inspiration but still a lot of chance.

For a truly prospective and more purposeful approach, identify and target specific customer satisfaction indicators by direct inquiry. One can design formal surveys to discover the needs, desires, merits, and actual level of satisfaction of all types of customers on a priority basis. It is easy to continually up-date, modify, and circulate periodic surveys to the targeted customer group.

Regardless of the method of monitoring and data collection, the findings from customer complaints, suggestions, and surveys can unmask opportunities for improvement, including operational problems that need to be solved. These findings should translate into quality surveillance indicators for scheduled monitoring.

Ultimately, the formation of a customer relations committee or advocacy group shows the greatest commitment to improving customer satisfaction and ferreting out the best, most meaningful indicators of quality improvement. A customer relations forum is a practical and effective method of deriving indicators of the quality of customer satisfaction. Because there are so many customers-suppliers served by the laboratory, such a committee should consist of representatives of all customer-supplier groups, including patients, attending physicians, other clinical staff, laboratory physicians, and other laboratory staff. Representatives of ancillary or lateral supporting activities, higher administrative echelons, the central source of organizational funding, sources of supply and equipment, licensing and accrediting agencies, and regulating agencies should also participate whenever necessary.

At times, it is helpful to convene very general, multidisciplinary groups; at other times, it is better to convene specially focused teams, depending on the scope of the intended QI activity. Regardless, if well-represented, motivated, and organized, these various teams can be a never-ending source of specific, focused quality indicators and their specific criteria. Whatever the group's composition, the resultant indicators are usually proactive and prospective, aimed at finding opportunities for improvement and heading off customer-related problems before they occur. The group methods should include brainstorming techniques, surveys, and other forms of active inquiry, along with analytical, fact finding, interpretive, and decision making tools.

Since customer satisfaction is of such a global nature (even more than "panorganizational"), one can target *any* aspect of laboratory operations and the path of work flow for QI scrutiny. Examples of general customer satisfaction indicator groupings include satisfaction with the quality of:

- Patient care outcome
- Laboratory employee satisfaction with the working and decision making environment, including safety
- Specific laboratory end products
- Reference laboratory end products
- Laboratory staff-customer-supplier relationships
- Customer-related research and development project results
- Laboratory location, size, and hours of access
- Customer education and training.

The next step is to rank and choose the specific indicators that deserve the highest priority attention. Then, design specially focused studies to monitor the best possible opportunities for improvement. Use task force groups to perform special studies and investigations when necessary.

Customer satisfaction can be a particularly problematic surveillance parameter for the nonhospital-based laboratory such as a physician's office laboratory (POL) or any other independent reference laboratory or diagnostic consultative center—including the blood center and the anatomic pathology consultative laboratory. Nonetheless, effort must be made to cultivate a meaningful relationship with all customers—no matter how small the operation (as with a POL) or physically removed from the customer (as with an independent reference laboratory). At the very least, surveys can be designed to query all customer groups on a periodic basis. Eventually, customer relations forums should be organized.[5-7]

Indicator Criteria and Thresholds. There are no nationwide indicator criteria (standards) or thresholds (assurance levels) for customer satisfaction other than the general JCAHO accreditation requirements. As with indicators and their criteria, thresholds for customer satisfaction are best determined through the joint effort of representatives of all laboratory customer groups.

The threshold for customer satisfaction can vary from a rate-based parameter to a sentinel event. This range of tolerance or assurance level depends on the degree of urgency of clinical or safety related repercussions and should be evaluated accordingly. Examples of thresholds, matching the above listing of general indicator groupings, include:

- Patient care outcome: there should be no adverse effects that threaten life or limb (sentinel event)

- Laboratory employee safety outcome: there should be no adverse events that threaten life or limb (sentinel event)
- Specific laboratory end products: the accuracy of serum calcium test results will be within ± 2 SD (comparative rate event)
- Reference laboratory end products: the turnaround time for a routine pediatric blood lead test result will be no greater than 3 days (comparative rate event)
- Laboratory staff-customer-supplier relationships: there will be no abusive behavior from either direction (sentinel event)
- Customer-related research and development project results: the trial survey of customer satisfaction following phlebotomy will be finalized no later than the end of the report quarter (comparative rate event)
- Laboratory location, size, and hours of access: the stat laboratory will respond to the surgical intensive care unit within 60 minutes of initial test request (comparative rate event)
- Customer education and training: all patients will be properly instructed of exercise restrictions immediately following blood donation (sentinel event).

Patient Care Outcome Management

The minimal outcome of laboratory resource management, process, and end product utilization is two-fold: patient care outcome and employee safety outcome. Data block 3 addresses customer outcome in terms of patient outcome in the fourteenth phase of work flow. A patient code number is used to refer to a specific patient case file while still protecting the anonymity of the individual in this public document.

3. Patient care outcome (work flow phase XIV):

Outcome Indicator: state patient code # if appropriate	Clinical Threshold	Observation
a. #____–______________	______________	________________________
b. #____–______________	______________	________________________
c. #____–______________	______________	________________________
d. #____–______________	______________	________________________

Evaluation:
Action/Action Person:
Assessment:

The clinical staff has traditionally measured this parameter of quality improvement—usually for risk management purposes. Aside from the study of blood product utilization and the tracking of tissue diagnoses, the laboratorian has not regularly, systematically scrutinized patient care outcome as related to clinical utilization of other laboratory products. In light of expanding JCAHO emphasis—and in the true spirit of comprehensive quality management—the laboratory must actively pursue patient care outcome surveillance on a prospective, preventive basis rather than as retrospective risk management, which is a form of damage control.

Indicators. This introduces the second indicator grouping of customer-related outcome, the first subset being patient care outcome—or clinical usefulness of a laboratory product. Until recently, the most common source of information concerning laboratory effect on patient care outcome has been the occasional incident report and sporadic patient record review. However, as with any other clinically-related work flow phase, patient care outcome indicators for the laboratory should be more prospective in nature, based on joint laboratory-clinical staff forethought and input.

The clinicians—and their patients—are best served by a joint monitoring and evaluation program enlisting the input of all involved customers-suppliers to identify laboratory patient care outcome indicators and evaluate the resultant data. Special joint task force groups can be formed to study the quality indicators of patient care outcome that have highest priority.

One approach to monitoring concurrent patient care outcome is using the so-called delta check. There are varying reports on the effectiveness of this approach. As is true of any statistical method, it is very dependent on the volume and accuracy of the data being studied. If used properly, however, delta checking can identify aberrant patient care outcome. An in-depth and timely study of the relation of laboratory results to changes in patient health status definitely requires computerized, relational data base management. If an adverse outcome does develop, then the QI process must determine whether it was due to a natural event (ie, out of the hands of the laboratorian or clinician), is caused by incorrect utilization of the laboratory end product (ie, work flow phase XIII), or is caused by incorrect selection of the laboratory product or service (ie, work flow phase V).

Modern times are creating new demands on quality management of patient care outcome as new types of laboratory testing products and services emerge. For example, direct patient access to laboratory services is, overall, requiring new approaches to patient care outcome surveillance. Also, with heightened regulatory interest in the quality surveillance of the small POL, the decentralized laboratory, and the large, independent reference laboratory, monitoring of patient care outcome is becoming an increasing challenge. Regardless of the type of laboratory, the method is the same for monitoring customer satisfaction; for example, the nonhospital-based laboratory must learn to cope with less direct contact with the attending clinical staffs, the clinical records, and the patient. In the case of direct access, all laboratories must cope with increasing contact with the patient. In any case, there still must be patient record review, written surveys of the attending clinical staffs, meetings with representatives of the attending clinicians, and even dialogue with the self-referring patients. Though the task of monitoring patient care outcome is more difficult for the subject laboratories, the difficulty does not ease the responsibility.[8,9]

Indicator Criteria and Thresholds. There are no nationwide indicator criteria or threshold levels for patient outcome other than the general JCAHO accreditation requirements. There is very little intralaboratory comparison information currently available to substantiate local criteria and thresholds. But national task groups are formulating indicators and are beginning to amass comparison data on which local indicator criteria and threshold levels will be more scientifically based.

Again, assessment of the quality of care, including the medical appropriateness of patient care outcome, requires a consensus between laboratory and clinical physicians regarding appropriate clinical goals and threshold levels for the desired outcome resulting from a particular laboratory end product used for a specific disease or diagnostic grouping. Monitoring and evaluation of these indicator data require peer level surveillance and exercise of the usual confidentiality in the public record.

The threshold for patient outcome—as well as for any other customer-related outcome—varies depending on the degree of relevant risk or danger. However, the prime directive must always be upheld: *non nocere primum*—above all, do no harm. If the outcome significantly threatens an individual's life or quality of life, then such an outcome becomes a sentinel event, requiring immediate investigative evaluation. Of course, the most serious danger usually applies to the patient and the employee, but the same threshold can apply to any other type of customer: the nature of significant harm must be interpreted for each customer type, eg, insolvent financial practices would be "harmful" to the central administrative, funding, or governing body.

Employee Safety Outcome Management

Data block 4 addresses customer-related outcome in terms of safety outcome, also in the fourteenth phase of work flow. Laboratory safety affects all customers—patients, physicians, and employees alike. However, laboratory management must focus on employee safety because that group is most immediately at risk. Since patient safety is inherent to the concept of patient care, the more rare case of patient mishap in the laboratory usually falls into the report category of patient care outcome or customer satisfaction—or becomes a risk management issue after the fact.

Indicators. Laboratory safety is the third indicator grouping and is the second major subset of the larger grouping of customer-related outcome. The entire laboratory environment—including the resources used, the

4. Laboratory safety/environment/security outcome (work flow phase XIV):

	Safety Indicator	Threshold	Observation
a.	______________	____________	______________________
b.	______________	____________	______________________
c.	______________	____________	______________________
d.	______________	____________	______________________

Evaluation:
Action/Action Person:
Assessment:

processes employed, and the products produced—must be safe for all laboratory employees and any other personnel who are even occasionally present, including visiting patients, clinical staff, and housekeeping staff.

Safety has been a cornerstone to laboratory quality management, as evidenced by its always being a highly visible CAP accreditation checklist item. Among other organizations, the Occupational Safety and Health Administration (OSHA), also has instituted comprehensive safety requirements for healthcare laboratories. These accreditation and regulatory requirements offer a rich source of potential QI indicators. Common QI indicators for the monitoring and evaluation of safe laboratory conditions include precautions against the hazards of:

- Biologicals
- Fire
- Electricity
- Chemicals, including carcinogens
- Radionuclides
- Waste disposal
- Facility design and environmental factors such as temperature control, ventilation, safety hoods, lighting, and physical and personnel security.

Monitor safety indicators by the same QI process as other indicators of outcome quality. Since there is at least one major customer directly affected by laboratory safety—the employee—there should be a concerted effort to enlist the employee as a key participant in choosing and evaluating safety indicators. Other customers to be included in joint deliberation over the safety program are the various safety and security agencies that are directly related to the laboratory safety program—at the very least, representatives of the facility engineers, the fire department, and the police or institutional security operations should be considered.

Indicator Criteria and Thresholds. The regulatory requirements of federal, state and local authorities are replete with indicator criteria and thresholds for employee safety, facility environment, and security. These sources would include the standards of national-level inspection and accreditating organizations, including OSHA, Food and Drug Administration (FDA), JCAHO, CAP, and the American Association of Blood Banks (AABB).

In keeping with the admonition to do no harm, the threshold for the occurrence of a violation of a safety standard should be that of a sentinel event: there needs to be 100% conformance to the design specifications, which are, in this case, the safety standards. Any occurrence of a discrepancy presents as an opportunity for improvement and requires immediate investigative evaluation.

POSTLABORATORY PROCESS WORK FLOW SEGMENTS

Laboratory Product Utilization Management

At this point of the report, the postlaboratory process work flow segments make their appearance. Data block 5 addresses the thirteenth phase of the work flow path: laboratory product utilization (usage or use). A provider code number is used to refer to a specific provider's case file while still protecting the anonymity of the individual in this public document.

5. Laboratory product utilization (work flow phase XIII):

Utilization Indicator: state Provider Code # if appropriate	Clinical Threshold	Observation
a. #____–______________	______________	__________________________
b. #____–______________	______________	__________________________
c. #____–______________	______________	__________________________
d. #____–______________	______________	__________________________

Evaluation:
Action/Action Person:
Assessment:

Indicators. This fourth major indicator grouping usually focuses on the utilization of laboratory testing, products, and services by physicians. However, the provider can also be a physician's assistant, a nurse practitioner, a therapist, or any other professional individual who is authorized to use a laboratory test result, diagnostic report, blood product, or other service for any form of patient care, no matter how ancillary or trivial it might seem.

Effective utilization of healthcare laboratories has been a concern for many years.[10] Based on JCAHO requirements, it has become common hospital administrative practice to organize review committees to monitor various aspects of laboratory product utilization. There is often a hospital-wide utilization review committee, but this forum has not always been effective in addressing laboratory product utilization in a comprehensive manner. Closer to the issue, the transfusion or blood use committee is another Joint Commission requirement better designed for specialized laboratory review of blood product utilization.

The JCAHO is now expecting the laboratory to perform broader utilization studies that are significantly beyond the scope of the traditional hospital-level utilization and transfusion committee activities. In keeping with this mandate, the laboratory should select utilization indicators for every important laboratory product—synonymous to every "important aspect of care" of the TSP. As with any clinically-related work flow phase, the key to successful utilization review is achieving joint laboratory and clinical physician agreement on what utilization indicators are important and how to specifically approach their quality surveillance.

As increased patient direct access develops, there is need to devise new means for quality surveillance of a patient's utilization of a laboratory product. This presents the challenge of establishing a new working relationship with a new form of customer. Surveillance of this work flow phase also promises to be problematic for the nonhospital-based POL and independent laboratory, but it still is an important avenue for QI surveillance.

Indicator Criteria and Thresholds. There are no nationwide criteria or thresholds for patient outcome other than the general JCAHO accreditation requirements. Until national standards become available, clinical indications and contraindications for the utilization of every important laboratory product for a given diagnostic grouping must be determined locally.[11,12,13,14] In deriving thresholds to guide the evaluation of laboratory utilization, the questions that need to be answered are:

- Was the laboratory product used correctly when its use ***was*** clinically indicated? This would include the timely use of a critical or alarm value that has been appropriately transmitted to the primary provider. This usage would be appropriate in a disease state.

- Was the laboratory product used incorrectly when its use ***was*** clinically indicated? This usage would be inappropriate in a disease state.

- Was the laboratory product used correctly when it ***was not*** clinically indicated? This is essentially a moot point since correct utilization of the product in work flow phase XIII is outweighed by the incorrect selection of the product in work flow phase V. This usage would be appropriate in a healthy state.

- Was the laboratory product used incorrectly when it *was not* clinically indicated? This fourth option—the double negative scenario—is least likely to occur, but it is still a possibility. This usage would be inappropriate in a healthy state.

The threshold for evaluating the answers to these questions is all-or-none: either a laboratory product is used correctly or it is not. It should be used correctly every time without fail. Consequently, any occurrence of incorrect utilization is a sentinel event requiring immediate investigative evaluation. However, just because an indicator is deemed a sentinel event, the need for investigation does not necessarily indicate the degree of corrective action—if any action is needed at all.

Utilization analysis requires medical chart review, which is greatly enhanced by computerized relational data base management. Computer support is particularly helpful in concurrently measuring utilization parameters such as delta checks.

Laboratory Throughput Management: Turnaround Time, Backlog, and Distribution

Data blocks 6 and 7 record the efficiency of laboratory "throughput," which make up the twelfth work flow phase. Throughput includes all factors that determine the accuracy and speed of distribution of the final laboratory product to the appropriate patient record or patient care location. This surveillance activity involves monitoring the actual delivery of the final laboratory product to its ultimate destination plus monitoring the efficiency of the overall work flow of the laboratory activity in terms of time. Throughput is an integral aspect of laboratory quality and is affected by the efficiency of managerial, interpretive, technical, clerical, and other supportive resources alike.

Indicators. Data block 6 introduces the fifth major indicator grouping. We measure the speed of throughput usually in terms of turnaround time

6. Laboratory product turnaround time/backlog (work flow phase XII):

Throughput Indicator	Threshold TAT/Backlog	Observation TAT	Observation Backlog
a. ____________	______ / ______	__________	__________
b. ____________	______ / ______	__________	__________
c. ____________	______ / ______	__________	__________
d. ____________	______ / ______	__________	__________

Potential Shift Opportunity? Yes___ No___ If so, attach analysis per shift
Evaluation:
Action/Action Person:
Assessment:

(TAT). The QI program can monitor any segment of the total work flow path for turnaround. There are four categories mentioned in Chapter Six: collection TAT, processing TAT, distribution or in-transit TAT, and overall TAT—all of which can vary widely from one laboratory procedure to another. Processing alone, can vary greatly depending on the specimen type, the technical methods, and the clinical urgency involved. Compare, for example, the processing turnaround for a stat chemistry analysis (30 min) to a routine surgical diagnosis (2 days).

The report format in data block 6 reveals a distinction between TAT and backlog, a second throughput indicator. Although the amount of turnaround usually correlates directly to the degree of backlogged laboratory work load, this is not always the case. One or the other parameter may be of greater importance in determining the extent and timing of the course of action.

Backlog, defined as workload volume yet to be done, can be a very informative statistic as it indicates the number of personnel required to resolve a throughput problem. Backlog is particularly valuable in the selection of priorities and allocation of corrective resources. This is especially true when dealing with labor-intensive technical procedures.

In a total quality management (TQM) and continuous quality improvement (CQI) environment, distribution volume might be a valuable improvement indicator, even when TAT and backlog are within their expected limits. In this case, it might be desirable to improve distribution in terms of increasing percent distribution or overall volume of distribution. This might be called "front log."

Data block 7 introduces the sixth major indicator grouping: laboratory product distribution. One can monitor and evaluate the accuracy of throughput in terms of the surety of delivery. For example, it is possible in some cases to almost instantaneously verify the unaltered distribution of the correct analytical or diagnostic written report to the correct patient "address" through electronic transmission of written reports. However, when electronic monitoring is unavailable, accurate and intact delivery requires much more complicated handling to reach the laboratory

7. Laboratory report or other product distribution (work flow phase XII):

	Distribution Indicator	Threshold	Observation
a.	____________	________	____________
b.	____________	________	____________
c.	____________	________	____________
d.	____________	________	____________

Potential Shift Opportunity? Yes___ No___ If so, attach analysis per shift.
Evaluation:
Action/Action Person:
Assessment:

product's intended destination; this is especially true in the case of distributing blood components. Concomitant quality improvement follow-up is also more complicated.

Regardless of the type of laboratory product or the mode of distribution, surveillance indicators of the accuracy of distribution must include verification of a match between the correct laboratory product and the correct patient. This verification also should incorporate an ascertainment of the physical state of the report or product at the time of delivery.

If adequate computer support is not available, the laboratory must survey this work flow phase by a more retrospective method. In the most passive monitoring mode, a distribution problem will surface as a specific complaint from a ward or clinic. The problem usually is that patient reports are not reaching the desired ward or clinic chart destination. One also can register such an event in data block 2 as a customer dissatisfaction or data block 29 as an incident or client complaint.

It is better to employ a more active approach to find opportunities to improve distribution and TAT. Return receipts (even by fax), written surveys, and telephone inquiries are available in a noncomputerized system. Computerized data analysis is, however, necessary for concurrent verification of test report distribution and "real time" measurement of throughput. Here is another example where bar coding and electronic mail provide innovative methods of follow-up and can be valuable to POLs and independent laboratories.

Indicator Criteria and Thresholds. There are no nationwide criteria or thresholds for throughput other than the general JCAHO and CAP accreditation requirements. It is necessary to determine quality surveillance standards or assurance levels for both turnaround and distribution for every important laboratory product. The extent of these guidelines depends on the nature of the laboratory product that has been selected, the specific diagnostic grouping at hand, the degree of clinical urgency, and the mode of transmission of the laboratory product to the ward or clinic physician and the patient record or patient bedside.

The CAP has clearly stated TAT accreditation standards for various laboratory products, especially for tissue diagnoses. In practice, however, it is necessary to tailor the interpretation of these standards to the technical and interpretive difficulty of the laboratory product in question. For example, certain analytical procedures, such as electrophoresis or flow cytometry, require more time than others for processing. Tissue diagnostic cases can also require additional time for special processing (ie, decalcification) or additional techniques (ie, special staining or electron microscopy). Under these circumstances, there should be a local agreement among laboratorians and clinicians that special exceptions for longer TATs are technically justifiable and clinically acceptable. Otherwise, a reference laboratory with a faster turnaround should be sought.

As another example, the transmission of a critical or alarm value should be considered as a sentinel event: the threshold must be 100% conformance to design specifications—meaning that all critical values must be transmitted within the standard time frame. In this case, any delay in throughput requires investigative evaluation.

INTRALABORATORY PROCESS WORK FLOW SEGMENTS

Postdeterminative Finalization and Handling Management

At this point, the intralaboratory process segments make their appearance. Data block 8 addresses the quality of the final "packaging" of the laboratory product as ascertained by a specific verification step. In addition, the data block includes data on the quality of postdeterminative specimen handling. All of these QI targets occur in the eleventh work flow phase of finalization.

8. Verification of postdeterminative product finalization/postdeterminative specimen handling and integrity flow (work flow phase XI):

	Finalization Indicator	Threshold	Observation
a.	____________	________	____________
b.	____________	________	____________
c.	____________	________	____________
d.	____________	________	____________

Potential Shift Opportunity? Yes___ No___ If so, attach analysis per shift.
Evaluation:
Action/Action Person:
Assessment:

Indicators. This portion of the narrative report introduces the seventh major indicator grouping. Verification occurs just before the laboratory product is officially released from the laboratory and is distributed to the appropriate patient record or site of patient care. It is performed as a 1) manual/visual inspection and recording or 2) computerized review and documentation. In the latter case, the actual verification and archival filing is instantaneous through electronic data management. The entering of a verification code into a computerized laboratory information record is also known as "certification."

Verification usually occurs at the last checkpoint before the laboratory product leaves the operative control of the laboratory environment. That final review should confirm that:

- All written information is clerically correct or accurate;
- An analytic or diagnostic report is supported by adequate quality control data;

- A blood component product is supported by adequate quality control data, including a final visual inspection;
- A diagnostic report is consistent with patient clinical information with adequate pathologist recommendations and supplemental comments; this verification is usually performed by the primary diagnostician (keeping in mind that peer control has already been accomplished and peer assurance is yet to be done);
- A donor/diagnostic/therapeutic service procedure (eg, apheresis) is supported by adequate quality control data;
- Specimen integrity has been maintained throughout the course of laboratory processing; this includes final handling and storage, as needed.

Any of these six general areas of concern can serve as general indicators that will reflect the quality of the final product at time of verification.

Indicator Criteria and Thresholds. There are no nationwide criteria or thresholds for verification other than the general JCAHO accreditation requirements, including those specifically designed for management of computerized records. Any postdeterminative evidence of disruption in the patient-request-specimen-product-patient (patient-to-patient) flow of integrity deserves evaluation as a sentinel event. Keep in mind that a disruption in the flow of integrity most likely reflects a systemic problem in the laboratory process, including the act of verification itself—rather than a problem with an individual employee's performance.

Reference Laboratory Quality Management

Data block 9 addresses the quality of reference laboratory support—also occuring in the eleventh or finalization work flow phase. This surveillance requires attention to a mixture of internal and external quality management activities with some overlap of work flow phases. It includes the monitoring of all types of reference laboratories, AP and clinical pathology (CP), alike.

9. Reference laboratory studies (work flow phase XI):

	Ref Lab Indicator	Threshold	Observation
a.			
b.			
c.			
d.			

Evaluation:
Action/Action Person
Assessment:

Indicators. Reference laboratory quality represents the eighth major indicator grouping. During the initial time that the patient specimen and request are in the hands of the primary laboratory, that laboratory can monitor the usual internal QI indicator groupings during the intralaboratory, predeterminative phases of work flow. However, after shipment of the specimen to the reference laboratory and for as long as the specimen is in the hands of that reference laboratory, it is still the responsibility of the primary laboratory to monitor the reference laboratory's performance to the best of its ability. After receiving the reference laboratory result or other product, the primary laboratory's responsibility should continue with follow-up of the effectiveness of the reference laboratory's process and the overall quality of the end product. Indicators of reference laboratory performance include:

- Reference laboratory testing volume
- Turnaround time
- Performance in accreditation inspections and proficiency surveys
- Patient care outcome
- Customer satisfaction
- Actual reference laboratory QC and QI data to document the quality of specific tests, if ever required.

As previously mentioned, quality surveillance of reference laboratory products involves an overlap of several process- and outcome-related work flow phases. One can address this surveillance information under each separate phase or combine it under one feeder report paragraph, as is shown in the accompanying example. There is some merit to organizing reference laboratory quality management information under one heading in finalization phase eleven—especially since the primary laboratory resumes responsibility for overall review and distribution of the laboratory test result upon receipt of the reference laboratory's report or other product. If ever needed, one can address individual QI issues under separate report paragraphs as special or focused study projects.

The volume of reference laboratory testing work load is a useful resource management indicator. Tests must often be sent to a reference laboratory when the test volume is too small for the primary laboratory and the method is too labor-intensive and costly. Eventually, a procedure can grow enough in volume that it is more cost-effective to perform in-house. This change can result in an improvement of the overall laboratory process, patient care outcome, and customer satisfaction through closer control, shortened TAT, and less customer expense.

Reference laboratory turnaround is the easiest reference laboratory indicator to monitor—and is perhaps the easiest to overlook in contradistinction to the perceived importance of a reference laboratory's analytical or diagnostic end products. The internal TAT of the reference laboratory should meet CAP accreditation requirements, but the shipping time—both to and fro—adds to the overall amount, and this is where inordinate delay often occurs. When it is a matter of returning a written report, electronic transmission (including facsimile transmission) can dramatically shorten that limb of the transit time.

Information regarding reference laboratory performance in accreditation and proficiency surveys can be harder to obtain. However, since it is required that for the primary laboratory to be CAP accredited, all reference laboratories must show evidence of that accreditation. That being the case, the reference laboratory should be willing to disclose information on their own QI program as confirmation that they are competitive and worthy as a professional business partner.

The laboratorian can specifically monitor the effect of reference laboratory products on patient care outcome, as well as their effect on customer satisfaction. Delta checking—or comparison of reference laboratory product utilization with concurrent clinical results—will indicate if reference laboratory value levels are concomitant with the clinical diagnosis, therapy, patient outcome, and customer satisfaction. Information on the latter parameter is available through the usual survey, questionnaires, interviews, and occasional customer letter or incident report. Again, this approach calls for adequate computer and information system support.

All of this postdeterminative special handling and scrutiny facilitates surveillance of the reference laboratory work being accomplished; but, it does not necessarily guarantee the reference laboratory's "in-house" accuracy since the primary laboratory has no immediate access to the reference laboratory's internal QC and QI data. Consequently, it is unfortunately the clinician who is often first to recognize a disparity between reference laboratory data and clinical response, raising the issue of reference laboratory quality through an incident report—a claim of untoward patient outcome and customer dissatisfaction. Effective laboratory quality management should thwart such customer dissatisfaction from occurring.

Indicator Criteria and Thresholds. There are no nationwide criteria or thresholds for reference laboratory outcome other than the general JCAHO and CAP accreditation requirements. Consequently, these parameters need to be established on the basis of local experience and clinical need.

Analytic Quality Management

Data block 10 can be applied against three aspects of the determinative work flow phase: qualitative/quantitative analytical determination, blood component preparation and other laboratory services (eg, phlebotomy, apheresis). Information reported in this data block is gleaned predominantly from analytical QC data, although other sources occasionally are available.

10. Analytical quality (work flow phase X):

	Quality Indicator	Technical Threshold	Observation
a.	______	______	______
b.	______	______	______
c.	______	______	______
d.	______	______	______

Potential Shift Opportunity? Yes___ No__ If so, attach analysis per shift.
Evaluation:
Action/Action Person:
Assessment:

Indicators. Analytical quality introduces the ninth major indicator grouping. This grouping exemplifies a phase in the laboratory work flow where the management of resources and processes can lead to significant quality improvement. Most often, such opportunities will be in the form of changing some aspect of workload volume, personnel strength or distribution, reagent stability, instrument stability, or procedural technique. QC data will be the bellwether that guides us to a means of improving the analytical process, pointing to the target for improvement.

To most clearly define an opportunity for improvement or a problem to be resolved, it is often necessary to monitor and evaluate a specific quality indicator for separate work shifts. Several data blocks in this feeder report purposefully ask if there is a possible work shift opportunity that should be investigated by stratification study. Two common discrepant issues arise among shifts: personnel distribution and instrument correlation.

First, a disparity between personnel staffing and workload volume can sneak up on the laboratory director or manager. Inadequate staffing may arise from too many staff vacancies or from too many authorized (or unauthorized) absences. On the other hand, the work load can slowly but significantly increase over a protracted period, the increase becoming perceptible but remaining imperceived if not carefully monitored. For whatever reason, an effective personnel shortage can develop, causing analytical quality to suffer because of excessive work load and employee stress.

Second, a disparity in instrument accuracy or precision also can arise between different work shifts when different instruments (eg, contrasting calibrations or methods) are used to produce the same laboratory tests. The subject instruments can be of identical manufacturer, model, and method or can be nonidentical. For example, the routine chemistry section might use one instrument during the daytime for creatinine analysis, and the stat laboratory might use a different instrument with a completely different method for creatinine analysis during the night time shifts. Consequently, comparing the QC data for creatinine testing might show a disparity or nonconcordance between the two instruments. Attending physicians are likely to first register this issue by reports of dissatisfaction, triggering investigative evaluation.

Quality surveillance of analytical procedures was once solely the role of the CP laboratory and did not apply to AP. In today's modern laboratory, however, it is not unusual to find analytical procedures being performed under the same roof as histotechnology and tissue microscopy. This change has resulted from the application of specialized receptor analysis, flow cytometry, and molecular analysis in support of tissue diagnosis. Consequently, the medical director/surgical pathologist must consider the quality management of these new analytical tools and follow appropriate QI indicators.

Indicator Criteria and Thresholds. There are no nationwide criteria or thresholds for analytical quality other than the general JCAHO and CAP accreditation requirements and what is being published for high visibility procedures such as cholesterol analysis. Criteria that apply to analytical laboratory performance include the traditional ± 2 SD control levels and normal reference ranges. These control criteria can be used as QI indicator criteria. Then, evaluation protocols such as Westgard's rules are useful in formulating threshold rules, levels, or ranges.

Based on modern CQI goals and objectives, analytical indicator criteria should eventually be improved by narrowing the traditional ± 2 SD control range, therefore increasing the degree of accuracy. In addition, the threshold or conformance to design specifications—which is equivalent to the degree of analytical precision—should be improved. That is, the analytical values for a given procedure should occur within the established indicator control range a greater number of times. Without specific national guidelines, these QI parameters must be established on the basis of local resources, technical experience, and clinical need.

Frequently, there is necessity to apply joint laboratorian-clinician attention to the identification of these analytical quality indicators, their criteria, and their thresholds. This is particularly true of analytical services for diagnostic groupings with the greatest severity of illness indices.[15,16,17] An example of such joint decision making is the identification of any analytical results that require alarm (or critical) values. These special values imply heightened patient risk and a significantly high severity of illness index. Such decisions would include determination of associated indicator criteria and thresholds—the tolerance ranges and assurance levels of quality management.

Diagnostic Quality Management

Data block 11 addresses the quality of the remaining determinative aspect of the tenth flow phase: interpretive diagnosis. A comparison of data blocks 10 and 11 reveals a distinctive difference between the two basic modes of laboratory decision making as described previously. On one hand, the

11. Diagnostic quality and peer review (work flow phase X):

	Quality Indicator: state Provider Code # if appropriate	Technical Clinical Threshold	Observation
a.	#____–____________	____________	__________________
b.	#____–____________	____________	__________________
c.	#____–____________	____________	__________________
d.	#____–____________	____________	__________________

Evaluation:
Action/Action Person:
Assessment:

quality management of analytical processing, blood component preparation, and laboratory services is usually very objective and instrumentally oriented. In comparison, the quality management of interpretive diagnosis is more subjective and cognitive in nature.

In either case, however, the same quality management principles should apply. Only the surveillance reporting is slightly different—as is shown by the report format. A provider code number is used to refer to a specific provider case file while still protecting the anonymity of the individual in this public document. Although the most frequently mentioned provider is the pathologist, there are other types of providers that might contribute to an interpretive diagnosis.

Indicators. Diagnostic interpretive quality introduces the tenth major indicator grouping. In the AP laboratory, the quality of the final diagnosis is dependent on two major factors. First, there is the adequacy of the technical preparation of the tissue specimen—similar to the needs for adequate preanalytical preparation. The screener or diagnostician should determine the quality of these prediagnostic steps. Examples of these histological technical indicators are similar to those listed under data block 12 for predeterminative specimen processing and include:

- Specimen security
- Preservation of the flow of patient-request-specimen-report-patient integrity
- Prevention of loss or destruction
- Prevention of introduction of extraneous material
- Specimen preservation and storage
- Specimen aliquot distribution, including shipment to a reference laboratory
- Specimen preparation for determinative analysis.

Second, there is the adequacy or medical appropriateness of the interpretive diagnosis itself, based upon the visual gross and microscopic inspection of the specimen by a qualified pathologist or other qualified individual who provides any part of the professional interpretation and diagnostic report. Therefore, quality surveillance of the work performed by the pathologist assistant and the cytology screener is also necessary.

The monitoring and evaluation of interpretive quality is done by peer review. Indicators of interpretive diagnostic quality apply to any type of tissue diagnosis in the AP or CP laboratory. Examples of these interpretive quality indicators include the concordance of:

- Tissue diagnosis with clinical history (applying to either intraoperative or permanent section diagnoses)
- Permanent section diagnosis with intraoperative (frozen section) diagnosis
- Permanent section diagnosis with cytologic diagnosis
- Peer review diagnosis with permanent section diagnosis
- Tissue committee clinical follow-up with permanent section diagnosis; this concordance represents a source of QI indicators and data other than those routinely scheduled.

Providers in the CP laboratory also perform some interpretive procedures that can be monitored by the same diagnostic peer review (ie, peer control and peer assurance) approach. These activities include any CP procedures involving the microscopic, interpretive appraisal of a tissue or fluid specimen. This category naturally includes bone marrow examination by a pathologist, which is identical to the process of tissue diagnosis in AP. However, it can also include other qualitative or semiquantitative interpretations by nonpathologists.

For example, CP procedures such as microscopic urinalysis, differential blood counting, and the assessment of microbiological stains of bronchial alveolar washings can be included in the nonpathologist group. The latter types of procedures are not typically "diagnostic" but are more qualitatively analytical and are usually rendered by a laboratorian other than a pathologist. Still, QI monitoring of these cognitive-type of analytical procedures easily adapts to the peer style of review used for the more traditional diagnostic procedures. In other words, peer review is applicable as a quality surveillance method for not only pathologists, but also laboratory nurses (usually in the blood bank), physician assistants (usually in AP), supervisors, and technologists—whoever may be performing a professional laboratory procedure where the employee is held personally accountable for an interpretive judgement.

The QI process for diagnostic type procedures exemplifies another juncture of laboratorian-clinician interface. Because of the relevance of the clinical history to an accurate tissue diagnosis and supplemental interpretive recommendations, there is need to include the clinical staff in the identification of diagnostic quality indicators. Clinical factors have to be considered in the quality management of both the technical and interpretive aspects of the diagnostic process.

Indicator Criteria and Thresholds. Diagnostic quality management at the national level is alive with identifying indicator criteria and thresholds for the monitoring of diagnostic indicators. Various specialty medical organizations are determining clinical indications and contraindications (ie, QI criteria) and tolerance levels or ranges (ie, QI thresholds) for a number of the most critical diagnostic groupings to ensure that 1) the clinician knows what information the pathologist needs to apply optimal technical and interpretive methods and 2) the pathologist knows what information the clinician needs to perform optimal patient work-up and therapy.

The clinical staff needs to better understand the importance of such items as adequate patient history and sampling when asking for a pathologist's diagnostic consultation. The clinical staff requires monitoring with reasonable criteria and thresholds just as the pathologists are monitored as to how they perform their diagnostic duties. Also, QI parameters need establishing at the national or local level for the nonpathologist practicing interpretive judgement in the AP and CP laboratory in support of the pathologist and the clinician in patient care.

Predeterminative Processing Management

Data block 12 addresses the ninth phase of the work flow path: intralaboratory, predeterminative specimen processing. Poor quality of predeterminative specimen handling and processing can lead to a break in the flow of specimen and data integrity that will affect all phases thereafter.

Indicators. This portion of the narrative report format introduces the eleventh major indicator grouping. This data block addresses quality surveillance of patient-request-specimen flow of integrity similar to that

12. Predeterminative specimen processing/integrity flow (flow phase IX):

	Processing Indicator	Threshold	Observation
a.	____________	____________	____________
b.	____________	____________	____________
c.	____________	____________	____________
d.	____________	____________	____________

Potential Shift Opportunity? Yes___ No___ If so, attach analysis per shift.
Evaluation:
Action/Action Person:
Assessment:

exercised in data block 8 for postdeterminative specimen handling, in data block 11 for diagnostic specimen handling, and in data block 13 for prelaboratory specimen collection. Similar indicators for integrity flow apply to both the AP and CP laboratories and include:

- Specimen preservation and storage
- Specimen aliquoting and distributing, including shipment to a reference laboratory
- Specimen security
  - preservation of patient-request-specimen flow of integrity
  - prevention of loss or destruction
  - prevention of introduction of extraneous material
- Specimen preparation for determinative analysis.

If there is any aliquoting of specimens, there must be surveillance of the quality management of all the specimen fractions. This includes monitoring the adequacy of transfer of patient-request-specimen identification data onto new labels and request forms. Whether those transcription procedures are performed by manual or automated methods, they are fraught with potential error. Bar coding will help alleviate many of these errors.

It is also in this phase that the primary laboratory prepares, packages, and sends patient testing requests and samples to the reference laboratory. Consequently, the QI program should direct special attention to the adequacy of these shipping procedures.

In the AP laboratory, there are similar histotechnical parameters that can be followed as quality indicators. These include:

- Specimen preservation and storage
- Specimen dissection, sectioning, and distribution, including shipment to a reference laboratory
- Specimen security during fixing, paraffinization, embedding, and mounting
  - preservation of patient-request-specimen flow of integrity
  - prevention of specimen loss, physical alteration, or destruction
  - prevention of the introduction of extraneous material into the specimen
- Specimen preparation for determinative analysis
  - temperature of processing solutions, baths, and ovens
  - replenishment of fresh processing solutions and baths
  - orientation of tissue in block
  - microtomy
    - proper thickness
    - section intact without fragmentation or chattering

- mounting of section on slide
  - proper fixing or gluing
  - section unwrinkled
  - absence of floaters
- staining of section
- labeling of slide.

Indicator Criteria and Thresholds. There are no nationwide criteria or thresholds for predeterminative processing other than the general JCAHO and CAP accreditation requirements. Programs such as CAP's Q-Probes® are beginning to formulate national-level QI standards and assurance levels. However, the laboratory still must empirically choose most local-level QI indicators, criteria, and threshold levels.

PRELABORATORY PROCESS WORK FLOW SEGMENTS

Prelaboratory Processing Validation Management

At this juncture of the feeder report, the prelaboratory process segments make their formal appearance. Data block 13 addresses the quality management of the eighth, seventh, and sixth phases of the work flow path—validation and accessioning; transportation-preservation-collection; and patient preparation. This block not only incorporates these three flow phases but also overlaps two segments: one intralaboratory segment (phase VIII) and one prelaboratory segment (phases VII and VI).

This merging of work flow segments occurs because the data for all three phases are (currently) most easily collected at the laboratory validation and accessioning point. The laboratory's actual review and acceptance (or

13. Validation of prelaboratory specimen integrity flow/specimen transportation/specimen preservation/specimen collection/patient preparation (work flow phases VIII, VII, and VI):

	Quality Indicator (index specimen/origin)	Threshold	Total Inval/Rcvd	Percent Invalid	Other
a.	__________	________	________	______	________
b.	__________	________	________	______	________
c.	__________	________	________	______	________
d.	__________	________	________	______	________

Potential Shift Opportunity? Yes___ No___ If so, attach analysis per shift.
Evaluation:
Action/Action Person:
Assessment:

rejection) of the provider request, patient preparation, and patient specimen for further processing is known as validation. This step focuses on the assessment of prelaboratory patient-request-specimen flow of integrity at the time of accessioning by the central laboratory system.

Indicators. This portion of the narrative report introduces the twelfth major indicator grouping. The laboratory should identify ongoing validation indicators for the most important aspects of laboratory patient care support; the data block refers to these indicators as index specimens or index sites of origin. The data points used in this block include the total number of index specimens invalidated versus the total number received (Total Inval/Rcvd) plus the percent of index specimens that have been invalidated (Percent Invalid).

An index specimen is used as a representative yardstick to assess key laboratory request preparation; patient preparation; and specimen collection, preservation, and transportation procedures over a lengthy baseline period. Aside from tracking these routine index cases, the QI program can also monitor special or focused study cases that spotlight special cases for investigation by a scheduled or nonscheduled QI process.

Validation indicators can be selected and followed on the basis of specific laboratory procedure; type of specimen; site of origin (eg, laboratory, ward, or clinic); or work shift. Most often, the key target of interest is the site of origin which can then be narrowed down to the general process practiced by a specific clinical service and, finally, to a specific individual provider, if necessary. Specific quality indicators within this grouping of combined work flow phases include:

- Laboratory request completeness
  - correct and unique patient demographics
  - laboratory procedure designation
  - specimen type
  - date and time of collection
  - patient preparation
  - designation and location of requesting provider
- Patient preparation adequacy
- Specimen collection adequacy
  - correct and unique patient identification
  - adequate sampling
- Specimen preservation
  - at time of collection
  - at time of transportation
- Specimen transportation
  - correct container and packaging
  - proper in-transit temperature
  - appropriate transit time.

Indicator Criteria and Thresholds. There are no nationwide criteria or thresholds for validation other than the general JCAHO and CAP accreditation requirements. Threshold levels are usually determined on a local empirical basis. A threshold for a validation indicator of an opportunity for improvement can be described as:

> the maximum, acceptable incidence rate (eg, percentage) of invalid specimens collected for an important laboratory analytical procedure, product preparation, or diagnostic consultation for the healthcare treatment of some specific disease or disease grouping. This incidence rate might pertain to a clinical service, ward or clinic, or specific practitioner.

It is important to recognize that validation thresholds vary among functional sections for substantive reasons—either technical or logistical. What might be an acceptable incidence of invalid specimens for one section may be too high or too low for another section, depending on the respective clinical setting, the technical method and instrumentation being used, and the clinical and laboratory resources that are available.

For example, the incidence of microthrombi in routine neonatal blood specimens for a complete blood count in the hematology section might warrant a threshold of > 10%, whereas the threshold for routine adult specimens might warrant a lower threshold of only > 2% because of the greater technical and clinical difficulty in obtaining repeat samples from neonatal patients. However, the higher validation threshold for neonatal specimens waves a red flag of warning that here lies an opportunity for improvement in collection technique that should result eventually in a lowered threshold.

For comparison, in the blood bank validation thresholds are most often 0%—at the sentinel event level—because of the life threatening effect of hemolytic transfusion reactions, regardless of what type of patient is involved. According to the principles of CQI, the challenge is to reduce all validation thresholds to their lowest absolute value (toward zero defects).

As previously noted for other work flow phases, validation of the quality of specimen integrity flow, transportation, preservation, collection, and patient preparation present a special challenge in dealing with direct patient access. This is because of the lack of direct control over patient compliance with preparatory procedures.

Likewise, the POL and the independent laboratory share similar difficulties in managing prelaboratory procedures—all for the same reasons: size (therefore, available QI resources) and lack of direct contact with the clinical arena. Regardless, as long as a nonhospital-based laboratory is being accessed directly by a clinician—or even a patient—for healthcare support, that laboratory is obliged to make some effort to ensure that the quality management of these three work flow phases are adequately addressed.

Bar coding and robotics will eventually revolutionize the monitoring of these three work flow phases, allowing actual on-site, real time surveillance and documentation of patient preparation and specimen collection. However, until such data automation is available, all of these validation QI parameters need monitoring indirectly at the accessioning point—whether that be at the level of the central laboratory or a specific section.

As an aside, the QI feeder report format design is easily adaptable to change. For instance, it should be very easy to divide data block 13 into its component parts if data automation; workload volume; and diversity of indexed, special, or focused indicators so dictate.

Laboratory Product Selection Management

Data block 14 addresses the fifth phase of the work flow path: selection of a laboratory product by a patient care provider. This indicator grouping applies to the selection of both AP and CP laboratory products or services. A provider code number is used to refer to a specific provider's case file while still protecting the anonymity of the individual in this public document.

14. Selection of laboratory test/product/consultation (work flow phase V):

Selection Indicator: state Provider Code # if appropriate	Clinical Threshold	Observation
a. #____–__________	__________	_______________
b. #____–__________	__________	_______________
c. #____–__________	__________	_______________
d. #____–__________	__________	_______________

Evaluation:
Action/Action Person:
Assessment:

Indicators. This portion of the narrative report introduces the thirteenth major indicator grouping. If specimen collection (phase VII) or patient preparation (phase VI) could be singled out as separate, concurrent indicator groupings, then the numbering of these major indicator groupings would be changed accordingly.

The QI monitoring of "test need" requires the surveillance of an activity that is almost entirely external to the physical boundaries of the primary laboratory and requires joint laboratory-clinical review and comparison of both laboratory and clinical data. As mentioned under the topic of laboratory utilization, this indicator grouping should invoke the peer review process.

Most often, surveillance of the selection process targets the clinical or attending physician, but there can be other primary providers involved such as physician assistants, nurse practitioners, or any other providers who are credentialed to request laboratory services for a patient, directly or indirectly. With direct access, the requestor even can be the patient, acting as a "self-provider."

QI indicators for laboratory product selection should target the requesting of specific products. General, blanket surveillance amounts to occurrence screening and is not systematically effective. A specific indicator can be initially defined in terms of a specific disease or diagnostic grouping. Then, it can be narrowed down to a specific selection process used by a provider group or even by a particular individual—if necessary.

Again, a reminder needs stating: indicator groupings that rely on laboratory-clinical cooperation and review of clinical records are a QI challenge for the POL and independent laboratory. As long as a nonhospital-based laboratory is being accessed directly by a clinician or patient, it is incumbent upon that laboratory to practice some degree of quality management of the selection phase through interdisciplinary dialogue—including communication with the patient self-provider, if direct access is being made available.

Indicator Criteria and Thresholds. First, there are the general JCAHO and CAP accreditation requirements. Second, Blue Cross and Blue Shield and the CAP have published clinical guidelines for laboratory test selection.[18,19] Also, journal offerings are increasing.[20] A Joint Commission task force and professional medical and surgical societies are actively engaged in formulating further standards of practice for laboratory service selection at the national level. Formulation of local standards are also encouraged.

In any case, the indicator criteria should be presented in terms of clinical indications and contraindications for the selection of a given laboratory product for a given clinical situation or diagnostic grouping. In general terms, criteria for laboratory product selection should answer these questions:

- Was the laboratory product selected when its selection was clinically indicated? Such selection would be appropriate in a disease state.
- Was the laboratory product not selected when its selection was clinically indicated? Such selection would be inappropriate in a disease state.
- Was the laboratory product selected when its selection **was not** clinically indicated? Such selection would be inappropriate in a healthy state.
- The fourth option—the double negative scenario—is a common possibility. Such selection would be appropriate in a healthy state and represents a corollary to the first option.

The determination of appropriateness of selection is based on a complex clinical profile that includes:

- Patient history
- Physical examination findings
- Diagnostic laboratory and radiologic findings
- Current clinical diagnoses
- Therapeutic course
- Postdiagnostic and posttherapeutic clinical and laboratory response.

The laboratory can formulate thresholds, or assurance levels, for laboratory product selection in terms of incidence rates or percentages of occurrence on a local, empirical basis at first. But, governmental, clinical, and laboratory specialty organizations are beginning to create national data banks that should allow for eventual interlaboratory comparison.

To establish a threshold, one must determine how often a provider can be allowed to exceed the criteria for selection of a given laboratory product before professional intervention. The allowed occurrence rate might be 0%—in other words, a sentinel event. Or, it might be a rate-based event—for instance 2% or 5% noncompliance—all depending on the clinical urgency of the patient care scenario and the availability of healthcare resources at hand to monitor, evaluate, and respond to the situation.

Since medical appropriateness of product selection is in question, the resultant QI data needs critiquing by the peer review process. In other words, physicians should provide the ultimate evaluation of laboratory product selection by other physicians. Additionally, other provider types should critique their own peers with physician overview. In the modern CQI environment, it will be interesting to see if the "other" providers eventually will have something to say about physician compliance with laboratory product selection criteria. Then, what type of peer review ultimately should there be to control and assure the selection of laboratory products and services by the patient "self-provider?"

Appropriately trained, authorized nonphysician personnel can assist in gathering the confidential data. The data and subsequent quality management records, however, must be kept strictly confidential, including the public identity of any patient involved or any provider under scrutiny. The feeder report format in this text allows disclosure of the minimal information necessary for documenting and tracking opportunities for improvement, including problems in product selection.

Although it would be ideal to monitor this aspect of care directly, or concurrently, there is no practical mechanism available to do so in most laboratories. For the time being, tracking of laboratory product selection must be a retrospective survey, often in concert with hospital-level utilization review.

Direct monitoring requires an extremely sophisticated, computerized laboratory information system and relational data base management programs that are not yet commonly available. However, it is not far away. As quality surveillance of test need becomes a target of increasing concern, patient care and data management will become more and more automated, clinical data will be increasingly linked to laboratory data, and direct monitoring of laboratory service selection will become a more practical reality.

LABORATORY STRUCTURE MANAGEMENT: OPERATIVE RESOURCE WORK FLOW SEGMENT

At this point of the report format, the operative resource management segment of work flow makes its appearance. As previously mentioned regarding laboratory resources, Donabedian's function of "structure" consists of two general subcategories: operative resources and organizational resources.[21]

- *Operative resources* encompass those laboratory assets that are required by any laboratory activity to accomplish routine day-by-day patient care-oriented and technically-based procedural requirements at the bench or desk top level.
- *Organizational resources* are the administrative management level, infrastructural components that are required to ensure that all laboratory sections function together in an integrated, systemically orchestrated manner.

The following portions of the feeder report (data blocks 15 through 24) address various targets for improving operative resource quality at the level of work flow phase IV.

Indicators. A complete QI program must focus on key aspects of the quality management of the operative resources since these nuts and bolts of laboratory processes directly affect the ultimate quality of the laboratory end product and any resultant customer outcomes—including patient care outcome. Examples of general indicator groupings for monitoring and evaluating the quality of operative resources include:

- Workload management
- Personnel strength
- Productivity measurement
- Personnel utilization
- Continuing professional education and training
- Procedural methods review
- Computer support

- Equipment—instrument and machine—procurement and maintenance
- Supply—expendable and nonexpendable—procurement and storage
- Facility maintenance and renovation/space utilization
- Budget status.

These indicators of operative resource management quality are easily incorporated into the indicator feeder report. They can be monitored and evaluated by means of the JCAHO ten-step process in the very same way as indicators of process and outcome. Monitoring and evaluating operative resource management, however, can be relatively complex. As with the process and outcome indicators, there are many interrelated facets to operative resource quality management. Just remember that each facet is an element of the work flow path and that all phases of the work flow can affect one another in both a feedback and cascade fashion.

Indicator Criteria and Thresholds. There are no nationwide criteria and thresholds for operative resource quality management other than the general JCAHO and CAP accreditation requirements. The clinical expectations for laboratory process and patient care outcomes plus the management expectations for employee safety or other customer-related outcomes should provide a substantial basis for resource quality indicator criteria and thresholds. Unfortunately, many guidelines for operative resource quality management must be based on local empirical determination.

Workload Management

The next eleven data blocks address the fourth phase of the work flow path: operative resource management. As shown in data block 15, work load

15. Workload management:

Workload Indicator (index procedures)	(in raw units) Threshold (quota)	Index Procedure Data Previous Period	Last Period	This Period	Current Raw Count: Weighted Work Load Ratio
a. ______	______	______	______	______	______
b. ______	______	______	______	______	______
c. ______	______	______	______	______	______
d. ______	______	______	______	______	______
Total (in CAP units)	______	______	______	______	______

Potential Shift Opportunity? Yes___ No___ If so, attach analysis per shift.
Evaluation:
Action/Action Person:
Assessment:

comes first. Workload surveillance offers a very logical baseline against which to compare the quality of all other laboratory resources. Workload data is useful as the basis for a number of "yardsticks" for measuring and demonstrating the efficiency and effectiveness of the entire operative resource/process/outcome management system. Thus, AP and CP work load should be carefully managed just as any other operational asset.

Indicators. This portion of the narrative report introduces the fourteenth major indicator grouping. It is advisable to monitor work load on the basis of total workload figures or on a sampling of the overall work load by selecting significant index procedures.

Index procedures are usually those routinely targeted, baseline procedures that are specifically chosen as high-volume, high-risk, or problem-prone. New indices also can arise during routine, scheduled or nonscheduled QI evaluation of any aspect of laboratory resource, operative process, product utilization, or outcome management. These latter *ad hoc* candidates surface as high-priority improvement opportunities or quality management problems.

It is useful to follow the same index procedures for reasonably long periods of time—from three to six months—to establish an adequate data baseline. These indices then can be reviewed on a more broadly scheduled rotating plan, if so desired.

This data block provides space for documenting work load in terms of both raw count and CAP workload weighted units. Tracking these two data points as comparative ratios provides an additional parameter for improvement surveillance. If the ratio between raw count and workload units significantly changes without explanation, there is need to evaluate the method of QI data collection. Also, the possibility of monitoring specific work shifts should always be considered.

Three reporting periods of data can be registered in this block to provide a cumulative record of trends or patterns. Space is available to enter an evaluation of upward or downward levels, trends, or patterns. The amount of space provided for indicator listings, data, evaluation, action, and assessment can be tailored to the needs of the laboratory. However, comments still should be kept as succinct as possible.

Indicator Criteria and Thresholds. There are no nationwide criteria and thresholds for workload management other than the JCAHO accreditation requirements and CAP indices. Increasingly specific examples of workload management guidelines are likely to appear in regulatory form; the criteria established for cytology screener work load by CLIA '88 are a recent example. The CAP workload recording (WLR) program—now curtailed—and laboratory management index program (LMIP) have provided detailed approaches to workload management. Ultimately, however, many workload criteria need establishing locally, predicated on the clinical requirements and available resources.

Regardless of the source of workload standards or control levels, one rule of thumb is that the laboratory manager should compare QI data of like sections only. For example, compare chemistry data to chemistry data; do not compare chemistry data to blood bank data.

A workload threshold for an index procedure can be described as a reasonable range of raw units or of CAP workload units—based on time-weighted or billable (ordered) tests—that can be accomplished with the resources on hand. Below that workload range, the resources at hand will be underutilized. Above that range, the resources at hand will be inordinately stressed to maintain acceptable and safe productivity.

If the observed workload level "exceeds" the threshold for any given index procedure or for all laboratory operations—either falling below or rising above the range limits—then a quality management decision to downgrade, stabilize, or upgrade resources, process, or outcome management should be considered to meet organizational objectives. From the QI administrative level of departmental/service managerial control, all three of the options might be exercised at the same time by shifting assets from one laboratory section to another in order to pursue an opportunity for improvement or solve an operational problem.

If workload variance is a one time occurrence, it is usually disregarded. If the variance continues over the span of several surveillance periods, or shows a continuous trend or pattern of variant (aberrant) levels, then there is reason to consider shifting personnel or other resource assets, cross-training personnel, or routing at least some work load to a reference laboratory. The extent of these decisions rests on the interpretation of a complex combination of cross-referenced, supporting data such as laboratory customer satisfaction, patient care outcome, laboratory safety, TAT/backlog, process indicators, productivity quotients, personnel strength, personnel utilization—or any other indicator groupings related to outcome, resource, and process quality that are significant.

Personnel Strength Management

Data block 16 addresses personnel strength. After work load, personnel are the laboratory's second most crucial operative resource.[a]

Indicators. This portion of the narrative report introduces the fifteenth major indicator grouping. Personnel strength QI data can be reported for any number of important job descriptions—eg, pathologist, supervisor, technologist—for any functional laboratory section or smaller operational laboratory unit. Several other examples of personnel positions are listed in the data block.

Personnel numbers are usually expressed in terms of the full time equivalent (FTE). One FTE represents one employee hired to fill one,

[a] Parenthetically, the budget is so all important an asset that it could be considered in a class of importance all of its own. As such, it warrants being discussed as the operative resource "bottom line" and is presented later as the last operative resource data block.

16. Personnel strength:

Personnel Indicator	# FTE Auth	# FTE On Hand	Net Gain-Loss Now	# of Current Hiring Actions	Threshold % Vacancy	Current % Vacancy	Net Gain-Loss Next Period
Pathologists	____	____	± ____	____	____	____	± ____
Managers	____	____	± ____	____	____	____	± ____
Supervisors	____	____	± ____	____	____	____	± ____
Nurses	____	____	± ____	____	____	____	± ____
Technologists	____	____	± ____	____	____	____	± ____
Technicians	____	____	± ____	____	____	____	± ____
Computer Ops	____	____	± ____	____	____	____	± ____
Secretaries	____	____	± ____	____	____	____	± ____
Receptionists	____	____	± ____	____	____	____	± ____
Maintenance	____	____	± ____	____	____	____	± ____
Supply Ops	____	____	± ____	____	____	____	± ____
Total	____	____	± ____	____	____	____	± ____

Potential Shift Opportunity? Yes___ No___ If so, attach analysis per shift.
Evaluation:
Action/Action Person:
Assessment:

authorized, full time position and expected to accomplish the work load that has been estimated for one full work period. The number of authorized personnel (# FTE Auth) is the number of full time staff positions officially awarded to a given laboratory unit; in the case of this report, the functional unit is the section. The number of authorized personnel on hand (# FTE On Hand) can be expressed as the number of full time staff personnel that are currently filling authorized positions or—in the negative mode—as the percent vacancy of authorized positions (% Vacancy).

Personnel strength can also be described in terms of current or projected net gains or losses (Net Gain-Loss Now or Next Period) and the number of current hiring actions (# of Current Hiring Actions)—as compared to authorized strength. In this case, a net "gain" is really meant to reflect an over hiring; whereas, a net "loss" reflects an under hiring. A net loss should equal the number of ongoing hiring actions.

Indicator Criteria and Thresholds. There are no nationwide criteria and thresholds for personnel strength management other than CLIA, JCAHO, and CAP accreditation requirements, WLR program, and LMIP guidelines. The total number of personnel authorized is usually determined by dividing the total work load by a staffing "yardstick" figure. The typical staffing yardstick represents the estimated, observed, or calculated amount of work that should be performed by one individual during one normal work shift (usually eight hours) for a normal work period (usually one month).

Staffing yardsticks can be fairly accurate criteria if some care is taken in their derivation and use. The calculation of authorized strength should then provide a reliable determination of the number of full time personnel required to operate a given section during its regular working hours, including specific shifts. Well-established national values for staffing criteria or standards are available from the JCAHO and CAP.

Derive the total FTEs on hand by an actual count of employees that are currently hired to work in a given section; then, measure the number of FTEs on hand against the criterion of the total FTEs authorized. The result is the net personnel gain or loss for the period, which is reported as either a positive (gain) or negative (loss) figure. Calculate the percent vacancy rate by dividing the net personnel loss by the total authorized FTEs and multiplying by a 100. Derive the number of current hiring actions, again, by a simple count; it should match any net loss. Space is available to note predicted changes in personnel strength for the next reporting period—usually projecting one to three months in advance.

A meaningful threshold for the percent vacancy rate should imply the "critical mass" of personnel required to complete the work load without significant compromise of patient care outcome and any other management objectives. Any vacancy rate level showing that the work force "mass" is below the threshold implies that there is a significant compromise of the quality of laboratory operations. Usually the laboratory must derive this threshold by an arbitrary, local, empirical decision based on the type of laboratory section at hand, the size of the section, the expected work load, and clinical expectations of laboratory performance.

Section size is a major determinant of critical mass. Consequently, a realistic threshold will usually vary from section to section depending on authorized strength: a larger section has more depth for cross training and substitution. For a larger authorized strength, the realistic threshold for percent vacancy rate might be 10%. For a very small section, the loss of just one individual can be so critical that the threshold might be 0% vacancy rate—in other words, loss of just one employee would be a sentinel event.

The shortage of medical technologists and cytotechnologists has been a nationwide problem in the recent past. This data block provides for an ongoing local commentary on the availability of a laboratory resource that has been increasingly scarce—so scarce that federal regulations have been changed to lighten requirements for certification of medical technology personnel. Such a staffing problem warrants significant organizational attention to recruitment and hiring activities. Administrative assistance in expediting hiring actions must almost always be stressed, requiring timely, aggressive followup. An inordinate delay in hiring should result in a QI evaluation comment with a recommended solution.

It is the personnel strength data block that deserves particular attention as a mechanism to alert management of a potential shift-to-shift maldistribution. Comparative analyses should be made of specific shifts by calculating numbers of FTEs required to accomplish the average work load per shift. It is surprising how often pockets of personnel become sequestered in one shift to the disadvantage of other shifts or sections, without an effective, ongoing surveillance program. One hidden FTE in excess or loss can be a managerial gold mine or an incapacitating albatross.

Productivity Management

Data block 17 addresses productivity measurement. A productivity quotient (PQ) is a typical productivity measurement tool derived from monitoring workload management data. A PQ represents the ratio between two important resource elements: work load to personnel (output to input). The CAP's WLR program provided computerized data management and interlaboratory comparison to its participating members. It was based on time-weighted workload units per worked time. In 1992, the CAP supplanted the WLR with the LMIP, based on billable tests per workforce FTEs.

17. Productivity management:

	Threshold (range)	Previous Period	Last Period	This Period	Trend or Pattern
PQ_p	____-____	________	______	______	________
PQ_w	____-____	________	______	______	________
PQ_{wl}	____-____	________	______	______	________
PQ_t	____-____	________	______	______	________
PQ_a	____-____	________	______	______	________
Workload Ratio	____-____	________	______	______	________

Potential Shift Opportunity? Yes___ No___ If so, attach analysis per shift
Evaluation:
Action/Action Person:
Assessment:

Indicators. This portion of the narrative report introduces the sixteenth major indicator grouping. Productivity management has been in a state of flux. Although no longer a formal program, the WLR remains important as an instructive model. Therefore, the basic precepts of time-weighted productivity measurement are used in this text along with billable test formulas for teaching purposes.

A PQ can be quite indicative of opportunities for improvement, including quality problems of staff management. Five WLR-based quotients have been followed in various laboratories[22,23]:

- Paid productivity (PQ_p)
- Worked productivity (PQ_w)
- Workloaded productivity (PQ_{wl})

- Total productivity (PQ_t)
- Available productivity (PQ_a).

In WLR and LMIP terminology, these quotients are calculated as follows:

$$PQ_p = \frac{\text{Output}}{\text{Input}} = \frac{\text{Work Load}}{\text{Personnel}}$$

$$= \frac{\text{Total Number of CAP Workload Units (in minutes)}}{\text{Total Paid Work Time (in minutes)}}$$

$$\text{or} \quad \frac{\text{Total Number of Billable Tests (in raw count)}}{\text{Total Work Force (in FTEs OR paid time)}}$$

Paid work time equals total paid time for all employees on hand during the reporting period. Paid time includes workload-weighted, nonworkload-weighted, and employee benefit time. The calculation of total paid work time amounts to X hours (per day) times N days (per work month) times the number of authorized FTEs on hand during the work month. The number of work hours per day or per week varies from one institution to another; 8 hours per day is used here as a common example.

As depicted in the above formula, the general definition of a PQ is the ratio of the work load to be accomplished compared to the number of personnel available to do the work. It is usual to measure productivity during a standard unit of time, usually a work hour. Thus the manager tracks productivity in terms of work hours, or converts the hours to work minutes, depending on personal preference. Also, one can express productivity in terms of percent productivity—that is as percent of a work hour.

PQ_p is the most broad based quotient since it embodies so many work related and nonwork-related elements. Therefore, this general measurement is most difficult to interpret as an indicator of probable workload stress.

$$PQ_w = \frac{\text{Total Number of CAP Workload Units (in minutes)}}{\text{Total Paid Work Time - Total Benefit Time (in minutes)}}$$

$$\text{or} \quad \frac{\text{Total Number of Billable Tests (in raw count)}}{\text{Total Actual Worked Time (in minutes)}}$$

Benefit time equals all authorized vacation, holiday, sick leave, compensatory time used, administrative absence (if the absence is for nonjob-related activity), and any other paid benefit time away from work. This PQ reflects the impact of paid employees' benefits on productivity.

Although these forms of authorized leave reflect officially paid time provided to the employee as work benefits, it is nonproductive time—in microeconomic terms, equivalent to an indirect, variable cost. After the subtraction of nonproductive employee benefit time from the total paid work time, all that should remain is work-related activities, both workload-weighted "bench work" and nonweighted support work, such as instruction and management. The latter support work is not truly "productive" in bench-level or microeconomic terms but is still considered directly related to effective productivity. When the PQ_w becomes inordinately elevated, the usual implication is that the work load is so stressful that the nonweighted work of support activities is often selectively ignored and paid short shrift.

$$PQ_{wl} = \frac{\text{Total Number of CAP Workload Units (in minutes)}}{\text{Total Paid Work Time - [Total Benefits Time + Nonworkloaded Time](min)}}$$

$$\text{or} \quad \frac{\text{Total Number of Billable Tests (in raw count)}}{\text{Total Actual Bench-Related Worked Time (in minutes)}}$$

Initially, PQ_{wl} was known as PQ_s or "specified" productivity. Nonworkloaded time (nonspecified time) equals work time that is spent performing official, nonworkload-weighted, usually nontechnical work.

Nonworkloaded time includes administrative or managerial tasks—such as quality management, education, and training. This work-related (but not truly bench work) time is considered as productive time, but it does it not contribute directly to truly workload-weighted, technical process-related productivity. An extensive list of nonworkloaded activities was provided by the CAP WLR manual—budget preparation, performance evaluations, inservice education, professional organizational meetings, and quality management are just a few of the many nonworkloaded activities that are still recognized. Nonworkloaded activities represent 22% to 30% of total laboratory staff paid work time.[22,24]

With benefit time and nonworkloaded time subtracted out, PQ_{wl} is a particularly sensitive indicator of staff overwork or stress since it specifically targets CAP workload-weighted (bench level) productivity. The nonworkload-weighted activities that have been removed to calculate PQ_{wl} provide some added flexibility in managerial interpretation of the other two quotients.

Note that the output numerator (total CAP workload units or billable tests) remains a constant in all three of the above calculations. Also, the denominator progressively diminishes from PQ_p to PQ_w to PQ_{wl}—that is, the paid time denominator becomes an increasingly precise measurement of technical work-related activities. As the denominator becomes smaller, the overall PQ increases in relative absolute value.

Two additional measurements of productivity were included in the CAP WLR program: total productivity (PQ_t) and available productivity (PQ_a). The CAP suggested that these two new parameters replace PQ_{wl}.[25]

$$PQ_t = \frac{\text{Total CAP Workloaded Time + Total Nonworkloaded Time (min)}}{\text{Total Paid Work Time (min)}}$$

$$PQ_a = \frac{\text{Total CAP Workloaded Time + Total Nonworkloaded time (min)}}{\text{Total Paid Work Time - Total Benefit Time (min)}}$$

Table II
Comparison of Productivity Quotients

Operational Description	Section Example	Quotient Level	Expected Productivity Quotients		
			PQ_p	PQ_w	PQ_{wl}
■ **Low work load-maximum work time section:**					
• 7 days/week • 24 hours (3 shifts) • Lowest workload volume • Manually intensive • Lowest productivity quotient values	• Blood bank • Stat lab • Immunology	Low	20-35	30-40	35-45
■ **Moderate work load-moderate work time section:**					
• 6-7 days/week • 16 hours (2 shifts) • Moderate workload volume • Still manually intensive but more automated or semi-automated • Moderate productivity quotient values	• Microbiology • Histology	Medium	30-40	35-45	40-50
■ **High work load-minimum work time section:**					
• 5 days/week • 8 hours (1 shift) • Night and weekend work done by stat lab • Highest workload volume • Most tasks are very repetitive • Most automated • Highest productivity quotient values	• Chemistry • Hematology • Cytology	High	35-45	40-50	45-55

In the two latter quotients, the output numerator remained constant but expressed total (workloaded and nonworkloaded) output in a given reporting period—compared to the workloaded (only) output numerator of the first three quotients. Expressed in such terms, these two parameters provided a more complete, true measurement of productivity and were accepted in lieu of PQ_{wl}. They provided an opportunity to quantify nonworkloaded activities. The LMIP does not address these two parameters since the numerators incorporate managerial work time unmeasured by the LMIP.

A "workload ratio" can also be used as a QI parameter. As expressed in the 1991 CAP Workload Recording Manual, it was calculated as follows[22]:

$$\text{Workload Ratio} = \frac{\text{Variable Hours x 100}}{\text{Variable + Constant Hours}}$$

where variable hours equal CAP workload-weighted hours and constant hours equal nonworkloaded hours. Again, the LMIP does not address this management parameter.

Indicator Criteria and Thresholds. There are no nationwide criteria and thresholds for productivity other than the general JCAHO and CAP accreditation requirements, productivity guidelines, and PQ ranges published for various laboratory functional sections (such as the AABB).

It is not reasonable to narrow a PQ down to exact criteria levels. It is more meaningful to define productivity in terms of threshold ranges or assurance levels, usually with a ten point spread. It is important to note that the range for any given quotient (paid, worked, workloaded, total, or available) will vary from one functional type of section to another—whether determined on the basis of time-weighted or test volume-weighted data. As is seen by the methods of calculation, there is a natural tendency for the threshold ranges to increase from PQ_p to PQ_w to PQ_{wl} and from PQ_t to PQ_a—or their billable test-based equivalents.

General threshold ranges for three example levels of laboratory productivity are compared in Table II. Using the "low work load-maximum work time" type of section as an example, the threshold for PQ_p is "exceeded" if the quotient reaches below 20 or above 35 minutes of productive time in 60 minutes of total paid work time. The average PQ_t is 44 to 48 minutes per paid hour or 73 to 83%. The average PQ_a is 53 to 57 minutes per paid hour or 90 to 95%. The normal workload ratio ranges from 65 to 75%.[24] The LMIP is providing similar benchmark ranges based on billable test data.

Personnel Utilization Management

Data block 18 addresses a potpourri of personnel management QI indicators aimed at measuring the quality of employee utilization. Singly, they are of limited usefulness. Combined, they can provide very supportive evidence in assessing the adequacy of personnel distribution, scheduling, and productivity and, thus, unmask opportunities to improve overall personnel staffing.

18. Personnel utilization:

		Hours			#16 Hr	
		Paid	Comp	Nonspec	Double	
Indicators:	% Avail	Overtime	Time	Duty	Shifts	Other
Threshold:	______	______	______	______	______	______
a. Technologists	______	______	______	______	______	______
b. Clerical	______	______	______	______	______	______
c. Other	______	______	______	______	______	______

Potential Shift Problem?: Yes___ No___ If so, attach analysis per shift
Evaluation:
Action/Action Person:
Assessment:

Indicators. This portion of the narrative report introduces the seventeenth major indicator grouping. One can align the various quality indicators in this utilization grouping against any imaginable assortment of employee types; the example data block lists only two, plus "other." Calculate the first indicator, percent availability, as follows:

$$\text{Percent Availability} = \frac{\text{Paid Work Hours - Total Work Hours Lost x 100}}{\text{Total Paid Work Hours}}$$

$$= \frac{\text{Net Hours of Actual Availability for Work x 100}}{\text{Gross Hours Scheduled To Be Worked}}$$

Net hours of availability = number of work days in the work period
x 8 hours per day
x number of FTE assigned
- all annual leave, sick leave, holiday hours exercised and, therefore, not worked

Gross hours = number of work days in the period
x 8 hours per day
x number of FTE assigned

The derivation and surveillance value of paid overtime, compensated (nonpaid) overtime, and nonspecified duty hours are straightforward and self-explanatory. The number of double (16 hour back-to-back) shifts is a particularly valuable statistic that can indicate staff overwork, potential or real staff "burnout," need for additional personnel, need for shifting of work load, or possible supervisory mismanagement. As can be imagined, there are other utilization indicators that can be designed for special QI surveillance circumstances, such as targeting the use of specific types of employee leave. The QI data for percent availability, paid overtime, compensated overtime, nonspecified work hours, and double shifts are also very helpful in supporting, analyzing, and interpreting employee staffing and productivity measurements.

As can be said for any other indicator grouping, all data points are only as reliable as the accuracy of collection and calculation. This is true for all QI indicators, but seems particularly true for workload recording, productivity quotients, and personnel utilization.

Indicator Criteria and Thresholds. There are no nationwide criteria and thresholds for personnel utilization other than the general JCAHO accreditation requirements and CAP workload guidelines for staffing. The laboratory must empirically derive the criteria and thresholds for the utilization indicators that are described here. Examples are listed in the following block.

	Ideal Criteria	Suggested Thresholds
Percent availability	Locally determined	80% and > 90%
Paid overtime	Zero paid overtime	> 10% of regularly scheduled working hours (total authorized work time)
Nonspecified duty time	Locally determined	<10% of regularly scheduled working hours
Compensated overtime	Zero "comp" overtime	Any occurrence (sentinel event)
Double shifts	Zero double shifts	Any occurrence (sentinel event)

A reasonable threshold for percent availability is < 80% to > 90%—a good example of a threshold that is expressed as a low-high range. Strictly an empirical decision, the range can vary depending on the laboratory section's authorized personnel strength, work load, and patient care mission.

On one hand, it is an unfavorable sign if staff availability drops below the 80% level. Data below that threshold suggest that an inordinate amount of annual leave, holiday hours, or sick leave is being exercised. Such a situation can be linked to poor scheduling on the part of a supervisor—that is, scheduling too many employees to take regular or holiday leave at the same time. However, in the face of excessive work load, it can also be caused by deteriorating employee morale with excessive leave being requested—especially sick leave. In the latter scenario, availability can be a predictive factor for staff burn out.

On the other hand, if availability exceeds 90%, then there is a possibility that employees are sacrificing their personal leave time to process an excessive amount of work load. Although an indicator of outstanding morale, too high a percent availability could also be a warning of staff overwork, stress, ultimate loss of productivity, and eventual attrition of personnel. With a normal amount of work load, if the staff is not taking its deserved leave, there is still a set up for growing fatigue, increasing mistakes, reduced quality, and ultimately decreased retention of employees. The latter scenario might denote poor supervisory management.

The laboratory can also empirically derive thresholds for the other utilization indicators.

- Regarding paid overtime, the threshold can be based on whatever number of paid work hours equals a 10% vacancy rate for the given section. Any excess of paid overtime can be a sign of over work and potential staff stress. In a tight fiscal situation, this indicator can be considered a sentinel event.
- Nonspecified (nonworkload-weighted) duty time is a similar type of indicator. If nonspecified time drops below 10% of the total authorized work time, then there is an indication that time allotted to management—including quality management—and continuing professional education activities is not being made available for these important supportive activities.

Compensated (nonpaid) extra duty time and double shifts can be treated as sentinel events where any occurrence serves as a red flag for investigative evaluation. The occurrence of either of these two indicators denotes the possibility of 1) excessive work load and employee fatigue or 2) mismanagement.

The above grouping of personnel utilization indicators demonstrates only one set of many possible choices. As for any grouping in this report format, many new indicators come to light in the process of QI surveillance. For example, measuring cost-effectiveness or product utilization is also possible.

Data blocks 19 and 20 appear together because they offer complementary information. Often, they can be supporting evidence for other personnel strength and productivity indicators. At the same time, the two subject indicator topics are of significant importance in their own right. Block 19 offers information on the quality of professional education and training; block 20 presents data reflecting the quality of review of procedural methods.

Continuing Education Management

Indicators. Data block 19 introduces the eighteenth major indicator grouping. Continuing medical (healthcare) education and training includes any instruction needed to maintain and upgrade any diagnostic, technical, clerical, managerial, or other required laboratory proficiency or skill. This program should orchestrate instruction that is provided both internally and externally to the laboratory. The intent of this ongoing instructional program is to keep all personnel up-to-date and proficient in their respective professional fields. This program is required for JCAHO and CAP accreditation.

19. Continuing medical education, training, and professional competence:

Education/Training/Competence Indicator	Threshold	Observation
a. ______	______	______
b. ______	______	______
c. ______	______	______
d. ______	______	______

Potential Shift Opportunity? Yes__ No__ If so, attach analysis per shift
Evaluation:
Action/Action Person:
Assessment:

Operative-level instruction does not include education and training in support of quality improvement, quality anticipation, and quality actualization. The latter programs shepherd their own instructional components—as is described later.

An indicator of operative education and training quality should ensure that the instructional effort is being made according to plan and that the effort is effective. One monitoring target is the instruction schedule: does an up-to-date schedule exist; is it being followed? It is important to include all work shifts in the monitoring of this instructional indicator grouping.

A second possible QI target is the primary product of the instructional program: employee competence. Operative instructional effectiveness should correspond to the resultant level of improved employee expertise. Some attempt should be made to measure that resultant combination of improved understanding and manual/visual facility through various testing instruments and to track those results by appropriate quality indicators. Proficiency testing results also indicate laboratory staff education, training, and resultant expertise.

Education and training are inextricably cross-linked with all other indicators of operative quality—for all interpretive, technical, and nontechnical laboratory activities at all levels of operative resource, process, and outcome management. In turn, instructional quality corresponds to indicators of internal (eg, QC and peer control) and external (eg, proficiency testing) quality management. Instructional indicators also relate to any indicator of nonspecified duty time productivity.

Methods and Procedures Management

Data block 20 introduces the nineteenth major indicator grouping. The quality of the review of procedural methods is another indicator that cuts across all laboratory operative activities—very similar to the scope of the instructional indicator: the written procedures are renewable scripts for practicing professional expertise. Thus, procedural review is exceedingly germane to maintaining total laboratory quality, including all operative resource management, all technical and nontechnical process, and all outcome management.

20. Procedural methods review:

	Review Indicator	Milestone Date	Threshold	Observation
a.				
b.				
c.				
d.				

Evaluation:
Action/Action Person:
Assessment:

Indicators. It is a requirement for the CAP and other accrediting organizations that all written procedural methods (also called the procedural manual, standing operating procedures, or SOPs) must undergo annual review. However, this policy does not mean that the written procedures are expected to be reviewed all at once at the end of the review year. Nor does it mean that all written procedures have to be completely retyped and pristine clean of handwritten notations. The policy means that there must be evidence of appropriate managerial level review ensuring that the operative guidelines are up-to-date, complete, legible (even with signed and dated handwritten annotation), and accessible by the appropriate employees.

Therefore, at every laboratory unit level (using the section as an example), it is helpful to divide and schedule the review of the written procedures on a monthly basis throughout the year. A realistic approach is to divide the total procedures into tenths, reviewing them over a scheduled ten month period, and leaving two nonscheduled months to allow for mid-winter holidays, mid-summer vacations, and review finalization. The review plan should be clearly scheduled and maintained on an ongoing basis. Spreading the requirements over such a broad period allows the review to be a substantive study of each method—not just a perfunctory perusal and meaningless signature on a universal cover sheet.

Indicator Criteria and Thresholds. Aside from the fact that JCAHO and CAP accreditation requirements mandate that both medical instruction and procedural review must be adequately maintained, there are no other, more precise national level standards. However, in the eyes of an accreditation surveyor, measurement of compliance to accreditation requirements (ie, conformance to quality design specifications) should amount to an all-or-none situation.

Therefore, take the same approach at the local level as the laboratory appraises its instructional and procedural maintenance processes. Plan and coordinate both instructional and procedure review schedules with serious intent on maintaining regular, ongoing programs. Any variance from a training schedule or procedural review milestone should warrant immediate investigative evaluation.

Information Management

Data block 21 addresses the quality of computer support. The computer has become inseparable from the modern, high-tech laboratory. Data automation has become an answer to the laboratorian's organizational prayer: finally, we have the means to build a reliable laboratory nerve center for data and information generation, transmission, and storage.

21. Computer support (specify total unscheduled down time in hours/days):

	Support Indicator	Threshold	Observation
a.			
b.			
c.			
d.			

Evaluation:
Action/Action Person:
Assessment:

First and foremost, laboratorians with adequate computer support can effectively communicate internally and externally with all laboratory customers-suppliers. Computer systems can generate, organize, utilize, and store data with lightening speed. An automated monitoring system is in place that will signal the occurrence of a critical clinical value or an outlying control value amidst the potentially hundreds or thousands of daily specimens and tens of thousands of daily data points. Of great importance, such a system can carry on the brunt of QC and QI monitoring and real time data analysis—allowing the laboratorian to more effectively coordinate and perform activities directly related to patient care.

Indicators. This portion of the narrative report introduces the twentieth major indicator grouping. What if the computer system fails because of some electrical, mechanical, or programming mishap? Then, the backup system usually is a reversion to manual data management methods—which have become archaic. Manual entry represents extra, unscheduled work load, usually with fewer FTEs available than can accomplish the extra task in the regularly scheduled time that is available. And, even after the computer is back on line, there still might be need for additional manual entry of backlogged data into the archival files—another stressful task under inadequately staffed conditions.

Consequently, a reasonable indicator of the quality of computer support is unscheduled time of nonavailability—computer downtime. The quality of system security as protection against software "viruses" and unauthorized tampering with patient records is another possible indicator. Many other indicators can be identified, depending on the nature of the local data automation system and its unique clinical, technical, and managerial requirements. For example, a large number of components of the computer system demand quality management, including printers, disk drives, and software programs. Look for opportunities to improve computer program relational data base capability, internal and external linkage (eg, computer-to-instrument or computer-to-printer/terminal or computer-to-computer), and general software program updating.

Indicator Criteria and Thresholds. Again, specific criteria or standards for computer support quality management are not currently available at the national level except for the requirements established for JCAHO and CAP accreditation. Many of these amount to the all-or-none criterion of a sentinel event.

The threshold for significant downtime also tends to be very arbitrary, needing local formulation. For example, the tolerable extent of unscheduled computer downtime can be limited to some empirically derived number of FTEs. How many personnel can be spared to:

- Manually generate and distribute laboratory results while the computer is inoperable?
- Manually enter backlogged results into the rejuvenated computer archives after the computer shut down or "crash" has been resolved?

Answers depend on the work load, staffing, and computerization characteristics of the given section. Those sections that are more heavily automated will be more dependent on the data management system and will have lower thresholds of tolerance for unscheduled computer downtime.

Equipment Management

Data block 22 addresses the quality of equipment management. This twenty-first major indicator grouping is concerned with the selection, procurement, and maintenance support of all equipment and includes both capital and noncapital expense items.

22. Equipment procurement and maintenance (capital/noncapital expense items):

	Equipment Indicator	Threshold (delay)	Observation
a.			
b.			
c.			
d.			

Evaluation:
Action/Action Person:
Assessment:

Indicators. Surveillance of the quality of equipment resources should begin with selection and procurement. This concern is especially important in regard to high-volume, high-cost instruments that must withstand extensive normal wear and tear and still produce consistently accurate and reproducible results, day in and day out.

On one hand, equipment quality management requires patience and a sense for long-range planning. Thus, equipment selection is one of several quality management issues that should be linked to planning (ie, QAn) activities. On the other hand, a common short term indicator is unscheduled equipment downtime. Monitoring the total time required for maintenance or repair is another way of looking at this quality surveillance issue. This indicator can be specifically defined as any malfunctioning instrument requiring repair over an inordinate amount of time—the length of time depending on the extent of repair; availability of replacement parts; and local, joint policy between laboratory, clinical, and medical maintenance personnel.

There is linkage between equipment management indicators and indicators of analytical and diagnostic quality. For example, the need for maintenance, repair, or replacement can be discovered or corroborated through the surveillance of determinative QC. Also, process TAT or backlog will increase if no backup instrument is available and laboratory throughput is significantly impeded.

Another subset of equipment indicators concerns safety. Various instruments and other pieces of equipment require special precautions so that employees avoid blunt or sharp trauma, electrical shock, inhalation of toxins and caustics, and burning.

Indicator Criteria and Thresholds. There are no specific criteria for equipment quality management available on a nationwide basis other than the general OSHA/FDA/JCAHO/CAP/AABB inspection requirements. More specific criteria must be established locally.

Threshold levels will also be quite empirical, usually derived by averaging baseline TATs. This is an issue of laboratory-clinical tolerance: how long can the laboratory or clinical staff wait for parts delivery, maintenance, or repair to be completed? For example, one QI reporting period could be the maximum acceptable downtime before a piece of equipment is returned from servicing. Beyond that time frame, some special coordinative action between the laboratory and medical maintenance is necessary. The length of the reporting period is then chosen accordingly; usually it is no greater than one to three months.

Supply Management

Data block 23 addresses the twenty-second major indicator grouping which covers the quality of supply management. This grouping is concerned with the selection, procurement (or preparation), storage, and inventory maintenance of all supplies, including both nonexpendable and expendable items.

23. Supply procurement and storage (nonexpendable/expendable items):

	Supply Indicator	Threshold (delay)	Observation
a.	____________	________	__________
b.	____________	________	__________
c.	____________	________	__________
d.	____________	________	__________

Evaluation:
Action/Action Person:
Assessment:

Indicators. The surveillance of the quality of supplies is similar to that for equipment. Individual indicators are identified by the description of the supply item and the quality under scrutiny. Supply delivery time and other aspects of supply quality after delivery, such as inventory shelf life, are typical targets for monitoring. These indicators are fairly straightforward but require a well-organized inventory and storage control data base at the operative QC level. One special aspect of supply quality concerns safety. Various chemical and biological supplies require special handling and storage to prevent hazardous contamination, inhalation, poisoning, caustic burning, fire, and explosion. All of these issues are targets for quality surveillance and are likely to warrant sentinel event status.

Another, unique subset of supply indicators revolves around the preparation and storage of transfusion (eg, blood components) and transplant (eg, bone marrow) tissue substances. On one hand, these usually fit into the category of laboratory end products. On the other hand, they fit into the category of clinical resources (supplies) to be applied for therapeutic purposes. These materials are unique in that the quality of preparation and storage can have direct, immediate, and life threatening effect on patient health. The preparation, handling, and storage of these substances offer targets for quality surveillance and usually warrant sentinel event status.

Indicator Criteria and Thresholds. There are no specific nationwide criteria for supply management other than general and safety-oriented OSHA/FDA/JCAHO/CAP/AABB inspection and accreditation requirements. Local, empirical criteria will need establishing. For example, baseline studies can generate average, routine and special order, supply delivery times. The laboratory can then create inventory criteria on the basis of the average delivery baseline data, clinical work load, and shelf life requirements.

The determination of thresholds can be based on clinical and operative resource contingencies. For example, it could be laboratory policy that all supply deliveries must be made within the established average time frame; that would be a 100%, zero defects supply delivery indicator. As an alternative comparative rate approach, only a certain percentage of deliveries for certain supplies might be expected to meet a given delivery time threshold. If that threshold is exceeded, then investigative evaluation is required as an immediate QI follow-up.

Facility Management

Data block 24 addresses the quality of facility and working environment management. This indicator grouping is primarily concerned with the maintenance, repair, and renovation of the laboratory facility, or working environment, including both capital and noncapital expense projects. Safety and space utilization are important subsidiary considerations here.

Indicators. This introduces the twenty-third major indicator grouping. The laboratory can identify appropriate quality indicators for facility design that require special scrutiny, including maintenance, repair, or renovation. Structural environmental factors such as fire control, electrical control, temperature control, ventilation (including positive and negative air balance), hood flow (including positive and negative air flow), lighting, and physical and personnel security are of particular importance. Several of the components listed here are integral to employee safety and serve as supporting evidence for the earlier mentioned topic of laboratory safety in work flow phase XIV.

24. Facility/working environment maintenance, repair, renovation, and space utilization (capital/noncapital expense items):

	Facility Indicator	Threshold (delay)	Observation
a.	______	______	______
b.	______	______	______
c.	______	______	______
d.	______	______	______

Evaluation:
Action/Action Person:
Assessment:

Facility space is one of the most coveted resources in a laboratory—few assets stimulate the visceral emotions of territorial imperative more readily. Still, space is almost always finite and allocation must be judicious. Often, changes in laboratory mission or method will dictate reassignment of space. Work flow and safety must be a part of any new space utilization design. Consequently, it is best for the organization to openly evaluate and decide on space allocation, using as participative a team process as possible. Thus, space management is an excellent candidate as a general QI indicator in this grouping.

Surveillance of the quality of facility management often requires the longest range of quality management perspectives because of the relatively long time required to accomplish the larger quality improvement projects. This temporal variable fluctuates widely depending on the scope of maintenance, repair, renovation, or even building anew. Again, we have a definite linkage between this indicator grouping, and those of the QI, QAn and QAc programs.

Indicator Criteria and Thresholds. There are very few nationwide criteria for facility management other than general and safety-oriented OSHA/FDA/JCAHO/CAP/AABB inspection and accreditation requirements. Other, specific criteria include federal, state, and local regulations, and these are often written into an architectural design, construction contract, or maintenance contract.

As with indicator criteria, performance thresholds are often written into a facility maintenance or construction contract. Otherwise, threshold determination is a local quality surveillance decision, usually empirically derived with very little or no baseline data available for reference. This is where the medical director or laboratory manager often has to make a judgment based on personal experience. If a threshold is not met, then there must be appropriate coordination and follow-up with the facility engineers, the facility contract management office, or the contractor.

Financial Management

Data block 25 addresses the quality of budget management. This twenty-fourth major indicator grouping is concerned with the adequacy of funding, allocating, dispensing, and spending of the laboratory budget, including management of all expense categories.

25. Budget management:

Budget Indicator	Non-Allocated	Allocated (contracts)	AIDS	CME	Total
a. % FY Completed (threshold)	______	______	____	____	____
b. Total $ Budgeted	______	______	____	____	____
c. $ Obligated by Contract	______	______	____	____	____
d. Total Nonobligated Expenditures	______	______	____	____	____
e. Total Expenditures (c + d)	______	______	____	____	____
f. % Budget Balance Expended (e divided by b x 100)	______	______	____	____	____
g. Projected $ Needed	______	______	____	____	____

Evaluation:
Action/Action Person:
Assessment:

Indicators. Although the budget is last on this listing of operative resource indicator groupings, it provides the appropriate fiscal "bottom line" of operative resources. As previously mentioned, the budget is almost in a resource class by itself because it is probably the single most important resource item: the quality of every other resource category hinges on adequate funding.

The choices of indicators will vary widely, depending on local budgeting practices. There are also likely to be special issues, that vary over time as indicators of importance. The example given in the data block, above, offers nonallocated (noncontractual), allocated (contractual), specific disease support (AIDS), and continuing medical education (CME) accounts as specified budget "line item" indicators. Even quality management budget figures could appear here; show the cost benefits of TQM and CQI.

Indicator Criteria and Thresholds. There are no nationwide criteria for budget quality management other than general JCAHO accreditation requirements. More specific criteria are usually available through local hospital or funding agency policy. Examples of indicator criteria for a controlled budget are that the:

- Working budget for each section should remain positively balanced during the course of the fiscal year on a monthly basis
- Overall budget at the department level should be at a positive balance by the end of the fiscal year.

These two criteria may seem identical but they can differ significantly in terms of their respective thresholds.

Thresholds for indicators of budget control quality should provide some managerial flexibility during the course of a fiscal year—as opposed to the more rigid indicator criteria that must be met at the end of the year. One useful working threshold can be expressed in terms of the percent of the budget expended compared to the percent of the fiscal year that has expired at the given reporting date. As used in this text, the amount of budget expended can be allowed to vary within a working range of ± 5% of the percent of the fiscal year expired. The latter range or spread is strictly an empirical decision and depends on local managerial discretion and operational budgeting constraints.

For example, if the QI reporting date is 30 June in a January to December fiscal year, then 50% of the planned budget should be expended and 50% of the fiscal year has expired. If the threshold for expended funds is a range of ± 5% of the planned expenditure, then the threshold range for 30 June will be 45% to 55% expenditure of the budget.

A working budget can be applied to individual sections. Its flexibility lies in the fact that section budgets can be balanced against each other on a department-wide scale. If a section encounters difficulty in meeting its ± 5% threshold and dips below that objective into a negative balance, the loss can be recouped from other sections. Thus, the overall goal to have a positive departmental balance at the end of the fiscal year is still possible. Therefore, the end-of-the-year threshold for the entire department could be a sentinel event, stated in a way that the balance must be positively balanced. A specific fiscal gain also could be added into the threshold at the section or departmental level. For example, the threshold for the end-of-the-year departmental budgetary balance must be ≥ 5%; any balance below a 5% gain must be investigated.

If budgetary constraints demand tighter control, the thresholds for the interim, working budget review periods also can be based on tighter adherence to budget design specifications. For example, the plan could require a consistently positive balance in every section.

In the evaluation of such expenditure indicator figures, consider the type of accounting system used. Remember that in a closed (forecasted) system, contractual costs can be "front loaded" with the brunt of the expenditures being made at the time of contractual renewals in the beginning of the first quarter of the fiscal year. In an open (reimbursable) system, such contractual "front loading" is not a major factor.

LABORATORY STRUCTURE MANAGEMENT: ORGANIZATIONAL RESOURCE WORK FLOW SEGMENT

As Donabedian has described, organizational resources include all administrative management components of the laboratory infrastructure that are required to integrate the functioning of all operative sections and other internal and external operational activities.[21] As this text emphasizes, the administrative infrastructure includes three specific managerial programs: quality improvement, quality anticipation, and quality actualization.

These three programs are crucially important in fostering an effective TQM operational system and CQI cultural process. Therefore, it is necessary to monitor the quality of these programs, including the overall improvement of each program. Surveillance of the quality and improvement of each program is addressed in the following portions of the QI feeder report.

Quality Improvement (QI) Work Flow Phase

Internal Quality Improvement Management

There are two components to the QI program: internal and external surveillance. Data block 26 introduces the quality assessment and improvement work flow segment. Internal QI management is defined as monitoring and evaluating the organization's own QI program and is performed by peers inside the laboratory. Therefore, this data block addresses the effectiveness and improvement of the internal QI program—the very program that is responsible for monitoring and evaluating the quality and improvement of all other operational activities.

26. Internal organizational quality surveillance:

	Internal QI Indicator	Threshold	Observation
a.	____________	________	____________
b.	____________	________	____________
c.	____________	________	____________
d.	____________	________	____________

Evaluation:
Action/Action Person:
Assessment:

The laboratory should provide evidence of its ability to monitor its own methods of improving operative and organizational quality. The monitoring and evaluating of all laboratory operations is considered in the overall program report—the feeder report helping to accomplish that purpose. This particular data block provides specific comment on the quality of the internal surveillance program based on QI surveillance of the QI program.

Indicators. This portion of the narrative report introduces the twenty-fifth major indicator grouping. How does one check on the checker or monitor the monitoring? Or evaluate the evaluator? Can it be legitimately done without an accusation being made that the fox is guarding the chicken coop—that is, that there is undue conflict of interest, bias, or prejudice? In a professional organization with proper documentation, yes, it can be done. It has to be done.

Such internal review is absolutely necessary for the TQM system and CQI process to be complete. The laboratory must select QI indicators that will reflect evidence that the quality surveillance program is, indeed, monitoring operational quality effectively and is, itself, improving continuously. To help identify such indicators—ask the same questions that would be expected of an inspector about to tackle the same task:

- First, is there a laboratory quality surveillance program plan?
  - Has the plan been *reviewed* and *updated* in the past year?
  - Has it been *distributed* to all functional laboratory sections and activities?
- Second, is there a formal, analytical QI process in use?
  - Using Shewhart's P-D-C-A cycle and the JCAHO *ten-step process* as primary examples, is the improvement process an integral part of the surveillance program?
  - Has there been recent review of the planning steps of that process with evidence of *systematic revision* of the essential QI components such as responsibilities, scope, important aspects, indicators, and thresholds?
  - Is the laboratory identifying new quality indicators through scheduled indicator monitoring and follow-up of *other QI indicator sources* such as incident reports, complaints, and customer advisory or other hospital-wide committee findings?
- Third, does the QI process emphasize a representative team approach using statistical tools of analysis?
  - Is there a *regular schedule* of QI committee or team meetings?
  - Is the QI committee or team membership *representative* of the laboratory quality management focus?
- Fourth, is there an ongoing education and training program aimed at instructing all employees in the state-of-the-art quality assessment and improvement, including:
  - the QI *plan*

- the QI *process*
- team *methods*
- analytical *tools*?

■ Fifth, is there evidence of ongoing indicator data collection.
  - Is there a laboratory indicator *monitoring schedule*?
  - Is the laboratory *following the schedule*?

■ Sixth, is there regular, ongoing exercising of the EvAAC limb of the surveillance process?

■ Seventh, is there evidence of adequate follow-up of lessons learned from the QI process?
  - Has there been any *operative improvement* in the form of new quality indicators, written procedures, methods, processes, policies, instructional topics, structure, or other operative changes?
  - Has there been any *organizational improvement* at some functional level during any work flow phase?

■ Eighth, does the laboratory adequately communicate the lessons learned from the QI program?
  - Has the laboratory communicated with all individuals and other groups—*all customers-suppliers*—who have any need to know?
  - Are *complete, uniformly formatted* QI data files, feeder reports, profiles, and committee/team minutes readily accessible?

■ Ninth, have the first eight questions provided any means of improving the QI program, itself?
  - In the course of monitoring the QI program, if there have been no opportunities to improve the program, has there been any reevaluation of the *quality improvement process*?
  - Is there a *continuous pattern* of improvement of the QI plan and process?

Answers to these questions should produce quality indicators to adequately monitor the overall QI program.

Indicator Criteria and Thresholds. There are no nationwide criteria or thresholds for monitoring internal quality surveillance programs other than the general JCAHO and CAP accreditation requirements and the *Agenda for Change*. Therefore, it often will be necessary to empirically establish indicator criteria (standards) and thresholds (investigative levels) at the lowest local level. Substantiate these surveillance guidelines on the best data base possible and—as usual— always have the background evidence on file to show their source or derivation.

The measurement of success for an internal quality surveillance program should center on evidence of effectiveness of the internal QI plan and process—as well as continuous improvement of the overall program. On most occasions, the criteria and thresholds will represent sentinel events, often presented as all-or-none statements—ie, yes or no; present or absent. For example, how does one measure if there is or is not an improvement plan or process? Either there is one or there is not one. How does one measure improvement of the program? Either there is evidence of substantive improvement or there is not.

All the QI indicators will begin in this general manner. However, as the surveillance of continuous improvement progresses, more specific, focused indicators will emerge.

Attempting to accurately measure and grade the degree of compliance to such quality surveillance requirements is unnecessary. It is a pattern of continuity that is most important. Instead of constantly striving for the one big improvement, establish a pattern of many small wins. Look on small accomplishments as giant steps toward continuous improvement. Create and sustain a pattern of learning and success that is consistent and systematic.

External Quality Improvement Management

Data blocks 27 through 29 address the external component of the quality improvement work flow. External quality surveillance, which is a subset of the overall QI program in work flow phase III, is defined as the monitoring and evaluating of the quality of a laboratory's overall operations, as provided by peers outside the laboratory.

Indicators. There are at least three major indicator groupings of interest regarding external quality surveillance. These include external inspections, proficiency surveys, and incident reports.

First, external inspections—the twenty-sixth major grouping—are routine experiences for healthcare laboratories. Many regulatory, licensing, accrediting, and certifying organizations perform on-site surveys, including OSHA, FDA, HCFA, JCAHO, CAP, AABB, other professional organizations, and various state agencies. Many of these programs are described as "voluntary" in nature, but in reality, they are mandatory if a laboratory wants to do business.

These surveys are usually on-site visitations, but they can also be in the form of an interim self-inspection, using an externally derived inspection checklist. In fact, completion of the CAP interim self-inspection is mandatory to satisfy the on-site accreditation survey that follows. Any inspection deficiency (on-site or interim) can serve as a valuable quality improvement indicator.

Second, participation in a proficiency testing (PT) program—the twenty-seventh major grouping—is another mandatory requirement for various certification and accreditation programs. These surveys offer a means for an outside, unbiased interlaboratory assessment of analytical and interpretive accuracy. Also, the results are refereed on the basis of interlaboratory comparison, providing a valuable—and compelling—peer measurement. The results of these PT surveys serve as surveillance indicators and can

27. Inspections (eg, FDA/JCAHO/CAP/AABB/interim self-inspections):

Inspection Indicator: (state inspection deficiency)	Threshold	Observation
a. ____________	________	____________
b. ____________	________	____________
c. ____________	________	____________
d. ____________	________	____________

Evaluation:
Action/Action Person:
Assessment:

28. Proficiency testing surveys:

Survey Indicator (state survey # with deficiency)	Threshold	Observation
a. ____________	________	____________
b. ____________	________	____________
c. ____________	________	____________
d. ____________	________	____________

Evaluation:
Action/Action Person:
Assessment:

29. Incident reports and complaints:

Incidental Indicator: state report or complaint	Threshold	Observation
a. ____________	________	____________
b. ____________	________	____________
c. ____________	________	____________
d. ____________	________	____________

Evaluation:
Action/Action Person:
Assessment:

uncover instructive opportunities for organizational improvement, including quality problems of a systemic, process-oriented nature. Very significant ongoing and focused quality indicators can be the result.

Third, incident reports and complaints—the twenty-eighth major grouping—are valuable sources of quality indicators when they occur. The problem is that they occur only sporadically and virtually nonsystematically.

Tracking these incidental reports is virtually identical to the occurrence screening employed in risk management. Thus, monitoring these reports is the most retrospective, retroactive, reactive approach to quality management. Still, when an incident or complaint arises, it should be approached as a unique external observation, and investigative evaluation should be activated. Lessons learned from these incidental reports frequently can develop into ongoing indicators.

In a sense, this report format has already addressed incident reports and complaints under the topic of the first indicator grouping for customer satisfaction. Incidental reports, complaints, and suggestions are included in the present external QI grouping as an option to the reader. The choice of placement in the structure of monitoring and work flow depends on how one interprets the relationship of these customer-related reports to the overall scheme of events. There are the lumpers and the splitters—they can each take their pick.

Overall, the questions asked in review of the internal QI program are applicable to an external surveillance program. Indicators of the quality of external QI should address the:

- Inclusion of external QI activities as part of the overall QI plan
- Integration of the overall QI process into managing external QI activities, including all the phases of the improvement cycle
- Follow-up and communication of lessons learned from external QI activities
- Improvement of the application or use of external QI activities themselves.

Indicator Criteria and Thresholds. There are no nationwide criteria or thresholds for external quality surveillance programs other than the general JCAHO and CAP accreditation requirements. Inspection findings and reportable incidents usually fit into the sentinel event category: any inspection finding or incident/complaint warrants immediate investigative evaluation and action. In the case of proficiency surveys, the criteria can be stated as $> \pm 2$ SDI (the usual CAP standard deviation index) or as a less than satisfactory rating, depending on whether it is a quantitative or qualitative type of survey.

Because of the gravity of their importance, the thresholds for any of these external improvement activities should demand 100% conformance or zero defects. As is true for internal surveillance, the measurement of success of external surveillance should center on evidence of overall program effectiveness—including improvement of the external QI activities themselves.

Quality Anticipation (QAn) Work Flow Phase

Data block 30 introduces the quality anticipation program. It addresses the effectiveness of the QAn program in work flow phase II. This data block should provide evidence of the organization's ability to plan for quality improvement. QI surveillance should provide information on the quality of current strategic plans, such as the relevance of project topics and the meeting of milestone dates. This feeder report monitoring is a snap shot of current planning effectiveness; it is not an in-depth QAn program status report.

30. Organizational research, development, and implementation
(review of reporting period's milestones for strategic planning):

	Research-Development-Implementation Indicator	Tasking Milestone (date)	Milestone Threshold	Observation
a.	____________	________	________	____________
b.	____________	________	________	____________
c.	____________	________	________	____________
d.	____________	________	________	____________

Evaluation:
Action/Action Person:
Assessment:

Indicators. This portion of the narrative report introduces the twenty-ninth major indicator grouping. There are three major phases of the quality anticipation process worthy of consideration: organizational research, development, and implementation. Indicators can be established for the monitoring of each of these three activities and can be further categorized for each individual section (or key operational areas) in terms of specific key management areas as well as short-, medium-, and long-range strategies. As a brief review, these indicators should address the:

- Presence of a QAn plan
- Presence of an ongoing education and training program aimed at instructing all employees in, state-of-the-art strategic quality planning
- Presence of an analytical, strategic planning process that incorporates the essential, basic elements of Shewhart's P-D-C-A

- Generation of short-, medium-, and long range strategies based on prioritized customer need
- Generation of research, development, and implementation phases to satisfy strategies for each phase
- Generation of goals, objectives, and taskings that are appropriate for each phase
- Presence of a QAn milestone schedule
- Overall effectiveness of all components of the QAn program, process, and schedule
- Improvement of the QAn program itself.

Indicator Criteria and Thresholds. There are no nationwide criteria or thresholds for quality anticipation other than the general JCAHO accreditation requirements and their *Agenda for Change*. Local criteria of success for a planning program should center on whether:

- The essential components of an effective QAn program are in place.
- Milestone events are occurring on time for each of the three anticipatory strategies and their phases.
- There is evidence of overall organizational improvement subsequent to the anticipation process—as well as improvement of the planning process itself.

If a tasking or milestone is missed, the target can be rescheduled, modified, or canceled as deemed appropriate by organizational management objectives. The option taken will depend on the quality issue and management resources at hand—remembering that time is also a resource. Such an approach guarantees up-to-date, concurrent review and measured, purposeful action.

All the QAn indicators will begin in a very general manner. However, as the surveillance of strategic planning progresses, more specific, focused indicators will emerge.

Quality Actualization (QAc) Work Flow Phase

Data block 31 introduces the quality actualization program. It addresses the effectiveness of the QAc program in work flow phase I—the very structural foundation of the entire path of work flow for all laboratory operations. This data block should provide evidence of the organization's ability to develop an effective organization that is committed to the concepts of TQM and CQI and capable of making effective quality improvement decisions. This final grouping represents the organizational "bottom line." QI surveillance of the QAc program does not produce an in-depth QAc program report. Rather, this data block provides just a snap shot view of the current quality of the program.

31. Organizational effectiveness:

Actualization Indicator	Threshold	Observation
a. Team morale	______	______
b. Team training:		
Medical staff	______	______
Supervisory staff	______	______
Technical staff	______	______
Resident staff	______	______
Clerical staff	______	______
Other	______	______
c. Personnel actions	______	______
d. Personnel incentives.	______	______
e. Commitment to CQI:		
Leadership commitment	______	______
General team commitment	______	______
f. Decision making	______	______

Evaluation:
Action/Action Person:
Assessment:

Indicators. This segment introduces the thirtieth major indicator grouping for this particular narrative report example. The grouping includes indicators of team effectiveness at the sectional level or lower. The organizational unit can be an operative section of the analytical/diagnostic type or an administrative support section of the clerical, computer, supply, maintenance type. Examples of such indicators are listed in the data block, but this is not a complete listing by any means.

Team morale needs monitoring by some method. The supervisor's empirical judgment is acceptable on occasion. However, it is much more accurate to directly ask the employees by interviews or written surveys. There are other supporting indicators of morale that have been discussed under the topics of analytical/diagnostic quality, productivity, and personnel utilization.

The next most critical indicator of QAc quality is training in organizational concepts, methods, tools, and skills. The organization must be very familiar with the concepts of TQM and the principles of the CQI process. All employees, including the leadership at every level, must be informed enough to be able to buy into those principles and programs. Only after adequate instruction can there be evidence of this all-organizational commitment. Thus, these specific educational requirements call for continuous monitoring and evaluation by the medical director, supervisor, and other section leaders to improve the organizational actualization process.

An organization is not naturally effective. Human energy and other resources have to flow into the organization if it is to prosper most effectively as a team. Similar to Newton's Third Law of Thermodynamics, if left to its own natural devices, any human organization naturally moves toward the direction of social entropy with constant diminishment of productive energy and effectiveness. Without specific education, training, and exercising of team methods, tools, and skills—smaller, less intercoordinated groups ultimately will emerge, forming around whatever leadership strength and functional and social identity there is at that new organizational level.

There is a reason for these natural tendencies. The natural organizational goal is to be most effective and to reach organizational actualization. However, without adequate input of direction and instructional resources, the organization naturally gravitates to its lowest denominator of team effectiveness as a means of maximizing its strengths and effectiveness with the resources that it perceives are at hand. This conceptualization of organizational behavior stems from Maslow's theory of survival and ultimate actualization—not McGregor's theory of "X-style" management.

A perverse spin-off of this natural tendency for a larger organization to split into smaller, independent units is that the smaller, subsidiary groups will work counterproductively to one another—ironically, in the spirit of a short-sighted sense of smaller group actualization. As a result, the familiar fiefdoms and mini-empires so common to classical (pre-TQM and CQI) healthcare organizations tend to flourish if not counteracted by purposeful team building at the larger organizational level.

Consequently, the most important energy that can be injected into an organization to counter this natural tendency toward entropy is the "force" of knowledge, skills, and exercise. Examples include:

- Knowledge of organizational values, mission, goals, and organizational behavior
- Skills in dealing with organizational communication, cooperation, negotiation, opportunity identification, and decision making
- Exercising those assets to reach maximal effectiveness.[26]

One major aspect of this instructional effort escapes experienced laboratory managers. After the first installment of education and training, there needs to be 1) continued orientation of new employees, 2) refresher training of the veteran employees, 3) new, in-depth study by the veteran employees, and 4) development of these organizational skills by real time problem solving. The result should be an endless cycle of orienting, instructing, and exercising the organizational expertise. The QI program can measure that QAc-level expertise through typical quality indicators or scheduling, follow through, and various outcomes.

The QI program also should monitor the quality of support provided to the employee as an element of QAc. This would include indicators of the effectiveness of 1) routine personnel actions, such as promotions, step increases, and bonuses, and 2) personnel incentives, recognizing quality performance. Are these actions timely, appropriate, innovative, and effective in building team morale and commitment to TQM and CQI?

Linked to the issue of morale is the question of commitment of the leaders and the other team members to TQM and CQI. The level of commitment needs ascertaining in some way. For example, has there been adequate empowerment exercised by the leaders and accepted by the other team members to bolster and sustain organization-wide commitment?

Finally, the laboratory should monitor the organization's effectiveness in making quality management decisions. Is there leadership support, including resources and personal involvement? Is there evidence of participative management and empowerment with assignment of responsibility? Is there evidence of accountability being delegated and accepted down to the lowest hierarchical, organizational levels? Is the team dealing with QI opportunities and problems expeditiously and effectively? If decisions have been identified that are too difficult to handle at the sectional level, is the team presenting these problems to the next appropriate, decision making level or forum for resolution in a timely manner? As a brief review, QAc indicators should address the:

- Presence of a QAc plan
- Presence of an analytical, actualization process, incorporating the essential basic elements of Shewhart's P-D-C-A
- Presence of an ongoing education and training program aimed at instructing all employees in the current, state-of-the-art of actualization, including organizational concepts, methods, tools, and skills
- Overall effectiveness of all components of the QAc program and process, including leadership support and involvement
- Improvement of the QAc program itself.

Indicator Criteria and Thresholds. There are no nationwide criteria or thresholds for quality actualization other than the general JCAHO accreditation requirements and *Agenda for Change*. However, the Joint Commission is explicitly clear regarding the requirement for commitment to the principles of CQI and organizational effectiveness—and that there be evidence to demonstrate it. As with QI and QAn, surveillance indicators will most likely be of the sentinel type, melding criteria and thresholds into an all-or-none, zero defect standard. Then, it becomes a matter of determining if the specific indicators of QAc are being met.

For example: is employee morale good? How does one quantify morale? One could answer the question most simply by yes or no; the indicator would become a sentinel event and answer no would trigger an evaluation. With a slightly more elegant approach, using a survey scale of 1 to 5 for example, morale is very bad (1) or very good (5), and that is about as precise as the measurement can be. Based on this scoring mechanism, however, the threshold for morale can vary just a little bit, and the indicator becomes a comparative rate type of event. Using written surveys, the threshold could be an average scoring of 4; any average score below 4 would trigger an investigative evaluation of team morale. For another example: is the team skill training program on schedule—yes or no?

All the QAc indicators will begin in a very general manner. However, as the surveillance of organizational actualization progresses, more specific, focused indicators will emerge.

FINAL NARRATIVE REPORT PARAGRAPHS

Summary of the Overall Improvement of Laboratory Operations

Data block 32 offers a closing summation of the effect of QI decisions on laboratory operations. This is a listing of any major change of organizational structure, policy, procedure, method, instrumentation, or other managerial approach that has occurred because of the overall improvement process during the reporting period. This information should reflect an emphasis on improving general processes, not individual performance. This information appears as an organizational "bottom line" statement to the feeder report, documenting continuous quality improvement. Data block 33 provides space for additional comments.

32. Laboratory structure policy/SOP/method/or other changes for improvement:

	Action/Change/Improvement	Assessment
a.	____________	____________
b.	____________	____________
c.	____________	____________
d.	____________	____________

33. Additional Comments:

Management Team Responsibility for Operational Quality Improvement

Information block 34 identifies the key quality management team members at the laboratory section (or any other unit) level who are responsible for quality surveillance and the feeder report. This group of signatures verifies the establishment of QI responsibilities as evidence of step #1 of the ten-step process and authenticates leadership support and involvement in the decision making process.

34. Signature block:

____________	____________	____________	____________
QI Technologist	Section Supervisor	Section Manager	Medical Director

35. Feeder report routing recommendation list (copies furnished):

a.
b.
c.
d.

Communication of Quality Improvement Lessons Learned

This final information block outlines to whom copies of the feeder report should be forwarded. There must be effective communication of any QI planning, monitoring, evaluating, action taking, and assessing that has occurred during the TQM and CQI processes. The recipients of the information should be laboratory customers-suppliers, including all internal, lateral, and higher echelons that have any need to know. Also, this information block helps to document step #10 of the JCAHO format.

In actual practice, the feeder report should be distributed only to laboratory service or departmental level since it is a preliminary report and deserves review and verification by at least one higher laboratory level. The sectional management team should exercise decision making throughout the feeder report, recommending all courses of action for the next laboratory QI level to consider including recommendations of the routing of information. At the service or department level, the same section quality management team should have a role in the final decision.

THE TQM SYSTEM AND THE CQI PROCESS AS SOURCES OF QUALITY INDICATORS

The foregoing discussion illustrates that judicious use of the TQM system and CQI process can generate a multitude of opportunities for improvement. Table III outlines the potential sources of quality indicators that are available from monitoring the three quality management programs of the system and the key elements of the process.

The system is a combination of three quality management programs for improvement, anticipation, and actualization—all reside at the administrative level of management. These three programs form the total infrastructure of organizational operations. The key elements of the process include the individual and team commitment built through continuous, systematic QI, QAn and QAc—as evidenced by customer satisfaction. Thus, TQM and CQI are inextricably linked, generating a countless number of opportunities for quality assessment and improvement.

The QI program offers two major sources of quality indicators for every section (or any other functional laboratory unit at any organization level): the important aspects of care and the path of work flow. Important aspects of care are identified in the third step of the JCAHO ten-step process and are typically characterized by their being high-volume, high-risk, or problem-prone. In their own right, the aspects of care are the source of an innumerable selection of indicators. We must remember, however, that there are other ongoing sources such as committee minutes and customer reports.

The path of work flow is also a plentiful source of surveillance indicators. The quality of every important aspect of care can be monitored during any one of the fifteen work flow phases—from QAc to customer satisfaction. Therefore, with the path of work flow acting as a multiplier of indicator possibilities, there is even greater potential for generating a myriad of quality indicators in any healthcare laboratory. In a CQI environment, there should also be indicators of improving the QI program itself.

The QAn program provides other sources of important indicators. These sources include key operational areas; key management areas (KMAs); organizational strategies; planning phases; and resultant goals, objectives, taskings, and milestones. The KMAs are especially helpful in focusing on specific quality indicators of all operational aspects of any functional laboratory section or other unit. Each KMA can then be addressed in terms of organizational strategies based on customer need. Any strategy can then be addressed in terms of the three-fold approach to phased planning: organizational research, development, and implementation. Each of these three phases can then generate prioritized goals, objectives, taskings—and potentially countless indicators of quality improvement for each KMA in each sectional unit. In a CQI environment, there should also be indicators of improving the QAn program itself.

The QAc program provides a third source of key indicators for each section, including: team morale, team skills, team support, and team

Table III
Sources of Indicators for Total Quality Management and Continuous Quality Improvements

QI Program

- ■ QI process (representing the basic P-D-C-A improvement cycle)
  - • All important aspects of care (per the JCAHO ten-step process)
  - • Any other source of QI information, eg minutes
  - • Criteria of importance
    - – High-volume
    - – High-risk
    - – Problem-prone
- ■ Path of work flow
  - • Outcome segments
  - • Process segments
  - • Structure segments
    - – Operative
    - – Organizational

- ■ *Continuous improvement*
  - • as evidenced by exercising the QI program overall
  - • by improving the QI program itself

QAn Program

- ■ Key operational areas
- ■ Key management areas
- ■ Strategies (short-, medium-, and long-range)
- ■ Planning phases
  - • Research projects
  - • Development projects
  - • Implementation projects
- ■ Scheduled goals, objectives, milestones, and taskings

- ■ *Continuous improvement*
  - • as evidenced by exercising the QAn program overall
  - • by improving the QAn program itself

QAc Program

- ■ Team morale and opinion
- ■ Team skills
- ■ Team support (personnel actions and incentives)
- ■ Team decision making
- ■ Team commitment to continuous improvement
- ■ Leadership effectiveness

- ■ *Continuous improvement*
  - • as evidenced by exercising the QAc program overall
  - • by improving the QAc program itself

decision making. In a CQI environment there are also potential indicators of team commitment, leadership effectiveness and continuous improvement of the QAc process itself. Considering all of these major actualization activities, there is an unending number of QAc indicators worthy of monitoring for quality improvement.

Between all three organizational programs, an inestimable number of quality indicators are potentially at hand. To have a manageable number of indicators to monitor, the laboratorian must limit the overwhelming number of possible QI indicators, using criteria for ranking and prioritizing the most valuable ones. Also the CQI-derived indicators are of the "bottom line" type, providing overall, summary information on a primary goal of the organization: quality improvement. They can be best answered in yes-or-no terms; has there been improvement or not?

The schematic diagram in Figure 7.2 displays an algorithmic approach to the identification of quality indicators based on the above discussion of all TQM and CQI indicator sources. The figure illustrates the three TQM administrative quality management programs—QI, QAn, and QAc—divided into their major, indicator generating components. All three programs begin at the level of separate, prioritized operative sections (A, B, C ...), remembering that such a "section" can reside at any organizational level, either operative or administrative.

Within each functional section, the QAc program (work flow phase I) generates prioritized quality indicators for the four key team activities of morale (1, 2, 3, ...), skills, support, and decision making. All QAc program components can be further evaluated in terms of the CQI criteria for continuous improvement—including team commitment and leadership effectiveness indicators for and incorporated with those already generated by the QI surveillance program itself.

Within each section, the QAn program (work flow phase II) identifies prioritized multiple key management areas. For each KMA (a, b, c, ...), short–, medium–, and long-range strategies can be planned, based on customer need and followed up by research, development, and implementation phases. Goals, objectives, and taskings then follow for each strategic phase. Specific indicators of the quality of each of these QAn components can then be developed. These QAn indicators are further evaluated in terms of CQI criteria for continuous improvement and incorporated with those already generated by the QI surveillance program.

Within each section, the QI program (work flow phase III) initially generates a careful selection of prioritized important aspects of care (a, b, c...), each important aspect being characterized in terms of volume, patient risk, or inherent technical problems (1, 2, 3, ...). Each important aspect of care indicator can be further characterized in terms of phases of path of workflow (I through XV). The potential result is innumerable possibilities of scheduled surveillance indicators that can be directed at all operational levels of outcome, process, and resource management. There also are the nonscheduled indicators generated from sources other than any

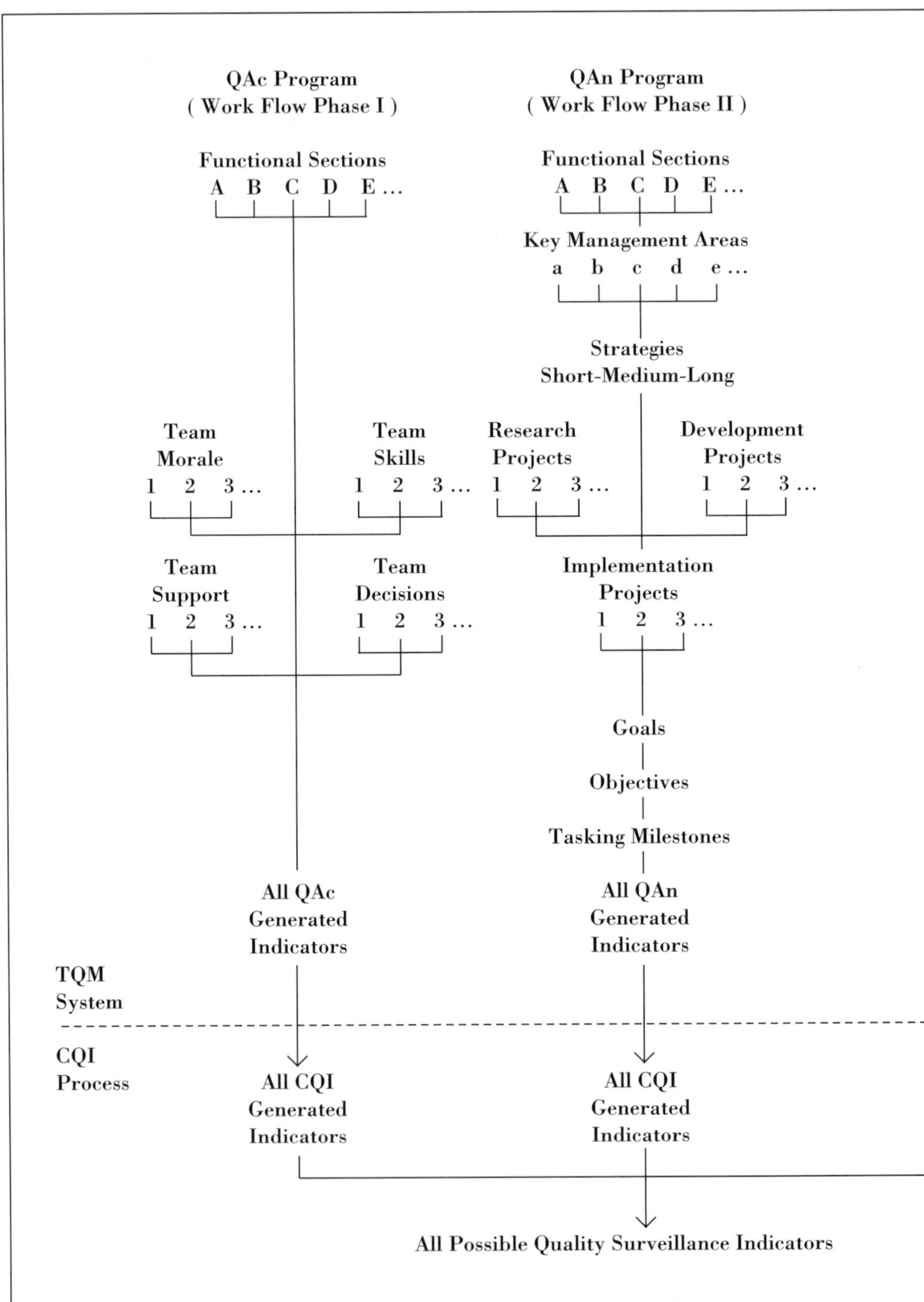

Figure 7.2 TQM and CQI sources of indicators

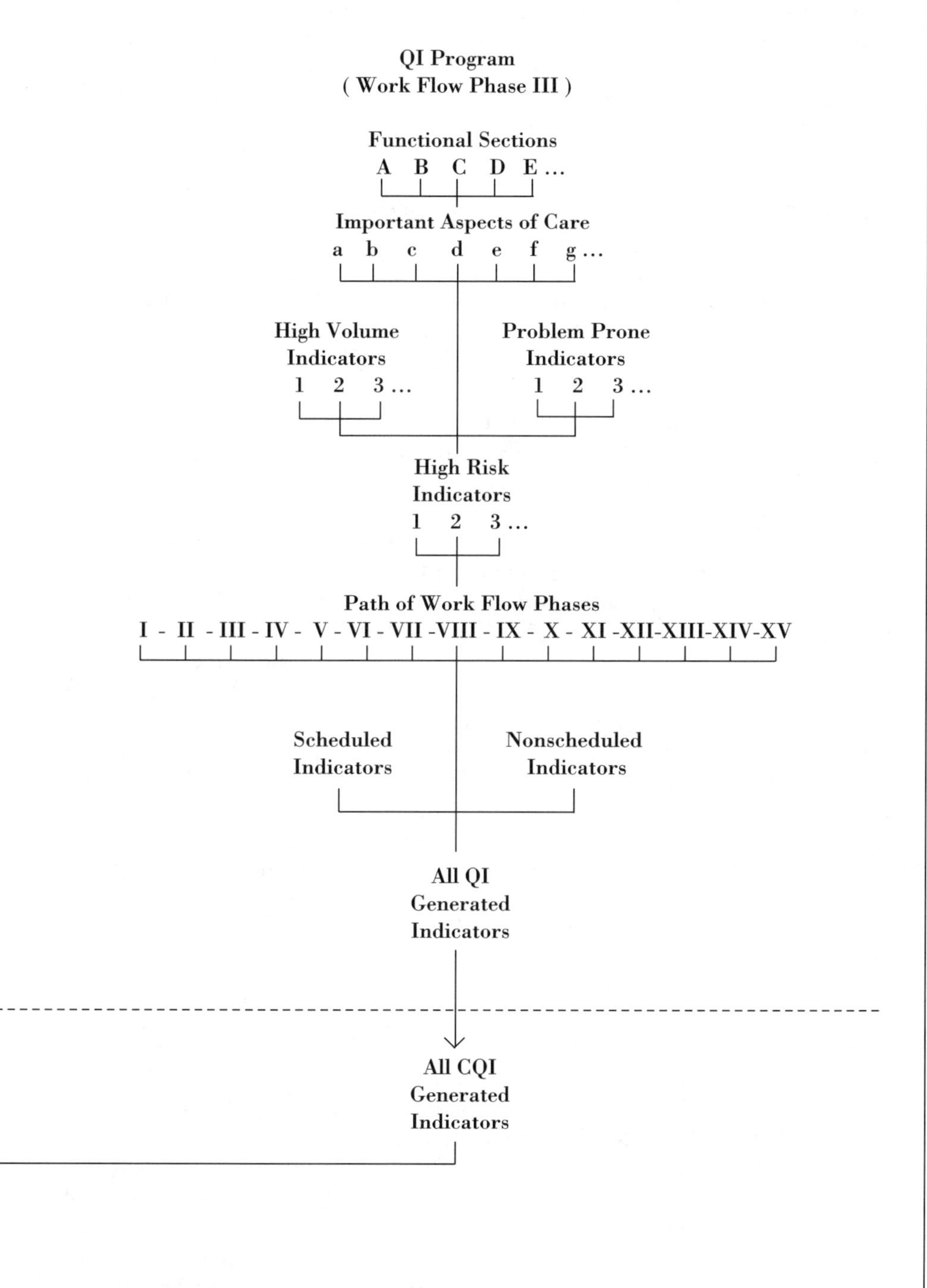
QI Program
(Work Flow Phase III)
Functional Sections
A B C D E ...
Important Aspects of Care
a b c d e f g ...
High Volume
Indicators
1 2 3 ...
Problem Prone
Indicators
1 2 3 ...
High Risk
Indicators
1 2 3 ...
Path of Work Flow Phases
I - II - III - IV - V - VI - VII -VIII - IX - X - XI -XII-XIII-XIV-XV
Scheduled
Indicators
Nonscheduled
Indicators
All QI
Generated
Indicators
All CQI
Generated
Indicators

formal QI process. These QI indicators can be further evaluated in terms of CQI criteria of continuous improvement and incorporated into the total pool of possible QAc indicators. The end result is all QI, QAn, and QAc indicators feeding into a surveillance pool of a potentially infinite amount of quality management data for continuous improvement.

USE OF THE SECTION QI FEEDER REPORT

This chapter presents a detailed description of the design and use of a narrative style QI feeder report at the sectional level. The discussion focuses on total operational quality surveillance, extending from the monitoring of customer satisfaction through all outcome, process, and resource management indicator groupings to quality actualization.

JCAHO accreditation guidelines have made singular impact on how a healthcare laboratory QI program should be designed, implemented, maintained, and orchestrated. Recent standards revisions have further crystalized these accreditation requirements, which are included in the design of the subject feeder report—providing a template for the development of TQM and CQI in the laboratory.

As implied by the narrative report model, the laboratory should pattern its QI process after some form of Shewhart's P-D-C-A improvement cycle; the model used in this text is the Joint Commission's ten-step format. Following such an improvement process should make for an effective laboratory QI program. At the same time, the program and its results become more standardized and easily understood by any JCAHO, CAP, or other inspector.

Such a report format offers an excellent, initial opportunity for sectional level personnel to establish a TQM-CQI based indicator monitoring plan, evaluate QI data, recommend actions, and assess the QI process at the lowest possible organizational level. Also the report mechanism should facilitate the actualization of team building and participative decision making at the operative managerial level. The structured, narrative report offered in this chapter also will guide healthcare laboratories in meeting their TQM-CQI strategic plans.

After its completion by the section management team, the section can submit the feeder report to the appropriate service or departmental QI committee for review. At that higher administrative level, the laboratory team (including sectional representatives) can make final decisions on the exercising of the EvAAC steps recommended by the section.

There understandably will be some difficulty for nonhospital-based POL and independent laboratories in accomplishing the QI surveillance of events that occur before receipt of the request and specimen and after release of the laboratory product for distribution to the healthcare provider. POLs have another challenge: being relatively small, they are still required to generate a QI program that meets the same requirements as those for larger laboratories; but, larger laboratories have more resources to accomplish QI surveillance particularly personnel. Still, by using the improved means of electronic communication and by using a systematic approach—taking one measured step at a time—these difficulties are surmountable. Any laboratory of any size can learn to work smarter.

REFERENCES

1. Joint Commission Primer on Clinical Indicator Development and Application. Measuring Quality in Health Care. Oakbrook Terrace, IL: Joint Commission on Accreditation of Healthcare Organizations, 1990.
2. Curry W. Outcomes management: new name for old idea. Phys Exec, 1989;15:2-6.
3. Ellwood P. Shattuck lecture: outcomes management. A technology of patient experience. NEJM, 1988;318:1548-1556.
4. Schwartz K, Cohen CG. Patient direct access to testing. Lab Med, 1990;21:589-590.
5. Kurtycz DFI. Pursuit of quality testing in the physician office laboratory. Lab Med, 1989;20:432-436.
6. Moser E. A support Program for physician's office labs. Med Lab Observer, 1989;21:59-62.
7. Tyler RD. Quality assurance in the ambulatory care setting. Phys Exec, 1989;15:17-20.
8. Koska MT. Outcomes management stresses patient outcome. Hospitals, 1989;63:32.
9. Chapman B. Pathologists, patients getting closer. CAP Today, 1991;5:1,24.
10. Murphy J, Henry JB. Effective utilization of clinical laboratories. Hum Path, 1978;9:625-633.
11. Check WA. Lab-use guidelines taking shape. CAP Today, 1991;5:1,22, 24-26.
12. Werner M. Attributes for parameters raise larger issues. CAP Today, 1991;5:28, 31.
13. Geehr EC, Salluzzo RF. Clinical practice guidelines: promise or illusion. Phys Exec, 1990;16:13-16.
14. Spath P. Joint commission unsnarls clinical indicator development. Hosp Peer Rev, 1989;14:76-79.
15. Goldschmidt PG. Severity-of-illness: red herring or horse of a different color: Parts 1, 2, and 3. Phys Exec, 1989;15(4):7-11;(5)12-17; (6):5-9.

16. Vanourny SE, Holtney S. Medical quality management: a comparative study of severity of illness indexes. Phys Exec, 1990;16:11-18.

17. Pine M, Smith DW. Severity-of-illness systems: an overview for medical directors: Part 1 and 2. Phys Exec, 1990;16(2):10-15;(3):19-22.

18. Sox HC, ed. Common Diagnostic Tests: Use and Interpretation. Philadelphila, Pa: American College of Physicians, 1987.

19. Effective Laboratory Testing. Skokie, IL: College of American Pathologists, 1987.

20. Campbell JA. Appropriateness of blood product ordering: quality assurance techniques. Lab Med, 1989;20:15-18.

21. Donabedian A. The quality of care: how can it be assessed? JAMA, 1988;260:1743-1748.

22. Workload Recording Method. Northfield, IL: College of American Pathologists, 1991.

23. Maffei LM. A new approach to workload recording. A contemporary approach to staffing analysis. Clin Lab Man Rev, 1990;4:105-108.

24. Maffei LM. Personal communication. 11 Oct 1991.

25. Koch J, Templin, J. Workload broadens scope. CAP Today, 1990; 4:1,5,53.

26. Pauker SG, Kassirer, JP. Decision analysis. NEJM, 1987; 316:250-258.

8. Using a Quality Profile at the Department Administrative Level: Postlaboratory Outcome Management

DESIGNING A QI PROGRAM TO SURVEY TQM AND CQI MOST EFFECTIVELY

This book describes the history, definitions, theoretical concepts, and suggested approaches to implementing quality healthcare laboratory management. The preceding chapter addresses one major approach, illustrating how to apply the Plan phase of Shewhart's improvement cycle at the sectional level: expanding that phase into the first half of the Joint Commission on Accreditation of Healthcare Organizations' (JCAHO) ten-step process (TSP). Now, we proceed into a detailed explanation of the Evaluation-Action-Assessment-Communication (EvAAC) steps of the TSP—representing the Check-Act phases of the Shewhart cycle—and a second major approach to implementing modern quality management.[a]

In real-life practice, can the active pursuit of total quality management (TQM) and continuous quality improvement (CQI) truly maximize laboratory management effectiveness and efficiency? Can modern management facilitate everyday laboratory excellence? This chapter illustrates how all of these quality management goals can be attained by following through with the EvAAC limb of the Joint Commission improvement cycle, using a profiling tool to organize, implement, and document all quality improvement activities.

In order to understand the EvAAC elements of the improvement cycle—and the structure of the quality

[a] "Plan" and "Do" phases of Shewhart's P-D-C-A cycle are incorporated into the "data collection" step of the TSP.

profile—there must be a clear understanding of how we select and prioritize the two essential elements of the quality assessment and improvement (QI) plan: the important aspect of care and the quality indicator. The nature of these two elements controls the extent of comprehensiveness and rate of success of quality management.

A key rate-limiting factor in successfully implementing both TQM and CQI is the QI program—to oversee and be aware of all that is really going on. It follows that actuating and maintaining comprehensive quality surveillance requires valuable operational resources—assets that must be used effectively and judiciously. The potential scope of surveillance in a laboratory would be staggering if the quality of *every* outcome, process, and resource management activity for *every* important aspect of care were to be verified. Consequently, complete quality management—particularly assuring total quality—is not managerially feasible from the perspective of resource availability, and that includes time as a resource.

First, all operational resources—including those necessary for quality management—are finite. Second, even if there were enough resources to support complete quality management, Pareto's Law is a compelling argument that total assurance is not statistically worthwhile—it is not cost-effective.[b] Hence, in the planning phase of the quality improvement cycle, the JCAHO has advised healthcare laboratories to collect a total inventory of the "scope of care" of laboratory services and select every important aspect of care (IAC) from that total inventory. Then, we must monitor the highest priority quality indicators for all of these most *important* laboratory products or services in some systematic fashion.

It is obvious that neither the Joint Commission nor any other regulating agency can stipulate how many important products and services there should be—that number is idiosyncratic for each laboratory. The JCAHO does require, however, that specific criteria (eg, high-volume, high-risk/benefit, and opportunity/problem-prone) be used to identify the IACs. Each individual laboratory must determine the reasonable number of aspects of care that can be ranked in some order of priority, characterized by specific indicators, and then monitored, evaluated, acted on (improved), assessed, and communicated—referring to the EvAAC steps of the TSP. Keep in mind that we must carry out these Check-Act or EvAAC activities by using the structural resources (operative and organizational) at hand—and, still, address all important aspects of care within a reasonable amount of time. Also, remember that the IAC listing must be a dynamic document: the individual elements of the inventory and their ranking of importance should change from one year's evaluation to the next.

The next step in the ten-step improvement process—selection of indicators—further clarifies what, otherwise, would be an overwhelmingly

[b] Pareto's Law is that 80% effectiveness of a given process is realized on expenditure of 20% of the resources. After reaching that point of initial logarithmic gain in effectiveness, the rate of gain of effectiveness tapers off dramatically, and the expenditure of resources becomes significantly less cost-effective.

complex matrix of essential elements of quality surveillance. This is especially true if the QI program embraces the total path of work flow for all operative and organizational activities.

As healthcare laboratories make the transition from the surveillance precepts of quality assurance (QA) to the more advanced practice of QI (quality assessment and improvement) then on to PI (improving organizational performance), laboratorians are challenged to choose quality indicators of greater managerial complexity. To facilitate this transition, it is helpful to identify monitoring targets that complement the TQM system of quality management programs and the continuous organizational quest for excellence.

In the course of the transition, several questions naturally occur as laboratorians grapple with the TQM system and CQI process in anticipation of inspection and accreditation. The most common questions are:

- How many potential indicators are there?
- How do we identify the most important indicators to monitor?
- How many indicators does the JCAHO want us to monitor?
- How many indicators should we monitor?

Local, regional, national seminars, workshops, and teleconferences by a growing number of professional organizations are offering up-to-date answers to these questions. Supporting literature also continues to emerge in journal and book form. Therefore, based on the current state of managerial understanding, consider the following approaches to choosing and using quality indicators in a TQM and CQI environment.

How many potential indicators are there?

Everyone cringes at the "how many?" question since we all realize that more quality indicators exist than can be realistically monitored by any one laboratory quality surveillance program. The JCAHO accreditation standards stipulate that *all* laboratory activities that have been identified as "important aspects of health care" are subject to surveillance.[c] If one considers all operational aspects in the chain of cause and effect, the quality management of all IACs involves all significant outcome, process, and resource management activities at both the operative and organizational management levels. As emphasized in the JCAHO *Agenda for Change*, one word that is key to understanding the full extent of the quality surveillance spectrum is "resource."

[c] The 1994 JCAHO accreditation standards for Improving Organizational Performance (PI) do not refer specifically to "important aspects of care" but will mention"those activities that most affect patient health outcomes" and "all important functions described in other chapters of the accreditation manual." Whatever we call it—an IAC or something less specific—these salient laboratory activities or functions need to be identified.

Table I
Sources of Quality Indicators Derived from Monitoring The Three Quality Management Programs

Quality Improvement Program (QI) for Organizational Surveillance

- Inventory of products and services
  - Scope of care
  - Important aspects of care and their indicators prioritized on basis of standard criteria, such as
    - High-volume
    - High-risk or benefit
    - Improvement- or problem-prone
- Alternative QI indicator sources of customer feedback, standing committees, task force groups, and other quality teams
- Path of work flow indicators covering all organization-wide operational segments of work flow, including:
  - All pre-, intra-, and postlaboratory activities
  - Customer outcome
  - Process
  - Structural resources
    - Operative resources
    - Organizational resources, including the QI program itself

Quality Anticipation Program (QAn) for Organizational Planning

- Key management area indicators
- Short-, medium-, and long-range strategy indicators
- Organizational research phase indicators
- Development phase indicators
- Implementation phase indicators
- Related goal, objective, tasking, and milestone indicators
- Improvement of the QAn program itself

Quality Actualization Program (QAc) for Organizational Effectiveness

- Team morale indicators
- Team skill training indicators
  - Team building
  - Opportunity identification and problem solving:
- Team maintenance indicators
  - Continued team skill training
  - Personnel actions
  - Personnel incentives
- Team effectiveness indicators
  - Organizational commitment
  - Leadership commitment to and support of TQM and CQI
  - Decision making
- Improvement of the QAc program itself

- Resource commonly alludes to all traditional, operative resource management activities, including workload, personnel, method, equipment, supply, facility, and budget management functions.

- Not as commonly considered, resource also applies to all nontraditional, organizational resource management activities, including all behavioral and cultural management functions. Such efforts underlie the programs for quality surveillance (quality assessment and improvement or QI), strategic planning (quality anticipation or QAn), and organizational effectiveness (quality actualization or QAc). These three programs are the administrative mainstay of any laboratory TQM system and CQI process.

Table I suggests how abundant each of the three administrative-level quality management programs can be as a source of operational quality indicators. First addressing the QI program, the JCAHO ten-step process initially addresses indicators in terms of "scope of care." By itself, such a complete inventory of all laboratory analytical-diagnostic products and services generates too prodigious a panoply of monitoring targets—including all customer (not just patient-oriented) outcome, all process, and all resource management activities. Consequently, we must reduce the total scope of care to a workable inventory of "important aspects of care" and their respective quality indicators based on standard criteria such as the high-volume, high-risk, problem-prone formula that stems directly from the ten-step QA process of the 1980's and current accreditation standards.

The JCAHO carefully reminds us that there are decision-making analogs other than their ten-step process (eg, PDCA, FOCUS-PDCA). Likewise, there are QI indicator sources other than the routine, scheduled laboratory improvement process. These alternative sources primarily represent various, nonprogramed means of obtaining customer satisfaction and patient care outcome feedback from standing committees, task force groups, other quality teams, and benchmark examples that are routinely identifying IACs and related indicators. Most of these alternative sources are customer/outcome-related, as opposed to process- or structure-related. No matter what the source, however, all emerging important laboratory functions and their indicators must still be prioritized along with those that are routinely derived using the same standard criteria formula.

Under the QI program, Table I also addresses the importance of the path of work flow. For further illustration, the quality indicator matrix in Table II demonstrates the relationship of the path of work flow to the important aspects of care. The laboratory path of flow forms the vertical axis; the important aspects of care comprise the horizontal axis of the matrix. The completed matrix expands the vista of potential indicators, the purposefully limited inventory of important aspects becoming a window to an infinite number of indicator choices.

First, the matrix enlarges each already prioritized IAC in terms of all relevant segments of the total path of work flow—including all post-, intra-, and prelaboratory outcome, resource, and resource management events. Second, the matrix amplifies each important laboratory function in terms of the surveillance approach, whether that approach be by general survey, indexed case study, or focused study approach. In fact, review of this matrix is an introductory step to understanding the structure of the quality profile.

For clarification, a general survey (GS) usually consists of the passive screening of incident reports, spot reports, suggestions, complaints, and acknowledgments. This surveillance approach is an ongoing process. As implied above, once an indicator grouping or specific indicator has been initially characterized by the general survey approach, establishing a substantial baseline, consider the more active surveillance of indexed cases or focused studies, which increase indicator sensitivity.

In contrast to the general survey approach, an indexed case study (IS) consists of monitoring characteristic indicators of important procedures, products, or services over a more lengthy, ongoing period. This form of QI study provides a continuous baseline against which critical operational levels, patterns, and trends can be gauged on an ongoing basis.

Using an even more proactive approach, a focused study (FS) consists of monitoring a specific operational event because a high-yield opportunity for improvement (OFI) is at hand. Such an opportunity usually demonstrates a high index of suspicion based on out-of-control QI data—routine or investigative data—or on a carefully made, deductive decision to improve the quality management system in the face of a lengthy history of consistently normal surveillance data. In the latter case, threshold levels, indicator criteria, or the choice of an IAC itself become candidates for revision.

- For example, a general, nonspecific survey of overall chemistry customer satisfaction could focus more precisely on the customer satisfaction level for electrolyte studies provided to surgical intensive care patients. Thus, the surveillance approach turns the spotlight of scrutiny from a general IAC topic to a specific laboratory end product provided and clinical activity served.

- As another example, a general survey of anatomic pathology routine surgical TAT could focus more specifically on the turnaround of a high priority source of surgical biopsy specimens, eg, male genitourinary cases, based on standard criteria and deductive or inductive rationale. Thus, our attention concentrates on a unique laboratory service (ie, IAC) provided to a defined patient care category and clinical activity.

Returning to Table I and considering the QI program overall, the consequent possibilities range from indicators of the quality of customer

Table II
Matrix of Essential Quality Indicator Elements

<table>
<tr><td rowspan="4">Path of Work Flow Divisions</td><td rowspan="4">Path of Work Flow Phases</td><td colspan="9">All Important Aspects of Care
Low Priority ⟷ High Priority</td></tr>
<tr><td colspan="3">High-volume Indicators</td><td colspan="3">High-risk/ High-benefit Indicators</td><td colspan="3">Opportunity-prone/ Problem-prone Indicators</td></tr>
<tr><td colspan="3">Approaches</td><td colspan="3">Approaches</td><td colspan="3">Approaches</td></tr>
<tr><td>GS</td><td>IS</td><td>FS</td><td>GS</td><td>IS</td><td>FS</td><td>GS</td><td>IS</td><td>FS</td></tr>
<tr><td>Outcome Management</td><td>• Customer satisfaction
• Patient care outcome
• Employee safety</td><td></td><td></td><td></td><td></td><td></td><td></td><td></td><td></td><td></td></tr>
<tr><td>Process Management</td><td>• Postlaboratory process
• Intralaboratory process
• Prelaboratory process</td><td></td><td></td><td></td><td></td><td></td><td></td><td></td><td></td><td></td></tr>
<tr><td>Operative Resource Management</td><td>• Workload
• Personnel
• Continuing education
• Methods and procedures
• Computers
• Equipment
• Supply
• Facility
• Budget</td><td></td><td></td><td></td><td></td><td></td><td></td><td></td><td></td><td></td></tr>
<tr><td rowspan="3">Organizational Resource Management</td><td>• Quality improvement (QI) program</td><td></td><td></td><td></td><td></td><td></td><td></td><td></td><td></td><td></td></tr>
<tr><td>• Quality anticipation (QAn) program</td><td></td><td></td><td></td><td></td><td></td><td></td><td></td><td></td><td></td></tr>
<tr><td>• Quality actualization (QAc) program</td><td></td><td></td><td></td><td></td><td></td><td></td><td></td><td></td><td></td></tr>
</table>

GS = General Survey IS = Indexed Case Study FS = Focused Study satisfaction to the quality of organizational effectiveness. It is important that indicators of the quality of the improvement program itself are included at the organizational resource management level. For example, major quality indicator groupings can target the effectiveness of the primary steps in the basic improvement cycle (eg, planning, doing, checking, and assessing)—whatever improvement process that is used. For example, these groupings could include surveillance of the effectiveness of any of the ten steps of the TSP. Thus, a truly systematic, total operational approach to indicator selection is achieved, capable of unmasking an unlimited network of potential quality indicators through the QI program.

Continuing with the next TQM program, Table I itemizes specific quality indicator sources derived from the QAn program for organizational planning. The extent of selections depends on the thoroughness of the strategic planning program. At the broadest operational level, the laboratory can choose indicators that target any key management area (KMA). A KMA represents an important management activity within a key operational area (eg, functional section), examples of which would include personnel, method, computer equipment, supply, facility, budget, and plans management. Then, the laboratory can identify indicator groupings within any KMA for each planning strategy, whether it be the short-, medium-, or long-range. Furthermore, the laboratory can establish specific indicators to monitor the progress of any QAn phase (ie, organizational research, development or implementation), goal, objective, tasking, or milestone—as well as improvement of the QAn program itself. Again, as a potential source of indicators, the planning program provides a source of theoretically limitless choices from the angle of organizational anticipation.

Table I outlines indicator sources derived from the QAc program for organizational effectiveness. One can identify QI indicators that reflect team morale, team building, team support, team decision making, and improvement of the QAc program itself—to suggest just a few of a potentially limitless number of QAc issues.

To summarize the answer regarding potential indicators, quality indicators are virtually myriad in kind and number. The matrix in Table II reminds us that the essential indicator ingredients include:

1) Important aspects of care identified by routine inventory methods or by alternative customer satisfaction, outcome-related approaches. All IAC are ranked for monitoring priority on the basis of appropriate criteria such as high-volume, high risk, and problem-prone.

2) Indicators for respective IAC, identified through the routine, intralaboratory QI process or by alternative means; they are ranked for monitoring priority on the basis of appropriate criteria and studied by general survey, index case, or focused study approaches.

3) Path of work flow divisions, segments, and phases, providing the managerial dimension by which we can scrutinize all key operational activities.

The matrix of quality indicator elements clearly reveals that any itemized listing, no matter how comprehensive, cannot cover all possible QI indicators. On the other hand, this vast range of potential indicators will not overwhelm a laboratory that is truly proficient in TQM and CQI practices; instead, the laboratory will select only the IACs and indicators that are most relevant to that laboratory's needs—thus, conserving managerial resources. This discussion repeatedly highlights the theme of judiciously using quality management resources—it is that important! So, the next challenge is to determine which quality indicators are most important in the modern quality management environment.

How do we identify the *most important* indicators to monitor?

There are straightforward methods for identifying the most meaningful indicators for the QI, QAn, and QAc programs within the laboratory path of work flow. First, we must follow a broad-based, analytical approach such as the ten-step process and identify each IAC from the overall scope of care. The JCAHO bases this advice on published guidelines: they want us to monitor indicators for *each* IAC over a reasonable period.[1,2] Otherwise, why would that product or service have been selected as important? If we have conscionably identified this inventory of unique laboratory activities, each of these activities must be critical enough to warrant some form of ongoing (ie, periodically repeated, regularly scheduled) surveillance. Weighed against this requirement of surveillance of each IAC are finite quality management resources.

Consequently, it is absolutely essential to first determine what feasible number of IACs can be assessed and improved with the available quality management assets. Then, select those important laboratory functions, keeping within the laboratory's IAC "budget."

Again, the chief suggestion is to choose the IACs by using the high-volume, high-risk or benefit, improvement or problem-prone selection criteria as previously discussed. Although other criteria are available, this JCAHO three-part formula is very basic and works well under ordinary QI circumstances.[d] These analytically-based guidelines allow the ranking and prioritizing of all important laboratory products and services for both internal and external laboratory customers. The more conservatively that these rules are applied, the more restricted and feasible the number of IACs (and their indicators) there will be.

The JCAHO is quite accepting in regard to how we reach these decisions. On one hand, they strongly advocate the precepts of TQM and

[d] In fact, these three criteria represent some of the very few hallmarks of the JCAHO standards of the 1980s that have withstood reconstruction over the past decade.

CQI. On the other hand, they deny endorsement of any particular mechanistic approach to achieving those precepts. Every healthcare organization must find their own way toward excellence—just as long as they do strive for it.[3]

For example, in deliberating over the choice of IACs, the JCAHO urges us to use various sorts of team composition, depending on the degree of multidisciplinary participation and the kind of problem solving that is *apropos*. Such team composition consists of several possibilities, including the following considerations:

TEAM COMPOSITION			
Internal Customer-Supplier		External Customer-Supplier	
Laboratory	Clinical	Support	Administration
Community		Industry	

The advice is that we use various TQM-oriented team approaches to stimulate participatory management at the lowest organizational level. These consensus reaching techniques consist of several possibilities, including the following:

TEAM PARTICIPATORY APPROACHES		
Panel	Committee	Task Force
Quality Team		Quality Circle
Majority Rule	Nominal Group	Delphi Group
Brainstorming		Benchmarking

Their advice is that we use various analytical processes to facilitate a consistent and logical approach to quality improvement. QI program processes, such as the JCAHO ten-step process, are very important to consider, but the TSP is only one of several different approaches that are available. These processes consist of several possibilities, including the following:

ANALYTICAL PROCESSES[e]					
Shewhart's PDCA	JCAHO's TSP	HCA's FOCUS-PDCA	Juran's Journey	Joiner's U-E-R-R-P	ODI's FADE

[e] PDCA = Plan-Do-Check-Act; HCA = Hospital Corporation of America; FOCUS-PDCA = Find-Organize-Clarify-Understand-Select-PDCA; Juran's Journey = Diagnostic and Remedial Phases; UERRP = Understand-Eliminate-Remove-Reduce-Plan; ODI = Organizational Dynamics, Inc; FADE = Focus-Analyze-Develop-Execute.

Finally, their advice is that we use various analytical tools to facilitate a thorough, statistically-based approach to decision making and quality improvement. These tools consist of several possibilities, including the following:

ANALYTICAL TOOLS				
Cause & Effect Chart	Pareto Analysis	Run Chart	Histogram	Fishbone Diagram
Check Sheet	Flow Chart	Control Chart	Scatter Diagram	Force Field Analysis

There is ample documentation of the successful use of these approaches to team composition, processes, methods, and analytical techniques.[3,4,5,6,7]

Next, identify the general indicator groupings and specific indicators for each IAC in the order of the latter's ranking and priority. Use the same team approaches, techniques, processes, and tools as suggested above. The algorithmic process for effective indicator characterization hinges on the discovery of "opportunities for improvement"—a direct link to the principles of the CQI process. An OFI needs not to be an operational problem with some adverse effect. Once all blatant problems have been addressed, any nonproblematic laboratory activity that is being performed acceptably within current standards can be studied for further improvement of the operative standards themselves, narrowing control levels and conforming closer to optimal design specifications.

A natural step in this decision-making process is relating indicator groupings and specific indicators to appropriate segments of the path of work flow. Algorithmic considerations for selecting the correct indicators and related path of flow segments are as follows:

- If there is a known or clearly suspected problematic OFI, follow Sutton's Law (ie, Willie Sutton) and "go where the money is." Since the problem (or OFI) is blatantly obvious, choose appropriate indicators that target relevant segments of the path of work flow for the given, problematic IAC, using quality team techniques and analytical tools.

- If there is no known problematic OFI, follow the Holmesian approach (ie, Sherlock Holmes) that requires deductive reasoning and informed analysis of all IAC and their path of work flow to determine the most potentially high-yield target for surveillance. Use selection criteria with analytical tools to isolate high-yield indicators and path segments. Incorporate general survey, indexed case study, and focused study approaches to reveal worthy QI targets, as discussed below.

Or, design a "most likely" or "worst case" scenario to target portions of the path of work flow that are worthy of closest scrutiny. The latter approach stresses a suspect process, program, or system to unmask important surveillance indicators.

- If no other approach is successful, systematically survey prioritized segments of the path of work flow of a given IAC over a reasonable period to determine if that laboratory function is really important enough to monitor. If it has changed significantly in relative importance, either select more sensitive indicators, relocate the IAC in the spectrum of priority, or delete the subject function from the inventory—in any case, there will have been some improvement of the QI process itself.

- Always be ready to react to an IAC or specific indicator that is identified by alternative, customer-related sources, such as committees, task forces, quality circles, other team types, and benchmark examples. These often require relatively rapid response as opposed to the more routine, deliberately planned, scheduled, and measured QI approach.

Now, is it surprising that the first step in identifying all important laboratory functions is to determine a workable number of aspects of care? The observation that the IAC total is beyond that feasible number reveals the very next OFI—that is to improve the QI program itself by reducing the size of the IAC inventory! In such a situation, options for subsequent action would be to:

- Bolster the quality surveillance assets to adequately support the number of IACs that have been identified:

- Reevaluate and tighten the IAC selection criteria to reduce the number of laboratory functions under surveillance to a workable level.

- Select another laboratory organization (internal or external) to administratively perform the quality surveillance of the excess IAC.

- Select a reference laboratory to perform the excessive IAC including the QI surveillance required.

Thus, laboratorians should avoid boxing themselves into a managerial corner; instead, they should carefully select each important laboratory function and its respective indicators! We need to be prudent in developing an IAC inventory that is manageable with our finite quality surveillance assets—and, at the same time, be resourceful in developing, tailoring, and using those assets more effectively. The IACs that are chosen influence which and how many indicators are monitored. Consequently, if we generate too many important functions with their respective indicators, we are apt to miss identifying an OFI that is exceedingly critical to customer satisfaction. This danger also crystalizes our responsibility to coordinate with clinical and other healthcare support colleagues in keeping with the precepts of TQM and CQI practice.

How many indicators does the JCAHO *require* us to monitor?

The answer to this question reveals the least number of indicators that is absolutely necessary to be fully accredited. When a JCAHO inspector walks through the door, how many indicators will that inspector require the laboratory to be monitoring? This question almost always arises at quality management workshops where the catalyst is the topic of preparing for accreditation.

Until recently, the most general answer has been that it always depends on the individual inspector's personal interpretation of JCAHO philosophy and policy. Well, thanks a lot! Anecdotal reports have set the usually acceptable minimum in an estimated range of four to ten indicators per laboratory per reporting period.[8] Fewer than four would not likely satisfy the "average" inspector. It would be nice if we could quantify the opinion of the average inspector within ± 2 SD—but, we cannot. So, until recently, "four to ten" has been a good rule of thumb. Such an acceptable level of ongoing monitoring largely has depended on the size of the laboratory: the larger the laboratory, the more ongoing indicators are expected to be scheduled. Now, these subjective guidelines no longer are supposed to apply.

To help solve the above quandary and provide more consistency to the accreditation process, the JCAHO has created a hospital accreditation program scoring system on which both healthcare organizations and the inspectors can rely as concrete guidelines to attain conformance to accreditation standards. As of this writing, the grading system is based on a scoring range of "1" to "5," which is explained as follows[9]:

1: *Substantial compliance*, meeting all major characteristics of a given standard

2: *Significant compliance*, meeting most characteristics of a standard

3: *Partial compliance*, meeting some characteristics of a standard

4: *Minimal compliance*, meeting few characteristics of a standard

5: *Noncompliance*, meeting none of the characteristics of a standard.

A score of "3" or lower is not flattering and requires an inspector's documenting the reasons for such a low score. Conversely, even a score of 1 does not necessarily signify that all major characteristics of all standards have been met since not all characteristics are awarded scoring guidelines.

According to the scoring guidelines as of this writing, the basic requirement for a score of "1" is that the laboratory monitors a *minimum* of two important aspects of care and two ongoing indicators; and how those indicators relate to the IACs can vary. In addition, the JCAHO requires monitoring of medical staff utilization of certain laboratory services—these special areas of interest include blood usage review and surgical pathology diagnostic correlations.

Since the standards and scoring guidelines, including the guidelines for the required type and number of specific indicators, are expected to change with the continued revision of the approach to QI, this text cannot go into any greater detail. Therefore, it behooves the laboratorian to be very familiar with the yearly-revised *AMH* and the scoring guidelines.[f]

How many indicators *should* we monitor?

This is truly the most important question from the viewpoint of laboratory management, if the intent of the organization is to make the precepts of TQM and CQI work best for maximum operational benefit. It is not a question of what minimal number of IACs and indicators we should monitor to satisfy an accreditation survey. Rather, it is a question of how many indicators we can monitor to practice best laboratory management.

From a benchmarking perspective, the answer to this question might be very surprising since many laboratories monitor more than the proverbial "four to ten" indicators in any given reporting period—sometimes as much as 20, 30, or more per section per reporting period.[10] Whereas the JCAHO establishes minimally acceptable standards for accreditation, quality indicators are actually so pervasive that they are just "naturals" for enhancing routine, administrative management of *all* laboratory operational activities at both operative and organizational levels, including traditional and nontraditional (behavioral and cultural) resource management activities. Thus, the maximum number of indicators that we are able to monitor rests on two major determinants:

1) How effectively laboratory managers integrate QI indicators with relevant management data already at hand, actualizing a truly TQM style of quality surveillance.
2) The availability of the laboratory's total quality management assets weighed against total operational workload requirements, which include all quality management duties.

Here we arrive at the fundamental determining factor—the linchpin that ties maximum effectiveness to any of the three quality management programs: the adequacy of quality management assets. How abundant and how effective are the personnel, the data management system, and all the other resources that are required to effectively perform quality management? We characterize the

[f] Any JCAHO policy or approach is subject to change. For the time being, however, these scoring criteria will hopefully remain stable while the JCAHO *Agenda for Change* is undergoing completion. As implied in the title of that healthcare initiative, however, the "name of the game" is change and the JCAHO accreditation standards—of which the scoring guidelines are a part—are the rules of that game.

capability of any given quality management effort by assessing these variable and finite resource elements. This structural capacity dictates the laboratory's ability to consistently pursue QI surveillance indicators, QAn planning projects, and QAc team building activities—executing all three programs of the TQM system—and to strive assiduously for continuous improvement.

Of course, the managerial beauty of TQM and CQI is that these systematic approaches inherently maximize the effectiveness of the personnel and other laboratory resources, vastly enhancing the organization's overall capacity to achieve excellence. Borrowing from Maslow's theory of hierarchy of needs, exercising systematic quality management ideally should bring an organization closer and closer to the ultimate goal of "team actualization." So the answer to "How many indicators can we monitor?" depends on the overall effectiveness of the organization and how successfully TQM and CQI are integrated into the laboratory culture—the everyday, routine way of doing business.

The JCAHO, ASCP, CAP, CLMA, and other professional organizations offer seminars, workshops, teleconferences, texts, and compendia that illustrate various approaches to indicator selection and display, including profiling.[11] Sample lists of indicators are becoming abundant. Still, it is absolutely imperative for every laboratory to formulate *its own* matrix of essential QI elements; each laboratory must select *its own* IACs and related indicators that are custom-fit to its unique internal and external operational environment, including the overall size of the laboratory, its scope of care, its managerial resources on hand, and its general management philosophy. That is the only legitimate path to continuous improvement. Therefore, it is the suggestion here to utilize more than the minimal two indicators: use QI as a total management tool and take powerful advantage of the copious management data that are already available.

Determine early in planning the QI program how many quality indicators the laboratory can realistically monitor on an ongoing schedule. Then, the monitoring schedule can be arranged on a monthly, bimonthly, quarterly, trimestral, biannual, or annual basis depending on the priority and other characteristics of the given indicators. The laboratory can begin modestly with as few as two indicators for the highest ranking aspects of care and then build a more comprehensive improvement program after time and practice. Assiduously seek improvement of quality, but be practical; go steadily for the small wins, stringing them together as pearls integral to a whole, elegant necklace.

The Structure of a Department-level Quality Profile Report

The next quandary to satisfy is managing multisectional data and reporting it economically at the department level. The preceding chapter addresses a vertically designed, narrative-style feeder report for use at the section level. Because of its proven effectiveness and completeness, the TSP is the skeletal support for that narrative model—although any other version of the PDCA model for analytical, decision making can be used in its stead. That discussion emphasizes the planning and development of indicators, their criteria, and thresholds. After accomplishing the first five steps in planning the ten-step process, the section QI team collects and manages the data, using the EvAAC steps of the ten-step process that are detailed below for the administrative, department level of quality management.

So, the next series of decision making steps are made at the service or department level, primarily to:

1) Condense all of the information gained from a number of subsidiary sections
2) Ensure a consensus of agreement over the EvAAC decisions
3) Ensure the provision of adequate resources to get the job done
4) Prepare a monthly or quarterly departmental summary for essential communication and documentation.

The quality profile report is a very useful tool for meeting all of these requirements at this higher managerial level.[g]

Therefore, this chapter concentrates on illustrating the use of the horizontally-designed, spreadsheet-style, profile report. While describing the profile format, the discussion centers on the practical aspects of evaluation, action, assessment, and communication (EvAAC) that can be exercised in response to the QI data.[12]

A quality profile report serves a number of purposes. It incorporates the ten-step process (or whatever improvement process or cycle that the laboratory has chosen), which facilitates consistent decision making department wide. It coordinates outcome, process, and operative resource management activities. It also ties together all three TQM programs: QI, QAn, and QAc—promoting the ongoing review and follow-up of quality surveillance, planning, and team building. The horizontal format of the report easily adapts to computerized word processing and forms publishing.

Figure 8.1 illustrates a schematic of the quality profile presented in this text as a matrix consisting of vertical and horizontal primary elements. The vertical component within the first column is a sequential listing of all the major work flow segments and their related indicator groupings. The figure refers to the top-most indicator grouping as the "top line" and lowest indicator grouping in the listing as the "bottom line." The natural path of work flow in this matrix moves from bottom to top; the path of analysis of the indicator groupings moves from top to bottom. The horizontal component of the matrix represents the flow of the data collection and EvAAC (Check-Act) steps of the QI process, moving sequentially from left to right.

[g] The quality profile described here utilizes elements of the JCAHO TSP. Any form of Shewhart's P–D–C–A improvement cycle will suffice, although the TSP does lend itself very well to such a profiling approach.

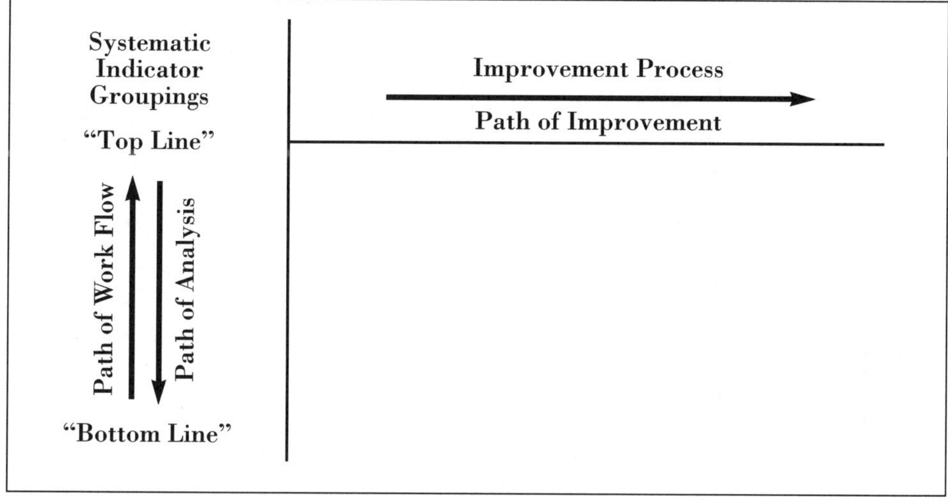

Figure 8.1 Schematic illustration of a Quality Profile

Figure 8.2 more explicitly illustrates that the vertical axis of the profile's first column consists of six major work flow segments, including the:

- Postlaboratory outcome segment
- Postlaboratory process segment
- Intralaboratory process segment
- Prelaboratory process segment
- Prelaboratory operative resource segment
- Prelaboratory organizational resource segment.

The horizontal axis consists of a sequence of QI process steps which include the reporting of data, evaluation, action, and assessment. The formulation of the profile itself and ultimate distribution of the profile to those who need to know completes the communication step of the EvAAC (Check-Act) phases of the improvement cycle.

The author cautiously emphasizes that the nomenclature used here—including that of the TSP itself—is optional. Although this approach and its operative terms have worked well in laboratories under the author's direction, one can certainly modify them to fit individual laboratory preferences and the continuously evolving healthcare industry parlance.

Figure 8.2 clearly illustrates how the vertical sequence of the quality profile segments and indicator groupings of the left-most column recapitulates the laboratory path of work flow. For example, the sequence of groupings is presented in reverse order compared to the normal path of flow (just as in the narrative-style sectional feeder report). For example, the

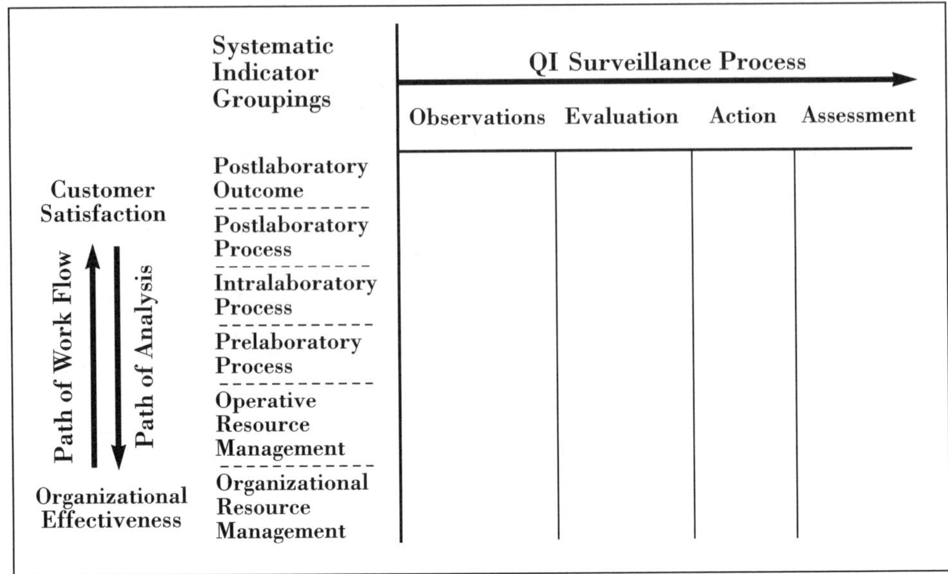

Figure 8.2 Basic components of a quality profile

profile report begins with the quality indicator grouping for postlaboratory outcome—customer satisfaction outcome being an example. Customer satisfaction is the ultimate goal of laboratory operations and represents the "top line" of the path of work flow; it is also the tip of a proverbial mountain of potential opportunities for improvement. If the customer is not satisfied, the organization has not fulfilled its primary mission—the organizational mission statement being an implied contract with <u>all</u> customers.

Following customer satisfaction and other outcomes, the profile indicator groupings consecutively address key aspects of operative process, operative resource, and organizational resource quality management in a retrograde fashion. Ultimately, the profile format symbolizes organizational effectiveness as the true "bottom line" of laboratory operations (as opposed to the hackneyed bottom line of the fiscal balance sheet). If an organization's staff is not adequately trained in quality improvement, not committed to quality improvement, or not adequately supported to meet that commitment, laboratory operations will not attain the standards that are required to provide *optimal* customer satisfaction and continuous improvement in an ever-changing technocratic environment. Table III (page 339) lists a more complete outline of the path of work flow segments and phases and their respective indicator groupings.

Table IV (pages 340-343) exhibits the structure and components of a typical quality profile—this sample being devoid of any QI data or EvAAC notation. As introduced earlier, the profile stands on a skeletal framework of path of work flow segments and their major indicator groupings, all located in the first column at the far left side of the profile.

Table III
The Organization of QI Indicator Groupings Within the Laboratory Path of Work Flow

- Postlaboratory Outcome Work Flow Segment
    - Customer satisfaction grouping
    - Patient care outcome grouping
    - Employee safety outcome grouping
- Postlaboratory Process Work Flow Segment
    - Laboratory report and product utilization grouping
    - Turnaround time throughput grouping
    - Report and product distribution grouping
- Intralaboratory Process Work Flow Segment
    - Postdeterminative product finalization grouping
    - Reference laboratory studies grouping
    - Analytical quality and diagnostic quality groupings
    - Predeterminative specimen processing grouping
    - Specimen and request accessioning grouping
- Prelaboratory Process Work Flow Segment
    - Specimen transportation grouping
    - Specimen collection grouping
    - Patient preparation grouping
    - Test and product and consultation selection grouping
- Operative Resource Work Flow Segment
    - Workload and productivity grouping
    - Personnel grouping
    - Continuing education grouping
    - Methods and procedures grouping
    - Computer support grouping
    - Equipment procurement and maintenance grouping
    - Supply procurement and storage grouping
    - Facility maintenance and renovation grouping
    - Budget grouping
- Organizational Resource Work Flow Segment
    - Quality Improvement (QI) Work Flow Phase
        - Internal QI indicator groupings (using the TSP as an example)
            - Responsibility
            - Scope
            - Important aspects of care
            - Indicator
            - Threshold
            - Data collection
            - Evaluation
            - Action
            - Assessment
            - Communication
        - External QI indicator groupings
            - Proficiency surveys
            - JCAHO, CAP, and other inspections
            - Incident reports, complaints, and suggestions
    - Quality Anticipation (QAn) Work Flow Phase
        - Organizational research grouping
        - Development grouping
        - Implementation grouping
    - Quality Actualization (QAc) Work Flow Phase
        - Team morale grouping
        - Team building, education, and training grouping
        - Personnel actions grouping
        - Personnel incentives grouping
        - Decision making grouping
        - Team commitment grouping
        - Leadership commitment, support, and involvement grouping

Table IV
Sample Quality Profile

Indicator Grouping/ Specific Indicator: Threshold (Periodicity)	QI Data Observations (Date trend started) J A S O N D	Evaluation of QI Data, TQM System, CQI Process	Action Action Person: (Date Initiated)	Assessment of Overall Improvement
POSTLABORATORY OUTCOME WORK FLOW SEGMENT				
Customer Satisfaction: any positive or negative report; sentinel event!!				
Patient Care Outcome: no threat to health status; sentinel event!! (Monthly)				
Employee Safety Outcome: no potential or actual hazard; sentinel event!! (Monthly)				
a. Biological				
b. Fire				
c. Electrical				
d. Chem/Carcinogen				
e. Radionuclide				
f. Waste Disposal				
g. Environmental				
POSTLABORATORY PROCESS WORK FLOW SEGMENT				
Laboratory Report Utilization: in keeping with joint laboratory and clinical standards!! (Quarterly)				
Turnaround Time of Index Procedures: (Quarterly)				
Report Distribution: no misdirected reports; sentinel event!! (Quarterly)				
INTRALABORATORY PROCESS WORK FLOW SEGMENT				
Postdeterminitive Product. Finalization and Specimen Handling: no loss of product or specimen integrity!! (Quarterly)				
Reference Laboratory Quality: no adverse effect on patient outcome!! (Quarterly)				
Analytical Quality: no major discrepencies!!				

Note: J A S O N D = Jul-Aug-Sep-Oct-Nov-Dec; : = threshold !! = sentinel event

Table IV: Sample Quality Profile (Continued)

Indicator Grouping/ Specific Indicator: Threshold (Periodicity)	QI Data Observations (Date trend started) J A S O N D	Evaluation of QI Data, TQM System, CQI Process	Action Action Person: (Date Initiated)	Assessment of Overall Improvement
INTRALABORATORY PROCESS WORK FLOW SEGMENT (CONTINUED)				
Diagnostic Quality (Peer Review): no major discrepencies! (______)				
Predeterminative Specimen Processing: no loss of specimen integrity!! (Monthly)				
PRELABORATORY PROCESS WORK FLOW SEGMENT				
Specimen Collection: >__% invalidation rate! (Monthly)				
Test Selection: in keeping with laboratory and clinical standards!! (Quarterly)				
OPERATIVE RESOURCE MANAGEMENT WORK FLOW SEGMENT				
Workload Management: a. Productivity quotients: within established limits!! (Monthly) 1. PQp (paid): ___ to ___ min/hr				
Personnel Management (Monthly) a. Work force: 1. Vacancy rate: Technologists: ≥ ___ % vacancy				
b. Utilization: 1. 16 hour shifts: none!! 2. Overtime: ≥ __ hours				
c. Availability: 1. % availability: ≤ __ %				
Continuing Education ≤ __ hour/mo!! (Monthly)				
Methods & Procedures Review: must be on time!! (Annually per Monthly Schedule)				
Computer Management: a. Unscheduled down time: ≥ __ hours (Monthly)				
Equipment: repair must be complete within __ days! (Quarterly)				

Table IV: Sample Quality Profile (Continued)

Indicator Grouping/ Specific Indicator: Threshold (Periodicity)	QI Data Observations (Date trend started) J A S O N D	Evaluation of QI Data, TQM System, CQI Process	Action Action Person: (Date Initiated)	Assessment of Overall Improvement
OPERATIVE RESOURCE MANAGEMENT WORK FLOW SEGMENT (CONTINUED)				
Supply: no potential for laboratory service limitations!! (Quarterly)				
Facility: no potential for equipment failure, biological spoilage or personnel stress!! (Quarterly)				
Budget: meet planned expenditure within ±5% of monthly target (Monthly)				
ORGANIZATIONAL RESOURCE MANAGEMENT WORK FLOW SEGMENT				
Internal Quality Improvement (QI)				
a. Improvement: there must be evidence of continuous improvement over a reasonable amount of time!! (Quarterly)				
b. Communication: there must be adequate sharing of lessons learned!! (Monthly)				
External QI (Monthly)				
a. Proficiency surveys: all results must be ≥ 2 SDI or found "Acceptable"!!				
b. JCAHO/CAP/other inspection: no unresolved findings!				
c. Incident report and complaints: every report is a sentinel event!!				
Quality Anticipation (QAn) (Quarterly)				
a. Organizational research: all milestones will be attained!!				
b. Developmental: all milestones will be attained!!				
c. Final implementation: all milestones will be attained!!				

Table IV: Sample Quality Profile (Continued)

Indicator Grouping/ Specific Indicator: Threshold (Periodicity)	QI Data Observations (Date trend started) J A S O N D	Evaluation of QI Data, TQM System, CQI Process	Action Action Person: (Date Initiated)	Assessment of Overall Improvement
Quality Actualization (QAc) (Monthly) a. Team morale: no adverse effect on team effectiveness!				
b. Team building , education, training: no skill lacking that adversely affects team effectiveness!!				
c. Personnel actions: none overdue!!				
d. Personnel incentives.none overdue!!				
e. Decision making: no problems too hard or unresolved ≥ __ months!!				
f. Leadership: no lack of commitment, support, or involvement that adversely affects team effectiveness!!				

Observe the first indicator grouping (ie, customer satisfaction). Similar to most groupings, it can include any number of specific indicators, depending on the type of outcome, process, or resource activity being monitored. Threshold and periodicity of monitoring are also noted in the indicator block.

The second column of the profile sample in Table IV is reserved for QI data under the title of Observations. This column provides space for the fruits of data collection—the "Do" phase of Shewhart's cycle of improvement. The "J-A-S-O-N-D" subtitle for the same column stands for "July-August-September-October-November-December"—a six month cumulative data period. This subtitle abbreviation changes each month as the months of the reporting period change. Additionally, one can note the date of initial observation of any particular observed event in this column.

QI profiles provide displays of quality management data that represent the functional status of an organization frozen at a moment in time. Even though they are stopped in "snapshot" form, these profiles can still convey a sense of the dynamics of a real laboratory managerial situation. For instance, many indicators in these profiles can include from three to six months of cumulative data points that allow the unveiling of significant trends and patterns at a glance.

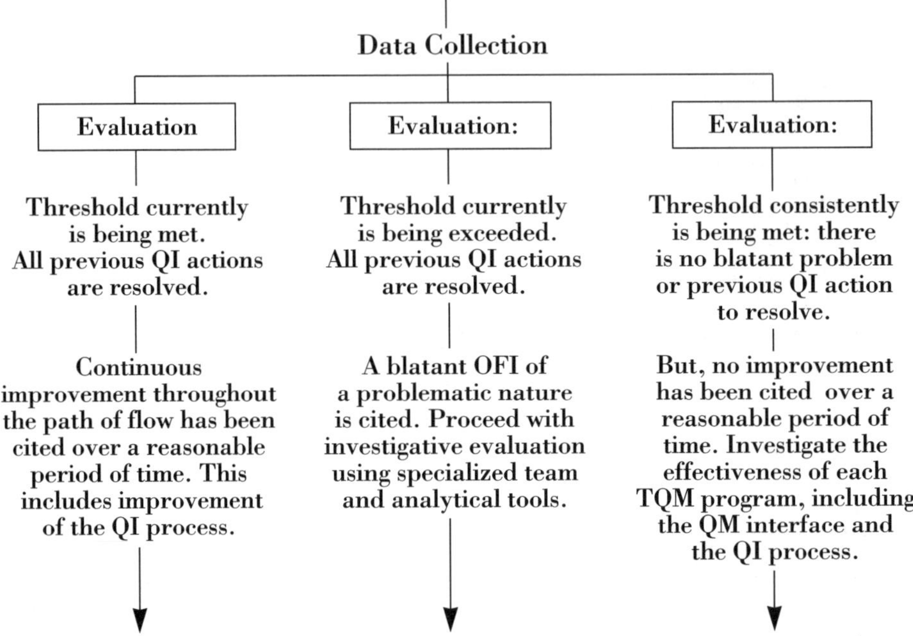

Figure 8.3 Algorithm of three options for evaluation in a CQI environment

The third column in Table IV is titled Evaluation; this step represents the "Check" phase of the Shewhart improvement cycle. This profile column provides space for a short comment on the evaluation of the data as compared to the nature of the indicator and its threshold.

Figure 8.3 illustrates the three-fold option that one must consider in exercising the evaluation step in a CQI environment (also addressed in Chapter Four). If all is normal, the evaluation can be "on target" for whatever number of months or reporting periods that there has been no change, as long as there is documentation in previous profiles of some improvement over the past six to nine months; this represents option one (the middle algorithmic branch in Figure 8.3).

If evaluation shows an obvious exceeding of the threshold, then option two (the right branch of Figure 8.3) is evident. Comment should be made if a threshold has been exceeded or if the cumulative data reveal an abnormal trend. Even if the threshold has not been exceeded, there might be a pattern still revealing an improvement opportunity. If there has been no OFI noted over an inordinate amount of time (six to nine months), then there is need to investigate the QI process for improvement, as well as the effectiveness of the other two TQM programs and the quality management (QM) interface. this situation represents option three (the left branch of Figure 8.3)

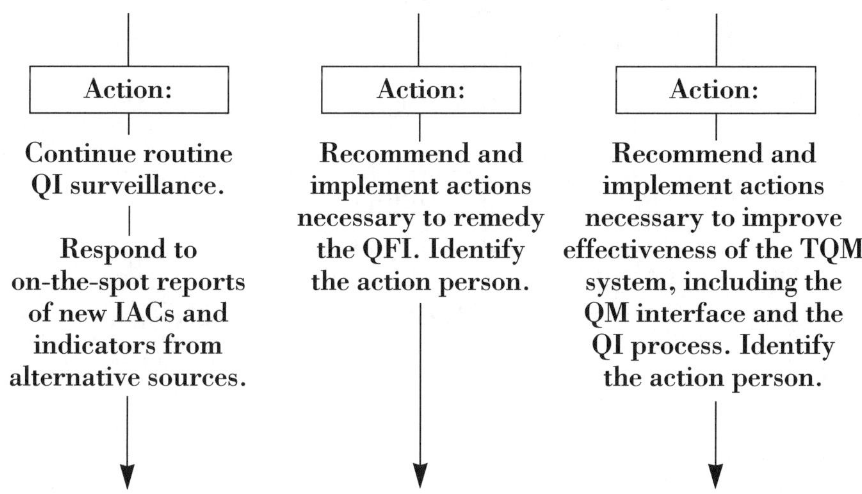

Figure 8.4 Algorithm of three options for action in a CQI environment

The fourth column in Table IV is titled Action, including a reminder to mention the action person and the date that action has been initiated. The action step represents the first portion of the "Act" phase of the Shewhart cycle for improvement. The preceding figure illustrates the continuation of the three-fold option that one must consider in exercising the action step in a CQI environment (also explained in Chapter Four).

Any action noted to be taken should mirror the evaluation findings and represent the most timely (but not necessarily the most expedient) and complete resolution of the problem—or improvement of the opportunity—at hand. If the evaluation is that the subject indicator is "on target" and that there is no need to investigate the QI process itself, the action comment is "none needed." Conversely, if there is need for investigative or resolving steps to be taken, the comment on the action should include whatever is needed to resolve the improvement opportunity at hand. Those directions should include any options of interim steps needed to be scheduled.

The action person is that individual responsible for effecting and following up on the required action. That individual is usually described by position title, not by name. Tracking the date that the action was initiated also can be useful in assessing the rate of success as time goes by.

In the interim until the next programed review, it is still possible that there will be a need to respond to on-the-spot reports of new IACs and indicators from alternative sources—as they occur. These alternatives include the derivation of nonprogramed, usually extradepartmental improvement targets for which we must be continually alert. The sources encompass various types of quality teams plus benchmark examples.

Table V
Table of Decision

Quality Profile: QI Report (month year)
Laboratory Section: (section name)

Indicator Grouping/Specific Indicator: Threshold (Periodicity)	QI Data Observations (Date trend started) J A S O N D
POSTLABORATORY OUTCOME IMPROVEMENT	
Customer satisfaction: any positive or negative report; sentinel event!! (Monthly)	PREFERABLY A PROSPECTIVE STUDY WITH CONCURRENT DATA • • • • CAN INCLUDE RETROSPECTIVE FOLLOW-UP DATA FOR PATTERNS AND TRENDS
Patient Care Outcome: no threat to life or limb; sentinel event!! (Monthly)	
Employee Safety Outcome: no potential or actual hazard; sentinel event!! (Monthly)	
a. Biological	
b. Fire	
c. Electrical	
d. Chemical/Carcinogen	
e. Radionuclide	
f. Waste Disposal	
g. Environmental	
POSTLABORATORY PROCESS IMPROVEMENT	
Laboratory Report Utilization: in keeping with laboratory and clinical stands (Quarterly)	
Turnaround Time of Index Procedures: Threshold stated per procedure (Quarterly)	
Report Distribution: no misdirected reports; sentinel event!! (Quarterly)	
INTRALABORATORY PROCESS IMPROVEMENT	
Postdeterminative Product Finalization and Specimen Handling: no loss of product or specimen integrity!! (Quarterly)	
Reference laboratory Quality: no adverse effect on patient outcome!! (Quarterly)	
Analytical Quality: no major discrepancies!! (Monthly)	
Diagnostic Quality (Peer Review): no major discrepencies!! (Monthly)	

Note: QFI = opportunity for improvement !! = sentinel event

Evaluation of QI Data, TQM System, CQI Process	Action Action Person: (Date Initiated)	Assessment of Overall Improvement
ON TARGET: QUALITY CONTROL IS EFFECTIVE, QI DATA ARE WITHIN THRESHOLD, THERE HAS BEEN SOME OFI OVER THE PAST 6 TO 9 MONTHS, AND ALL IS RESOLVED OR DESCRIBE ALL PAST OFIs THAT ARE STILL CURRENTLY UNRESOLVED • • • • • • HAVE ALL PREVIOUSLY RECOMMENDED ACTIONS BEEN EFFECTIVE ? OR DESCRIBE THRESHOLDS THAT ARE CURRENTLY EXCEEDED, WITH TRENDS, OR ABNORMAL PATTERNS • • • • • • INDICATE DEGREE OF: IMPACT, FOCUS, AND SEVERITY • • • • • • CONSIDER: WHAT? / WHO? / WHERE? / WHEN? / WHY?	NONE NEEDED OR DESCRIBE ACTION NEEDED • • • • WEIGH OPTIONS AND CONSIDER: INTERIM FIX PRIORITIES PHASING • • • • IDENTIFY ACTION PERSON	NO IMPROVEMENT NEEDED: TQM SYSTEM AND CQI PROCESS ARE EFFECTIVE OR CONTINUOUS IMPROVEMENT DOCUMENTED OR IMPROVEMENT IN PROGRESS OR IMPROVEMENT NEEDED • • • • EMPHASIZE INEFFECTIVE PROCESS OR ACTION WHEN SIGNIFICANT • • • • EMPHASIZE NEED FOR SPECIFIC EXTRA-DEPARTMENTAL SUPPORT WHEN SIGNIFICANT
CONCENTRATE ON IMPROVING PROCESS AND FUNCTION—NOT INDIVIDUAL PERFORMANCE • • • • • • CONSIDER MODIFYING THE QI PROCESS TO INCREASE SENSITIVITY TO DETECT OFI IF THERE HAS NOT BEEN ANY OFI OVER A 6 TO 9 MONTH PERIOD • • • • • • ARE ALL OTHER TQM PROGRAMS (ie, QAn and QAc) INTACT? • • • • • • REVIEW SUPPORTING INDICATORS • • • • • • IS THE ROUTINE QM INTERFACE INTACT? • • • • • • WHAT TEAM COMPOSITION, TECHNIQUES, AND TOOLS ARE RELEVANT AND WILL FACILITATE EVALUATING THE OFI AT HAND? • • • • • • IF AN OFI IS TOO HARD TO RESOLVE: DESCRIBE LATERAL OR HIGHER ECHELON SUPPORT NEEDED AT THE QM INTERFACE		

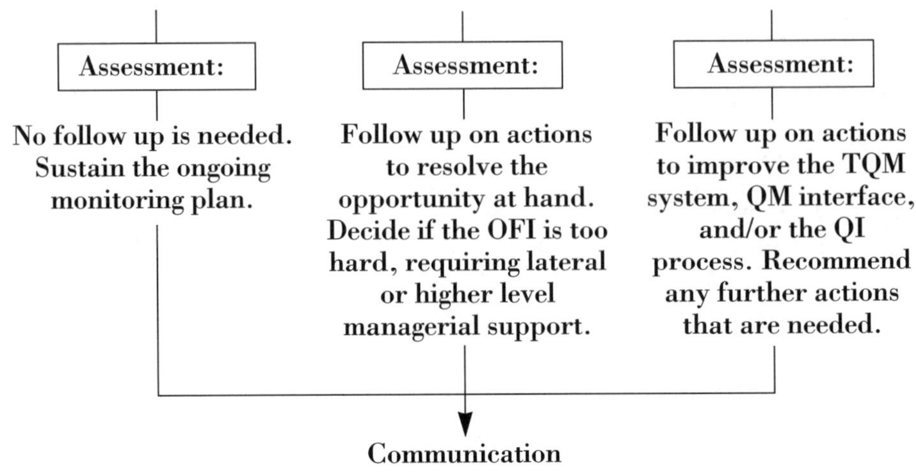

Figure 8.5 Algorithm of three options for assessment in a CQI environment

The fifth column is titled Assessment. The assessment step represents the second portion of the "Act" phase of the Shewhart cycle for improvement. Figure 8.5 illustrates the continuation of the three-fold option that one must consider in exercising the assessment step in a CQI environment (also addressed in Chapter Four).

Practicing the assessment role is predicated on 1) there having been action recommended to resolve an OFI and 2) there having been an adequately long period for that action to become effective. In one case, if an action has been determined in the present monitoring period, there is usually nothing that can be said for assessment except "improvement in progress" or "improvement pending." However, under these circumstances, it is helpful to note when results of the action are expected to occur for the sake of further follow-up.

In another case, if an action was determined in an earlier reporting period, one must decide if there has been appropriate implementation, follow-up, and resolution of the OFI at hand. In other words, has the action been effective in capitalizing on the opportunity? If not, what is the reason for lack of improvement?

As another possibility, if the required action has been ineffective for an inordinate amount of time (three to six months), one must decide if there is a need for lateral or higher echelon support? Is the problem or OFI at hand too hard to resolve at the laboratory level without extradepartmental assistance? The need for such support should be identified in a timely fashion without inordinate delay—that is, without "spinning of the organizational wheels" or becoming "wrapped around the organizational axle."

In any case, there should be evidence of a logical progression of decisions being made from evaluation to action to assessment. The evaluation should adequately reflect the QI data provided, including comment if there is not adequate data; the action should complement the evaluation; and the assessment should provide a follow-up perspective of the data, evaluation, and action.

The final step in the EvAAC limb of the QI ten-step improvement cycle is titled Communication in Figure 8.5. This represents the third portion of the "Act" phase of Shewhart's improvement cycle. The laboratory should communicate lessons learned by using the profile as it is designed—as a report format for distribution to all personnel at all organizational levels who have a need to know.

Table V (pages 346 and 347) provides a table of decision (TOD), superimposed over the first two pages of the quality profile format. The TOD summarizes the key considerations for satisfying each major EvAAC element of the profile that are discussed above, including a number of short definitions, questions, and options. This chapter—as well as the complete profiles provided in the appendices—illustrate examples of how this decision table can be useful during the improvement cycle.

Cross-Linkage of Supporting Indicator Groupings

Using a spreadsheet-style format can aid in the revelation of cross-linkages between indicators of different operative and organizational activity levels—spanning the entirety of outcome, process, resource, QI, QAn, and QAc managerial activities. Table VI (pages 350 and 351) is a complicated matrix, but it does show how each quality profile indicator grouping correlates with 24 other groupings.[h] Although there is not 100% cross-reference, there still is extensive correlation. Such surveillance redundancy adds great strength to the profile as a quality management tool in the form of supporting documentation, especially when a subtle OFI must be detected. At times, it is not until reviewing supporting indicators that the proverbial light bulb of sudden discovery turns on and underlying causes suddenly illuminate their related effects. Additionally, cross-correlation generates an understanding of the full complexity of a given opportunity, helping to ensure complete plans for resolution and follow-up of the opportunity.

Table VII (pages 352 and 353) illustrates schematic examples of various major cross-correlations for the first 13 sample groupings (through the prelaboratory process segment of the path of work flow). The 13 vertical bar lines symbolize probes measuring the state of integrity of an organization's management system. This table clearly spotlights the common denominator for all healthcare quality as evidenced by whatever outcome (ie, vertical column 1) is being scrutinized. That mutual factor is

[h] There is no limit to the number of possible indicator groupings. Depending on the laboratory's managerial philosophy and personality mix (eg, the predominance of "lumpers" versus "splitters"), there might be fewer or greater than the 26 that are ultimately presented in this text. For example, there could be reason for creating specific groupings for patient or physician satisfaction with related focused studies. On the other hand, tables VI and VII lump internal and external QI together.

Table VI
Cross-Correlations of Indicator Groupings

Indicator Groupings	Outcome			Process							
				Post-laboratory			Intralaboratory				
	1	2	3	4	5	6	7	8	9	10	11
1. Customer satisfaction outcome	–	O	)	C	E	E	E	L	I	I	I
2. Patient care outcome	O	–		C	E	E	E	L	I	I	I
3. Employee safety outcome	O		–								
4. Report/product utilization	C	C		–							
5. Turnaround time/backlog	E	E			–	E	E	L	I	I	I
6. Report/product distribution	E	E			E	–					
7. Postdeterminative finalization	E	E			E		–	L	I	I	I
8. Reference laboratory studies	L	L			L		L	–	L	L	I
9. Analytical quality	I	I			I		I	L	–		I
10. Diagnostic quality	I	I			I		I	L		–	I
11. Predeterminative processing	I	I			I		I	I	I	I	–
12. Patient-request-spec validation	P	P			P	P	P	P	P	P	P
13. Test/product selection	C	C		C							
14. Workload/productivity review	R	R	R		R	R	R	R	R	R	R
15. Personnel management	R	R	R		R	R	R	R	R	R	R
16. Continuing medical education	R	R	R		R	R	R	R	R	R	R
17. Methods and procedures review	R	R	R		R	R	R	R	R	R	R
18 Computer management	R	R	R		R	R	R	R	R	R	R
19. Equipment management	R	R	R		R	R	R	R	R	R	R
20. Supply management	R	R	R		R	R	R	R	R	R	R
21. Facility management	R	R	R		R	R	R	R	R	R	R
22. Budget management	R	R	R		R	R	R	R	R	R	R
23. Quality improvement (QI)*	A	A	A	A	A	A	A	A	A	A	A
24. Quality anticipation (QAn)	A	A	A	A	A	A	A	A	A	A	A
25. Quality actualization (QAc)	A	A	A	A	A	A	A	A	A	A	A

O = outcome correlation
C = clinical laboratory process correlation
E = endproduct laboratory correlation
L = reference laboratory correlation
I = intralaboratory process correlation
P = prelaboratory process correlation
R = operative resource managerial correlation
A = administrative (organizational) resource correlation

* Includes both internal and external

resources—operative and organizational resources: the *structure* of Donabedian. And, the most consistently necessary of all of these structural elements are the organizational programs for QI, QAn, and QAc. Improvement, planning, and actualization of quality are the most common threads that course through the fabric of healthcare management at the most fundamental organizational levels. If there is any weakness in any of these three programs, then operative resource, process, and outcome management will suffer fundamental shortcomings.

The specific pattern of indicator cross-correlation is not immutable but varies among different laboratories; thus, the constellation of cross-linkages in Table VI or VII is not fixed. The matrices provided in this text suggest

Pre Lab		Operative Resources									Organizational Resources		
12	13	14	15	16	17	18	19	20	21	22	23	24	25
P	C	R	R	R	R	R	R	R	R	R	A	A	A
P	C	R	R	R	R	R	R	R	R	R	A	A	A
		R	R	R	R	R	R	R	R	R	A	A	A
	C										A	A	A
P		R	R	R	R	R	R	R	R	R	A	A	A
P		R	R	R	R	R	R	R	R	R	A	A	A
P		R	R	R	R	R	R	R	R	R	A	A	A
P		R	R	R	R	R	R	R	R	R	A	A	A
P		R	R	R	R	R	R	R	R	R	A	A	A
P		R	R	R	R	R	R	R	R	R	A	A	A
P		R	R	R	R	R	R	R	R	R	A	A	A
–		R	R	R	R	R	R	R	R	R	A	A	A
	–										A	A	A
R		–	R	R	R	R	R	R	R	R	A	A	A
R		R	–	R	R	R	R	R	R	R	A	A	A
R		R	R	–	R	R	R	R	R	R	A	A	A
R		R	R	R	–	R	R	R	R	R	A	A	A
R		R	R	R	R	–	R	R	R	R	A	A	A
R		R	R	R	R	R	–	R	R	R	A	A	A
R		R	R	R	R	R	R	–	R	R	A	A	A
R		R	R	R	R	R	R	R	–	R	A	A	A
R		R	R	R	R	R	R	R	R	–	A	A	A
A	A	A	A	A	A	A	A	A	A	A	–	A	A
A	A	A	A	A	A	A	A	A	A	A	A	–	A
A	A	A	A	A	A	A	A	A	A	A	A	A	–

only one way of looking at the major phases of the total operational path of work flow. Each laboratory must determine a path of work flow, a quality profile, and indicator matrix that is most representative of its own organizational and patient care milieu.

Comparison of Two Sectional Quality Profile Examples

This remainder of this chapter and the next three chapters offer a comparative analysis of two simulated quality profiles for a Chemistry Section and a Transfusion Service Section. These profiles illustrate the

Table VII
Schematic Outlines of Major Indicator Cross-Correlations

CORRELATIVE INDICATOR GROUPINGS	TARGET INDICATOR GROUPINGS				
	# 1	# 2	# 3	# 4	# 5
1. Customer satisfaction outcome	x	—	—	—	—
2. Patient care outcome	—	x		—	—
3. Employee safety outcome	—		x		
4. Product utilization	—	—		x	
5. Turnaround time/backlog	—	—			x
6. Product distribution	—	—			—
7. Postdeterminative finalization	—	—			—
8. Reference laboratory studies	—	—			—
9. Analytical quality	—	—			—
10. Diagnostic quality	—	—			—
11. Predeterminative processing	—	—			—
12. Patient-request-spec validation	—	—			—
13. Product selection	—	—		—	
14. Productivity	—	—	—		—
15. Personnel management	—	—	—		—
16. Continuing medical education	—	—	—		—
17. Methods and procedures review	—	—	—		—
18 Computer management	—	—	—		—
19. Supply management	—	—	—		—
20. Equipment management	—	—	—		—
21. Facility management	—	—	—		—
22. Budget management	—	—	—		—
23. Quality improvement (QI)*	—	—	—	—	—
24. Quality anticipation (QAn)	—	—	—	—	—
25. Quality actualization (QAc)	—	—	—	—	—

Note: Each horizontal bar represents a direct correlation with its respective target indicator grouping. Using the target grouping of product utilization (#4) as an example, patient care outcome is directly correlated (see bar at correlative indicator grouping level 2); whereas, employment safety is not directly correlated with patient care outcome (there is no bar at level 3 for target indicator #4). The lower case "x" indicates the position of each primary target grouping on its own respective schematic barline.

* Includes internal and external

extent to which TQM programs and the CQI process can promote effective laboratory management and how extensive an amount of managerial information can be brought together in compact form to yield a practical advantage. Appendices C through G offer complete, simulated profiles for *chemistry, hematology, microbiology*, and *transfusion service* from CP and *histopathology* from AP in their entirety.

The two section profiles that are primarily highlighted illustrate how differing QI data can be evaluated, acted on, assessed, and communicated through this condensed reporting formula. They also illustrate the importance of cross-indicator correlations that provide supporting evidence of improvement

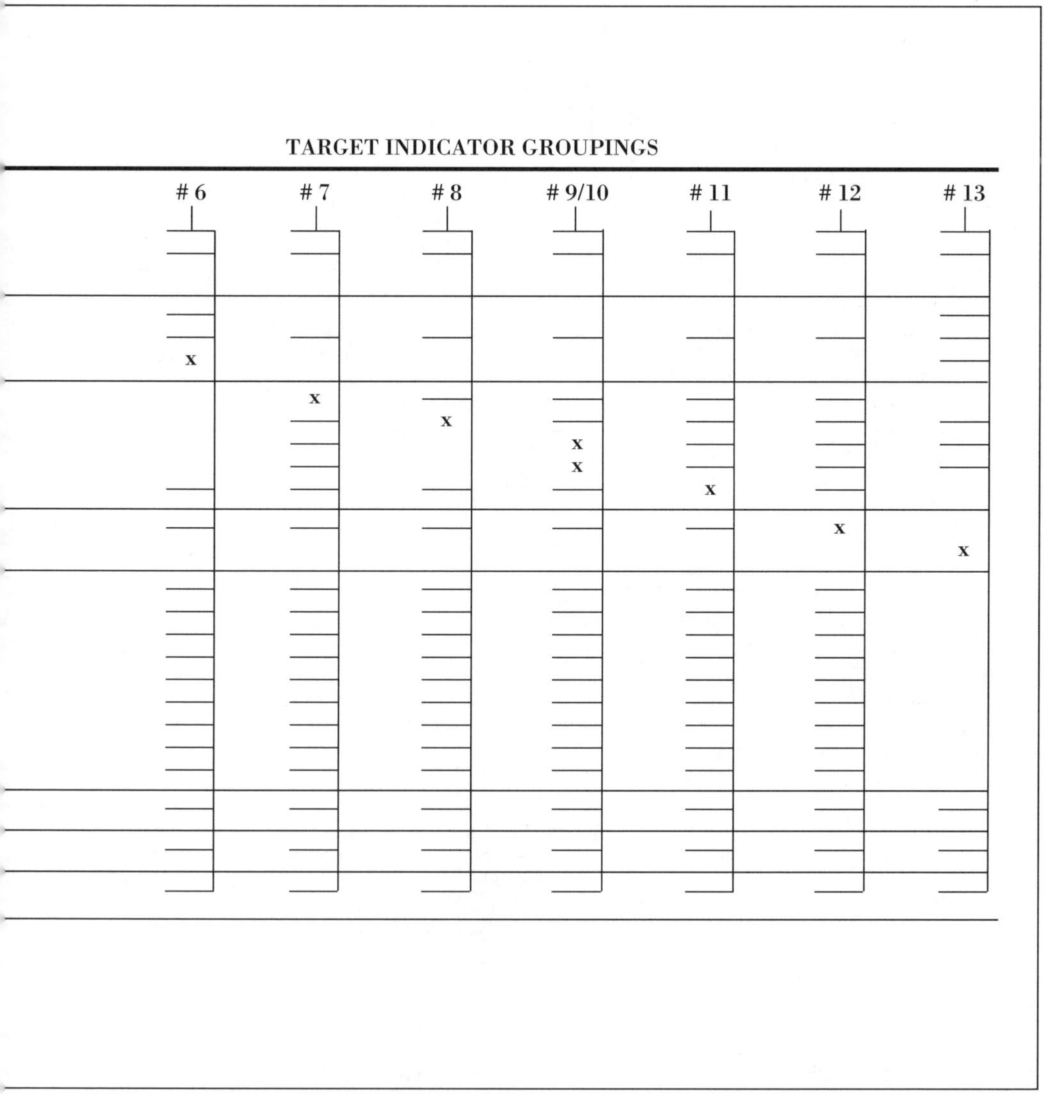

TARGET INDICATOR GROUPINGS

# 6	# 7	# 8	# 9/10	# 11	# 12	# 13
x						
	x	x	x x	x		
					x	x

opportunities. While the chemistry and transfusion section profiles are discussed in detail, the three other sample sections (hematology, microbiology, and histopathology) also are briefly addressed, revealing relevant aspects of quality management—some general and some specifically related to the given section.

All sample profiles in this text demonstrate a *maximum* amount of QI indicator groupings generated from the *entire* path of operative and organizational work flow. This comprehensive presentation provides as many teaching examples as possible to portray the intricacies of TQM and CQI.

Yet, even these detailed examples are not exhaustive in terms of the number or identity of specific indicators that are actually possible within

Indicator Grouping 1
Customer Satisfaction
Quality Profile: QI Report Dec 95
Section: Chemistry

Indicator Grouping/ Specific Indicator: Threshold (Periodicity)	QI Data Observations (Date trend started) J A S O N D	
POSTLABORATORY OUTCOME WORK FLOW SEGMENT		
Customer satisfaction: any positive or negative report; sentinel event!! (Monthly) a. Overall review	Section nominated by Med Dept for Hosp 1996 Quality Management Award; lab's establishing Lab-Nursing Teams was leading factor	
b. Thoracic surgery study: to be determined (TBD)	Protocol being coordinated with Thoracic Surgery Service (Nov 95)	

Quality Profile: QI Report Dec 95
Section: Transfusion Service

POSTLABORATORY OUTCOME WORK FLOW SEGMENT		
Customer satisfaction: any positive or negative report; sentinel event!! (Monthly)	1a. Due to clinical staff complaints, hospital has formed an administrative task force to assist the Trans Service in filling staff vacancies (Dec 95)	
	1b. Patient had a hemolytic reaction on Ward 22; See Patient Care Outcome and Utilization Indicators	

!! = sentinel event

these general work flow segments and indicator groupings. Surprisingly, as comprehensive and complex as the sample profiles in this text might appear, they still are not all-inclusive: they provide only a representative sampling of the myriad of actual possibilities of individual aspects of care, indicators, criteria, thresholds, and subsequent opportunities for improvement. No text, seminar, or workshop could ever be expected to produce an exhaustive listing of all imaginable specific indicators. Thus, the models presented here provide only guidelines for indicator selection.

These profiles might seem impractical because of their sheer ponderosity. To ease any misapprehension in this regard, the reader should understand first that the quality profile format in this text was originally developed in a large pathology department where it was found to be useful in providing an understandable road map to quality

Evaluation of QI Data, TQM System, and CQI Process	Action Action Person: (Date Initiated)	Assessment of Overall Improvement
Continuous quality improvement over the last year has been recognized	Continue the good work!! ACTION: Section team	Continuous improvement cited
Coordination in progress	To be ready for QI review by Mar 96 ACTION: Medical Director	Improvement of QI process is ongoing
Evidence over several months has shown that QI, QAn, and QAc programs/QM interface/CQI process are ineffective	Coordinate with the Hospital Task Force (HTF) ACTION: Section Medical Director	Ineffective TQM system, QM interface, and CQI process: Section needs improved intra- and extra-departmental support
Hospital assistance is being provided to perform QI functions thru the Task Force	Design focused study of blood utilization on Ward 22 for Jan 96 ACTION: Task Force	

management—thus, it has been tested by practical application. Second, in that trial setting, the profile format was clerically feasible by either manual or automated word processing—albeit, dedicated clerical resources were necessary. Third, the profiles presented in this text are purposefully comprehensive, and various managerial points have been deliberately exaggerated for teaching purposes, illustrating as many examples of indicator selection and evaluation as possible.

Finally, one ought not to be deterred by such misapprehension since each laboratory must still design a constellation of its own important aspects of care and respective indicators of quality that are tailored specifically for that laboratory's own unique ecology of operational characteristics and working environment. In real practice, each laboratory always must tailor such profiles to fit specific operational needs, administrative (including clerical) resources, and management objectives—the key ingredient being resources.

All five sectional profiles offered in this text portray a wide range of varying operative and organizational opportunities for improvement. However, there is one central theme: all sample profiles—including the chemistry and transfusion examples—are designed to portray the effect of personnel shortage in a progressively decremental fashion. Each section lacks six full-time personnel; however, those six vacancies represent a wide percentage range of vacancies among the five simulated sections. For example, the chemistry section profile shows the least effect from personnel shortage, which would be a "best case" scenario. Conversely, the transfusion service shows the greatest effect derived from personnel shortage—definitely a "worst case" scenario.[i]

POSTLABORATORY OUTCOME WORK FLOW SEGMENT

This first segment of the example Quality profile format involves three indicator groupings—remembering that there could be other choices for outcome surveillance, as well. Each grouping includes one or more specific quality indicators, each specific indicator addressing some measurable outcome event at the terminus of the laboratory path of work flow. The profile begins with the most important and general QI topic: customer satisfaction outcome. Patient care outcome and employee safety outcome follow sequentially.

Customer Satisfaction Management (Indicator Grouping 1)

Chemistry profile interpretation:
The evaluation of the collected data for this outcome grouping of the Chemistry profile is that there is excellent customer satisfaction. First, as a general observation, this evaluation is accurate from the viewpoint of the Department of Medicine and the hospital staff from whom there has been a very positive, substantive response to laboratory quality management. Medicine's laudatory action stems particularly from the effectiveness of a laboratory-nursing team program established by the Chemistry Section. The laboratory department quality management leadership cites the section team for keeping up the "good work"—a congratulatory comment. The assessment of effective control and improvement is appropriate. The communication step for this general indicator appears to be entirely intact, based on the apparent success of the section's QI program.

[i] Especially in the case of the Transfusion Service example, none of the scenarios depicted in any of the example profiles in this text is intended as models of any particular operative or organizational managerial style. In fact, they are occasionally quite exaggerated for the sake of emphasizing certain teaching points.

In addition, Chemistry is coordinating a protocol for a focused study with the Thoracic Surgery Department. The profile lists the medical director as being responsible for establishing the protocol, since the coordination is at the doctor-to-doctor level and requires joint clinical-laboratory criteria. There is a specific milestone date for implementation of the project. The assessment of ongoing improvement of the QI process is accurate since the newly scheduled, focused study is supplementing the general survey approach. Communication appears to be effective, so far.

Overall, this profile grouping provides an example of an excellent customer satisfaction "top line," reflecting very effective quality management and ongoing improvement at this terminus of the path of work flow. All EvAAC steps appear to be in concert with the observations at hand.

Transfusion profile interpretation:
This laboratory section's profile presents the data solely in the form of general survey observations. The "top line" evaluation is that the Transfusion Service has significant customer satisfaction problems—grand opportunities for improvement, to say the least. These customer satisfaction statements set the stage for a series of problematic indicator groupings that will reveal themselves as the profile is analyzed, for this is the tip of a proverbial and menacing iceberg.

The most profound evaluative statement is the summation that all three TQM programs (QI, QAn, and QAc), the QM interface, and the CQI process have deteriorated to the point that a hospital-level task force has been formed to resolve the overriding problem (a giant, multidepartmental opportunity for improvement) of staff vacancies. Even though it is customer dissatisfaction that is highlighted, the greater portent of the evaluation is that this Transfusion Service has serious operative and organizational problems that weave through the entire fabric—into the very depths—of their laboratory operations. The responsibility for coordinating the action rests on the section medical director, the chief quality team leader. The hospital-level concern regarding the Transfusion Service and subsequent task force formation comprises an apparently new indicator topic freshly generated from a committee or task force minutes—rather than the more deliberately programed and scheduled intradepartmental QI process.

Equally alarming, the second indicator reports that a hemolytic reaction has occurred, to be further explained and followed under the Patient Care Outcome and Laboratory Product Utilization indicator groupings (Groupings 2 and 4). The evaluation relates that the newly formed task force is providing hospital-level assistance for QI follow-up of the transfusion reaction. As meted out at the section QI level, the action is understandably knee-jerk in nature but matches the facts at hand, recommending that the task force carry on an additional focused study of blood utilization, including transfusion practice, on ward 22 where the reaction occurred. There is no focused study of customer satisfaction being carried on at this section level; rather, a hospital level focused study in the form of a joint task force has just been established.

The overall assessment mirrors the evaluations and actions for both indicator topics presented. The assessment points out that, while there is great customer dissatisfaction at the top line, a major contribution to the section's resource problem is an inadequate CQI process at the hospital support level. Resolution of this improvement opportunity requires improvement of personnel hiring and improved quality management at both departmental and extradepartmental levels—managerial echelons above the operative level of the Transfusion Service.

Communication calls for extensive coordination between section, service, and department quality management teams. The profile implies that there is a need for enhanced feedback with extradepartmental activities as well, such as the specially focused, interdisciplinary task force, personnel management office, and the hospital administration.

All of these customer-related events introduce an ominous sign at this section's "top line" for quality. Although, the root of the problem allegedly is a severe personnel shortage, Transfusion's top line is a small tip of a very large mountain of improvement opportunities.

Additional profile interpretations

Hematology (Appendix D). Since there has been no evidence of significant customer surveillance activity over at least 6 months, the customer satisfaction QI process is improving by establishment of some specific focused studies. These studies are aimed at known problematic process indicators that are more fully described later in this profile.

Microbiology (Appendix E). Similar to Hematology, customer satisfaction is generally on target with not only a general survey being reported, but a new focused study protocol also is being coordinated with internal medicine department.

Histopathology (Appendix G). Administrative levels above the laboratory have created a hospital-level task force to improve customer satisfaction regarding surgical pathology report turnaround time. In addition, there is establishment of a study focused on dermatology service customer satisfaction.

Discussion:

The quality profile begins with surveillance of outcome improvement. As demonstrated earlier by the TQM and CQI models, the peak of the hierarchical model represents the most important element of overall laboratory quality assessment: organizational actualization of continuing quality improvement as evidenced by customer satisfaction. This is the top line of organizational excellence—rather than the entrepreneur's proverbial "bottom line" of profit.

Indicator grouping. There are several real or potential types of customer-supplier relationships that can be monitored and evaluated.

These customer types include the patient, the physician, the laboratory and other hospital employees, other hospital departments, the hospital administration, and external organizations or agencies all with whom the laboratory does business—the laboratory serving as a supplier of one sort of a product or service and receiving some sort of product or service in return. Although employee satisfaction is partially considered later in the profile under the employee safety indicator grouping, any aspect of employee satisfaction can be addressed in this first, global grouping if it is deemed important enough.

In a TQM and CQI-oriented organization, working relationships should be different than are ordinarily encountered in a classical hierarchical, bureaucratic organization. The top administrator-middle manager, employer-employee, producer-customer type of relationships should be all two-way—not one-way, as Max Weber might have envisioned in his early theorizing on organizational hierarchy. With TQM programs and the CQI process in place, all organizational communication is two-way and free flowing; all relationships are of the interactive supplier-customer type. Within the organization, every employee position is included in both the decision-making and communication processes. Each organizational position at every operational level has to develop "supplier-customer relations" with all other positions—all organizational positions or units serve each other in some reciprocal fashion. All business relations outside the organization also deserve similar supplier-customer status since they are all served by, as well as support, the laboratory mission.

Healthcare laboratory customer satisfaction is directly related to the degree of quality of the health care provided. Whether the customer be the patient, physician, or some other clinical or laboratory staff member, a quality manager can ascertain the degree of satisfaction on the basis of the customer's subjective interpretation or perception of the quality of health care as much as on the basis of objective analysis.

For example, the simulated profiles demonstrate two types of indicators of customer satisfaction. The first is in the form of very generic customer satisfaction outcome data that are passively gathered by occurrence screening of several sources, including incident reports, questionnaires or surveys, and committee findings. Much of this information surfaces naturally as subjective data.

The second indicator type is in the form of a more objective, actively pursued focused study, such as the one proposed for Chemistry on thoracic surgery patients. Such a study requires close collaboration with the attending physician and other clinical staff to develop a study protocol, establish the method of the study, choose indicators and thresholds, collect the data, and perform the remaining EvAAC steps of the improvement process—all at the joint laboratorian-clinician level. The potential number of indicators of the quality of customer satisfaction is limited only by the number of important aspects of care and the customers affected by the quality of any of these IACs—as is true for any indicator grouping.

Supporting Indicators. As illustrated in Table VI and VII, customer satisfaction is a global type of indicator grouping; it interrelates with all the other 25 indicator groupings actually listed in the profile. It is global because the extent of cross-correlation is inestimable in scope since all customers—both internal and external—are involved. This vast scope of correlative possibilities is greater than "panorganizational," often extending far beyond the laboratory organization and, quite possibly, even beyond the hospital. Only the term "global" or "universal" is an adequate description here.

Therefore, any of the other quality profile groupings can potentially support the customer satisfaction interpretation. In the case of the Chemistry profile, review of all 25 other quality indicator groupings will reveal a consistent pattern of excellence with only occasional outliers. Sporadic, random, and occasionally systematic error appear to be under control and in some phase of continuous improvement. The section is closely watching, controlling, containing, and resolving known weaknesses, such as the multichannel analyzer. All of these supporting indicators confirm what is reflected under the customer satisfaction grouping.

In the case of the Transfusion profile, further analysis will show that the situation seems almost hopelessly the opposite. There are severe problems in many phases of the section's path of work flow, a significant number of groupings are out of control, and all of this is clearly presaged by the customer satisfaction indicator grouping.

Threshold. As is true for every other aspect of the quality profile model, the threshold provided in the example for customer satisfaction is:

1) Only one possibility of many; although this threshold statement was useful in the author's laboratory, it is not the only option and is not necessarily the right statement for every laboratory to use.

2) Extremely brief as a documentary reminder; it is not necessarily the complete threshold statement. The entire statement, including all its specific conditions, should be on file under the respective indicator title.

The example threshold—"any positive or negative report; sentinel event"—mandates that any occurrence screening report of any type that reveals an opportunity for improvement must be mentioned in the quality profile report. Therefore, since there must be "zero defects," the indicator qualifies as a sentinel event. The threshold for the focused study in Chemistry is still under consideration, annotated as "to be determined" (or TBD) and to be included in the profile when the study protocol is finalized.

Monitoring Periodicity. A section can monitor and report the general topic of customer satisfaction as an ongoing survey every reporting period (usually monthly) if it is so critical to the entire CQI process—incident reports, congratulatory and complaint messages, committee minutes, and any other possible sources might need to be documented, evaluated, and followed-up without delay. On the other hand, a section can monitor focused studies of specific target groups with regular periodicity but with less frequency—usually quarterly. As is true for every major indicator grouping, the periodicity of monitoring and evaluating depends on the managerial ecology of the laboratory in its unique operational resource dependent environment.

Evaluation. Because of the cross-linkage of customer satisfaction with all other outcome, endproduct process, intralaboratory process, operative resource, QI, QAn, and QAc groupings, the evaluation of customer satisfaction should always focus on one other segment of the path of work flow as the actual target for improvement—at the very least. There often will be more than one segment or grouping that requires supporting evaluation.

Based on the three standard options for evaluation in a CQI environment, the Chemistry profile cites data that are currently on target with respective thresholds with continuous improvement over a reasonable period of time. The Transfusion Service profile evaluation is that of blatant OFIs of a problematic nature requiring immediate investigation and follow-up.

Action. Based on the three standard options for evaluation in a CQI managerial milieu—keeping to the middle course of simply continuing the improvement process as scheduled (just "good quality management as usual") is best for Chemistry, with no action needed except to keep up the excellent QI work, overall. In Transfusion, the option requires immediate action to solve several blatant problems of a systemic process nature.

Because of the global nature of customer satisfaction, required actions will often involve extradepartmental coordination. Always establish an action officer and a milestone date for final completion or an interim review.

Assessment. Conducting the process of assessment is always in two stages:

1) Set milestones for assessment of a new action when there has been too little time for a recommended action to produce any improvement.

2) Determine effectiveness of a previously established action after there has been adequate time for results.

Additionally, when assessing the effectiveness of any action always consider the three standard options for assessment in a CQI environment. Of those three options, it is especially important to recognize if there has been no significant improvement over a reasonable amount of time. If so, it is necessary to determine what aspect of the QI process should be adjusted to increase sensitivity to improvement opportunities.

Communication. The two indicator grouping examples provide their own models for communicating QI information. First, the Chemistry profile segment illustrates that there is a need to continue to communicate customer satisfaction lessons learned with all laboratory operative and administrative levels, as well as with other hospital departments involved and with the hospital QI system. In the second example, there is a need to communicate Transfusion Service customer <u>dis</u>satisfaction with the same general addressees, as well as the specially appointed hospital level task force.

Indicator Grouping 2
Patient Care Outcome

Chemistry Section Quality Profile

Indicator Grouping/ Specific Indicator: Threshold (Periodicity)	QI Data Observations (Date trend started) J A S O N D
Patient Care Outcome: no threat to health status; sentinel event!! (Monthly) a. Overall review	0 = no adverse outcome Last incident in Dec 94 .....Patient Code #..... 0 0 0 0 0 0
b. Pediatric lead level (Quarterly)	- - 0 - - 0 Chart review study began in Mar 95 after incident - = no report scheduled 0 = no adverse outcome

Transfusion Service Quality Profile

Patient Care Outcome: no threat to life or limb; sentinel event!! (Monthly) a. Hemolytic transfusion reaction: none!!	0 = no adverse outcome .....Patient Code #..... 0 0 0 0 0 53* * = Nonfatal hemolytic transfusion reaction (pt #53) on Ward 22 (Med) during 12-8 shift: nurse mistakenly mixed the identity of 2 brothers on the same ward

Note: OT = overtime; HTF = hospital task force !! = sentinel event

These sample scenarios suggest the intra- and extralaboratory routes of information dissemination that are so essential to affect sustained quality improvement. It is important to remember that general QI information can be dispersed without divulging the actual identity of a specific provider, clinical service, or patient that is involved.

Patient Care Outcome Management (Indicator Grouping 2)

Chemistry profile interpretation:
Evaluation of this second outcome indicator grouping demonstrates that no patients are reported to have suffered any untoward event secondary to any Chemistry laboratory end product. We derive this evidence from data gathered from a general survey of incidents, as well as from a focused study of pediatric lead testing.

Evaluation of QI Data, TQM System, and CQI Process	Action Action Person: (Date Initiated)	Assessment of Overall Improvement
On target x 12 mo; general survey has not detected any OFI over an inordinate amount of time; a focused study has been in progress	Change periodocity of evaluation to quarterly ACTION: Supervisor	Improvement of QI process is in progress
On target x 3 qtrs; baseline established	1. Review this study to ensure that it is adequately sensitive 2. Select new study topic for Jan 96 ACTION: Supervisor	Improvement of QI process is in progress
Reaction was non-fatal; serious problem with Ward 22 staff, especially the 12-8 (night) shift. who are not receiving training in patient identification and transfusion techniques; tng may require OT $	1. Coordinate with C, Nurse and C, Med regarding training and supervisory responsibilities 2. Study use of "floating" staff 3. Study pt identification process ACTION: Medical Director	Ineffective QI process: Needs improved response at HTF level to a known operative-level training requirement

The general survey shows an "on target" pattern extending from December 1994; the last reportable incident of adverse patient outcome occurred twelve months before this quality report. The general survey has not detected any OFI over a lengthy period. Since a focused study approach is already in progress, the recommended action for the survey is to change the periodicity of reporting the general indicator from monthly to quarterly for routine review; this is to simply keep the general topic alive for periodic review and questioning. Of course, if any adverse incident ever arises, it is reportable immediately during the month of occurrence without waiting for the scheduled reporting date.

The special study of pediatric lead testing offers nine months of cumulative data. The evaluation and action for this study seem in synchrony with the data at hand. Since this focused process has established a nine month baseline, one might surmise that a first quarter 1992 incident stimulated this pediatric study. Nevertheless, without any adverse incident or process failure detected over the past three quarters, the entire process of pediatric lead testing (from clinical selection to clinical utilization) seems to be intact.

At this point, either 1) the study is flawed and is not sensitive enough to reveal an OFI or 2) the study has truly documented that the QI process is indeed intact and there is an effective laboratory-clinical testing dynamic. If there is any way of improving the study by focusing on any particular part of the path of work flow yet untouched or improving indicator definition, criteria, or threshold levels, then those changes in the study should be analytically determined on a joint laboratory-clinical team level and acted on accordingly. Thus, the laboratory will have addressed an OFI, improving the improvement process itself.

Conversely, if the design of the current focused study is adequate and does not show promise for any further improvement, then it is time to select a new focused study topic based on established prioritization criteria—in other words, reprioritizing all related IACs and reselecting the most likely candidate for improvement. Depending on the priority of other indicator groupings and the amount of quality management assets available, the patient outcome grouping—like any other grouping topic—also is always a candidate for no reporting at all. It depends on how critical the laboratory considers monitoring the patient care grouping as a generic or global, ongoing, proactive QI activity.

Continuing with review of the Chemistry profile, assessment of both the general and the focused indicators reveals an effective improvement process—so far. However, after such lengthy periods with no discovery of any opportunity for improvement, the section is improving the process by ensuring the sensitivity of the two surveillance approaches, reducing the frequency of reporting of the general survey to a quarterly periodicity, (ie, phasing out the passive, general survey approach), and moving on to a new focused study topic of higher priority than pediatric lead testing. In both cases, the assessment is accurate: improvement is in progress.

Transfusion profile interpretation:
This laboratory section reports that an adverse patient outcome has occurred in December—a nonfatal hemolytic reaction. The observations column anonymously identifies the patient by code number 53. The data relates that a ward staff member allegedly caused the problem by mistaking the identity of two brothers who were patients on the same ward; there has not been any investigation and proof of this allegation, so far.

Evaluation of the data reveals that one improvement opportunity at hand is to upgrade the ward staff training in transfusion technique, particularly those who work the nondaytime hours. Team analysis of the situation reminds us that transfusion problems can also occur because untrained "floater" personnel might work on the ward during shifts that are difficult to staff—and train. If this is the current practice, then here is an opportunity to improve the selection or training of the floater personnel.

The evaluation also raises the issue of need for additional training funds, possibly in the form of overtime remuneration.

The investigative and follow-up action requires coordination with the clinical leaders involved in management of the ward and the medical director of the Transfusion Service—the latter being primarily responsible for the clinical level of healthcare decision making within the laboratory section. There is a need to study the adequacy of clinical training and proficiency, as well as supervisory effectiveness.

Also, other possibilities require consideration. For example, the patient identification process requires investigative study. The transfusion mishap could be related to the physician's ordering of blood, the laboratory's crossmatching of blood, or the nursing staff's administering blood for the incorrect patient because of a flawed identification process.

The overall assessment is that the QI process in the Transfusion Service has been ineffective because of inadequate follow-up to a known training need. Allegedly, there has been some neglect of the training of ward personnel that are assigned to work during nondaytime hours. There is a need for support at a higher echelon of support, namely the newly formed hospital task force. Supporting indicators located further into the body of the profile will substantiate all of these needs.

Additional profile interpretations:

Hematology (Appendix D). Quality surveillance shows that patient care outcome is on target with an intact QI process.

Microbiology (Appendix E). Patient care outcome, including the QI process, is on target.

Histopathology (Appendix G). Patient care outcome surveillance shows evidence that the QI process is effective.

Discussion:

This indicator grouping is aimed at the quintessential customer of health care: the patient. For many laboratorians as well as other healthcare professionals, patient care outcome has been the ultimate grouping, superseding any other "top line" topic. Assuredly, this end result is the key focus of most laboratory mission statements. However, although the patient is of uppermost importance in a healthcare facility, there are a great number of other potential customers—any of whom can take QI precedence under certain circumstances.

Hence in this sample quality format, the patient care grouping is second in precedence of listing to the broader outcome topic of general customer satisfaction and higher in precedence than employee safety. In certain situations, however, the order of priority for patient care and employee safety might be in reversed order. For example, when health-threatening bacterial contagion or toxic fume intoxication breaks out in a laboratory section due to inadequate engineering controls, employee safety can become a critically important grouping—superseding the importance of any other customer. And, this can happen!

Indicator Grouping. Ongoing patient care outcome indicator data can be available from incident reports, questionnaires or surveys, and committee findings. Focused studies require both laboratory and medical record review. Patient anonymity must be maintained. Any number of indicators are available as focused study topics.

The patient outcome indicator grouping affords the key opportunity to evaluate the parameters of clinical relevance, the parameters being sensitivity, specificity, predictive value, and efficiency.[13] These very important characteristics are linked to the probability of positive and negative test results occuring by chance in a clinical setting.

It is relatively easy to determine clinical relevance after one has established criteria for true positive (TP), true negative (TN), false positive (FP), and false negative (FN) test results. Obviously, the test method must be well controlled, a normal reference range must have been established, and clinical criteria for related clinical symptoms and signs must have been determined on a joint laboratory-clinical basis. It is the latter three conditions that require most time and effort.

- *Sensitivity*, or the incidence of true test positivity in a diseased patient population is calculated from $\frac{TP}{TP + FN} \times 100$
- *Specificity*, or the incidence of true test negativity in a healing patient population is calculated from $\frac{TN}{TN + FP} \times 100$
- *Predictive value* of a true positive test result in a mixed healthy and diseased patient population is calculated from $$\frac{TP}{TP + FP} \times 100$$
- *Test efficiency*, or the percent of all results that are true results (either positive or negative) is calculable from $$\frac{TP + TN}{TP + FP + TN + FN} \times 100$$

Any of these parameters are useful as specific QI indicators of clinical relevance. Thus, this indicator grouping can be indispensable in meeting FDA and CLIA requirements for high complexity methods. Any of the four parameters can serve as specific indicators under this major grouping.

Supporting Indicators. Patient outcome is another indicator with global cross-linkage. For the Chemistry profile, a review of all other indicators of quality—such as customer satisfaction, test utilization, test selection, internal and external QI, QAn, and QAc—will corroborate that there are no adverse patient events during the reporting period. Thus, the redundancy inherent in the profile model helps to confirm that the quality of patient outcome is indeed accurate as stated.

Regarding the Transfusion profile, review of blood utilization, specimen collection, personnel (vacancies and continuing education), external CAP inspections, incident reports, QAn, and QAc reveals a multiplicity of interlinked problems. The seed of all these problems seems to be personnel shortages in both the Transfusion Service and the nursing staff on ward 22 with subsequent lack of follow-up on required training.

However, though the nurse's mistake is professionally a red flag denoting a serious lack of individual proficiency, it is the overall process involved in administering blood transfusions that is most important and must be addressed first and foremost by the QI program—and part of that process includes the support provided by the leadership at several operative levels of responsibility. For example, the question remains to be answered if the transfusion reaction arose from a flaw in the process/function of patient identification or staff training. Thus, a systemic process could be at fault, redirecting quality management's attention from the immediate target of individual proficiency.

Threshold. Since the general indicator grouping is, again, that of a sentinel event, the threshold is an all or none statement—no threat to life or limb; sentinel event. If there should be any latitude to the degree of the threat, that should be a joint laboratorian-clinician decision. The profile does not state the threshold for the focused study on pediatric lead testing, but it should be explicitly clear in the study protocol that is on file.

Monitoring Periodicity. In both examples, the general survey of patient care outcome is monitored every month because it is so critical for the subject laboratory. As demonstrated by the Chemistry Section, however, the scheduling of both the general and focused studies can be less frequent to allow more time for data collection and analysis and to relieve the QI workload. This decision takes into account the relatively low rate of high-risk factors involving most chemistry tests compared to the Transfusion Service.

Evaluation. As with any global outcome indicator grouping, the cross-linkage between patient outcome and the other 25 groupings adds grounds for explaining the roots of a given problem and providing the opportunity for a substantive improvement. Consequently, there should be more than just a superficial, quick fix at the top line level of quality surveillance.

Compared to the customer satisfaction indicator grouping, however, the laboratory should not evaluate patient care outcome solely on the basis of a subjective perception on the part of an observer. Base the evaluation of patient care outcome predominantly on the analysis of valid, objective data elements.

Evaluation of the Chemistry data reveals a section actively searching to find improvement opportunities. This is a sign of anticipatory quality management and is predictive of a relatively brief quality profile with comparatively few really high priority, crisis-oriented indicators being

Indicator Grouping 3
Employee Safety

Chemistry Section Quality Profile

Indicator Grouping/ Specific Indicator: Threshold (Periodicity)	QI Data Observations (Date trend started) J A S O N D	
Employee Safety Outcome: no potential or actual hazard; sentinel event!! (Monthly) a. Biological	Biohzd labels dc'd IAW CDC universal precautions; now technologists' concern over control of HIV specimens has been raised at the management-employer relations level; dept-level task force confirms that contagion is under control	
b. Fire	No OFI identified x 12 mo	
c. Electrical	No OFI identified x 12 mo	
d. Chemical/Carcinogen	No OFI identified x 12 mo	
e. Waste Disposal	No OFI identified x 12 mo	
f. Radionuclide	No OFI identified x 12 mo	
g. Environmental	No OFI identified x 12 mo	

Transfusion Service Quality Profile

Employee Safety Outcome: no potential or actual hazard; sentinel event!! (Monthly) a. Biological	Recent concern of technologists over HIV has unmasked their perception that there is need for improved control (Nov 95)	
b. Fire	No OFI identified x 12 mo	
c. Electrical	No OFI identified x 12 mo	
d. Chemical/Carcinogen	No OFI identified x 12 mo	
e. Waste Disposal	No OFI identified x 12 mo	
f. Radionuclide	Not applicable	
g. Environmental	The staff complained of heat in Room A03 (platelet storage) in Dec; usually is a problem in the summer	

IAW = in accordance with !! = sentinel event dc'd = discontinued

Evaluation of QI Data, TQM System, and CQI Process	Action Action Person: (Date Initiated)	Assessment of Overall Improvement
Contagion is in control. There is need for greater training and worker awareness of the philosophy and intent of universal precautions	Enhance biohazard training program by Jan 96; coordinate with section volunteers and hosp infection control service ACTION: Laboratory Safety Officer	Biohazard training needs improvement: A more complete assessment to be made in Feb 96
These four indicators have been on target x 12 mo; there has been no improvement over an inordinate amount of time	Select a focused study for each of the six safety indicators to be scheduled over the next six months ACTION: Supervisor	Ineffective response to general survey: Improve sensitivity of QI process

There is need for increased training and worker awareness of universal precaution rationale	Enhance biohazard training program by Jan 96; ACTION: Hospital Infection Control (Nov 95)	There is effective contagion control BUT infection control training needs to be improved
These 4 indicators have been on target x 12 mo; there has been no improvement over an inordinate amount of time	1. Exclude any immediate problems ACTION: Dept Lab Safety Officer 2. Establish focused studies over the next year ACTION: Acting Supervisor	Improvement has been stalled due to staffing problems; prioritize QI carefully until section is rebuilt
QI Note: Ineffective TQM system, QM interface, and CQI process overall; see notes under Blood Product Utilization, Postdeterminative Finalization, and Facility indicator groupings		

scheduled for ongoing monitoring. Also in such a quality management posture, there are likely to be relatively more *ad hoc* (nonprogramed) indicators being generated through committee and other quality team efforts at the multidisciplinary, operative support, and peer level lateral to (not higher than) the laboratory. Thus, there will be plenty of time for invention and innovation in quality management.

Conversely, the Transfusion Service data characterizes a section that is overwhelmed by crisis management with no time to seek out opportunities proactively. This "worst case" example will rapidly reveal that the occurrence of an adverse patient care outcome is linked to many other problematic clinical and nonclinical laboratory activities—all of which can be associated with the fundamental lack of technical personnel.

The Transfusion Service profile portends grave trouble, predictive of a much longer, more complex quality profile with many high-priority, crisis-laden indicators. In such a quality management posture, resolution of such problems will require intensive, quality team efforts involving administrative, organizational management echelons higher than the laboratory.

Unfortunately, there will be minimal time for innovative planning for improvement. Instead, quality management will consist mostly of implementation and concentration of management processes and techniques already in place. Any consequent planning of innovative approaches will require snap decisions and no time for trial runs. Whatever new courses of action are decided must work correctly the first time because of the criticalness of the patient care services that are under scrutiny.

Action. The Chemistry example demonstrates straightforward action requirements without complications. In stark comparison, the Transfusion Service example requires multiple actions involving the highest levels of responsibility. The laboratory personnel shortage allegedly is the leading contributory factor in the section's inability to effectively interface with other hospital activities such as ward 22—and effectively execute needed, already recognized actions such as the training of ward personnel in transfusion technique. The need for intensive, interdisciplinary support and action justifies the hospital-level action of formulating a joint task force to solve the root of the personnel shortage problems—as well as resolving the patient care outcome problem which is only symptomatic of an immense ripple effect from lack of adequate section staffing.

For the sake of effective resolution of the key issues at stake, Transfusion's personnel shortage has gone far beyond the "critical mass" of workload management and staffing terminology. For this section and the hospital, overall, the situation has evolved into "survival of the managerially fittest," making expedient action—and effective results—absolutely necessary.

Assessment. The Chemistry example provides a strong managerial image of controlled, continuous improvement; the profile might show several problems on further review, but none isof a truly critical nature. In the Transfusion Service profile, typical of all their indicator groupings, the underlying assessment challenge is not to answer how the personnel shortage or training problem can be resolved. Rather, it is to answer how the precepts of TQM and CQI have been neglected throughout all aspects of the QI, QAn, and QAc programs and allowed to go so awry.[j]

Communication. Comparing these two examples, Chemistry has no apparent difficulty in communicating effectively at the patient care outcome level. However, special effort must be made by the Transfusion Service and all other related laboratory managerial echelons to communicate and coordinate with the clinical leadership on ward 22 as well as the new task force. Management of patient care outcome, being such a global indicator grouping, often requires a department-wide and hospital-wide multidisciplinary communication network. The laboratory should always be able to openly disseminate important information without divulging the identity of a provider, clinical service, or patient that is involved.

Employee Safety Outcome Management (Indicator Grouping 3)

Chemistry profile interpretation:

This is the third outcome indicator grouping. There can be a varying number of specific indicators included in this outcome grouping, depending on the types of employees and other customers-at-risk and their unique safety needs.

The observed data for employee safety outcome reveals that there is a problem in communicating biohazard policy—while no hazard secondary to specific organism contagion actually exists. The laboratory's adopting universal precautions for all biohazardous samples, including the discontinuation of the use of biohazard labels, has created the situation. There is a report that the management-employee relationship is potentially at stake, but the problem can be solved with adequate education and training.

> *Using compliance with universal precautions as a teaching example might seem arguable to some readers since the transition to the CDC universal precautions should have occurred in the mid-to late 1980s However, it is not impossible that there are certain localized bastions of "pre-HIV" policy still in existence, based on differences of medical management opinion regarding patient population-at-risk and resource limitations. Second, as the incidence of HIV infection and other causes of acquired immunosuppression increases, there will be a concomitant*

[j] Happily, this Transfusion Service scenario is just an example that is designed to dramatize how ineffective quality management can become, to what extreme lengths ineffective management might go—and how to improve it. As a real life portrayal, it cannot be taken too seriously. Besides, fact can be even stranger than fiction.

increase in the associated communicable diseases—such as is already being experienced with tuberculosis—that will threaten all laboratorians-at-risk.

In addition, national policies will continue to change as time goes on. For example, OSHA standards have already begun to eclipse the earlier CDC policies. OSHA now requires that phlebotomy trays and other patient specimen containers need to be labeled as containing potentially contaminated patient specimens—although CDC universal precautions have eliminated biohazard labeling of individual specimens. According to OSHA, specimens can also be labeled, but they still must all be handled by the same precautionary measures, including protective barriers. The end result is the same: the environment is protected through these engineering controls by removing the hazard from the work place or isolating the hazard from the employee.

The action statement cites the laboratory safety officer for the responsibility of managing and follow-up of the training requirement. Some intermediary negotiation might be required and some compromises in immediate compliance might be in order while the new program is being phased into operation, allowing the employees some time to become accustomed—and buy into—a changing philosophy and practice of laboratory safety. Implementation of any action for improvement can be phased to facilitate training and overall acceptance.

The adroit manager can orchestrate all of this planning by inviting members of the section to participate in the decision making. Such volunteers can serve as representatives of the section, forming a quality circle type of team along with representatives of the hospital infection control service who can perform the actual facilitating and teaching. As the project action officer, the laboratory safety officer can also serve as an unbiased quality management facilitator.

In contrast to the participatory approach, the senior manager can issue a dictatorial, authoritarian mandate of a grand, sweeping nature. But, that could easily result in selective counterproductivity and dangerous noncompliance. The assessment of this biohazard problem will not be ready for ascertainment until after the next QI reporting date to allow time for the training to take place and cause some effect. Then, conduct the assessment by employee interview, written survey, or visual observation of employee adherence to biohazard precautions.

The remainder of the safety indicators show 12 months of monitoring with no opportunity for improvement identified and no action required. The appropriate follow-up response is to establish focused studies in some order of priority over the next six months. The assessment is accurate that there is need for improved sensitivity of the QI process. In this case, the process needs improvement by choosing focused studies rather than depending on a general occurrence screening. Of course, this monitoring is all predicated on whether the safety indicator in question is of high enough priority to warrant any surveillance attention at all.

Transfusion profile interpretation:
Under the biohazard indicator, this section's profile reveals—as in the Chemistry Section—that the same general problem of technologist concern over changing philosophy on control of biohazardous specimens. This issue is one of many examples of common problems that might be shared among various departmental sections. The evaluation, action, and assessment are basically the same as for the Chemistry Section. However, compliance will be much more difficult in the Transfusion Service because of the more profound problems that are at hand. Consequently, the entire biohazard problem is in the hands of the hospital infection control service.

Under the environmental indicator, there is evidence of an opportunity to improve the ambient temperature control and staff comfort in Room A03 (which is used for platelet storage). It will eventually become more clear that there is a linkage between this problem of temperature control and the problem with platelet storage that is documented under blood product utilization, postdeterminative finalization, and facility management groupings.

As with the Chemistry Section, several other safety indicators have undergone general monitoring for at least 12 months without discovery of any improvement opportunity. Thus, quality management must be broken! Under normal circumstances, the evaluation provided would be correct with subsequent action to select focused study topics and improve the sensitivity of the QI process. However, as the assessment indicates, Transfusion's improvement of the quality surveillance of the areas of fire, electrical, chemical/carcinogen, and waste disposal hazards needs to be approached gingerly due to lack of quality management resources. Thus, the section has the entire year of 1996 to regroup and revitalize this portion of the QI program. As an interim step, the department (or service) level safety officer is to conduct an intense survey for any blatant problems and report those findings immediately.

Additional profile interpretations:

Hematology (Appendix D). These employees do not have any problem in coping with universal precaution policy—presumably because of effective communication through education and training. There is a chronic occurrence of excessive seasonal temperatures causing employee stress and instrument malfunction that requires immediate facility engineer attention. In addition, there is need to improve the QI process for several inactive safety indicators.

Microbiology (Appendix E). There is the prevalent problem regarding employee concern over adoption of universal precautions and discontinuation of using biohazard labels on individual patient specimens.

Much more disconcerting, however, is the occurrence of two technologist skin test conversions due to inadequate biological hood performance. There is also the same department-wide reoccurrence of seasonally high temperatures. The latter two problems demand facility engineer remedial attention—perhaps, even, major structural renovation. The assessment for the environmental indicators highlights the need for improving lateral department (eg, facility engineer) support. Neither the hood (requiring guaranteed negative air pressure) or ambient temperature (requiring appropriately conditioned air exchange) problem should endure any further delay in resolution. Finally, there is need to improve the QI process for several inactive indicators.

Histopathology (Appendix G). This section is alerted to a different type of OFI: the need to upgrade the fire alarm system. For a laboratory operation that routinely involves use of flammable substances, fire hazard is a major threat. This profile is doubly problematic since a CAP inspection finding (two years ago) identified the need to upgrade the ventilation serving the gross specimen examination area. Finally, there is need to improve the QI process for several inactive indicators.

Discussion:

The main teaching point in addressing this indicator grouping is that employees are internal customers of the laboratory. Although employee safety is used here as a third and final outcome phase indicator grouping in this demonstration quality profile, there can be other employee-related outcome indicators as suits the individual laboratory QI program. There are other aspects to employee satisfaction that can be a part of a profile, such as technical process quality, pay, promotion, methods and procedures, continuing medical education, and team building—just as a few examples. Such issues are normally followed deeper in the quality profile but still might become so important—as a "quality improvement stopper"—to warrant being highlighted under employee satisfaction outcome.

Second, the specific issue concerning implementation of universal precautions and other controls will continue to be relevant as long as laboratorians and government regulatory agencies engage in the potentially emotional arena concerning HIV infection, as well as contact with other serious contagious, biohazardous agents. Philosophies and policies will wax and wane; local philosophy will continue to vary with national policy, creating variances in compliance and employee satisfaction.

Indicator Grouping. The key management area of safety has always been of great importance in laboratory quality management and accreditation inspections. At least seven types of employee safety indicators can be monitored under this major grouping. These indicators mirror seven safety issues covered by the CAP accreditation inspection checklist, including the following laboratory hazards:

- Biological
- Fire
- Electrical
- Chemical/carcinogen
- Radionuclide
- Waste disposal
- Facility/environmental.

Display of these indicators connotes that there should be a formalized safety program with appropriate plans, procedures, ongoing training, and responsible personnel. New topics will continue to emerge from the burgeoning regulatory activity of OSHA, HCFA, JCAHO, and CAP, including new engineering controls, safe work practices, and personal protective equipment and procedures.

Supporting Indicators. The strength of any finding made under this major grouping can be corroborated by review of other QI data—although indicator cross-correlation is less pervasive than with the previous two profile groupings. Because of its greater specificity, employee safety is less global in nature as an indicator grouping.

Indicators that support employee safety findings are predominantly resource-related. They include quality indicators of customer satisfaction, operative resource management, internal and external QI, QAn, and QAc. Purposefully designed into the system, profile redundancy guarantees confirmation of the quality of the safety statement and the identification of causes and effects of an immediate safety threat.

Threshold. Again, the threshold for this indicator grouping is that of a sentinel event because of the high risk of the subject matter—"no potential or actual hazard; sentinel event." The actual occurrence rate of opportunities for improvement will be very low on the basis of general occurrence screening; but, evidence of any opportunity to improve employee safety must be evaluated by further investigation.

Although this profile model segment does not demonstrate focused studies, such an approach is usually more practical and cost-effective. Thresholds for such studies would be set according to the respective study protocols. They would not necessarily be sentinel event thresholds but could just as likely be comparative rate-based—depending on case-by-case, laboratory-by-laboratory priorities.

Monitoring Periodicity. All seven specific employee safety indicators in this indicator grouping example represent ongoing surveillance activities being monitored monthly because of perceived high criticalness. However, priority and periodicity for these surveillance topics will vary from one laboratory section to the next.

For example, the Transfusion Service resources are so overwhelmed, it is physically impossible to effectively monitor all of these general surveys on a monthly basis. Thus, if managerial resources are so limited, monitoring of these safety-related indicators can be on a less frequent schedule. Any indicator is still reportable as a salient event if a problem or opportunity for improvement suddenly becomes apparent, no matter whether that indicator is being actively monitored or not. There is also ample justification to pursue focused studies on a periodic schedule as long as they do not merit immediate priority, monthly attention.

As another example, in a microbiology section biological hazards might require monthly monitoring and reporting. In a chemistry section, however, biohazards might warrant only occurrence screening—in this case, the indicator subject being reported only when an incident is anticipated through astute data surveillance and prudent planning.

Evaluation. The priorities for evaluating specific aspects of employee safety data will vary from one section to another. For example, a Microbiology Section profile should be evaluated with particular concern over the threat of biohazards and waste disposal. A Chemistry Section has comparatively higher risk of chemical, carcinogen, and radionuclide dangers and should emphasize those targets with highest priority compared to biohazards—although, the guard against biohazards cannot be let down in any laboratory section that encounters any type of patient specimen. Chemistry and Histopathology both utilize greater volumes of volatile solvents with a higher probability of fire, explosion, and toxicity risk. On the average, all sections share an almost equal risk of electrical, facility, and environmental opportunities for improvement, all depending on the organization's structure, its mission, its procedural methods, and its resources on hand.

Action. Regarding the subject profiles at hand, there are various options for accomplishing biohazard training. Aside from utilizing laboratory personnel—many of whom are very well trained and capable of the requirement—hospital infection control or preventive medicine personnel can also be used to provide such training. Use of personnel from outside the laboratory can be advantageous because of the added professional expertise, extradepartmental peer review, and unbiased facilitation that nonlaboratory professionals can provide the laboratorian. There must be unfettered multidisciplinary dialogue to facilitate the most effective quality management.

Assessment. On the basis of general occurrence screening, the safety indicators appear to be in overall control, including the technical control of biohazardous procedures for both profiled sections. However, as we are seeing again and again, general surveys are much too passive to provide any sense of assurance of being in control.

Both example sections need to improve biohazard training to improve employee awareness of the rationale behind changing regulatory policies. While choosing one of the three major options for action in a CQI environment, each section still needs to delay the assessment of the required training for at least one QI reporting period until after the training has been coordinated, scheduled, and implemented. Conduct the subsequent assessment by a number of direct and indirect means, including written exams, on-the-spot inspections and drills, and questionnaire surveys.

The remaining nonproblematic, noncontributory indicators call for exercising the third option of improving the QI process through prioritized focused studies—since there have been no opportunities for improvement discovered in six to nine months. Follow-up assessment should detect improved sensitivity of the process.

Communication. The transmission of lessons learned from employee safety QI surveillance is as crucial as ensuring the health and welfare of any patient: the healthcare employee must not become a healthcare patient. Therefore, there should be every reasonable effort to ensure that lessons learned from employee safety quality management are shared with all laboratory employees and nonlaboratory support activities that have any need to know. Similar to practicing preventive medicine, we must practice preventive management.

REFERENCES

1. The Joint Commission 1992 Accreditation Manual for Hospitals. Oakbrook Terrace, IL: Joint Commission on Accreditation of Healthcare Organizations, 1991.
2. Joint Commission Primer on Clinical Indicator Development and Application. Oakbrook Terrace, IL: Joint Commission on Accreditation of Healthcare Organizations, 1991.
3. The Transition from QA to CQI: An Introduction to Quality Improvement in Health Care. Oakbrook Terrace, IL: Joint Commission on Accreditation of Healthcare Organizations, 1991.
4. Simpson KN, Kaluzny AD, McLaughlin CP. Total quality and the management of laboratories: implementation strategies and challenges Clin Lab Man Rev, 1991; 5:448-456.
5. Westgard JO, Barry PL. Total quality control: evaluation of quality management systems. Lab Med, 1989; 20: 377-384.
6. Westgard JO, Barry PL, Tomar, RT. Implementing total quality management (TQM) in healthcare laboratories. Clin Lab Man Rev, 1991; 5: 353-5, 358-9, 362-6.
7. Brassard M. The Memory Jogger. Methuen, MA: GOAL/QPC, 1988.
8. Schweighoefer H. Managing total quality: JCAHO compliance. Clinical Laboratory Management Association Hot Topic Seminar. Philadelphia, PA: Mar 1990.
9. Hospital Accreditation Program Scoring Guidelines: Quality Assessment and Improvement Standards. Oakbrook Terrace, IL: Joint Commission on Accreditation of Healthcare Organizations, 1992.

10. Clark GB. ASCP Workshop Survey. Unpublished data.
11. Compendium of Clinical Indicators. Oak Brook, IL: University Hospital Consortium, 1991.
12. Clark GB. Quality assurance, an administrative means to a managerial end: Part IV — Choosing quality improvement indicators in a TQM and CQI environment. Clin Lab Man Rev, 1992; 6(5):426-7, 430-432, 434-436, 438-440..
13. Galen RS, Gambino Sr. Beyond Normality: The Predictive Value and Efficiency of Medical Diagnosis. Toronto, Canada: John Wiley and Sons, 1975.

9. The Quality Profile: Laboratory Process Management

POSTLABORATORY PROCESS WORK FLOW SEGMENT

Following the postlaboratory outcome segment (described in the preceding chapter), there are three major portions of the path of work flow that address the unique aspects of laboratory process: the post-, intra-, and prelaboratory segments, listed in their order of analysis in the quality profile. This chapter presents each segment as it appears in the profile.

Postlaboratory process is the second major profile segment; it includes three prominent indicator groupings in this example. Each grouping directs attention to a laboratory process activity that usually occurs outside the confines of the laboratory after release of the laboratory product to a clinical healthcare location. The groupings in this profile example include 1) laboratory product utilization, 2) report, product, or service throughput, and 3) report or product distribution.

Maintaining the format of the previous chapter, the numbering of these indicator groupings is in keeping with the analytical format of the quality profile—remembering that they are in the reverse order of their natural, chronologic sequence of occurrence. Notwithstanding, regular use does not necessarily limit this segment solely to these three particular groupings. There could be less or more—the same number and topics or not—all depending on how one decides to delineate postlaboratory process activities. Likewise, each individual grouping can include any number of more specific quality indicators.

Indicator Grouping 4
Laboratory Product Utilization

Chemistry Section Quality Profile

Indicator Grouping/ Specific Indicator: Threshold (Periodicity)	QI Data Observations (Date trend started) J A S O N D	
POSTLABORATORY PROCESS WORK FLOW SEGMENT		
Laboratory Report Utilization: in keeping with joint laboratory and clinical standards!! (Quarterly) a. Liver profile	- = not scheduled 0 = no provider identified .....Provider Code #..... - - 73 - - 0	

Transfusion Service Quality Profile

POSTLABORATORY PROCESS WORK FLOW SEGMENT		
Blood/Component Utilization: in keeping with joint laboratory and clinical standards! (Monthly) a. Packed red blood cell utilization: threshold on file	0 = no provider identified .....Provider Code #..... 0 0 0 0 0 46* * = on-the-spot report re "nurse # 16" and XF rx from Ward 22: 12-8 shift	
b. Frozen blood utilization: threshold on file	0 0 0 0 0 0 0% Baseline started in July	
c. Fresh frozen plasma (FFP) utilization: threshold TBD	Clinical indicators being determined for study of FPP in coordination with Med Dept	

TBD = to be determined !! = sentinel event XF rx = transfusion reaction

Laboratory Product Utilization Management (Indicator Grouping 4)

Chemistry profile interpretation:
This laboratory section's product utilization indicator grouping consists of a focused study of the clinical use of liver profiles. In this example, evaluation of the collated data reveals no problem or other opportunities for improvement for the October-November-December quarterly monitoring period.

Earlier profile data reminds us that a provider (code number 73) was identified in the July-August-September quarter for having overutilized (or underutilized) liver profiles; the exact facts should be on file. However, it is apparent that the same provider did not repeat inappropriate utilization of any laboratory product or service in the fourth quarter. Since there is no obvious trend, the follow-up improvement has apparently been successful.

Evaluation of QI Data, TQM System, and CQI Process	Action Action Person: (Date Initiated)	Assessment of Overall Improvement
On target ; no repeats or new occurrences since September	Coordinate a new study topic for Jun 96 ACTION: Section Medical Director	Improvement of the QI process is in progress
The OFI at hand is related to the transfusion reaction on ward 22; "nurse # 46"on 12 to 8 shift is cited as responsible	1. Appraise training needs for all ward 22 shifts ACTION:Chief Nurse 2. Schedule refresher training for all ward 22 shifts per appraised needs 3. Investigate all systemic causes ACTION: Medical Director	Ineffective QI process: Needs improved follow-up on training requirement, especially for 4 to 12 and 12 to 8 ward shifts
On target x 6 mo	None needed, yet	QI process is effective to date
QI Note: Improvement of this IAC is not as critical as for other operational activities such as Staffing and Analytical QC: postpone this indicator for now.		

Consequent to the Chemistry Section's evaluation, there is need for action. The recommended action is to replace the liver profile indicator with a higher priority topic—setting a new study topic into motion to improve the overall quality assessment and improvement (QI) process. As usual, the basic rationale for selection of any new indicator is the ranking and prioritizing criteria, eg, high-volume, high-risk (benefit) problem (opportunity)-prone. Remember, also, that general occurrence screening, as well as committee and other alternative quality team activities, are always sources for new indicator topics.

The profile documents that the section medical director is assigned the action under this grouping. The overall gauging of clinical utilization remains a physician responsibility since the issue involves the question of medical appropriateness—a chief dimension of healthcare quality.

The indicator assessment is that the subject study has demonstrated effective quality management. With selection of more productive study topics, there is continuing improvement of the QI process.

Transfusion profile interpretation:
This sections's profile grouping reveals that three, ongoing focused laboratory utilization indicator activities are in progress. It is not surprising that the Transfusion Service is so active in blood utilization studies since the Joint Commission on Accreditation of Healthcare Organizations (JCAHO) has specifically required these studies for all blood products for so many years.

The hospital transfusion committee (also called the blood components utilization or usage committee) usually shepherds these studies. However, responsibility for collection and organization of the data routinely rests with the Transfusion Service staff: hence, the data is easily available for including in the quality profile. This section's profile grouping targets the clinical utilization of 1) packed red cells, 2) frozen blood, and 3) fresh frozen plasma.

First, the monthly red cell utilization study registers provider (code number 46) on ward 22 as associated with the patient mix-up and hemolytic transfusion reaction. The evaluation summarizes the situation at hand.

The recommended actions imply that there has been joint laboratory-nursing staff dialogue facilitating the remedial process and resulting in a bimodal action plan. The recommended action for the nursing department director is to appraise the ward 22 nursing staff regarding their understanding of transfusion techniques; the situation might, in fact, necessitate surveying staff of other wards as well.

At the same time, the Transfusion Service medical director is to schedule refresher training on ward 22 for all shifts and to investigate all other possible systemic causes for the patient misidentification.

The assessment reflects that the quality management system is broken and needs fixing. This concern includes both the Transfusion Service and ward 22. The need for improvement might possibly ripple out to all shifts on all wards.

Second, in the six months that the frozen blood utilization study has been reported monthly, the evaluation of the data is that there has been no evidence of inappropriate clinical utilization practice. The recommended action is to stay the current course of routine surveillance for the time being. In another three months, it will probably be reasonable to focus more specifically on the utilization of frozen blood units by a specific clinical specialty. The assessment is accurate that the QI process is operating smoothly in regard to this particular indicator.

Third, the Transfusion Service is coordinating the establishment of a fresh frozen plasma utilization study with the internal medicine department staff. This choice is presumably due to some perceived high priority warranting the expenditure of precious quality management resources.

Although the study is not yet fully implemented to provide data for evaluation or action, establishing a new study is progress toward improvement of the QI process itself. However, the question at assessment is whether or not the section really has the quality management resources needed to venture into a new surveillance topic at this operationally critical time. The answer is that such *de novo* improvement of the improvement process at this instant is not prudent and that it should either progress along "at all deliberate speed" or, bluntly, resume scheduling when it is more organizationally feasible. A departmental-level "QI Note" attests to this dilemma.[a]

Additional profile interpretations:

Hematology (Appendix D). This section's profile demonstrates two focused studies, one on clinical utilization of platelet counts and the other on manual differential counts. Neither study reveals any opportunity for improvement (OFI) over six and eight month periods, respectively. The evaluations, actions, and assessments are all appropriate. It is of note that the platelet study shows that one way to improve the QI process is by reducing the periodicity of review (eg, from monthly to quarterly).

Microbiology (Appendix E). A general survey reveals that, although some sort of laboratory product malutilization occurred in June 1995, there has been no citing of any repeat or new incident. It is reasonable to establish increased QI sensitivity through selection of a focused study—as attested to by the action and assessment statements.

Histopathology (Appendix G). Two focused studies are in progress. One study following clinical utilization of frozen-sections shows that it was initiated in September after discovery of inappropriate utilization by a provider (code number 85) with no repeat or new occurrences after a four month baseline. The second study of rush surgical utilization is being established—the new study being an improvement of the QI process. Respective actions and assessments for these two studies are appropriate.

Discussion:

Indicator Grouping. Clinical utilization of laboratory products and services is a surveillance topic that is a proven leader in providing opportunities for quality improvement. There have been various reports of physicians ordering laboratory tests and then failing to address abnormal results—or addressing either normal or abnormal results inappropriately. Citing only a few representative reports, physician noncompliance to laboratory-clinical standards of practice in response to laboratory results has been noted to range as high as 66% to 73% of tests ordered, regardless of the specific diagnoses or diagnostic related groupings (DRGs) reviewed.[1,2]

[a] On occasion, the section's initial recommended actions can be somewhat short of the mark, requiring an additional departmental comment or emphasis under "QI notes," especially regarding adequate action follow-up and QI process improvement. This aspect of the various profile scenarios presented here might be a little nebulous until remembering that the quality profile is intended as a department-level report format. As such, it should include departmental emphasis where needed. Such departmental comment should imply section-level consensus.

Utilization could be inappropriate because of the use of incorrect selection criteria from the very beginning for either the healthy or diseased states. There could be nonutilization by virtue of the laboratory product not being delivered to the point-of-care. Failure of appropriate clinical follow-up of an abnormal laboratory determinative result (ie, analytical or diagnostic) could also be due to incorrect charting of test results.

Utilization can be inappropriate based on incorrect clinical interpretation of a laboratory test result. Or, it could be a case of mistaken laboratory product-patient identification at the time of selection—or at the time of utilization. In either case, the subsequent treatment provided will be incorrect.

Utilization also can be inappropriate because the requesting clinician has not matched initial laboratory product selection criteria with a changing clinical situation. The clinician's initial justification could have been correct in respect to the patient's clinical status at that particular time. But, the patient's status could have changed between time of selection and time of laboratory product delivery and charting. This scenario could easily happen in the intensive care unit milieu. The clinician could have waited too long to respond to the charted laboratory result. Or, the patient's clinical condition could have changed too rapidly for anyone to adequately keep up. These many possibilities could be brought to light by using several analytical techniques such as brainstorming, force field analysis, and flow charting.

The two major profiles described in this grouping remind us of a central issue regarding the quality management (QM) interface: every laboratory section needs to establish technical and clinical standards for utilization of laboratory services at the *joint* laboratorian-clinician level.[b] This is exemplified by the liver studies profiled in the Chemistry Section and the three blood products profiled in the Transfusion Service.

Also, the practice of utilization surveillance implies that there should be a system for review of medical records, including both clinical and laboratory archival data. This system should provide a reliable means of correlating provider utilization of specific laboratory tests or services with preestablished standards of practice.

Whereas the additional profiles offered in this text are ancillary examples, remember that other laboratory sections can be subjects of a quality profile. Those candidates include clinical toxicology, therapeutic drug monitoring, special chemistry (eg, radioimmunoassay, spectrophotometry, electrophoresis), diagnostic immunology, diagnostic molecular biology, and cytogenetics, just to mention a few in clinical pathology (CP). Surgical pathology, autopsy pathology, and cytopathology are major anatomic pathology (AP) possibilities.

The sample profiles expressly mention "provider"—not just physician—utilization. As demonstrated by the transfusion incident on fictitious ward 22, the action of a healthcare provider other than a physician is *allegedly*

[b] The QM interface is the laboratory-clinical juncture for any of the three organizational programs of QI, QAn, and QAc that are integral to continuous quality improvement.

associated with the aforementioned hemolytic reaction; in this case, a nurse working on the ward during the 12 to 8 shift is being held responsible.

On the other hand, there is not yet unequivocal proof that the incident was a provider mistake in administering the blood unit. It could have been a systemic problem in the process of patient identification during transfusion selection (by a physician), of sample collection (by ward or laboratory technical personnel), of blood unit crossmatching (by a laboratory technologist), of blood unit release (by a laboratory technologist), or of blood unit delivery to the point-of-care (by some individual or mechanical system).

There could even be other possibilities, depending on the complexity of the blood distribution and interim blood storage system in use. In other words, first there must be a joint investigative evaluation of all relevant systemic processes before any responsible individual is held directly accountable. Team analytical methods are invaluable in this situation.

As a related point, it is absolutely imperative that this profile model preserves provider and patient anonymity. For example, the QI document details certain information such as the patient (code number 53) under the patient care outcome grouping, provider (code number 73) under the subject indicator grouping, the transfusion incident, related training, and other relevant aspects of the transfusion incident in general terms to facilitate quality management communication and resolution of the OFI.

However, the specific details, especially those having to do with individual identities, can discreetly remain on file in the department, available for review only by legally appropriate personnel. Generally speaking, there must be detailed file information on any issue mentioned ever so briefly in any portion of the quality profile report.

Additional indicator topics are plentiful. First, consider the inventory of all important aspects of care (IACs) identified for any given laboratory section. As a second alternative, look at the utilization topics generated by other committees, task forces, and other quality teams.

Using the Transfusion Service scenario as an example, look at all the possibilities for the clinical utilization of any blood component offered by the Service. Then, consider the routine parameters used for tracking the clinical use of blood units ordered for type and crossmatch—eg, the crossmatch-transfusion ratio. Also, entertain the use of other major utilization criteria that are regularly followed in blood utilization committee minutes. Remember, also, that other Blood Bank laboratory subsections or units can target the utilization of donor and patient services (as compared to products) such as donor or therapeutic phlebotomy and apheresis.

Supporting Indicators. Referring back to Tables VI and VII in chapter eight, there can be correlation of the laboratory utilization grouping with other indicator groupings for customer satisfaction, patient care outcome, laboratory product/service selection, internal and external QI, quality anticipation (QAn), and quality actualization (QAc) organizational programs. The degree of correlation is relatively limited for this utilization grouping compared to that of indicator groupings with more global cross-linkage.

However limited the correlation with utilization might be, the review of supporting indicators for the subject indicator grouping reveals two significant concepts. First, outcome data are very important. Second, if clinical staff are jointly involved in the designing and review of this aspect of the laboratory QI program, the laboratory also should directly incorporate the clinical staff into the laboratory QAn and QAc programs! Just as there is joint laboratorian-clinician effort in quality surveillance through the QI program at the organization-wide level, there is a legitimate need for joint anticipatory planning and joint team effectiveness activities. Of course, the "flipside" is also true: clinicians should be inviting laboratorians to participate in clinical QI, QAn, and QAc activities as well. The corroborative importance of these three activities would be documented by their respective profile groupings for the QI program (ie, indicator groupings 23 and 24), QAn program (ie, indicator grouping 25), and QAc program (ie, indicator grouping 26).

Threshold. The threshold that is stated for both major profile examples—ie, "in keeping with clinical and laboratory standards; sentinel event"—implies that joint clinical and laboratory standards of practice for utilization of liver profiles and blood products have been established for specific patient populations, diagnoses, DRGs, or clinical specialties. This very general threshold describes conformance of this QI indicator with its design specifications as an all or none event: the standards cannot be ignored; they must be met precisely as they are written.

Of course, how the standards are written will determine what specific exceptions to the rule can be tolerated, including whatever important mitigating circumstances affect a given patient population. Such details are better suited for less strict, comparative-rate type threshold statements. The more specific the QI focus, the more lenient the threshold limitations likely will be.

Monitoring Periodicity. Usually, one follows a general survey indicator on a monthly basis—remembering, however, that incident reports, usually being serendipitous in their occurrence, are not effective as a systemic measure of a systematically-oriented QI program. However, the sectional quality management team must always immediately address any such report if ever it surfaces—its subsequent periodicity of follow-up monitoring to be determined on a case-by-case basis as the target for improvement develops.

In comparison to the general survey, a systematically selected, focused study approach frequently serves the utilization grouping indicator much better. The frequency of monitoring and reporting can be monthly, quarterly, trimestral, or even less often depending on the criticalness of the related IAC, the indicator subject, the indicator criteria, and the quality management resources on hand.

Evaluation. The JCAHO and its surveyors are increasingly emphasizing utilization studies beyond the well-established blood utilization and surgical case review. Now, according to the Joint Commission standards and their accompanying scoring guidelines, the laboratory should ultimately schedule many other IACs (ie, important laboratory products and services) for utilization study. By definition, the laboratory deems these important products or services to be significantly important enough to warrant expenditure of quality management resources. Therefore, by Joint Commission guidelines all laboratory functions designated as important enough must be monitored by the QI program at some time or another, using some indicator or another. The section's quality management team must orchestrate such a scheduling over a lengthy period, using acceptable criteria for ranking and prioritizing the appropriate IACs. Thus, the QI monitoring of many IACs should target clinical utilization for continuous improvement on a scheduled, anticipatory basis—not as a knee jerk reaction to an incident report.

Furthermore, quality evaluation of clinical utilization must survey not only physicians, but also all other types of healthcare providers practicing in the laboratory customer-supplier system. A healthcare provider is anyone with the potential authority to clinically use or administer any important laboratory end product. Thus, the choice of providers should include all nonphysician personnel legitimately credentialed by a healthcare organization to utilize a laboratory product or service for clinical diagnosis or treatment; in turn, all such providers are subject to peer review. These nonphysician providers would include psychologists, nurse practitioners, physician assistants. Ironically, as the practice of direct access progresses, the "provider" can even be a patient.

It is important to consider one further point regarding evaluation of these quality data. All supporting indicator groupings are invaluable in corroborating the effectiveness of clinical utilization of laboratory products and services.

Action. It is very natural for any organization to direct remedial steps that will afford improvement of laboratory product utilization by some individual healthcare provider—whether that be by a physician or another type of healthcare provider. However, the organization should direct its approach toward improving processes that affect laboratory product/service utilization—instead of focusing on individual accountability and rehabilitation or discipline. Do not single out individual providers except to facilitate the identification and concentration on generic provider groups.

For example, rather than aiming at immediate correction of the nurse on ward 22, the entire nursing staff should be the target for evaluative investigation and remedial action. The individual nurse should not be the focus of organizational improvement, unless all other possibilities of aberrant operative- and organizational-level processes have been systematically ruled out, including continuing education.

As demonstrated by the Transfusion Service profile, QI action can be bimodal. In this scenario, there are action requirements for both the ward and laboratory staff. On one hand, the nursing staff (and possibly the physician staff) responsible for ward 22 must appraise the details of the incorrect administration of blood to the ill-fated patient. They must curtail

Indicator Grouping 5
Turnaround Time And Backlog

Chemistry Section Quality Profile

Indicator Grouping/ Specific Indicator: Threshold (Periodicity)	QI Data Observations (Date trend started) J A S O N D
Throughput of Index Procedures: (Quarterly)	See Analytical Quality, Personnel, and Equipment groupings; selection of new analyzer began in Jan 95 due to QC problems; there are 6 FTE vacancies
a. Multichannel analyzer " X" TAT: > 3 hours avg TAT	2.5 - - 2.0 - - h h= averaged hours
b. Stat test TAT: > 60 min avg TAT	- 50 - - 45 - m No OFI identified x 12 mo m = averaged minutes

Transfusion Service Quality Profile

Indicator	J	A	S	O	N	D	
Throughput of Index Procedures: (Monthly)	h = averaged hours						
a. Type and crossmatch TAT: > 4 hours average TAT	3	3	3.5	4	4.5	5	h
b. Type and crossmatch backlog: none > 4 hours TAT per day	0	0	0	0	32	64	c
	c = averaged backlogged cases per day						

immediate emphasis on the performance and accountability of the suspect nurse and redirect their attention to the processes involved on the ward throughout the entire path of work flow from blood transfusion selection to blood unit utilization. Individual disciplinary action should be the last resort exercised in resolving an improvement opportunity.

On the other hand, in either of the two major example profiles the section medical director should be responsible for the recommended laboratory actions because of the relevance of the quality dimension of medical appropriateness. And, in every case these examples demonstrate that, by the very nature of this indicator grouping, every action involving laboratory utilization requires extensive laboratory-clinical dialogue.

Assessment. Again, the options are mixed, depending on the nature of the particular profile indicator under scrutiny. Any of the three improvement options for a continuous quality improvement (CQI) environment might be

Evaluation of QI Data, TQM System, and CQI Process	Action Action Person: (Date Initiated)	Assessment of Overall Improvement
1. On target for at least 6 mo in spite of QC problems and 6 staff vacancies 2. Threshold of 3 hr is too long — too insensitive; can be improved if clinically important	1. Maintain QC vigilance 2. Negotiate reduction of threshold with clinical staff 3. Resolve staffing and equipment problems ACTION: Supervisor	Improvement of TAT is in progress BUT good TAT is masking QC, equipment, staffing, and QAn/QAc improvement needs
On target x 12 mo; but no significant improvement over an inordinate period	Select a more focused study on ER TAT for Jan 96 ACTION: Supervisor	Improvement was stalled but now is in progress
1. There is excessive TAT and backlog with progressive deterioration associated with severe staff shortage, loss of supervisor, and increasing signs of employee stress 2. Dec backlog represents need for 1 additional FTE	1. Basic human resource problems have to be solved 2. Innovative staffing and motivation approaches are needed 3. Begin use of reference lab ACTION: Acting Supervisor	Ineffective QC, QI, QAn, and QAc, processes are worsening: Needs improvement of severely critical systemic problems

appropriate: stay the QI course, 2) improve any blatant OFI, or 3) improve the improvement process itself.

Communication. The unique nature of this indicator grouping requires that there be effective communication of QI lessons learned to all appropriate laboratory personnel and all clinical staff who are part of the laboratory improvement process. General information can be disseminated without divulging the identity of the providers, clinical services, or patients that are involved—whenever anonymity is prudent.

Laboratory Throughput Management: Turnaround Time and Backlog (Indicator Grouping 5)

Chemistry profile interpretation:

This profile grouping example for monitoring laboratory throughput introduces a surveillance tool described as the *index study*. This QI tool is further described under this grouping's discussion.

Evaluation of data for two quarterly index studies reveals no explicit problems for the throughput parameter of total, average turnaround time (TAT). In the first study, however, there is implicit information available from subsequent supporting indicator groupings that the multichannel analyzer TAT data have remained "on target" in spite of significant chronic analytical quality control (QC), technical staff shortage, and equipment maintenance problems. In other words, throughput for the subject chemistry tests has remained within normal limits only through extra bench and supervisory work that has maintained control of the errant analyzer—but, only through expenditure of extensive extra effort in the form of repetitive minor instrument repairs and repeated test, control, and calibration runs.

The lack of a workload backlog accumulation supports the evidence of a well established TAT baseline of at least six months. Additionally, the supporting data for outcome indicators—particularly customer satisfaction—confirm the stability of the turnaround process even in the face of such extensive QC efforts.

The actions recommended for the multichannel analyzer index study are concomitant with the available facts, including a reevaluation of the threshold value; the supervisor is assigned the action. The premise for suggesting reduction of the multichannel analyzer TAT threshold is twofold. It is based on:

- First, the opportunity for improvement of turnaround and customer service with faster instrumentation and, especially, with more effective electronic communication between the laboratory and points of health care
- Second, the revelation that the current threshold is being handily met in the face of resource consuming control efforts—a major resource being time.

The latter aspect of this scenario could be reminiscent of the adage, "If it ain't broke, don't fix it." In this case, however, the data actually evoke a key precept of CQI, "If there has not been improvement over a reasonable period, consider whether or not the quality management process is broken and needs fixing."

In the earliest years of batch, multichannel analysis, a QI threshold from 12 to 24 hours was acceptable as a standard of practice. Yet, in the intervening years, it has become possible that each, individual chemistry multianalyzer request actually can be processed immediately on receipt by the laboratory section. Consequently, it is conceivable that a laboratory can respond to every routine multichannel analysis request just as an erstwhile "stat" request used to be handled. Effectively, some laboratories can process all requests as if they are all marked stat. Therefore, improvement of clinical customer satisfaction and the QI approach to managing multichannel chemistry TAT actually might be possible.

However, QI assessment of this indicator of Chemistry throughput quality reminds the reader of evidence gleaned from supporting indicator groupings, including those for analytical QC (instrumental performance), staffing, QAn (plan implementation) and QAc (decision making). At this point of quality profile analysis, the favorable TAT is masking problems in those supporting laboratory activities. Particularly, the overall improvement of multichannel analyzer effectiveness still rests on expediting the procurement of a new instrument; this amounts to improving the section's decision making process. Thus, the excellent multianalyzer turnaround and even the opportunity to improve on it take on secondary importance.

The second index study provides QI data on stat test TAT evaluated as "on target for 12 months." The action selected at the sectional level is definitely overdue since 12 months have passed without any earlier identification of opportunities for improvement. The recommended action is for the supervisor to redesign the QI approach by focusing on a more specific study topic; emergency room turnaround is the improved surveillance target.[3] The indicator's assessment highlights the delay in response to nonimprovement over an inordinately long period.

Transfusion profile interpretation:
This profile demonstrates an ongoing focused study of type and crossmatch TAT and backlog. Evaluation of the six month cumulative data record shows progressive deterioration of the index study data for TAT. As shown by supporting groupings, this quality management problem coincides with several other system-wide outcome, process, and operative-organizational resource management problems. The major, underlying resource factor is a severe personnel shortage.

Additionally, over the last two months there has been documentation of the averaged backlog of type and crossmatch cases. The definition of this backlog is the averaged daily number of cases that have exceeded the TAT threshold of four hours during the reporting period—in this case, monthly. During the November reporting period, the average backlog was 32 cases; in December there were 64 backlogged cases.

As further explanation, in December there was a daily average of 64 cases with a TAT greater than four hours (separate shifts not being specified). Assume for the sake of discussion that this laboratory has established a staffing yardstick guideline that one technologist should perform eight type and crossmatch cases per hour. If so, the December backlog represents a need for one additional technologist per work day just to absorb the type and crossmatch backlog.

Knowing this section's staffing problem, one could easily ask to what extent other procedures are backlogged on a given day requiring more FTEs. This example is of an averaged backlog; in comparison, the hematology profile grouping for reference laboratory quality (ie, indicator grouping 8) demonstrates a total cumulative backlog recording approach.

Additional profile interpretations:

Hematology (Appendix D). This example profile demonstrates the use of index studies to track TAT over a lengthy period. Taking the first three studies together [ie, complete blood count (CBC), coagulation, and urinalysis] and considering their overall trends, there is borderline acceptability with one indexed TAT actually being exceeded in December when the average CBC turnaround was five hours. This is particularly important when remembering that these are *averaged* TAT values, usually calculated over a month's time. Thus, during any given monitoring period there could be a significant number of absolute occurrences when turnaround events exceed the maximum threshold level—even when the averaged reported values are borderline high "normal."

In the latter situation, the "average" customer might be satisfied while a notable number of "outlier" customers might be very unhappy with consistently prolonged turnaround that is being masked by the laboratory QI process of averaging TAT indicator data. A managerial question must be how many such dissatisfied customers are significant; how many can be allowed to be dissatisfied but not recognizable to the laboratory quality management system. Many laboratory and clinical healthcare managers would say, "NONE!"

These vagaries of averaged turnaround data become especially noticeable when considering the need to ensure adequate preservation of various types of samples. Consider urine samples, for instance. In the face of a normal average TAT overall, who knows how many outliers for urinalysis turnaround represent samples that have undergone suboptimal refrigeration or prolonged storage before analysis—attributed to a delay in transit or in predeterminative processing? For any of the "outlier" patients, theirs is a 100 percent problem being obscured by normative statistics.

This hematology profile also offers a new twist on stating and interpreting TAT—using the "negative percentile" notation. Consider the fact that a threshold can be expressed with the usual < or > limitation symbol. In most cases, the threshold is noted as a symbolic expression, most commonly using the > symbol; this convention denotes that the threshold for the subject event is exceeded if a certain value is greater than the stated threshold value. As such, the threshold is a limiting normal value *above* which the subject indicator level must rise before an investigative evaluation is required.

Occasionally, the indicator criteria or threshold definition mandates evaluative investigation when the indicator level falls below the threshold limit value; this characterizes an inverted threshold statement. In the subject hematology profile, the indicators of routine and special bone marrow diagnosis TAT reveal a variation of the inverted threshold (or negative percentile) threshold theme.

For example, consider the routine diagnosis TAT: the threshold statement conveys that the section expects that at least 95% or more of all routine diagnoses will be completed in an average of two days or less. In other words, if less than 95% of routine diagnoses are completed with an average turnaround of two days, there is an "exceeding" or violation of the threshold, mandating an investigative evaluation. The evaluation is that the cumulative profile data indicate an actual improvement of the routine (and special bone marrow) diagnosis TAT.

This form of inverted threshold (and the use of threshold percentages) demonstrates how the < and > symbols can cause problems in interpretation of threshold and associated QI data; these problems are basically a "matter of semantics." Usually, such interpretive differences are not academic; rather, they usually are based on differences between normal intuitive versus objective personality reasoning skills—or right versus left brain predominance. And, any of these differences of opinion should be resolvable through the practice of an effective QAc program.

Overall, the major secret to a laboratory's interpretive success is to be consistent with the use of the limitation symbols—no matter how the local laboratory finally agrees to use and interpret them. Further discussion of TAT and backlog is offered under the groupings for reference laboratory quality and secretarial staffing for this hematology profile.

In regard to the three index cases at hand, all evaluations point to a "borderline adequate" TAT, raising questions about the effect of staffing shortage. In the case of the urinalysis turnaround indicator, there is some concern over the adequacy of preservation. Supporting indicator groupings such as personnel management enhance the credibility of the primary evaluation.

The combined recommended action is to approach these borderline TAT patterns from the standpoint of improving staff effectiveness by hiring and innovative scheduling. A third action is to investigate the adequacy of specimen preservation, vis, urinalysis.

The assessment is that the borderline patterns stretching over a five to six month period represent turnaround performance of marginal effectiveness. These TATs must improve, primarily by addressing the barrier of protracted staff shortage. The assessment emphasizes the importance of the QM interface between the laboratory and the hospital-level personnel office.

Microbiology (Appendix E). This laboratory section provides several examples of index case studies for ongoing TAT surveillance. Evaluation reveals that the indicator levels are consistently but minimally excessive, and the trend is generally that of a variable plateauing. The use and relative value of modifiers such as borderline, marginal, minimal, moderate, and severe are all dependent on local laboratory managerial philosophy and should be defined in each laboratory's QI procedure manual and used with consistency.

In the Microbiology Section, there is a distinct correlation between TAT and laboratory staff vacancies, although other possibilities require investigation (eg, the length of the prelaboratory transportation contribution to turnaround). Also, there is the question of whether the thresholds are, in fact, inappropriately too low, or if there is increased (but not necessarily excessive) clinical utilization creating a greater than normal workload. The laboratory needs to rule out all possibilities by investigative evaluation as testified by the recommended actions. The TAT assessment states that improvement of the QI process in progress.

Histopathology (Appendix G). This section's TAT profile segment provides another version of the use of the inverted threshold, using the averaged, percentile approach similar to that explained for the Hematology Section profile. There has been a disastrous worsening of the routine surgical diagnosis TAT with some improvement of the special diagnoses turnaround—though still exceeding the expected threshold. The improvement in the special diagnoses throughput is explained by the section's simply placing a higher priority focus on the special cases; but, the data corroborates that this approach has been at the expense of the routine case TAT—truly a Pyrrhic victory!

The laboratory manager assumes all action responsibilities. The section supervisor and medical director are left alone to concentrate on other problems such as predeterminative processing. This scenario provides a perfect example of an operative-level quality management decision to "degrade" in-house conformance to procedural design specifications in order to meet healthcare management objectives. In this case, the routine diagnosis TAT is so deplorably inadequate, the decision is to send the routine surgical pathology cases to a reference laboratory—at least the histotechnical work; this is a curtailment of in-house procedures. Sending these cases to an outside laboratory represents acceptance of a longer TAT than the in-house criteria and thresholds would allow—but, the overall result still will be an acceptable improvement in service to the clinical customer—a managerial compromise in the name of quality improvement reached by joint laboratory-clinical quality management decision making. The shifting of this workload to a reference laboratory is an interim option only until the histotechnical staffing problems are resolved.

Due to the interdepartmental aspects of interfacing the AP services with the hospital points-of-care through an automated information system, the laboratory manager for the AP service definitely is to assume responsibility for the fourth action. Otherwise, it would be the responsibility for the laboratory manager at the departmental level.

This sample profile does not mention the potential QI targets for tracking TAT and backlog indicators for cytopathology cases and complete autopsy reports. Autopsy report TAT often proves itself to be problematic, even for routine cases with a 30 day CAP turnaround requirement.

The indicator assessment points to the need to improve the QM interface between the Histopathology Section and the hospital personnel office regarding the hiring of needed technical and secretarial staff. There also is mention of the hospital Task Force as a reminder of their newly established role.

Discussion:

Indicator Grouping. The use of *index procedures* can be a fruitful QI monitoring approach in lieu of general surveys or focused studies. By definition, an index procedure, case, or topic is a standing indicator (ie, ongoing but subject to periodic review and modification) that is consistently characteristic of the given grouping in the subject section's operational milieu. Index procedures provide a steady baseline profile of some key laboratory activity on a continuous basis—as opposed to a serendipitous, general survey that just plods along or the snapshot-style of a focused study that runs only for a limited period. Thus, index procedures serve as constant operational yardsticks that provide a consistent stream of data against which a specific quality of a section's current operation can be continually measured over a lengthy series of monitoring periods. Deviations from an index baseline are easily recognizable as shifts, trends, or patterns of indicator levels. Index TAT studies are particularly important as heralds of changes in workload volume and staff strength.

Regarding the throughput in general, the definition of total TAT can vary from one laboratory to another. In this text, total average turnaround extends from the time of specimen collection to report distribution to the medical chart. It could even start before or after collection, depending on the laboratory's quality management objectives. In any case, its exact laboratory definition needs to be spelled out in the QI plan and in the individual method procedures. It is a definition that should have joint laboratory-clinical input.

Total TAT is a very general parameter that is affected by a number of diverse pre-, intra-, and postlaboratory factors. Therefore, this quality indicator potentially affects—and is affected by—the evaluation of many segments of the path of work flow. In some cases, the total turnaround concept needs expanding to include not only operative resource management activities but even organizational structural activities such as QI, QAn, and QAc. This is especially true for the latter since the turnaround of every laboratory product always begins at the fundamental level of team building and actualization. And those organizational effectiveness activities often must include both laboratory and nonlaboratory personnel.

A prolonged total TAT suggests that there is some systemic problem in the laboratory process warranting further investigation through a focused study. Compared to an index study, a focused study would address specific elements of TAT, triggered by questions raised through the routinely scheduled QI process or from alternative QI sources. The use of a focused approach is often necessary to single out the cause for an unduly extended—or inordinately diminished—TAT. Compared to an index study, a focused study is not indeterminate in duration; usually, in selecting a focused topic, the section sets a target of limitation as to when the study shall cease.

To concentrate on a specific throughput OFI, the section can analytically divide the total TAT for the subject IAC into all of its component parts. This analysis can be for the entire section, for specialized work centers, or for specific shifts within the section. Remember that there are both intralaboratory and extralaboratory segments of the path of work flow. Through this analytical approach one can isolate opportunities for improvement that are otherwise masked by the total value.

Backlog, the second type of throughput modality, is more controversial; some agree with the practicality of its use as a quality indicator, and some do not. However, it can be especially valuable in judging the number of full time equivalents (FTEs) that might be necessary to expeditiously resolve a throughput problem.

Additional indicator topics include all the various components of the total TAT and backlog. Ferreting out these ancillary surveillance targets requires the entire panoply of analytical QI tools, including flow charting, Pareto analysis, and others suggested earlier in this text.

Supporting Indicators. Throughput is very much a global indicator. Corroborative data are available from most outcome indicators, such as customer satisfaction and patient care; almost all process indicators, such as product distribution, reference laboratory studies, analytic/diagnostic QC; all resource indicators—especially productivity, personnel strength, computer downtime, supply, equipment, budget; and indicators of all three organizational programs for QI, QAn, and QAc.

Threshold. The scope of TAT threshold requirements tends to vary for different laboratory procedures based on the complexity of technique and the degree of patient care risk. For example, the three index studies that are presented in the two major sample profiles demonstrate a wide range of turnaround threshold—ranging from 60 minutes to 3 hours. For more complex, in-house reference and consultation studies, turnaround time often must be in terms of days.

The expression for TAT limitations is usually in terms of "greater than (>)" a given time value; occasionally, it is in terms of "less than (<)" or a range that combines the two. An "inverted" threshold and a negative percentile approach also are useful in certain instances, as described above. Also, the turnaround threshold can be in terms of averaged figures for the entire reporting period or maximum or minimal single events occurring within the reporting period.

There are several means of expressing threshold for backlog. It can be a tabulation of cases exceeding the threshold on a daily or routine workshift basis; those results would then be averaged for the overall reporting period. Or, it can be a tabulated count of unfinished cases that have accrued at the end of the reporting period. Also, it could be in terms of the percentage of unfinished cases.

Monitoring Periodicity. Again, the character of this QI topic depends on the criticalness of the aspect of care being monitored and the adequacy of the quality management resources on hand—for either throughput modality.

Evaluation. TAT and backlog comprise the essential elements of a key indicator grouping that need to be evaluated with an eye kept toward balancing workload and resources—the most significant resource usually being personnel strength. However, there are other resource constraints that can cause delayed throughput, such as instrumental failure, computer downtime, and increased clinical utilization—any of these representing sources of increased workload. In comparison, a prolonged normal baseline TAT—or even diminished, subnormal data—could indicate that there is an opportunity for improving the turnaround criteria, increasing the workload, or reducing (or redistributing) the work force.

Likewise, backlog is especially helpful as a means of judging what additional numbers of FTEs would be necessary to resolve an excessive-workload/limited-resource imbalance. For example, many laboratories have employed this QI surveillance tool, especially in cytopathology when faced with a retrospective look-back project. This backlog provides the means to predict the number of personnel needed to expedite a massive "look-back" requirement and to monitor the progress of the quality management task.

There can be some subtlety in interpreting turnaround data that requires supporting indicator data. For example, the most important evaluation of the subject Chemistry profile segment is veiled by misleading TAT data. At first glance, the multianalyzer throughput data appear to be consistently on target—the process is performing just the way it is supposed to be and is coinciding with an excellent customer satisfaction record as discussed above. However, supporting indicator groupings show that:

- The excellent TAT record exists in spite of significant QC problems are being contained on a routine basis requiring a substantial amount of FTE work units (ie, analytical QC—indicator grouping 9).
- The staff is maintaining a superb TAT record in spite of six vacancies (ie, personnel management—indicator grouping 15).

Thus, the more informed evaluation of the multichannel analyzer TAT threshold is that it is too long or insensitive to opportunities for improvement. This evaluation is further substantiated in view of the potential capability of multianalyzer turnaround when the instrument is linked to a modern, computerized laboratory-hospital information management system. In this case, thorough analysis of even a normal TAT can unmask substantiation for improving a related laboratory operational process.

Action. As usual, the preceding evaluation begs the proceeding action. Improving throughput can be very straightforward or quite multifaceted, depending on the complexity of the underlying causes for operational delay. The required action might be immediate or there might be need for further investigative study along with interim remedial steps; any such fix—whether immediate (the proverbial "quick fix"), interim, or long term—is a substantive improvement as long as it is orchestrated toward the mending of systemic processes with some degree of permanency and stability.

Most important: through the QI process, the quality management team should design actions that will definitively resolve the OFI at hand—in this case, a TAT control management problem; the team should not merely contain the problem, as the "quick fix" is usually limited to accomplishing. Thus, the work force that is usually inordinately consumed in quick fix, containment activities will remain available to perform more productive and truly proactive activities—such as reducing turnaround, absorbing backlogged workloads, or improving some other procedural quality in an anticipatory fashion.

Regarding the Chemistry Section TAT threshold, presumably the three hour threshold for multichannel analyzer results was originally a joint laboratorian-clinician decision. Such an action decision probably rested on the assumption that batch runs could be serially scheduled no more frequently than every three hours during any staffed shift.

Modern technology and, especially, modern laboratory information computerization and electronic dissemination are overtaking previous medical management decisions such as the one described here. Consequently, a three-hour TAT now might be considered as being a rather cavalier decision in view of just how quickly modern technology can facilitate analysis and reporting of chemistry results. Thus, the section's recommendation to reduce the multianalyzer turnaround threshold figure to less than three hours is cogent in attempting to meet the laboratory's perception of clinical needs in the light of continuously mounting technological advances.

Ultimately, the feasibility—even the desirability—of a reduced threshold needs confirmation at the joint laboratory-clinical level. The irony is that such an improved change in laboratory service might not be clinically desirable enough to warrant the extra expense or staff effort—regardless of the advanced instrumentation or information management systems that might be available to make it so.

The Transfusion Service TAT/backlog data and evaluation definitely call for action dealing with a throughput problem, requiring some sort of supplemental assistance over at least a short term. Sending routine ABO blood typing and prenatal screens to a reference laboratory is propitious; establishing automation is an even more long term consideration fraught with technology that is not yet fully effective.

Assessment. As wends the action step, so goes the assessment of previous, unfinished actions and the current overall QI process. For example, in considering various avenues of potential action for the Chemistry Section, the review of supporting indicators generates an ancillary point. Although the section has no overt TAT problem—it is evident elsewhere in the profile that there are QC problems requiring replacement of the multichannel analyzer.

However, instrument procurement has become inordinately prolonged—the selection process itself needing immediate improvement. Ultimately, if the instrument fails before replacement, there will be a need for considering a degradation of management objectives—that is, by resorting to the use of a reference laboratory while tolerating a slightly longer TAT than originally determined by joint laboratory-clinical coordination. Again, the laboratory should reaffirm such an action that impinges on the integrity of the established threshold goals by a joint laboratory-clinical decision. Thus, the overall assessment for the multichannel analyzer TAT indicator registers an appropriate admonishment that a normal turnaround record is masking problems in QC, instrument procurement, staffing, QAn, and QAc.

Additionally, Chemistry's assessment for the indexed stat test TAT is that—for at least 12 months—the baseline survey has remained steady and within the threshold limits. The lesson here is that even an index procedure cannot run indeterminately without evidence of some improvement. Consequently, the assessment notes that by careful selection of a focused study there should be an increased sensitivity to QI opportunities. Hence, improvement that has been stalled will be reenergized.

In the Transfusion Service example, the assessment paints a picture of increasing loss of quality control and anticipatory management. It alludes to a need to address several systemic problems in order to catch up.

Communication. As illustrated by the Chemistry profile example, all QI lessons learned need to be transmitted to all intra- and extralaboratory personnel that are involved with the laboratory QI process. Specifically, data and decisions concerning the multichannel analyzer need to be shared with all concerned clinical personnel.

Likewise, the Transfusion Service must share its QI turnaround information globally, to include the hospital QI organization, the hospital task force, and the hospital administration. One lesson learned here is that TAT and backlog indicator data almost always affect nonlaboratory personnel at many organizational levels who have a "need to know" so that they can participate in the decision-making and improvement processes.

Laboratory Throughput Management: Distribution (Indicator Grouping 6)

Chemistry profile interpretation:
Evaluation of the subject data demonstrates no opportunities for improvement of laboratory report distribution identified over a six month period—as reflected by this general survey of incident and other occurrence screening feeder reports. Also, evaluation of the supporting indicators for laboratory product distribution confirms this inactivity: there is no customer complaint, adverse patient care outcome, increased TAT or backlog, or externally created incident report (ie, indicator grouping 24) alluding to poor distribution.

Under ordinary circumstances, no action would be necessary and the section would wait for another three months for reevaluation. However, it seems to this section's quality management team (knowing the laboratory system as it really is), that in any six month period there should have been some general complaint of inadequate distribution from somewhere in the hospital. Accordingly, after such apparent indicator inactivity, the question

Indicator Grouping 6
Laboratory Product Distribution

Chemistry Section Quality Profile

Indicator Grouping/ Specific Indicator: Threshold (Periodicity)	QI Data Observations (Date trend started) J A S O N D
Report Distribution: no misdirected reports; sentinel event!! (Quarterly)	0 = no OFI identified - = no report required - 0 - - - - Survey began in Jul 95

Transfusion Service Quality Profile

Indicator Grouping/ Specific Indicator: Threshold (Periodicity)	QI Data Observations
Report/Component Distribution: no misdirected reports or products; sentinel event!! (Quarterly)	No OFI identified x 12 mo

!! = sentinel event

must be whether or not the QI program is adequately sensitive to detect the distribution improvement opportunities that are discoverable but that are not being detected.

Thus, the section quality management team recommends selection of a focused study. The analytical approach to making such a choice is by using the usual high-volume, high-risk (benefit), problem (opportunity)-prone trilogy for ranking of all IACs and their specific indicators for priority. All the usual analytical tools are at the section's disposal.

Transfusion profile interpretation:
The data amount to a general statement without specific cumulative information. Evaluation of that data summarizes that no opportunities for improvement have been discovered for 12 months. Knowing the ward and laboratory problems as they are, the accuracy of a consistently negative finding is definitely arguable. As cited in the profile, the recommended action is to select a focused study for the next monitoring period. The assessment mirrors that of the Chemistry profile—with the additional remonstration that there has been a much more substantial delay in the Transfusion Service's decision-making process, a fundamental facet of the QAc program—a key supporting indicator grouping.

Additional profile interpretations:

Hematology (Appendix D). Evaluation of this profile's distribution data reveals that there has been no identification of any OFI for eight

Evaluation of QI Data, TQM System, and CQI Process	Action Action Person: (Date Initiated)	Assessment of Overall Improvement
On target x 6 mo; this seems unrealistic; QI process must lack sensitivity	Select focused study for Feb 96 ACTION: Supervisor	Improvement of the QI process is in progress
On target x 12 mo; no improvement over an inordinate amount of time	Select a focused study for Jan 96 ACTION: Acting Supervisor	Improvement decisions were stalled but now are in progress

months of monthly reporting. Although control of distribution quality seems to be "on target" for almost three quarters, the monitoring of that aspect of laboratory quality has been on the basis of occurrence screening, only. Thus, the action for the section supervisor to select a focused study seems more prudent quality management. The assessment is that improvement of the QI process is ongoing.

Microbiology (Appendix E). Evaluation of the microbiology data for distribution reveals that ward 22 has registered a complaint of nonreceipt of several Gram stain reports scattered over several days during the reporting period of December. The recommended action is for the supervisor to investigate the OFI at hand. The assessment is that improvement is needed in the Gram stain distribution process somewhere between the microbiology section and the ward.

The fact that there is an apparent disconnect at the distribution interface between the laboratory section and the clinical ward is a probable tip of the proverbial mountain of causative possibilities. There are the following "what ifs":

- *What if* the original Gram stain requests and specimens never reached the laboratory?
- *What if* they were received; then were the specimens analytically processed?
- *What if* they were processed; then were the reports released for distribution?

- *What if* they were released; is there confirmation that the reports were delivered and accepted by the ward?
- *What if* they were accepted, were the reports correctly placed in the appropriate patient charts?

The preceding list suggests the process by which the section quality management team should investigate their distribution problem. First, the team should perform a flow chart analysis of the entire path of work flow for the Gram stain requests and specimens. Then, there needs to be a verification of the integrity of each procedural step and branching step for all pre-, intra-, and postlaboratory Gram stain events.

For example, one possible scenario presumes that the laboratory correctly received, processed, released, and delivered the request-specimen-report "package." If so, then, the question remains as to how the process of charting the results on ward 22 might have broken down? If this is a problem; has it spread systemically to any other wards and clinics?

Histopathology (Appendix G). Evaluation of the distribution indicators data reveals no OFI identified since the general survey was begun six reporting periods ago in July. Although the general survey data are "on target," there is perceived need to select a focused indicator topic within the next five months (there are other surveillance activities with greater precedence). The assessment is that the QI process is undergoing improvement.

Discussion:

Indicator Grouping. In a general medical laboratory that provides the usual wide scope of healthcare support, this indicator grouping usually concentrates on the monitoring of the distribution of written data or diagnostic reports. However, in sections such as the Transfusion Service, the laboratory end product will be in another form—usually a blood component of some kind. Other services such as blood donor phlebotomy, therapeutic phlebotomy, apheresis (donor and therapeutic) and bone marrow storage are also available, but usually the laboratory provides (ie, delivers) them on-site within the laboratory's own area. Still, if any of these services are deliverable to the bedside or other points of health care, the section also should prioritize those distribution activities for monitoring.

One main point is that it is not satisfactory to simply release a CP or AP report or other end product and rely blindly on subsequent delivery to a patient chart. Unfortunately, it is not uncommon for the laboratory to "pigeon-hole" reports in distribution boxes (the classical in-and-out box), or a robotic conveyer—or even be entered into a computer for electronic transmission—without adequate follow-up, acknowledgement or confirmation of proper transmission or transportation and receipt. This monitoring should include tracking the adequacy of telephonic and "hard copy" transmission of critical values.

The method of distribution can vary in sophistication throughout the laboratory, from AP to CP service and from section to section. However, confirmation of receipt is still necessary by some means (whether it be by ongoing monitoring or periodic sampling) depending on the criticalness of the aspect of care. For example, alarm values, Pap smear reports, and blood components are clearly contributory to heightened patient risk if these laboratory products do not arrive at the correct patient care "address" in an accurate and timely manner. Consequently, an up-to-date record of appropriate addressees would be an initial step toward ensuring high quality distribution for all laboratory products.

The patient chart is usually the primary destination for written laboratory reports. With the aid of advanced computerization, electronic mailing, and bar coding, the laboratorian can directly forward a legible and complete hard copy to the appropriate attending clinical provider at the correct point-of-care. In turn, this service ensures that timely diagnostic and therapeutic decisions are made with all the necessary data at hand. Otherwise, delivery must be done mechanically or manually, still as correctly and expeditiously as possible.

In the case of blood components, not only delivery of the blood product but also return of the used blood bag and associated paperwork is mandatory to ensure adequate follow-up of appropriate distribution. These steps also facilitate the monitoring of laboratory product utilization and patient care outcome.

For blood products, effective distribution also connotes maintenance of proper preservation and storage—meaning sustained temperature control within all extremes of prescribed limits. This QC information should also be a part of the distribution documentation.

Leave nothing to chance; use every practical way to facilitate success. Assume nothing. One cannot *guarantee* good quality management; but one can *assure* whether there has been good management or not by timely, assiduous follow-up surveillance.

The laboratorian can easily design focused studies to survey all the various methods of laboratory report/product distribution. As for any of the 26 suggested indicator groupings in the profile, the quality management team should plan appropriately targeted QI studies of laboratory product distribution by employment of the QAn program for organizational research, development, and implementation. The QAc program for effective organizational decision making will facilitate the quality of these planning decisions resulting in a final QI plan for scheduled assessment and continuous improvement.

Additional indicator topics are as plentiful as there are numbers of laboratory IACs, types of laboratory end products, means of distribution, and sites of delivery. It is absolutely imperative to choose judiciously. Use all the analytical QI tools available for an informed and decisive ranking and prioritizing of the most appropriate monitoring objectives.

Supporting Indicators. As pointed out in the Microbiology Section profile interpretation, opportunities for distribution improvement correlate well with most other groupings, especially overall TAT and all phases of post-, intra-, and prelaboratory processing. Additionally, in any of the latter process phases, secretarial and technologist staffing can be a decisive factor. Other strongly potential contributory groupings include physician and other clinical staff satisfaction outcome, patient care outcome, other aspects of operative resource adequacy, and QI, QAn, and QAc activities.

Threshold. As the stated threshold for both profile examples implies—"no misdirected reports; sentinel event." Ergo, the laboratory has deemed product distribution to be an all or none event. All distribution must be perfect—the laboratory will not tolerate any imperfect distribution. This is a zero defects endeavor. Any problem in the distribution process warrants an immediate investigative evaluation, seeking every reasonable remedy to capitalize on the OFI present.

However, as for almost every other QI concept illustrated in this text, determination of the threshold is a judgment for each individual laboratory to make. Consequently, the threshold also can be a comparative rate event, depending on the aspect of care, local resources, and management objectives.

Monitoring Periodicity. As is always the case, the periodicity of monitoring depends on the criticalness of the aspect of care that is under scrutiny. In the case of this grouping, the general survey warrants no more than a quarterly review—while still maintaining monthly collection of data. If a critical opportunity for improvement is discovered by either general survey or focused study, then a more frequent schedule would be clinically, technically, or administratively appropriate.

Evaluation. A laboratory often will inadvertently overlook the importance of the distribution indicator grouping as an important element in the path of work flow. In some instances, conditional myopia evolves from systemic distribution resource problems existing in the institutional memory from time immemorial (eg, the institutionalized "in-box/out-box" distribution syndrome). In other cases, nonlaboratory distribution activities—some operating even outside the primary hospital—become directly involved in laboratory distribution activities. These are assumably out of the purview of the primary laboratory's power of control or assessment.

However, such a rationale represents a self-fulfilled prophecy and is not an acceptable reason to omit evaluation of nonlaboratory distribution processes. The laboratory must remain cognizant of what happens to its end product even beyond its physical boundaries.

Action. Resolving laboratory product distribution process problems often involves many nonlaboratory resources, including physicians, medical students, nursing personnel, hospital volunteers, the patients themselves, computer operation personnel, facility engineers, the local telephone company, postal and other shipping facilities, and others. Thus, any required action must include all appropriate laboratory and nonlaboratory personnel involved in the decision-making and implementation processes.

The need for such an effective interdepartmental interface implies that the laboratory is exercising all aspects of QI, QAn, and QAc to adequately affect the appropriate action. These three programs are important at the QM interface because:

- QI is the source of improvement opportunity identification and resolution.
- QAn is the source of improvement action checks and resource balances.
- QAc is the source of organizational energy that fuels the other two programs in the continuous quest for quality improvement; thus, quality actualization is the most fundamentally important of the three programs.

Assessment. For this indicator grouping, the follow-up of action and overall QI process effectiveness also must reach beyond the laboratory doors. Because of this, the options for assessment must promote a sensitivity and continued commitment to joint improvement in a systematic, timely manner. Always keep in mind the three assessment options important in a CQI environment.

Communication. Just as there is need for joint planning and implementation, there is equal importance of joint communication in order to implement and sustain distribution improvement. This process should include open, two-way dialogue in support of participative decision making by all customers and suppliers who are involved and have a need to know.

INTRALABORATORY PROCESS WORK FLOW SEGMENT

This is the third major segment of the quality profile format and includes five prominent indicator groupings in this sample profile report. Each of the groupings addresses a chief intralaboratory process event of the work flow path. By definition, each of these groupings usually occurs within the confines of the laboratory after initial accessioning of a patient's specimen and before release of a laboratory product for distribution.

In the usual order of profile analysis, these groupings include 1) postdeterminative finalization, 2) reference laboratory studies, 3) analytical quality, 4) diagnostic quality, and 5) predeterminative processing. In actual practice, there can be fewer or more groupings; each grouping can include one or more specific quality indicators. Remember that the profile presents these groupings for analysis in the reverse order of their natural sequence of occurrence in the path of work flow.

Indicator Grouping 7
Postdeterminative Product Finalization and Specimen Handling

Chemistry Section Quality Profile

Indicator Grouping/ Specific Indicator: Threshold (Periodicity)	QI Data Observations (Date trend started) J A S O N D	
INTRALABORATORY PROCESS WORK FLOW SEGMENT		
Postdeterminative Product Finalization and Specimen Handling: no loss of product or specimen integrity!! (Quarterly)	No OFI identified x 3 qtrs	

Transfusion Service Quality Profile

INTRALABORATORY PROCESS WORK FLOW SEGMENT		
Postdeterminative Report/Component Finalization and Specimen Handling: no loss of product or specimen integrity!! (Quarterly) a. Special study:* platelet storage ambient temperature: < 20 to > 24°C (°C = degrees Centigrade)! *Ordered by med director after an on-the-spot report on 21 Dec. Jul-Nov temps are archival monthly averages. Dec temp is month's high.	25 25 24 23 23 27 °C 1. 27°C was high temp on 21 Dec 2. Staff complaints over xs temperature in the platelet storage Room A03 began in mid Dec 95 3. A new frozen blood freezer was moved into Rm A03 on 15 Dec without attention to the additional heat produced. The freezer was removed on 21 Dec 4. Lab discarded 5 platelet units (10%) after 21 Dec report of 27°C temp 5. Ambient temp has been in control since 21 Dec	

xs = excess !! = sentinel event

Postdeterminative Finalization and Handling Management (Indicator Grouping 7)

Chemistry profile interpretation:
The data column proffers a general statement that there has been no opportunity for improvement of postdeterminative product finalization or specimen handling for the last nine months. The evaluation is equally general. Under the circumstances, the section has deemed that the QI process has been ineffective at the level of sensitivity practiced. Therefore, pursuing a focused study is advisable. The indicator assessment intimates that nine months of nonimprovement should begin to give any objective observer an uneasy feeling.

Evaluation of QI Data, TQM System, and CQI Process	Action and Action Person: (Date Initiated)	Assessment of Overall Improvement
On target x 9 mo; there has been no improvement over an inordinate amount of time	Select focused study for Mar 96 ACTION: Supervisor	Improvement was stalled but now is in progress
1. Temp QC is off target!! Bimodal pattern 2. Seasonal problems abated but not resolved: inadequate response by QI team 3. Dramatic increase in the last month without adequate response by QI team 4. There is no recording alarm system for the ambient platelet temperature 5. There might be a need for a lock box on wall thermostat	1. Install temp recorder/alarm 2. Investigate need for thermostat lock 3. Consider use of storage incubator versus another room 4. Hold inservice tng on QC and QI re platelet storage 5. Coordinate with Fac Engineers to resolve summer temp problem 6. Report temp as a maximum, not as an average ACTION: Acting Supervisor	Ineffective QC and QI processes!! Improvement of QC and QI processes is needed immediately QI Note: conduct an investigative evaluation of QC and TQM programs immediately

Transfusion profile interpretation:
The Transfusion Service reports data for a focused study that began in December. There is one month of concurrent data for December and five months of "look-back" data for July through November. The profile notes that the section medical director ordered the retrospective review of platelet storage temperatures on the basis of an on-the-spot incident report on 21 December. The section obtained the look-back data for those five months by reviewing archival ambient temperature control charts for Room A03, the platelet storage room. The December data demonstrates that the single, highest temperature spike (27°C) occurred on 21 December.

The threshold states specifically that the ambient temperature should range within 20°C to 24°C. Even though the threshold is expressed as a bimodal range, it still demonstrates an all or none condition, a sentinel event. For example, the profile data demonstrate that five months (July through November) of averaged ambient temperatures ranged from 23°C to 25°C! It also illustrates that the maximum ambient temperature recorded in December reached the high level of 27°C on 21 December.

The section's evaluation pointedly purports that there is something terribly wrong in this area of laboratory quality management—platelet storage has been out of control for at least six months! In fact, on careful examination this profile demonstrates a bimodal (multifactorial) temperature control problem. The abnormal pattern (in this case, not really a trend) is that of borderline-high average ambient temperatures in the July-August reporting periods and a significantly higher temperature spike in the December period.

First, the retrospective look-back portion of the study reveals that the section allowed an averaged ambient temperature of > 24°C to occur during the hottest summer months of July and August. Even when the *average* temperature was exactly 24°C in September, there had to be untold highs exceeding the threshold on certain days. The profile alludes to the inordinately high temperatures in July and August as a "seasonal" temperature control problem, which has probably occurred yearly because of inadequate facility ventilation, cooling, or air exchange.

As it turns out historically, the indicators for environmental (ie, indicator grouping 3) and facility (ie, indicator grouping 21) quality also support that the summer months are seasonably hot. In fact, all other section profiles provided in this text attest to that fact that excessive ambient room temperatures in the summer are a general facility shortcoming for this entire, albeit fictitious, laboratory department.

The staff has endured these excessive, seasonal temperatures, but especially inappropriately so in Room A03 without proper attention to the platelets stored in that area. Yes, capital expense facility repair or renovation is often a hurdle to overcome because of budgetary constraints and the need for long-range planning. However, such administrative barriers are no excuse for this section's tolerating such aberrant platelet storage temperatures. Seasonal or not, there are always relatively inexpensive methods of solving the problem aside from major facility repair or renovation.

Nor is there any mention in the profile report of the inordinately high temperatures triggering an alarm. In fact, investigative evaluation has brought out that there has been no alarm present capable of immediately signaling a disparate ambient temperature occurrence—not even a relatively inexpensive, commonly available low-to-high-range recording thermometer to register maximum temperature swings.

As for the second portion of the bimodal trend in this postdeterminative platelet handling and storage study, evidence has suddenly dawned of 1) the ambient temperature in Room A03 spiking to 27°C and 2) the laboratory discarding five platelet units (10% wastage) during the December reporting period. Blood component wastage usually involves loss on the clinical side as a laboratory product utilization topic, but in this case the loss has occurred in the laboratory.[c]

Investigative evaluation of the December data unmasks this second difficulty to be of similarly grave proportions as those in the summer months. After a three month lull of normal ambient temperatures, the maximum temperature in the platelet storage room suddenly shot up to a recorded high of 27°C in late-December. Also, there was some delayed recognition of the problem: the temperature spikes probably began on 15 December, but the medical director did not receive a report until 21 December. The sectional staff finally exercised investigative evaluation and took corrective action after the on-the-spot report on 21 December.

Further investigative evaluation has revealed that the temperature spikes and subsequent platelet loss were directly related to someone "inadvertently" (a familiar managerial euphemism) installing a frozen blood component freezer in Room A03, the platelet storage room, on 15 December. The presence of this heat-producing freezer caused the sudden increase of the ambient temperature in the room used for platelet storage. Concordant with the reporting of the elevated temperature on 21 December, the section had to discard the entire inventory of five units of platelets on that day—which represented 10% wastage of the month's total inventory.

Review of the supporting grouping for personnel strength (ie, indicator grouping 15), reveals that there has not only been a serious technologist vacancy rate, but there has also been a loss of a full-time supervisor, with an acting supervisor assuming responsibility in November. Other supporting indicators provide corroborating evidence of suboptimal performance in analytical quality, proficiency tests, and the QI, QAn, and QAc programs. All these supporting groupings substantially show that there are other very important operative and organizational activities within the section that are suffering from the same staff shortage and overwork.

The most unsettling aspect of either of the two temperature problems or the platelet mishandling is that the section apparently exercised no effective QI reporting or evaluation of platelet storage temperature abnormalities in the summer or in December until a crisis was reported. The section routinely recorded and filed the monitoring data but never officially reported it until the "look-back" portion of the study was performed. In addition, no one in the section took any effective action in response to the blatantly high temperatures in July to reinstate and ensure a controlled platelet storage temperature—even the response to the December event was too much delayed.

From the very beginning, the section could have taken steps to gain control of their ambient temperature. At the very least, they could have gained temporary, local temperature control by installing portable fans or

[c] Laboratory wastage at the site of preutilization storage could be a topic for surveillance under the postdeterminative specimen handling grouping or under the supply indicator grouping in the general profile segment for operative resource management. Stored platelets are a supply item, especially in the eyes of the clinical primary user.

air conditioners. Or, they could have simply transferred the platelets to a more controlled environment—eg, to another, cooler room or a properly controlled enclosure in the same room. The ultimate remedy would have been to institute plans for facility repair or renovation jointly with the hospital administration, facility engineers, and contracting office. As a last resort, they could have curtailed production and storage of platelets.

However, there is no mention of any restitution of temperature control or platelet storage integrity by taking any of the above actions until late in December. So, we must assume that no substantive remedial steps were taken to guard the integrity of the ambient temperature or platelet products until the December crisis.

The prescribed action for the December QI period is to resolve the temperature and platelet handling control problems and to resolve any other problems in any related operational process. As described under evaluation, immediate and long-range action decisions match the QC and QI managerial problems at hand. Along with improving routine temperature control and quality surveillance, the section will improve the platelet storage threshold definition and reporting style (an element of the QI process) to alleviate sporadic temperature highs from being masked by averaged data.

The overall assessment is that there is need for immediate improvement of the subject QC and TQM programs. The overall situation is not at all flattering to the section, service or departmental quality management program. First, there has been sorely ineffective action in identifying and resolving these blatantly serious temperature control and platelet storage control problems at the operative, hands-on, real time level. For example, the section staff's response to the summer QI data was not at all adequate; the July-November surveillance data was not even present in the profile until after a retrospective, look-back, investigative study.

Additionally, the QI process itself has not been adequately sensitive or responsive to the several opportunities for improvement that have been literally right in front of the laboratory quality team's noses—at both the section and department/service levels. The performance of responsible individuals is not as important compared to the importance of the effectiveness of the entire organizational surveillance (QI), planning (QAn), and decision making (QAc) system of programs—all of which are in significant disrepair due to severe staff shortage.

Additional profile interpretations:

Hematology (Appendix D)*:* Evaluation of the QI data reveals that there have been no improvement opportunities for three quarters. The recommended action is for the supervisor to select a focused study. The assessment is accurate.

Microbiology (Appendix E)*:* There has been no OFI identified for 12 months, an extremely long time to wait for remedial action and improvement of the QI process. The recommended action is for the supervisor to begin quarterly reporting of the general review, along with selection of a focused study. The assessment reflects that the appropriate action has been unduly delayed.

Histopathology (Appendix G)*:* There have been no OFI identified for seven months of QI monitoring. The recommended action is for the supervisor to select a focused study topic. The assessment is accurate.

In the AP service, product finalization has traditionally involved accurate transcription of a dictated or handwritten examination, diagnosis, and clinical-pathological correlative comments. High quality finalization implies that there has been careful review of the final, written product with verification by handwritten signature or electronic registration by the primary diagnostician. This verification should ensure that the final report accurately and completely reflects what the primary diagnostician originally intended to convey to the clinicians at the point-of-care. Becoming familiar with the finalization of more CP-like, analytical procedures is already occurring on the AP scene, as more analytical approaches become adopted to supplement the more traditional anatomic diagnoses.

Discussion:

Indicator Grouping. In any laboratory, the postdeterminative finalization phase of the path of intralaboratory process work flow is replete with pitfalls that can be easily overlooked. Consequently, this indicator grouping promises many possible targets for quality improvement. Regarding either written test or diagnostic reports, problems can range from a transcriptional error in patient identity data to the inaccurate typing of the final analytical or diagnostic results to the omission of critical clinical-pathological correlative comments. Considering the preservation of a laboratory product until time for clinical utilization, the Transfusion Service profile suggests the extent of potential problems.

The satisfactory compliance with postdeterminative indicator criteria and threshold levels should cover quality expectations for diagnostic procedures. Wherever interpretive reports are produced, the postdeterminative finalization process requires peer review and verification of final written reports and appropriate peer control data before embarking on the next step of product distribution.

If a patient specimen is to be preserved for future study, the section still has to maintain postdeterminative specimen integrity. In this light, ensuring postdeterminative processing integrity is really a final confirmation of the chain of request-patient-specimen-product integrity.

Except for the addition of the product to the chain, the subject grouping represents a mirror image of the predetermination processing and validation groupings that are also part of the chain of request-to-product integrity and are analyzed later in the profile.[d] Thus, there are many surveillance indicators available in this work flow phase or indicator grouping for ongoing, indexed or focused studies.

[d] But, they occur earlier in the natural order of the path of work flow.

The Transfusion Service sample profile provides an example of one particular variance in profile notation. Many indicator data are expressed as averages, some are expressed as grand or cumulative totals. In the subject profile, the ambient temperature for December is expressed as an all-period high. The laboratorian must be aware that, in some cases, the use of averaged data can dangerously mask important sentinel events.

Additional indicator topics for the postdeterminative profile segment are as myriad as the number of IACs, specific laboratory products and services, and laboratory customers. One telling indicator topic for this grouping would be the absolute number or percent of results or other products that are modified after release of the original by the laboratory. Such changes can result after postrelease discovery of analytical QC, clerical transcription, or delta check discrepancies. They afford us a measure by which to gauge the effectiveness of the postdeterminative finalization and verification/confirmation process that is supposed to be performed before release of products to the point-of-care.

Supporting Indicators. These are fairly global in scope. They include customer (physician and patient) satisfaction, patient care outcome, overall TAT (or postdeterminative processing turnaround specifically), analytical-diagnostic determinative quality, intralaboratory-prelaboratory processing, and operative resource management, plus the QI, QAn, and QAc activities. Probably of greatest corroborative importance is analytical-diagnostic determinative quality.

Threshold. As demonstrated by the example profiles, the threshold for postdeterminative finalization and end product/specimen handling can vary widely in its range of limitations and mode of expression. As a QI range of sensitivity, the threshold depends on patient risk and technical complexity inherent to the important aspect of care being monitored.

Monitoring Periodicity. This scheduling depends upon the criticalness of the aspect of care being monitored and the adequacy of the quality management resources on hand.

Evaluation. Postdeterminative (predistribution) product finalization, including end product and specimen preservation and handling, can be a "sleeper" in its perceived importance in quality management. Only by purposefully directing systematic scrutiny on this segment of the path of flow can the quality management team be consistent in discovering opportunities for improvement. This endeavor involves the review of the finalization processing and disposition of a diverse collection of reports and other laboratory products and services—such as apheresis—along with patient specimens requiring further preservation and storage.

Of special note, it is during the postdeterminative stage that the primary laboratory also verifies or confirms reports and other products from reference laboratories before their release to the patient's point-of-care. However, the quality profile scheme used in this text specifically addresses all reference laboratory quality management in the next indicator grouping (ie, indicator grouping 8).

Action. The action required in response to postdetermination finalization opportunities can involve the entire laboratory quality management team. This includes not only the technological staff, but also the diagnostic and the clerical staff. In some instances, when a final review uncovers predeterminative need for improved clinical data or other support to complete the laboratory product, then even the clinical staff must become involved in quality management and QI dialogue.

Assessment. Postdeterminative finalization, end product management, and specimen handling and storage comprise one of the key workload phases for which the effectiveness of both remedial action and the long range QI process needs ascertaining. By virtue of its complexity, this grouping easily provides the occasion to exercise all three QI assessment options in the CQI environment at one time or another. Additionally, assessment of postdeterminative finalization should reflect whether the QAn or QAc programs need improving because of their importance in related team planning and decision making activities.

Communication. In keeping with the postdeterminative finalization indicator's global nature and inherent complexity, communication requirements can be quite extensive throughout the laboratory. These open dialogue requirements even extend beyond the laboratory to lateral and higher hospital managerial and administrative echelons. Such nonlaboratory players and potential communication addressees include clinical departments, ancillary support departments (eg, facility engineers and personnel management), the hospital QI system, and the hospital administrative echelon.

Reference Laboratory Quality Management (Indicator Grouping 8)

Chemistry profile interpretation:
The subject data report, based on a general survey of section feeder reports, summarizes that there have been no opportunities for improvement over an 11 month cumulative period. The evaluation, action, and assessment for this general profile segment are all in keeping with the facts at hand. Instead of being discontinued (as it could be), the general survey continues on a quarterly reporting schedule. The primary laboratory still considers monitoring the reference laboratory quality to be significantly relevant to customer satisfaction—rather than omit the general survey approach entirely.

The focused study denotes that the reference laboratory's alpha fetoprotein (AFP) turnaround time was prolonged to eight days in July 1992. Consequently, the primary laboratory section decided to pursue a special review of AFP testing TAT over the last six months—this heightened scrutiny being exercised above and beyond the level of a general survey.

The data, evaluation, action, and assessment are concomitant with the apparent resolution of the reference laboratory's AFP turnaround, the averaged data returning to its acceptable normative operable threshold of

Indicator Grouping 8
Reference Laboratory Quality

Chemistry Section Quality Profile

Indicator Grouping/ Specific Indicator: Threshold (Periodicity)	QI Data Observations (Date trend started) J A S O N D
Reference Laboratory Studies: no adverse effect on patient outcome!! (Quarterly)	- - 0 - - 0 Gen survey began Feb 95 - - = not scheduled 0 = no OFI identified
a. α fetoprotein TAT: > 4 days from primary lab submission to return receipt by primary lab	8 3 3 4 3 3 d This study began in Jul 95 Last clinical complaint Jul 95 d = averaged days

Transfusion Service Quality Profile

Reference Laboratory Studies: no adverse effect on patient outcome!! (Quarterly)	No OFI identified x 3 qtrs

!! = sentinel event

>4 days TAT.[e] With the establishment of this data baseline, the primary laboratory can track the indicator with a more widely spaced follow-up schedule. Since this reference laboratory activity seems to have resumed its control of throughput, a completely new, focused study topic for reference laboratory testing is advisable for the near future. The new study would address a different reference laboratory test procedure, or some other high-priority phase of the path of work flow influenced by reference laboratory quality, or a completely separate segment of the quality profile. The section can deemphasize reference laboratory quality as a scheduled grouping altogether since it has shown recent, substantive improvement, and other portions of the path of flow could easily demand the attention of limited laboratory quality management resources.

On another note however, if deemed necessary the grouping could become more extensive with backlog of AFP cases serving as a valuable coindicator. Monitoring backlog can provide a much better idea of the numbers and actual identities of all dissatisfied customers and thwarted patient care cases.

[e]In this example, the normal operable range of actual TAT can vary between zero and four days, whereas the section expresses the TAT threshold limitation as > 4 days. The use and interpretation of the < and > symbols are an important distinction in quality management shorthand.

Evaluation of QI Data, TQM System, and CQI Process	Action Action Person: (Date Initiated)	Assessment of Overall Improvement
1.On target for at least 6 mo; good baseline for this general survey	Continue with quarterly periodicity ACTION: Supervisor	Effective QI process
6 month baseline is established after initial ref lab TAT of 8 d; problem appears to be resolved	1. Change periodicity to quarterly review 2. Consider a new study topic ACTION: Supervisor	Improvement of the QI process is in progress
On target x 3 qtrs; no improvement over an inordinate amount of time	Select a focused indicator for Mar 96 ACTION: Acting Supervisor	Improvement was stalled but now is in progress

Transfusion profile interpretation:
The data are in the form of a summary statement without individual reporting period figures—being dependent on only a general survey of incident feeder reports. Evaluation of the data reveals that no opportunities have been discovered during the past nine months. No focused study is under way. Thus, the action and assessment are in keeping with the summary findings.

Additional profile interpretations:

Hematology (Appendix D): This section profile segment example reveals an interesting aspect of reference laboratory quality monitoring. In this case, the average TAT and backlog for cytogenetic studies are under focused study. The throughput data reveal both excessive turnaround on the part of the reference laboratory and inconsistent reporting of the indicator data on the part of the section quality management team. The excessive TAT is corroborated by the growing number of backlogged cases (ie, the number of uncompleted, unreported cases tallied at the end of the reporting period). The backlog data provide an added dimension that aids in characterizing the severity of the problem at hand.

The recommended action decisions follow the evaluation. First, there needs to be improved reporting of QI data by the section—team QAn and QAc activities must address this reference laboratory QI issue. Second, the reference laboratory must be more expeditious in reporting its results—or the section must select a more responsive reference laboratory. Both actions are the section supervisor's responsibility. The assessment points out the need for improvement at the two quality management levels for both section and reference laboratory processes.

Microbiology (Appendix E): There has been no identification of any OFI for six months. The action is for the supervisor to select a focused study topic. The assessment is that focusing QI efforts reflects an improvement of the QI process.

Histopathology (Appendix G): Two focused studies of TAT are in progress: one for tissue diagnosis consultation by "ABC" Laboratories and the other for estrogen receptor assay by "XYZ" Laboratories. Evaluation reveals that the former turnaround indicator has been "on target" since its inception four months ago. The latter has been slightly off target by about one day over the past three months.

More revealing is that, although the latter receptor turnaround delay has been relatively low in severity, the total number of backlogged cases has been demonstrating a subtle, "subacute" trend of creeping growth; in this case, the section defines backlog as the accumulation of unreported cases that extend beyond the TAT threshold at the end of each reporting period. Although a low-level, plateaued turnaround belies a low priority OFI, the reference laboratory performance is not at all stable but is slowly yet surely falling more and more behind in serving its customers as evidenced by the slowly growing backlog.

The decision that no actions are needed for the ABC Laboratory study is appropriate in answer to the nonproblematic evaluation. The assessment is accurate.

The action for the XYZ Laboratory study demands improvement—or else. Otherwise, the laboratory manager is to select a new reference laboratory. The assessment is accurate that this indicator study is providing evidence that the section is on the verge of losing operative-level control—and the quality management team is about to lose administrative-level assurance. By recognition of the OFI and establishing remedial action, the section is making progress toward improving patient care support. But, the laboratory cannot afford to allow this poor quality of reference laboratory service to continue.

Since each reference laboratory used by a CAP-accredited primary laboratory has to earn accreditation in its own right, the reference laboratory should be adhering to the same general requirements for internal TAT for routine analytical and diagnostic procedures. The CAP requirement for routine tissue diagnosis from accessioning to distribution is 48 hours.

The five day threshold used in this example for ABC Laboratory is from the primary laboratory's perspective. It takes into consideration that the "average" consultation case might require:

- Shipment of tissue, blocks, or slides to the reference laboratory
- Processing of tissue or blocks by the reference laboratory
- Diagnosis and finalization
- Distribution of the hard copy consultation diagnosis by either electronic or regular mail.

Relatively little time should be necessary for transmission of the final report in this era of electronic mailing.

Various anatomic cases will take less or more than five days for consultative completion, depending on the shipping and distribution system and the inherent technical and diagnostic complexity of the case. In the more complicated cases, although interim reports can alleviate the violation of routine TAT thresholds, there ultimately have to be separate threshold limits for the more complex cases.

Thus, the primary laboratory often finds it worthwhile to track several classes of diagnostic cases, each with its own threshold level. For example, there are the routine and special cases. There also are the rush cases that might even require an immediate telephonic reply with an expedited hard copy follow-up. All of these classifications warrant individual TAT threshold limitations.

Discussion:

Indicator Grouping. This grouping demonstrates that reference laboratory quality can be a vexing challenge to monitor as a QI indicator. TAT is one major reference laboratory quality that frequently requires improvement—for any number of reasons.

In the eyes of the laboratorian, reference laboratory TAT might be defined as extending from the time that the primary laboratory sends a specimen to the reference laboratory to the time that the primary laboratory receives a written report or some other product from the reference laboratory. However, in the clinicians' eyes as the ultimate customer, reference laboratory turnaround begins when the initial laboratory request and specimen are sent to the primary laboratory and ends when the desired report is charted at the point-of-care.

In terms of the laboratorian's definition, reference laboratory TAT problems are usually caused by some systemic delay in the clerical, analytical/diagnostic activities of the reference laboratory itself or in the logistical process responsible for transporting the request-specimen to the reference laboratory and transmitting the final report to the primary laboratory. In view of the clinicians' definition, delay in reference laboratory testing or diagnosing might easily involve the primary laboratory's speed in processing the request and specimen prior to submission to the reference laboratory.

For example, is the primary laboratory sending the request-specimen on clinical demand, with immediate processing and shipping to the reference laboratory on a case-by-case basis? Or, is the primary laboratory practicing batch shipping, expending inordinate clinical waiting time prior to actual shipping?

What about other aspects of reference laboratory quality? Can the primary laboratory monitor reference laboratory analytical or diagnostic proficiency on an ongoing basis or by periodically scheduling focused studies? How can one proprietary laboratory track the quality of proficiency of another?

- First, there always should be some up-to-date, publicly available documentation that the subject reference laboratory is appropriately accredited and, thus, is performing consistently well on external proficiency surveys. The reference laboratory really should divulge its performance on proficiency testing at the request of any primary laboratory customer.
- Additionally, although at some expense, split samples can be sent to the subject reference laboratory and to a second, known-to-be-credible reference laboratory for comparative studies.
- Third, delta checks can be used to compare the efficacy of reference laboratory testing with clinical events occurring at the point-of-care.
- Finally, the primary laboratory can proactively survey the opinion of the clinicians regarding a reference laboratory's quality—rather than wait retrospectively for an incident report.

Unfortunately, it is clinical staff members who quite often are the first to detect technical trouble with a reference laboratory result through clinical correlation, then registering the problem verbally or in a written report. Therefore, the primary laboratory must continuously "keep an ear to the ground," remaining always alert for clinical customer input. This requirement implies that the laboratory must always ensure to the best of its ability that there is a sensitive enough mechanism for facilitating dialogue between the laboratorian and the clinician.

A major lesson learned here is that, although seemingly out of reach, the performance of a reference laboratory can be systematically scrutinized through several phases of the path of work flow. Hopefully, this surveillance is in a prospective, anticipatory (ie, continuous quality improvement) fashion—and not in a retrospective, reactive risk management (ie, damage control) mode.

As a special note, it is worthwhile considering that reference laboratory activities deserve much more attention than afforded by a single indicator grouping interleaved within a whole laboratory section quality profile. Should we limit reference laboratory quality management to the dimension of a single grouping profile segment? On the contrary, a reference laboratory could easily justify attention as a completely separate work center, warranting a completely unique profile. This expanded approach is similar to the quality management recommended for monitoring point-of-care or ancillary testing activities as separate work centers, receiving total QI surveillance on the same scope as a primary laboratory section.

Additional indicator topics are easily identifiable as one considers the entire spectrum of the path of work flow and all of the indicator groupings that potentially relate to reference laboratory quality management. The potential indicator topic candidates span most of the entire profile gamut, ranging from outcome indicators, to operative process indicators, to organizational process indicators.

Operative resource management indicators are of particularly limited value in the primary laboratory's monitoring of a reference laboratory's quality. That limitation rests on the lack of direct reference laboratory management data input into the primary laboratory's QI process and lack of the primary laboratory's direct influence on the quality of the reference laboratory's operative resources. This is especially true in view of the fact that, in most instances, we are talking about two private, competitive organizations. However, one important reference laboratory operative resource that the primary laboratory directly affects is the reference procedure workload type and volume. It is also worthwhile to correlate the cost of reference laboratory procedures as a primary laboratory operative resource, ie, budgetary, element.

Supporting Indicators. These indicators include all phases of work flow that directly affect—or are directly affected by—reference laboratory function. They include outcome indicators of physician and other clinical staff satisfaction and patient care outcome, all primary laboratory pre- and postdeterminative process indicators, primary laboratory operative resource management indicators of reference laboratory procedure workload volume and cost, as well as personnel staffing, and all internal and external organizational indicators for both primary and reference laboratories. It is advisable, in fact, that both laboratories perform the three organizational-level programs of QI, QAn, and QAc on a joint basis to at least some degree.

Threshold. A wide range of possibilities exists in selecting thresholds for reference laboratory QI surveillance. The criticalness of such a threshold depends—as usual—on the high-volume, high-risk (benefit), problem (opportunity)-prone factors of patient risk, procedure difficulty, workload volume, procedure cost, and the given phase of work flow under scrutiny.

Monitoring Periodicity. Again, this aspect of the QI process depends upon the priority ranking of the aspect of care being monitored, the extent of the quality management resources on hand, and the related patient severity index.

Evaluation. Much of the surveillance of the quality of a reference laboratory is dependent on limited, indirect observations—although a few direct routes of inquiry are available. To a large extent, the amount of direct observation possible will be dependent on the degree to which the two laboratories are linked through joint QI, QAn, and QAc program activities. Consequently, any evaluation of reference laboratory quality must be couched in terms that evenly weigh the degrees of subjective and objective observation.

Action. The options for immediate action depend on the nature of the opportunity for improvement at hand. The ultimate choice of selecting a new reference laboratory—or having the primary laboratory assume a new workload—are examples worth consideration. The feasibility of either option might be gauged on the degree of clinical need for improved quality or on the basis of a shift in workload that dictates more cost-effective use of the primary laboratory's resources.

Consequently, the volume of reference laboratory testing workload can become a useful resource management indicator. The primary laboratory must often request a reference laboratory to perform a test when the subject test workload volume is too small to be cost-effective for the primary laboratory to perform itself. In this case, the method is too labor-intensive or too inherently costly for some other reason. Eventually, that reference procedure volume can grow large enough that it becomes more cost-effective to perform the procedure in-house. This change also can result in an upgrading of the overall laboratory process, including providing improved patient care support, by being able to use more up-to-date methods and to exercise more direct control of the entire process. On the other hand, the primary laboratory might have to request reference laboratory support if the workload overwhelms the number of primary laboratory staff that is available.

A secret to success for any action directed at improving reference laboratory quality rests on the caliber of joint communication between the primary and reference laboratory. The value of unimpeded, two-way dialogue becomes quite evident when there is need to follow up on remedial action and monitor subsequent improvement of reference laboratory quality. It is possible for both laboratories to be jointly involved in QI, QAn, and QAc programs to further their mutual advantage and to enhance QI action.

Assessment. As usual, the three options for assessment depend on the effectiveness of whatever resolving action has been taken and the effectiveness of the QI process practiced in the CQI environment.

Communication. The communication of lessons learned must often carry far beyond the boundaries of the primary laboratory, its client hospital or physician offices, and any reference laboratory. However, the follow-up of lessons learned from this indicator grouping is slightly different compared to other groupings because it involves dealing with another, usually proprietary, competitive laboratory operation.

Other "customers-suppliers" potentially involved could be local, state, and national professional licensing and regulatory organizations. Such extensive communication might be necessary to determine or clarify the accreditation, proficiency, and licensure status of a reference laboratory. Also, follow-up of adverse incidents might involve communication with the same types of external organizations for peer review purposes. Therefore, always consider the value of seeking the advice of legal counsel when regarding any external QI communication involving another laboratory.

Analytical Quality Management (Indicator Grouping 9)

Chemistry profile interpretation:
The general threshold for this grouping is that of a sentinel event. Evaluation of six months' cumulative data reveals two opportunities to improve two separate sets of analytical instruments. First, the multichannel analyzer "X" is known to be aged and difficult to maintain since a service contract is no longer available; the ion-specific electrode is a common source of difficulty. Consequently, the section must closely monitor the analytical quality of this instrument. There must be continuously documented assurance of patient results, accomplished by repeated runs, parallel testing, assiduous on-the-spot, in-house maintenance and repair. Such an ambitious control effort comprises a great deal of extra bench and supervisory effort.

The recommended action—since January 1995—has been for the section supervisor to maintain QC while obtaining a new instrument. On-site visits and contracting are under way, but the overall remedial process needs immediate expediting. Other interim options include obtaining a loaned or leased instrument—or deferring certain tests to a reference laboratory. The sustaining of satisfactory clinical outcome weighs heavily on the requirement that these laboratory quality management decisions be implemented as soon as possible.

The subsequent QI assessment is that the required action has been only marginally satisfactory—if not blatantly ineffective. This assessment rests on the basis of a 12 month delay in obtaining a new instrument for absolute improvement of the situation.

This Chemistry Section profile segment offers a second opportunity to improve disparate results that are being generated by two different instruments that measure the same analytes. Analyzer "A" is located in the general Chemistry laboratory serving the overall hospital, while analyzer "B" is located in the stat laboratory unit in support of surgical intensive care.

As is often the case, a clinical incident report in the November reporting period brought the alleged disparity to light. In response, the section has appropriately decided to perform parallel studies to ascertain the respective accuracy and precision of the two instruments. If the clinical impression is proven accurate, the section's ultimate objective is to replace one of the two instruments to meet the goal of providing equal technical quality for both surgical and all other hospital patients. In the interim, the Chemistry Section must ensure maintenance of QC and assure the correctness of all

Indicator Grouping 9
Analytical Quality

Chemistry Section Quality Profile

Indicator Grouping/ Specific Indicator: Threshold (Periodicity)	QI Data Observations (Date trend started) J A S O N D
Analytical Quality: no major discrepancies!! (Monthly) a. Multichannel Analyzer X	Service contract is not available for Analyzer X Selection of new analyzer began in Jan 95! • = no problems cited x = major QC problem cited
Acid Phos	x • • • • x
BUN	• x x • x •
CO2	• • • • x •
Glucose	x • • • • x
Na/K	x • x • • •
ALT (SGPT)	x • • • • x
b. Analyzer A and B disparity in alk phos test results; analyzer A is in general chem lab; analyzer B is in ICU stat lab: no major disparity!!	- - - - x x This disparity in alk phos tests was first noted in Nov 95 through a clinical incident report - = no study in progress x = disparity reported

Transfusion Service Quality Profile

Analytical Quality: no major discrepancies!! (Monthly)	0 0 1 1 2 4 These occurrences represent mistakes in interpretation of crossmatch and other antibody-antigen reactions at the bench by more than one individual One incident report in Dec involved a case of inaccurate temperature recording for the blood reefer (refrigerator)

!! = sentinel event

Evaluation of QI Data, TQM System, and CQI Process	Action Action Person: (Date Initiated)	Assessment of Overall Improvement
Constant imprecision due to aging instrument; patient studies remain in constant control through constant maintenance, recalibration and repeat runs; on-site visits to observe best replacement candidate have been scheduled	1. Maintain QC and patient result assurance 2. Replace the instrument immediately or obtain loaned/leased instrument or defer to reference lab NLT 1 Feb 96 ACTION: Supervisor (Jan 95)	Ineffective QI process; instrument selection is excessively prolonged: EXPEDITE procurement of new analyzer!
Disparity between two different methods in General Chemistry Lab and Stat Lab causing confusion in clinical diagnosis and therapy; results are currently under control	1. Standardize the alk phos methods 2. Coordinate with medical maintenance and suppliers 3. If neccessary obtain new analyzer ACTION: Supervisor (Nov 95)	Improvement is in progress; improved control is only temporary until disparity is resolved
1. Increasing incidence of major discrepancies over 4 mo; not limited to any one person. 2. Supervisor resigned in Nov; acting Supervisor is in place 3. Critical staff shortage persists	1. Increase overview of bench QC 2. Consider automation of hi vol procedures ACTION: Acting Supervisor 1. Fill staff vacancies; place priority on supervisory job 2. Determine interim processing options: ie, curtailment and referral! ACTION: Medical Director	Ineffective QC and QI processes! Resolving personnel shortage requires support of Hosp Admin, Personnel Office, and Task Force Ineffective QI process to date

test results being issued for patient health care. This is all possible only through significant extra effort (ie, FTE expenditure) on the part of the technical and supervisory personnel.

By comparing the two indicators in this grouping, it is apparent that the section must accomplish the solution of this second improvement opportunity faster than has been the experience with the multianalyzer. They must handle both situations expeditiously; they must judiciously choose appropriate interim solutions that will ensure the best quality of test result for the patient and physician with the least stress on laboratory resources—particularly human resources. Both situations exemplify extra quality management workload demands at the operative-level, causing decreased technical productivity, overall.

Transfusion profile interpretation:
The general threshold for this grouping describes it as a sentinel event (note the !! marks). Evaluation of six months' cumulative data reveals unsettling evidence of progressively increasing QC discrepancies over the last four months. These errors include the misreading of blood typing reactions—implying inaccurate visual inspection and cognitive interpretation—and lack of attention to other QC details such as temperature control. The profile reports that the errors involve more than one individual at the section level.

There are several supporting indicator groupings that corroborate the analytical quality data. These topics include customer satisfaction, throughput, platelet storage, staffing, QI (eg, proficiency testing and external inspections), QAn and QAc. For example, in addition to a severe staff shortage, the loss of a full-time supervisor has undoubtedly magnified the potential incidence of errors since November.

The Transfusion Service and supporting departmental/service quality managers have determined a bimodal action plan. First, the acting supervisor must direct his or her full attention toward bench QC.

Second, the staff vacancy rate is so crucially high that the shortage is quite seriously affecting section effectiveness at the technological and clinical-interface level. Since the acting section supervisor is so overwhelmed, the section medical director has assumed the responsibility for overseeing the filling of the existing staff vacancies in coordination with the hospital Task Force. Ordinarily for less critically staffed laboratory sections, the section supervisor, laboratory manager or administrative officer routinely handles the follow-up of staff hiring actions.

In addition, with the staffing constraints that are so apparent, there is ample argument that the acting supervisor and other quality management team members must consider eventual automation of the most high-volume procedures—if the staffing problem cannot be readily remedied.[4] Furthermore, a recommended action is for the section medical director to determine interim options to ensure quality service to the patient. For example, a major alternative is to curtail certain in-house transfusing service (or blood bank) procedures and defer them to a reference laboratory. This duty is a medical director assignment because of the inherent importance of medical appropriateness as a key quality dimension.

Assessment of this sample profile segment is painfully obvious—the immediate QI actions required to quell QC disparities and to fill staff vacancies have been woefully ineffective. Under these circumstances, the overall opportunity for improvement must become the immediate combined concern of the section medical director, the departmental leadership, and the hospital administrative leadership—including the personnel management office and the newly established task force.

Additional profile interpretations:

Hematology (Appendix D): There has been no identification of any opportunities for improvement of analytical quality for four months, but the establishment of a baseline is in progress. The action is to continue establishing the baseline. The assessment is that of stable pursuit of the QI process. Savage is one of several authors to report on quality management in the hematology laboratory. He addresses surveillance of not only process, but also outcome and operative resources. Of salient importance, he describes organizational "interface" indicators that can affect analytical quality.[5]

Microbiology (Appendix E): There has been no identification of any OFI for seven months. The action is to select a focused study within the next quarter. For example, such a study could address the degree of technical compliance with the laboratory manual for any important procedure, eg, the accuracy of isolation of clinically significant pathogens or the accuracy of testing for antimicrobial susceptibility. As an alternative, the quality management team should be searching current laboratory-clinical committee minutes for high priority indicator candidates. In any case, the usual source of these indicator data would be QC records. The assessment for this profile segment is accurate. Richardson has compiled a concise collection of quality management guidelines for diagnostic microbiology analytical quality.[6]

Histopathology (Appendix G): This section's profile demonstrates that histopathology—primarily a diagnostic determinative activity—entails some technical (but not usually analytical) QC as part of the predeterminative process in support of the diagnostic process. The proficiency of these histotechnical steps is the subject for discussion under predeterminative process (ie, indicator grouping 11) presented later in this chapter.

On the other hand, increasing numbers of anatomic pathology services are embarking on performance of CP-like analytical procedures in support of the traditional, tissue diagnostic approach. For example, flow cytometry and molecular biological analyses are becoming common in the AP arena. Under these circumstances, the anatomic laboratorians who have elected to perform these analytical determinative procedures should be following the same CP-like quality management steps. These analytical procedures would be reportable under this indicator grouping for analytical quality.

Discussion:

Indicator Grouping. This indicator grouping focuses on the analytical mode of the determinative phase of laboratory work flow (as compared to the diagnostic mode addressed in indicator grouping 10). In the infancy of laboratory quality management, it was this work flow phase on which laboratorians concentrated because of their familiarity with statistical analytical process control at the bench. Even today, the analytical quality profile grouping provides a preponderance of possibilities for QI monitoring, evaluation, and assessment.

It cannot be denied that the usual healthcare laboratory probably performs more analytical QC management than any other form of quality management. This is because process control is so much integrated into every analytical procedure. However, the QI program cannot focus solely on the effectiveness of traditional analytical control. There are other facets to analytical quality management besides classical, statistical process control. Especially in this age of high-technology and super-automation, we continually must ask what other aberrant operative and organizational functions are responsible for divergent analytical results?

For example, laboratory analysis is especially prone to operative-level variance where the determinative process is nonautomated—and especially if the analysis depends on a laboratorian's visual examination and cognitive interpretation. Laboratory sections in which these conditions are frequently encountered are the transfusion service, hematology, urinalysis, and microbiology. In any high-volume and (instrumentally speaking) low-technological workload situation, there is possibly greater risk of serious analytical mistakes occurring and going unnoticed—if there is not some concomitant mode of QC available. This is particularly true if human resource problems are creating additional stress for the laboratory staff. Consequently, nontraditional QI methods such as "peer control" and "peer assessment" provide improved quality management of these particular low-technological, high workload laboratory procedures. There is more discussion of these nontraditional quality management methods for interpretive analysis under diagnostic quality (ie, indicator grouping 10).

Any laboratory section can generate additional topics for analytical quality by prioritizing all IACs and matching those leading functional procedures against the prioritized elements of the related path of work flow. The resulting matrix can afford an abundance of indicators to schedule for monitoring in the order of their respective importance.

Supporting Indicators. These include quality indicators of patient and physician satisfaction and patient care outcome, laboratory product utilization, throughput, postdeterminative process, predeterminative process, laboratory product selection, and all operative resource management activities. All three infrastructural programs—QI, QAn, and QAc can also provide important QI information that supports analytical quality indicator data.

Whereas any of these supporting indicators can corroborate opportunities to improve analytical QC, the predeterminative process grouping can be particularly contributory. Also, it is a common experience that accuracy and precision easily suffer if there is inordinate work stress, resource constraints, or some other systemic aberration. Thus, indicators of the adequacy of operative resources are frequently of great supporting value for interpreting analytical QI grouping data. The Transfusion Service profile provides an example of diminishing analytical quality supported by indications of insufficient laboratory section support of ward training, inadequate section quality management of platelet products, decreasing section technical productivity, diminishing section performance with external proficiency testing, and disabled section organizational programs for planning and team effectiveness. The basis for all of these supporting OFIs is a fundamental lack of staff members—the ultimate operative- (and organizational-) level resource.

As just noted, supporting indicators of proficiency testing, including external and internal surveillance, have grown to be of exceedingly great importance to the assessment and improvement of analytical quality. The emerging regulatory requirements of CLIA '88 especially have singled out these confirmatory tests of human analytical skill and instrumental capability as key tools for managing the quality of all analytical (and diagnostic) competency. Thus, their supporting data have gained essential value in interpreting analytical quality—and a laboratory's success or failure in the eyes of HCFA.

Further study of the network of supporting indicator groupings reminds us that QC does not involve the analytical process alone: QC in some mode or another must be an integral part of all outcome, process, and operative and organizational resource management activities. Thus, the greatest body of ready-made quality management data resides in the operational-wide QC system, where more operative-level and organizational-level management decision making occurs than anywhere else in the laboratory. Consequently, this abundant control data should be judiciously used for QI purposes, with a balanced, systematic approach applied between management of outcome, process, and all structural resource activities. It follows, then, that statistical process control (traditional and nontraditional) is equally important to every indicator grouping at any phase or segment of the entire path of workflow—QC is not unique to determinative analysis.

Threshold. The profile threshold statement for this overall grouping—"no major discrepancies"—is rather general but will be more specific for a focused or index study. The most precise parameters against which to measure analytical performance are the QC standards and control levels established for each individual important aspect of laboratory healthcare support, ie, for each analytical laboratory test procedure or service.

Therefore, QC standards serve as the basis for quality indicator criteria. Likewise, various analytical control evaluation rules and control limits, such as Westgard's rules, are adaptable as QI thresholds for monitoring analytical quality. Otherwise, each section must determine thresholds for the analytical grouping indicators on an IAC-by-IAC basis.

Monitoring Periodicity. This element of the QI process depends on the nature of the laboratory section being considered, the criticalness of the aspect of care being monitored, and the adequacy of the quality management resources on hand. For example, the Transfusion Service profiled in this text is inherently more problem-prone with much more patient-risk fundamentally at stake than the routine Chemistry Section scenario. Thus, Transfusion Service indicators of analytical quality might require more frequent monitoring and reporting on a regular, ongoing basis than Chemistry Section indicators.

Evaluation. Healthcare laboratorians are expert in the evaluation of operative-level, analytical quality data. The preponderance of this data is produced by sections of the CP service, although the AP service is becoming increasingly involved in objective, analytical measurement. The latter change will rapidly emerge as modern technology bridges the procedural gap between histopathology and molecular biology. Each laboratory section will provide different varieties of indicators, ranging from the automated quantitative and objective to the more qualitative and subjective analytical QC data. In addition, there is ample cross-linkage between several supporting indicator groupings that can provide direct and indirect clues to aid in the interpretive evaluation of analytical opportunities for quality improvement.

Action. Compared to certain other profile groupings, it is relatively easy to discern opportunities for improvement of process in this laboratory indicator category. This is especially true for implementing improvement of high-technological procedures, supported by traditional statistical QC for initial characterization and follow-up. Actions can be more complex when they are in response to improving low-technological, nonautomated, more subjective, analytical procedures supported by nontraditional peer review control for initial characterization and follow-up.

Care must be taken, however, to improve the analytical process at hand—whether it is the technological process of analysis, the training process, or the QI process itself—rather than to mistakenly concentrate on reacting to individual personnel performance by way of disciplinary action. Instead, pursue the improvement of processes that enhance personnel proficiency, eg, procedural method updating, continuing education, balancing staff strength with the workload, providing timely personnel actions and incentives, and promoting two-way communication with employees. Then, individual disciplinary action becomes an approach of last resort.

Thus, the best action to improve analytical quality is usually direct with relatively few subtleties and is generally confined to within the laboratory. Occasionally, however, interim steps need to be considered in order to maintain the highest control of laboratory end product quality. These interim options may involve temporarily borrowing or leasing instruments, equipment, or supplies, or temporarily deferring workload to an outside reference laboratory. Also, there may be need to enlist the support of other departments such as medical maintenance or the facility engineers. Occasionally, joint action needs to be coordinated between the laboratory and clinical departments, especially when analytical standards of performance affect clinical standards of practice.

In the case of improving low-technological, nonautomated procedures, actions often will center on assessing and upgrading individual laboratorian proficiency, inservice education and training scheduling, and access to external educational programs. Improvement of peer control is a very essential beginning. Also, workload to individual stress correlation might need improvement as experienced in the AP arena of cytopathology screening. Likewise, all appropriate CP sections need to apply the same importance of workload limitation to their own low-technological, nonautomated, more subjective analytical procedures.

Assessment. The Chemistry profile assessment provides a good example of a prescribed action being allowed to take too long to come to fruition. In this scenario, there is no apparent resource management constraint that justifies the described delay of that particular QI process; the only "constraint" could be lack of adequate planning (ie, an inadequate QAn program) and decision making (ie, an inadequate QAc program). However, the QI assessment should have been stressing this point long before this particular December profile report.

The Transfusion Section example illustrates how analytical quality can reflect the severity of personnel shortage and accompanying stress with blatant burnout. The assessment is accurate: this combined matrix of related problems is, indeed, "too hard" a problem for the section or laboratory department to handle alone. The hospital administration and combined Task Force must provide the needed assistance.

Communication. Again, the section should disseminate lessons learned to all individuals and all organizational levels that are involved. This includes communication throughout the laboratory department as well as all concerned hospital activities lateral and higher than the laboratory department—such as the personnel management office and the hospital administration who need to know the functional repercussions of a significant staff shortage.

It is fitting that we consider the dimension of clarity of communication under this overall grouping of analytical quality. There is no question that for communication to be effective, it must be efficient; there must be clarity in broadcasting QI information. Characteristics of this dimension include not only accuracy of facts (as one would expect in addressing the analytical grouping) but also succinctness aided by a standard format and nomenclature. This dimension of communication applies to all groupings throughout the quality profile.[7]

Indicator Grouping 10
Diagnostic Quality

Chemistry Section Quality Profile

Indicator Grouping/ Specific Indicator: Threshold (Periodicity)	QI Data Observations (Date trend started) J A S O N D
Diagnostic Quality (Peer Review): no major discrepancies!! (– – – – – –)	Not applicable; no semiquantitative or qualitative interpretive analysis performed

Transfusion Service Quality Profile

Indicator Grouping/ Specific Indicator: Threshold (Periodicity)	QI Data Observations (Date trend started) J A S O N D
Diagnostic Quality (Peer Review): no major discrepancies!! (– – – – – –)	No documented peer control or assessment is being performed

!! = sentinel event

Diagnostic Quality Management (Indicator Grouping 10)

Chemistry profile interpretation:
This indicator grouping is not always applicable to a Chemistry Section since interpretive analysis is used less often in the modern chemistry laboratory in lieu of the usual instrumental approach. Thus the subject profile states that this indicator grouping is "not applicable for the given scenario."

In fact, it could be applicable in other situations! As mentioned under the preceding grouping, wherever visually interpreted semiquantitative or qualitative tests are employed in the CP service, the subject diagnostic grouping can be employed rather than using the regular analytical quality indicator approach—interpretation of electrophoretic patterns in the Chemistry Section or in the Diagnostic Immunology Section being an example. In such a case, reporting peer review of these interpretive reports at both the QC and QI levels would be quite appropriate. Therefore, any section describing this indicator grouping as "not applicable" essentially is reporting that the section is not performing any interpretive procedures. The quality management team needs to regularly appraise the IAC inventory to always be sure of the validity of this observation.

Transfusion profile interpretation:
Although deemed "not applicable" in the subject profile, this indicator grouping could, in fact, be useful in characterizing the quality of routine Transfusion Service bench activities. If immunohematology is performed

Evaluation of QI Data, TQM System, and CQI Process	Action Action Person: (Date Initiated)	Assessment of Overall Improvement
------	------	------
------	QI Note: It is the opinion of the departmental quality management team that peer control and assessment must be implemented in the transfusion service	

manually—as it usually is—then the technologist visually inspects cellular agglutination reactions and makes an interpretive judgement as to whether a test is positive or not. In fact, the final immunohematology report often cites semiquantitatively the degree of strength of agglutination that the reaction exhibits.

Thus, this section could be practicing some form of peer review of these interpretive analyses for the purpose of quality control and quality assessment and improvement. Although stated as "not applicable" in this section's profile report, the fact is that the subject Transfusion Service has not established any conditions for such review—even though they should have. Thus, a "QI Note" renders a departmental assessment that the Transfusion Service must implement some form of analytical-interpretive peer review at both the operative (QC) and administrative (QI) levels.

Additional profile interpretations:

Hematology (Appendix D): The Hematology Section is a prime candidate for QI surveillance of indicators of the preceding analytical quality grouping by virtue of its wide-ranging use of instrumental procedures. But, the section is also an active arena for surveillance of analytical-interpretive and diagnostic-interpretive quality by virtue of the several morphologic characterization and differentiation procedures that are commonly performed. This is true wherever individual laboratorians are interpreting cellular morphologic characteristics through blood and body fluid microscopy.

On one hand, the analytical-interpretive approach is routine in the examination of differential blood cell count smears and various centrifuged body fluid preparations. In many hematology (also known as clinical microscopy) sections, these examinations include semiquantitative and microscopic urinalysis as an analytical-interpretive procedure. Usually, non-physician, technologically-trained laboratorians perform these procedures. The quality management of interpretive microscopic urinalysis is similar to that described for classical hematology analysis. Practical parameters for peer control (ie, QC) and peer assessment (ie, QI) are easy to establish.

On the other hand, there is a division of hematology known as hematopathology. This interpretive activity is set apart from the other routine hematology analytical procedures by virtue of its being diagnostic-interpretive in nature. Key dimensions of general proficiency of the hematopathologist are the education, training, skill, and expertise required of a physician diagnostician; the key dimension of diagnostic-interpretive quality is medical appropriateness.

In either case, the laboratorian should consider all of these microscopic procedures as targets for analytical-interpretive or diagnostic-interpretive quality control and quality assessment and improvement. In view of the subjective nature of these laboratory activities, this text describes the related form of quality management in terms of peer review at the dual quality surveillance levels of peer control and peer assessment.

The subject Hematology Section report exemplifies how a periodic quality profile can identify individual laboratory healthcare providers when peer control at the day-to-day, operative-level reveals significant nonconcordance that warrants further investigative review at the peer assessment level. The providers who might be targeted include physicians and technological personnel, alike. The profile utilizes a provider code, protecting individual anonymity.

The example profile segment reports by general survey that there has been no identification of any major discrepancy for any interpretive procedure after six months of establishing a baseline. With the perceived need to increase the sensitivity of the QI process, the recommended action is for the section supervisor to establish a focused study of differential count morphologic analytical-interpretive quality. If the study were to focus on bone marrow diagnostic- interpretive quality, the section medical director would be responsible for implementing the study; in this case, the deciding quality dimension would be medical appropriateness.

Caution: The peer review QI surveillance approach is not intended to address, supplant, or supplement any internal proficiency testing program (ie, using the distribution of unknown samples as an internal proficiency surveillance device). Proficiency testing is addressed later in this discussion as well as under external surveillance of the quality assessment and improvement program (indicator groupings 23 and 24).

The recommended action for this Hematology profile grouping example is simply intended to focus by means of peer assessment review on the quality management of the day-to-day performance of differential counting as evidenced by routine QC-like methods—in this case, peer control review of the daily work. Such peer control can consist of partial sampling (eg, 10%) or a complete 100% review, depending on the judgment of the quality management team. Choosing the peer control parameters should involve not just the section supervisor who is responsible for implementing this level of quality management but also the medical director and the technologists who are actively participating in the differential counting. The administrative QI-level of peer review (ie, peer assessment) should consist of a complete review of all operative-level, peer control findings during a given monitoring period—just as any other form of nonpeer QI surveillance consists of a review of all available forms of nonpeer QC findings.

As mentioned under supporting indicators for the analytical quality grouping, proficiency testing (PT) has become an especially hot topic in the wake of CLIA 88. Subsequent to these new federal requirements, there is increased regulatory scrutiny of individual and overall organizational competence. This growth of federal micromanagement of laboratory quality is so important as to weigh distinctly on individual licensing and credentialing, as well as laboratory licensing, certification, and accreditation. Unfortunately, the establishment of the National Data Bank, CLIA '88 regulatory requirements, and similar personnel proficiency rules are forcing laboratorians to shift from the JCAHO's more organization-wide emphasis on process improvement towards the more disciplinary policing of individual performance. There has to be a reasonable balance between process and individual performance surveillance.

For example, as a result of the National Data Bank's and CLIA's strong disciplinary approach to the results of peer review (as evidenced especially by proficiency testing), the professional community is evolving a typical knee-jerk response as an understandably natural attempt at self defense. The consequent results of peer assessment practiced in the quest of proficiency improvement are unmistakably threatening to an individual's career, vis, credentialing and litigation—greatly overshadowing any rationale for organizational-level process improvement. In any event, we must continue to minimize the effect of the reactive approach of individual discipline and maximize organizational actualization of the more proactive approach of process improvement.

Microbiology (Appendix E): This section also lends itself to the practice of QI surveillance of analytical-interpretive activities. For example, broncho-alveolar lavage provides a good target for such an interpretive indicator. Again, this microscopic, interpretive procedure is subject to timely peer control and periodic peer assessment.

In the example profile segment, a general survey has not identified any OFI for at least six months. If there had been any nonconcordance initially detected by peer control review, the peer assessment monitoring process would document the responsible provider by a code number with some description of the type and degree of nonconcordance on a feeder report. A peer assessment panel would then review the event as a part of the quality profiling process. Without any discrepancy on record in the subject example, the action is for the supervisor to select a focused study on broncho-alveolar lavage interpretations. The assessment infers that improvement of the QI process is in progress.

Histopathology (Appendix G): This laboratory section epitomizes the quintessential model of diagnostic-interpretive quality management. This particular sample profile segment is designed to denote the total number of occurrences of peer control nonconcordance over the reporting period, including both major and minor discrepancies—the report format befitting the very general threshold statement. Remember, this example format represents only one of many possible designs that are possible.

Thus, the cited occurrences include <u>all</u> the nonconcordances found during routine peer control review of all primary diagnoses positive for malignancy during the reporting period; they also include <u>all</u> nonconcordances found during peer control review of a sampling of diagnoses negative for any malignancy (eg, a 10% review of all normal laboratory diagnoses for a potentially clinically malignant condition). The example report data do not differentiate between minor and major discrepancies. Instead, the peer quality management team rules on the significance of those differences during the evaluation step.

The profile format presents ongoing index studies of three specific types of concordance reviews. For each of these studies, code numbers anonymously symbolize individual diagnosticians. These might be staff pathologists but could also be other qualified physicians credentialed to render anatomic diagnoses by the same institution—all under the peer purview of the AP service or department. Dermatologists and various pathology-trained surgeons could fit into the latter category.

The evaluation of the peer control data by the peer assessment panel cites that there were no <u>major</u> discrepancies during the current reporting period—only minor ones—and there was no trend or repeat occurrence by any diagnostician. Thus, the recommended action is for the section (or service) medical director to review the minor findings with the appropriate diagnosticians as follow-up communication, only.

The second recommended action is to improve the QI process by dropping the combined focus on minor diagnostic discrepancies and reporting only the major ones that significantly affect patient life, limb, or other welfare. At the same time this decision allows those physicians practicing peer control at the operative-level to exercise more direct influence on minor discrepancies. The latter decision should be a "team" product involving all participating diagnosticians. Finally, the accompanying assessment of improving the QI process is accurate.

Discussion:

Indicator Grouping. As is especially exemplified by the hematology-hematopathology, microbiology, and histopathology profiles, this indicator grouping focuses on peer assessment of the diagnostic-interpretive mode of the determinative work flow phase. Peer control and peer assessment are commonly practiced in the quality management of tissue diagnoses in the AP service and of bone marrow and peripheral blood diagnoses for hematopathology in the CP service; peer review is also the means of quality management for the less diagnostic, more analytical-interpretive procedures.

However, as pointed out under the preceding indicator grouping for analytical quality, there are analytical-interpretive procedures scattered throughout CP for which a similar form of peer review is most effective. These procedures occur wherever analytical technique rests on visual examination and cognitive, interpretative judgement to render a semiquantitative or qualitative determination. Aside from the two sections already cited, immunohematology and diagnostic immunology also exemplify work centers where interpretive reporting is an everyday occurrence and should be supported by some type of peer surveillance, assessment, and improvement. For reporting these analytical-interpretive procedures, the subject diagnostic grouping also can be quite useful.

Peer assessment of diagnostic quality indicators can easily glean data from peer control records. As with any other QI grouping, tracking the quality of diagnostic or interpretive activities helps to assure not only procedural quality, but also the integrity of the peer assessment and improvement process itself. Keep in mind that there are always alternative sources of peer review data available from committee minutes and incident reports—mostly of an outcome nature.

Diagnostic or interpretive quality management terminology deserves particular attention. For example, throughout the laboratory diagnostic QI process, most of the peer surveillance derives its information from QC-like activities that mirror the very subjective nature of the diagnostic-interpretive procedures, themselves. Instead of being called QC in the interpretive environment, this text refers to these methods for direct control at the operative-level as peer control—as described in the earlier chapter on concepts and definitions.

In the same interpretive vein, the literature often has referred to the diagnostic QI-like surveillance (vis, the subject profile indicator grouping) as peer assurance, borrowing from earlier Joint Commission QA terminology. However, the more up-to-date term used in this text is "peer assessment" as befits the changes in the JCAHO quality management approach since 1992. This terminology should stand the test of change as we continue to experience the coining of new QI nomenclature in response to the JCAHO *Agenda for Change*, their revised accreditation standards for 1994, and the advent of their "improving organizational performance (PI)" approach to quality management.

In any case, the terms peer assurance or assessment connote an administrative-level, QI activity of the peer review type. This remains as an administrative managerial follow-up of the conformance of laboratory performance to desired quality management specifications.

The word "assurance" brings up some other specific teaching points. First, quality assurance (or assessment) is not synonymous with quality control. It must seem strange to some readers for that to be said here. But even today, authors commonly use quality assurance in their titles, articles, and texts in a misleading way when they really mean operative-level quality control. In many of these publications, quality assurance is a major discriminator in the title but is actually paid extremely little attention (or none at all) in the body of the text. Instead, the vast majority of the text focuses on QC.[8]

Second, assurance has been misconstrued by some healthcare managers as a guarantee; it is not a guarantee. The word only implies an administrative-level follow-up by peers of desired quality specifications. As used in this context, the word connotes overview surveillance to determine whether or not an operational process control system has worked—a means of double checking to make sure that desired results have been achieved.[f] If those results have not occurred as originally expected, then there are the investigative and remedial QI steps that must follow to minimize immediate damage and to improve the appropriate operative- or organizational-level process so that the desired quality will be realized thereafter.

Thus, the terms assurance or assessment or improvement will never guarantee quality. At best, these terms will indicate only a concerted approach to continuous systematic follow-up through the practice of a QI program or whatever the JCAHO decides to call it in the future.[g] To come closest to any "guarantee" at all, both the QAn and QAc programs must all be in concert with the improvement program—and, still, there will never be any guarantee to any dimension of quality. In a CQI environment, there must always be on-going quality surveillance, follow-up, and appropriate improvement to deal with institutional change and inherent random/systematic error in operational processes.

Indicator Standards. Because of the very subjective nature of peer control and assessment (ie, one visual interpretation matched against another as a second diagnostician peers "over the shoulder" of the first), QI evaluation of any of this data must be carried on very carefully. Otherwise, unwarranted bias can result in an unfair, inaccurate evaluation: either it can be too strict (ie, unfair to the primary diagnostician) or not strict enough (ie, unfair to the patient).

Therefore, we must establish judicious as well as appropriate thresholds and make accurate evaluations of diagnostic-interpretive peer control data. The key to achieving these objectives is to base assessment judgments on well-established, *joint* laboratory-clinical standards of practice. Such standards are equivalent to any other indicator criteria

[f] Throughout this text, the term operational includes operative- and organizational-level processes.

[g] The most recent change in JCAHO nomenclature was in the 1994 edition of the *Accreditation Manual for Hospitals* when "quality assessment and improvement (QI)" became "improving organizational performance (PI)."

that are used for the characterization of any other type of grouping of specific indicators.

Another, fairly rigorous approach to diagnostic control and assessment of anatomic pathology quality is emerging in the form of standardized checklists[9,10] and report formats.[11,12,13] Major professional societies and individual laboratories are beginning to devise these lists to facilitate accuracy, completeness, and uniformity in diagnostic reports. In effect, these checklist and reporting methods will enhance diagnostic procedures, providing a new dimension of reproducibility or precision—already a well-established concept of analytical quality. These methods also are applicable to cytopathology—in fact, to any interpretive-determinative procedure whether diagnostic or analytical.

Additional indicator topics for this diagnostic-interpretive indicator grouping can include index or focused studies of any interpretive IAC that has been identified in the anatomic arena of surgical,[14-24] cytological, or autopsy[25,26] pathology. Adding to this matrix of possibilities, the laboratory quality management team can study any interpretive aspect of care in terms of a specific customer (or generic group of customers) that supplies the laboratory with a request and specimen for that IAC. In addition, the quality management team can establish concordances of clinical outcomes for any interpretive IAC. The latter approach definitely calls for joint laboratorian-clinician dialogue—that dialogue also being a candidate for improvement in the process.

In the arena of clinical pathology, additional indicator topics should address gauging the effectiveness of the less traditional means of controlling quality of low-technological, high-workload procedures. The latter approach could include monitoring the effectiveness of peer control of the individual laboratorian's semiquantitative or qualitative analyses. There must be a means for administrative-level monitoring of indicators of the quality of a laboratorian's ability to accurately differentiate and identify the morphologic characteristics of blood and other body fluid specimens. This type of analytical quality surveillance indicator must rely on the monitoring of operative-level peer review reports (ie, peer control as contrasted with quality control) at the bench during procedural, "real time" analysis.

Supporting Indicators. Sources of corroborative QI data include the groupings for customer satisfaction and patient care outcome, TAT and end product finalization processes, predeterminative processing, all operative resource managerial activities, and QI, QAn, and QAc. This constellation is a mirror image of the groupings that support evaluation of analytical quality. Predeterminative intralaboratory processing and prelaboratory processing are of particular importance to the quality of diagnostic-interpretive determination; the example histopathology profile demonstrates this.

For example, adequacy of clinical information (ie, an element of prelaboratory processing) is a very common QI monitoring target that can be monitored under this diagnostic quality grouping, as well as under postdeterminative finalization (ie, indicator grouping 7), predeterminative processing (ie, indicator grouping 11), and prelaboratory process validation (ie, indicator grouping 12).

Threshold. If the indicator of diagnostic-interpretive quality is of the comparative rate type, by definition the threshold will vary according to the given diagnostic (or analytical-interpretive) procedure. Other possible determinants of threshold limits include the individual patient diagnostic or demographic grouping or the specific DRG involved. In contrast, these various patient-related factors might be so critical as to warrant that the indicator be of the sentinel event type, requiring an all-or-nothing threshold level. The various profile scenarios in this text provide examples of these two different approaches.

Monitoring Periodicity. This always depends on the criticalness of the aspect of care being monitored and the adequacy of the quality management resources on hand. Each factor can vary in the due course of time requiring changes of monitoring schedules.

Evaluation. This step of the QI process for this determinative indicator grouping should follow along quite naturally once indicator standards, their criteria, and thresholds have been established. Then, it is just a matter of comparing the QI surveillance data against their respective QI limitation parameters. Additionally, the cross-linkage of supporting indicators can be of great value since the QI data tends to be so subjective. Customer satisfaction and patient care outcome are critical in substantiating peer control and peer assurance information and in identifying indicator topics for focused study candidates. Peer evaluation of diagnostic-interpretive quality almost always becomes a joint, laboratory-clinical endeavor when taken to the ultimate administrative level of credentialing review.

Action. Almost any effort to actualize an improvement opportunity for diagnostic-interpretive quality also must involve the clinical physicians to a significant degree. At the very least, the clinicians need to provide follow-up from their unique vantage point to affirm that there is the expected improvement of the diagnostic-interpretive process and outcome—or not.

It is in this QI arena of diagnostic-interpretive quality that some of the most resource-intensive repercussions can occur in response to the discovery of poor quality; one example is the emergency option of 100% "look back" or retrospective survey of previous diagnoses. On occasion, the latter action is necessary in cytopathology and, less often, in assessment of the surgical or autopsy pathology quality. If it is found that a screener or diagnostician has issued a significant number of seriously inaccurate diagnostic interpretations, peer assessment might be obliged to dictate that all of the cases handled by the alleged individual during the past several weeks—up to even a year—be reviewed by a competent diagnostician. This "look-back" amounts to being a form of "damage control"—or risk management in the guise of QI—hopefully to find any other misdiagnoses that could significantly affect patient welfare before it is too late. This is one of those few instances where anticipatory quality improvement and reactive risk management can overlap.

Assessment. The same three standard options for assessment in a CQI environment need to be considered in assessing the adequacy of recommended action and the QI process for diagnostic-interpretive determinative quality.

Communication. The key concept in communication is joint ... *joint* ... **JOINT** dialogue. Laboratorians must communicate lessons learned concerning diagnostic-interpretive quality to the clinical side if there is to be any semblance of an operable, "fail safe" anticipatory QI system. Neither side, laboratory or clinical, can afford to practice in isolation from the other.

During the process of peer surveillance review, an involved laboratory section must communicate any occurrences or trends of diagnostic problems to facilitate managerial and administrative action and to provide documentation suitable for follow-up and accreditation review. Like it or not, in the due course of events a QI report of some sort must signify the provider of a discrepant diagnostic interpretation as well as the patient who is involved.

However, it is easy for the identity of a screener, diagnostician, or patient to remain anonymous in any public quality management record—such as a quality profile—by employing an alphanumeric code. Actual identities (ie, discoverable evidence) must be available only to confidential peer committees, quality surveillance teams, or credentialing activities. The laboratory must keep such sensitive, confidential information secure since all quality surveillance records are considered nondiscoverable. This precaution is not to shield anyone but to guarantee all involved individuals the due process of law that they justifiably deserve. Ultimately, the subject of the extent of controversial data reporting must be managed according to local policy based on legal counsel.

Predeterminative Processing Management (Indicator Grouping 11)

Chemistry profile interpretation:
Evaluation of the data reveals that there has been no opportunity for improving predeterminative specimen processing for seven months. In this scenario, the sectional evaluation cites not only a relatively long period of quiescence, but also the need to revise the QI process.

The recommended action is to improve the improvement process by initiating a focused study: the topic would be adequacy of any processing procedure required in preparation for a given analytical chemistry procedure. For example, these topics could include:

- The frequency of hemolytic specimens encountered in preparation for serum potassium analysis
- The length of time allowed before centrifuging and aliquoting a blood glucose specimen
- The frequency of grossly bloody or hemolyzed lumbar puncture taps submitted for cerebrospinal fluid chemistry analysis.

Indicator Grouping 11
Predeterminative Processing

Chemistry Section Quality Profile

Indicator Grouping/ Specific Indicator: Threshold (Periodicity)	QI Data Observations (Date trend started) J A S O N D	
Predeterminative Specimen Processing: no loss of specimen integrity!! (Monthly)	No OFI identified x 7 mo	

Transfusion Service Quality Profile

Predeterminative Specimen Processing: no loss of specimen integrity!! (Monthly)	No OFI identified x 4 mo	

!! = sentinel event

The assessment reflects sectional-departmental consensus that the section's evaluation and action meet the requirements on an effective surveillance process.

Transfusion profile interpretation:
Evaluation of the data attests to there being no opportunity for improvement of predeterminative specimen processing for four months. The action and assessment that follow are all in keeping with establishing a data baseline.

Additional profile interpretations:
Hematology (Appendix D): Evaluation of the QI data reveals that there has been no identification of any OFI for predeterminative processing for ten months. The action is to select a focused study indicator topic such as:

- Frequency of microclots impeding instrument function
- Adequacy of bone marrow aspirate smears
- Adequacy of differential smear staining
- Adequacy of centrifuging body fluid cytological preparations
- Adequacy of any other preanalytical processing procedure in meeting analytical (or diagnostic) procedural requirements.

Whatever the indicator topic becomes, it must be carefully chosen by

Evaluation of QI Data, TQM System, and CQI Process	Action Action Person: (Date Initiated)	Assessment of Overall Improvement
On target x 7 mo; there needs to be a more sensitive QI approach	Initiate a focused indicator in Feb 96 ACTION: Supervisor	Improvement of the QI process is in progress
On target; baseline being established	None needed	Effective QI process to date

established prioritization criteria (eg, high-volume, high-risk/benefit, problem/opportunity-prone). The profile segment's assessment is that improvement of the QI process is in progress.

Microbiology (Appendix E): There has been no identified OFI for three months as a baseline is being established. The action and assessment are appropriate.

Histopathology (Appendix G): Since a major portion of this sample profile's grouping happens to be predeterminative processing, the brunt of this presentation focuses on a unique laboratory activity—prediagnostic histotechnological processing. This is a laboratory activity where operative and organizational dimensions of quality can be easily overlooked.

The listing of specific, focused study indicators under this specific profile's grouping is quite extensive—much more than usually would be expected for index studies. These indicators range from the extremely serious (eg, lost specimens) to those that are usually less crucial but occasionally can confound accurate diagnosis (eg, section too thick).

Such a lengthy panoply of ongoing QI studies usually denotes that the histotechnology predeterminative processing activities are a current hot spot of quality concern. One would immediately suspect this with so many indicators selected for monitoring and investigative follow-up.

Evaluation reveals the definite need to remedy certain predeterminative processes; there could be more than one operational process needing improvement. For example, the incidence of lost (versus destroyed) specimens was a significant problem from July through October. In addition, the poor orientation of tissues in blocks began to appear in November, although with fewer occurrences in December; this is another, more recent significant problem. Also, slide mislabeling appears to be a rather consistent (and serious) problem throughout the six month profile. Problems with the other histotechnical indicators are very sporadic and random.

Evaluation of supporting indicators discloses that there is a known insufficiency of technical staff numbers. In addition, there has been lack of sufficient supervisory support, training, team planning, or team actualization. The profile action recommendations intimate that at least part of the OFI at hand has been inadequate supervision.

For example, since the recent arrival of a new medical director there has been apparent resolution of several problems in handling and processing tissue specimens. However, a new "hot spot" has become evident in the area of tissue embedding.

The predominant action is for the section supervisor to monitor QC daily to maintain control of recurrent processing problems, begin new QI indicator baselines if needed, and work with the hospital Personnel Office to fill the staff vacancies. The medical director is to provide "close support" in tandem with the section supervisor.

Sometimes, instead of improving a systemic process, we cannot escape having to emphasize improving individual performance. In this case, in fact, it could still be a matter of improving the process of managerial supervision overall rather than disciplining the section supervisor individually.

As with all the sample profiles provided in this text, the section is lacking six staff FTEs. The assessment points out that, as usual, the staff shortage is magnifying all other operational problems. Whereas the section and its supporting department/service are doing almost everything possible with the management resources available, the hospital QI process has not been adequately responsive in helping to fill the six staff vacancies. Tying the personnel shortage with crippled predeterminative processing grouping, extensive TAT, and dismal customer satisfaction, the necessity for forming a hospital-level task force becomes even more clear—not just to resolve the TAT problem, but also to enhance processing, supervision, and overall team effectiveness.

The profile treats the slide mislabeling indicator separate from the rest. In this case, the section's quality management is very suspect. Whereas, the other problems have been brought under control, this OFI has persisted consistently over at least the last six months. The recommended action is for the supervisor to resolve this problem. Is this a last chance offer? The assessment is that the section's follow-up action and overall QI process are ineffective. A final "QI note" is submitted by the AP service or pathology department chairman. It requests the new section medical director to systematically evaluate the OFIs at hand and seek out new or alternative paths to remedy them.

Discussion:

Indicator Grouping. Some might argue that discriminating between pre- and postdeterminative specimen processing is excessive splitting of managerial hairs. Such disagreement is academic, and those who do not want to use either indicator grouping have an open choice. The subject grouping is included in this text in an attempt to leave nothing to false assumption or chance, ie, the example profile format covers all the bases. In trying to design the best quality assessment and improvement system, the laboratorian should leave nothing to chance in prioritizing and scheduling key QI indicators. Thus, at certain times predeterminative specimen processing might be a reasonable juncture at which to confirm request-patient-specimen-product integrity as an indicator of operational quality. Just as at other crossroads in this sample format, not all groupings are intended to be used at all times; that would not be resourceful.

Opportunities to improve predeterminative specimen processing will usually surface as a disruption in the chain of request-patient-specimen-product integrity. In either the CP or AP laboratory, these breaks in the stream of integrity are often in the form of transcription or labeling errors, especially in the less automated, less computerized laboratory. Even less frequently, such breaks can be much more grave in the form of lost or destroyed specimens or introduction of extraneous (foreign) material.

The selection of additional indicator topics is straightforward. The usual matching of sectional IACs against numbers and types of physician customers, patient customers, and diseases encountered will provide a decision matrix. By constructing this type of matrix, the quality management team should be able to anticipate and identify all possible important indicator topics, using standard rules for prioritization. Also, one always needs to consider the alternative sources of relevant QI indicators, including various laboratory, clinical, and nonclinical work groups and quality teams.

Supporting Indicators. Being that the predeterminative processing indicator grouping is uniformly global, corroborative QI data is potentially available from essentially all the other 25 indicator groupings addressed in this text; if the reader thinks about it, this correlation even includes employee safety. However, most directly related would be those groupings for customer satisfaction, determinative quality, operative resources, and organizational resources (ie, the programs for QI, QAn, and QAc).

Threshold. This indicator grouping centers around the issue of consistent request-patient-specimen-laboratory product integrity. Since maintenance of this train of integrity is the very foundation of effective laboratory function, an all-or-none standard of practice is mandatory. This is the rationale for taking such special care in monitoring at least two major milestones for laboratory operative integrity along the path of work flow: predeterminative processing and postdeterminative finalization.

Thus, the threshold—"no loss of specimen integrity"—rings the bell as a sentinel event.

Often, if we do not ask the question, we do not see the opportunity. In this case, we always ask the question "Why?" if there is any break in the mainstream of laboratory processing.

Monitoring Periodicity. This scheduling depends on the criticalness of the aspect of laboratory healthcare support being monitored and the adequacy of the quality management resources on hand. It is better to pinpoint the most likely targets of opportunity for regular, periodic monitoring, rather than being forced by an unanticipated disaster to implement an emergency, prospective review—including "look-backs" and other costly retrospective studies. This can happen in especially susceptible laboratory sections, such as histopathology and cytopathology in AP or other work centers where diagnostic-interpretive procedures predominate such as hematopathology and cytogenetics in CP.

Evaluation. Since this grouping for predeterminative processing represents a zero defects issue, the laboratory ideally should not have to improve on specimen integrity—it always should be perfect. Consequently, almost any opportunity for improving this aspect of laboratory quality QI indicator will be a matter of solving the mystery of the derailment of the train of systematic integrity. Such problems lurk in the system of multiple, intrinsically complex laboratory processes, can go undetected, and will work insidious operational damage.

Adding to this difficulty of evaluation, several preparatory steps that feed the integrity of predeterminative processing lie outside the boundaries of the laboratory, eg, including adequate clinical history with the laboratory request for microbiology procedures. Thus, as with any analytical or diagnostic quality management, all possible clues pertaining to the "integrity connection" need to be kept in proper operational perspective. Reviewing all supporting indicators can aid immeasurably in evaluating such an integrated QI target and maintaining the proper systemic perspective.

Action. As usual, action should answer to the evaluation. Whether it is a simple, direct remedy or if there are interim steps to be taken along the way to the ultimate (but never final) improvement, the quality management team must determine the appropriate actions and those responsible for timely follow-up. Although actions in the predeterminative processing arena usually involve the section team, sample profiles provided here demonstrate that there are instances when action requires extradepartmental coordination.

It is important to remember that the request-patient-specimen-product chain of integrity usually begins outside the laboratory in a ward or clinic and, then, ends there. Thus, action to maintain the chain usually requires some coordination with the clinical side of the house. Quite often, the action of choice is training ... *training* ... **TRAINING**—to meet the needs for continual reinforcement and revision because of changing personnel, need for repetition, and new technologies, methods, and managerial policies. This training can be given by laboratory or nonlaboratory personnel. A direct reward to expect from such bolstering of laboratory and clinical team actualization is an improved chain of process integrity.

Assessment. The same three standard options for assessment in a CQI environment apply to this indicator grouping, as is demonstrated by the sample profiles.

Communication. As illustrated by earlier steps in the improvement process for this grouping, lessons learned need to be transmitted up and down the entire chain of laboratory process integrity. This includes sharing QI information throughout the laboratory and beyond to the ward and clinic and other nonlaboratory personnel. Wherever management of training and compliance of any nonlaboratory personnel is concerned, effective communication requires the involvement of the nonlaboratory leadership.

PRELABORATORY PROCESS WORK FLOW SEGMENT

This fourth major segment of the quality profile format can consist of several indicator grouping options. Any grouping incorporated into this phase should address some aspect of the laboratory work flow path that usually occurs outside the laboratory's physical confines. Examples of such groupings include 1) laboratory validation,[h] 2) request-specimen transportation, 3) specimen preservation, 4) specimen collection, 5) patient preparation, 6) request submission, and 7) laboratory product selection.

The sample quality profiles in this text demonstrate the combined surveillance of the quality of the first six activities under the auspices of the laboratory-clinical interface phase of validation and accessioning. Thus, the only two major indicator groupings included under the prelaboratory process portion of the example profile format are 1) request-specimen validation and 2) laboratory product selection. Especially with the aid of more advanced computerization support, it should eventually be feasible to concurrently monitor the first six specific indicators as separate, "real time" prelaboratory activities or work flow phases—instead of combining them all under validation retrospectively.

As with any other distinct work flow phase, it should be clear that there can be any number or combination of separate major indicator groupings. Likewise, each grouping can consist of one or more specific quality indicators.

[h] Although validation occurs within the laboratory, it is usually performed at the physical interface between the laboratory and the outside processing activities at the time of inspection before accessioning. Therefore, this interface activity provides a key monitoring point for surveillance of prelaboratory processing.

Indicator Grouping 12
Prelaboratory Processing Validation

Chemistry Section Quality Profile

Indicator Grouping/ Specific Indicator: Threshold (Periodicity)	QI Data Observations (Date trend started) J	A	S	O	N	D	
PRELABORATORY PROCESS WORK FLOW SEGMENT							
Validation: > 1% invalidation rate* (Monthly)	This data represents only daytime shift performance of specimen collection						
a. Ward 22 staff	3	2	3	3	4	5	%
b. Ward 49 staff	2	3	2	3	2	1	%
c. Ward 71 staff	3	2	3	2	3	2	%
d. Ward 73 staff	2	3	2	3	2	3	%
e. Lab staff	1	2	2	1	1	2	%
*adjusted from 5% in July	QI note: Ward 22 is not performing well in other section QI reports						

Transfusion Service Quality Profile

Indicator Grouping/ Specific Indicator: Threshold (Periodicity)	J	A	S	O	N	D	
PRELABORATORY PROCESS WORK FLOW SEGMENT							
Validation: > 0% invalidation rate (no cases invalidated)!! (Monthly)	Because this is a sentinel event, invalidation is reported on a case-by-case basis						
a. Ward 22 staff	0	0	3	3	3	4	c
b. Ward 49 staff	0	0	1	0	0	0	c
c. Ward 71 staff	0	0	0	0	1	0	c
d. Ward 73 staff	0	0	0	1	0	0	c
e. Lab staff	0	0	0	0	0	0	c
	c = number of seperate cases invalidated These cases represent various examples of improper specimen collection rejected by the lab						

!! = sentinel event

Prelaboratory Processing Validation Management (Indicator Grouping 12)

Chemistry profile interpretation:

Based on statistically-based team analysis and decision making, the section

Evaluation of QI Data, TQM System, and CQI Process	Action Action Person: (Date Initiated)	Assessment of Overall Improvement
Overall, slightly increased; demographics (patient name, number) are still main problem Ward 22 is performing poorly in other lab sections No data on evening/night ward shifts	1. Maintain vigilance at specimen receipt window, especially Ward 22 2. Continue teaching on the wards 3. Focus study on each of the three ward shifts 4. Reduce periodicity from monthly to quarterly ACTION: Supervisor	Improvement of validation and QI process is in progress
QI Note: There is a need for improvement of validation at the accession point with establishment of a new indicator grouping for patient preparation		
Ward 22 has a severe problem with unabated occurrence of validation discrepancies in spite of 3 inservice training sessions; problems are restricted to night (12-8) shift; are temporary "floaters" involved? Ward staff shortage persists. Training problem was noted in Sep 94 CAP interim inspection. See related notes under Patient Outcome and External Inspection indicator groupings	1. Maintain vigilance at specimen receipt window 2. Teach on the ward intensively 3. Schedule meeting with MD and RN directors regarding processing training and supervisory improvements ACTION: Section Medical Director	Ineffective QC and QI processes: out of control on ward 22! Since 1994 interim CAP survey deficiency, no effect of external QI on QC: Needs extensive improvement at interdept QM interface

has decided to monitor the first six steps of prelaboratory processing through the general indicator grouping of request-specimen validation. This is a fairly general topic that encompasses a multitude of potential improvement opportunities. However, monitoring validation does help to initiate concentrating on more specific characteristics of prelaboratory processing practices of individual wards and clinics. Even the laboratory phlebotomy staff is a candidate for surveillance under this grouping.

The section has selected an ongoing indexed study of prelaboratory processing performed by four wards as well as by the laboratory phlebotomy staff. Again, one can base the choice of wards or clinics on any number and type of prioritization criteria.

In their own right, the indicator criteria should include specific aspects of specimen adequacy as well as laboratory test/consultation request form completeness. Much more specific indicators with more limiting criteria are available for focused study indicators, if such an approach is necessary.

It is noted that six months before the date of the current profile the Chemistry Section reduced the threshold from 5% to 1%. Apparently, the section quality management team decided on this modification after a reasonably long period during which invalidation rates were consistently below the former 5% threshold level. The various wards and laboratory staff could have caused this improvement in prelaboratory processing by providing enhanced demographic information or specimen preservation—but, that information is appropriately filed elsewhere. Whatever the reason, reducing the threshold was an act of improving the QI process itself.

Evaluation of the subject profile data reveals that all four indexed wards have exceeded the modified threshold of 1%, scoring invalidation rates ranging between 1% and 5%. This variable excess has been consistent over several months of ongoing monitoring—but ward 22 has shown the greatest excess which also seems to be trending upward.

It is of particular importance that the Chemistry Section is aware by involvement in the department-wide QI program that ward 22 is performing poorly in this particular phase of work flow, as cited by "other lab sections," particularly the Transfusion Service. This awareness speaks well for intralaboratory communication of lessons learned from QI activities. Evaluation also reveals that there is an absence of monitoring data from nondaytime shifts.

The section's combination of actions is reasonable, considering that the readjustment of the threshold has been recent without enough time to reach a new baseline or for ward or laboratory behavior to adjust in return. Continuing with the current threshold along with continued emphasis on education, the desired result should be small but steady "wins" in improving ward personnel proficiency and awareness. Studying the separate work shifts could pinpoint focal problems in prelaboratory processing.

Chemistry's action includes an interesting new twist. They have verified that there are indicator groupings deserving higher priority of closer scrutiny while their QI surveillance resources remain limited. Therefore, to conserve their resources but still provide adequate attention to critical validation indicators, they are reducing the periodicity of reporting from a monthly to a quarterly basis. Chemistry's assessment for this general indicator grouping is accurate.

A special "QI note" reflects sectional-departmental dialogue during the monthly QI review that produces the quality profile report. This profile exhibits a QI note that expresses some concern over the lack of control and surveillance of patient preparation as a more specific monitoring target. This early phase of the laboratory path of work flow often goes unattended and easily warrants attention as a separate indicator grouping. This new indicator could be inserted as a specific indicator for the validation major grouping in the profile format.

Transfusion profile interpretation:

It is virtually impossible to maintain absolutely zero defects in request-specimen validation for any section of any sized hospital; too many weak links exist in the overall system. Although we must live with the fact that Murphy's Law is inherent to this world of Brownian movement and systematic variance, still we must never let down our managerial guard.

However, in transfusion medicine where the patient is so much at risk, the *desired* goal must always be absolute perfection in maintaining patient-request-specimen-product integrity. This mandate implies that adequate organizational and operative resources must always be available to back up the desired guarantee of operational quality.[i]

Evaluation of the proffered profile reveals that three ward prelaboratory request-specimen processing activities have experienced rare, sporadic, random, nonsystematic problems. Reported on a case-by-case basis, the profile records single invalid cases occurring rarely.

Ward 22, however, demonstrates serious problems of a continuous, increasing nature; in the last four months, thirteen cases have had to be invalidated. As reflected by the laboratory section's evaluation, preliminary investigation narrows the cause of these variances on ward 22 to inadequate training of the nondaytime shift work force and inadequate ward supervision. On review of supporting indicator groupings, it also is very troublesome that there is evidence that a 1994 interim CAP self-inspection noted inadequacies in ward support of prelaboratory processing training on the wards—particularly for the nondaytime work shifts.

The prescribed actions for the section medical director address the chief evaluation findings. These include increasing accessioning vigilance, improving laboratory teaching of all ward shifts, and working conjointly with ward directors to establish training and supervision objectives. The laboratory profile does not mention disciplinary action; this is a low priority CQI concern. Whether it is a chief matter for the ward's quality management leadership to consider or not is primarily their decision; they might, at least, have to take some interim measures until all the relevant operational processes have been investigated. The medical director is the action officer, based on the importance of the quality dimension of medical appropriateness.

[i] In this case, the desired managerial outcome is a guarantee—not just "assurance." We try to assure that the guaranteed quality is met by practicing the surveillance process of quality assessment and improvement (QI).

The section profile's assessment ties ineffective staff QC with ineffective laboratory QI. It also links external QI to this indicator grouping by citing the 1994 CAP accreditation, interim self-survey finding. There is an emphasis on improving the interdepartmental QM interface, highlighting the importance of all three programs for QI, QAn, and QAc at the joint level.

Additional profile interpretations:

Hematology (Appendix D): Hematology's validation threshold is 10%. The section quality management team has chosen a QI limiting value that is much higher than for any other section discussed in this text. Their approach combines validation at the accessioning "window" plus that which occurs at the point-of-analysis. Their rationale is that there is a relatively greater incidence of invalidation problems inherent in handling certain hematology specimens.

In the usual hematology section, many problems with invalidation do not occur so much at the initial point-of-accessioning; rather, many occur at the point-of-analysis, ie, at the various instruments. Hematology cell counters are particularly infamous for requiring adequately collected and preserved specimens since microclots can cause aberrant results. Although these microclots are not readily discernible at accessioning, the specimen insufficiency becomes evident during actual CBC analysis. At this point and time a laboratorian must reconsider the specimen for invalidation and request a repeat collection.

Thus, the subject profile evaluation includes the observation that the major problems causing invalidation are inadequate specimen labeling (found at the accessioning window) and inadequate specimen collection resulting in microclot formation (found at the cell counter). Also, it is noted that there is no QI information for specific shifts: all data has been averaged for all three shifts combined.

Consequently, the section quality management team has decided that 10% should be the overall, general threshold. But, that does not mean that they are obliged to stay at that level. On the contrary, after working with that parameter for a while, they should work toward reducing the threshold by improving the collection methods or instrumental procedures in order to reduce the number of specimens needing repeat collection, reduce the TAT of those specific procedures, reduce patient morbidity—and improve the validation rate. Another approach would be to revise threshold determinations for specific patient populations (thereby, for specific wards or clinical services, as well) since various populations exhibit varying frequencies of invalidation problems in hematology—further described below under thresholds.

Also, the Hematology Section already has decided to focus on ward 22. The section might have experienced problems with ward 22 on its own (these details being on file) or because of department-wide dissemination of lessons learned. For example, the Transfusion Service already has ample evidence of ward 22 as an OFI in this segment of the path of work flow. And, the Chemistry Section displays ample suspicion of ward 22 as a high-priority OFI.

The recommended action is for the section supervisor to try new, innovative educational methods on the ward. In addition, the section is to target all shifts for continuing education instead of just the daytime ward work force.

The assessment directs attention to the fact that the cumulative data reveal that the problem has been documented since August. In spite of remedial steps currently being taken as of the December reviewing and reporting period, the section's action is definitely delayed. It is better to anticipate, recognize, and respond to an adverse pattern in the QI data with immediate improvement before it becomes a blatantly problematic trend requiring immediate reaction, resource-demanding damage control, and delayed improvement.

Microbiology (Appendix E): Evaluation of the data reveals that there has been no identification of any OFI for five months. However, even this section has become aware of problems on ward 22 through the departmental communication of QI lessons learned. Thus, their action is for the supervisor to coordinate the preparation of a focused study on ward 22 for the next reporting period—not to wait any longer. The assessment is that the improvement process is being improved. In the process of improving their approach to monitoring ward 22, the section is likely to learn how to better identify opportunities in the other wards and clinics.

Histopathology (Appendix G): This section is monitoring invalidation rates on a quarterly basis; the next reporting period is in January. However, the cumulative and narrative data on hand do show that there has been no identification of any OFI for the past three quarters of scheduled reporting. Under these circumstances, the recommendation is for the section supervisor to design a focused study on the adequacy of clinical information on Dermatology Service surgical pathology requests; the study should be ready for presentation in three months—ie, within the next scheduled QI monitoring quarter. The assessment implies that the section is successfully exercising the improvement process with overall improvement of the quality management approach.

Discussion:

Indicator Grouping. The laboratory can monitor several major activity areas to demonstrate the quality of prelaboratory processing. A very general indicator parameter for this surveillance is the invalidation rate which is usually determined at the point of laboratory accessioning.[j] As demonstrated by the Hematology Section profile, however, some request-specimen validation can occur at the point-of-analysis (or diagnosis).

[j] There really is not a satisfactory substitute term that more precisely describes the general QI monitoring target of "all prelaboratory processing activities except laboratory product selection" without directly targeting each subelement of the process.

Examples of specific indicators that are available as elements for this grouping include the adequacy of:

- Patient identification
- Specific demographic information on the request
- Clinical history relevant to the laboratory test/consultation requested
- Patient preparation
- Specimen collection
- Specimen type and amount
- Specimen labeling
- Specimen preservation
- Specimen transportation/time in transit.

Bar coding and palm top computer terminals are providing great assistance in the surveillance of prelaboratory processing at the very point of health care. As these modern devices continue to develop in their sophistication and communication capabilities, compliance with correct laboratory procedure will become a matter of real time (instantaneous) surveillance, evaluation, action, assessment, and communication. As a result of technological advances, all of the specific indicators listed above will ultimately become available for direct monitoring.

Additional indicator topics include the usual matrix of sectional IACs matched against numbers, types, and priorities of clinical customers, patients at risk, diseases at hand, and quality management resources on hand. Consequently, this grouping has the potential for being quite extensive in terms of numbers of specific indicators. Also, the section quality management team can organize entirely new general groupings using the topics listed above with even more specific indicators incorporated under each of those new groupings.

Supporting indicators: As demonstrated in Table VI and Table VII of the preceding chapter, indicators of the validation grouping directly link with all other indicator groupings in either a cause or an effect relationship—including employee safety and excluding laboratory product selection and utilization. For example, the Transfusion Service profile shows a tangential link between the issue of prelaboratory processing quality and the 1994 CAP interim survey citing of the need to train laboratory techniques on the wards; improvement surveillance of the external QI program (ie, indicator grouping 23) is the source of this corroborative data.

Threshold. The validation rate threshold can vary greatly from one laboratory section to another, each having its own unique technical requirements for prelaboratory processing. The criticalness of the threshold will depend largely on the given patient diagnostic category and current clinical status and the laboratory product on request. The strictness of limitations of the threshold determines the subsequent EvAAC activities that will ensue at the validation point.

The Transfusion Service provides a perfect example in which laboratorians can legitimately insist on an absolutely perfect match of specimen and accompanying request documentation to the sentinel-type threshold requirements. Every step must be flawless before preparing a blood unit and while transfusing a patient. Complete conformance to procedural (ie, design) specifications is mandatory because a hemolytic transfusion reaction must be preventable at all possible costs. Consequently, if a laboratory request or specimen is inadequate, the appropriate action is often to repeat the collection of a proper specimen with a new request. Rarely, extenuating circumstances based on clinical urgency arise where the goal of 100% conformance is not feasible. The laboratory must consider all such exceptions on a case-by-case basis, supported by appropriate documentation.

In most other sections, the threshold for error in request-specimen submission is usually less rigid, varying with the technical nature of the section's function. For example, the usual chemistry section might realistically expect to achieve a controlled validation rate of 1% or less. As a contrasting example, a hematology section might be forced to work with a rate as low as 1% for adult patients along with one as high as 5% for neonatal patients. The section would base these differences on the varying difficulty of obtaining a nontraumatized specimen and the propensity of formation of microclots with their causing dysfunction of modern-day flow cell counters. Such a relationship between QI threshold and instrument function can change with the improvement of the collection procedure or the instrumental procedure—more likely it will be the former.

A laboratory just beginning to monitor this QI target might easily have significantly higher validation threshold levels. Then, after a little time and practice, their intention should be to gradually improve and continually whittle down those threshold levels. In comparison, the laboratory that is more experienced in the improvement process usually will have improved to the point of using much lower thresholds for this grouping.

In the latter vein, the Chemistry profile provides a good example of the process of adjustment of a improvement threshold. The indicator suggests, in fact, that the section might have reduced its threshold so recently that a good baseline and period of ward and laboratory adjustment has not yet taken place. Similar to all other comparative rate indicators, this section can continually—slowly but surely—strive to move toward zero defects. The section can accomplish this objective by carefully scheduling continuing education and assiduously shepherding the QI, QAn, and QAc organizational-level programs for both the laboratory and related wards and clinics.

Monitoring Periodicity. The two main example profile segments illustrate the differing needs of the two subject sections. Chemistry is adjusting its periodicity from monthly to quarterly to conserve QI resources. The Transfusion Service must maintain monthly scrutiny to monitor a high priority indicator—in spite of a severe personnel shortage.

The latter management judgement call hinges on the high-risk/benefit prioritization criterion that is inescapably important to the practice of transfusion medicine. Ironically, the Transfusion Service's staff shortage and its increasing analytical error rate are even more reason to monitor specimen submission on a monthly basis. The fact is that they must obligingly increase vigilance on a problem-prone activity; at the same time, they burden their already overwhelmed staff with QI responsibilities that they simply cannot curtail because their effectiveness (along with their patients' welfare) is already so much at risk. The consequent monitoring requirements indeed create a "Catch-22" situation for the Transfusion Service, unless staffing improves by an increase or workload improves by some curtailment.

Evaluation. The validation of prelaboratory processing quality (along with the impact of the hemolytic reaction) has unmasked a bimodal OFI for the Transfusion Service. The first portion of the opportunity deals with the needs of the Transfusion Service in upgrading its support of the ward system teaching program. This improvement should include the targeting of all appropriate ward personnel on all work shifts. The Transfusion Service unquestionably needs outside help to support any ward training at this time. There are several alternative sources of capable laboratory and nonlaboratory personnel for accomplishing this training requirement.

The second portion of the processing OFI involves the ongoing nursing staff shortage on ward 22 with lack of time, supervision, and inservice training. The remedy to their problem also reinforces the concept that ward and clinic personnel should be evaluating laboratory quality management decisions that affect the clinical side—preferably this is being done jointly with the laboratory.

In the case that is presented, the nursing personnel on ward 22 must decide how to increase their staffing or reduce their workload and improve their own training and supervision on all work shifts—to make themselves more effective so that prelaboratory processing technique is improved and patient care is no longer compromised. Actually, in a proper joint TQM and CQI environment with properly functioning QI, QAn, and QAc programs, the nursing and laboratory staff should have already accomplished these quality management goals and objectives long before the crises in processing and blood administering ever occurred.

Action. If the laboratory product request, patient preparation, or specimen is not totally adequate, the usual options are to:

- Flag the procedure for close scrutiny but continue with the laboratory determination; resolve and confirm whatever is in question.
- Run the determination as requested but repeat with a new, adequate request and specimen as soon as possible.

- Hold the specimen, notify the attending clinical staff of the specific problem in specimen integrity, and negotiate an *apropos* remedy to the problem.
- Modify the extent of the procedure and perform only whatever is medically appropriate; repeat request and specimen collection for whatever cannot be performed with the initial submission.
- Destroy the specimen and request resubmission of a new request and specimen to the laboratory.

Again, any solution to an opportunity to improve any aspect of the laboratory process that affects validation almost always extends beyond the confines of the laboratory to the halls of the wards and clinics. This includes joint improvement of the QI process itself, along with all relevant QAn and QAc activities.

For example, one action for the Transfusion Service—although not cited in the profile—would be for other laboratory sections to provide supporting personnel to assist the section in certain duties such as bench analysis, ward training, and QI surveillance. Even experienced nursing staff from adequately staffed wards or clinics could support the ward training until the laboratory section is staffed well enough to support the training endeavor on the clinical side. The laboratory manager at the service or departmental level might even take on the coordination of this multidisciplinary approach as a special assignment.

Assessment. Adjustment of QI indicators, criteria, thresholds, data collection methods, or data analysis methods might become necessary if the surveillance data consistently shows no improvement. The data can be extremely abnormal (as demonstrated by the Transfusion Service), low grade abnormal (as demonstrated by the Chemistry Section), or completely normal.

In the case of the Chemistry Section, regardless of how good the data looks no improvement over a significant period of time indicates a problem with the QI system, itself. The adage, "If it ain't broke, don't fix it" does not apply in CQI, where instead continuous improvement is the central theme. The working adage must be, "If the quality management system doesn't produce some improvement over a reasonable period of time, the system must be 'broke.'"

Communication. The Transfusion Service example particularly demonstrates the multidepartmental nature of the validation indicator grouping. By definition of the prelaboratory processing phase of the path of work flow, the quality of all of these activities is predicated on the competence—or compliance—of many laboratory and nonlaboratory individuals, to include even the patient. Consequently, any lesson learned through this grouping needs to be communicated throughout the entire train of involved personnel, keeping the total scope of the laboratorian-clinician-patient connection unbroken—informing whomever has a need to know.

Indicator Grouping 13
Laboratory product Selection

Chemistry Section Quality Profile

Indicator Grouping/ Specific Indicator: Threshold (Periodicity)	QI Data Observations (Date trend started) J A S O N D
Chemistry Test Section: in keeping with joint laboratory and clinical standards!! (Quarterly) a. Serum calcium	- = not scheduled 0= no provider identified Survey started in Jul 92 .....Provider Code # ..... - - 0 - - 0

Transfusion Service Quality Profile

Blood Product/Procedure Selection: in keeping with joint laboratory and clinical standards!! (Monthly) a. Packed red blood cells	0= no provider identified - = not implemented .....Provider Code # ..... - - - 0 0 0
b. Fresh frozen plasma (FFP); the standards are TBD	Blood utilization committee (BUC) requests the lab establish this indicator to focus on the Thoracic Surgery Service practice of selecting FFP based on findings reported in BUC committee minutes

!! = sentinel event TBD = to be determined

Laboratory Product Selection Management (Indicator Grouping 13)

Chemistry profile interpretation:
This profile grouping demonstrates that a focused study is under way and that no improvement opportunity in clinical selection of serum calcium testing was detected for, at least, two quarters. It is important to note that the selection data are reported in terms of a provider code number. The profile should identify any provider that has over selected (or under selected) a laboratory product according to preestablished, joint, laboratory-clinical standards of practice.

Based on only a six-month baseline, the action is appropriate. The assessment is that the action and QI process are under good management

Evaluation of QI Data, TQM System, and CQI Process	Action Action Person: (Date Initiated)	Assessment of Overall Improvement
On target x 6 mo; baseline established	Continue for one more quarter; THEN Select a new study for Mar 96 ACTION: Supervisor	Improvement of the QI process is in progress
On target x 3 mo; baseline is being established	Continue baseline ACTION: Blood Bank Manager (if there is one) or Medical Director	Effective QI process
BUC has identified a need for improvement of FFP selection by the Thoracic Surgery Service (TSS); joint selection standards need to be established	Coordinate with C, TSS, to establish improved clinical indications for requesting FFP; to begin monitoring in Mar 96 ACTION: Medical Director	Improvement of the FFP selection process is in progress

and improvement is in progress.

If after the next quarter the calcium study remains nonproductive, the section is to select a new focused study based on analytical prioritization. The new study could be a modification of the current calcium topic, narrowing it down to a more concise target, such as selection of serum calcium determination by the surgical intensive care unit. Or the topic could change to a completely different laboratory testing parameter (ie, IAC).

Transfusion profile interpretation:
Evaluation of this section's profile reveals that a focused study of clinical selection of packed cells has produced a three-month baseline. No opportunities have been noted yet. Based on such a short baseline, the

actions and assessments are appropriate. The mention of a "blood bank manager" as action officer responsible for continuing the packed red cell selection study reminds us that there are many laboratory job positions that might actually fit the bill, depending on the laboratory's size and organizational structure. Delegate a given responsibility according to span of control and influence.

A second study of fresh frozen plasma (FFP) selection is in the embryonic stage of implementation. In this case, the listing of the medical director as action person for the FFP study points out the need for a laboratory physician to be involved in actions involving the establishment of joint laboratory-clinical standards of practice and dealing with medical appropriateness as the key dimension of quality.

Compared to other profile groupings for this section, this Transfusion Service profile grouping seems to be reasonably successful. It is ironic, however, that one must question how much effort the transfusion personnel can realistically expend on this second selection indicator at this time. Perhaps the FFP study should be postponed as a new QI project until there is more staff available. This is a judgement call on the part of the section and the joint quality management team; the decision depends greatly on the clinical need for improving the <u>clinician's</u> selection process.

Additional profile interpretations:

Hematology (Appendix D): The profile for this laboratory product selection grouping shows that a general survey indicator has been ongoing for four months. The resultant baseline reveals no identification of any OFI. With the baseline still in its formative stage, there is no further need for action except to wait a little longer before deciding if an index or focused study is appropriate.

Microbiology (Appendix E): This section's profile is one developmental step beyond that of the preceding one in that a monthly baseline has now been established over a six month period. The action is to 1) change the general survey to a quarterly reporting scheduling and 2) select a focused study within the next quarter. The assessment is accurate in that there is improvement being made in the QI process.

Histopathology (Appendix G): This profile segment for anatomic consultation selection represents another developmental step beyond the others already described. It reveals that a general survey indicator has been ongoing for nine months. Evaluation of this survey's results reveals that there has been no OFI identified during the period of active monitoring.

The recommended action is to discontinue the general survey and rely on the already established focused study. This action will facilitate more efficient use of quality management resources and gain more effective results from the monitoring effort.

The focused study has been in progress for only three months. Although aimed at a specific laboratory IAC, the topic is still fairly general: clinical selection of frozen-section diagnoses. In December, the third month of the study, the report notes that provider #24 exceeded joint laboratory-clinical standards of practice in requesting the frozen-section procedure. Evaluation of this occurrence reveals that provider #24 from the otolaryngological (*ie*, ENT) service submitted tissue to the AP service with the request for a frozen-section diagnosis following a routine tonsillectomy without justification.

The recommended actions are bimodal. On the laboratory side, the medical director of the surgical pathology service must 1) discontinue the general survey and 2) sharpen the focus of the specific indicator study by looking solely at the selection of frozen sections by the ENT surgical service. The main question is whether or not there is a systemic element in the selection process that can be improved.

On the clinical side of this joint QI process, the recommendation is for the chief of the ENT service to 1) counsel provider #24 in the appropriate selection of frozen-section procedures and 2) participate in a joint laboratorian-clinician effort to determine how to improve the frozen-section selection process, vis, otolaryngological surgical requests.

The overall assessment is accurate in that a joint laboratory-clinical effort is improving the frozen-section selection process in the specific area of ENT service requests. In pursuing this OFI, there also is improvement of the joint improvement process at the organizational-level of the QI, QAn, and QAc programs.

Discussion:

Indicator Grouping. This indicator topic of laboratory test, product, or service selection is a corollary—although not quite a mirror image—of the indicator grouping for laboratory product utilization. Over several years, the JCAHO and other accrediting organizations have placed major emphasis on documenting surveillance of effective utilization of laboratory end products (especially blood products and surgical pathology reports). A tangential spin-off from that scrutiny has been modification of product selection in a retrospective fashion. However, there is no reason we cannot exercise direct oversight of laboratory product selection, nipping the basic issue of "malutilization" in the bud, concurrently as it happens—and before any further prelaboratory processing occurs.

As an immediate response, many laboratorians object to this QI approach of monitoring clinical selection of a laboratory product or service. Their reasoning is that we are placing ourselves in the position of policemen; Diamond clearly warned the laboratory community of this adverse possibility.[27] Since the days of Codman, however, we have never really had much of a choice in this matter: Codman was a clinician asking for the "police work" to be done, and laboratorians have a definite role to share in this endeavor. Even today, the Codmans are still speaking out—again, mostly on the clinical side—and the laboratorians must respond.[28]

It is an economic reality: as supply creates its own demand, imperfections in the market will follow. Even the healthcare marketplace can become distorted; in fact, such distortions are well known. For example, Taffel, et al, have recently pointed out that about 25% of all U.S. births are surgically intervened by cesarean section. Of those, less than half are medically appropriate.[30] Similar studies have revealed the inappropriateness of selection of laboratory studies—these being the flip side of studies showing the inappropriate nonuse of laboratory studies after they have been requested, performed, and charted.[1,2,29]

Thus, the discouraging incidence of laboratory product "malselection" characterizes a major distortion in the healthcare marketplace; this is predicated on the inappropriate use of too plentiful (or too easily obtainable) a supply of the commodity of healthcare laboratory products. The healthcare "commodity" can be a surgical, or medical, or pediatric, or laboratory, or radiological, or pharmaceutical, or insurance, or any other imaginable healthcare product or service. Regardless, any such commodity can represent a distortion of not only economics but also professional practice if malselected and misused. The prediction is that the healthcare share of the gross national product will be greater than 15% by the year 2000.[31] As customers in the national marketplace, we all are experiencing this distortion in the guise of this monetary backlash of runaway costs accompanied by some significant degree of unnecessary patient morbidity.

Diamond had an answer to his admonition not to be policemen. The answer is to build a solid foundation of mutual trust and substantive dialogue between the laboratorian and the clinician: to police-up the distortions in healthcare through joint effort. We can sufficiently achieve this foundation only through joint QAc, QAn, and QI programs.

In fact, nowadays the concept of a joint quality surveillance program receives some reasonable amount of popular credence. However, the value of joint strategic planning and team building is still given no more than passing lip service in many healthcare organizations. Ironically, it is only through the latter two programs that the greatest strides can be continually taken toward a truly successful and sustained quality improvement. Currently, the JCAHO deserves credit in being the only nation-wide healthcare voice in support of organizational planning and actualization; almost all the other organizations are following along (or are being dragged)—and not without complaints and lack of full endorsement.

The profile format exemplified in this grouping allows that the "provider" requesting the laboratory product might not be a physician. Other providers such as nurse practitioners, physician assistants, and psychologists might be involved in the ordering of laboratory products. In this new era of "direct access," even the patient might be making the request.

The very essence of laboratory product/service selection mandates that there is joint laboratory—clinical staff agreement over standards of practice for the selection of important laboratory products/services (ie, important aspects of care). These standards are equivalent to indicator criteria.

The laboratorian can approach quality surveillance for this indicator grouping from at least three levels of sophistication. The first level would be the tried and true method of laboratory consultation. A form of peer review, this approach requires that all requests for certain preselected laboratory products be reviewed by a laboratory physician or other qualified laboratorian before collection of the specimen is allowed.

This first level of approach is usually the action of last resort only when resource constraints—such as personnel shortage, instrument accessibility, or inherent expense of the requested laboratory procedure—prevail. Use of this first level of approach also can imply that computer resources are limited. This first approach can supplement either of the next two levels of approach.

The second level of sophistication requires that adequate clinical information be provided as a part of the informative data in the laboratory request. There needs to be at least some indication of the patient's leading diagnosis, physical signs, or symptoms (including preliminary laboratory reports) that justifies a product selection. The laboratory can monitor the quality of product selection at this second level during accessioning as described under the validation profile grouping.

As an example, in most cases "for admission" or "for screening" would be inadequate as a sole justification for requesting a laboratory product or service, and a blank entry for appropriate clinical data should be frankly inadmissible. The diagnostic category plus the patient's sex and age—as a minimum—could easily fit into a computerized or noncomputerized, algorithmic matrix that would assist in concurrent monitoring of appropriate laboratory product selection. The advent of bar coding and palm top computer terminals already are beginning to facilitate this surveillance effort at the actual time and point of the laboratory product selection event.

The third level of sophistication is application of a delta check at the time of validation and accessioning of the product request-specimen. Such an immediate follow-up, scanning, and comparison of current laboratory data with the request in hand can 1) detect whether or not there is an indication for requesting a given laboratory product, 2) alert the laboratory-clinical team that additional options of laboratory products need to be considered, or 3) alert laboratorians and clinicians that the ordering of a laboratory product is contraindicated and is unacceptable without further clinical input. The laboratory can exercise all of these options as part of a "real time" quality management program.

Delta checking requires an adequate computerized laboratory information system. The eventual application of such advances as backpropagation neural networks continue to enhance the effectiveness of the delta check procedure.[32] Again, bar coding and other more advanced devices linking the laboratorian and clinician to computerized data archives will greatly enhance laboratory product selection and the joint laboratory-clinical QI process.

Additional indicator topics are as plentiful and varied as there are numbers and types of IAC for either the AP or CP service sections, along with the usually related determinant resource factors. The resultant decision matrix, the same as described for any other indicator grouping in this chapter, will produce more indicator possibilities than is feasible for fitting into the QI monitoring schedule. Thus, the secret to a realistic QI program is to exercise the prioritization and decision criteria very judiciously.

As mentioned above, the Toffel article is a good example of many relevant outcome-oriented reviews that point the way to timely laboratory product selection quality indicator topics.[30] It brings to mind that the QI process is a matter of monitoring the concordance of requests for laboratory procedures with joint laboratory-clinical standards of laboratory-clinical practice.

In the case of the inappropriate cesarean sections cited by Toffel, one laboratory link that could aid *joint* laboratory-clinical QI monitoring of the appropriateness of the surgical procedure would be the concordance of requests for type and crossmatch with appropriate clinical data justifying a cesarean section. In other words, "for cesarean section" would not be adequate clinical information. There would have to be some justifiable rationale included that would satisfy the Transfusion Service medical director of the medical appropriateness of the blood request, eg, " for cesarean section due to cephalo-pelvic dysproportion." The surgeon and clinical assistants would have to put a little conscionable effort into composing the blood request—substantiated by adequate documentation, including an appropriate examination.

Supporting Indicators. These are relatively limited to indicators of customer satisfaction and patient care outcome, laboratory product utilization, and QI, QAn, and QAc activities. The latter three organizational programs are especially important for a successful joint surveillance venture into quality selection.

Monitoring Periodicity. This scheduling depends upon the criticalness of the aspect of care being monitored and the adequacy of quality management resources on hand.

Threshold. The range of tolerance of variance from the subject clinical and laboratory standards depends on the degree of patient risk, difficulty of the laboratory procedure, health care resource constraints, and joint quality management goals and objectives. The resource constraints might not necessarily be solely laboratory resource limitations: there also can be clinical resource constraints.

Evaluation. As noted in Table VI and VII of the preceding chapter, there is comparatively limited cross-linkage of supporting indicator groupings to assist in this evaluation. Thus, a great deal of effective evaluation rests on an adequate computerized data management system, whereby the collection of data and evaluation can be largely automated. Otherwise, it would involve very time-consuming medical record review, limiting the scope and timeliness of any study. In any case, there certainly would be a need for laboratory-clinical evaluation at a joint peer review level. The secret to an effective and efficient evaluation is developing a strong mutual trust and dialogue between the laboratorians and the clinicians—as only can be fostered by strong joint QI, QAn, and QAc programs.

Action. As shown by the example histopathology profile, the brunt of the action for this profile grouping rests on the quality management leadership on the clinical side of the house—amongst the primary healthcare providers. Resolving a selection problem is theoretically a 50-50 proposition with the laboratory leadership sharing half of the responsibility for coordinating remedial action with the clinical staff. But, if any opportunities do exist to improve laboratory product selection, realistically they predominantly depend on modification of the processes that affect clinical staff behavior—which is a direct responsibility of the clinical quality management leadership. The best that the laboratorian can do is teach ... *teach* ... **TEACH** and continually foster mutual trust and dialogue.

Communication. As clearly implied above, lessons learned from selection surveillance must be disseminated to both the laboratorians and clinicians who are involved and are responsible for quality management. "Clinicians" includes more than physicians. For example, dentists, podiatrists, psychologists, nurse practitioners, physician assistants, and any other healthcare provider who is credentialed to select and order laboratory products and services are a part of the clinical team. In this burgeoning era of direct access, even the patient as a "self-provider" and as the ultimate customer in any case should be a recipient of these QI lessons learned.

Remember, also, that the laboratory can disseminate general follow-up information regarding the quality management of laboratory product selection without divulging the identity of a provider, clinical service, or patient that is involved. Communication of quality management information can and should protect individual anonymity.

Quality Profiling of Decentralized Testing And Other Ancillary Testing Activities

The advent of formal surveillance of decentralized laboratory testing (DLT) occurred with the JCAHO announcement of the importance of these decentralized activities and the CAP publication of the checklist for inspecting ancillary testing sites.[k] An ancillary testing activity provides a very limited extent of laboratory products or services and is located in a ward or clinic separate from the primary or central laboratory. Usually, nursing and medical staff perform the testing procedures. If DLT exists in a hospital in which the primary laboratory is CAP accredited, then the ancillary testing site must be inspected along with the primary laboratory.[34,35]

All of the outcome process, operative resource, and organizational resource management requirements for QC and QI that are expected of the

[k] This type of testing is also known as "out-of-laboratory testing" in Canada.[33]

primary laboratory also apply to DLT. The usual proviso is that the appropriate primary laboratory staff provide the QI oversight of ancillary QC through their primary quality surveillance program. Therefore, under these circumstances it is reasonable for the primary laboratory to incorporate the DLT into its QI, QAn, and QAc programs at the joint laboratory-clinical level. Thus, joint surveillance of the ancillary laboratory is manageable through the use of a complete quality profile—just as in the regular laboratory-section profile approach. This concept is worthwhile sharing at this juncture of this text, since the main topic of the current chapter is overall organizational laboratory process control and assessment—a major topic of concern in the CAP ancillary checklist.

Another quality profile target—it is also worthwhile remembering that the same option exists to expand QI surveillance of reference laboratory quality to the same level and scope as a regular primary laboratory section or DLT. Again, this approach provides the reference laboratory with a surveillance status warranting the entire scope of operative and organizational segments of an entire quality profile. This would encourage the primary laboratory to look at the reference laboratory with a wider perspective, especially from the vantage point of effective TQM and CQI. Such a managerial position would enhance joint performance of QI, QAn, and QAc programs.

REFERENCES

1. A compendium of peer review data and information. 1990 Pro Abstract Naperville, IL; Crescent County Foundation for Medical Care, 1990
2. Bate W. Inappropriate readmission. Iowa Medicine, 1989;79:126-30.
3. Howanitz PJ, Steindel SJ, Cembroski GS. Emergency room stat test turnaround times. Arch Path Lab Med, 1992;116:122-8.
4. Plapp FV, Rachel JM. Automation in blood banking: machines for clumping, sticking, and gelling. Am J Clin Path, 1992;98 (supplement 1):S17-S21.
5. Savage RA. Suggestions for quality assurance routines in the clinical hematology laboratory. Lab Med, 1989;20:556-559.
6. Richardson H (ed). Quality Management of Diagnostic Microbiology. Toronto, Ontario: Ontario Medical Association, Laboratory Proficiency Testing Program, 1992.
7. Polesky HF. Clarity in communication (editorial). Am J Clin Path, 1992;98:148-149.
8. Harrison HH, Miller KL, Dickinson C, Daufeldt JA. Quality assurance and reproducibility of high-resolution two-dimensional electropheresis and silver staining in polyacrylamide gels. Am J Clin Path, 1992;97:97-105.

9. Kempson RL. The time is now. Checklists for surgical pathology reports (editorial). Arch Path Lab Med, 1992;116:1107-1108.
10. Zarbo RJ. Interinstitutional assessment of colorectal carcinoma surgical pathology report adequacy. A College of American Pathologists Q-Probe study of practice patterns from 532 laboratories and 15,940 reports. Arch Path Lab Med, 1992;116:1113-1119.
11. Frable WJ, Kempson RL, Rosai J. Editorial: Quality assurance and quality control in anatomic pathology: standardization of the surgical pathology report. Mod Path, 1992;5:102a-102b.
12. Rosai J, Bonfiglio TA, Corson JM, Fechner RE, Harris NL, LiVolsi VA, Silverberg SG. Methods in pathology: standardization of the surgical pathology report. Mod Path, 1992;5:197-198.
13. Rosai J, Bonfiglio TA, Corson JM, Fechner RE, Harris NL, LiVolsi VA, Silverberg SG. Methods in Pathology: Recommendations on quality control and quality assurance in surgical pathology and autopsy pathology. Mod Path, 1992;5:567-568.
14. Legg MA. What role for the diagnostic pathologist? N Engl J Med, 1981;305:950-951.
15. Schwartz WB, Wolfe HJ, Parker SG. Pathology and probabilities. A new approach to interpreting and reporting biopsies. N Engl J Med, 1981;305:917-923.
16. Macartnery JC, Henson DE, Codling BW. Quality assurance and surgical pathology. Pathologist, 1983;37:788-792.
17. Whitehead ME, Fitzwater JE, Lindley SK, Kern SB, Ulrisch RC, Winecoff WF. Quality assurance of histopathology diagnoses: a perspective audit of three thousand cases. Am J Clin Path, 1984, 81:487-491.
18. Rickert RR. Quality assurance in anatomic pathology. Clinics in Lab Med, 1986;6:697-706.
19. Cook RE. A quality control system for anatomic pathology. Lab Med, 1987;18:391-392.
20. Travers H. Quality assurance in anatomic pathology. Lab Med, 1987;18:85-92.
21. Penner DW. Quality assurance diagnostic surgical pathology (editorial). Arch Path Lab Med, 1987;111:513.
22. Kaufman Z, Lew S, Griffel B, Dinbar A. Frozen-section diagnosis in surgical pathology. A prospective analysis of 526 frozen sections. Cancer, 1986;57:377-379.
23. Rogers C, Klett EC, Chandrasoma P. Accuracy of frozen-section diagnosis in a teaching hospital. Arch Path Lab Med, 1987;111:514-517.
24. Howanitz PJ, Hoffman G, Zarbo RJ. The accuracy of frozen-section diagnosis in 34 hospitals. Arch Path Lab Med, 1990;114:355-359.

25. Anderson RE. The autopsy as an instrument of quality assessment. Classification of premortem and postmortem diagnostic discrepancies. Arch Path Lab Med, 1984;108:490-493.

26. Schned AR, Mogielnicki RP, Stauffer ME. A comprehensive quality assurance program on the autopsy service. Am J Clin Path, 1986;86:113-138.

27. Diamond, I. Quality assurance and/or quality control. Arch Path Lab Med, 1986;110:875.

28. McClendon WW. Ernest A. Codman MD (1869-1940), the end-result idea, and *The Product of a Hospital*: the challenge of a man ahead of his time and perhaps ours. Arch Path Lab Med, 1990;114:1101-1104.

29. Caplen RL. Health care reform: should the marketplace reign? Clin Lab Man Rev, 1992;6:490,488-489.

30. Taffel SM, Placek PJ, Moien M. 1988 U.S. cesarean-section rate at 24.7 per 100 births—a plateau? N Engl J Med, 1990;323:199-200.

31. Hilborne LH. Piecing together the quality puzzle. Laboratory medicine's role in medical practice. Arch Path Lab Med, 1992;116:815-816.

32. Astion ML, Wilding P. The application of backpropagation neural networks to problems in pathology and laboratory medicine. Arch Path Lab Med, 1992;116:995-1001.

33. Ogram D (ed). Out-of-laboratory testing. Can J Med Tech, 1992;54(suppl 3).

34. The Joint Commission 1992 Accreditation Manual for Hospitals. Oakbrook Terrace, IL: Joint Commission on Accreditation of Healthcare Organizations, 1991.

35. Inspection checklist. Ancillary testing (VolumeXXX). Skokie, IL: College of American Pathologists, 1992.

10. The Quality Profile: Laboratory Operative Resource Management

ABORATORY OPERATIVE RESOURCE WORK FLOW SEGMENT

Following the three process-related segments, the next major portion of the laboratory path of work flow addresses operative resource management. This fourth segment of the quality profile format consists of nine suggested indicator groupings; each grouping focuses on a key operative resource management activity. All of these activities primarily occur within the confines of the laboratory—although there are many external support elements related to these main laboratory operative resource functions. The nine groupings include management of 1) (workload) (productivity), 2) personnel, 3) continuing medical education, 4) methods and procedures, 5) (computer operations) (information), 6) equipment, 7) supply, 8) facility, and 9) budget.

It is important to remember that these are only example groupings and indicators. A laboratory can select any number and type of operative resource groupings, just as each segment and grouping can include any combination of general or specified quality indicators.

Productivity Management (Indicator Grouping 14)

Chemistry profile interpretation:
Workload is a unique operative resource, and it should be managed as such—not just allowed to "be." A well-established method for managing workload is carefully recording the work accomplished and monitoring productivity measurements.

Indicator Grouping 14
Productivity Management

Chemistry Section Quality Profile

Indicator Grouping/ Specific Indicator: Threshold (Periodicity)	QI Data Observations (Date trend started) J A S O N D
OPERATIVE RESOURCE MANAGEMENT WORK FLOW SEGMENT	
Workload Management:	
a. Productivity quotients: within established limits!! (Monthly)	m = minutes/hour
1. PQ_p (paid): 40 to 45 min/hr	56 52 51 49 46 41 m
2. PQ_{wl} (workloaded): 50 to 55 min/hr	112 104 104 98 92 71 m

Transfusion Service Quality Profile

Indicator Grouping/ Specific Indicator: Threshold (Periodicity)	QI Data Observations (Date trend started) J A S O N D
OPERATIVE RESOURCE MANAGEMENT WORK FLOW SEGMENT	
Workload Management:	
a. Productivity quotients: within established limits!! (Monthly)	m = minutes/hour
1. PQ_p (paid): 30 to 38 min/hr	39 45 49 52 56 61 m
2. PQ_{wl} (workloaded): 46 to 51 min/hr	50 59 64 69 72 83 m

!! = sentinel event

This example profile grouping consists of index studies of two productivity quotients: one for the *paid productivity quotient* (PQ_p) and the second for the *workloaded productivity quotient* (PQ_{wl}).[a] Evaluation of six month's cumulative data for PQ_p reveals that the paid productivity generally exceeded its upper threshold limit between July and November. However, the overall trend was that of a gradual return to an acceptable level by December. In comparison, the PQ_{wl} levels are consistently excessive—but still demonstrate a trend toward reduction.

[a] CAP Workload Recording (WLR) Program quotients appear in these profiles as examples. One can use CAP Laboratory Management Index Program (LMIP) quotients based on billable tests, but average ranges are not easily obtained. There is no LMIP manual as of this writing. Refer to Chapter 7 for the derivative formulas for these productivity quotients.

Evaluation of QI Data, TQM System, and CQI Process	Action Action Person: (Date Initiated)	Assessment of Overall Improvement
1. PQ_p is improving with a successful hiring program 2. PQ_{wl} is consistently excessive; but this stress indicator is improving; the PQ ratio is 1.7 in Dec	Continue to pursue hiring to fill remaining vacancies ACTION: Supervisor	Improvement of the hiring process is in progress
PQ_p is excessive and increasing, suggesting severe employee stress situation	Pursue the hiring for vacant staff positions ACTION: Dept Administrative Superviser (if there is one) or Dept Lab Manager	Ineffective hospital QI process: This section needs Hospital Admin and Personnel Office support
PQ_{wl} is consistently excessive; a steadily worsening trend		

All that can be construed directly from this productivity information is that there has either been an inordinate increase in workload or a decrease of available work force. In fact, the supporting grouping for personnel management (ie, indicator grouping 15) corroborates that there has been a significant shortage of technical personnel. The vacancy rate information parallels the present grouping's productivity data showing progressive improvement over the past six months—with a shortage of only six full-time equivalents (FTEs) in December. Compared to the Transfusion Service example, however, the Chemistry Section staffing level has not exceeded its "critical mass"—that is the staff level at which productivity and quality of product are significantly compromised.

Comparison of PQ_p with PQ_{wl} data exemplifies how much more sensitive the latter is to a shift in the balance of workload versus work force.

This is due to the PQ_{wl} being calculated to measure workload-weighted (ie, strictly analytical/interpretive) procedures by excluding nonworkload-weighted (nonbenchwork) duty time and benefit time.

Also, the ratio of PQ_{wl} to PQ_p was 1.7 for December compared to the ratio of 2.0 during the earlier months. Since the overall work force strength is constant during a given reporting period, this comparative shift between the two quotients suggests a decrease of specified (workload-weighted) analytical/interpretive workload (ie, as evidenced by a relative decrease of the size of the output PQ numerator). Such a workload decrease would be expected during the December holiday season. In comparison, an increase in this ratio would suggest a relative increase of specified workload in a given reporting period. The action and assessment are appropriate for the occasion.

Transfusion profile interpretation:
Compared to the Chemistry Section, the productivity quotients show that this less automated Transfusion Service activity is moving in the diametrically opposite operational direction. Both the PQ_p and PQ_{wl} are significantly elevated over their respective threshold limits and the general cumulative trend toward ineffective productivity is worsening dangerously.

Review of corroborative work force data (ie, indicator grouping 15) provides another major lesson. Even though this section lacks six technologists—just as do all of the other example sections—those six FTEs represent 55% of the authorized Transfusion Service work force in December (compared to 21% in Chemistry). In fact, this section's staffing level has exceeded its "critical mass" for effective productivity and ability to deal with the workload at hand.

Such an adverse development is further substantiated by what we already know about the Transfusion Service in regard to customer satisfaction, patient care outcome, throughput, quality control, and analytical proficiency. We can see further supportive evidence under other operative and all organizational resource management indicator groupings that essentially all operational functions are severely crippled.

The recommended action to remedy the staffing situation is accurate. The overall assessment emphasizes the need to improve the quality management (QM) interface between this laboratory section and the hospital administration, its personnel managerial support assets, and the special task force.

Additional profile interpretations:

Hematology (Appendix D): Evaluation of both the PQ_p and PQ_{wl} data reveals a steady increase over the last six months. This trend would indicate either a steady increase of workload (ie, the output numerator of the productivity quotient) or a decrease of the technical staff (ie, the input denominator of the quotient). In this case, the supporting indicator grouping for personnel management and work force strength corroborates a steady loss of technical personnel—there being six FTE vacancies in December.

The recommended actions are typical responses to adverse productivity in a constrained work force environment, aimed at resolving the underlying personnel and resultant workload problems. There is need to 1) use still available staff through innovative scheduling and motivating approaches; 2) consider interim mitigating options to relieve workload stress; 3) recruit and hire; and 4) even consider long-range plans for increasing automation and reducing work force need if none is available. The assessment accurately points to an ineffective QM interface between the laboratory and the hospital personnel management in filling staff vacancies.

Microbiology (Appendix E): Evaluation reveals that there was a brief period of excessive paid productivity in August through October, but the quotient returned to the normal range in November and December. In contrast, the PQ_{wl} has been consistently excessive throughout the last six months—although, the downward trend has been approaching normalcy. The cumulative data also show a spurious distortion in the August-October time frame, similar to that seen with PQ_p.

Corroborative work force data under indicator grouping 15 demonstrate a staffing shortage extant throughout the six month period—six full positions being vacant in December. This shortage has also improved over the profiled period coincident with the same overall trends in productivity. The work force data confirm that the August-October "spike" is most likely related to increased workload during that three month period.

Comparing PQ_p to PQ_{wl} data demonstrates that the former is much less sensitive to work force/workload dysequilibrium than the latter. PQ_p incorporates nonworkload-specific time that tends to absorb low magnitude decreases in work force and increases in workload; whereas, PQ_{wl} excludes nonworkload-weighted time from its calculation, making it much more sensitive to changes in work force strength or specified workload volume. The actions and assessment are appropriate to the somewhat stressful but improving workload management situation.

Histopathology (Appendix G): Evaluation of the productivity quotient data reveals a significant decrease in production effectiveness for both PQ_p and PQ_{wl} throughout the six month profile period. The overall trend for PQ_p is toward improvement; in fact, it returned to within its normal range from October through December. The PQ_{wl}, however, is consistently high, implying chronically ineffective workload management; though there also has been a trend toward improving the PQ_{wl} indicator level, it has plateaued over the last three months.

Corroborative work force information shows significant staff shortages over the last six months. The overall trend has been toward improvement, but that has also plateaued at six vacancies over the last three months. The action and assessment are appropriate, aimed at increasing technical staffing and improving the QM interface between the laboratory and hospital administrative support.

Discussion:

Indicator Grouping: Workload recording and productivity measurement have proven to be extremely helpful tools for managing workload and staff resources. In essence, they normalize workload and personnel resource data so that meaningful comparisons can be made for any given section from one monitoring period to the next. In addition, productivity quotients can be useful for comparing the same type of sections on an interdepartmental—laboratory to laboratory—basis.

However, the laboratorian cannot compare workload data between functionally dissimilar laboratory disciplines since laboratory methods and analytical/diagnostic disciplines, workload units and QI threshold ranges will differ. Such cross-comparisons are not at all meaningful.

For example, any chemistry section usually warrants a relatively higher threshold range for productivity quotients because increased automation and greater processing volume in that section cause higher total workload unit values. In contrast, any transfusion service usually is much less automated, and it processes a relatively lower workload volume—while often still obliged to maintain a work force twenty four hours a day. Thus, the normal productivity levels and threshold ranges for the latter section tend to be lower in value.

Productivity quotient calculation is discussed in Chapter Seven and elsewhere.[1] Basically, the quotients are founded on establishing uniform time units (unit values) that are assigned to each individual technical procedure. Then, the laboratory quantifies the volume of work performed in units of time—usually minutes—or as a percentage of available time.

If one divides the total number of workload-weighted minutes that have been performed in a given surveillance period by the total number of paid work minutes, the result is the PQ_p—the paid productivity quotient. Of course, the total number of paid work minutes includes a significant amount of time allotted for legitimate but "nonproductive" duty activities, including routine supervisory activities, quality management, continuing education, and procedure review.[b] Based on its calculation, PQ_p also incorporates all paid benefit time such as regular vacation time, sick time, and personal time.

The College of American Pathologists (CAP) Workload Recording (WLR) Program also identified the importance of personal, fatigue, and delay (PFD) time, underlining the difficulty in measuring it.[1] Laboratorians frequently overlook "personal" time as a significant workload management parameter. However, it is important enough that there should be some means for systematically monitoring and managing PFD at the supervisory level.

Focusing on the Transfusion Service as the most dramatic example in this text, it is normal that as workload stress increases, the tendency is for some staff members to spend more time attending to their personal needs,

[b] "Nonproductive" duty activities are not directly related to the hands-on production of a laboratory end product, but they are still essential to the achievement of necessary laboratory management and training tasks.

eg, taking more frequent and more lengthy breaks. Although this sounds like McGregor's Theory X of behavioral management, taking such personal time can be a natural, human response to a chronically stressful situation—especially when there is inadequate incentive and motivation.

The same phenomenon also can occur when significant stress is not a factor. In this case, the supervisor can be so lax or unobservant that employees might learn that they can simply abuse their normal personal time privileges (eg, lunch time, other break time, and errand time). In either case, such personal behavior is manageable—but, quality measurement (ie, quality assessment and improvement or QI), quality planning (ie, quality anticipation or QAn), and team building (ie, quality actualization or QAc) are essential ingredients in the solution process.

Through further calculation, if one eliminates all "nonproductive" activities from the denominator—including nonworkloaded duty time and paid benefit time—the result is the PQ_{wl} (the workloaded productivity quotient). The laboratorian can consider the PQ_{wl} as a much more specific measurement of "hands-on," analytical/diagnostic productivity.

Workload can become excessive when either there is an increase in the absolute workload or a decrease in the amount of personnel time (number of FTEs) available to accomplish the workload at hand. In each case, there is more flexibility in managing the total paid time available to perform all operative and organizational tasks, compared to managing the less flexible specified work time required to solely perform the specific analytical/diagnostic workload. Thus, in any of the profile examples, the PQ_p quotient shows greater tolerance to increased workload (or decreased work force), compared to the less tolerant PQ_{wl} that represents the truly absolute, specified workload.

In the case of the Chemistry Section profile, the December PQ_p is within normal limits while the PQ_{wl} is still excessive. This bimodal constellation of quotients suggests that there is a need to fill the six vacancies, but it is not an overwhelming priority—especially since the situation is improving.

In stark contrast, the current Transfusion Service staffing constraints are so severe as to cause both PQ_p and PQ_{wl} to be excessively high; the trend is also rising at an alarming rate as a result of relentless staff attrition. Such a unimodal constellation of quotients combined with such a deteriorating trend provides additive evidence of the stressful workload management situation in this section. Additionally, a 55% personnel vacancy rate in the Transfusion Service obliterates any staffing flexibility that could be represented normally by the PQ_p quotient.

Workload data are very useful for developing and monitoring staffing requirements in collaboration with the monitoring of staff strength. First, identify all factors that affect workload and personnel requirements. Then, derive personnel requirements to accomplish specific workloaded and nonworkloaded tasks. Next, develop a staffing plan for a given position according to the expected workload for that position. Project personnel requirements for changes in number of inpatient days (ie, occupied beds, length of stay, and discharges) and outpatient visits. Calculate and project varying effects of a reduction in FTEs or a reduction in the salary dollar budget. Next, calculate strategies ahead of time for managing variable laboratory workload scenarios, using workload data and productivity quotients. Finally, monitor workload in real time or billable (ordered) tests and match the ongoing results against the already developed staffing models. In these days of changing personnel regulations and the effect of modern total quality management-continuous quality improvement (TQM-CQI) managerial practice, there also could be a need to consider a mix of technologist versus technician, as well as a remodeling (usually a reduction) of the number of managerial FTEs.[2]

There are various methods to ensure the integrity of the workload data—a form of workload management quality control (QC). For example, the laboratorian can convert workload data to ratios of workload units per day or per FTE. One can then graph and monitor these workload parameters on a Levy-Jennings chart just as is used to monitor the control of an analytical procedure. It logically follows that the laboratory section can monitor these workload QC parameters as indexed or focused QI indicators. In order to utilize this surveillance information, the laboratory manager must understand the effects of allocating work hours and know when to reallocate staff and then recompare target utilization levels amongst various work centers within the section.

Additional indicator topics include a number of alternative productivity quotients and other ratios. The nature of these QI targets partially depends on the workload managerial approach: whether it be from the traditional CAP workload management method typical of the laboratorian or from the management engineering approach typical of the hospital administrator. An example of the difference between the two approaches is that the WLR method excludes PFD from time studies and awards a flat amount of time in each worked hour for all nonworkload-weighted activities, including PFD. In comparison, the management engineering method inflates the specific workload-weighted count by a percentage adjustment specifically for PFD; the LMIP also has to approach personal, fatigue, and delay time, indirectly at least. In either case, the laboratorian can devise a quality indicator to target actual PFD by monitoring the time taken for personal breaks. Other potential QI workload management topics include the monitoring of worked productivity (PQ_w), total productivity (PQ_t), available productivity (PQ_a), the workload ratio, raw workload volume, and the workload QC data.[1]

We must direct special consideration to the development of alternative workload management indicators. Many of the QI indicator topics suggested above might be moot in light of the CAP's curtailing their nation-wide WLR program and discontinuing their publishing of updated unit values for specific laboratory procedures. Subsequently, the CAP has shifted its workload management methods to those of the Laboratory Management Index Program. The LMIP relies on nonworkload-weighted parameters as measures of workload management and productivity; it focuses on accounting data such as billable (ordered) tests.

Without being updated, published time-studied workload values will quickly subside in accuracy as new laboratory procedures and techniques continue to emerge. As this attrition of published CAP data occurs, healthcare laboratories will have to rely increasingly on workload measurements based on either 1) locally developed time studies or 2) raw counts and other, more easily derived measurements of both bench procedure-specific and nonprocedure-specific (eg, training and quality management) laboratory activities.

In lieu of the WLR program, the LMIP is providing interlaboratory comparison. As long as each local laboratory practices a consistent QI monitoring approach, its ability to accurately measure workload and staff productivity should be reasonably successful.

Supporting Indicators. Productivity quotients are global quality indicators—as are all operative and organizational managerial activities. The only indicator groupings that are not cross-linked are laboratory product selection and utilization, as is shown in Table VI and VII in Chapter Eight. Consequently, cross-linkage can exist with any of the 25 other groupings used in the quality profile example of this text.

One unique supporting indicator for the productivity grouping that is frequently overlooked is adequacy of facility space. Sufficient physical space is necessary to permit an efficient, logical flow of work from specimen receipt to the interim sequences of the analytical and diagnostic procedures to the final dispatching of the end product. Limited space is not an uncommon detractor from the optimal effectiveness of laboratory resource usage, particularly the use of the human resources.

Commonly, the laboratory poorly plans, studies, or remedies effectiveness of facility space. In fact, it is likely to be one of the most neglected factors in the management of healthcare laboratories. While new technologies, methods, and instrumentation are continually emerging and absorbing space, the laboratory seldom pursues appropriate modification of the work environment.

Such shortsightedness is the result of giving short shrift to the quality measurement, strategic planning and organizational effectiveness programs of an effective TQM system. The result often is a lack of optimizing the true capabilities of new technical developments, the potential productivity of the work force, and the needs of the clinician and the patient.

Threshold. An unusual aspect to productivity quotient thresholds is that they present as a minimum to maximum range. A productivity quotient falling below the minimum level suggests there are more FTEs present than are needed to perform the workload at hand. A quotient exceeding the maximum threshold level suggests that there is more workload to be performed than the number of authorized staff present can accomplish safely in a reasonable amount of time while still maintaining the desired level of end product quality.

Another aspect of these optimal QI ranges is that they vary according to the type of laboratory section being addressed. Regardless of what the productivity measurements are based on (time-weighted or billable tests), they tend to become higher in value as a given section becomes more automated and volume-intensive. The less automated/volume-intensive section will be relatively less productive with a lower value of tolerable limits. This variance of threshold ranges is a reminder that only functionally similar sections can be compared against one another and that quality surveillance thresholds must be appropriate for the type of section being studied.

Monitoring Periodicity. This scheduling depends on the criticalness of the laboratory section or aspect of care and the adequacy of the work force on hand to accomplish the workload. If there is significant personnel workload stress with other danger signs of burnout—such as decreased analytical or diagnostic accuracy—then the periodicity should be more frequent.

Evaluation. Workload recording and productivity measurement are generally "supply and demand" dependent (ie, staff-rich or staff-poor versus high-volume or low-volume). This characteristic is opposed to other QI indicators that are more high-risk or problem-prone in nature. Thus, the evaluation of workload and productivity data greatly depends on the accuracy of the workload data gathering. This collection process can be problematic if the individuals involved in the gathering, organizing, and calculating are not knowledgeable, experienced, and assiduous in their task. In addition, if workload weighting is also part of the program, the unit values must be correct and up-to-date.

Also, productivity measurements are indicators of a dual nature, obviously reflecting both personnel strength and workload volume (ie, the "supply and demand" of laboratory management). Adding further complexity to the picture, staff "strength" is expressible in terms of either work force numbers—or the inherent capability of the absolute work force to perform proficiently (ie, both efficiently and effectively). Posing such a duality, the laboratory cannot evaluate these productivity indicators independently. They can alert the laboratorian to a production bottleneck, but they will not characterize the true impediment.

The critical problem can be personnel strength (ie, either too low or too high) or an inordinate workload volume (ie, either too high or too low). Or, it could be personnel capability based on any number of underlying problems, including inadequate maintenance of proficiency, instrumentation, supplies, or other operative or organizational resources. Consequently, it is imperative that a productivity indicator be used only as evidence in support of other indicators that are more resource-specific in nature.

Action. Quite often, multifaceted opportunities for improving productivity require action that is multiphased with interim options and panorganizational targets. For example, there might be need for the interim reduction of workload by using a reference laboratory or a tightening of the laboratory-clinical criteria for the ordering of certain tests. There might be need for temporarily shifting cross-trained personnel from one section to another. There could be a need for revising instrumentation, allowing for higher specimen volume throughput or increased data automation and transmission. These interim remedial steps would focus on improving a number of different laboratory or clinical activities over a short term while medium- and long-range actions are going into effect. But, the laboratorian cannot rely on just the short-range remedy to resolve a chronic institutional problem.

Also, the laboratory might need to mobilize lateral and higher hospital echelons to help expedite laboratory workload. These nonlaboratory hospital activities echelons might be able to assist in securing personnel or capital expense items needed to resolve an opportunity to improve productivity. Whatever the recommended action might be, the laboratory must select it based on more than just productivity data.

Assessment. Whereas the assessment for the Chemistry Section profile example is benign, the assessment for the Transfusion Service profile is very blunt and critical of the hospital administration and ancillary support activities. However, if QI is going to work—especially in such a crisis as described in the latter profile—the quality manager cannot mince words. In such critical situations, there is neither time nor paper to waste. Determine the assessment and get on with the quality management work at hand. If the hospital and lateral department leadership has bought into the TQM-CQI precepts, there should be some mutual understanding. Not everyone will necessarily like the facts as published—but, they should understand and cooperate to their best ability.

Communication. Again, the sharing of lessons learned from the productivity indicator grouping must be as global as possible. The laboratory needs clinical as well as nonclinical, administrative support to solve serious problems of productivity. Consider all customers-suppliers as potential QI correspondents.

Personnel Management (Indicator Grouping 15)

Chemistry profile interpretation:

This example indicator grouping lists several specified indicators that reflect the effect of personnel strength matched against current workload. The grouping incorporates indicators of actual work force strength (ie, percent vacancy rate) and staff utilization including 16-hour (back-to-back) shifts, overtime hours, and percent availability.

First regarding personnel strength, evaluation of this specified indicator reveals that although there are six technologist vacancies, the vacancy rate

Indicator Grouping 15
Personnel Management

Chemistry Section Quality Profile

Indicator Grouping/ Specific Indicator: Threshold (Periodicity)	QI Data Observations (Date trend started) J A S O N D
Personnel Management (Monthly)	
a. Work force:	
1. Vacancy rate: Technologists: > 10% vacancy	55 50 45 38 31 21 % 6 FTE vacancies in Dec 95
b. Utilization: 1. 16 hour shifts: none!!	s = 16 hour shifts 18 15 17 14 12 11 s
2. Overtime: > 429 hours	532 496 497 477 419 407 h h = hours
c. Availability: 1. % availability: < 80%	84 78 85 90 83 85 %

Transfusion Service Quality Profile

Indicator Grouping/ Specific Indicator: Threshold (Periodicity)	QI Data Observations J A S O N D
Personnel Management (Monthly)	
a. Work force:	- = no vacancy to report
1. Vacancy rate: Supervisor: no vacancy allowed; sentinel event!!	- - - - 100 100 % 1 FTE vacancy since Nov 95
Technologists: > 10% vacancy	21 31 38 45 50 55 % 6 FTE vacancies in Dec 95
b. Utilization: 1. 16 hour shifts: none!!	s = 16 hour shifts 6 8 9 10 11 12 s
2. Overtime (OT): > 126 hours h = hours	419 450 477 532 655 702 h 30% of OT performed in Dec was performed by crosstrained personnel
c. Availability: 1. % availability (technologists): < 80%	90 85 84 83 79 78 %

!! = sentinel event

Evaluation of QI Data, TQM System, and CQI Process	Action Action Person: (Date Initiated)	Assessment of Overall Improvement
Six staff vacancies! BUT trend is steadily decreasing as positions are being filled	Fill 6 positions ACTION: Supervisor	Improvement of hiring is in progress
Excessive but decreasing!	Continue innovative staffing ACTION: Supervisor	Improving
On target and decreasing	Continue innovative staffing ACTION: Supervisor	Improving
On target; superb motivation!!!	Keep up with personnel actions and incentive awards ACTION : Supervisor	Effective total QI process
Supervisor position vacated in Nov 95 There are six vacancies and the trend is increasingly alarming	1. Fill 7 positions with priority on supervisory position 2. Request class action pay raise ACTION: Acting Supervisor 1. Determine interim staffing options 2. Send routine abo and prenatals to reference lab 3. Increase technical automation ACTION: Acting Supervisor 1. Transfer cross trnd staff from other sections ACTION: Dept Lab Manager	Ineffective QI process: Obtain emergency assistance from Hospital Admin and Personnel Office to relieve staff vacancy problem
Excessive and increasing Excessive; has become increasingly severe	Implement more innovative staffing providing more crosstrained staff from other sections ACTION: Acting Supervisor with Dept Lab Manager	Ineffective QI process: Requires Hospital Admin and Personnel Office assistance
Off target!! TREND: technologist availability is steadily decreasing.	1. Fill vacancies 2. Increase incentives ACTION: Action Supervisor	Has been effective BUT this QI parameter began to deteriorate in Nov

significantly decreased over the last six months. This diminishing vacancy rate corresponds to the trend of improving productivity demonstrated in the previous indicator grouping.

In addition, the utilization indicators demonstrate secondary effect. Even though 16-hour work shifts are still shown as being necessary, the trend for this specified QI indicator—as well as the indicator for overtime—is toward reduction. Also, personnel availability for work is at a reasonable level, reflecting positive motivation and reasonable morale.

The concomitant actions and assessments are all appropriate for the facts at hand. Overall, the total indicator grouping is very positive, showing continuous improvement over the six month cumulative period.

Transfusion profile interpretation:
Evaluation of every specified indicator in this grouping spells out trouble for this section. First, the vacancy rate is astronomically high and is steadily increasing. Thus, there is a correlative answer to the quandary presented by the supporting workload and productivity quotient grouping. Not only are there six technologist vacancies, but the full time supervisor position is also empty! It is of interest to note that a comparison of Chemistry Section and Transfusion Service total vacancies reveals that each section lacks six technical FTEs.[c]

The impact of the six laboratory technologist "bench" vacancies is much more devastating for the Transfusion Service because of its smaller authorized size and consequent lack of staffing depth. Plus, the loss of one full time, trained, and experienced supervisor is catastrophic!

Evaluation of the utilization indicators reveals that they are very distorted. For example, the use of back-to-back, 16-hour shifts is increasing beyond imagination; at the same time, the use of overtime is dramatically accelerating. The interpretation is that these utilization indicators are very excessive based on the severe personnel shortage, furthered by inexperienced supervision, and worsened by continuing staff attrition.

In the face of the preceding indicator data, it is a tribute to the positive motivation of the section staff that they have maintained the percent availability at such a high level; still, even this indicator finally deteriorated in the month that the supervisor left. This utilization indicator reflects the amount of sick time and regular vacation time being taken by the employees. Under the degree of duress shown by the workload and work force strength data, it would not be surprising if the section staff used more personal leave time—as well as personal time on the job, ie, PFD.

The laboratory is leveling the planned actions at a diverse group of action persons: the departmental administrative supervisor (or laboratory manager), the section's acting supervisor, the section medical director, and the departmental laboratory manager. These delegated duties range from

[c] All five section profiles exemplified in this text demonstrate a lack of six technological FTEs. The varying impact of this fixed number of staff vacancies depends on the overall authorized strength of each section and the matching workload.

the coordinative activities at the hospital task force level, to cross-sectional staffing at the department/service level, further down to the staffing actions within the section itself. The assessment (made at the department level for this departmental report) focuses on the need for assistance from the hospital administration and the personnel management office.

Additional profile interpretations:

Hematology (Appendix D): Evaluation of this profile reveals two specified indicators for staff vacancy rate—one for technologists and one for secretaries. The technologist vacancies have been creeping upward to six in December—which is above the 10% threshold level. The secretarial vacancy rate has been diminishing over the last six months to one vacancy in December—which is below the 10% threshold level.

The ancillary utilization indicators are listed only for technologist positions. The 16-hour shifts, overtime, and % availability are all showing adverse trends. The recommended actions and assessments are appropriate for the situation. There is need to improve technologist motivation at the section level. Also, there is need to improve the QM interface regarding technologist recruitment and hiring at the hospital administrative support level.

Microbiology (Appendix E): With six vacancies noted in December, the overall trend has been a slow but sure strengthening of the technologist work force. However, the plateauing over the last three months indicates a lull in effective recruitment and hiring activity.

The ancillary utilization indicator for 16-hour shifts reflects absolutely no back-to-back shifts being performed over the last six months, in spite of a significant staff vacancy rate ranging from 23 to 21 percent. Compared to the previous section examples, this observation suggests that the Microbiology Section requires a smaller work force during nonworkday shifts to handle a smaller, albeit mostly hands-on (nonautomated) workload. The use of overtime, albeit still necessary, also has been decreasing over the cumulative period.

At the same time, personnel availability has fluctuated, reaching a "low water" mark in December. The latter could at least partially reflect supervisory authorization of a greater amount of vacation time during a holiday month with a traditionally lower workload. Still, incentives might be improved. The actions and assessments are appropriate.

Histopathology (Appendix G): This section has experienced a stormy six months with a significant technologist staff shortage that has improved but also has plateaued at a total of six vacancies over the last three months. At the same time there has been a worsening secretarial shortage with three vacancies in December.

Ancillary utilization indicators indicate no 16-hour shifts being performed. In this case, the reason is because the AP service operates on only a daytime shift schedule. In spite of the current technologist shortage, the use of overtime is also minimal because of the daytime schedule and limited technical and secretarial staff. Although the staff availability was below the threshold limit in the late summer and fall months, it improved over the last month. The evaluations, actions, and assessments are appropriate for the situation.

Discussion:

Indicator Grouping. Personnel management is of crucial importance to effective laboratory quality management, including the entire TQM system and CQI process. As presented here, this grouping illustrates the use of specified indicators of personnel authorization, recruitment, hiring, allocation, utilization, retention, and attrition. As either personnel attrition or workload expansion becomes excessive, personnel management indicators can help portray the imminence of staff stress and fatigue ("burn out") and foretell the subsequent loss of productivity and proficiency.

As a shrinking laboratory staff becomes increasingly burdened by overwork, the time available for rest, operative and administrative managerial duties, continuing education, and participatory decision making also diminishes. The staff becomes more prone to committing errors all along the path of work flow. The Transfusion Service profile clearly demonstrates this destructive progression of events.

As briefly mentioned under the workload management grouping, there is a concept of critical mass in balancing workload against personnel strength. One definition of critical mass is "the degree of reduced staffing beyond which a section cannot function without demonstrating some significant degradation of operational quality."[d]

For example, the productivity, personnel strength, and utilization data for the Chemistry Section suggest that there is still substantial operational depth and that they have not even come close to reaching their critical mass. Obviously, this section's use of paid workloaded (technical) overtime and nonworkloaded (nontechnical) paid time has helped to accomplish the workload at hand. Still, various minor compromises of the normal duty schedule have probably been necessary to stay within the normal limits of the PQ_p. Besides the use of overtime, there has probably been some borrowing of nonworkloaded (nonbillable) duty time—such as from routine supervisory activities, quality management, and procedure reviews—to provide time for bench work, without cutting short the allotted time for producing a quality end product. Still, review of profile groupings such as customer satisfaction, analytical quality, CME, procedure review, QAn planning, or QAc effectiveness reveals that there has not been any substantial degradation of those important activities.

In comparison, the Transfusion Service profile reveals that the section has reached its critical mass with almost all profile groupings showing some evidence of adverse effect. This is a portrait of blatant organizational decompensation.

[d] Another definition of critical mass could be "the degree of balance between staffing and workload beyond which a section cannot function without demonstrating some significant degradation of operational quality." Any definition of critical mass must assume optimal productivity of all staff members at hand, including the managers.

Regarding additional QI indicator topics, the laboratorian need not restrict personnel management quality indicators to those listed in the sample profiles. For example, personnel strength and utilization indicators are available to monitor various work (or cost) centers of any type or size—including specific work shifts. Laboratory personnel requirements also are correlative to the raw volume of specific laboratory tests, products, and services processed. These correlations to laboratory-specific function and outcome are much more meaningful than matching laboratory personnel requirements to the number of hospital patient discharges, inpatient days of stay, or outpatient visits.

Supporting Indicators. Personnel management activities are as global in effect as the productivity indicator grouping; thus, they are supported by the same 23 other indicator groupings. Only product selection and utilization groupings do not apply since the latter depend on nonlaboratory personnel complying with standards of clinical practice. Of special importance, as staff strength shrinks one must remember employee safety.

Threshold. Each specified indicator used as an example in this grouping requires its own, individual criteria and threshold. In most cases, the laboratory must derive these thresholds empirically, based partly on national guidelines but mostly on local experience and organizational makeup. The laboratory rationale for determining the limiting levels used in this example are as follows:

- The vacancy rate for technologists was arbitrarily established at 10% of the authorized strength. The laboratory considered this as the maximum vacancy level that would be tolerable without significant degradation of laboratory quality. This threshold rate can easily vary, depending on a laboratory unit's authorized strength. For example, if the staff position in question is section supervisor, no vacancy is tolerable—this being a zero defect, sentinel event.

- Any 16-hour shift was considered a sentinel event. No individual should be expected to routinely work back-to-back shifts.

- The acceptable amount of overtime was calculated as the number of overtime hours that are equal to 10% of the total monthly paid work hours. This amount of overtime is comparable to the number of FTE hours represented by the 10% vacancy rate threshold.

- The break even point for percent availability was determined empirically by experience at a large medical center laboratory to be about 80%, which seemed to be the minimally tolerable level. Below that level, there was increased evidence of excessive scheduling of regular vacation time and the taking of excessive sick time. This parameter can also vary significantly depending on the authorized strength and operational milieu.

Indicator Grouping 16
Continuing Medical Education

Chemistry Section Quality Profile

Indicator Grouping/ Specific Indicator: Threshold (Periodicity)	QI Data Observations (Date trend started) J A S O N D
Continuing Education: < 3 hour/mo!! (Monthly)	3 3 3 3 3 3 h h = hours

Transfusion Service Quality Profile

Continuing Education: < 3 hour/mo!! (Monthly) a. Trans Svc staff	1 1 0 1 0 0 h Reflects hrs of immunohematology inservice training
b. Ward 22 staff	Ward 22 evening and night shifts have not been involved in routine or special inservice training re transfusion technique (see External QI notes)

!! = sentinel event

Evaluation. With such an expanse of supporting indicators, there should be ample sources of QI data for evaluating, substantiating, and characterizing any adverse (or positive) effect of workload volume or personnel strength on laboratory function. Personnel strength and utilization also comprise a key management area that requires evaluation of the effectiveness of the quality management (QM) interface between the laboratory and other departments or higher administrative echelons; such managerial coordination can be crucially important.

Action. As shown in the example profiles, the required action for this grouping might involve any laboratory section, service, department, other (lateral or support) department, or higher hospital level of management. There is commonly a need for lateral or higher echelon support of recruitment and hiring actions. Also, there often is need for interim, phased steps to resolve an opportunity to improve personnel management. Remedies include obtaining cross-trained or ancillary support personnel or temporarily diverting workload to a reference laboratory.

Assessment. In assessing the effectiveness of personnel management improvement, the laboratory must consider the three standard options for assessment in a CQI environment. The various specified indicators

Evaluation of QI Data, TQM System, and CQI Process	Action Action Person: (Date Initiated)	Assessment of Overall Improvement
Consistently on target x 6 mo; no improvement of performance noted	Select a focused study for Apr 96 ACTION: Supervisor	Improvement of the QI process is in progress
Off target on regular schedule! Are nondaytime personnel being trained??	Maintain the CME goal of 3 hours/mo ACTION:Acting Supervisor	Inffective CME and QI process: Improvement needed
Educational and training program is not serving nondaytime shifts on wards	Coordinate with Chiefs of Nursing and Medicine to facilitate Ed/Tng Program ACTION: Medical Director	Ineffective followup of CAP requirements for improvement!

exemplified in the various profiles under this grouping demonstrate ample means of exercising all three possibilities.

Communication. In keeping with the potentially broad scope of action that might be necessary to improve personnel strength and staff utilization, the laboratory must transmit lessons learned to all personnel at all echelons involved.

Continuing Education Management (Indicator Grouping 16)

Chemistry profile interpretation:

Evaluation of this example profile's data seems very straightforward: the section has been consistently "on target." Even with six or more FTEs absent, the section team has been able to provide three hours of continuing medical education (CME) every month. This information connotes that the section has established a written CME schedule that has been continuously reviewed and consistently followed. However, even in the face of this superb training record, the evaluation notes that there has been no improvement of any sort over the entire cumulative period.

Could this apparent inattention to lack of improvement be due to the section's proximity to reaching its critical mass? No, it is more likely that the indicator inactivity is due to an insensitive QI process.

Consequently, the quality management team recommends that the supervisor design a focused study topic within the next quarter. Again, this action points out that QI surveillance is not effective in a CQI environment unless there is some indication of improvement along the path to excellence. How does the supervisor go about selecting such a focused study?

First, the supervisor could survey the section work force to determine their opinion of CME topics that they most crucially need and can monitor by the QI process. The laboratory could also target specific topics of instruction, particularly those that are mandatory (eg, universal precautions and fire safety). A focused study could consist of monitoring the percentage of total work force in attendance or monitoring the participation in CME by specialized work centers or work shifts. The profile assessment is appropriate.

Transfusion profile interpretation:
This section's QI data remind the reader that laboratory-related CME is not necessarily restricted to laboratory personnel. For example, this profile segment includes CME monitoring data for both the Transfusion Service and ward 22.

Evaluation of the CME data reveals that it mirrors the current staffing crisis: the section has not met the threshold of three hours of training per month in the last six months; during three of those months (including November and December) the section did not provide any CME at all! One would wonder if a training schedule even exists! Surely, this CME situation—compared to all the others profiled in this text—provides supporting evidence of a section's reaching its critical staffing limitations.

Regarding evaluation of ward 22 CME, the joint observations are in the form of a narrative data statement—there being no numerical data presented. The statement relates what has already been learned under the patient care outcome and laboratory product utilization groupings: nondaytime shifts are lacking training in laboratory-specific techniques. This need is also corroborated under the grouping indicator for external QI (ie, indicator grouping 24).

The sectional-departmental recommendations for action correlate with their evaluation. Besides addressing the surveillance of the intralaboratory CME, there is also the need to coordinate with laboratory customers-suppliers—namely the nursing and medical staff on ward 22. The assessment is appropriate for the actions, QI process, and QM interface requirements at hand.

Additional profile interpretations:

Hematology (Appendix D): Evaluation of the narrative-style data reveals that the section's CME program has been within the three hour threshold for five months, during which a baseline has been in the making. The action and assessment are appropriate.

Microbiology (Appendix E): For comparison, evaluation of this section's narrative-style data reveals that the CME program has been within the three hour threshold for 12 months. An additional observation is that the section has not identified any improvement opportunity during that extensive period. There is no indication that the section has reached its critical mass. The summation is that, in a CQI environment, the section is long overdue in choosing some course of action that would achieve some degree of improvement.

One approach would be to decide that CME is not currently critical enough in priority for monitoring at this time and to curtail surveillance of this indicator as nonproblematic. This would be reasonable as long as it is clear that the CME program is appropriately serving all aspects of laboratory function as planned. Another major approach would be to increase the sensitivity of the grouping by using more specific index or focused studies. In this profile example, the decision is to select a focused study. The assessment is accurate.

Histopathology (Appendix G): This section reports that their surveillance of CME has only been ongoing for two months; a baseline is in its earliest stage of development. The action and assessment are correct for this situation.

Discussion:

Indicator Grouping. In using the term continuing medical education, the word "medical" receives deliberate consideration in this text. Many different healthcare professional groups refer to their own brand of educational programs by their own specialized phrases. In some cases, physicians seem to have claimed the use of the term "medical." Other groups use their own modifiers, such as continuing nursing education. Also, laboratory technologists can earn continuing medical laboratory education credits, assigned specifically to "non-physician associate and clinical scientists."

In reality, we are <u>all</u> medical (or healthcare) professionals. Whoever works on the healthcare "team" should receive continuing medical education when it is in support of patient care. Thus, "medical" should not be considered an elitist term, especially in the CQI environment. Thus, in this text all healthcare professionals are included under the term of CME; college degrees and job descriptions can be sorted out elsewhere.

The Chemistry and Transfusion Service examples illustrate that CME can be a significant QI indicator grouping. The provision of continuing professional training is of crucial importance to staff proficiency, safety, motivation, and morale and should stand alone—rather than being, for instance, a subelement of the personnel management grouping as a measurement of critical mass.

Also, it is advisable that a laboratory differentiate CME from the teaching of organizational programs and skills in its QAc program. As illustrated, the quality profile format stipulates that a section will perform three hours of CME per month. As is shown under the grouping for QAc (ie, indicator grouping 26), the section also has planned an additional *one hour per month for organizational skills training*. All of this amounts to a total of four training hours per month (or one hour per week) for one type of training or the other. Yes, this is an ambitious goal—for instructional purposes—or to set an example.

Additional indicator topics are as replete under this CME indicator grouping as the list of potential educational subjects is long. As suggested by the above profile example, the laboratory can use multiple indexed or focused studies.

First, monitor the inservice schedule and any laboratory-specific training earned by laboratory personnel outside the facility. Second, bring QI attention to bear on laboratory-related CME activities provided to nonlaboratory personnel. Although the wards and clinics are important, that does not leave hospital support activities off the hook.

For example, it is usually the fire marshal who comes into the laboratory to instruct laboratorian in fire safety, but why not *vice versa*? Why not invite the fireman to learn more about laboratory-unique operations relevant to fire hazards and discuss the resolution of current OFIs for which the fireman might have some answers? Does the fire marshal know everything there is to know about the laboratory that would make the marshal's job more effective? What does the fire marshal *need to know*? Or the personnel administrator? Or the facility engineer? Or the custodial engineer? Consequently, there is a wealth of CME focused study topics that any laboratory section can rank and prioritize as important for QI surveillance.

Supporting Indicators. As is shown in Table VI and VII of Chapter Eight, laboratory CME is a global indicator—it affects or is affected by all other 25 indicator groupings in the profile format. Except for workload and personnel, all seven other operative resource management groupings are totally global in nature.

Threshold. The example indicator grouping threshold symbolically states that "there should be at least three hours of CME training per month"—less than three hours violates the threshold. In-service education is important not only as a means of sharing QI information but also as a team building and team sustaining activity. Therefore, considering the way that the requirement is couched, an unmet scheduled requirement is virtually a sentinel event; there must be at least three hours of CME per month, 100% of the time.

Even though CME is so fundamentally important, unfortunately it is almost always the first of the operational mission requirements to fall by the wayside in times of resource constraints and operational curtailment. It seems that managers often think that they can catch up on the training schedule later. This is a fallacy; a laboratory cannot catch up on lost training time without experiencing some degradation to the organization's effectiveness.

Monitoring Periodicity. This scheduling depends on the criticalness of the aspect of care being monitored and the adequacy of the quality management resources that are at hand.

Evaluation. Considering how globally germane CME is to the entire scope of laboratory operational effectiveness, evaluation of the QI data should include a perusal of all supporting indicators. Consequently, the laboratorian can direct a keen eye and ear to any overt or covert clue of opportunities to improve the CME effort—to make the organization more effective.

CME is so closely linked to the tenth QI process step of communication that each is an important corollary of the other.[g] Monitoring the data for both groupings provides mutual feedback of information at all intralaboratory and interdepartmental QM interface levels. Thus, the laboratory should pay heed to cross-sectional laboratory educational needs, as well as the needs for laboratory-clinical cross-disciplinary training in regard to adequate coverage of QI lessons learned; the two schedules can merge.

Action. Since CME is a universal linchpin between staff capability and operational effectiveness for all sections, services, and departments, any recommendations for action should cover <u>all</u> the appropriate functional targets. Consequently, there is often need to delegate implementation and follow-up responsibilities to several individuals working at multiple intralaboratory and nonlaboratory focal points. The laboratory should include all involved work centers and all shifts in the training program—ie, the late night shift workers cannot be orphaned. Subsequently, CME often requires phasing and repetition.

It is important that joint coordination is frequently needed for combined laboratory and clinical CME. Also, the laboratory needs to target *nonclinical support* activities for combined education such as hospital administrators, hospital personnel managers, medical maintenance managers, fire fighters, safety officers, contractors, and suppliers.

Assessment. The three standard options for assessment in the CQI environment also apply to the CME indicator grouping. The quality profile can include statements directed at follow-up of previously recommended QI action—such as the Transfusion Service's inadequate meeting of the continuing education threshold and their ineffective follow-up of an earlier CAP inspection recommendation related to ward 22. Likewise, sectional-departmental assessment ends up as a query as to whether there is need for improving the QI process or the QM interface.

Communication. As already noted under Evaluation, the CME grouping embodies the very essence of the tenth step of the QI process. Dissemination of any QI lessons learned <u>is</u> CME, in one form or another—whether it be by a memo or policy statement that is broadcast throughout

[g] This statement alludes to the surveillance of the internal QI process under profile grouping 23. The laboratory can use that profile grouping to study the effectiveness of QI communication of lessons learned. Often, however, that type of communication is best suited as an up-dating of laboratory and nonlaboratory personnel on improved operational procedure during in-service CME training.

Indicator Grouping 17
Methods and Procedures Review

Chemistry Section Quality Profile

Indicator Grouping/ Specific Indicator: Threshold (Periodicity)	QI Data Observations (Date trend started) J A S O N D
Methods & Procedures Review: must be on time!! (Annually per Monthly Schedule)	Monthly review schedule is up-to-date

Transfusion Service Quality Profile

Methods & Procedures Review: must be on time!! (Annually per Monthly Schedule)	SOPs have not been reviewed per schedule for 6 mo

SOP = standing operating procedure !! = sentinel event

the organization, informal comments made during a staff meeting, or some type of formal inservice presentation.

Methods and Procedures Management (Indicator Grouping 17)

Chemistry profile interpretation:
Based on the threshold statement, the section has designed its review schedule by dividing all of the operational procedures into calendar month groups and performing a substantive review of each procedure during the allotted time frame. From this report, one would surmise that there is an up-to-date schedule for reviewing all laboratory section procedures—including all pre-, intra-, and postlaboratory written procedural guides for clerical, technical, analytical, diagnostic, operative resource management and organizational management operations.

Evaluation of this section's narrative data reveals that the annual review of methods and procedures is right on schedule. The action connotes that the yearly review cycle begins in March with a new schedule due at that time. The assessment for this ongoing process is appropriate given such an excellent record.

Transfusion profile interpretation:
Evaluation of this section's narrative data reveals that the review process is significantly off schedule—another indication of this section's exceeding its

Evaluation of QI Data, TQM System, and CQI Process	Action Action Person: (Date Initiated)	Assessment of Overall Improvement
Consistently on target	Finalize new review schedule for Mar 96 ACTION: Supervisor	Improvement of the review process is in progress
Off target because of staff shortage	Resume review schedule, using cross-sectional support ACTION: Acting Supervisor	Improvement of the review process is in progress

critical mass. This serious breach of procedural review is not surprising in view of the documented staff shortage and other indicators of personnel stress and overburdening workloads.

In reviewing supporting indicators, the procedure review indicator is a good example of how nonworkload-weighted operational requirements can receive short shrift in favor of the workload weighted bench duties. Referring to indicator grouping 14 as an example, the PQ_{wl} for December theoretically implies that the equivalent of 71 minutes worth of analytical, directly patient-related workload was accomplished for every 60 minute work hour during the reporting period. For that seemingly impossible achievement to be the case, the section had to ignore practically all nonworkload-weighted laboratory duties—thus, procedure review, CME, and other crucially important (but "nonproductive") operative and organizational activities were left unattended. Mirroring the lack of time to address procedure review, analytical proficiency has become significantly impaired.

The PQ_{wl} of 71 minutes is statistically possible if one can imagine that the usually allotted time for technical procedures is being truncated in order to squeeze the amount of workload at hand into the relentless limits of the amount of time left in a day—all because of personnel shortage. In other words, the staff is taking managerial and technical short cuts to get the work done. A number of other indicator groupings in the Transfusion Service profile also attest to the ripple effect of the excessive staff vacancy rate. The action and assessment for this procedure review grouping are appropriate.

Additional profile interpretations:

Hematology (Appendix D): Evaluation of the narrative report reveals that the procedure review schedule is consistently on target. But, in the face of a relatively serious staff shortage, who is doing the review and when? This profile suggests that, if the procedure review is really to be accomplished, there are many ways to delegate the scheduled review workload in order to achieve the objective. The action and assessment are appropriate for a nonproblematic situation.

Microbiology (Appendix E): Evaluation of this narrative statement reveals an example of a section accepting "on target" QI indicator data for too long a period. The options in a CQI environment are as usual in this situation: 1) deem that the indicator is not high enough in priority to warrant attention at this time or 2) select a more specific indexed or focused study. The section has chosen the latter action. The assessment is accurate considering the new course of action.

Histopathology (Appendix G): This section's profile report provides a numerical data base. It is evident that there was a slight lull in effectiveness during August when the section was experiencing its most severe personnel shortage. However, the two procedures that were missed in August were reviewed in September and October. Thus, the current evaluation, action and assessment are all accurate.

Discussion:

Indicator Grouping. This grouping fits into the suggested profile and path of work flow because of the fundamental importance of using up-to-date laboratory methods and procedures. Thus, the laboratory quality management team should periodically monitor every functional section for its adherence to its procedure review schedule. This QI requirement includes reviewing the written procedures for all operative as well as organizational resource managerial activities. Every active operational procedural method is of importance.

The quality management team at the section level is responsible for this review. At a minimum, the review team for a given procedure should consist of the employee working closest to the procedure (ie, the lead technologist or resource "operator"), the chief supervisor or manager, and the medical director. The employee closest to the given procedure should perform the review—if at all possible.

Additional indicators are easy to identify. First, the laboratorian can divide the major indicator grouping into more specific monitoring targets for pre-, intra, and postlaboratory procedures. These indicator topics are further divisible into categories for analytical/diagnostic (ie, technical and interpretive), clerical, operative resource management, and organizational resource management (ie, QI, QAn, and QAc program) plans and schedules. One or more of these specific categories might be of critical-enough priority (based on the usual volume/risk/problem-prone criteria) to warrant QI attention over the others.

Also, this indicator grouping offers a splendid opportunity to utilize backlog as a throughput-like indicator parameter. In this sense, the reviewing task at hand is very similar to that experienced at the technical bench: there is an established volume workload to process in a finite time frame. Whereas the review threshold describes the TAT required to accomplish the task, the section can also define and monitor a backlog restriction—as with any other throughput situation.

Supporting Indicators. As mentioned in the profile interpretation, this indicator grouping is clearly global in impact—as are almost all the operative resource management indicators. In other words, method and procedure review can affect every one of the 25 other groupings in one way or another.

Threshold. Is procedure review an all or none indicator—as much, for example, as the indicator grouping for CME or determinative quality is a sentinel-type event? Under ordinary circumstances, the answer is "No."

For one thing, there is greater flexibility in procedure review; there is greater tolerance in organizational variance from the ideal of a completely on-schedule review. Since other indicator groupings—such as customer/patient satisfaction, employee safety, laboratory product utilization—usually have higher priority, it is reasonable to provide some flexibility in meeting procedure review schedules in order to provide time for addressing higher priority issues.

Performing laboratory-wide procedure revision takes time and word processing resources; thus, the laboratory needs to parcel out those resources judiciously. Therefore, the threshold demonstrated in this example quality profile format states that every procedure should be reviewed within the calendar year that it is scheduled (ie, "annually per monthly schedule"). The section could tighten this limitation by stipulating "semiannually per monthly schedule," "quarterly per monthly schedule," or "monthly per monthly schedule." Definitions of these threshold options are as follows:

- Annually per monthly schedule—as long as the overall monthly review quotas are met over the course of the entire review year, the threshold limitation is satisfied. If one or more scheduled reviews are missed in a given month, there is no investigative evaluation as long as the section catches up within the allotted year.
- Semiannually per monthly schedule—the grace period for accomplishing the monthly schedule is six months.
- Quarterly per monthly schedule—there is a three month grace period.
- Monthly per monthly schedule—there is no grace period; the monthly schedule must be precisely met. This exacting threshold defines a sentinel event; it is an all or none requirement: all scheduled procedures must be reviewed; if even one is missed, an investigative evaluation is warranted.

Given the quarterly-based threshold for example, if a written procedure for routine urinalysis is scheduled for review in February, as long as it is reported as being reviewed sometime in January, February, or no later than the end of March, the review process has met the QI threshold limitation. Of course, a well-organized, adequately supported section will review each procedure during the target month, as scheduled—no sooner, no later.

Keep in mind that the quality management team can always change the threshold requirements. If a given section is continuously falling behind with a growing backlog of unreviewed procedures, the team can revise the threshold to be less flexible—for example, allowing for only a six month window of flexibility instead of one year. Thus, a threshold is a dynamic monitoring tool—just as all elements of the QI process should be.

Monitoring Periodicity. The scheduling of procedure review deserves some explanation. A CAP accreditation requirement is that every laboratory procedure should be reviewed annually.[h] This requirement does not necessarily specify adherence to the Gregorian calendar year or fiscal calendar year. Rather, it refers to a specific procedure review calendar year as designated by the laboratory quality management team. The span of this review year can be totally separate from any other operational cycle and is often dictated by the timing of a CAP, Joint Commission on Accreditation of Healthcare Organizations (JCAHO), American Association of Blood Banks (AABB), or other accreditation survey.

In the worst of cases, the section accomplishes its procedure review in one "fell swoop," very perfunctorily at the last minute just before a scheduled accreditation survey. Thus, any chance for a substantive review is lost because of poor planning, lack of interest, and expediency—"just to get it done before the ultimate external QI deadline."

In the best of cases, each section (either technical, diagnostic, or administrative support) will inventory all plans and procedures and then schedule each one for a thorough review, spaced out over a 10- or 12-month period. Each procedure has a specific monthly anniversary date for review. A 10-month review schedule is helpful for providing two extra months for final administrative polishing of the procedures.

Evaluation. A written procedure is a miniplan. And—as with any other plan—mission, goals, objectives, methods, and means (resources) are always subject to change. Thus, each section must periodically revise its plans and procedures to keep up with the times.

Of particular relevance to up-to-dating methods and procedures is the continuously changing work force due to the gaining of new personnel. All personnel—including those that are new—must periodically review all procedures which are important to their laboratory role. In fact, orientation review is a reasonable QI indicator worth monitoring on occasion. At the very least, up-to-date procedures must be readily available to them "at the bench."

[h] For CAP (and other accreditation agency) purposes, the laboratory usually interprets this requirement as referring to only technical/analytical/diagnostic-related procedures. This text recommends that the review include all laboratory plans and procedures.

Now, what if an employee goes to the procedural manual and finds some critically important step crossed out with faintly hand-scribbled changes? A new individual, especially, then has to go out of the way to seek accurate, clarifying information—or resort to using the outmoded or poorly handwritten directions at hand.

Thus, the poor quality of written procedures can reach out to dissatisfy the employee, the attending physician, and even the patient. In the flow of events, several other aspects of laboratory operative and organizational quality also can suffer. Therefore, the laboratory has to consider all of the peripheral aspects of procedure review during the evaluation of the related QI surveillance data.

To assist in the evaluation, the procedure review grouping is typically cross-linked with all other 25 supportive indicators. Thus, evaluation of the effect of procedure review can be greatly facilitated by perusal of all supporting indicator groupings. Their indirect contributing action—as well as their own "down stream" externality effect—can be as subtle as those noted for the CME or QAc grouping (indicator grouping 26) and as perniciously dangerous, if neglected.

Action. Although this indicator topic might be global in effect, its immediate sphere of influence and, thus, the main target for investigative and follow-up action is at the sectional level. If there is a serious delay in procedure review, the quality management team must direct its action toward improving the education and motivation of the supervisor and staff, while also addressing any other underlying factors such as personnel shortage.

These actions should emphasize improving the procedure review process, not disciplining some individual. There are many steps along the path of work flow worthy of addressing before an individual has to be singled out for corrective action. This philosophy is true when the laboratory is acting on the improvement of any QI indicator grouping.

The procedure review issue is another area where it is easy to become "clinophobic" and ignore the input of the clinicians in seeking the resolution of an OFI at hand. Whenever a laboratory procedure rests on 1) the adequacy of analytical or diagnostic clinical standards of practice or 2) clinical information to assist in the interpretation of a laboratory test result, it is mandatory to include appropriate clinical and other nonlaboratory staff in the review of the relevant portions of the subject laboratory procedure. Just make a copy and send it to an appropriate clinician for review. This approach not only ensures the integrity of the procedure audit process, but also enhances essential communication between laboratorians and clinicians.

Assessment. The section must consider the three standard options for assessing procedure review effectiveness in the CQI environment. First consider the effectiveness of recommended actions. If the QI surveillance process does not achieve improvement over a reasonable time, then the assessment should consider whether or not the threshold is sensitive enough, the reporting data is accurate enough, or the action warrants a

Indicator Grouping 18
Information Management

Chemistry Section Quality Profile

Indicator Grouping/ Specific Indicator: Threshold (Periodicity)	QI Data Observations (Date trend started) J A S O N D
Computer Management: a. Unscheduled down time: > 24 hours (Monthly)	No OFI identified x 6 mo

Transfusion Service Quality Profile

Indicator Grouping/ Specific Indicator: Threshold (Periodicity)	QI Data Observations (Date trend started) J A S O N D
Computer Management: a. Unscheduled down time: > 24 hours (Monthly)	No OFI identified x 2 mo

more focused study. Also, the assessment should consider the QM interface effectiveness.

Communication. Much has already been said about sharing the procedure review—including QI lessons learned—with the clinical staff and hospital administrative staff. Therefore, transmission of QI information regarding this indicator grouping is fairly straightforward: it should reach all laboratorians and nonlaboratorians involved in the subject review.

A good example of the unconventional intricacies of such global communication is provided by the review of procedures for department and section level supply procurement, storage, and inventory. In this case, the process of communicating lessons learned could include all supply managers not only within the laboratory but also at the extralaboratory level, including the hospital-level administration and external supply and manufacturing organizations.

Information Management (Indicator Grouping 18)

Chemistry profile interpretation:
Evaluation of the QI data for a general survey of unscheduled computer down time reveals that no opportunities for improvement have been identified over a six month baseline. This general survey of incident and other sectional feeder reports has not brought any opportunities to the surface, either positive or adverse. This rather passive approach—ie, just

Evaluation of QI Data, TQM System, and CQI Process	Action Action Person: (Date Initiated)	Assessment of Overall Improvement
On target x 6 mo; general baseline has been established	Establish a focused study for Feb 96 ACTION: Supervisor	Improvement of the QI process is in progress
On target x 2 mo; baseline is being established	None needed	Improvement of the QI process is in progress

waiting for something to happen—can be effective only if there is a significant amount of indicator event activity.

A general baseline can be valuable for the record. However, after six to nine months of indicator inactivity it is prudent to modify the QI process and select a topic for a focused study—or curtail the computer management grouping altogether in favor of a higher priority quality issue. Consequently, the action established by the section to select a focused study and increase the sensitivity of the QI process is justifiable—just as is the section-department quality team assessment.

Transfusion profile interpretation:
This section's computer management profile demonstrates a general survey that has only begun to establish a baseline. The evaluation, action, and assessment are all quite in order with the beginning of such a survey.

Additional profile interpretations:

Hematology (Appendix D): Whereas the former two profiles present data in a narrative form, this profile example demonstrates numerical data for unscheduled down time. The general indicator threshold expresses down time as total hours over a month's time. Down time has been in excess of the 24 hour threshold limit for the last three months, purportedly due to hard drive failure. This computer malfunction has resulted in adding workload at the bench by forcing technologists to manually report, distribute, and file laboratory results. In the face of an increasing personnel shortage, this added workload is critically important to an already overburdened laboratory staff.

The section is aiming its action at improving communication with the hospital computer operations activity. The assessment of the adverse trend and the overall need for improvement of lateral department support is accurate.

Microbiology (Appendix E): This section's report offers numerical data. Aside from sporadic unscheduled computer down time that was below the threshold but scattered over the six month cumulative period, significant down time has occurred in October and December. This seems to be a random occurrence but it also could be slowly increasing in its severity. Although this much less automated section might be somewhat less affected by computer malfunctioning than a more automated section, still the section's handling of final results requires computer assistance. Thus, an already reduced section staff is being randomly stressed by computer malfunction.

Action is more thoroughly outlined than in the Hematology profile report: improve liaison with the Computer Operations Department and upgrade the section's plan for backup response when the computer system is inoperable. The assessment is accurate regarding the overall state of improvement and the importance of the QM interface between the laboratory and the computer operations activities.

Histopathology (Appendix G): Evaluation of this section's narrative report reveals that there is need to establish an AP laboratory information service—from scratch! The action is appropriate.

The assessment that the QI process has been ineffective is due to the inordinate amount of time that it has taken for the AP quality management team to recognize the reality of their situation. It is also accurate that there is need for improved hospital-level support to facilitate a speedy remedy of the situation at the QM interface.

Discussion:

Indicator Grouping: Ordinarily, computer operations departments plan scheduled down time for routine maintenance with advance notice and during low volume hours without significant effect on laboratory operations. It is unscheduled computer down time that can significantly deter laboratory staff productivity and effectiveness—both clerical and technical.

Many modern laboratory sections have become totally dependent on an automated laboratory and hospital information system. Computers of various types are used for automated analysis, report (word) processing, report distribution, other types of electronic communication, quality management activities, and archival storage. Laboratory-specific instruments and smaller computers can be on-line within a local laboratory network or laboratory information system—or they can be integral to a large-scale, hospital-wide hospital information system.

Implementing and upgrading computerization usually results in the enhancement of any laboratory operational process. The trade off is that a computer malfunction at any economy of scale spells trouble. A malfunctioning (the proverbial "crash") of any portion of a computer system can adversely affect almost any laboratory activity. Resultant unscheduled computer down time can cause delayed TAT and even lost data at virtually every step of the laboratory path of work flow. It can also result in unwarranted workload stress on personnel and other resources.

The general indicator grouping for computer management opens up a unique world of QI surveillance possibilities. The specific quality indicators that can be included under this grouping span the entire breadth of computer technology and application.[i] Topics for consideration include the need to improve

- Archival capacity
- Various passive and interactive—as well as intermediate and peripheral—devices such as bus interfaces, printers and monitors
- General and specialized software programs not on-line
- Programs that are already on-line
- Hardware malfunctioning with unscheduled mainframe or peripheral device down time.

For demonstration purposes, the quality profile format unscheduled down time as a specified quality indicator for computer management.

Supporting Indicators. Computer management indicators of quality are global in cross-linkage with other profile groupings, a characteristic of almost all operative resource activities. Thus, any of the 25 other indicator groupings listed in the sample profile can easily reflect some effect secondary to a change in computer system function.

Threshold. The criticalness of computer system effectiveness can range from that of a sentinel event to a rather flexible comparative rate indicator activity. This all depends on the nature of the computer malfunction, the nature of the involved laboratory section, the level of patient-risk inherent to the affected laboratory aspects of care, and the depth of backup computer resources at hand. Data entry backlog thresholds can be of key importance to signal critical mass of staff overload if manual entry is necessary.

Monitoring Periodicity. This scheduling depends on the criticalness of the important aspects of laboratory healthcare support affected and the adequacy of all relevant backup resources at hand.

Evaluation. There is an extensive amount of corroborative evidence available from cross-linked indicator groupings as well as multidisciplined laboratory sections. This supporting evidence can substantially facilitate the evaluation of the status of computer operations and their comprehensive

[i] Review of the CAP accreditation general inspection checklist for computer operations requirements will provide numerous surveillance topic candidates.[3]

Indicator Grouping 19
Equipment Management

Chemistry Section Quality Profile

Indicator Grouping/ Specific Indicator: Threshold (Periodicity)	QI Data Observations (Date trend started) J A S O N D
Equipment: resolution of any opportunity must be complete within one quarter!! (Quarterly)	1. Multichannel Analyzer X is under constant QC scrutiny 2. Analyzers A (routine chemistry) and B (ICU) show disparate results

Transfusion Service Quality Profile

Equipment: repair must be complete within one quarter!! (Quarterly)	0 - - 0 - - 0 = no OFI identified - = no report scheduled

!! = sentinel event

effect on related laboratory functions. Computer support activities are of such a pervasive nature that evaluation of their effectiveness might reveal not only intralaboratory but also pre- and postlaboratory clinical components to any related OFI. Backlog of data entry can indicate the staff and time required to resolve a computer downtime situation.

Action. Any action necessary to resolve the effects of computer down time and improve computer operations should include consideration of interim options or phased backup steps. For example, if there is an inordinate amount of unscheduled down time, the laboratory must take steps to resolve the computer maintenance or repair problem and—in the interim—identify actions to mollify the lack of computer support in the laboratory work area. Written backup plans should be in place and should be a part of the procedure review mentioned earlier. These plans should include critical thresholds to ensure operational stability.

Assessment. The laboratory must exercise the standard three options for assessing remedial actions, QI process, and QM interface in the CQI environment, however appropriate.

Communication. Based on the global nature of this computer management grouping, lessons learned should be disseminated to all intra- and extralaboratory personnel involved in or affected by laboratory computer function. Often, a computerized laboratory information system is operated, maintained, and repaired by a specific nonlaboratory computer

Evaluation of QI Data, TQM System, and CQI Process	Action Action Person: (Date Initiated)	Assessment of Overall Improvement
Replacement of Analyzer X is prolonged; on-site visits are scheduled in Jan 96; eval of analyzers A and B is in progress	1. Replace multichannel Analyzer X 2. Resolve Analyzer A and B disparity immediately ACTION: Supervisor	Improvement needed; too prolonged decision making re Analyzer X
No report scheduled; next report due Jan 96	---------	---------

operations activity. In such a case, there should be effective two-way dialogue between the laboratory and that hospital-level support activity.

Equipment Management (Indicator Grouping 19)

Chemistry profile interpretation:
The equipment management grouping for this section consists of a general indicator. The QI indicator definition encompasses maintenance, repair, or replacement of all section equipment. The wording of its threshold is in equally general terms: "resolution of any opportunity must be complete within one quarter." The periodicity of review is also quarterly.

Evaluation of the Chemistry Section data reveals, that a multichannel analyzer X and two disparate analyzers (A in the routine chemistry laboratory and B in the intensive care unit laboratory) require managerial attention. It is the process of resolving the multianalyzer problem that is off target—and it is the quality of organizational decision making that is most wanting. The earlier mentioned profile grouping for analytical quality already has corroborated the status of both improvement opportunities. Later in the profile, further substantiation of the organizational level problems at hand will be evident under the groupings for quality planning (ie, indicator grouping 25) and quality decision making (ie, indicator grouping 26).

The recommended actions address remedies for both equipment management opportunities. The assessment is in keeping with all the facts at hand—many of which have already been made available through other supporting indicators.

Transfusion profile interpretation:
The equipment management grouping for this laboratory section is still of the general type but consists of a slightly more specific definition regarding repair. The threshold is worded in equally limited terms: "repair must be complete within one quarter." Thus, compared to the Chemistry Section, this section's equipment manager grouping consists of an indicator that encompasses only repair, excluding maintenance and replacement and lacking mention of any particular piece of equipment.

An evaluation of this quarterly scheduled indicator reveals that no report is due for the month of December. Subsequently, there is no action or assessment statement required.

Additional profile interpretations:

Hematology (Appendix D): Evaluation of the narrative data reveals that there has been no OFI identified for the last three quarters. There is no indication as to whether the cumulative data represent a nine month baseline or a much longer data record. However, there is a dual revelation that 1) due to indicator inactivity and 2) due to the threshold being too lenient, there is need to develop a more sensitive QI process and select a focused study—or spend quality management time on a higher priority indicator grouping altogether. The action and assessment are appropriate.

Microbiology (Appendix E): This section demonstrates three specified indicators; each indicator focuses on one piece of equipment that has required some sort of maintenance support. The first issue relates to a need for support by the Computer Operations Department since April 1995; the other two issues involve Medical Maintenance Department support needed since July 1994 and September 1995. The computer support has been delayed for six months; medical maintenance for one major project was delayed for one and a half years (finally being resolved in December) and the second, more minor project has been delayed for four months.[j]

The chief lesson provided here is that the laboratory quality management team must deal with problems at the QM interface between the laboratory and lateral (or higher echelon) support departments. This issue is often a QI consideration to some degree or another; in this example, it is a problem of a major degree of importance. The actions for the three separate issues are appropriate in attempting to continue coordinated resolution of the various problems with two separate hospital support activities.

[j] The safety hood problem is already adequately addressed under the employee safety and facility grouping. But, it could be listed under this equipment grouping as well.

The assessment points out the ineffectiveness of the laboratory <u>and</u> hospital-level QI process in dealing with poor equipment maintenance support; even though one medical maintenance initiative was finally resolved in December, it was after an inordinately long time. A special "QI Note" emphasizes the need for the laboratory department leadership to become involved in the improvement process by dealing with the hospital administration directly.

Histopathology (Appendix G): This section's profile demonstrates the use of numerical data to portray the effectiveness of equipment management. Based on the quarterly review schedule, there is no report planned for December. However, in spite of there being no need for a report this month, the quality management team has decided that there has already been insufficient indicator activity for this general survey approach, warranting the scheduling of a focused study. The assessment is accurate.

Discussion:

Indicator Grouping: The quality of laboratory equipment performance, including analytical and diagnostic instruments, can affect the entire chain of laboratory processes that ultimately proceed to customer satisfaction. It is important to remember that there are many significant pieces of laboratory equipment aside from the most expensive, "centerpiece" analytical instruments. Some equipment are not so glamorous but still serve critically important functions. Safety hoods are a chief example of the latter; they might be ugly and sit in an obscure corner, but they are extremely important in safeguarding the health and welfare of the employee (ie, indicator grouping 3).

There is a procurement, maintenance, and repair life cycle for all pieces of laboratory equipment. First, equipment/instrument function has to match laboratory-clinical need. Next, the laboratory satisfies that need by procuring an appropriate device—either by loan, lease, reagent rental, or direct purchase. Then there must be sustaining of equipment performance by routine calibration, maintenance, and repair. Finally, the equipment life cycle is complete when the piece has to be replaced through new procurement.

The effectiveness of all of these events in the life cycle of any piece of equipment are potential targets for QI surveillance. Each event is a candidate as a quality indicator topic—either general or specified (ie, indexed or focused); this is illustrated as follows:

- Instrument down time is an example of a *general* indicator topic.
- Multichannel analyzer X down time is a *specified* indicator.
- Following the routine maintenance of the multichannel analyzer X over an indeterminate time as a general baseline is an *indexed* study.
- Scheduling the repair of the multichannel analyzer X until the specific problem is resolved constitutes a *focused* study.

Regarding repair, positive rapport must be fostered with the medical maintenance and repair service—this being a typically reciprocal customer-supplier relationship. Consequently, while instrument down time is a very specific, direct indicator, the quality of QAc and team building between the laboratory and medical maintenance (or other departments such as computer operations) is also potentially important. A similarly mutual interdepartmental relationship should exist between the laboratory and the hospital activities responsible for contracting and purchasing. Even mutual CME is worthwhile entertaining. All of these relationships are grist for the laboratory QAc program.

Additional indicator topics include all the potential QI targets of the equipment procurement, maintenance, and repair life cycle. An alert quality management team can direct general or specified QI indicator attention to any of these cyclic elements for any piece of laboratory equipment for any laboratory section.

Another additional topic is monitoring equipment safety and protecting the employee from any harm. Although this overlaps the employee safety grouping under the outcome segment, the general topic still is approachable at this level of the quality profile. The quality management team can define this issue on the basis of the usual high-volume of use, high-risk to the patient, and problem-prone to the employee (or patient) criteria inherent to a given piece of equipment. The nature of threat might include biological, electrical, ionizing radiation, electromagnetic/radio wave radiation, thermal (hot or cold), auditory, visual, or sharp and blunt injury hazards.

Supporting Indicators. Although there is a global relationship amongst the supporting indicators for this equipment management grouping, there are some particularly important ones. Key outcome indicator groupings are customer need satisfaction and employee safety; a key process indicator grouping is analytical/functional quality; equally key ancillary operative resource groupings are work force strength and budget and the three organizational-level groupings for QI surveillance, QAn planning, and QAc coordination.

Threshold. The quality tolerance level for equipment management depends on the nature of the laboratory-clinical aspects of care affected by equipment performance, as well as the adequacy of the supporting operative and organization resources at hand at both the laboratory and hospital levels.

Monitoring Periodicity. This scheduling depends on the criticalness of the laboratory-clinical aspects of care served by the subject equipment and the adequacy of supporting resources. Usually, this indicator is well enough served by a quarterly review, based primarily on the "reasonable amount of time" that is often necessary for major repair of a high technology instrument. Obviously, this timing depends on the caliber of the medical maintenance or any other organizational activity providing support to laboratory equipment.

Evaluation. There is ample cross-linkage of supporting indicators and a wealth of substantive direct indicators to afford easy evaluation of equipment/instrument quality—throughout its entire life cycle. This evaluation will vary in nature from one section to another because each laboratory work center offers unique equipment and environmental characteristics, including those of employee safety. Aside from the quality management of analytical/diagnostic instruments, there is a multitude of other mechanical devices that require equally careful QI surveillance.

Action. Calibration, maintenance, repair, or replacement of instruments—and all other mechanical equipment—must be accomplished in a timely and cost-effective manner. There should be a cost analysis to decide whether to perform an instrumental procedure in-house ("to make") or to utilize an outside reference laboratory ("to buy"). If the former, then there is the decision to acquire the needed instrument either by loan, by direct purchase, by lease, or by reagent rental.

It may be necessary to observe the on-site operation of a candidate instrument in an environment similar to one's own laboratory. In the interim, the laboratory must maintain careful observance of QC, possibly reduce the workload, and even consider short term use of a reference laboratory in order to maintain patient care quality. Again, resolution of equipment management problems requires joint laboratory-clinical coordination to ensure the most informed decision making—and to maintain the integrity of the joint organization.

Regarding the disparate analyzers A and B, such lack of correlative results must be resolved or credibility among the clinicians will plummet for *both* instruments. This problem must be resolved immediately. Use a reference laboratory, if at all necessary, before the clinicians start sending their patient specimens to the same reference laboratory!

Assessment: The laboratory must consider the three standard options for assessing remedial actions, the QI process, and QM interface in managing laboratory equipment in the CQI environment. Both the follow-up of recommended action and the improvement process, itself, need to be determined as effective or not. It seems universal that the equipment management indicator grouping requires special emphasis in assessing the effectiveness of the quality management interface between the laboratory and supporting department activities (eg, medical maintenance).

Communication. The laboratory needs to disseminate QI lessons regarding equipment/instrument quality improvement not only throughout the appropriate section, service, and departmental levels of the laboratory but also to the other supportive hospital-level departments such as the medical maintenance, computer operations, and contracting and purchasing activities. The quality profile for Microbiology exemplifies one approach to monitoring and reporting opportunities to improve medical maintenance support.

Supply Management (Indicator Grouping 20)

Chemistry profile interpretation:
Under this general grouping for supply management, the section has elected

Indicator Grouping 20
Supply Management

Chemistry Section Quality Profile

Indicator Grouping/ Specific Indicator: Threshold (Periodicity)	QI Data Observations (Date trend started)	J	A	S	O	N	D
Supply: no potential for laboratory service limitations!! (Quarterly)	0 = no supplies overdue None overdue since Jun 95						
a. Overdue supplies: none > 14 d		-	0	-	-	0	-

Transfusion Service Quality Profile

Indicator Grouping/ Specific Indicator: Threshold (Periodicity)	QI Data Observations (Date trend started)	J	A	S	O	N	D
Supply: no potential for laboratory service limitations!! (Quarterly)	0 = no supplies overdue None overdue since Apr 95						
a. Overdue supplies: none > 14 d		-	-	0	-	-	0

QI Note: Lab product storage (eg, rbc, platelets, cryo) could be reported here as a "supply" indicator

!! = sentinel event

to follow a general survey of delay in supply receipt (ie, overdue supplies). Evaluation of the numerical data reveals that the section has not identified any OFI over the past five months.

Since the reporting schedule for this specific quality indicator is on a quarterly basis, the next month for reporting will be February 1996. However, an additional narrative QI control statement relates that there have been no overdue supplies since June (ie, two quarters of negative reports). Consequently, the section has determined that at least six months of monitoring with no OFI is unsatisfactory; thus, the general approach is too insensitive.

The recommended action is to select a more focused study, choosing a high priority supply target (ie, high-volume, high-risk, or problem-prone). The assessment is accurate.

Transfusion profile interpretation:
Quarterly evaluation of supply delay reveals that there have been no opportunities for improvement for three quarters (since June 1995). The recommended action is to select a focused study, and the assessment reflects effective action and overall QI process. There is no forced time for completion due to staffing constraints.

The one question to be answered is whether or not the section has sufficient personnel strength to devote time to such a quality management

Evaluation of QI Data, TQM System, and CQI Process	Action Action Person: (Date Initiated)	Assessment of Overall Improvement
No report scheduled; next report due Feb 96; on target x 2 qtrs; general survey is too insensitive	Select a focused study for Mar 96 ACTION: Supervisor	Improvement of the QI process is in progress
On target x 2 qtrs;	Select a focused study as soon as possible ACTION: Acting Supervisor	Improvement of the QI process is in progress

objective. Some might say that it would be prudent to just maintain the general survey until more adequate quality management resources are available with improved levels of supervisory and technical staffing.

Additional profile interpretations:

Hematology (Appendix D): Evaluation of the narrative data statement reveals that there has been no identification of any OFI for two quarters. The action to select a focused study and the assessment of continuous improvement are accurate.

Microbiology (Appendix E): This profile is a mirror image of the Hematology profile.

Histopathology (Appendix G): Evaluation of the numerical data reveals that a report is not due until January 1993. On the other hand, the section has still decided in this month of review that there is a need for a more sensitive, focused study. The assessment is accurate.

Discussion:

Indicator Grouping: As for any of the indicator groupings listed in this profile, this grouping can include a variety of general or specified and indexed or focused indicators of supply resource management quality. The general indicator demonstrated here is aimed at surveillance of the overdue delivery of supplies. Examples of more specific targets for surveillance of the quality of supply management might include:

- Supply/reagent function: for manufacturing, storage and usage quality
- Supply/reagent storage stability: for manufacturing, storage, and usage quality
- Inventory level adequacy: for ordering, delivery, and usage quality
- Shelf-life expiration: for ordering, inventory,and usage quality
- Compliance with safety precautions in storage, handling, and usage: for employee safety quality
- Compliance with storage and preservation requirements: for usage quality.

Of course, applying any of the above general themes against more specific supply types (ie, reagents, expendables, and nonexpendables) would act as a multiplier of the number of potential indicators available for surveillance consideration.

An additional supply topic to consider under this grouping is the storage of any healthcare product that is manufactured in the laboratory. Blood components such as blood units or platelets are a leading example. Once produced by the laboratory, these items are a healthcare supply item that require inventory and storage maintenance just like any other supply item. This subject also is discussed under the postdeterminative finalization grouping.

Supporting Indicators. Once supplies are delivered (or produced in the laboratory—such as blood components), they must be stored correctly. Delay in supply and delivery or inadequate supply maintenance integrity can cause a progressive series of problems as evidenced by quality indicators of customer satisfaction, patient care outcome, and employee safety; laboratory product and other laboratory process TAT and backlog; determinative quality problems, all other operative resource activities; and all QI, QAn, and QAc activities. Of all of the above, determinative (analytical/diagnostic) quality is the key supporting indicator for reagent-type supplies.

Threshold. The QI tolerance levels for supply management indicators will vary with the patient care criticalness of the aspects of care that are under surveillance, the storage stability of the subject supply or reagent, and the impact of supply management on other laboratory resources. Usually, supply management warrants a comparative rate threshold.

The threshold for the general grouping in this sample profile is "no potential for laboratory service limitations." The more specific the indicator becomes, then the more specific the threshold should be. For example, the threshold for the more specified indicator of overdue supplies is "none will be any more than 14 days overdue from the date originally expected." Now, the latter stipulation might seem cavalier in its allowing such tardy supply delivery—but that is a decision for the individual laboratory to make. Certainly, tightening up on the threshold definition would be an improvement in the QI process.

In regard to the quality of managing supply delivery, first, the exact threshold definition depends on the delivery time definition. For example, is "overdue" delivery measured from the date of ordering to the date of actual delivery or from a date of expected delivery to the date of actual delivery?

Second, there are a number of other variable elements in determining an exact supply management threshold. For example, the timeliness of delivery to the laboratory storage shelf might have to meet a threshold of 15 days delivery time for an item that also has to meet a 30 day inventory shelf-life requirement and a 60 day manufacturer's expiration shelf-life.

Monitoring Periodicity. This scheduling depends on the criticalness of the aspects of care affected and the adequacy of the quality management resources at hand.

Evaluation. Healthcare laboratorians are expert in the QI monitoring and assessment of analytical quality data. However, laboratorians and other healthcare managers are not as well versed in applying the analytical steps of the same improvement process to the quality management of logistically-oriented operative resources such as supply, equipment, and facility. However, the QI approach is very useful in integrating all laboratory management activities under the precepts of TQM and CQI.

A major point to remember is that most organizations already generate a plethora of management data relating to supply—as well as all other key resource management areas. There is substantial reason to take advantage of all of that data and incorporate it into a total operational QI process. In so doing, quality management can be integrated into all segments and phases of the laboratory path of work flow, including operative resource management. Even organizational resource management can be included, as is specifically addressed in the next chapter.

At the same time, the laboratory should curtail collecting and discard all information that is <u>not</u> useful for quality management purposes. Make the overall QI process as streamlined and resource-effective as possible. In fact, such a reduction approach could constitute another valuable quality monitoring target.

Evaluation of the quality of supply management should include any additional ramifications contributed by supporting indicator groupings. Wherever there is an opportunity to improve supply management, that modification is almost always linked to the improvement of process and outcome.

One important supporting indicator grouping calls for special attention. Namely, employee safety requires that laboratory supplies be stored, handled, and used with appropriate safeguards.

Action. This rather specialized indicator topic calls for actions that might involve any portion of the chain of supply procurement, delivery,

Indicator Grouping 21
Facility Management

Chemistry Section Quality Profile

Indicator Grouping/ Specific Indicator: Threshold (Periodicity)	QI Data Observations (Date trend started) J A S O N D
Facility: no potential for equipment failure, biological spoilage or personnel stress!! (Quarterly)	No OFI identified x 2 qtrs

Transfusion Service Quality Profile

Indicator Grouping/ Specific Indicator: Threshold (Periodicity)	QI Data Observations (Date trend started) J A S O N D
Facility: no potential for equipment failure, biological spoilage or personnel stress!! (Quarterly)	- x - - - x* x = an adverse incident - = no OFI identified Staff complaint of excess heat in platelet storage room (A03) in Dec; occurs routinely in the summer months, eg, Aug

!! = sentinel event

storage, and usage both inside and outside of the healthcare laboratory. Improving supply management outside the laboratory requires direct coordination with hospital supply management and even with suppliers and manufacturers.

Assessment. The laboratory must consider the three standard options in assessing supply management in a CQI environment. Through appropriate QI follow-up, recommended actions, the improvement process, and the QM interface need deeming as being effective or not.

Communication. Lessons learned from the supply management QI process should be transmitted to all individuals in the chain of direct and indirect supply effects—whoever will benefit from any opportunity to improve supply management. The addressees include those who are both inside and outside the laboratory organization.

Facility Management (Indicator Grouping 21)

Chemistry profile interpretation:
Evaluation of December's narrative report indicates that there has been no identification of any OFI for six months. Under the circumstances, the sectional-departmental quality management team has decided to select a focused study during the next quarter by April 1996. The action and assessment are appropriate.[k]

It is of interest that the Chemistry Section does not comment anywhere in

Evaluation of QI Data, TQM System, and CQI Process	Action Action Person: (Date Initiated)	Assessment of Overall Improvement
On target x 2 qtrs; no OFI identified for six months	Select a focused study for Apr 96 ACTION: Supervisor	Improvement of the QI process is in progress
Room A03 (Plat Storage Room) has seasonal ventillation or air balance problem; See Postdeterminative Finalization notes re platelet storage problem	Schedule engineer study to assess cause and feasibility of resolution of hi ambient summer temp ACTION: Acting Supervisor (Dec 95)	Ineffective QI process: Needs improvement of QM interface

its profile on seasonally elevated ambient temperature. Compared to the other sections in the department, this section might be protected from such seasonal highs. On the other hand, this issue might be an excellent candidate for the focused study that is being planned—if deemed appropriate through the usual preliminary ranking and prioritization methods.

Transfusion profile interpretation:
According to the quality profile schedule, this grouping would not be reported ordinarily until February 1996. However, there has been an incidental remark in reference to the platelet room ambient temperature. This problem has been partially evaluated as a seasonal temperature spike in need of immediate attention. Evaluation of the December occurrence is deferred to profile notes found under the postdeterminative finalization grouping in Chapter Nine. The action and assessment statements for this grouping are appropriate.

Additional profile interpretations:

Hematology (Appendix D): It seems that seasonally high temperatures in the summer months are plaguing almost the entire laboratory

[k] It should be noted through all the various sample profiles that the scheduling of new studies is spread out over a wide calendar time frame so that undue demands are not being made on laboratory quality management resources at any one time.

department—as is the case for this Hematology section. The earliest citing of the problem was July 1994—also highlighting what seems to be institutional inattention to the overall problem! The lack of remedial response stands out in the face of reports of personnel heat stress and equipment failure. The action and assessment are appropriate but are mild considering the blatant ineffectiveness of the departmental and hospital QI process—and an apparently total breakdown at the QM interface.

Microbiology (Appendix E): Evaluation of this section's narrative data echoes what has already been said for other sections in this department. However, this section has an additional problem related to the location of an autoclave in the mycobacteriology unit area. Review of employee safety as a supporting indicator grouping reminds the reader that this laboratory activity also has a safety hood problem, which might involve facility renovation.

The action for this grouping states that any major ventilation renovation should also address the effect of the autoclave location. The assessment is appropriate.

Histopathology (Appendix G): This section's facility management profile segment is a final substantiation of what has already been documented for almost the entire department: there is a department-wide heat control/ventilation problem. The evaluation, action, and assessment are appropriate.

Discussion:

Indicator Grouping: The facility management indicator grouping often consists of protracted improvement opportunities since the process of major facility repair and renovation is often so complex: facility management is frequently contractual and heavy construction-oriented—and <u>very</u> expensive. Thus, the grouping might include a number of general and specified indicators. Compared to focused indicators, indexed indicators are not as applicable to the quality surveillance of facility management but still might be occasionally useful, eg, tracking ambient temperature. An example of a specified indicator of the focused type might address any inordinate delay in renovation of the autoclave location in the mycobacteriology unit, requiring the construction of a new wall with special ceramic heat shielding.

Because of its inherent complexity and lengthy time lines, facility management remedies often require phased planning with interim corrections of primary and secondary problems. Thus, additional indicator topics for this grouping might include any aspect of primary or secondary problems, along with the duration or TAT of engineering studies, contractual negotiations, and the actual repair or renovation—or new construction.

Supporting Indicators. These corroborative groupings include outcome indicators of customer satisfaction, patient care, and—especially—employee safety; all laboratory process activities; all operative resource activities; and all QI, QAn, and QAc organizational activities.

Threshold. Because facility work is often performed on a contractual basis, a contract should stipulate the time phasing for the accomplishment of a project. These milestones can then serve as quality indicator criteria or standards. Then, the laboratory can base QI thresholds on these contractual criteria, usually providing some flexibility before investigative evaluation needs to begin.

Monitoring Periodicity. This scheduling depends on the criticalness of the laboratory section or function involved and the adequacy of laboratory resources at hand needed to absorb whatever inconvenience there might be during facility repair or renovation.

Evaluation. The need for facility improvement is almost always initiated or substantiated by one or more supporting indicators; the Transfusion Service profile segment is a good example of this. Evaluation of facility quality data is often substantiated by an extensive array of retrospective data as compared to the more concurrent or prospective data typical of many other QI groupings. It would be advantageous to be able to discover opportunities for facility improvement by evaluating prospective data—that is, data collected to anticipate an untoward facility-related event before it occurs. However, the expense of facility repair, renovation, or new construction usually dictates extensive, time consuming, and heavily documented justification—unless the problem at hand is health or life threatening.

Action. Actions required to improve the physical plant usually require negotiation and coordination with the hospital administration, the chief financial officer, contractors or a contract management office and the facility engineers. These are complex projects that require adeptness at coordinating many nonlaboratory activities.

Assessment. The quality management team must consider the three standard options for assessing facility management in a CQI environment regarding effectiveness of recommended actions, the improvement process, and the QM interface.

Communication. QI lessons learned in facility management need sharing throughout the laboratory as well with all nonlaboratory activities that are involved. The addressees might include intralaboratory managers and employees, the hospital administration, the chief financial officer, contractors or a contract management personnel, and the facility engineers.

Financial Management (Indicator Grouping 22)

Chemistry profile interpretation:
At first glance, evaluation of the six months of cumulative data reveals that the threshold of ±5% variance from the amount expected to be spent during the elapsed fiscal year (FY) has been exceeded in the last two months. For instance, since the year is noted to begin in October of each year:

- One-twelfth or 8.3% of the budget should be expended during October

Indicator Grouping 22
Budget Management

Chemistry Section Quality Profile

Indicator Grouping/ Specific Indicator: Threshold (Periodicity)	QI Data Observations (Date trend started) J A S O N D	
Budget: meet planned expenditure within ± 5% of monthly target (Monthly)	+3 +4 +3 +4 +10 +9 % Fiscal year (FY) starts in Oct; major contracts are front-loaded in the first months of the FY	

Transfusion Service Quality Profile

Indicator Grouping/ Specific Indicator: Threshold (Periodicity)	QI Data Observations (Date trend started) J A S O N D	
Budget: meet planned expenditure within ± 5% of monthly target (Monthly)	+4 +5 +3 +2 +9 +11 % FY starts in Oct; a front-loaded budget is in use; data does not include wage expenditures	

B 16.7% should be expended through November

B 25% should be expended by the end of December.

Consequently, the data show that 12.3% (+4%) was spent through October, 26.7% (+10%) by the end of November, and 34% (+9%) by the end of December.

However, this seemingly adverse trend of overexpenditure, although factual, does not trigger undue alarm in the example quality profile. The final evaluation by the laboratory is that payment into front-loaded contracts for instrument services and supplies has caused the overexpenditure of the planned budget during the first few months of the fiscal year. This was anticipated.

The cited action is in response to the laboratory quality management team's becoming interested in an alternative accounting system that would approach front-loaded expenditures on a more balanced, prorated fashion: find an alternative method of budgeting.

The assessment leaves the specifics of balancing the accrual accounting system in the hands of the laboratory manager. Yet, it also notes that the section still might improve the system.

Transfusion profile interpretation:
Evaluation of this section's profile segment reveals the same general picture

Evaluation of QI Data, TQM System, and CQI Process	Action and Action Person: (Date Initiated)	Assessment of Overall Improvement
Over expenditure due to front-loaded contracts; this has been anticipated but it skews the data	Investigate use of an alternative accounting system Action: Lab Manager	Budget system is being improved

Overexpenditure at the start of fiscal year causes a skewing of the budget data; and, there is a need to capture wage data	Seek an alternative accounting system to even out contract expenditures and capture wage data Action: Lab Manager	Improvement of the budget process is in progress

as shown in the Chemistry profile. The same comments apply to this section's budget management profile's action and assessment, as well.

Additional profile interpretations:

Hematology (Appendix D): Evaluation of this section's budget management indicator grouping reveals that there was a perfect rate of expenditure during the months of July through October, ie, there was a 0% variance from the budget management objectives. This perfect record also could be due to the transfer of end-of-the-year (ie, July through September) surplus hematology funds to other sections that needed money in order to meet their separate management objectives. There is evidence of the same front-loading in November and December as has been noted in the two profiles above. The action and assessment are similarly appropriate.

Microbiology (Appendix E): Evaluation of this section's budget grouping echoes what has been shown above. This profile demonstrates a slight variation of the reallocation theme by indicating a slight underexpenditure in July and August. The budget manager apparently reallocated this "pool" to other, more needy sections in September. October being the beginning of the new fiscal year was apparently a zero balance month: no excess, no surplus—simply perfectly on target. The action and assessment are appropriate as discussed above.

Histopathology (Appendix G): Evaluation of this section's profile demonstrates a slightly different budget management situation. Until

October of the current fiscal year, the AP Service did not have a budget reporting system at all. Although it should have been implemented and reported in October and November, it was not. After some delay, the section submitted its first report in December, which still was on target at the threshold cut off point of +5% expenditure of the planned accrued expenditure. The action to establish a six-month baseline and the assessment of an improved QI process are all appropriate.

Discussion:

Indicator Grouping: The budget management indicator grouping is aimed at the entrepreneur's or accountant's "bottom line"—which is not the laboratorian's quality management bottom line.[1] The above examples for this grouping demonstrate that it is possible to establish QI indicator criteria and threshold limits to monitor the quality management of the laboratory budget program.

Aside from total sectional budget expenditure, there are a myriad of additional specified indicator topics that can be followed under this grouping. First, the quality management team can aim indexed or focused studies at more specific laboratory work centers within a given section. The adequate funding and judicious spending for any one of these activities would serve as an appropriate QI surveillance topic—as long as it is correctly ranked and prioritized in importance.

Second, all laboratory-wide activities include workloaded technical bench activities and nonworkloaded operative and administrative managerial activities. All of this work requires funding to some extent or another—and that includes the quality management functions. Thus, all laboratory activities, processes, and products of any type can be "priced" and monitored for cost-effectiveness. The quality management team can measure the quality of cost-effectiveness at whatever level of exactness it wishes—even down to a specific analytic procedure performed by a specific instrument on a specific shift. Diagnostic procedures are equally applicable. Costs can be monitored in terms of fixed, variable, and other accounting components.

Third, the appropriation, allocation, or expenditure of special funds is also worth targeting if it is of a high enough priority. Funds earmarked for HIV-related laboratory activities would be one example of an attempt to ensure control of an emerging and potentially out-of-control budget topic through the QI process. Fourth, the budget accounting system, itself , can be a target for improvement.

Supporting Indicators. The budget management indicator grouping is as global as any profile grouping imaginable. Every outcome, process, and resource management activity (at every operative and organizational level) is

[1] The laboratory quality manager should be more concerned about the organizational "top line" of customer satisfaction and the organizational "bottom line" of team actualization. The fiscal bottom line will be maximized by optimal organizational effectiveness and productivity.

affected by the budget. Consequently, there is total cross-linking of this indicator grouping with all of the 25 other groupings.

Threshold. A laboratory section ordinarily will derive the threshold used in these examples on an empirical basis. In the case of the sample profiles, the budget expenditure threshold allows a 5% variation from the budget for the QI report period; thus, it is a comparative rate threshold. In reality, the potential threshold for this grouping's indicators can vary from 0% to greater than 5% deviation, depending on the organization's financial status, accounting system, management objectives, and administrative policy. Breakeven points can also be used as the basis for threshold parameters.

Monitoring Periodicity. This indicator characteristic depends on the criticalness of the aspects of care and laboratory activity involved and the adequacy of the operative and organizational resources on hand.

Action. Any action required to improve appropriation, allocation, or expenditure of the budget must involve all laboratory managers as well as all quality managers involved at the hospital level. It is usual for QI action resolving budgetary issues to involve joint laboratory-clinical-nonclinical decision making.

Assessment. The section must exercise the three standard options for assessing budget management effectiveness in the CQI environment in followup of any remedial action, the QI process, and the QM interface.

Communication. Lessons learned from the quality management of the budget must be shared with all laboratory managers as well as all other nonlaboratory personnel involved in the budget management process.

REFERENCES

1. Workload Recording Method and Personnel Management Manual. Northfield, IL: College of American Pathologists, 1991.
2. Barros A. Improving productivity: the administrator's point of view. Med Lab Obs, 1990;22:21-22.
3. Inspection Checklist. Laboratory General (Section 1). Northfield, IL: College of American Pathologists Laboratory Inspection Program, 1994.

11. The Quality Profile: Laboratory Organizational Resource Management

LABORATORY ORGANIZATIONAL RESOURCE WORK FLOW SEGMENT

The path of work flow is the basis for the sequential structure of the quality profile format and offers an area of interest for every laboratory managerial role.

- There is the postlaboratory outcome management portion that attracts those interested in ensuring the healthcare end result of patient care, employee safety, and overall customer satisfaction—the "top line" type of people.
- There are the three post-, intra-, and prelaboratory process management portions that intrigue those interested in ensuring the elements of hands-on, patient-request-specimen-product processing.
- There is the operative resource management portion that draws the attention of those interested in ensuring direct support activities.
- And, there is the earliest portion of the path that captivates those "bottom-line" people interested in ensuring the organizational-level programs for quality improvement, anticipation, and actualization—the foundation of all operational endeavor.

The programs for implementing quality improvement (QI), anticipating quality improvement (QAn), and actualizing quality improvement (QAc) constitute the fountainhead of excellence for all laboratory activities discussed in the previous three chapters. These organizational programs fuel the human effort of operative enterprise. In retrospect, all opportunities for improvement (OFIs) detected in the preceding profiles ultimately stem from the quality of the organizational activities that occur in this initial segment of the path of work flow and final segment of quality profile analysis.

This chapter addresses the organizational resource management segment of the path of work flow. This sixth and final segment of the profile consists of four indicator groupings. Each grouping focuses on a key organizational-level management activity that originates within the laboratory—remembering, however, that there are a myriad of related nonlaboratory elements.

The four groupings focus on the three organizational resource management programs that comprise the total quality management (TQM) system. The QI program provides two groupings; the QAn and QAc programs consist of individual groupings. Thus, the four indicator topics are 1) internal QI activities; 2) external QI activities, 3) the QAn program, and 4) the QAc program.

It is important to remember that the groupings and indicators used in this text's profile model are only examples. A laboratory can select any number and type of organizational groupings, just as each grouping can include any combination of general or specified quality indicators. The laboratory must judiciously select these monitoring devices on the basis of valid ranking and prioritizing criteria.

Internal Quality Improvement Management (Indicator Grouping 23)

Chemistry profile interpretation:

This section's quality profile grouping for internal quality improvement consists of one general indicator for assessment and another for communication. These indicators measure the quality of the last two steps of the Joint Commission on Accreditation of Healthcare Organizations' (JCAHO) ten-step process, which is the QI process exemplified throughout this text. These indicator topics could just as easily cover the individual elements of Plan-Do-Check-Act (P-D-C-A), FOCUS-P-D-C-A, Juran's Journey, or any other improvement process that the quality management team happens to choose.

Considering the grouping's first indicator, the laboratorian must satisfy three key questions regarding the effectiveness of the assessment step in the continuous quality improvement (CQI) environment. Is this ninth element of the QI process adequately assessing the effectiveness of:

1) Previously recommended actions?
2) The overall quality management system?
3) The QM interface?
4) The QI process, itself?

Indicator Grouping 23
Internal Quality Improvement Management

Chemistry Section Quality Profile

Indicator Grouping/ Specific Indicator: Threshold (Periodicity)	QI Data Observations (Date trend started) J A S O N D	
ORGANIZATIONAL RESOURCE MANAGEMENT WORK FLOW SEGMENT		
Internal Quality Improvement (QI)	Continuous improvement is documented, overall; section has received the 1996 hospital QI award indicating effective QI assessment, overall	
a. Assessment: there must be evidence of continuous improvement over a reasonable amount of time!! (Quarterly)	HOWEVER, see Analytical Quality and Equipment Management groupings for data on instrument replacement problem	
b. Communication: there must be adequate sharing of lessons learned!! (Monthly)	No OFI identified x 8 mo Data reveal at least 1 hour of QI inservice training per month x 8 mo	

Transfusion Service Quality Profile

ORGANIZATIONAL RESOURCE MANAGEMENT WORK FLOW SEGMENT		
Internal QI (Monthly)		
a. Assessment: there must be evidence of continuous improvement!!	There is a lack of effective assessment in several key management areas as shown by their respective indicators	
b. Communication: there must be adequate sharing of lessons learned: > 1 hr training per month!!	Communicating QI lessons learned is greatly limited by staff shortage and lack of time for nonworkloaded activities; there has been < 1 hr per mo of QI in-service training exercised in the last 3 months	

!! = sentinel event TAT = turnaround time

Adequate assessment requires that enough time must have passed to allow remedial actions, the QI process, and the QM interface to respond to whatever opportunity is at hand. Yet, assessment must always be accomplished in a timely manner.

Evaluation of the Chemistry Section's narrative data reveals that the section has performed effective assessment—in most cases. Review of the

Evaluation of QI Data, TQM System, and CQI Process	Action Action Person: (Date Initiated)	Assessment of Overall Improvement
On target in most operational areas, BUT there is a problem in the process of assessing instrument replacement; this QI step needs improvement within a reasonable period	1. Begin a focused study of the instrument selection process for Jan 96 ACTION: Dept Lab Manager 2. React more readily to periods of nonimprovement by fine tuning the QI assessment process ACTION: Supervisor	Overall, very effective QI process EXCEPT FOR assessment of equipment selection process effectiveness and related QI process sensitivity
On target x 8 mo; there has been no improvement over an inordinate amount of time	Select focused indicator study for Mar 96 ACTION: Supervisor	Improvement of the QI process is in progress
Both indicators support the need for improving the assessment and communication steps of the QI process. This is particularly evident under the customer satisfaction, patient care, postdeterminative product handling, TAT, analytical quality , workload management, and staffing groupings	1. Improve staffing 2. Start team rebuilding (QAc) 3. Begin quality planning (QAn) 4. Bolster training of improvement process (QI) ACTION: Medical Director	Ineffective internal QI process: Improving staffing requires hosp admin assistance!! Improving section team integrity requires department facilitation

preceding profile groupings substantiates this general observation. For example, the organizational "top line" of customer satisfaction (ie, profile grouping 1) exemplifies how well the Chemistry Section has succeeded in communicating QI lessons learned to the clinical staff by establishing laboratory-nursing teams.

Granted, the Chemistry Section is not absolutely perfect in its ability to assess improvement needs in a timely manner. In fact, review of the preceding 22 groupings reveals that there are still some opportunities to improve the assessing of certain operational functions along the profile sequence. The groupings that exhibit obvious aberrant assessment function include employee safety, turnaround time (TAT), postdeterminative product finalization, analytical quality, and instrument procurement. The single major flaw is in the delayed replacement of the multichannel analyzer. In the other cases, the problem has been tardy recognition of "indicator inactivity." Nevertheless, this section is still light years ahead of the Transfusion Service example in assessing overall effectiveness of quality improvement activities.

The first recommended action for this internal QI indicator is to focus on improving the assessment of equipment selection and procurement—there is a definite OFI to resolve here. This initiative will entail a combined section/service/department-level quality management team analysis of the QI process with emphasis on effectiveness of the assessment step, vis, the equipment replacement process. Consequently, the department-level laboratory manager is responsible for the overall coordination and follow-up of this new study.

A second overall recommendation is for the section to react more readily to inordinately long periods of nonimprovement, ie, indicator inactivity. The section supervisor is responsible here—just as the section medical director (the quality management team leader) could be. The assessment for this CQI profile indicator is appropriate for the facts and actions presented.

Considering the second indicator for effectiveness of the QI communication step, evaluation of the narrative data demonstrates the last point regarding timely response to indicator inactivity. The Chemistry Section has not detected any opportunities to improve communication of QI lessons learned for at least eight months.

While the profile corroborates that at least one hour of QI-related inservice training has been given every month, the section-department decision is that eight months still is too long a period to rely on a general survey without any specific improvement of the communication step. Therefore, it is either time to 1) improve the approach to this surveillance activity and design a focused study of the communication process, 2) replace this indicator with a higher priority internal QI issue, or 3) eliminate this indicator entirely, reduce the total number of monitoring targets, and focus on higher priority topics elsewhere along the path of work flow.

The section chooses the first option with the supervisor being responsible. Without a more specific OFI to resolve, the first step is to study the section QI plan and determine how well it defines and describes the communication step. How well does the section plan for the communication step dovetail with the service and department-level improvement plans? Is the section adequately teaching the communication step through its QI training program? Are intradepartmental improvement program plans adequately merged with interdepartmental training of the communication step?

The next step is to determine how lessons learned are actually being disseminated and if that process is effective. How well is the laboratory integrating the dissemination of QI lessons learned with the intra- and interdepartmental inservice training programs (ie, CME indicator grouping 16), including all relevant lateral departments and higher administrative echelon levels? Certain lessons learned from this indicator could also be topics to include in the QI program training schedule.

Finally, the laboratory can select more specified operational targets to focus on QI effectiveness. For example, there can be a review of the communication of lessons learned for any of the 25 other indicator groupings listed in this quality profile example. Since there is always some overlap between indicator groupings, condense the target and eliminate duplicate quality management effort. The assessment for this second indicator is appropriate.

Transfusion profile interpretation:
A combined evaluation of this section's profile grouping addresses both of the indicator topics since their respective deficiencies are founded on mutual operative and organizational resource constraints. The evaluation of the narrative data for both the assessment and communication steps of the QI process reveals that there is need for enhancing the assessment and communication steps in several very crucial management areas. Review of the 22 preceding groupings highlights several that call for immediate attention, including customer satisfaction, patient care outcome, analytical quality, workload management, technical staffing, and continuing medical education (CME). These deficiencies in both assessment and communication stem from excessive staff shortage and workload stress. The organizational top line of customer satisfaction particularly exemplifies how poorly the Transfusion Service has performed in communicating lessons learned to the clinical, operative resource support, and hospital administrative staff.

The recommended actions also are combined for both indicator topics. The actions target both staffing and organizational management issues. It is obvious that there must be improved staffing. But, it is also important for the section to address improvement of the organizational, or administrative-level, managerial programs affecting these two indicator topics. In this case, the laboratory must substantially strengthen all three organizational-level programs—QI, QAn, and QAc.

First, even with the lack of sufficient staff on hand, the section must initiate an effort at team rebuilding through the QAc program. It is imperative that the laboratory service, the department, and even the hospital provide the reduced workload, the extra time, and people for such a section-level rebuilding project to be successful. Second, the section must reactivate its QAn program, focusing on longer-range plans to rebuild the team and rejuvenate its operational effectiveness.

Third, there needs to be a bolstering of QI program training to improve the execution of all the elements of the improvement process within the section. This training process should include the supporting service and department, along with the section. Remember that the most important QI elements requiring improvement might not even be the assessment or communication steps exemplified in the sample profile. This transfusion service will undoubtedly have to go back to the beginning—reidentifying scope, responsibility, and important aspects of care—and then proceed from there. The immediate improvement surveillance targets must be the QI steps having the highest priority as determined by careful analysis of the data at hand using valid criteria.

As the final follow-up for this profile segment, a combined assessment for this section's internal QI grouping pinpoints the ineffectiveness of previous actions and of the improvement process itself. Also, it underlines the need for laboratory department and hospital administrative assistance to improve the QI program of this belabored Transfusion Service at the QM interface, implying joint, interdepartmental QI *and* QAn *and* QAc efforts.

Additional profile interpretations:

Hematology (Appendix D): There are two specified indicators used for surveillance of this section's internal QI program. They are measurements of the effectiveness of 1) the overall improvement process and 2) the communication step.

Evaluation of data for the first indicator topic reveals that there has been identification of "several opportunities" for improving the QI process over the last six months. There are no itemized details under this indicator; however, the narrative statement indirectly relates to discovery of opportunities to enhance the improvement process under several outcome, process, or operative resource management profile groupings. These improvements could have been in the form of enhancing the effectiveness of remedial actions, redefining indicator criteria and tightening thresholds, or improving QM interface effectiveness. Review of the 22 preceding profile indicators reveals actual examples under the groupings for employee safety (ie, environmental), TAT, reference laboratory quality, prelaboratory process validation, workload management, personnel strength, computer management, and facility management.

In spite of the overall success of the present QI process, the recommended action is for the department-level laboratory manager to identify alternative improvement processes other than the JCAHO ten-step process. Apparently, the section-department quality management team has decided to investigate other approaches to continuous quality improvement—but, using the same TQM system and CQI philosophy. The section might be seeking an alternative QI approach that increases the emphasis on specified team analysis (as in FOCUS P-D-C-A) or simplifies the approach when team and analytical analysis are least necessary (as in Shewhart's P-D-C-A). Perhaps the section wants more than one option available, just to be more flexible. The section's personality composition and management objectives will weigh heavily on this decision. Finally, considering the data, evaluation, and action that are profiled, this first indicator's assessment is appropriate.

Evaluation of the second indicator's data on QI communication reveals that the section has consistently communicated improvement lessons learned through the CME inservice program. However, the section has not identified any opportunities to improve this improvement process step for nine months. Under the circumstances, the section-department quality management team recommends that the section supervisor coordinate a more focused analysis of the effectiveness of communication of lessons learned. The assessment for this indicator is appropriate.

Microbiology (Appendix E): Similar to the Chemistry Section profiles, there are two indicators: one following the assessment step and the other covering the communication step of the QI process. First, on review of the 22 preceding profile indicators, evaluation of the effectiveness of the assessment step reveals that there are several current opportunities to improve follow-up of remedial actions, the QI process, or the QM interface. The most important path of flow phases requiring improvement of the assessment step include employee safety (ie, biohazard and environmental), report distribution, personnel management, equipment management, and facility management. The recommended action is for the supervisor to coordinate the monitoring of these identified opportunities through some form of focused study of the assessment step.

The object of this action is not to monitor groupings already being monitored, just to increase the "indicator count." The object is for the laboratory to discern a way by which the assessment step of the QI process can be improved to provide more timely improvement follow-up and to 1) decrease delays in the improvement process and 2) reduce the number of indicators to only those that are of the highest priority. The assessment for this indicator is appropriate.

Second, evaluation of the surveillance data for the communication step reveals that there has been no identification of any OFI to improve communication of QI lessons learned over the past nine months—which is an inordinate period of inactivity. For the same reasons as given above, the recommended action is for the section supervisor to select a focused study to find a way in which the communication step can be improved. The assessment of this profile's indicator is appropriate.

A special QI note from the section-department quality management team recommends that the team identify an alternative quality evaluation process to use adjunct to the ten-step process. One approach might be useful, for instance, when an OFI is of such a straightforward nature that the forming of a complex team or using extensive statistical analysis is unnecessary (eg, P-D-C-A); a more extensive approach might be appropriate when the OFI is so complex that an enhanced team approach, a joint effort, or statistical analysis is absolutely necessary (eg, FOCUS P-D-C-A). In seeking alternative processes, the quality management team is seeking added flexibility in the improvement process.

Histopathology (Appendix G): Similar to the Chemistry Section profile, there are two indicators under the internal QI grouping: one addresses the assessment step and one covers the communication step of the ten-step improvement process. Evaluation of the data for the assessment indicator reveals that currently there are "several problematic opportunities" without significant improvement over an inordinate time—where assessment has failed to effectively bring the problems to resolution. It appears that the QM interface at the hospital level is particularly weak, requiring the formation of a special task force at the hospital level.

Review of all 25 accompanying indicators reveals that the most important examples of ineffective assessment are under the groupings for employee safety (ie, fire, chemical, and environmental), TAT, predeterminative specimen processing, workload management, personnel strength, computer management, and facility management. In looking ahead to the next chapter, quality planning and team actualization will require attention under the assessment step. For example, the QAn and QAc groupings will show that there needs to be an improvement of the assessment for those organizational groupings.

Consequently, the recommended action is for the section medical director (the quality management team leader) to 1) coordinate with the hospital task force to improve the QI process and the QM interface and 2) revitalize planning and actualization programs. The assessment for this indicator is appropriate.

Discussion:

Indicator Grouping: When considering the effectiveness of the internal QI program, we must confront the issue of whether or not the laboratorian must play the role of policeman within the laboratory organization. If the answer is "Yes, we have to," it follows that employing an organizational indicator grouping directed at the internal QI program is a tool to "fine-tune" the fine-tuning program—that is, to check the checkers. It is a means of internally "policing" the laboratory's quality surveillance, measurement, and improvement mechanisms. As with peer review in general, it is a role that we cannot escape as professionals. We must be assiduous in peer reviewing ourselves internally, just as we must be ready to accept peer review by others externally.[a]

One major concern is likely to surface at this point. It relates to the possible misinterpretation of the entire purpose behind the overall QI program—including both its internal and external components. Again and again, professionals throughout the laboratory community ask, what does the JCAHO mean by the term improvement? Does it intend to focus entirely on improvement of organizational performance—or does it really have

[a] The main target of interest for this grouping is effectiveness of the internal QI process; the external QI process is addressed in the next grouping (ie, indicator grouping 24).

improvement of individual performance in mind? Although, at times, the latter questions smacks of paranoid hysteria, there is legitimate professional concern over any improvement program that could possibly swing regulatory and accreditation forces towards any more stringent peer review, including recertification testing.

As a perfect example, during the first JCAHO field review of the proposed revisions for the 1994 *Accreditation Manual for Hospitals*, the proposed title for the revised chapter on quality improvement was "Performance Assessment and Improvement." Even with extensive advance preparation and education on the part of the Joint Commission, there was an immediate reaction with the voicing of great consternation over the new title's perceived implication that individual performance and competency was being assailed. Although the JCAHO had clearly explained that the intention behind the title and its chapter was to emphasize the improvement of *organizational process* performance, the chapter was subsequently renamed between the first and second field review. The new title became "Improving Organizational Performance." Hopefully, this change will result in less misunderstanding as to what the chief target for those accreditation standards really is.

In studying the present grouping for internal QI, one must also maintain the same overall focus on improvement of organizational—not individual—performance. An individual only comes under scrutiny in this QI process when review of all related organizational processes is exhausted. And even then, with an individual's competency under review, the questions still must be asked as to how organizational processes should have detected any individual's aberrant performance earlier—or should have prevented any trained individual from losing competency in the first place.

Up to this point, we already have taken care of analytical and diagnostic quality peer review under their respective groupings (ie, indicator grouping 9 and 10). So, how does the organization—as a team entity—check the checkers, manage the managers, and lead the leaders under the peer umbrella of the basic management system? It is easy! The laboratory accomplishes these organizational-level peer surveillance tasks just as all other workflow elements are measured: by using the same systematic QI program plan and the same analytical approach.

In this text, the QI model used in the quality profiles series is the JCAHO ten-step model. However, any other systematic analytical approach could suffice—ie, P-D-C-A, FOCUS P-D-C-A, Juran's Journey, as well as any number of other conceptual models available in the literature. Therefore, any advice in this discussion applies generically to any approach or method for measuring the effectiveness of any internal improvement plan, process, or analytical tool.

The indicator grouping for surveillance of the internal QI program can consist of indicators for any or all of the steps or goals of whatever improvement process is at hand. In this series of sample profiles, the example groupings illustrate the monitoring of two steps of the ten-step model as more specified indicators.[b] Considering the various alternative approaches, candidates for internal QI indicators might include any of the improvement process elements listed in Table I. As the laboratory approaches these topics from a systematic perspective, they all deserve ranking and prioritizing in their candidacy for monitoring.

Additional indicator topics are as plentiful as the operational scope of the internal QI program. For example, one potential indicator topic is the effectiveness of the written internal improvement plan. Although the plan should parallel the structure of the process, it might include more than one improvement process and usually will include other important structural or organizational elements worthy of consideration for improvement. Other indicator topics might include the effectiveness of remedial action follow-up, as well as the effectiveness of the QM interface.

Another candidate as an indicator topic is the effectiveness of the QI training process. There should be periodic scheduling of training sessions to introduce the concepts and methods of the improvement program for new employees or to bring veteran employees up-to-date. Also, the laboratory can meld this training series with the organizational training mentioned under QAn (ie, indicator grouping 25) and QAc (ie, indicator grouping 26), bringing the effectiveness of these other team-oriented activities into the internal QI spotlight.

Supporting indicators. This internal QI indicator grouping is so global that any of the other 25 groupings can potentially provide corroborative evidence of an opportunity to improve the overall internal QI program.

Threshold. As shown in the quality profile examples, the QI threshold can be very general—for example, "there must be evidence of continuous improvement over a reasonable amount of time" or "there must be adequate dissemination of lessons learned." The degree of tolerance to variance (ie, conformance to design specifications) actually allowed for communication of the QI data depends on the inherent patient or employee risk from any related laboratory aspect of care and the quality management resources available.

Peters speaks well in regard to the use of thresholds as a QI tool in the TQM and CQI environment where there is a need for promoting creativity and empowerment in the improvement process.[3] The main point is that creativity and empowerment are usually more important than attempting for zero defects. Of course, the degree of potential customer risk is higher in healthcare than in most other business endeavors. However, managing sentinel events is necessary on a relatively limited number of occasions when patient health or employee safety is clearly threatened. So, creativity and empowerment should be major managerial themes in dealing with most thresholds.

Monitoring Periodicity. If the remedial actions, the QI process, and

[b] To show some variation, the Hematology Section profile monitors the overall QI process along with one specified step.

Table I
Possible Indicator Topics for Monitoring Improvement of the Overall QI Process Using Three Process Models

Shewart's P-D-C-A[1]	JCAHO's Ten-step Process[1]	HCA's FOCUS P-D-C-A[2]
■ Plan ■ Do ■ Check ■ Act		■ Find a process to improve ■ Organize a team ■ Collect data ■ Understand the process in question ■ Select improvements
■ Plan	■ Scope ■ Responsibility ■ Important aspects of care ■ Indicators ■ Threshold	■ Plan and initiate a change
■ Do	■ Collection of data	■ Do what is needed for full implementation and monitor
■ Check	■ Evaluation ■ Action	■ Check results of the change implementation
■ Act	■ Assessment ■ Communication	■ Act to fine-tune the implementation and find new opportunities for improvement

the QM interface are effective overall, the periodicity can be relaxed, as shown in the quarterly scheduled Chemistry Section profile segment. If any of these improvement process elements are not effective, then the scheduling of the internal QI grouping should be more frequent—as is shown in the monthly scheduling for the Transfusion Section profile.

Naturally, the more frequent scheduling demands more time spent on quality management. This is a good example of how a QI program can represent a real cost to the laboratory in terms of numbers of involved personnel and their nonworkloaded time. If a section is overwhelmed as they are in the Transfusion Section example, the quality management team might have to allocate resources from some other section, service, department, or from outside the laboratory, in order to accomplish the quality management task. If there are just not enough people, then laboratory production or the QI process will have to be modified, downgraded, or curtailed in some way to meet the laboratory's management objectives. There should always be a balance between workload (including the inherent quality management elements) and the work force (including quality management resources).

Evaluation. The indicator grouping for internal QI should afford straightforward evaluation of all important elements of the improvement program and its processes. Examining the 25 other profile groupings and their individual indicators facilitates this evaluation—to determine whether or not there is corroborative evidence of any opportunity to improve any internal QI program component in question. Instead of relying on general surveys, the laboratory should direct more specified studies at high priority elements of internal QI quality to generate objective data for more effective evaluation.

Action. Recommendations for resolving any OFI in this grouping should be directed to improving elements of the laboratory department, service, or section QI plan and processes. In some cases, there is need to dovetail internal improvement plans between departments, including joint laboratory-clinical or laboratory-administrative support activities. If so, there should be some mutual agreement to modify internal plans. Depending on the severity of the problem, the scope of responsibility for remedial action can vary from the level of the hands-on operator to that of the quality management team leader.

Assessment. As usual, the laboratory needs to consider the three standard options for assessing the internal QI program in the CQI environment. This would include assessing the effectiveness of remedial actions, the QI process, and the QM interface. The second option—asking if the QI process is effective—offers a unique opportunity to improve the internal QI process by using the same improvement process to look at itself. Because of the possible masking of a "dual flaw" in both the internal QI process being studied and the same QI process being used for the study, it might become necessary for an outside consultant to assess the in-house improvement process by an external QI process.

Communication. All lessons learned need to be effectively shared with all laboratory and nonlaboratory activities and personnel that are involved in the laboratory internal QI program. There should be appropriate integration of this new information with the CME program, as well as with the individual training programs established to serve the QI, QAn and QAc programs.

External Quality Improvement Management (Indicator Grouping 24)

Chemistry profile interpretation:
Evaluation of the data for this section's external QI grouping entails a review of general indicators for three major activities: 1) proficiency testing (PT) surveys; 2) JCAHO, College of American Pathologists (CAP), and other

accreditation or licensing inspections; and 3) incident reports, complaints, and suggestions.

First, regarding external PT surveys, the data lists two specific survey reports, both received in December. The subject analytes—serum human chorionic gonadotropin (HCG) by radioimmunoassay (RIA) and serum glucose by the multichannel analyzer—are slightly off target from the CAP standard deviation index (SDI) threshold of 2.0.

Evaluation of the first survey reveals that the HCG (RIA) deficiency of a 2.2 SDI was a borderline error, caused by inadequate bead washing. This was a single occurrence; no trend or pattern was noted.

The action in response to the HCG survey result is for the supervisor to initiate an immediate investigative evaluation of the analytical process—paying special attention to the bead washing portion of that technical process. This focused study should include an audit of related QC data for the next quarter. Any correcting, remedial training, or disciplining of the involved technologist should be a last resort consideration—only after all other possibilities of process improvement are exhausted.

The overall assessment of the HCG survey is that improvement of the analytic process is needed, but the immediate actions cannot be reviewed for effectiveness until after the next three months. Only when there has been time for the investigative evaluation and resultant action to take their course can the laboratory truly assess the effectiveness of any remedial actions, the QI process, or the QM interface.

Evaluation of the second survey reveals that the multichannel glucose deficiency of a 2.6 SDI is reminiscent of earlier discussions in this section's profile regarding the need to replace the aged instrument. It is not surprising that a similar proficiency survey result occurred in the reporting period of July, representing an expected adverse trend of repeated deficiencies.

The action at the operative managerial level in response to the multichannel glucose PT results is for the supervisor 1) to continue strict QC management at the operative bench level and 2) to replace the analyzer. Because of a protracted record of deficient proficiency testing—and the recognized ineffectiveness of the internal QI process to replace the instrument—the assessment is that both the external <u>and</u> internal QI processes require study and improvement.

As an added "QI note," the departmental QI review committee recognizes the need to address "internal proficiency testing" per implications of the Clinical Laboratory Improvement Amendments of 1988 (CLIA '88). "Nonregulated" tests (those not covered by commercial PT providers) should be assessed every six months by accuracy verification. This can be done by practicing split testing and blind testing.

Second, regarding JCAHO, CAP, and other external inspection programs, the Chemistry Section reports no opportunities for improvement in the form of unresolved deficiencies. The evaluation and action are appropriate. Regarding the assessment—as further discussed below—this indicator provides an example of an "opportunity-limited" QI topic. It is only when an

Indicator Grouping 24
External Quality Improvement Management

Chemistry Section Quality Profile

Indicator Grouping/ Specific Indicator: Threshold (Periodicity)	QI Data Observations (Date trend started) J A S O N D
External Quality Improvement (QI) (Monthly) a. Proficiency surveys: all results must be ≤ 2 SDI* or found "Acceptable"!! 1. HCG (RIA)	* SDI = Standard Deviation Index (Interval) - = no survey scheduled 0 = no deficiencies - - 0 - - 2.2
2. Glucose (Multi-channel Analyzer X)	- - 2.8 - - 2.6
b. JCAHO/CAP/other inspection: no unresolved findings!	No unresolved findings from any previous inspections
c. Incident report and complaints: every report is a sentinel event!!	Liver profile report cited as inaccurate by physician on Ward 17 (Male Medicine)

Transfusion Service Quality Profile

External QI (Monthly) a. Proficiency surveys: all results must be ≤ 2 SDI or "Acceptable"!! 1. Antibody screen profile	SDI = Standard Deviation Index (Interval) - = no survey reported 0 = no deficiencies UA = "Unacceptable" - - UA - - UA
b. JCAHO/CAP/other inspection: no unresolved deficiencies!!	1. Ineffective training of evening (4-12) and night (12-8) nursing shifts 2. The training problem re evening and night nursing shifts cited in 1994 CAP interim survey is still unresolved
c. Incident report and complaints: every report is a sentinel event!!	0 0 1 2 2 3 Adverse complaints re xs TAT in Sep, Oct, Nov, and Dec. One report in Dec concerned the hemolytic transfusion reaction on Ward 22

!! = sentinel event XS = excess CAP = College of American Pathologists

Evaluation of QI Data, TQM System, and CQI Process	Action Action Person: (Date Initiated)	Assessment of Overall Improvement
Bead washing error in Dec; no trend	1. Investigate the analytical process 2. Audit QC data for any trend of repeated HCG (RIA) inaccuracies for the next 3 mo 3. Assess remedial actions in Mar 93 ACTION: Supervisor	Improvement of the analytical process is in progress
Daily QC acceptable with repeated maintenance and repeat runs; aging multichannel analyzer X is being replaced	1. Watch QC carefully 2. Replace the problematic analyzer ACTION: Supervisor	Internal and external QI processes need improvement
QI Note: per CLIA 88, section supervisor is to survey entire scope of procedures to identify need for internal proficiency testing		
On target	None needed	Effective QI process
Calculation transcription error; no trend	Investigate the transcription process ACTION: Supervisor	Assessment of improvement is to be determined

This recent trend of inaccuracy appears related to staff shortage and workload stress; poses as a problem in view of CLIA '88 requirements; lab could be closed! See Analytical Quality Grouping data	1. Correct the staffing problem 2. Review this report with the technical staff 3. Send portion of workload to reference lab immediately ACTION: Acting Supervisor	Ineffective QI process; QI, QAN, and QAc programs all need improvement: Assessment is pending on follow-up of remedial actions
1. Ward 22 training is ineffective; the need to enhance ward staff tng is critical; 2. Followup on CAP inspection, including interim survey, has been ineffective	1. Upgrade the plans for education and training on ward 22 2. Review the process of inspection follow-up ACTION: Department Chairman (Dec 95)	Ineffective follow-up of external QI findings: Entire external QI process needs improvement
Hemolytic reaction due to mistaken patient identity on ward 22; see data under Customer Satisfaction, Patient Outcome, and invalidation groupings	Same as mentioned under Customer satisfaction, Patient care Outcome, and Invalidation groupings	Ineffective QI process requires improvement at the interdeptal Qual Impvt/Risk Mgmt level!

JCAHO = Joint Commission on Accreditation of Healthcare Organizations external (or internal, interim) inspection occurs that there might be generation of any OFI.

Third, regarding external incident reports, complaints, and suggestions, a physician has initiated an incident report, citing a perceived occurrence of liver profile inaccuracy. The evaluation reveals that the inaccuracy was due to a transcription error without evidence of any repetition or trend.

The action consists of a plan for the supervisor to investigate and ensure the effectiveness of the test result transcription process. Only as a last resort should there be consideration of any technical or clerical personnel correction. After the true source of the problem is determined and there are some initial results from the investigative evaluation, then the laboratory can make plans for appropriate follow-up assessment.

Transfusion profile interpretation:
The external QI data is organized under the same three general indicator topics. First, regarding external PT surveys, evaluation of the data reveals that two surveys reported in October and December were unacceptable. It is clear that this recent trend is related to the severe staff shortage and resultant workload stress. Whatever the cause, in view of CLIA, JCAHO, and CAP standards it is equally clear that this PT performance record poses a serious threat to maintaining accreditation and Medicare payment eligibility.

The action and assessment are appropriate, echoing approaches similar to those of earlier indicator groupings. The main message is to remedy both technical and resource management processes and support the technical staff as soon as possible.

Second, regarding JCAHO, CAP, and other external inspection programs, the QI data corroborate the ineffective training of transfusion technique on ward 22 as evidenced by an unresolved 1994 CAP survey deficiency. The subject inspection was an interim self-inspection—in contrast to an on-site inspection by an external inspection team; regardless, the overall impact of the deficiency should be the same. The evaluation, action, and assessment steps appropriately focus on the need to improve the entire external QI process in terms of internal follow-up of external inspections. The delay in effective follow-up suggests that the usual internal QI remedial action process has been hampered by an ineffective QM interface in resolving the staffing crisis.

Third, regarding external incident reports, complaints, and suggestions, the report cites a reiteration of the hemolytic transfusion reaction on ward 22. Evaluation of the data corroborates what has already been reported under the customer satisfaction and patient care outcome groupings; the profile report makes reference to those earlier groupings. The recommended action and assessment are appropriate.

Additional profile interpretations:

Hematology (Appendix D): The same three specified indicators prevail as above for this section's external QI grouping. Evaluation of the data reveals that 1) three correct external PT survey results were received in the last month, 2) there are no unresolved external inspection deficiencies, and 3) there have been no external incident reports for eight months. These externally generated assessments of laboratory quality match the overall record provided by the earlier profile groupings. The action and assessment for the indicator are accurate—although the Hematology Section could learn some QI lessons from the following Microbiology Section profile.

Microbiology (Appendix E): Regarding external PT surveys, evaluation of the narrative data report reveals excellent performance with the last two surveys. In fact, the narrative relates that the external proficiency survey program has been on target for, at least, the past 12 months.

Since the external proficiency testing program is "opportunity-limited in the CQI environment," it is unnecessary to consider the lack of OFIs over a 12 month period as a matter of an insensitive QI process. Thus, there is no reason to respond to this indicator inactivity with a more specified monitoring approach.

Subsequent to CLIA requirements, however, this section's evaluation concludes there is a need to consider instituting an internal proficiency testing program. Thus, the recommended action is for the section supervisor to ascertain the actual need. The profile further suggests that follow-up of this <u>internal</u> proficiency testing can be continued under this same external QI grouping as a subsidiary, related indicator topic—or under analytical quality (ie, indicator grouping 9) or diagnostic quality (ie, indicator grouping 10) as a new external peer review indicator topic. The assessment is appropriate.

Regarding JCAHO, CAP, and other external inspection programs, evaluation of the narrative data reveals that there are no outstanding deficiencies since the last inspection. The action and assessment are appropriate for this opportunity-limited indicator.

Regarding external incident reports, complaints, and suggestions, evaluation of the narrative data reveals that the indicator has been "on target" for twelve months. The evaluation further cites that this extensive record without any adverse reports equates to indicator inactivity over an inordinate period—typical evidence that a general survey can easily be too passive. In contrast to the two earlier mentioned indicator topics, this indicator topic is "opportunity-<u>un</u>limited" in the CQI environment. It is independent of any external organization's schedule or resources and dependent only on the number and type of customer-suppliers as potential correspondents. Thus, the laboratory has the means to actively approach customer-supplier opinion—instead of just waiting for a complaint to surface—and tailor the incident-complaint-suggestion report as a more specified indicator.

Subsequently, the recommended action is for the supervisor to select a focused study on the basis of an active survey questionnaire directed at key customers, inquiring about their major concerns of laboratory quality. Many customers (internal or external) will not tell—unless they are asked. Instead, they will be inclined to "vote with their feet" and seek another laboratory's support—or go to a higher administrative echelon requesting better laboratory management. Therefore, it pays to be proactive and to anticipate customer-supplier reaction to laboratory products and services and new needs. The assessment for this indicator is appropriate.

Histopathology (Appendix G): This section's external QI profile provides a look at the same three specified indicators as above. Regarding external PT, there is a narrative record of one acceptable proficiency survey returned during the monitoring period, along with excellent results reported for all surveys in the last six months. The evaluation, action, and assessment are appropriate for the data on hand.

The recommended action is two-fold: first, the department laboratory manager is to coordinate with the hospital engineers and administration to resolve the protracted resolution of the CAP deficiency. Second, the section medical director is to evaluate the cause of the internal QI process's failing to effectively follow-up on the CAP (external QI) deficiency. The overall assessment appropriately refers to a failed improvement process with need to improve the laboratory- facility engineer QM interface.

Another indicator deficiency relates to an August 1995 fire inspection, citing inadequate fire alarm coverage. The investigative action for this indicator is appropriate for the OFI at hand with a five month delay—there should be no delay when it comes to fire prevention. The assessment relates to the already cited ineffectiveness of the laboratory QM interface with the hospital engineers, who must install all of the required alarms.

Regarding external incident reports, complaints, and suggestions, evaluation of the numerical data reveals that there has been an inordinate number of recurrent complaints concerning the TAT of surgical pathology reports spanning the six month cumulative period. This record matches what has already been reported under the customer satisfaction and turnaround groupings. The diminishing trend matches the corroborative evidence of improved management of the TAT process and technical staffing under earlier profile groupings. The favorable assessment is accurate—but, there is still need for substantial improvement.

Discussion:

Indicator Grouping: This indicator grouping for ensuring external quality improvement can include any of the three specified indicators demonstrated in the example profiles. These topics include externally generated proficiency testing, inspections, and incident reports. The first two indicator topics are opportunity-limited.

Just as the preceding grouping for internal QI attests to the laboratory's need to monitor itself, this grouping for external QI points to the fact that the laboratory cannot escape being monitored by others. Both internal and external peer review requirements are inexorably driven by governmental regulations and professional standards that are beyond individual laboratory control. All of these standards are to protect the laboratory's customer supplier.

An obvious distinction is made in this text between internal and external QI activities. There has been a popular trend to consider external QI (ie, proficiency testing and accreditation inspections) as a form of QC.[4] Recently, however, the distinction has been made even more clear by the CLIA requirements for both internal and external proficiency testing. These regulatory requirements recognize external peer review to be at an administrative level quite distinct from that of operative, bench-top QC.[5]

Referring back to earlier comments regarding professional concern about the peer review of individual competence, it is inevitable that this subject will arise whenever external peer review programs such as PT surveys or inspections are at hand; but, that is what peer review is all about. For example, there is evidence that accuracy of PT test results does correspond to laboratory staff qualification's. One study suggests that the use of ASCP certified technologists correlates with a "significantly higher probability of achieving 80% accuracy across all (PT) surveys."[6]

Quick mention of the CLIA requirement for internal proficiency testing also is appropriate at this point. Since CLIA '88 makes provisions for internal PT when an alternative laboratory testing method is not covered by external PT, where would the internal peer review fit into the quality profile? The laboratory can monitor internal PT results under the external QI grouping or under the analytical or diagnostic quality groupings (ie, indicator grouping 9 or 10), as it would any other internal peer review of the determinative process. The author prefers following internal PT under external QI since the former is externally driven.

The proficiency testing survey program can be administered by the CAP or any other peer organization that is able to provide valid analytes or tissue samples for participant analysis/diagnosis and accurate peer review with interlaboratory comparison. The main condition is that the external PT program has to be acceptable by accrediting organizations.

In regard to tissue diagnosis, finding an appropriate provider of proficiency survey material can be more problematic. This is particularly true when the primary laboratory is of academic stature. Occasionally, such a high caliber laboratory perpetuates the mistaken notion that it "has no peers." Well, every laboratory has its peer group. All that a laboratory of this caliber needs to do is look within the academic laboratory community-at-large and coordinate with a peer program that can produce the desired tissue samples and a credible proficiency review. Even where several elite subspecialties are involved in the parent laboratory, a separate academic-level peer program can serve each subspecialty. Still, whatever external PT program is chosen, it must meet the requirements of whatever accrediting programs are also involved.

The external peer inspection indicator can monitor any outside program that periodically inspects or surveys the primary laboratory. This on-site inspection process is usually necessary to meet requirements for accreditation, licensing, or some other type of formal certification. There are several national, state, and local accrediting, certifying, and licensing agencies that might be involved. Health Care Financing Administration (HCFA), Food and Drug Administration (FDA), military Offices of the Inspector General, state agencies, JCAHO, CAP, and American Association of Blood Banks (AABB) are some examples—and there are others associated with specialty and subspecialty laboratories. All are subjects for monitoring under this indicator grouping.

The laboratory should consider any inspection finding or deficiency as a subject to be followed under this portion of the quality profile. At the QC level, for example, the laboratory can establish a date by which all inspection findings must be resolved and reported back to the inspecting organization. For administrative-level follow-up, the laboratory can then monitor any inspection finding not completely resolved by the QC date under the external QI grouping. The QC target date then becomes a QI indicator criterion at this higher quality management level. The threshold would then be a comparative rate or sentinel event type, depending on how critical the deficiency is to patient care, employee safety, or laboratory cost-effectiveness.

The Transfusion Service profile illustrates how an interim CAP inspection finding can become an external QI issue. This teaching point reminds the laboratorian that interim self-inspections are based on the same inspection checklists used for the on-site, external inspections. Interim self-inspections are extremely valuable, and the laboratory should exercise them to their maximum advantage. Philosophically, follow-up of the self-inspection process might seem to fit under an internal peer review grouping. However, since the interim inspection is required and reviewed by the external peer organization for accreditation purposes, it is more appropriate to monitor the interim inspection under the indicator grouping for external QI as part of the sequence of externally generated events.

Regarding incident reports, complaints, and suggestions, this quality indicator topic is an example of what often is referred to as "occurrence screening." Often monitored as a general survey, this opportunity-unlimited indicator is easily tailored to be a more specified, focused or indexed topic. This potpourri of customer comments might be a serendipitous catch-all—but, it is still an important one that cannot be forgotten as a potential source of opportunities for improvement. Most often, the reports cited under this indicator originate from clinical staff and patients. But, we also must include opinions from employees and all other customers-suppliers, including those representing lateral support departments and higher hospital administrative echelons. Every customer-supplier is important.

Should the laboratory include comments from the "suggestion box" under this general indicator? The laboratory can include suggestions here or under the first indicator grouping for customer satisfaction, depending on the quality management philosophy. In the author's opinion, it is helpful to isolate all specific external comments—pro or con—under the external QI grouping, leaving the customer satisfaction grouping as a more globally-related, "top line" summary.

Ordinarily, additional indicator subtopics become an issue at this juncture of the indicator grouping discussion. As mentioned above, the first two indicators under this grouping are of a unique type—the opportunity limited type. As further described under the topic of assessment, the proficiency testing and external QI indicators do not commonly afford additional indicator topics because of this interesting characteristic. On the other hand, since incident reports are "opportunity-unlimited," the laboratory can proactively direct focused studies at any combination of customers-suppliers, thus generating a potentially unlimited number and type of additional indicator topics.

Another candidate for an indicator topic is the effectiveness of the external QI portion of the overall improvement program. Also, there is the potential question of effectiveness of scheduling lessons learned.

Supporting Indicators. As a global indicator, the external QI grouping enjoys cross-linkage with all 25 other groupings. The laboratory should take advantage of this level of corroborative information. In effect, studying any of the supporting indicators during a quality profile review of external QI equates to a laboratory "mini" self-inspection.

Threshold. Threshold levels for indicators under the external QI grouping can vary the full spectrum—from a sentinel event to a fully relaxed comparative rate indicator. This scope of variation depends on the criticalness of the laboratory management issues under external scrutiny.

Monitoring Periodicity. The periodicity for monitoring external QI indicators will also vary widely, depending on the criticalness of the quality management subject at hand.

Evaluation. External QI is a global indicator, as are all four of the organizational groupings. Consequently, evaluation of external QI data should correlate very well with all other supporting indicators.

There can be great variability of findings amongst individual sections. Comparing the two major examples, Chemistry is in much better condition than Transfusion in the eyes of more than one external reviewer—and both sections lack six FTEs. Again, the comparative differences in staffing depth and critical mass come to our attention through this indicator grouping, even though it is not specified for personnel strength.

Action. By virtue of the global nature of external QI indicators, any major element of laboratory operations—outcome, process, or structural resource—is subject to improvement program scrutiny. Consequently, required actions can target any level of intralaboratory or extralaboratory responsibility for any operative- or organization-level key management area.

There is an added element to an already heightened sense of urgency for remedial action and resolution of any OFI under this profile grouping. Secondary to the CLIA rules for proficiency testing, there must be rapid resolution of any PT or inspection deficiency. Repeat deficiencies are sure grounds for disenfranchisement from Medicare payment eligibility by HCFA.

Assessment. As always, the three standard options apply to the assessment of external QI in the CQI environment. The second option—asking if the improvement process is effective—offers a unique opportunity to use the internal QI process as a mechanism to improve the external QI process (both being part of the overall improvement program). Proficiency testing surveys and interim CAP inspections provide two common examples of this unique possibility.

In the first example, a laboratory can fall into the trap of not subscribing to a PT program of sufficient caliber that matches the primary laboratory's extent of patient care support. In routine follow-up, the "second option" assessment would be that the external QI process is insufficient as an overall means for detecting systemic laboratory error. Thus, subscribing to a more complete PT program will expand the potential monitoring targets and improve both the internal and external improvement processes.

In the second example, it is very common for a laboratory to pay short shrift to interim inspections, glossing over the prescribed check list. Again, the assessment would be that the external improvement process is insufficient. Considering the internal QI requirements for assessment, the laboratory should take better advantage of the opportunity to improve itself through a more careful, thorough self-inspection. Thus, performing a more complete self-inspection will expand the scope of potential monitoring targets and improve not only the external but also the internal improvement process.

However, practice of the second option is limited when it comes to assessing the effectiveness of the external QI grouping in respect to prolonged indicator inactivity in the CQI environment. The main point is that this grouping is essentially opportunity-limited, all other quality indicator groupings being opportunity-unlimited. With any other grouping, if there has not been any improvement over a reasonable period, then the quality management process needs improvement due to its lack of sensitivity or ability to detect OFIs that actually exist—but have not been discovered. But, in the case of external QI—once a PT survey or an inspection deficiency is resolved, there is no mechanism available until the next scheduled, externally-generated observation (including external or internal PT survey or on-site or interim inspection) can reveal any further opoprtunity for improvement.

For example, only when a scheduled inspection uncovers a deficiency can the laboratory establish a reasonable time limit for resolution of the opportunity. Once all inspection deficiencies are satisfied, there are no further OFIs to monitor—until the next inspection. The primary laboratory can do nothing more than wait for the next survey mailing or inspection visit.

Under the external QI grouping, only incident reports, complaints, and suggestions qualify as opportunity-unlimited indicators. The laboratory can practice the assessment "second-option" with this external QI topic on an unlimited scale. If not enough complaints or suggestions surface spontaneously, the laboratory can go out and actively elicit them from the customers-suppliers, thus improving the QI process through improved indicator activity.

Perhaps incident reports and complaints are as good a laboratory example, as any, of Kriegel and Patlers' admonition that "If it ain't broke—break it!" Without delving into the QI process and actively eliciting customer opinion, the laboratory will only hear the bad news—and, then, only after it is too late.[7]

Communication. The transmission of QI lessons learned from this external QI grouping should match its global nature. All customers-suppliers who are involved in the laboratory QI program have a need to know and should receive lessons learned relating to the external QI grouping.

Quality Anticipation Management (Indicator Grouping 25)

Chemistry profile interpretation:
There are three general indicators chosen for this profile grouping. They cover the three phases of strategic planning: research, development, and implementation.

- In the organizational research phase, the laboratory surveys customers-suppliers. This amounts to the typical internal and external market assessment of strengths, weaknesses, opportunities, and threats (ie, SWOT analysis) regarding customer-supplier special needs for product-service improvement—and regarding internal and external barriers to the laboratory's meeting those needs.
- In the development phase, the laboratory uses information from the research surveys to design and test new or improved laboratory products and services.
- In the implementation phase, the laboratory takes successful developmental products and services and places them into full-scale production or operation.

There should be a smooth, continuous flow of action from one anticipatory phase to the next. When a project is not successful after an adequate trial, it simply drops out of the overall plan, and the laboratory generates new planning projects to maintain the momentum of satisfying customer needs (both internal and external).

Evaluation of the QAn numerical and narrative data for the Chemistry Section's QAn profile reveals that only the research phase was scheduled for reporting in December. The laboratory section attained only one of two research survey milestones in December and only one of three in September. The profile measures the successful attainment of these planned research projects by whether or not they result in usable data. Not attaining this goal suggests faulty design, inadequate execution, or too little time for completion of a research project. The evaluation summarizes that research surveys have not been totally effective in producing usable data due to faulty survey designs.

Indicator Grouping 25
Quality Anticipation Management

Chemistry Section QualityI Profile

Indicator Grouping/ Specific Indicator: Threshold (Periodicity)	QI Data Observations (Date trend started) J A S O N D
Quality Anticipation (QAn) (Quarterly)	3/3 = 3 out of 3 attained - = report not scheduled
a. Organizational research: all milestones will be attained!!	- - 1/3 - - 1/2 Interpretation: only 1/3 attained in Sep & 1/2 in Dec resulted in usable data due to faulty survey designs
b. Development: all milestones will be attained!!	- 0 - - 0 - 0 = no milestones missed; all attained
c. Implementation: all milestones will be attained!!	3/3 - - 2/2 - -

Transfusion Service Quality Profile

Quality Anticipation (QAn) (Quarterly)	
a. Organizational research: all milestones will be attained!!	No new survey projects have been scheduled x 6 mo
b. Development: all milestones will be attained!!	No new projects scheduled x 6 mo
c. Implementation: all milestones will be attained!!	- - 2/3 - - 0/1 - = no report scheduled 2/3 = 2 of 3 milestones attained

!! = sentinel event

Although the other two planning phases are not scheduled for reporting in December, evaluation of their cumulative records reveals that these parameters have been on schedule with no adverse trends over the last two monitoring periods. However, because of the lack of research phase effectiveness exhibited by the first indicator, the section quality management team is concerned about the sensitivity of the development

Evaluation of QI Data, TQM System, and CQI Process	Action Action Person: (Date Initiated)	Assessment of Overall Improvement
All research surveys are reported as completed on time, BUT effectiveness of approach has been spotty	1. Establish focused studies and analyze effectiveness of all projects 2. Proceed to developement phase with successful projects 3. Report in Jan 96 ACTION: Supervisor	Internal QI process and QAn research processes need improvement
No report scheduled; above comment raises concern over focus of this indicator	Report due in Feb 96; comment on project effectiveness ACTION: Supervisor	To be determined (TBD)
No report scheduled; consider improving the focus of this indicator	Report due in Jan 96; comment on project effectiveness ACTION: Supervisor	TBD
This phase of the QAn program has been neglected	Reprioritize and reschedule QAn as part of QAc team building effort ACTION: Medical Director Staff vacancy problem must be solved to bring QAn back on track or dept must provide ancillary support ACTION: Admin Supervisor	Ineffective QAn and QI processes: Vacancy problem must be solved to realize effective infrastructural programs such as strategic planning
This phase of the QAn program has been neglected		
Increasing failure to meet milestones without QI follow-up due to supervisor and staff shortage		
QI Note: The implementation project missed in December was designed to enhance Ward 22 staff training in transfusion techniques, including nondaytime staff; the missed project in September to establish a new technique for thawing FFP was not critical.		

and implementation indicators, as well. Thus, their evaluation suggests the possible need to improve the focus of the indicators for development and implementation.

Under normal circumstances, the recommended action for each planning phase should consist of a fairly routine, straightforward progression of follow-up events. The action for research should link the initial survey activities with the generation of development projects. The action for development should link those projects with final implementation activities. The usual action for follow-up of implementation projects should call for establishing project target dates and reporting their progress through other general or specified studies until the subject plan or procedure, technique or method, or product or service is fully institutionalized.

In actuality, the subject profile's concern over research effectiveness is stimulating a recommendation to establish focused studies for all planned research projects. First, the section quality management team is to analyze the reasons for research survey ineffectiveness; the supervisor is responsible for follow-up. Under the given circumstances, there is a recommendation that the section team also determine whether or not the development and implementation indicators are accurately reflecting project effectiveness.

Assessment of the research phase reveals that remedial action has been tardy, thus the QAn process lacks effectiveness and needs improvement. Assessment of the other two indicators is "to be determined" since December is not a scheduled reporting month and the immediate action results will not be available until at least the next month.

Transfusion profile interpretation:

Evaluation of the QI data for the same three general indicators reveals that all three phases of this laboratory section's QAn program are sorely in need of improvement. For the organizational research phase, the section has scheduled no survey projects for half a year; the same holds true for the development phase. Planned implementation projects have dwindled in numbers and effectiveness. In summary, the section has demonstrated ineffective execution of the QAn plan and ineffective follow-up of missed opportunities for all three phases.

The combined action for repairing all phases of the actualization program connects the success of QAn with the QI and QAc programs, as well as with staff recruitment and hiring. The assessment cites ineffective QAn action and QI follow-up along with an ineffective improvement process at the QM interface.

A special QI note explains that a planning project that was designed to enhance ward staff training in transfusion techniques, (including the nondaytime staff) was one of the missed implementation projects in December. This would have been the section's answer to the 1994 CAP interim survey finding which might have prevented this month's hemolytic transfusion reaction on ward 22. However, the project did not materialize because of the burdens of staff shortage. That particular ward accident links several of this section's profile indicator groupings, including customer satisfaction, patient care outcome, laboratory product utilization, workload management, personnel management, internal and external QI, quality anticipation, and, as is later seen, quality actualization.

Additional profile interpretations:

Hematology (Appendix D): Evaluation of this section's QAn grouping reveals a perfect record for all research, development, and implementation phase indicators with successful completion of all their scheduled projects over the last six months. Whereas December is the month for reporting the development phase profile, and this phase demonstrates six months of indicator inactivity—one recommended action is for the supervisor to select a focused indicator for the development phase to improve the sensitivity of the QI process. All assessments are accurate.

Microbiology (Appendix E): Evaluation of this section's QAn grouping reveals another perfect record. All actions and assessments are appropriate.

Histopathology (Appendix G): Evaluation of this section's QAn grouping reveals that the section has missed several research survey projects with a worsening trend over the past two reporting periods; the surveys are simply not being done. The section has attained all development projects in follow-up of previously completed research projects. No new implementation projects have been planned for the last two quarters. This means that several fully developed projects—although waiting as back-up—have not been transformed into implementation plans and action. One could interpret this situation as a throughput problem with a decreased TAT of research and implementation projects and a backlog of development projects. QAn throughput needs to be expedited accordingly.

Similar to the Transfusion Service scenario, this section has been short staffed—but, also, has been poorly supervised. As a result, the QAn schedule has stalled in generating new research and implementation projects and in transforming development projects. The respective actions are all aimed at improving follow-up, especially to take advantage of already developed improvements just waiting for full implementation. One way of improving the QAn process would be to review the section's planning goals and modify them according to the current staff strength—reducing research and development expectations and catching up on implementation of those projects already developed and just waiting for implementation.

Discussion:

Indicator Grouping: Of the three infrastructural programs that comprise the TQM system at the organizational, administrative management level, strategic planning can probably be considered the most "traditional." Planning is a well-established process of anticipatory improvement that has been a part of managerial theory, concept, and practice since the beginning of the industrial age—at least. However, although planning is well established as a managerial concept, it is deplorably underestimated in value, misunderstood as a process, and underutilized by many organizations and their leaders. Often when there has been substantial effort to formulate a "Strategic Plan," it is published and left to languish on a dusty bookshelf or in an obscure file drawer—without adequate follow-up until the next annual planning conference.

The laboratory should periodically consider every key management program, key management activity, and individual procedure for improvement by a disciplined anticipatory process of:

- Organizational research (including internal and external assessments)
- Development (including pilot decisions and project trials)
- Full-scale implementation.

The laboratory can monitor the achievement of milestones for each QAn phase, as demonstrated by the three QI indicators in the quality profile format.

The microbiology profile example provides a good example of fertile ground for the three planning phases. In the research phase, the laboratory can query all employees (the internal customer) by a written survey regarding their biohazard exposure experience. Questions could include types of personal protective items used, as well as the frequency of use and under what circumstances they are used. The laboratory can then correlate blood and body fluid exposures, including percutaneous injuries, with the use of personal protection.[8]

This research project could then feed into the development phase where the laboratory could test new protective approaches for overall effectiveness. Then , these results would feed into full implementation projects.

In regard to additional indicator topics, the laboratory can multiply the number and type of potential QI indicators by applying focused studies to any phase and its individual projects on a prioritized scale of importance. Also, review of the quality of the QAn plan itself can serve as a specified indicator topic, phasing the review as has been suggested for the reviewing of all the other written laboratory procedures. Also, there could be QI monitoring of the effectiveness of the teaching of QAn lessons learned.

Supporting Indicators. Quality anticipation is a totally global indicator. All 25 other indicator groupings can provide QI data to corroborate the evaluation of the QAn data.

Threshold. QI variance limits for QAn indicator data depend on the criticalness of the subject indicator topic and the adequacy of the quality management resources on hand. The Elizabethan quality management puzzle always remains: to be a sentinel event—or not to be? This is a case-by-case decision.

Monitoring Periodicity. As usual, this scheduling is linked with the indicator criteria, the degree of threshold freedom, the subject aspect of care, and quality management resources on hand.

Evaluation. If any quality indicators are global in nature, QAn surely is at the top of that list. *Every laboratory activity*—every operational procedure in every program at every organizational level—should arise from an up-to-date written plan. We should not operate a laboratory department without a current strategic plan any more than we should not perform an electrolyte analysis without an up-to-date technical procedure—the only difference is the economy of scale. Consequently, QI evaluation of the QAn program will often reveal linkage between planning program effectiveness and findings in other groupings of the quality profile.

Such an evaluation should be a matter of weighing "*process* cause" against "*process* effect"—as opposed to "*person* cause" versus "*person* effect." The Transfusion Service QAn profile segment provides a good example of how evaluation of the state of the planning program interlinks with the most problematic process causes and effects that plague this section and related clinical ward operations. In this case, the section staff has really been trying—with all the good intentions—of formulating anticipatory action to prevent poor transfusion techniques and adverse patient care outcome. The section's quality managers have known how to orchestrate organizational research, development, and implementation—but they have not had the quality management resources by which to institute a successful operational program—including ward training. As a probable consequence, a hemolytic transfusion reaction has occurred on ward 22.

Action. A global indicator calls for an equally broad scope of action to resolve laboratory-scale opportunities for improvement. Thus, any organizational research, development, or implementation plan can be very focused on a specific aspect of one technical operating procedure or it can reach out and focus on section-wide, service-wide, department-wide, or hospital-wide activities. Therefore, all involved individuals need to participate in the strategic planning process, and such planning should include joint laboratory-clinical or laboratory-administrative input, whenever appropriate.

The actions for any of the three planning phases should reflect some progression of anticipatory events. For example, actions to improve organizational research should include some impetus toward progressing to the development phase. Likewise, actions to improve the development phase should include some movement toward full scale implementation.

On some occasions, the need for improvement can be so blatantly critical that one must begin planning for immediate full-scale development or implementation. Consequently, the first or second planning phase must be abbreviated or completely dismissed in the process. This truncated approach presumes that 1) adequate baseline data are already at hand to preclude need for the research phase or 2) patient care, employee safety, or operational cost-effectiveness is so critical as to demand an emergency short cut with no time left to do otherwise. The laboratory should undertake the decision for such truncated QAn action advisedly with documented justification—lest either of the first two, very valuable phases become habitually ignored in favor of the conveniently expedient quick-fix.

Often, the QAn action personnel are at a higher level of laboratory leadership responsibility than usual. In the Chemistry Section profile example where QAn is on track, the section supervisor has proven the

Indicator Grouping 26
Quality Actualization Management

Chemistry Section Quality Profile

Indicator Grouping/ Specific Indicator: Threshold (Periodicity)	QI Data Observations (Date trend started) J A S O N D
Quality Actualization (QAc) : (Monthly)	
a. Team building: 1. Morale: no adverse effect on team effectiveness!!	Morale is excellent based on the review of Nov team survey and supporting indicators; this has been a consistent observation for 12 mo
2. Skills training (TST): no skills lacking that adversely affect team effectiveness!!: < 1 hour/qtr for QAc Training!!	Training schedule is on time; at least 1 hour per month; all work shifts have been consistent for 12 months
b. Team maintenance: 1. Continuing TST	As noted above
2. Personnel actions: none overdue!!	0 0 0 0- 0 0 None overdue x 12 mo 0 = no action overdue
3. Personnel incentives: none overdue!!	0 0 0 0 0 0 None overdue x 12 mo
c. Team effectiveness: 1. Decision making: no problem too hard or unresolved > 3 months!!	Most OFI have been adequately addressed by the section team; if too hard, they have been correctly submitted to the appropriate higher echelon or lateral dept; HOWEVER, there has been 1) insuffïcent attention paid to the replacement of the multichannel Analyzer X and 2) prolonged response to indicator inactivity
2. Leadership committment: TBD	

!! - sentinel event TST = team skills training

capability to carry on with the QAn tasks at hand. In the Transfusion Service example, however, the resource constraints and priorities are of such grave importance that the assignment of direct QAn responsibilities has escalated to the level of the section medical director and the departmental administrative supervisor (or laboratory manager, whatever the case may be).

Assessment. The three standard options for assessing the quality anticipation program effectiveness in a CQI environment are still at play. This includes assessing the effectiveness of remedial action follow-up, the effectiveness of the overall QI surveillance of QAn opportunities for improvement, and the effectiveness of the QM interface related to planning activities.

Evaluation of QI Data, TQM System, and CQI Process	Action Action Person: (Date Initiated)	Assessment of Overall Improvement
On target x 12 mo; there has been no improvement over an inordinate amount of time	Select a focused study for Feb 96 ACTION: Supervisor	Improvement has been stalled but now is in progress
On target x 12 mo; there has been no improvement over an inordinate amount of time	Select a focused study for Mar 96 ACTION: Supervisor	Improvement now in progress)
As noted above	As noted above	As noted above
On target x 12 mo; no improvement over an inordinate amount of time	Select a focused study for Apr 93 ACTION: Supervisor	Improvement now in progress)
On target x 12 mo; no improvement over an inordinate period	Select a focused study for May 93 ACTION: Supervisor	Improvement now in progress
Generally on target EXCEPT FOR 1. delayed decision to replace analyzer X and 2. poor reaction to prolonged indicator inactivity in several key management areas	1. Start focused study on decision making for instrument replacement for Jan 96 2. React more readily to indicator inactivity ACTION: Medical Director	QI process and decision making improvement has been stalled but now is in progress
QI Note: Begin reporting on "Leadership committment" as a new QAc indicator grouping for Jan 96		

Communication. Just as global as a QAn opportunity might be, the need of transmitting the lessons learned from the planning process to all involved customers-suppliers can be equally widespread.

Quality Actualization (Indicator Grouping 26)

Chemistry profile interpretation: Evaluation of the data for this section's QAc grouping reveals evidence of an excellent actualization program—aside from just a few relatively minor aspects needing improvement. This grouping highlights the three major program phases of team building, team maintenance, and team effectiveness. Six, more specified indicators include

Indicator Grouping 26 (Continued)
Quality Actualization Management

Transfusion Service Quality Profile

Indicator Grouping/ Specific Indicator: Threshold (Periodicity)	QI Data Observations (Date trend started) J A S O N D
Quality Actualization (QAc) (Monthly) a. Team building: 1. Morale: no adverse effect on team effectiveness!!	1. Morale is poor based on anecdotal evidence, causing documented ineffectiveness; two more resignations have been threatened 2. There are obvious signs of staff "burn out"as borne out by several supporting indicators 3. Main cause of morale problems is staff shortage and excessive workload
2. Skills training (TST): no skills lacking that adversely effect team effectiveness!!: < 1 hour/qtr for QAc training!!	1. Lab staff needs special attention to improve morale and effectiveness 2. Ward 22 evening & night shifts need educ/tng in team skills building (plus instruction in transfusion technique)
b. Team maintenance: 1. Continuing TST	As noted above
2. Personnel incentives: none overdue!!	0 0 0 0 1* 1 0 = none overdue * = resolved late
3. Personnel incentives: none overdue!!	0 0 0 0 0 0 No new incentives have been initiated in 6 mo
c. Team effectiveness: 1. Decision making: no problem too hard or unresolved > 3 months!!	All three infrastructural programs (QI/QAn/QAc) are crippled; the platelet storage problem is a good example of disabled quality management and poor organizational team decision making

!! - sentinel event TST = team skills training

team morale, team skills education, personnel actions, personnel incentives, decision making, and leader commitment. Generally speaking, the narrative and numerical data reports are favorable—mirroring the Chemistry Section's overall satisfactory quality profile in its entirety.

Under the team building phase, the quality management team reports section morale to be excellent. The section derives this narrative observation from a written section survey or questionnaire received from all section employees in November plus a review of all other indicator groupings. This

Evaluation of QI Data, TQM System, and CQI Process	Action Action Person: (Date Initiated)	Assessment of Overall Improvement
Staff shortage and the resultant overburdening workload are crippling team morale and effectiveness There are no objective data obtained from direct employee input	1. Determine reasons why techs have been leaving (other than staff shortage); run a survey of current staff; review exit surveys 2. Resolve workload- staffing burdens ACTION: Medical Director	Ineffective QAc and QI processes: Staffing action requires highest level assistance
1. Time for team bldg in Trans Service must be made available by innovative staffing and scheduling in lab and ward 2. Coordination is needed between interdepartmental leadership re Ward 22 tng	1. Increase tm bldg in Trans Service 2. Coordinate with Chiefs of Nursing and Med re trng in tm bldg and trans technique on Ward 22 ACTION: Medical Director	Ineffective QAc and QI processes in Trans Svc and Ward 22
------	------	------
One promotion action overdue this month; trend developing	Meet personnel needs on time ACTION: Admin Supervisor	Ineffective QAc and QI processes:
No new incentives provided for 6 mo when they have been especially needed	Institute new incentives by Jan 96 ACTION: Lab Manager	QAc and QI processes need improvement
Team decision making is currently grossly ineffective due to staff shortage and excessive workload	1. Coord with HTF & fill all vacancies 2. Rebuild the team 3. Reprioritize all organizational activities 4. Hire a TQM consultant ACTION: Medical Director	Seriously ineffective QI, QAn, & QAc processes: Several problems are "too hard" for this section to improve
QI Note: Begin monitoring "Leadership commitment" as a new, ongoing monthly QAc indicator grouping for Jan 96; target departmental-, service- and selection-level leadership involvement in support of the QI, QAn, and QAc programs		

high level of morale has been the general observation for one year with no alleged opportunities for improvement noted.

The evaluation reveals that, although this consistent QAc record of high morale seems impeccable, there has been no documented improvement over an inordinate period. Thus, in a CQI environment such indicator inactivity suggests an insensitive improvement process. The recommended action is to design a focused study within the next two months that will improve the sensitivity of the QI surveillance process. This might result in a more specified questionnaire or survey instrument; a different approach such as group or individual interviews; or an interactive suggestion program, or a reprioritization of this indicator in favor of a more important target for monitoring. The assessment is accurate.

Again under team building, the profile demonstrates that the laboratory has consistently provided education of organizational skills as evidenced by a perfectly maintained training schedule of at least one hour per month. This educational effort coincides with the other three hours per month of CME that have already been noted as being on schedule (ie, CME indicator grouping 16). The profile notes that personnel on all laboratory shifts have been involved in the training. Again, this is a pattern of success that the section has established over a full year of quality surveillance, even with a significant staff shortage.

The evaluation notes that the indicator has been "on target for 12 months." In spite of such a successful record, the evaluation recognizes that there has been no improvement of the QAc training for over a full year. Thus, the recommended action is to select a focused study to improve the QI process within the next quarter. The assessment is accurate.

Under the team maintenance phase, the personnel actions and personnel incentives indicators both demonstrate equally impeccable QI data records for 12 months of cumulative data (6 months of which are specifically shown). Since there has been no improvement of either of these two QAc team maintenance processes for a full year, the recommended actions are to select focused studies for each indicator within the next four to five months, covering both personnel actions and personnel incentives. The individual assessments for the two indicators are accurate.

Under the team effectiveness phase, the profile describes decision making in terms of most opportunities having been adequately addressed; also, most OFI that have been "too hard" have been shifted to supporting departments or higher echelons. However, the narrative data point out that there has been some delay in the follow-up of remedial actions (ie, the multichannel analyzer replacement). There have also been many instances where there has been prolonged indicator inactivity without an appropriate QI response, including the QAc grouping.

Evaluation of the decision making data reveals that section decisions have generally been on target; however, the quality management team recognizes that decisions regarding instrument replacement were unduly delayed, as well as there having been poor response to prolonged indicator inactivity.

The recommended actions are for the section medical director, as team leader, to initiate a focused study on the section's decision making process related to instrument replacement. A second overall recommendation is for the section to respond more readily to indicator inactivity. The assessment is appropriate with emphasis on follow-up of remedial actions and the need to improve the quality surveillance process.

A separate section-department QI note states that the section quality management team must initiate a new indicator of leadership commitment under the general topic of team effectiveness. This would stimulate surveillance of the effectiveness of leader training in quality management theory, concepts, and tools; leader involvement in the improvement process; and leader support of quality management by ensuring adequate resources.

Transfusion profile interpretation:
Evaluation of this section's organizational "bottom line" reflects all the ominous information that has been portrayed throughout the body of this quality profile—if "ominous" is even an adequate word.

Under the team building phase, the morale indicator reports team spirit as poor, caused by severe staff shortage and workload stress. Although there has not been any active surveying, the narrative data cite word-of-mouth and supporting indicators as evidence of staff ineffectiveness and overload. Two more staff members have announced plans to resign.

The recommended action is for the medical director to determine reasons for the technologists' leaving the section—however, reviewing old exit interviews is the worst way to be learning about staff morale—when the proverbial horse already is out of the barn. There is also to be a survey of the current staff to determine their immediate needs, to start team rebuilding, and to begin to improve morale. The assessment is accurate in that both the QAc and QI processes are broken and ineffective, along with the QAn process.

Team skill education is in need of concerted attention. As a note of joint QI-QAc concern, this segment indicator also reports that the clinical staff on ward 22, particularly the nondaytime shift personnel, also require team building—in addition to their CME requirements. The recommended action is for the medical director to 1) begin team building and skill training (ie, start from scratch) and 2) coordinate with the nursing and medical leaders of ward 22 to begin team building and blood transfusion training. The whole point is that team morale on ward 22 impacts on the laboratory's ability to serve the patient—just as the laboratory's own team morale affects the ward's ability to serve the same patient. The assessment is accurate.

Under the team maintenance subgrouping, the personnel actions indicator reveals that promotion actions have been inordinately delayed. The promotion due in November was late but is noted as resolved. One due in December was late without resolution to date. An adverse trend is developing with this indicator. This beleaguered section is under the control of a new, acting supervisor who needs to cope with an immense operative managerial task—plus dealing with the paperwork of personnel actions. Considering the immense resource constraints, the recommended action to "do better" and assessment of ineffective processes are appropriate; under better circumstances, there would be a more concerted attempt at analyzing and improving the personnel action process—there are "bigger fish to fry."

The personnel incentives indicator data demonstrate no overdue actions. On the other hand, no new incentives have been developed for the past six months to improve the motivation of a highly stressed team. The recommendation to institute new incentives and the assessment of ineffective processes are appropriate, considering the current circumstances.

Under the team effectiveness phase, the decision-making indicator narrative data say it all—all three infrastructural programs are crippled: all which provide the organizational energy and the fundamental focus for effective decision making. The platelet storage problem is used as a key example. The overall evaluation is that the staff shortage and excessive workload are the chief causes.

The recommended action is for the medical director to, first, concentrate at the hospital level on rebuilding the section's staff in terms of numbers; the work force is the underlying operative resource problem. Second, in terms of revising the section's process for decision making, there must be team rebuilding, along with reorganizing and reprioritizing all organizational activities at the section level—deciding how to accomplish the workload with the number of staff available. This calls for prioritization of needs and some tough decision making in regard to what must be done and what cannot be done, including what some other department or administrative echelon must do.

The section's actions as documented throughout this section's entire QAc grouping resemble a series of knee-jerk responses; but considering the operational circumstances (ie, human resources versus workload), there is not much more that can be expected. Actions are directed at the medical director, administrative manager, and laboratory manager, reflecting the necessity for the highest level of leadership involvement—if quality actualization is to mend as is needed in this Transfusion Service. As with QI and QAn actions, QAc actions are often so global as to require the involvement of section personnel who have the highest authority and who control the most resources.

The assessment for the decision making indicator cites ineffective QI, QAn and QAc processes. In regard to the QM interface, it points out that there are several problems that are too hard for the section to improve, requiring department-wide as well as hospital-wide assistance.

A special section-department editorial QI note cites that, within the next month, there will be a need to begin monitoring leadership commitment in support of all three quality management programs of the TQM system. In the face of such serious operational ineffectiveness, this new indicator is important enough to add to the quality profile—but, only after reprioritization and reduction of all other QI surveillance targets.

Additional profile interpretations:

Hematology (Appendix D): Under the team building phase, this section's morale indicator reveals that there is no overt lack of morale.[c] However,

[c] This grouping demonstrates one of the few management areas where an "opportunity for improvement" infers a problem in which there is only too little—and not an opportunity for improvement in which also there could be too much. For example, it is virtually unheard of for there to be too much morale or too great an *esprit*.

supporting groupings substantiate that there is an inordinate imbalance in staff strength versus workload; this suggests a stressful work environment.

The evaluation is that, although there is a perception of good personnel morale, there has been no attempt at actively measuring personnel esprit in the face of mounting workload stress. The recommended action is for the supervisor to initiate a focused indicator study of morale by means of an active survey of all employees on all shifts and to ensure that there is adequate team building and maintenance activities within the next month. The assessment is accurate in that the effectiveness of the current methods of measuring morale are questionable; there really are not any effective methods in active use.

Regarding the team skill training indicator—in spite of the data reflecting this program as being consistently on target—there has been indicator inactivity for a full year. The recommended action is for the section supervisor to select a focused study for measurement of the effectiveness of the current QAc training program. First, there should be a survey of the employees to ascertain their perception of training needs; second, there should be reevaluation of the team skills training and team building plan and schedule. The assessment is accurate.

Under the team maintenance phase, evaluation of the indicators for both personnel actions and personnel incentives reveals similar situations. In either case, there has been indicator inactivity for over half a year, in spite of the data reflecting these programs as having been consistently on target. The first recommended action is for the supervisor to select a focused study and improve the management of personnel actions. The recommended action for improving management of personnel incentives is for the supervisor to develop new incentive awards recognizing personnel working under heavy stress; there is also to be selection of a focused study to follow the effectiveness of the personnel incentive program. The assessment is accurate.

Under the team effectiveness phase, there are two general indicators: one measuring decision making effectiveness and the other measuring leadership commitment. Evaluation of the decision making data reveals that there has been inordinate delay in deciding how to resolve several quality management issues. The recommended action is for the medical director (the quality management team leader) to review the decision making apparatus regarding these key problematic issues.

The second action is for the quality management team to select a focused indicator for studying the effectiveness of interdepartmental coordination at the quality management interface between the laboratory and the facility engineers, medical maintenance, and one reference laboratory. The assessment that decision making skills are flawed, requiring improvement at the QM interface level is accurate.

A specified indicator addresses the topic of leader commitment. The indicator focuses on leader support of quality management by measuring the extent that the leader provides adequate resources. Evaluation of the narrative data reveals that the method of measuring leader support has been very passive, depending on voluntary comments through a general survey approach. The recommended action is for the medical director to determine the section team's consensus opinion on leadership commitment. The method is not specified but could include any combination of a written survey, interviews, or nominal group techniques. The assessment of there being ongoing improvement of the QI process is accurate.

Microbiology (Appendix E): Under the team building phase, this section's morale indicator reveals a definite morale problem in the mycobacteriology unit based on a November survey and supporting evidence through the employee safety grouping. Evaluation reveals the source of discontent to be two technologists' recently experiencing tuberculin skin test conversion and the subsequent discovery of a malfunctioning safety hood. Aside from actions directed at improving biohazard control within the subject laboratory area—the recommended action under this QAc indicator is for the medical director to bolster team building in the mycobacteriology unit and to assure the employees that the laboratory is in control of contagion hazards.[d] The assessment is accurate.

Evaluation of the team skill training indicator reveals that the program has been consistently on schedule for 12 months. In the CQI environment, this is an inordinately long period of indicator inactivity. The recommended action is for the supervisor to select a focused study of the effectiveness of team skill training. The assessment is accurate.

Under the team maintenance phase, evaluation of both indicators for personnel actions and personnel incentives reveals two similar situations. In either case, the data reflect that the program has been consistently on target for ten and eight months, respectively; these have been inordinately long periods of indicator inactivity. The recommended actions are for the supervisor to select focused studies to improve the management of both personnel actions and personnel incentives. The assessment is accurate.

Under the team effectiveness phase, evaluation of the decision making indicator data reveals overall favorable consistency—except for making decisions related to coordinating facility engineer and medical maintenance support. The recommended action is for the supervisor to initiate a focused study to measure the laboratory's coordination of facility renovation and equipment maintenance at the QM interface level. The assessment is accurate.

A special QI note announces two improvements for the QAc program (and the QI process). First, the section is to initiate monitoring leadership commitment as a new indicator under the team effectiveness grouping. Second, it is to evaluate changing the periodicity of review of the QAc indicators from monthly to quarterly.

Histopathology (Appendix G): Under the team building phase, this section's morale indicator reveals anecdotal evidence of favorable morale and

[d] This is the best use of the word "assure" in healthcare quality management—not to document quality performance (as in quality assurance) but to truthfully guarantee (pledge) to human beings that they are being treated fairly and safely.

a record free of complaints for ten months. However, there have not been any active surveys, interviews, or team fact-finding activities to substantiate this favorable impression. Evaluation of all the data at hand, including supporting evidence of decreased staff with subsequent increased workload stress, provides a strong suggestion of threatened morale. The recommended action is for the supervisor to survey all section employees—with support of the section medical director. This latter condition of medical director involvement ensures team leader involvement in a section that has been weakened by lack of strong supervision. The assessment is of ineffective past remedial actions and an ineffective QI process that needs an improved, more active measurement of morale.

Evaluation of the accompanying team skill training indicator reveals that this program is not on schedule due to staff shortage—or ineffective supervisory attention to maintaining the QAc program—or inadequate medical director leadership—or all of the above. Additionally, QAn, QI, and several operative indicators suggest a developing environment in which these organizational skills would be very valuable in handling the current work stress. The recommended action is to reestablish an effective team skills training schedule; this step is of such great importance that the medical director is responsible for this action. The assessment notes that the QAc program and QI process need improvement; it also strongly suggests that leader involvement must be improved in support of the actualization program.

Under the team maintenance phase, evaluation of the indicators for personnel actions and personnel incentives reveals two similar situations. In both cases, the data reflect that these programs have been inconsistent in meeting their threshold targets. The record shows that four personnel actions (eg, promotions) and two incentive actions (eg, special pay awards for excellent service) were missed during the last six months. The recommended actions are for the supervisor to select a focused study to improve the management of the personnel action and personnel incentive programs. In addition, the supervisor is to enhance the incentive award program in recognizing outstanding staff motivation. The assessment of an improving QI process is accurate for both indicators.

In spite of the apparent supervisory incapabilities, the laboratory still must investigate process problems before processing problems. The former situation alludes to a systemic issue unrelated to individual performance. The latter situation alludes to an individual inadequately performing required duties. In resolving any OFI, pay attention to the process as a cause before investigating the processing.

Under the team effectiveness phase, evaluation of the decision making indicator data reveals that the section has missed several, critically important improvement opportunities through faulty or stalled decision. Additionally, the section has demonstrated inability to transfer "too hard" problems to the appropriate supporting lateral department or higher echelon. As one major result, the section's ineffective coping with too hard problems has resulted in severe customer dissatisfaction, causing the hospital to form an interdepartmental task force to resolve the delayed throughput of surgical pathology reports.

The recommended action under this decision making indicator is for the AP service medical director to form a service-level task force to determine the management needs of the histopathology section and reestablish appropriate organizational skill levels and techniques to improve decision making in the Histopathology Section. The assessment is that execution of the QAc and QAn programs and the QI process has been ineffective in providing and maintaining basic team actualization skills.

Under the leadership commitment topic, review of the general indicator data reveals that this is a new QI initiative—and very much needed. The section is developing the plan, format, and collection methods and will report for the first time in the next month. Thus, there is no evaluation, action, or assessment baseline available.

Discussion:

Quality actualization is
the last quality profile segment,
the beginning of the path of work flow,
and the organizational "bottom line,"
—the source of organizational energy and synergy—
the fountainhead of excellence.

Indicator Grouping: When the entrepreneur refers to the financial "bottom line," it is a term often used as an expedient short cut to focus on the monetary values of productivity and profit. The accountant's bottom line does characterize a specific type of quality. Yet, this is a quality that usually is of primary importance only to the profit sharing supplier—not to the healthcare customer.[e]

In contrast, the quality profile progresses from the organizational "top line" of customer satisfaction, through all the outcome, process, and structural resource management phases, to finally reach the organizational "bottom line" of team effectiveness. As an infrastructural, administrative management program, QAc is the fundamental basis for all other organizational and operative events' building toward the ultimate goal of continuous quality improvement as evidenced by customer satisfaction.

The various profile examples of this indicator grouping illustrate six specified indicators. These are just suggestions as to how to approach an objective analysis or measurement of team effectiveness. Considering the topic of team skills training, alone, one might address any of the following basic actualization skills:

[e] It is at this level of the monetary bottom line that the somewhat altruistic dualism of the customer-supplier concept abruptly ends—where the customer and supplier part company on separate paths; where reciprocity no longer means a guarantee of the two reaching a *quid pro quo*; instead, the accountant's bottom line infers potential liability for the former and monetary gain for the latter.

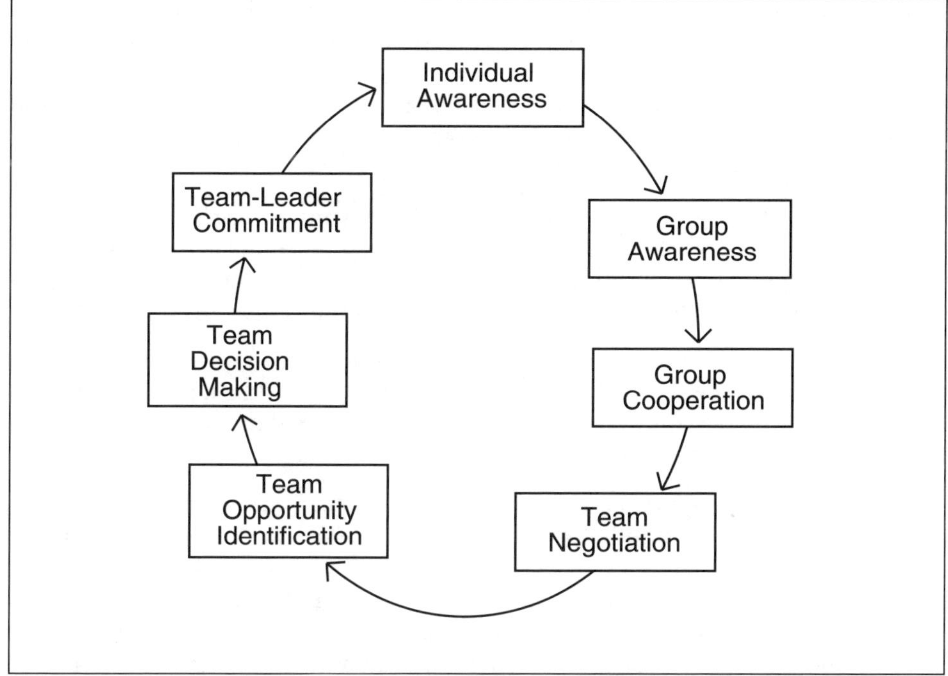

Figure 11.1 Model of team skills integration through the actualization cycle

- *Individual awareness* of personalities and values
- *Group awareness* of interpersonal dynamics and cultural diversity
- Intragroup and intergroup ability to *cooperate*
- Team ability to *negotiate* to a mutual yes or win
- Team ability to identify, characterize, and prioritize *opportunities for improvement*
- Team ability to perform differential *decision making* and choose best options
- Team and leader ability to buy into TQM-CQI practices and make a *commitment* to continuous improvement.

A model of the integration of these seven, basic, team analytical skills is conceptualized in Figure 11.1. In interpreting this model, consider the following definitions and conceptsof team skills.

Group formation occurs whenever two or more individuals decide to provide laboratory services together. This group has the potential to become a team.[f] The group begins as a loosely coalesced gathering of

[f] On occasion, an organizational unit consists of only one individual; that single person must function in lieu of a group or team.

individuals. Only after learning certain actualization skills can that group become a cohesive team. Some of those individuals might already have some of those skills from past experience and training; some of the individuals might intuitively learn some of the skills as the group works together; but all of those individuals will have to learn some of the skills through formal QAc training. Those skills might include:

- *Individual awareness* occurs in the actualization cycle when the individual members of a laboratory group become aware of their own value and personality make-up—and the values and personalities of all the rest of the group members. This is the first analytical skill set.
- *Group awareness* occurs when the individuals become aware of their identity as members of the group and are able to identify and cope with interpersonal dynamics, including cultural diversity. This is the second analytical skill set.
- *Group cooperation* occurs when the group members realize the reasons and methods for interpersonal cooperation, working together toward a common goal. This step includes learning skills to facilitate ethical bargaining and compromise within the group and between combined groups. *It is at this point that the group becomes a team.* The JCAHO emphasizes the use of improvement teams at intra- and interdepartmental levels.[9] This is the third analytical skill set.
- *Team negotiation* occurs when the team learns to negotiate controversial issues within the group and among combined or diverse groups. The object is to reach a common "yes" or a win-win conclusion and resolve conflict—if nothing else "to agree to disagree." This is the fourth analytical skill set.
- *Team opportunity identification* occurs when the team learns to identify and characterize opportunities for improvement—either problematic or nonproblematic. This is the fifth analytical skill set.
- *Team decision making* occurs when the team learns to differentiate between low and high priority opportunities and establish decisions for action. This is the sixth analytical skill set.
- *Team and leader commitment* occurs when each member at each respective level of authority and responsibility buys into and becomes committed to TQM and CQI practices. The member will manifest this commitment by actively participating in 1) continued quality management training, 2) actual quality management activities, and 3) providing resources for quality management from whatever level the member is able to participate. Leader committment ensures adequate resource allocation. The leader's empowering the employee—and the employee's accepting that empowerment—occurs in this step. This is the seventh analytical skill set.

Leadership in the TQM and CQI environment is a fundamentally critical issue. In analyzing the actualization cycle in Figure 1, the proverbial question is: who appears first on the quality management scene, the rank and file individual or the leader? Or, at which step does the actualization cycle really begin: with individual awareness or leader commitment? Realistically, quality management cannot begin without leader support—as a top-down process. Each leader must receive training in the seven skill sets before becoming fully capable of an adequately informed commitment—a buying in. Thus, the quality actualizationcycle must begin with the leader.

The precepts of TQM and CQI always converge on the concept of empowerment. But, always *there has to be a leader.* Ultimately, all the delicate QAc activities and actions require trained and talented maestros at every organizational level. It is in discussion of this caliber of sensitive, knowledgeable management at the participative level, that Dr. David Brown's analogy of the derivation of the word management comes into play. He talks of the Italian root derivation "*manegg(iare)*" meaning to handle, train which stems from the earlier Latin word "*manus*" meaning hand—as the hands of a jockey who recognizes the subjective and objective subtleties of handling a magnificent race horse to be first across the finish line.[10,11]

Yes, in healthcare quality management, it also helps to be somewhat of a poet as well as a musician to grasp the subjective values of the handling and orchestration process. These "right brain" skills do not absolutely require inherent talent; they can be learned by anyone who is truly interested in good management, willing to modify certain behavioral traits, and accept a constantly changing world.

Maffetone and others apply the term "passion" as a primary characterization of quality leadership in the orchestration of the combined QI, QAn, and QAc program activities.[12] For example, a successful QAc program does not require charismatic influence. But, it does require sincere, motivated, and energetic leader commitment; commitment to not only the traditional aspects of healthcare management but also to the nontraditional aspects of behavioral management of all organizational customers-suppliers.

Additional topics for the QAc indicator can concentrate on the seven basic aspects of actualization that are described above. The laboratory can enlarge on each basic actualization component by applying various magnifiers. The chief amplification methods include measuring the steps of actualization against the laboratory's important aspects of care and the individual steps of the path of workflow.

As another indicator topic example, one of the elements of effective QAc in the TQM and CQI environment is leadership capability. The laboratory is supposed to measure this component by the leaders' evaluating their own effectiveness, as well as by the staff's providing honest feedback to the leader. This QI monitoring should all be part of the quality profile.[13] Another possible indicator topic would be the effectiveness of the QAc plan.

Supporting Indicators. Since QAc is the most global indicator grouping of all, its supporting indicator groupings are theoretically legion. Any profile grouping that can be conjured up in the laboratorian mind has the potential to support the QAc grouping with relevant data—for QAc is the fountainhead of all other laboratory operational events.

Threshold. An analogy could be used here of the "little girl with the little curl right in the middle of her forehead"—when the quality of QAc is good, it is very, very good; but, when it is bad, all the laboratory operations are horrid. Anyone experienced in intralaboratory personality conflicts and corridor politics should agree. Thus, the threshold for QAc indicators can swing wildly from relaxed and very composed (of the comparative rate type) to a very tight and emergent nature (of the sentinel event type).

Monitoring Periodicity. As usual, periodicity is linked to the criticalness of the given threshold. This scheduling can be easily paced at a quarterly schedule or very rapidly run at a monthly schedule.

Evaluation. QI evaluation of the QAc data must be made after careful review of all other profile grouping information. By virtue of the perfectly global extent of laboratory actualization and its impact on all organizational operations, the quality management team needs to carefully correlate between the specialized actualization indicator data and the supporting evidence of laboratory and nonlaboratory (clinical and operative support) QI lessons learned of the remaining profile.

Action. As with any global organizational grouping, action to improve organizational actualization can be aimed at any level of laboratory management as well as at supportive departments lateral to the laboratory and administrative echelons higher. As a correlation, action personnel might represent any portion of that entire spectrum of involved managerial levels with the appropriate amount of joint coordination. Actions required to bolster QAc often are of the most interactive, person-with-person type—not person-on-person, person-at-person, or person-to-person.

The skills of handling interpersonal and group dynamics, cooperation, negotiation, opportunity identification, decision making, and commitment are professional skills that must be mastered, providing any number of improvement opportunities for any laboratory organization size or type. Actions need to be continually identified and directed toward enhancing those skills. Decision making is at the pinnacle of the hierarchy of group actualization (deferring to Maslow's theory of self actualization), and is a quintessential organizational skill that must be continuously honed to a razor's edge.[14] The challenge is not easy when the goal is appropriate decision making that is compassionate while still mindful of all resource constraints and all customer needs.

The team building phase provides an example of how a QAc action can meld with the QAn program. Besides monitoring for the level of employee morale, there can also be an indicator for conflict resolution. As one author relates, the successful organization can "harness the positive energy of conflict."[15] Through the QAn program research phase, employees can provide information regarding current causes and effects of conflict within the laboratory. This dialogue can be very helpful—if not even partially therapeutic in its own way by providing an opportunity for individuals to ventilate. Based on the research data, the laboratory can design development projects to test various in-house remedies to resolve the ongoing conflicts. After test results, the laboratory can place the best solutions into full implementation. This QAn approach to a QAc opportunity for improvement is a model that is applicable to resolving issues in any phase of the actualization program.

Assessment. As with the other 25 groupings, the QAc grouping requires attention to all three standard options for assessment in the CQI environment. Effectiveness of remedial actions, the QI process, and the QM interface are the options. It is at this point of QAc assessment that the "too hard" quality management situation really comes to the laboratorian's attention. As exemplified under some of the profile interpretations, an OFI may become so difficult to resolve at the laboratory section (or service or department) level that it is indeed too hard. Such an opportunity requires quality management resources from outside the laboratory to reach final resolution.

Mismanagement of the "too hard" situation can be closely akin to Harvey's Abilene Paradox.[16] An old joke is, "So, you want to go to Innisfree? Well, you can't get there from here!" Harvey's Abilene Paradox is a little more complex: "So, we are all together on our way to Abilene. Well, we might all be going to Abilene—but, none of us really wants to go to Abilene from here!" Harvey would explain this paradox on the basis of the team lacking fundamental awareness and agreement skills.

In this "too hard" situation, the laboratory section has a problem to solve (ie, they have a common destination). However, because of resource constraints, work overload, and faulty communication, the team is unable to reach an accurate consensus of agreement. Even though the individual team members see the good in reaching a solution to the problem, they do not want to exert the effort to solve it. Going the distance to Resolution would take too much of their already overtaxed time and effort—so they all embark on a trip to Nonresolution (ie, Abilene), instead. Each participant has assumed that this is the way that the group wants to travel without any effective team agreement.

As a result of false assumption and lack of actual team agreement, the "too hard" goal typically remains on the quality improvement agenda for month after month, the problem growing in severity with all good intentions still written under the action and assessment columns as if the section is really going to get the job done some day. If the section really wants to get to the right destination, they must learn to agree to transfer their problem to another laboratory echelon, a nonlaboratory department, or a higher administrative echelon that has adequate resources to resolve the quality management problem.

Communication. As the epitome of global indicator groupings, the QAc grouping requires the widest of dissemination of QI-based lessons. This definitely includes communication between laboratory-wide and nonlaboratory clinical and administrative support elements. This must be a dynamic, two-way sharing between "customer" and "supplier"—not just one-way transmission of managerial data as has been traditional in the typical hierarchical, productivity-oriented organization.

THE QUALITY IMPROVEMENT COMMITTEE REPORT FORMAT

After the improvement process has been initiated at the operative section level, the indicator feeder report is usually submitted to the department (or service) QI committee. That committee should review the sectional indicator planning, data, and EvAAC decisions, preferably with the participation of each section management team. At that time, both section and department-level staff can inject relevant information, including information that might be available from other sectional reviews or from administrative echelons lateral to or above the laboratory. Final evaluation, modification, and decisions should then be documented by means of a formal QI committee report and communicated to all appropriate intra- and extralaboratory QI activities, vertically and horizontally—to all personnel who are involved and have a need to know lessons learned.

A quality "profile" can be a useful format for the department-level QI committee report. Written to provide the equivalent of a snapshot profile, the report can provide a means of easy comparison of multi-section data and decisions as gleaned from several indicator feeder reports. Such a profile format can be designed to portray, at a glance, the status of quality of a section's laboratory product in terms of structure, process, and outcome. It can also be organized to present data and decisions in logical terms of the laboratory path of work flow and whatever improvement process is being used, which can be extremely helpful at the time of accreditation survey visits.

The quality profile best serves as a committee report if accompanied by an appropriate cover memo or letter. The memo should document:

- The committee participants
- The profile, itself
- Any salient, protracted problems, requiring assistance of other departments or higher administrative echelons
- Each individual who is directly involved in action follow-up of an indicator as the "action officer"
- All individuals who directly or indirectly need to be aware of the identified problems and recommended actions; this includes anyone who is indirectly involved at a nonlaboratory level in supporting the remedy of a salient laboratory indicator problem.

Examples of complete quality profiles are illustrated in the appendix. A profile incorporates the same general organization and headings as used for the section feeder report introduced in Chapter Seven, but it definitely can be more complex, covering all sectional operational resource, process, and outcome activities—if necessary. Although the sample profiles attempt to include all possible categories of indicator groupings, the format is extremely flexible, allowing any modification that might be desirable for a given laboratory. The QI committee report can be greatly shortened to report only the essential opportunities. Normal baseline data can be presented to illustrate stability after an opportunity is resolved, if so desired.

CQI PROFILE SUMMARY

After such an extensive review of the quality profile, a key point must be driven home. The profile, as presented, is a complete, comprehensive listing of all possible groupings with many example indicators. This is a model for teaching purposes. To be effective, a laboratory profile must be shaved down to the most essential quality management issues.

As mentioned in Chapter Eight, the questions that the quality manager must ask to tailor a profile to a specific laboratory's needs are:

- How many potential indicators are there?
- How do we identify the most important indicators to monitor?
- How many indicators do the accrediting agencies want us to monitor?
- How many indicators are we able to monitor?
- How many indicators should we monitor?

The ultimate answer is to systematically monitor as few indicators as are neccessary to manage the quality of laboratory operations as effectively as possible. The laboratory must analytically determine that indicator total in relation to what the highest priority customer satisfaction issues are and what quality management assets are on hand to handle the quality management workload.

ANTICIPATING FUTURE CHANGES IN QUALITY MANAGEMENT

In this final summation, it is important to reinforce two important points. The previously discussed quality profile segments, specified indicators, indexed indicators, and focused study indicators are not hard and fast. The design of the laboratory path of work flow and structure of a profile are unique decisions for each individual laboratory. These schemes need to be based on each laboratory's local working environment—the laboratory-clinical-administrative support "ecosystem." In fact, the last four chapters provide a description of the ecology of the request-patient-specimen-product-patient complex in quality management terms. Two major indicators of the overall quality of that complex is the operative "top line" of customer satisfaction and the organizational "bottom line" of organizational actualization.

The second point is that there is an abundance of managerial data generated and collected for all kinds of uncoordinated administrative reasons. Examples of these data sources include workload, personnel management, and accreditation activities. It makes practical sense to take advantage of that data for the purposes of QI surveillance and use it to identify opportunities for improvement.

Finally, as healthcare quality management matures, there will always be *avant-garde* buzz words and theories to emerge, only to be replaced by others earning current popularity. However, except for replacement of names and perceptual concepts/models, the basic system portrayed in the quality profile will never really change. The fundamentals of human enterprise have been and always shall be the same. Major fluctuations to anticipate will be in:

- The cultural environment—usually a matter of institutional versus generational values
- The specific laboratory discipline under scrutiny—usually a matter of social, political, or economic special interest
- The economy of operational scope and size under consideration—usually a matter of national versus local issues
- The conceptual approach to quality management—usually a matter of individual perspective versus technological development
- The nature of quality management resource constraints—usually a matter of supply and demand.

The quality profile demonstrated in these last four chapters provides a model by which all operative- and organizational-level laboratory functions can be systematically organized at the team level, planned, monitored, and improved. The processes for managing healthcare quality might direct attention to varying portions of the profile—depending on the individual laboratory's unique characteristics But, the profile's skeletal structure (ie, the laboratory path of work flow) will remain basically unchanged for the foreseeable future.

REFERENCES

1. Simpson KN, Kaluzny AD, McLaughlin CP. Total quality and the management of laboratories: implementation strategies and challenges. Clin Lab Man Rev, 1991;5:448-456.

2. Joint Commission Primer on Clinical Indicator Development and Application. Measuring Quality in Health Care. Oakbrook Terrace, IL: Joint Commission on Accreditation of Healthcare Organizations, 1990.
3. Peters T. TQM and the music that stirs the soul. CAP Today. October 1992;6:94.
4. Howanitz PJ, Howanitz JH. Laboratory Quality Assurance. New York, NY: McGraw-Hill, Inc, 1987
5. A Summary of Major Provisions of the Final Rules Implementing the Clinical Laboratory Improvement Amendments of 1988. Northfield, IL: College of American Pathologists and American Society of Clinical Pathologists, 1992.
6. Lunz ME, Castleberry BM, James K. Laboratory staff qualifications and accuracy of proficiency test results. Arch Path Lab Med, 1992;116:820-824.
7. Kriegel RJ, Patler L. If It Ain't Broke—Break It. New York, NY: Warren Books, 1991.
8. Jagger J, Detner DE, Cohen ML, Scarr PR, Pearson RD. Reducing blood and body fluid exposure among laboratory workers. Clin Lab Man Rev, 1992;6:415-417, 420-424.
9. Improvement teams key to quality improvement efforts. Joint Commission Perspectives. 1992;12:11-12.
10. Brown DS. Management Concepts and Policies. Washington, DC: National Defense University, 1989.
11. Webster's Third New International Dictionary of the English Language. Springfield, MA: Merriam Webster, Inc, 1984.
12. Maffetone, MA. TQM: passion and process. Clin Lab Man Rev, 1991;5:476-478,480,482.
13. Nowlin DL, Hickok C. Executives look in the mirror. Healthcare Forum Journal. Jul/Aug 1992;35:64-69.
14. Massie JL. Essentials of Management. Englewood Cliffs, NJ: Prentice-Hall, Inc, 1987.
15. Hunt LB. Management in action: here's how you can harness the positive energy of conflict. Clin Lab Man Rev, 1992;6:456-459.
16. Harvey JB. The Abilene Paradox and Other Meditations on Management. San Diego, CA: University Associates, 1988.

12. Why Should We Practice Quality Management: Because It Is Mandated or Because It Is Good Business?

LABORATORIANS PRACTICE SOME form of quality management daily—whether it be quality control at the operative level or the most complete quality profiling at the administrative level. The extent of this effort ranges between two extremes.

- On one hand, there are the externally-derived regulatory requirements for practicing quality management. These rules and standards codify a reasonably safe, efficient, and efficacious laboratory product or service that meets the most critical customer needs. The intent of such guidelines is usually to protect the norm and ensure the minimal yet acceptable effort.
- On the other hand, there are internally derived ethics and standards. Most laboratorians inherently want to practice the most effective quality management. Their intent is to provide the best possible product or service to all customers by anticipating future customer needs and ensure the maximum, optimal effort.

Somewhere in the middle of these two extremes, the reality of professional peer opinion and common-sense practicality holds sway.

Considering the spectrum of potential performance, how do we choose between the bare minimum and the absolute optimum performance? We usually end up weighing each of the two extremes on the mental balance of decision making. First, we apportion our quality management efforts in accordance with the amount of resources that we have on hand. Next, we weigh those resources against the various government-imposed regulations and self-imposed standards. Then, we decide how much further we can extend our resources to reach our optimal goals. Let's examine the nature of the diverse regulatory forces that influence our style of quality management, because they are such important ingredients in the crucible of quality management effort.

FOR INTRO

REGULATORY EMPHASIS ON QUALITY MANAGEMENT

Regulatory forces include all federal, state, and local government requirements—as well as all subsidiary peer-level accreditation, licensure, certification, and inspection activities that enforce the regulations. These various technocratic stipulations are constantly evolving to match shifts in socioeconomic and political reality.

Looking at the panoply of regulatory and subsidiary organizations, we have an acronym soup. DHHS, HCFA, CLIA, FDA, OSHA, JCAHO, CAP, and AABB are some of the leading components of the regulatory broth.[a] Some of these programs approach the laboratory on a global basis; others focus more on laboratory subspecialty practice. Some are more reactive and outcome-limited in promoting quality management; others are more anticipatory and comprehensive in nature.

To illustrate, we can compare the CLIA to the JCAHO and their respective approaches to quality management. Both programs are under the auspices of DHHS and HCFA; however, they are quite different in their influence on healthcare quality management.

CLINICAL LABORATORY IMPROVEMENT AMENDMENTS OF 1988

The CLIA inspection and certification program is much more widespread in its span of influence than the JCAHO survey and accreditation program. This is because all laboratories throughout the United States are subject to CLIA requirements. Its range of influence extends from the smallest physician's office laboratory to the largest hospital-based or independent reference laboratory.

However, the quality management aspects of CLIA requirements are much more focused on outcome and process control; they pay very little attention to the management of structural quality. As a brief overview, the program requires moderate- to high-complexity laboratories to have a "system, mechanism, or some other means" to[1,2]:

[a] DHHS (Department of Health and Human Services), HCFA (Health Care Financing Administration), CLIA (Clinical Laboratory Improvement Amendments of 1988—a program administered at state level), FDA (Food and Drug Administration), OSHA (Occupational Safety and Health Administration), JCAHO (Joint Commission on Accreditation of Healthcare Organizations), CAP (College of American Pathologists, and AABB (American Association of Blood Banks)

- Establish comprehensive policies and procedures to monitor and evaluate the ongoing, overall quality of the total testing process through a written plan
- Monitor, evaluate, and revise all the "systems" required under CLIA as a part of the quality management process
- Assess the effectiveness of revisions or corrective action policies and remedy any ineffective policies and procedures
- Identify, evaluate, and remedy patient test results that appear inconsistent with clinical data
- Identify, monitor, evaluate, and remedy the relationship between test results from different instruments, systems, or sites
- Monitor, evaluate, and remedy proficiency testing (PT) performance, particularly where there have been unsatisfactory results
- Identify, evaluate, and remedy its policies that ensure employee competence, including that of consultants
- Identify, evaluate, and remedy breakdowns in communication between the laboratory and individuals who order or receive test products
- Identify, document, evaluate, and remedy all complaints and problems reported to the laboratory
- Document, assess, and remedy problems arising from quality management reviews and prevent their reoccurrence
- Document all corrective actions and make them available to HCFA.

At first glance, familiar buzzwords such as *comprehensive*, *ongoing*, *total*, and *systems* leap from the above listing. But, one also recognizes the QA-like (ie, quality assurance) approach of these CLIA guidelines. They are more reactive than anticipatory. Also, they predominantly focus on outcome and process. Although the program alludes to a comprehensive, systematic approach, there is no explicit mention of the importance of structural resources—except written plans, policies, instruments, proficiency testing, and individual competence at the operative-level. No other aspects of organizational-level programs are obvious; instead, they are lumped together under the general concept of "systems".

The CLIA program is a vast, nationally mandated program that incorporates an immense number of participating laboratories. However, limited governmental assets are available to operate the inspection process. Thus, it is predictable that the CLIA program will continue to remain primarily outcome- and process-focused. Federal and state government will have enforcement resources to direct only meager attention to the quality management of the structural elements of laboratory operations.

In time, CLIA's enforcement capabilities will change if peer organizations such as the Joint Commision take on deemed status responsibilities. Also, computer enhancement of reporting to HCFA will eventually enhance CLIA's administrative capabilities.

Given CLIA's truncated approach to surveillance of quality management, is there a more effective alternative? The JCAHO program is voluntary; therefore, it is not as universally subscribed to as CLIA. It too has some resource constraints. However, it is the premier regulatory enforcement organization in the United States healthcare industry when it comes to addressing the whole span of quality management.

JOINT COMMISSION ON ACCREDITATION OF HEALTHCARE ORGANIZATIONS

The JCAHO's mission is to enhance the quality of health care provided to the public.[3] The Joint Commission has endeavored to meet that aim through a steady progression of quality management programs over the past several decades. These programs have included various forms of medical audit, peer review, and systematic quality surveillance.

During the 1980s, the JCAHO chose two planning strategies to achieve its mission—one was short-ranged and the other was long-ranged. As a short-range strategy, the commission formalized ongoing quality surveillance under the aegis of quality assurance (QA) and instituted its ten-step improvement process to ensure uniform monitoring and evaluating of healthcare quality.

As a long-range strategy, the JCAHO introduced its *Agenda for Change*. This far-reaching plan has become significantly important for all healthcare quality management, including the medical laboratory. The *Agenda* has already led to substantial changes in the Joint Commision standards—these revisions have hallmarked the transition from formalized QA to a more modern approach of quality surveillance—quality assessment and improvement (QI). The QA program of the 1980s served as an introduction to the modern principles of quality management, including those of total quality management (TQM) and continuous quality improvement (CQI). In turn, the QI program of the early 1990s has served admirably as an industry-wide introduction to the more refined approach of improving organizational performance (PI).

THE JCAHO *AGENDA FOR CHANGE*

The JCAHO first published its *Agenda* in 1987 as a major organizational research, development, and planning effort. It mapped out the approaches by which the Joint Commission would accomplish the following long-range strategies[3]:

- To create a healthcare environment that focuses on the quality of patient care, whereby every healthcare organization's governing, administrative, managerial, and clinical leadership is committed to continuous quality improvement
- To develop a national performance measurement database system that stimulates assurance of quality improvement and provides risk-adjusted, comparative feedback to all healthcare facilities.

By modifying its accreditation standards and survey methods, the JCAHO is creating a more desirable healthcare environment for organizational commitment to improvement. Also, it is creating a national database by standardizing and computerizing the monitoring, evaluating, and feedback system. Both initiatives are immensely complex, costly, and challenging; and they will require several years before substantial success is realized.

The *Agenda* has become the JCAHO's master plan for improving the quality of all patient care in the United States, including laboratory patient care support. This plan is based on Juran's and Deming's management principles of TQM and CQI, emphasizing that[3]:

- All key activities of an organization should further its mission
- Continuous improvement of quality should be a major, ongoing priority for the entire organization, including its leadership
- The importance of process improvement is favored over that of correcting individual performance
- Customer needs should be a chief focus for data collection, requiring effective communication with both internal and external customers
- A comprehensive, systematic approach should integrate clinical and managerial processes, with emphasis on cross-disciplinary teamwork
- Measurement of quality should consist of monitoring objective, valid indicator data; adjusting for natural variation; and investigating targets of opportunity for improvement and underlying causes of problems or barriers to improvement.

It must be clear that, as much as the JCAHO based its *Agenda* on TQM and CQI principles, it has not endorsed any particular method to implement those principles. The Joint Commission does not mandate the use of any specific school of management, improvement process, or quality management tools. These choices are up to the individual healthcare organization, including each laboratory. From the viewpoint of the Joint Commision, the phrases "total quality management" and "continuous quality improvement" must remain in lower case type—not to be reified as a managerial icon in capital letters.[4] Of utmost importance is improving operational processes to satisfy anticipated customer needs. Each organization should choose its own means toward improvement—as long as it attains that end goal.

The *Agenda* projected how the JCAHO is going to tailor its accreditation process to provide a more objective and precise means of evaluating healthcare resources, processes, and outcomes. Commission's aim is to insure that all healthcare organizations achieve maximum clinical excellence—and that includes medical laboratories. The *Agenda's* goals for achieving that degree of excellence have been threefold[5]:

- To develop more relevant clinically-based quality surveillance indicators for objective screening and identification of improvement opportunities or problems
- To develop new standards for organizational management for monitoring the effectiveness of the governance and management of the laboratory
- To develop *improved accreditation survey methods* by more accurately and speedily comparing and assessing the ability of healthcare organizations to provide patient care.

To achieve its goals, the *Agenda* has offered five major research and development objectives for the continuous improvement of patient care. Those five objectives have been to[3]:

- Identify and select standardized clinical indicators
- Identify and select standardized organizational management indicators
- Develop risk adjustment methods
- Establish an ongoing monitoring and evaluation process
- Modify survey and accreditation procedures.

Objective One: *to identify and select standardized clinical indicators*

The Joint Commission has sought to create a more uniform, better orchestrated system for monitoring and evaluating the overall quality of clinical activities and to foster a more balanced assessment of structural resources, processes, and outcomes. Through the JCAHO-sponsored Performance Evaluation Procedure or PEP audits of the 1970s, hospital committees retrospectively studied the quality of clinical outcomes. The attention paid to process (versus outcome) often depended on the location of the audit center. For example, process was usually emphasized in the laboratory while outcome was preferentially addressed in medicine or surgery; the quality of structural resources was largely ignored as a target for quality surveillance by most healthcare activities.

As JCAHO-directed QA programs developed in hospital clinical pathology (CP) laboratories during the early 1980s, there was still a tendency to concentrate on process because of an inherent laboratory preoccupation with process control. Ostensibly, assessment of the laboratory effect on clinical outcome was limited to the JCAHO-required study of blood utilization. Full-fledged review of clinical outcome was approached with trepidation because of the personnel hours required for manual patient record reviews and a lack of effective clinical criteria (or standards of practice) for most important aspects of laboratory service. Again, there was limited interest in assessing the quality of structure because of lack of precedence and incentive.

In anatomic pathology (AP) laboratories during the 1980s, the primary emphasis was on peer review of the quality of the pathologist's diagnosis. This effort complemented the JCAHO-required study of surgical outcomes through tissue and tumor board committees. Traditionally, the professional importance of the diagnostic outcome tended to overshadow interest in the more comprehensive quality assessment of process and structure in AP.

In some isolated instances, the practice of quality assessment in AP or CP was unduly restricted to solving inspection and survey deficiencies. Such myopic attention to external peer review findings was the epitome of incremental, quick fix, crisis management. Thankfully, such quality management has remained the exception and not the rule.

In any case, quality management in the 1980s was not well balanced. Despite JCAHO's intentions, quality assurance became problem-oriented and did not evenly address outcome, process, or structure.

Regarding the first element, this situation was really quite understandable. Hospital-wide QA programs inherited a great deal from the clinical mindset and methods of the earlier days of retrospective, outcome-oriented audits. In the laboratory, however, deriving clinical outcome indicators or standards of practice seemed too complex—largely because of the lack of effective communication with the attending clinical staff and effective computerized data retrieval.

Laboratorians have always been reticent to approach clinical standards and indicators without clinician input—and rightfully so. At the same time, there have been significant barriers to effective laboratorian-clinician exchange. The list of causes is lengthy, but, if nothing else, everyone involved—on either side—has just been "too busy" to communicate. Also, improving these relationships has not been a major part of either side's strategic plan—if they have had any long-range plan at all.

Regarding the second element, it was always easier to implement QA in the laboratory by using process-oriented quality control (QC) data elements as sources of quality indicator data elements. This was the path of least resistance because QC data were so readily available—especially in the CP laboratory where process control had developed into such a fine art and science. Regarding the third element, laboratorians paid minimal attention to the surveillance of resource quality because it was not a traditional source of patient care quality indicators.

In contrast, truly effective quality management requires a more balanced approach to the assessment of Donabedian's three aspects of healthcare function. It also requires improved laboratory and clinical management styles—along with computer support to provide the extensive data automation needed to meet the challenge.

In addition, carefully designed national standards of practice rather than empirical local estimates—are necessary for establishing uniformity in selecting clinical indicators. At one time, it was the JCAHO's intent to incorporate pretested clinical standards of practice into the accreditation requirements. These standardized indicators would provide critical measures of the quality of clinical structure, process, and outcome for important aspects of care. For laboratory quality surveillance, these same clinical guidelines would generate indicators of quality for salient segments of the operational path of work flow—including organizational and operative resource management activities that affect patient care outcome and customer satisfaction.

In the late 1980s, the JCAHO formed a Clinical Indicators Task Force to answer the need for indicator standardization. The task force consisted of carefully chosen clinical experts whose purpose was to formulate valid and reliable clinical indicators at the national level. For example, in 1989, indicators for obstetrics, anesthesia, and hospital-wide care were pilot tested at 17 hospitals; clinical performance data on cardiovascular, trauma, and oncology care were collected in 17 other test sites in 1990.[6] Various clinical specialty associations have been simultaneously developing indicators on their own initiative in concert with the JCAHO developmental activities.

Members of laboratory specialty associations have provided laboratory expertise to the various JCAHO and clinical specialty task force groups. For example, the American Society of Clinical Pathologists (ASCP) has formed a Practice Parameters Committee, and the CAP has its Practice Guidelines and Clinical Indicators Committee; both provide laboratory liaisons to the Joint Commission clinical specialty standards groups. How the resultant clinical indicators are ultimately put to use will rest in the success of the JCAHO's indicator monitoring system or IMS.

Additionally, the CAP *Q-Probes* Program is establishing an important national database that will provide more information on laboratory support of clinical outcomes. At the same time, each laboratory is being encouraged to identify local, in-house indicators and to incorporate them into the local quality improvement process.

Major concern continues about the validation of performance measures such as indicators. We must be confident that such quality measurements do, in fact, measure what they are intended to measure.[7]

Regardless of the source of quality management indicators, the JCAHO intends to collect and compile local organizational data into a national data bank through its nationwide computerized IMS network.[3] Ultimately, JCAHO and CAP guidelines for monitoring and evaluating clinical indicators will become more uniform, and the laboratory's approach will be better aligned with the clinical staff quality assessment activities.

Objective Two: *to identify and select standardized organizational management indicators*

Organizational management activities must also be effective. These functions include both administrative- and operative-level management of all structural, process, and outcome events that affect patient care. Establishing management standards that support high-quality hospital and laboratory patient care will meet this objective.

Early in the *Agenda for Change* process, the JCAHO divided organizational management into traditional and behavioral categories. *Traditional management* included activities such as:

- Instituting organizational-oriented research, development, and planning
- Allocating operative resources
- Managing personnel
- Managing supplies, equipment, and facility
- Managing finances
- Monitoring and evaluating quality.

All of these activities are potential QI indicator groupings. Because these indicators are so objective and interwoven into the everyday management of a laboratory, they are relatively easy to monitor and evaluate. Thus, methods for the evaluation of these traditional management activities are well-established. A workload recording and evaluation program is a classic example of a traditional resource quality assessment approach.

The second category, *behavioral management*, represented a nontraditional, more modern approach. It included activities such as:

- Establishing an effective staff organization
- Setting and assessing internal performance standards
- Resolving personality and transactional conflicts
- Promoting participative decision making
- Providing feedback to employees and other customers
- Monitoring, evaluating, and assessing quality improvement.

These behavioral management indicators are much more subjective and, therefore, are more difficult to measure. Most of the difficulty in dealing with this indicator category, however, is that it is so often ignored. Behavioral management activities have not been adequately scrutinized because concern about such indicators has not been characteristic of the

American industrial culture, including the healthcare industry. Actually, behavioral management is relatively easy to monitor and evaluate.

In the late 1980s, the JCAHO formed an Organization and Management Indicators Task Force to address this area of interest. The task force identified 11 key organizational principles. A combination of traditional and behavioral precepts, they focused on continuous improvement of the quality of patient care. These guidelines required evidence of[3]:

- An *organizational mission* that expresses commitment to the CQI of patient care. This mission should encompass measurable objectives and action plans, including resource, program, and strategic planning.
- An *organizational culture* that exhibits widespread commitment to CQI. This culture should encompass open communication, participative decision-making, and ongoing self-assessment.
- *Organizational change* that reflects continual improvement of patient care quality. This attribute should encompass the cultural and managerial abilities to recognize, accept, and implement substantive improvements in operative and administrative management. This organizational ability should be based on the active assessment of the external environment; patient access to healthcare; and the adequacy of patient volume to support clinical competence, the satisfaction of patients, their families, healthcare providers, other employees, payors, the community, and other associated healthcare organizations. Organizational response to these variables should include changes in the plans, programs, resources, and methods.
- *Leadership commitment* to CQI. This commitment should be written into the job descriptions of the governing body and the managerial and clinical leadership. Ongoing performance evaluations should show that every leader systematically seeks, measures, and uses the judgments of all individuals involved in monitoring and promoting an integrated TQM-CQI program.
- *Leadership qualifications* for managing CQI. These qualifications encompass continued development and evaluation of the proficiency of the governing body and key managerial and clinical leaders. Quality management skills should be manifested by regular evaluation of the vision, attitudes, commitment, knowledge, and skills of the leadership for continuously assessing and improving the quality of patient care.
- Independent *practitioners' qualifications* in managing quality improvement of patient care. These qualifications encompass continued development and evaluation of practitioner proficiency. Clinical and managerial effectiveness should be supported by a sufficient number of competent practitioners—including

pathologists—who demonstrate commitment and active involvement in the continuous improvement process. "Sufficient number" connotes an adequate staff strength weighed against the patient workload volume.

- *Human resources* that support and sustain CQI. Adequate personnel assets encompass recruitment, development, evaluation, and retention policies and practices that ensure an adequate number of healthcare professionals (weighed against the workload volume) who are competent, committed, and actively involved in CQI.
- *Operational resources* that support and sustain CQI. Adequate operational resources encompass facilities, equipment, and technology that are regularly evaluated and maintained and provide an appropriate patient care environment. This support system should provide flexible resources and procedures that are responsive to quality improvement changes.
- *Evaluation and improvement* of patient care quality. The quality surveillance program encompasses an organization-wide assessment process that integrates data from quality management, risk management, and utilization review activities and that facilitates ongoing feedback on the quality of care between all involved individuals. This surveillance and analysis system should be used to develop short- and long-range plans for CQI of patient care.
- *Organizational integration* and coordination that facilitates improvement of patient care. These aspects of organizational culture encompass an effective interdependence of all persons, clinical disciplines, and organizational units related to laboratory support of patient care. There should be evidence that all personnel recognize their responsibility to work together to continuously improve the quality of patient care.
- *Continuity and comprehensiveness* of patient care provided both internally and externally, including laboratory patient care support. These attributes encompass the development and maintenance of effective communication between internal and external healthcare providers. Such communication should support CQI patient access and the continuity and comprehensiveness of patient care.

Subsequent to the establishment of these 11 principles, the Joint Commission recognized that organizational and management indicators should evolve naturally in the course of the systematic follow-up of clinical indicators. Thus, the Joint Commission dissolved the Organization and Management Indicators Task Force. Still, their principles remain as important statements that should be incorporated into any quality management program. The JCAHO has attested to this by melding them into the most recent editions of its own accreditation standards as high priority issues.

Objective Three: *to develop risk adjustment methods*

At least six types of variable factors influence the quality of the events that occur during the total laboratory operational path of work flow. These factors include:

- Healthcare policy
- The overall healthcare organization
- The healthcare team
- The individual practitioner
- Clinical care
- The patient.

Overall interpretation of the effect of these variables (as represented by quality surveillance data) requires adjusting indicator targets to the severity of illness—or risk for illness—into which a given patient or group of patients fits. Most often, variations of quality management indicators are natural and random. Occasionally, clinically significant variations in quality surveillance data occur because of a specific problem in the quality of laboratory practice. However, misinterpretation of these variations can also result from a lack of risk adjustment. For example, a patient grouping that includes individuals being treated for the same disease may represent a mixture of different clinical settings. Consequently, any quality management data derived from this diverse patient grouping will be imprecise for statistical purposes.

Each clinical setting represents a unique degree of statistical risk that is reflected in any indicator data variation. Consequently, risk adjustment methods are required to normalize variations of QI indicators among different clinical settings for the sake of intra- and interlaboratory comparison.

For example, a diagnostic related grouping (DRG) portrays a loosely defined cohort of patients with mixed risks of variability. The problem with this method of prospective payment is that every grouping is so broad in scope that it does not adequately take patient risk into account—the least ill are mixed with the most ill. The severely ill become statistical outliers as reflected by their laboratory QI data. As a result, diagnostic and therapeutic expenses can exceed the averaged expenses officially allotted to that DRG for reimbursement. The converse is true of the least ill.

Nationwide, healthcare facilities of all sizes and in all geographic locales are assessing patient care indicators. Practitioner, healthcare team, clinical care, and organizational variables of structure, process, and outcome significantly affect the comparability of these indicator data. Thus, interpreting these inherent variables becomes very complex—especially when amassed on such a grand scale. Even when assessing laboratory performance, we must compare apples to apples; but, that can be difficult.

Consequently, the JCAHO intends to tailor its standards, surveys, and other quality surveillance processes to cope with these risk-associated variations. The commission is developing risk adjustment methods to sort and compare complex indicator data in a meaningful manner. For example, work groups are characterizing patient covariants such as severity of illness and case complexity for specific clinical indicators.

Eventually, risk adjustment formulas will be available. Then, intra- and interorganizational comparisons of the indicators can be made more accurately. The JCAHO intends to facilitate the development of these formulas and methods of comparative study.

Objective Four: *to establish an ongoing monitoring and evaluation process*

The *Agenda* established that the JCAHO and accredited institutions will participate in a continuous-flow monitoring system. Eventually, there will be ongoing transmission of clinical and organizational data from all accredited healthcare organizations to a computerized Joint Commission database—known as the IMS. The JCAHO will then transmit its analyses of the feed data back to the participating organizations. The feedback will take three forms:

- Comparison of the participating healthcare organization to *internal expectations* as an "early warning system"
- Comparison of the organization to *external expectations* based on national performance criteria or thresholds
- Comparison of the organization to *similar organizations' actual performance* using normalized interorganizational data.

Of course, while the JCAHO describes these plans in terms of the hospital-wide organization, medical laboratories will naturally be incorporated into the IMS database system.

Objective Five: *to modify survey and accreditation procedures*

Modification of Joint Commission survey and accreditation procedures is being driven by the need for improved analysis of increasing amounts of clinical and organizational data. The exact modifications and their effect on the medical laboratory are yet to be determined. It is quite clear that the standards are already in a great state of flux—changing from a specialty-specific, operative-level focus to a more generic, function-oriented, organizational-level orientation. In addition, surveillance procedures will become increasingly computerized and dependent on electronic exchange of information to supplant the current on-site survey visitation process. It is also likely that the medical technologists on the survey teams will become more involved in the examination of the laboratory's quality management program.

Clearly, this summary of the JCAHO *Agenda's* goals and objectives reveals how much work needs to be accomplished. The Joint Commission has scheduled full implementation of the *Agenda* for the 1990s. Whether they can meet all of their objectives is yet to be seen. However, the Commission will inevitably establish the basic principles of TQM and CQI in all accredited healthcare facilities.

REVISIONS TO THE 1992 JCAHO STANDARDS

True to the *Agenda for Change*, significant changes to JCAHO accreditation standards appeared in the *1992 Accreditation Manual for Hospitals (AMH)*.[8] The Joint Commission's aim was to stimulate voluntary transition from QA toward continuous improvement of organizational performance—the quality management hallmark of the 1990s.

There were several salient features of the 1992 revisions. For example, the JCAHO changed the title of the quality surveillance chapter from "Quality Assurance" to "Quality Assessment and Improvement." The abbreviation for the latter title shifted from QA to QI in the 1993 *AMH*.

They wrote a new preamble for the entire chapter and deleted the preamble for Standard QA.3.[b] Compared to its predecessor, the new preamble did not emphasize the ten-step process. Instead, it deemphasized any specific surveillance process in lieu of promoting more general quality improvement activities that better reflect the principles of continuous performance improvement. Also, it addressed the major trends leading toward QI, as well as pointing out various barriers to continual improvement.

Did this change in emphasis portend JCAHO's abandonment of the ten-step process? Not completely. The ten-step process has remained unchanged in other Joint Commission publications such as the *Monitoring And Evaluation Series* and the *Primer on Clinical Indicator Development and Application*. However, it is likely that the process will continue to change in content and importance following further managerial experience with continuous performance improvement. For example, the threshold step is not as viable a concept in a continuous improvement environment.[9,10]

The revised quality management chapter introduced one new standard for leader involvement in quality surveillance and improvement. At the same time, there were slight modifications of the remaining standards. One change involved the phrase "monitoring and evaluation of the quality and appropriateness of care" seen throughout the QA chapters of preceding years. In 1992, the words "and appropriateness" were deleted—thus erasing the JCAHO's first attempt at formulating specific dimensions of quality.

[b] The chapter title was changed in 1992, but the standard designation remained "QA" until it was changed to "QI" in the 1993 *AMH*. It changed to "PI" in the 1994 *AMH*.

An important implication of the 1992 Standard QA.1 was that the healthcare organization's leadership is expected to provide the assets required to mount an effective QI effort. These assets were to include personnel and other tangible operative resources as well as time. Standard QA.2 included the QI responsibilities of each department/service director, as well as the responsibilities for surveillance of outside sources of patient care services. Also added was a comment on the primary *use of quality assessment results for study and improvement* of processes that affect patient care outcome.

Although titled the same, the revised Standard QA.3 mentioned the improvement of governance, managerial, and support activities, *adding both traditional and nontraditional structural elements as targets for improvement*—rather than targeting just process and outcome. Selected elements of the ten-step process were mentioned; however, the emphasis was beginning to shift from problem solving to opportunity finding.

The revised Standard QA.4 emphasized establishing *"operational linkages" between "professional disciplines"* such as between risk management functions and QI functions. There was also an added emphasis on finding opportunities for improvement.

Of lasting importance, the JCAHO designed the 1992 quality management standards and requirements to overcome certain barriers to continuous improvement. The new QI chapter itemized the following suggestions:

- AVOID an exclusive focus on clinical aspects of care; consider the full extent of interrelated activities that affect patient outcome, including governance, management, support, and clinical processes

- AVOID an exclusive compartmentalization of QA activities; consider organizing quality improvement activities around the entire flow of patient care, including interrelated, cross-disciplinary, and cross-departmental processes

- AVOID an exclusive focus on the performance of individuals—especially performance problems; consider focusing on how well the process in which an individual participates is performed, coordinated, integrated, and improved

- AVOID initiating action only when a problem is identified; consider finding better ways to carry out processes

- AVOID separating clinical appropriateness and technical effectiveness from the efficiency (cost-effectiveness or value) of patient care; consider integrating the parameters for improvement of patient outcome with those that improve efficiency.

The latter guidelines apply even to the current time.

REVISIONS TO THE 1994 JCAHO STANDARDS

The overall design of the 1994 *AMH* format differs significantly from any preceding edition, reflecting striking improvements in its general approach.[11] The manual now consists of chapters that focus on the overall care of the patient and emphasize the quality of performance of organizational processes. Most chapters address important organizational functions that are generic to clinical and nonclinical departments/services.[c] The Joint Commission divided the 1994 *AMH* into four sections, including:

- Patient care function chapters on patient-specific activities and procedures
- Organizational function chapters on leadership, human resources management, information management, environmental management, organizational performance improvement, and infection control
- Essential structural component chapters on the governing body, administrative management, medical staff, and nursing—all structures of important functions
- Other department and service requirements that are still in transition.

Whereas the JCAHO designed the 1992 standards to stimulate voluntary movement to continuous performance improvement, the 1994 revisions pointedly mandate adoption of organizational performance improvement as the keystone of healthcare quality management. The goals for the 1994 standards are five-fold:

- Increased leadership responsibility
- More formalized techniques for improving the quality of performing organizational processes
- Enhanced education and training
- Broadened communication and collaboration
- More effective use of lessons learned from the improvement process.

As a result of the field review process, the title reverted from "Quality Assessment and Improvement" to an interim title of "Performance Assessment and Improvement"(PI). There was such a ground swell objection to the latter title's potential inference to individual performance or competency that it finally became "Improving Organizational Performance" (also PI).

If the JCAHO has any influence on the preferred nomenclature of quality management, the term "quality assurance" should become outdated in most

[c] The JCAHO has separated specific laboratory accreditation requirements from the *AMH*, creating a separate *Accreditation Manual for Pathology and Clinical Laboratory Services*.

quality management circles. QA is too reminiscent of the problem solving of the 1980s. The term has always seemed teleologically unsound; it is arguable that any measurable characteristic of quality can be presumed to be "assurable" or guaranteed in a continuous performance improvement environment where there is always potential for improvement.

Another revision, the 1994 quality management preamble is shorter with less direct instruction or explanation. It emphasizes the importance of improving organizational performance by operational processes. It also introduces nine dimensions of performance, which include:

- Respect and caring
- Safety
- Appropriateness[d]
- Efficacy
- Effectiveness
- Availability
- Timeliness.
- Continuity
- Efficiency.

Appropriateness and efficacy characterize doing the right thing; the other seven are dimensions of doing the right thing well. The preamble also highlights the importance of the principles of CQI and TQM, especially those regarding the responsibilities of the leadership role.

The quality improvement standards remain at five in number. They are identified by the abbreviation for the title, PI. They include:

- PI.1 Plan an overall improvement strategy (Plan)
- PI.2 Design specific improvement approaches (Plan)
- PI.3 Measure process performance (Do)
- PI.4 Assess process performance (Check)
- PI.5 Improve process performance (Act).

Although the 1994 manual packages these standards in a slightly different way, they echo the same overall intent as the 1992 standards. Their format or flow (ie, plan, design, measure, assess, improve) is that of a typical improvement process. As pointed out by the parenthetical reminders in the above listing, these JCAHO standards prove that it is impossible to escape the pragmatism of Shewhart's P-D-C-A cycle. Standard PI.2 reinforces the importance of Shewhart's first or "plan" phase of the improvement cycle.

[d] The JCAHO deleted medical appropriateness as an important dimension of quality in 1992 but has reinstated it with the eight other dimensions of performance—or quality.

There is one other major characteristic of the 1994 PI standards that deserves mention. The quality management standards emphasize the importance of planning, measuring, and assessing the improvement of outcomes and processes. It is the organization of the entire manual that elevates structure to the highest level of importance. Almost all chapters focus on the most important organizational functions—which are structural in nature.

As predicted by their 1987 *Agenda for Change*, the Joint Commission will continue to develop and improve their accreditation standards in the *AMH* and other accreditation manuals. Over the past decade, the JCAHO standards have definitely proven themselves to be "moving targets;" hopefully, this rapid generation of competing terms and abbreviations will subside. However, neither their general format nor specific content can ever be written in stone; the Joint Commission standards must continually evolve with the times. It is understood, however, that they must always focus on the principles of good management and common sense. Why? Because that is the best way to do business.

IT'S THE BEST WAY TO DO BUSINESS

The 1994 JCAHO standards, their intent statements, and scoring guidelines easily corroborate the quality management approaches described throughout this text on systematic quality management. If one follows the principles of TQM and CQI as described in the preceding chapters, all CLIA, JCAHO, and any other organization's regulatory or standards requirements will be easily achieveable.

So—addressing the original question posed at the beginning of this chapter—why practice quality management? Should it be to satisfy the minimal operational requirements of regulatory and peer review organizations? Or should it be to satisfy our inherent desires to do the very best that we possibly can, above and beyond the norm imposed on us by government?

Predictably, most laboratorians match McGregor's description of the Theory Y worker, and they will choose the latter style of motivation.[12] Why? First, because it is our inherent nature. Second, because, business-wise, it is the smartest approach. If meeting the customer's needs is a chief driving force in any business, the modern quality management principles of TQM and CQI should be most attractive because they are, by that very definition, the best way to do business. This should be true no matter if the altruistic goal of service or the entrepreneurial goal of profit is more important organizationally.[e] Each of these two goals should serve the other. If it is our business to practice good laboratory medicine—as well as to run our medical laboratory practice as a good business—then meeting most regulatory and accreditation requirements should occur naturally as we practice the principles of TQM and CQI.

[e] This entrepreneurial goal includes meeting operating expenses by the non-for-profit healthcare organization.

Summary

It is important to understand the differences between CLIA and JCAHO quality management guidelines. It is equally helpful to understand why and how the Joint Commission has been revising its quality management standards over the past two decades. As a testimony to these changes, the revisions of the 1992 and 1994 standards appear in this chapter in brief outline form. The laboratorian can refer to the most recent edition of the JCAHO *AMH* to study the current standards in detail.

Considering the current surge of reform in the public administration of this nation's healthcare system, significant regulatory change is likely to be ongoing for some time to come. Subsequently, accreditation requirements have been and promise to continue to be "moving targets." However, the anticipatory nature of the JCAHO *Agenda for Change* on laboratory quality management has been, overall, "on target"—and it promises to continue to be so.

Establishing QA and the ten-step process in the 1980s was worthwhile in introducing the principles of quality management to pathology and the clinical laboratory. The recent transition from QI to PI is even more timely as we prepare to meet the challenges of the next decade and century.

In the long run, quality assurance and organizational performance improvement will prove to have been a valuable administrative means to an improved clinical end. However, symbols such as QA, PI, TQM, and CQI are all destined to be passing mileposts on the never-ending journey to managerial excellence. New, better, and more exciting managerial developments will always be coming into our view from just over the horizon.

However, any "new" revolutionary approach, process, system, or school of managerial thought is not likely to really be new; most of these concepts have been around for the past millennium, at least. Most new paradigms just represent shifts in managerial emphasis that fit changing socioeconomic and political times. So, do not become sidetracked trying to meet popular (and minimal) technocratic requirements. Avoid hip shooting at moving targets. Instead, carefully aim for optimal quality management. In the long run, it's the best way to do business. Then, all the regulatory requirements will fall naturally into place by doing the right thing and doing it the right way.

REFERENCES

1. Foster HS. Leaked CLIA '88 regulations. CLMA Management Briefs, 1991;13:1-11.
2. A Summary of Major Provisions of the Final Rules Implementing the Clinical Laboratory Improvement Amendments of 1988. Northfield, IL: College of American Pathologists and American Society of Clinical Pathologists, 1992.

3. A brief overview of the Joint Commission's *Agenda for Change*. A Joint Commission briefing paper. Oakbrook Terrace, IL: Joint Commission on Accreditation of Healthcare Organizations, 1989.
4. Schyve PM. Personal communication. Oakbrook Terrace, IL: Joint Commission on Accreditation of Healthcare Organizations, March 9 1992.
5. Overview of the Joint Commission's *Agenda for Change*. Chicago, IL: Joint Commission on Accreditation of Healthcare Organizations, August, 1987
6. Koska MT. JCAHO: Pilot hospitals' input updates *Agenda for Change*. Hospitals, 1990;64:50-52,54.
7. O'Leary DS. President's column. Joint Commission Perspectives, 1989;9:1-2.
8. 1992 Joint Commission Accreditation Manual for Hospitals. Oakbrook Terrace, IL: Joint Commission on Accreditation of Healthcare Organizations, 1991.
9. Monitoring and Evaluation: Pathology and Medical Laboratory Services. Chicago, IL: Joint Commission on Accreditation of Healthcare Organizations, 1987.
10. Primer on Clinical Indicator Development and Application. Chicago, IL: Joint Commission on Accreditation of Healthcare Organizations, 1990
11. The Joint Commission 1994 Accreditation Manual for Hospitals. Vol I and II. Oakbrook Terrace, IL: Joint Commission on Accreditation of Healthcare Organizations, 1993.
12. McGregor D. The Human Side of Enterprise. New York, NY: McGraw-Hill Co, Inc, 1960.

13. Developmental Quality Improvement

THIS TEXT RAISES several questions regarding the implementation of modern quality management.

- "How can I develop these quality management concepts in my own laboratory; through what phases must I go to put the theory into practice?"
- "How can the practice of quality management affect my laboratory's organizational structure?"
- "Who can take the lead in implementing quality management?"

In Figure 13.1, the hierarchical model for total quality management (TQM) and continuous quality improvement (CQI)—developed in Chapter Two and Three—reminds us how the essential building blocks of a complete quality management system fit into place. This model demonstrates that the two quality management approaches require a substantial organizational infrastructure. Quality actualization (QAc)—as evidenced by total organizational commitment—is the very foundation of that system.

The *ideal* approach to implementing TQM and CQI theory would be to begin as soon as one or more individuals decide to form a laboratory organization. Their first step would be to plan, develop, and sustain a QAc program through a written program and a facilitated team building approach. Thus, from the very onset, the new organization would learn and practice the skills of effective team decision making—including all leadership levels. The next steps would be to plan, develop, and sustain the quality anticipation (QAn) and quality improvement (QI) programs, in that

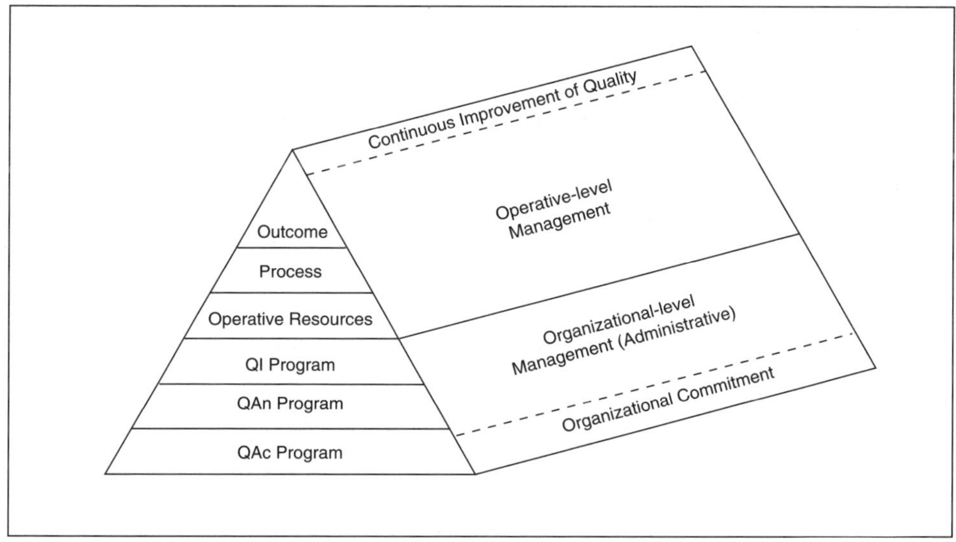

Figure 13.1 Model of essential elements of TQM and CQI

order; then, all organizational functions would be in place.

Once all three, interactive quality management programs are functioning at the *organizational-level* of operations, that infrastructure would steer the laboratory toward the next level of operational activities: planning, developing, and sustaining *operative-level* quality management. These activities would include the control oversight of all operative resources, processes, and outcomes. Thus each operational process—at both organizational and operative levels—would be integrated into the TQM system and CQI process.

Unfortunately, we seldom (if ever) experience the luxury of such an ideal progression of organizational development. Laboratory operations are almost always already ongoing at the time that we want to implement TQM and CQI practices. However, we can approximate the ideal approach by implementing a tri-phased schedule of actualizing, planning, and measuring the quality of operational events that are already under way. This requires shoring up whatever infrastructure that already exists and remodeling (or reengineering) the laboratory organization from the bottom up—with close support and involvement of all leaders from the top down.

There are many variations to this multi-phased approach to implementing modern quality management. No matter which one a laboratory chooses, it is helpful to understand the concept of developmental quality improvement for long-range planning purposes.

Developmental Quality Management

"How can I develop these quality management concepts in my own laboratory; through what phases must I go to put the theory into practice?"

This first question introduces the concept of *developmental quality management*. A developmental approach can help us understand how to build a managerial system of TQM programs and a CQI process when we already have an institutionalized laboratory organization and an established organizational culture. In this setting, the building of a quality management system usually moves through two major phases: implementation and actualization. Specific management and documentation styles characterize each phase.

The *implementation phase* usually consists of a centralized management style and an archival type of documentation. At the onset of this initial developmental phase, most organizational members ordinarily have little to no experience with modern quality management practices. Thus, they need basic team skills training and a hands-on introduction to quality management. It is during this first phase that the organization discovers and unleashes its positive cultural forces that will be dedicated to continuous improvement of customer satisfaction. Of key importance, the participants must achieve their new management skills while still performing their routine laboratory operative procedures that require the highest caliber of proficiency.

Centralized management allows a small cadre of leaders to perform most of the key, initial administrative activities—including training and exercising the total organization in the practice of TQM and CQI. The usually limited personnel assets on hand and an unrelenting laboratory workload require stringent planning, scheduling, and orchestrating of all operational activities. A successful introductory phase requires an efficient leadership style, which is best served by a small group in a typically hierarchical (pyramidal) organization. This staff cadre, however, should include the key leaders from all organizational levels down to the section level or lower.

Archival documentation consists of collecting a relatively large volume of quality information on the most important aspects of patient care (ie, all important laboratory products and services). The laboratory then profiles the data in cumulative form during three to six months of initial surveillance.

Despite the time and other resource constraints encountered, the implementation phase requires a significant amount of baseline data. All organizations require a basic fund of operational information to fuel their initial TQM and CQI processes and to stimulate the second phase of mature quality management development. Ironically, amassing such baseline information is a substantial drain on already taxed operational resources. Nevertheless, we must do it! Such an archival effort is possible if we pursue it one bite (or byte) of information at a time.

Archival documentation can drain energy from the organization because more data are gathered from the organization than lessons-learned information is transmitted back to the organization. However, it is necessary to pay this initial price so that informed decisions can be made by the limited leadership cadre at the very beginning—and by the organization-wide leadership in the second phase.

As the organization matures in its basic knowledge, skills, and use of TQM and CQI, there should be a natural progression from the implementation phase to the *actualization phase*. This transition involves a gradual, coordinated shift from a centralized to a decentralized, participative management style and a shift from an archival to an informative type of documentation.

A key to the actualization phase is encouraging *participative* management, a style that is germane to the most basic understanding of TQM and CQI. This "company-wide" approach to management is based on delegating decision making to the lowest possible levels of the organization. To some degree, all workers should share in the management, decision making, and accountability responsibilities—not just the chairs, chiefs, directors, managers, and supervisors. Thus, empowered decision making (eg, quality circles) should become the norm, incorporating the various investigative and decision making tools of Shewhart, Juran, Deming, Ishikawa, and others.

Even though participative management should largely supplant centralized management, there remains a need for some form of central leadership. A managerial rule of thumb is that *there has to be a leader.* This maxim does not call for an autocrat; on the contrary, it requires a sensitive leader who is an accomplished facilitator and decision maker, committed to total organizational improvement and empowerment, but still capable of making decisions whenever needed. The ability to "command the wisdom of Solomon" would be appropriate in such a leader's job description.

During the organization's metamorphosis into the second developmental phase, the treatment of quality management information should also shift from the archival to the *informative* type. The laboratory needs to carefully orchestrate this documentary shift in cadence with its transformation in management style.

Once an adequate amount of baseline information has been gathered, the archival type of documentation should diminish in volume as the alternative informational approach emerges. Thus, as participative management burgeons, so should its companion style of informative data management, because there is a greater need for the most current news of QI lessons learned. A mature quality improvement organization thrives on sharing its own success stories.

Informative documentation is a less resource-intensive form of data collection and is characterized by reduced gathering of cumulative data. Rather, its focus is on disseminating more selectively gathered and evaluated information throughout the organization—both horizontally and vertically. There should be concordant changes in monitoring periodicities, report formats, and communication methods.

However, as informative documentation supplants the archival mode, there will still be a residual need for some archival documentation. It is always necessary to substantiate new indicator levels, patterns, and trends

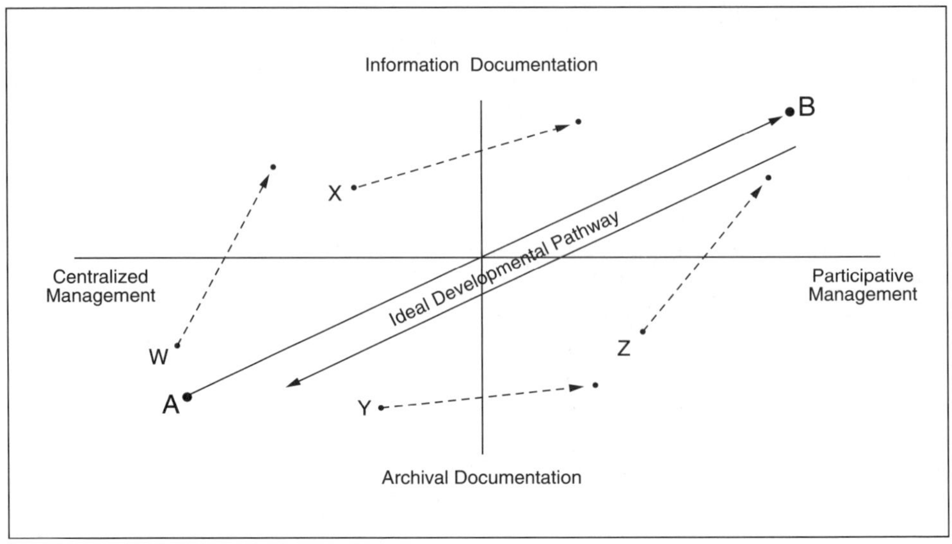

Figure 13.2 A model of the implementation and actualization phases of developmental quality management

with new baselines and cumulative data. Thus, archival documentation never disappears entirely.

As one futurist, Korpman, points out, health care is an information (not a data) industry—and will become even more so as the new century unfolds. This evolving healthcare information system will become increasingly patient-centered and functionally integrated, optimizing all operational processes and functions. It will incorporate electronic medical record keeping and point-of-care, bedside-based automation. There will be extensive control functions, integrating expert systems, advanced digital and data imaging, robotics, and barcoding with a proliferation of point-of-care, interactive terminals.[1] Thus, there will be ample operative- and organizational-level information to assimilate and manage on a carefully prioritized basis.

Figure 13.2 models the progression of developmental quality improvement from the first to second phase. Mapped out on the X and Y axes, this model demonstrates a four-quadrant or four-dimensional spectrum of possible management and documentation styles.

The double solid line (A-B) depicts the most ideal path of development. The reverse element (B to A) represents the partial return to more disciplined management practice when the need arises. The implementation phase extends from point A to the graph's origin (the X-Y intersect); the actualization phase extends from the origin to point B.

In actuality, a laboratory can commence from any point of the model and arrive almost anywhere in any quadrant, depending on the laboratory's commitment to developing TQM and CQI. Laboratories "W, X, Y, or Z" and their broken lines of pathway depict such less-than-ideal possibilities. Each laboratory must determine its own position on the model and follow the general guidelines according to its current organizational values, mission, vision, goals and objectives—as well as its management resources.

The Evolution of Organizational Structure

"How can the practice of quality management affect my laboratory's organizational structure?" This second question introduces the concept of the evolution of organizational structure. How might an organization's structure change to reflect the phases of quality management development? As TQM and CQI develop, the typical laboratory should make a transition from the traditional form of organizational structure toward a more modern one—at least, to some degree.

Figure 13.3A illustrates the traditional rank and file, hierarchical organization modeled after 19th century concepts of bureaucratic organizations—a structure very typical of any healthcare laboratory in the implementation phase of quality management. The figure is a very familiar wiring diagram that depicts the highest level of department leadership at level A, middle management (service or section) at level B, supervisory management at level C, and operative technical, hands-on work at bench level D. Theoretically, these position designations could go on to include all employee groups, if space in the model permitted. This traditional organizational model clearly displays the lines and span of control and communication.

One universal lesson implied by any organizational structure is that to communicate *is* to control. A second lesson is that any organizational design that facilitates communication also potentiates more efficient and effective outcomes. Paradoxically, excessive control of an organization's transmission of information (ie, micromanagement) is seldom conducive to fully actualized organizational efficiency and effectiveness. So, how does the traditional, hierarchical organizational structure of Figure 13.3A treat communication?

First, the bureaucratic model hinges on the leadership and authority being centralized at the top of each echelon (ie, the epicenter of decision making). As experience and studies demonstrate, this structural arrangement tends to enforce strategy from above and draw information from the bottom echelons to the top—rather inadequately—without a reciprocal flow of lessons learned back to the lower echelons.

As a consequence, operational control—including control or power over communication—becomes concentrated among a relatively few individuals; this favors rapid but not always accurate decision making. Data management in such an organizational structure is traditionally more archival (unidirectional) than informative (multidirectional).

Second, this model favors division of labor and subspecialization by both managers and hands-on workers alike. Is this model beginning to

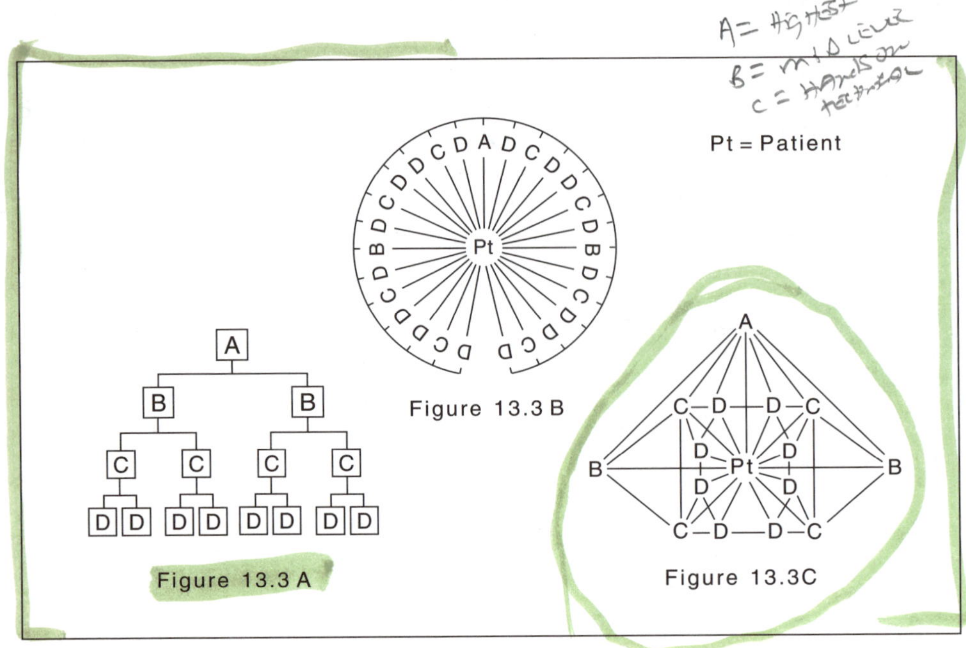

Figure 13.3 Development of organizational structure

resemble a typical government bureaucracy or the military? Or a healthcare laboratory?

Third, there is no traditional position for the customer (ie, consumer, client) in this organizational structure. Neither the patient nor any other external (or internal) customer is visibly evident—and that includes the employee as the internal customer. A vital participant in total operational quality improvement process is missing from the model. Thus, the central authority is limited in envisioning all possible contingencies encountered at the operative level.

Fourth, information is easily modified as it passes through so many hierarchical levels. Whereas some bits of information can be lost or deleted, other pieces can be unduly modulated or biased. This classical, organizational structure of Figure 13.3A is usually in place at the onset of the centralized management/archival documentation phase of TQM and CQI implementation.

Figure 13.3B depicts a sweeping change from the organizational wiring diagram of the traditional hierarchy to a more idealized example of a participative organizational model. This nontraditional, organic structure stems from the more modern, behavioral school of management. The same leadership and other job positions still exist: the highest, titular position of department leadership is still at block A; middle-level managerial positions are in place at blocks B; and operative-level supervisory and hands-on technical positions are in place at blocks C and D respectively. Again, these position designations could go on indefinitely to include all employee groups, if space permitted. Figure 13.3C depicts a more three-dimensional rendition of the same organic model, also reminiscent of a stylized atomic shell structure.

Models B and C are "organic" because all constituent elements enjoy the same access to the communications network—similar to a multicellular organism. Also, all employees are linked to the primary customer, the patient. The organic model favors a working environment in which employees—managers and workers, alike—are more apt to be more multiskilled (compared to the traditional hierarchy).

These two models enjoy one distinguishing difference from the traditional, rank and file model. All organizational employees (including all leaders, managers, supervisors, and operative-level workers) are virtually at the same communication level. There is a common level of communication where all information flows freely along the same plane and at the same degree of intensity in all directions. In fact, this two-dimensional diagram does not adequately portray the networking potential because all the players really work in a three-dimensional world; electronic communication devices even add a fourth dimension. Everyone does not have to be the primary addressee for every piece of information; however, everyone who has a *need to know* has access to all pertinent information—medico-legal confidentiality withstanding.

Being part of the mainstream of information—and being able to freely enter into the operational dialogue—empowers all employees as potential decision makers. Yes, communication is control; information is power; and that power is influential over decision making. In more modern structural models, everyone in the organization is equally informed—and, therefore, is equally empowered. The key to ultimate control in this model is that some leader-employees are just more empowered than others.

In the organic model of figures 13.3B and 13.3C, there is no top-heavy epicenter of information collection and decision making. In fact, a distinguishing characteristic of this model is that the patient (or any other key internal or external customer) represents the informational/decisional epicenter or focus for this participative, multicellular, organizational matrix. Thus, all employees are theoretically in a position of decision making to some degree and each is in relative proximity to or in actual contact with the patient (ie, each is linked closely enough to the operative work level that he or she can listen to the customer).

Additionally, less modification of information is apt to occur between one echelon and the next. This is because everyone has access to the same information through the same communication system at the same organizational access level in real time. Potentially, the entry of one piece of data or information from any input terminal can simultaneously reach all read-out terminals. Such a universal information-link is possible through computerized data management and electronic communication.

An organic network can promote the sharing of information regarding patient health status, healthcare outcome, and customer satisfaction between the patient and all those in the organization who need to know.

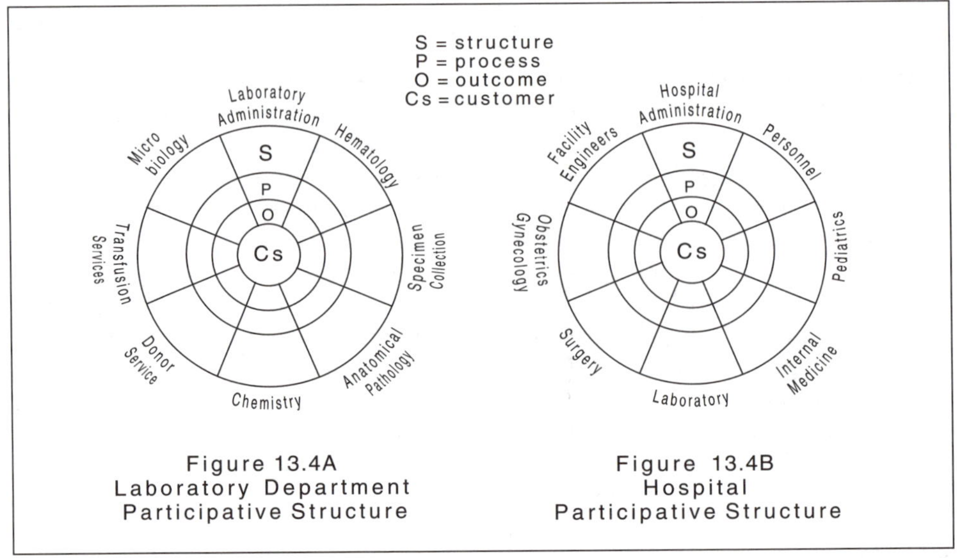

Figure 13.4 Variations of the participative structure in the laboratory and hospital

Through such a facilitative organizational matrix, the focus on patient care can easily transfer to any other aspect of customer satisfaction, including employee health and welfare. The organizational structure of figures 13.3B and 13.3C approximates what could be ideally expected to evolve in the typical participative management/informative documentation phase of TQM and CQI actualization.

Whether one envisions this organizational paradigm as analogous to an organic or atomic structure, remember that it is just a model. The best aspects can be adopted and merged into the traditional organizational scheme. There still has to be leadership and decision making. There still have to be job descriptions and performance evaluations, all typical of a planned, hierarchal structure. This merging of the two paradigms into an acceptable hybrid structure will come about primarily through the aid of computerization and electronic networking.

Figure 13.4 illustrates variations of the organic model that incorporate the TQM and CQI model presented earlier. Figure 13.4A highlights the relationship of the various anatomic and clinical pathology services and sections in a hospital laboratory department. Figure 13.4B portrays that a healthcare laboratory organization mirrors the entire parent hospital organization. The hospital model is a natural expansion of the departmental model; the hospital is just larger in scope.

Every hospital department (eg, surgery, medicine, administration) enjoys the same general internal operational relationships that the laboratory department enjoys. Likewise, each departmental organization should have similar working relationships with all associated departments, sharing information with equal facility—as in a three-dimensional game of managerial chess. In either case, the laboratory department or hospital administration unit is on an equal operational plane with its respective lower echelons in terms of information flow and patient/customer relations.

Of utmost importance, all healthcare departments link with one common external customer—the patient. Both figures 13.4A and 13.4B depict such intra- and interdepartmental, three-dimensional relationships that include the customer as a central focus.

The organic model is much more a functional than a physical representation of an organization. Also, it should be clear that a participative organizational structure of any size and any kind must be supported by an automated information network of adequate dimensions and complexity. A complex organization of departmental and hospital dimensions depends on the computerized transfer of information for its multi-dimensional communication capability.

Please understand that the structural models illustrated in this chapter are for demonstration purposes; they are idealized structures. No laboratory or hospital can hope to exactly emulate these models—neither physically nor functionally. At the present time, most laboratories are probably patterned after the traditional, rank and file model. It is likely, however, that the practice of TQM and CQI will stimulate hierarchical laboratories to function more like modern, organic structures—whether they really intend it or not.

THE IMPORTANCE OF LEADERSHIP

Champions of Innovation

"Who can take the lead in implementing quality management?" This third question introduces the concept of *champions of innovation*, *creative-responsive organizations*, and *all-in-all communication networks*. In a nutshell, anyone can successfully take the lead if they adequately understand themselves, modify their own managerial behavior or management style to fit their organization's needs, and can overcome the cultural barriers at hand.

The literature is replete with testimonial evidence that successful quality management starts from the top. Without leadership that is involved both in decision making and resource support, the practice of TQM and CQI is doomed to only piecemeal success, at best—and abject failure at worst. Thus, what is needed to seal the success of continuous improvement is a fair share of creative leaders: champions of innovation.

Problems in implementing and sustaining good quality management clearly reflect an inherent inability—even a conscionable unwillingness—on the part of both the top-level leaders and the bench-level employees to cross over industrial-cultural borderlines. Therefore, it is imperative that "champions of innovation" within our healthcare organizations and laboratories help to overcome those barriers.

Who are these champions? Parker describes them as individuals having the vision, the commitment, and the courage to succeed in the countercultural endeavor of fostering change. These are men and women who are willing to go where no one has ever gone before in laboratory management and quality improvement.[2] In a sense, a champion of innovation fits the mold of an organizational entrepreneur—an explorer, researcher, developer, and general operator of new ideas for quality improvement.

Such champions are essential for the sustained *implementation* and *actualization* of modern quality management practices. This is somewhat paradoxical in that we are talking about the institutionalization of a quality management system that accepts *continuous change*. Thus, a champion of innovation must be able to promote antithetical managerial models and paradigm shifts. Under such unique circumstances, what sort of individuals seem to make good champions?

Regarding the vision: a champion has vision that is based on both objective observation and subjective intuition. He or she is committed to making that vision a reality. He (or she) "does not guide his actions with economic rationality" but "keeps trying until he achieves his goal or reaches exhaustion."[2] Such an individual must be courageous, willing to take calculated risks, unafraid of making mistakes along the way, and ready to face peer criticism—even ostracism.

A champion of innovation understands and can apply complex, technical concepts and abstract ideas to healthcare systems. He or she is able to identify and prioritize the most important aspects of the healthcare system at hand and deal with the highest ranking priorities accordingly.

Regarding commitment and courage, Parker describes these champions as having a significant need for achievement; a moderate need for power; a bull dog tenacity; and a driving, aggressive, dynamic personality. He or she must be adventuresome—ready to accept the avant-garde, the rash, the risky, and even the hazardous. He is not discouraged by failure. In the eyes of his critics, his could be perceived as an irrational commitment, an inordinate energy, even a combative skill akin to a guerrilla warrior—none of which is really all bad.

What sort of personality type might be most successful? Parker's profile of a champion of innovation best fits two of the 16 types described by Myers.[3] The most appropriate categorizations include the introvertive and extrovertive intuitive-thinking-judging (ie, INTJ and ENTJ) Myers-Briggs types. Based on Jungian theory of personality development, these two types theoretically represent the most originally innovative thinkers.

Table I illustrates the prevalence of INTJ and ENTJ personality types among both male and female college preparation, high school students. Myers' data suggests that approximately 11% of the general college preparatory high school male population are of the INTJ or ENTJ type.[3]

Table I
Prevalence of Selected Myers-Briggs Personality Types among College Preparatory High Students*

Type	Men	Women
INTJ	4.4%	1.8%
ENTJ	6.2%	3.3%
	10.6%	5.1%
ISTJ	8.2%	3.3%
ESTJ	16.3%	9.7%
ISFJ	4.0%	6.9%
ESFJ	6.4%	17.6%
	34.9%	21.5%

*Note: These figures are compiled from data presented by Myers.[3]

There is supporting evidence that these percentages are even less among the general laboratory workforce population because of even more self selection.[4]

Table I suggests that there are relatively few men who fit the champion profile by innate personality type alone. It is a blessing, then, that individuals representing the other 14 Myers-Briggs types can modify their inherent behavior—some with greater ease than others. Thus, a few more of these other individuals are also prone to step forth as champions. Still, there are precious few who overcome the cultural barriers—whether they be men or women.

The data in Table I support Parker's observation that even fewer champions of innovation are women. Considering Myer's studies of college preparatory high school students, women represent approximately half (5% versus 11%) the number of INTJ and ENTJ personality types—the two types that are most likely to prefer the role of champion. In addition to the smaller prevalence of this inherent trait among women in a self-selected population of college preparatory high school students, there are well recognized, traditional socio-economic barriers that make championing an even greater challenge for those women who already have the natural constitution to take a risk further down the professional pathway.[a]

There is also a shadow side of our personality types with which we must contend. As is true for any type, both INTJs and ENTJs have their inherent, counterproductive weaknesses that they must master. These adverse traits are most likely to surface in times of stress.

For example, as an introvertive-intuitive-thinking-judging type, the

[a] Demographics have changed since these studies were performed and, therefore, warrant restudy. However, the relative prevalence of the INTJ and ENTJ types is unlikely to be significantly different.

INTJ is probably the most cerebral of all the 16 possible Myers-Briggs types. This does not have anything to do with innate intelligence; it has to do with the INTJ's preference or style of processing and using information. Ordinarily, these cognitive traits can be very advantageous to the individual and the organization. However, having a cognitive bent along with a strong introvertive streak, the INTJ *potentially* has to work at being a team builder and team player. In fact, he or she might have to ward off natural tendencies of suspiciousness, defensiveness, and self-righteousness in the course of doing business with all other types.[5]

Additionally, the INTJs must guard against a quiet arrogance and overconfidence that they can master the complexity of any system at hand.[5] Metaphorically, here is the rub: the INTJ might easily grasp the complexity of the entire forest, but he or she might as easily miss the significance of a specific tree—or, more likely, of an important flowering plant hidden among the brush.

The ENTJ shares many of the same potentially counterproductive weaknesses as the INTJ. Many of the ENTJ's adverse characteristics are accentuated by that individual's streak of extrovertism. He or she must always work at developing a sensitivity to other people's feelings and their reactions to the extrovertive champion's enthusiasm—especially the reactions of introvertive colleagues. The ENTJ champion of innovation must exercise caution against displaying undue impatience and blatant arrogance. The good news is that the INTJ or ENTJ champions of innovation usually learn to modify and control the shadow-side tendencies of their behavior—as do all other personality types.[b]

Just as we need to develop and nurture champions of innovation, these key individuals also need to work within a "creative-responsive" organization that will support the innovator's successes and momentum. Parker, as well as Deming, characterize such an organization as having the following attributes.[2,6]

- Member awareness of and commitment to the organization's mission, vision, and goals
- Lack of a well-defined hierarchy as evidenced by its routine functioning
- A multi-directional communication system that serves as an "interactive network" for the champions of innovation within and outside of the organization.

First, member commitment to the organization's strategic plan is a matter of education, communication, and empowerment. Thus, the

[b] Use these MBTI characterizations only as the general guidelines that they are. Do not pigeon-hole any individuals, vis., personality type. For example, some NTs do not fit the general innovative "mold"; other non-NT types can modify their behavior and become great innovators.

champion of innovation must also be a leading proponent of motivation, incentive, and team building.

Second, the absence of a *functional* hierarchy does not preclude there being an organizational wiring diagram in someone's drawer. However, functionally, there should be blurred distinctions between senior and junior members and a lack of restrictive chain-of-command requirements between so-called superiors and subordinates. There should be a clear emphasis on the free exchange of ideas without fear of adverse repercussions. These relationships should extend down to the levels of production workers nearest to the testing bench and the word processing work center—and even further to all types of customers.

Third, Parker's "creative-responsive" organization mirrors the decentralized, participative model described under the concept of developmental improvement. In almost all cases, our current laboratory structures are centralized, polarized, and extremely hierarchical. Most administrative—and innovative—power for QAc, QAn, and QI purposes is concentrated at the top of the pyramid. Usually, the only way for the organization to deal with significant internal or external change is for someone to wrest control of that power away from those at the top by a *coup d' etat* of one form or another.

In the more decentralized organization, there are equally ambitious champions of innovation at all organizational echelons. In such an environment, it is natural for these champions to build their own fiefdoms without having to struggle or compete with an entrenched central authority. We should be able to use these natural tendencies of fragmentation and energies of innovative leaders at all organizational echelons to our advantage.

Fourth, Parker's "all-in-all," organic communication system should promote both formal and informal exchange of data, information, and ideas. This network should incorporate both horizontal and vertical organizational dimensions—again, including all customer types.

In reality, the participative phase of developmental quality improvement will hopefully generate a happy mixture of both worlds of centralized and decentralized authority and innovation. In this hybrid environment, the central or top leadership portion of the organization should function mostly as a clearinghouse and switching station for the dissemination of ideas. However, we must always keep in mind that, ultimately, *there has to be a leader*—no matter how flexible or innovative the overall organization's structure might be. A decentralized laboratory is not a leaderless organization. The buck has to stop somewhere. Keeping human nature in mind—and being wary of any personality type's potential shadow side—an umpire-type always has to watch the clock and keep the rule book at arm's reach. This leader persona must incorporate, in fact, a multiplex, umpire-coach-player-cheerleader capability—each aspect under control but at instant recall.

Experts in the practice of quality management widely attest to the importance of leadership during any organization's journey toward quality improvement; it all begins with the leader. Often, the leader's personal journey begins with a curiosity that develops into intensive self-education—an education that is never ending. The next steps for these individuals are revising their own management styles, modifying their own managerial behavior to include clinical patient management, reallocating budgets to include quality management, revamping their own schedules to include all three quality management programs, and redesigning their own performance evaluations to include their involvement and support of systematic quality management.[7,8]

In the healthcare industry, the most important and likely candidate as lead champion is the primary healthcare provider. There is widespread agreement that the physician champion is absolutely essential to any healthcare quality management effort—including efforts within the laboratory. However, cardinal supporting roles—both clinical and administrative—also rest on the shoulders of all other healthcare providers. There must be innovative champions of improvement at all levels of the laboratory organization.

Ernest Codman, a prime example of a healthcare champion of innovation, demonstrated all of the appropriate traits. In turn, the medical community pilloried Codman for his views on outcome measurement in the form of extensive professional ostracism. Nonetheless, Codman lived to see the earliest advances of healthcare reform and quality improvement. Perhaps he was somewhat vindicated for the sacrifices that he paid for such personal commitment to a profound vision. Semmelweiss experienced much worse.[10]

Barriers to Innovation

There has always been cyclical interest in quality management throughout all industries in the United States. Overall, our society is very fickle when it comes to managerial approaches; it is clearly reluctant to have any long-term relationships with any management system—we lack corporate patience. A faltering popularity of TQM and CQI has been particularly characteristic of the healthcare industry in the United States.

At each onset, so-called "new" paradigms, concepts, models, and acronyms initially seem to fill some void and make good sense.[c] But cultural barriers usually slow implementation, especially in any good-sized operational system. Often, the organizational learning and practice curves quickly begin to lag far behind initial expectations. Before long, the new miracle system either languishes through a slow demise or immediately disappears as key leaders rotate. In fact, this is the litmus test for any quality management system: does it survive when key individuals rotate?

There are many, diverse cultural barriers to quality management implementation and sustainment in healthcare, including in the

[c] Ironically, most of the so-called "new" management paradigms and concepts are not really new at all; they are just common sense presented in new wrappings.

laboratory. The preponderance of these obstacles are not financial. It is true that top management might not recognize the importance of quality management compared with financial success—but that is the subject of the next chapter.

Most often, the key barrier to innovation is lack of trained and committed leadership. For example, a recent study reveals that physicians—who are of key importance—are the least enthusiastic of all the primary players in healthcare quality management. The study cites only 2.9% being really enthusiastic.[11] This latter trend has to reverse or someone other than the physician leader will be orchestrating innovation in healthcare quality management.

What are the reasons given by healthcare providers for opposing innovation in quality management? Here is what some say[12, 13]:

- Health care is too unique for its quality to be quantified.
    - Health care deals with biological systems that consist of too many variables for accurate measurement of quality.
    - In a biologically-based system, a management concept that strives through unlimited opportunities for improvement toward zero defects is unrealistic.
    - Patients are not "widgets;" they are flesh and blood.
    - We cannot quantify health care's huge emotional cost to patients, families, and providers in terms of human suffering.
    - Medicine is an art, not a science.
- Quality management infringes on sacrosanct rights or privileges, including:
    - The provider's professional rights and privileges
    - The patients rights and privileges
    - The provider-patient relationship.
- Quality management smacks of "the administration" and their bean counters whom healthcare providers often perceive as natural, sworn enemies.
    - The quality management of healthcare and nonhealthcare industries is different.
    - Hospitals are not like factories.
    - Health care is not an industry; it is a profession.
    - Health care is a service industry and the quality of services are not measurable.
    - The jargon of nonhealthcare quality management is foreign and, therefore, offensive.

- Quality improvement will reduce the quality of health care.

In their own right, some of the issues listed above are actually very important; and some are outrageous. However, none of them truly justifies exclusion of quality management from healthcare. Now, where have such questionable, even contradictory, notions come from?

Some of these adverse reactions spring from medicine's early guild heritage and its penchant for a closed professional society. In most cases, these opinions and feelings arise from the way that healthcare providers are traditionally trained.

For example, there is a strong, ingrained professional machismo attitude against failure, not withstanding a realistic concern for patient health and welfare and humanistic effort to do no harm. Although support systems account for at least 80% of the patient care process, the primary provider's singular competence is paramount in terms of accountability. The provider is taught to be in control; and the provider cannot lose control. This professional work ethic creates a "control or shielding paradigm" for the provider—a mindset in which only the function of provider skill ultimately counts. Support personnel are taught to accept the same paradigm. Thus, providers and support personnel tend to reject systematic quality management principles and, in fact, violate them every day.[12]

For example, as a result of such a professional work ethic, there is a significant fear of peer criticism and ostracism. Such a fear of retribution is common cause for the mishandling of outcome data requiring peer review and eventual dissemination of lessons learned. Here is a perfect opportunity to practice one of Deming's 14 points: drive out fear in the workplace.[6] Or, as Berwick has said, alluding to the "bad apple," fix the process, don't fix the blame.[14]

It is an inherent profession-wide feeling that a physician's or other provider's professional performance cannot be questioned through some impersonal TQM system. Why? Because a professional pays too great a price in long years of education and training. Afterwards—at least in some cases—they work until they are done, sometimes waging truly mental and physical heroic struggles against insurmountable odds, saving lives and healing. These hard and long hours of work drain healthcare providers, physically and emotionally. As a result, they perceive that there is no extra time available for quality management—their plate is too full. Besides, quality management is a job for an administrative bean counter—just as long as they do not count "*my* beans."

In fact, this adversarial relationship between healthcare providers and administrators must cease! Many providers perceive administrators as foisting quality management on the practitioners' back just to improve the financial bottom line. The facts are that the provider's luxury of having such an arrogant opinion of quality management no longer exists. Yes, measuring the quality of processes in a service industry is more difficult—but it is not impossible. And providers reluctant to adjust their schedules and practices to improve patient outcomes will have to change their attitudes, learn a little more about team skills, and modify their own behavior.

This misperception regarding the role of administration is why the physicians and other providers must become more involved as leaders in healthcare quality management. The medical staff must "own" the TQM system and CQI process. That ownership must be earned by their total involvement and support. There can be a sharing of rewards and recognition among all healthcare providers; there should even be recognition of the administrators as providing certain aspects of health care.

What about the "jargon?" Because medical directors and other healthcare leaders within the laboratory are not enthusiastic and not well trained in quality management, the jargon often seems alien. Yes, TQM and CQI originated in a nonhealthcare language that can be offensive to a healthcare professional. In many cases, providers accurately perceive that it is the language of the assembly line and efficiency time-motion-study experts. In the providers' view, such an approach depersonalizes the services in a caring, personal environment. Ironically, in these days of high technology, the problem of low touch care actually is a more prevalent threat. One suggestion to making management language more palatable is to continue to present TQM in terms of patient satisfaction and internal customer welfare.[13]

If there really is a so-called "bottom line," it is that we must teach quality management to physicians and other providers and encourage them to step forward to serve as the innovative champions they need to be. As implied in the discussion of different personality types, this change in behavior is learnable—if it is not already inherent. For the physicians, this process should begin as early as their internship and specialty training—perhaps even earlier while they are still in medical school.[15] In other words, "Physician, heal thyself!"

Otherwise, as poorly trained and disinterested medical leaders become more and more turned off to quality management, they begin to wallow in the morass of dysfunctional organizational dynamics and poor business practice. Often, theirs is a subjective, intuitive lack of comprehension of healthcare management concepts. Eventually, they begin to offer unsubstantiated opinion and rumor from the podium, *ex cathedra*, that the current quality management model is failing—that it is falling from popular favor. This becomes a repetitive cycle of self-fulfilled prophecy.

For example, common sense should not be dismayed by the pseudo-hysteria generated by the Chicken Littles of the laboratory community, saying: "Its going to fail; its going to fail!" Otherwise, the folk tale allegory might become the self-fulfilling prophecy. Instead, the practice of common sense in good quality management must prevail.

At the other end of the organizational spectrum, the bench level workers—those closest to the work and to the patient—are often offended by being given more to do. In other words, empowerment is not always what it is cracked up to be. The truth is that many employees do not want to be "empowered"—

especially if they (as potential leaders) have not received adequate preparation or the necessary resources. In some cases, this even becomes a negotiation issue between labor union and laboratory management.[16] Thus, all healthcare employees from top to bottom must undergo cultural changes to overcome:

- Fear of providing empowerment—with a potential loss of top management power or positions
- Fear of being empowered—with a potential increase of work to be done or a flattening of the organizational structure and loss of middle management or lower echelon positions.

There is another generic cultural barrier to innovation and quality improvement that can exist organization-wide. This potential problem consists of a personality backlash based on the general makeup of all of the laboratory employees other than the innovator types. This basic cultural barrier rests on the very foundation of the combined personality of the laboratory workforce. As noted in Table I, Myers found that a large portion of college preparatory students fit into the sensory-judging (SJ) personality temperament (ie, ISTJ, ESTF, ISFJ, and ESFJ). In the student population, as many as 35% of the men and at least 22% of the women could be SJs.[3] Another study has shown that more than 50% of laboratorians are SJs.[4] This all suggests self-selection by laboratory workers into a preferred profession and work environment.[4] When confronted by the ideas and efforts of the INTJ/ENTJ champions of innovation and improvement, the SJ personality types (who tend to be very conservative) can band together and resist change.

Another TQM and CQI concept of contention among healthcare providers involves the use of the terms customer, customer-supplier, user, or client—as opposed to the time-honored reference to the patient. Again these management terms generate semantic differences that are offensive to healthcare traditionalists.

In fact, health care provides a perfect example of the customer-supplier connection. In traditional, nonhealthcare industries, suppliers provide raw materials for manufacturing use. In the healthcare industry, it is easy to accept the patient as the primary customer. However, the patient is also the basic supplier of the most quintessential raw material to be processed: the patient's own physical and mental health condition.[13,17]

In summation, this chapter has covered developmental quality improvement. Inextricably linked to these developmental processes are organizational structure and leadership, including the barriers to innovation and change. Healthcare leaders need to reframe health care in terms of modern quality management. Begin with a general perspective of modern TQM and CQI, and slowly but surely turn quality management tools, techniques, and bench marks into successful healthcare managerial approaches.[18]

It is helpful to consider the developmental needs of the laboratory organization, just as we have learned to consider the individual's needs. To paraphrase Maslow, whether we are considering the ultimate actualization of an individual or that of an organization, *"Become all that you can be!"*

REFERENCES

1. Korpman RA. New technologies and laboratory medicine: four paradigms for the future. Lab Med, 1992;23:396-404.
2. Parker LA. Interactive Networks for Innovational Champions: A Mechanism for Decentralized Educational Change. Harvard University, Ed.D, 1971. Ann Arbor, MI: University Microfilms International, 1981.
3. Myers IB. Gifts Differing. Palo Alto, CA: Consulting Psychologists Press, Inc, 1989.
4. Clark GB. Laboratory MBTI survery. Unpublished data.
5. Kroeger O, Kroeger J. Type Talk at Work: How the 16 Personality Types Determine Your Success on the Job. new York, NY: Delacorte Press, 1992.
6. Walton M. The Deming Management Method. New York, NY: Putnam Pub Group, 1986.
7. Eubanks P, Grayson M. TMQ/CQI: The CEO Experience. Hospitals, 1992;66:24-8,30-2,34-6.
8. Larson K. Hospital trustees lead quality efforts. Qual Prog, 1990;23:31-34.
9. McClendon WW, Ernest A, Codman MD (1869-1940). The end-result idea and *The Product of a Hospital:* the challenge of a man ahead of his time and perhaps ours. Arch Pathol Lab Med, 1990;114:1101.
10. Lyons AS, Petrucelli RJ. Medicine. An Illustrated History. New York, NY: Abradale Press, 1987.
11. Koska MT. CEOs say hospitals must learn from each other for TQM success. Hospitals, 1992;66:42,44,46,48,50.
12. Morison PE, Heinke J. Why do health practitioners resist quality management? Qual Prog, 1992;25:51-55.
13. Mueller RA. Implementing TQM in health care requires adaptation and innovation. Qual Prog, 1992;25:57-59.
14. Berwick DM. Continuous improvement as an idea in healthcare. NEJM, 1989;320:53.
15. Valenstein PN, Burke MD. Teaching pathology and laboratory medicine: teaching pathology residents to evaluate the quality of laboratory testing. Arch Pathol Lab Med, 1987;111:571-4.
16. Clinical indicators require drastic cultural changes. Hosp Peer Rev, 1989;14:53-5.
17. Stratton B. Health care (editorial). Qual Prog, 1992;25:19-20.
18. Fried RA. Crisis in health care. Qual Prog, 1992;25:67-69.

14. Is Quality Management Cost-Effective?

WESTGARD AND OTHERS generally describe the various costs of implementing and sustaining total quality management (TQM) and continuous quality improvement (CQI). Also referred to as "barriers," these costs include time, people, equipment and supplies.[1] For example:

- Time for training personnel in team skills such as group dynamics approaches, consensus techniques, analytical tools, and opportunity identification and problem solving skills
- People to participate in team projects as team members, quality facilitators, coordinators, and directors
- Equipment and supplies for computerization, automation, and communication.

It is reasonable that we expect some reciprocal benefits in return for our investment in quality management. However, most reports of such cost-benefits are very general and anecdotal. In addressing the economics of healthcare quality management, three questions regarding specific operational costs and benefits arise:

- "How much will the practice of quality management cost my laboratory?"
- "How much will the practice of quality management save my laboratory in terms of non-costed operational benefits and costed financial savings?"
- "Will quality management remain viable in this era of increasing socio-economic constraints?"

THE COST OF QUALITY MANAGEMENT

"How much will the practice of quality management cost my laboratory? This first question addresses quality costs. Its answer lies in the theory of the value of quality plus the macro- and microeconomics of health care in the United States.

Theory of Quality, Its Cost and Value

The theory of quality, its cost, and its value bring us back to basic definitions provided in initial chapters of this text. We need to define the quality of a product or service as it is perceived "in the eye of the customer." Futhermore, our definition of quality should embrace the perspectives of a number of different players in the healthcare system—from the viewpoint of the patient, the provider, and the purchaser or payer.

First, we can consider the definitions of well-versed students—the so-called gurus—of quality, such as Shewhart, Deming, Juran, Crosby, Shector, Wollschlager, and others who have formulated the following dimensions of quality[2-7]:

- Competitiveness through a superior product or service as established by the customer; meeting customer expectations (ie, doing the right things)
- Conformance of a product or service to design specifications as established by professional/industrial standards (ie, doing things right the first time)
- Freedom from deficiencies (ie, zero defects)
- Fitness for use
- Reliability and yield.

The importance and scope of these parameters of quality will vary depending on which type of customer is making the quality assessment.

One benchmark example is the Joint Commission on Accreditation of Healthcare Organizations' (JCAHO) updating of its definition of healthcare quality:

> The degree to which patient care services increase the probability of desired patient outcomes and reduce the probability of undesired outcomes given the current state of knowledge. Potential components of quality include the following: accessibility of care, appropriateness of care, efficiency of care, timeliness of care, patient perspective issues, and safety of the care enviroment.[8]

The JCAHO has also identified a chain of critical events that links performance of process with outcome (including cost) with assessment of

Table I
Estimated Costs of Quality [9]

	Ideal	Actual
Overall Quality Costs (as a percent of total revenue)	3%-7%	25%-35%
Categories of Quality Costs		
Prevention costs	45%	5%
Appraisal costs	25%	20%
Internal failure costs	20%	45%
External failure costs	10%	30%

quality (including costed and non-costed value). Again, this assessment has to be in the eyes of the patient, provider, or payor—whoever happens to be the primary customer.

As shown in Table I, Daigh has demonstrated a system for the itemized cost analysis of quality.[9] The costs of quality can fit into one of three categories: prevention, appraisal, or failure. Thus, total quality costs equal the sum of the costs of[8-10]:

- *Preventing* nonconformance to performance requirements
- *Appraising* a product or service for conformance to standards
- *Failing* to meet said standards.

Prevention costs stem from the integration of quality building and defect avoidance into all operational processes. These include costs of ongoing assessment and improvement, strategic improvement, and cultural improvement.

Appraisal costs stem from monitoring product or service conformance and customer satisfaction. These include costs of internal operative-level quality control, and organizational-level assessment and improvement plus external inspections and surveys.

Failure costs stem from any correction of a flawed outcome of a defective operational process. Internal and external costs can result from production or service failure. *Internal costs* include paid time wasted in the course of reinspection, idleness or suspended operations, reworking or repeating production or services, changed orders, wasted or scrapped raw materials and supplies, and evaluation and correction of defects and errors. *External costs* include those associated with lost customers and referrals plus liability or malpractice expenses.

As shown in Table I, Daigh compares the ideal with actual quality costs.

Actual quality costs can be inordinately severe—greater than one-quarter of total revenue. Such a burden is usually due to excessive failure costs. Ideally, quality costs should be less than 10% of the total revenue with greatest emphasis on prevention.

As to the value of quality, the full value equals the total cost of quality management weighed against the total-costed and non-costed benefits of subject quality improvement as judged by the customer. Crosby has written that successful quality management can result in, at least, a 5% to 10% increase of profit; in fact, he likes to say that quality is free.[5] Juran predicts a potential six-fold return on a quality investment in prevention.[4] And, Deming discounts the importance of the cost of quality, entirely.[3] No wonder there is confusion about the value of quality management! As usual, the truth lies somewhere in the middle.

The Macroeconomics of Healthcare Quality

Modern day efforts to improve the quality of national healthcare access and costs initially began with the Hill-Burton (Hospital Survey and Construction) Act of 1946. This law promoted a vast expansion of healthcare facilities during the postwar years. That *laissez faire* era began to fade with John Kennedy challenging institutionalized medicine in the early 1960s. As a result of changing public opinion, Public Law 89-97 of 1965 amending the Social Security Act of 1935 established Medicare for public funding of health care of the elderly and Medicaid for care of certain indigent people.[11] This legislative innovation created sweeping changes in healthcare economics. However, a major untoward result was the generation of an unprecedented wave of runaway healthcare costs nationwide. The JCAHO responded by revising its standards to stem the tide of healthcare overutilization and cost overruns.[12]

In 1972, Professional Standards Review Organization (PSRO) programs were established by law in a further attempt to improve health care utilization and peer review. At about the same time, the JCAHO began its Performance Evaluation Procedure (PEP) medical audit program to organize prospective outcome audits by member hospitals. The PSRO and PEP programs were short-lived. Both programs failed due to lack of voluntary cooperation and ineffective application of proficiency criteria. Costly, serendipitous, prospective outcome studies often were pursued instead of more cost-effective, retrospective-concurrent, problem-oriented audits. Most recently, the Health Care Financing Administration (HCFA) has created Peerl Review Organization (PRO) programs to focus more directly on cost containment audits.

In 1975, the judicial case, *Corleto v Shore Memorial Hospital*, established a legal precedent that hospitals and their medical staffs have responsibility for quality assurance (QA) peer review.[13] In 1979, the JCAHO introduced its requirement for a hospital-wide, systematic QA program. Subsequently, in 1984, they introduced their ten-step monitoring and evaluation process. This process provided a mechanism for setting priorities for QA activities, the increased use of quality measurements called indicators, and an increased focus on the quality of care provided by healthcare professionals.[14]

In 1982, Congress provided another answer to the national problem of escalating healthcare costs with the passage of the Tax Equity and Fiscal Responsibility Act (TEFRA), Public Law 97-248.[11] TEFRA placed hospital laboratories under reimbursement limitations and changed the basis of pathologist reimbursement. HCFA received authority to limit pathologists' reimbursement to a reasonable compensation equivalent or RCE. TEFRA set the legislative stage for enactment of the Social Security Amendments of 1983, Public Law 98-21, which replaced the RCE basis for Part A Medicare reimbursement with a prospective payment system (PPS). This system rested on the diagnosic related grouping (DRG) as a categorization and prioritization tool. Medicare reimbursement for laboratories had been based on a retrospective assessment of the reasonable cost of providing services; instead, the PPS became an incentive for hospitals (and their laboratories) to budget spending more cost-effectively.[11]

TEFRA, PPS, and DRGs set the stage for a more competitive healthcare industry. Such medical competition had been a long time coming since the days when hospitals first transformed from being charitable institutions with socially granted legal immunity. Of specific concern to clinical laboratory managers, healthcare administrators rapidly responded to regulatory reality and began practing a new brand of cost-effectiveness. Hospital laboratories—formerly considered sources of institutional profit—became cost centers.

By the time of the passage of TEFRA, at least 70 years of a mostly voluntary healthcare improvement process had transpired. During those decades, there had been a gradual realization of the necessity of quality management and various surveillance methods. By 1992, the JCAHO could show that about 90% of the hospitals in the United States were accredited by one healthcare accreditation program or another. Although such success in standardization deserved high praise, the effectiveness of health care remained short of the mark in the stern gaze of public and federal scrutiny. National healthcare expenditures still remained excessive, and the quality of some aspects of health care still remained suspect.

In 1988, Congress passed the Clinical Laboratory Improvement Amendments (CLIA), stimulated by a series of adverse incidents caused by poorly managed medical testing. Now under enforcement, there is no question that this law can cause improved quality as well as greater laboratory operational costs. However, like most laws, CLIA and its future regulatory clones will add to the cost burden of laboratory quality management.[15]

Other cost-related regulatory changes are occurring parallel to expanding federal and JCAHO quality management requirements. Striving to meet mounting Medicare, Medicaid, DRG, and Relative Value Scale (RVS) reimbursement constraints, hospital and laboratory managers are

Table II
National Healthcare Statistics[a]

	1980	1990	1992	2000
Total healthcare cost	$250.1B	$666.2B	$838.5B	$1600.0B
Private insurance	$73.4B (29%)	$216.8B (33%)		$507.6B (31%)
Medicare	59.5B (24%)	136.1B (20%)		302.8B (19%)
Out of pocket	37.5B (15%)	111.2B (17%)		290.3B (18%)
State/local	33.2B (13%)	87.3B (13%)		238.8B (15%)
Medicaid	26.4B (10%)	75.2B (11%)		243.8B (16%)
Other	12.1B (5%)	30.6B (5%)		61.6B (4%)
Percentage of GNP	9.2%	12.2%	14.0%	16.4%
Cost per capita	$1063.00	$2566.00		$5712.00
Total laboratory cost nation-wide			$30.B[25]	
Estimated total laboratory error cost[b]			$0.9B[20]	
Number of uninsured			37.0M[24]	39.0M

[a]Because these figures are rounded off, they do not add up exactly to their respective totals
[b]Error cost equals 3% of total laboratory cost
GNP = gross national product; M = million; B = billion

having to use increasingly limited budget and personnel resources to implement and improve continually expanding quality management programs. In addition, recessionary and inflationary changes will persist to complicate the control of healthcare costs.

Table II illustrates in macroeconomic terms how the nation is faring in its struggle with healthcare cost and access.[16-18,20-22,29] From 1980 to 1990, healthcare cost rose nearly twice as fast as for any other nonhealthcare consumer needs. By 1990, United States health care cost equaled twice those of competing countries in terms of percentage of gross national product (GNP).[21] There was also a growing segment of noninsured and underinsured customers.[22]

According to United States Commerce Department statistics, healthcare costs rose in 1992 at a rate of 11.4% (versus the anticipated 10.5%) to

$838.5 billion (versus the predicted $817 billion) and represented 14% of the GNP.[17] Projections of total healthcare costs for the year 2000 vary from $1600 billion ($1.6 trillion) to $1700 billion and 16% to 18% of the GNP.[17,23]

Perhaps as revealing as any of these statistics is the estimated burden of health care per capita. In 1980, the cost was $1063.00 per capita; in 1990, it was $2566.00 per capita; and in 2000, it is projected to become $5712.00 per capita.

As of 1992, the number of uninsured was cited as 37 million; this figure is expected to increase to, at least, 39 million by the year 2000.[24] Actually the 1992 figure varies from 37 million to 57 million, depending on the criteria used. The 57 million figure includes the noninsured plus the underinsured. The uninsured tended to be the working poor, more than 50% of whom earned below $20,000 annually and one-third of whom met the federal poverty definition—but who were not poor enough to meet poverty definitions for Medicaid.

In comparison, Medicare in 1993 covered 35.2 million people 65 years or older and Medicaid insured 23.2 million people (mostly women and children). The latter standards vary from state to state. Regarding Medicaid age groups, 9.5 million were children, 11.1 million were 18 to 29 years old, and 2.6 million were 55 or older. Of all these groups, the children were in greatest need of preventive care.[24]

What does the big picture reveal about laboratory costs? Costs for laboratory tests and services amounted to $30 billion in 1992, which represented a doubling from 1985 figures.[25] According to one estimation, the cost of laboratory error was 3% of the total laboratory cost or $900 million in 1992.[20] The latter figure is hard to come by because costs of laboratory error are not very well documented.

In view of the above statistics, it is apparent that the various healthcare laws passed in the preceding 12 years have curbed escalating costs by no more than five GNP percentage points. Granted, this degree of stabilization has occurred in spite of continual inflation; increased technological research and development costs, drug costs, insurance costs, and other healthcare entrepreneurial costs; and decreased healthcare resources in some sectors. In other words, the regulations have been somewhat successful in containing public expenses. However, we are not yet in control when one percentage point of the GNP equaled $8 billion in 1992, and the healthcare share continues to escalate.

Ironically, these same cost-containment regulations also are playing a role in increasing the cost of health care. The price of the administrative support, the increased number of inspectors, and other additional quality management requirements typical of a bureaucracy are being forced on the laboratory. CLIA is an excellent example of a statute that is adding significant quality management costs to healthcare laboratory operations. One estimate is that this statute will require $540 million a year in fees alone to cover the costs of enforcing the law, and those costs will be passed on to the patient and third party payors—the government and insurance companies.[26]

Another cost-raising activity related to new regulations and standards is quality management training and the hiring of consultants. As new rules are made, facilities invite consultants to help implement a quality management system, provide training, prepare for accreditation or licensing inspection, or solve actual problems that have been discovered during a recent inspection. But these consultation, training, and facilitation fees can be quite expensive—adding even further to the overall national cost of healthcare that is passed on to the patient.

Also related to individual laboratory quality management costs are new JCAHO standards designed to ensure that adequate resources will be applied to the infrastructural programs that cause TQM and CQI to happen. The usual practice has been to channel only minimal time, money, and people to those efforts. This practice is in keeping with the common traditional observation that *the allocation of resources to quality management has been inversely proportional to the importance of these activities*. Thus, the Joint Commisson requirements of the 1990s are intended to reverse the perception and practice of quality management resource allocation.

Finally, we will incur additional quality management costs in meeting computerization and communication requirements—such as those being established by the JCAHO for their indicator monitoring system (also known as the IM system or IMS).[27] When fully implemented, the IMS will create an enormously complex data management system designed to process quality management information on a national scope. No matter how useful this program or how gradually its implementation, it is going to be expensive. And, as usual, the cost will be passed on to the customer.

One major approach to reducing healthcare costs is to practice preventive health care—to improve the lifestyles of the United States citizenry. Considering that the patient's health status is the raw material for the healthcare industry, we need to continue to upgrade the quality of the basic raw resources that feed into the healthcare system. It could be construed thatunhealthy lifestyle is associated with 50% of all deaths in this country, including:[28]

- Smoking is related to 16% of total deaths.
- Alcohol is related to 4.5% of all deaths.
- Drug abuse is seen in 7.5% of women in labor.
- Obesity is seen in 20% of the population.
- Sedentary living is seen in 55% of the population.
- Seat belts are not used by 30% of the population.
- HIV/AIDS is the third leading cause of death in men ages 25 to 44.
- Homicide is the twelfth leading cause of death.

Thus, there is much to be accomplished in the public health arena to improve the quality of the patient population that is at risk and reduce healthcare costs. Judicious use of laboratory testing is one major healthcare component to resolving several of the lifestyle problems listed.

Microeconomics of Laboratory Quality

How do the *macro*economics of national health care translate into the *micro*economics of the individual laboratory? In facing the microeconomic challenges, laboratorians must realize what Shewhart taught in the 1930s: systematic quality management undeniably enhances the quality and cost-effectiveness of a product or service, especially over the long run. However, the quality management process cannot be achieved without expending finite resources—not only during the initial implementation phase of quality development but also throughout the sustained actualization phase.

Ideally, a significant share of operational activities should focus on the support of the infrastructural, administrative programs of quality assessment and improvement (QI), quality anticipation (QAn), and quality actualization (QAc) (Figure 14.1). Nonhealthcare organizations (eg, IBM, Xerox, Ford Motor Company) spend 3% to 7% of their annual budgets on quality management (Table I).[20] In comparison, healthcare organizations spend less than 1%.[9,29]

Getzen defines profitability as the cash value of a laboratory operation. This value is equal to the amount of discounted cash flow that the laboratory generates.[30] As a more specific example, Fantus describes laboratory profitability in terms of ten QI indicators and standards.[31] His approach is to "prune the amount of quality management information to the core," including the flow of reports, analyses, and financial statements. In his estimation, one can expect 10% profit if all of his ten benchmarks are met. Fantus' strategy is to enhance the efficiency of processing billable tests, since only these produce revenue. His indicators (and their standards) include:

- Total labor costs per net sales (<40%)
- Cost of supplies per net sales (<15%)
- Indirect costs per net sales (<35%)
- Tests per month per number of all FTEs (>310 tests)[c]
- Monthly tests per production FTEs (>1000 tests)
- Monthly tests per support FTEs (>535 tests)
- Monthly tests per management FTEs (>2550 tests)
- Billable (ordered) tests per total tests (>80%)
- CAP WLU per paid hours (>85%)[c]
- Net profit per net sales (>10%).

[c] Full time equivalent (FTE), College of American Pathologists (CAP), and workload unit (WLU) are all laboratory management terms that are common to the CAP workload reporting (WLR) program. Although discontinued, the WLR approach remains a useful quality management concept for some laboratories.

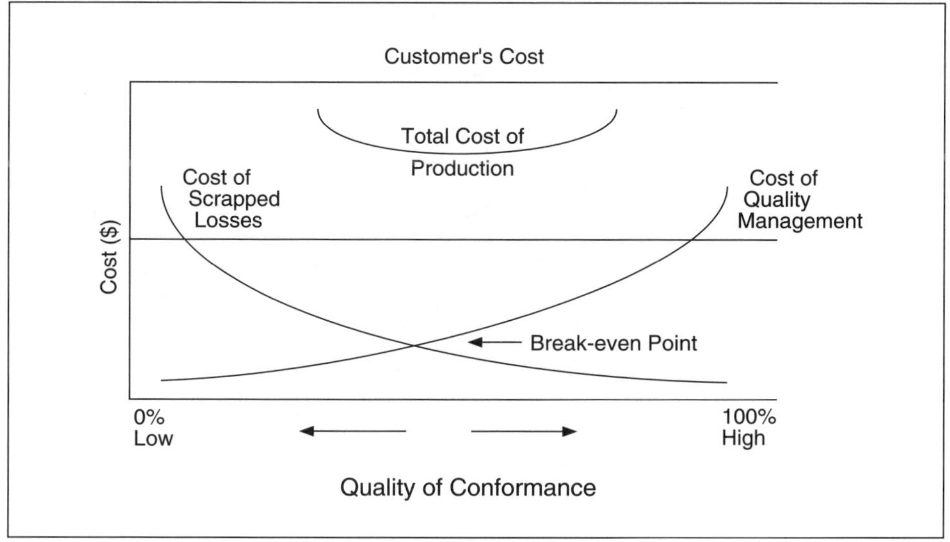

Figure 14.1 Shewhart cost of quality model

Because quality management is a mixture of indirect, fixed, and variable costs, it does not neatly fit into such a bottom line-oriented profitability formula. Besides, such formulas do not recognize quality investment as the profit multiplier that it truly is.

There is a financial break-even point between the dollar value of quality benefits and quality costs, and there is a Pareto-like statistical limit to cost-effective quality management. As laboratorians, we are obliged to meet regulatory and accreditation requirements for quality management to the best of our ability, but we must do so by judiciously establishing TQM and CQI priorities and scheduling those activities appropriately for the resources on hand. Even the JCAHO supports this point: establish a systematic approach to quality management but be practical and efficient.

Figure 14.1 illustrates an expenditure analysis model of quality management based on Shewhart's work on statistical quality control. He based his approach on such pragmatic observations as "variations of process cause inferior products" and "the better the quality, the lower the manufacturer's cost."[32] His themes of the cost-effectiveness of efficient quality management are echoed in Crosby's book, *Quality Is Free*.[5] Shewhart's was a preventive processing approach that promoted the best quality of effort along the entire assembly line—or path of work flow—and doing the right thing correctly the first time.

The graph in Figure 14.1 compares various *costs of production* (which include quality management) against *conformance to design specifications*. For the sake of discussion, we assume that operative resource costs (eg, raw materials, parts, and labor) and consumer costs remain constant.

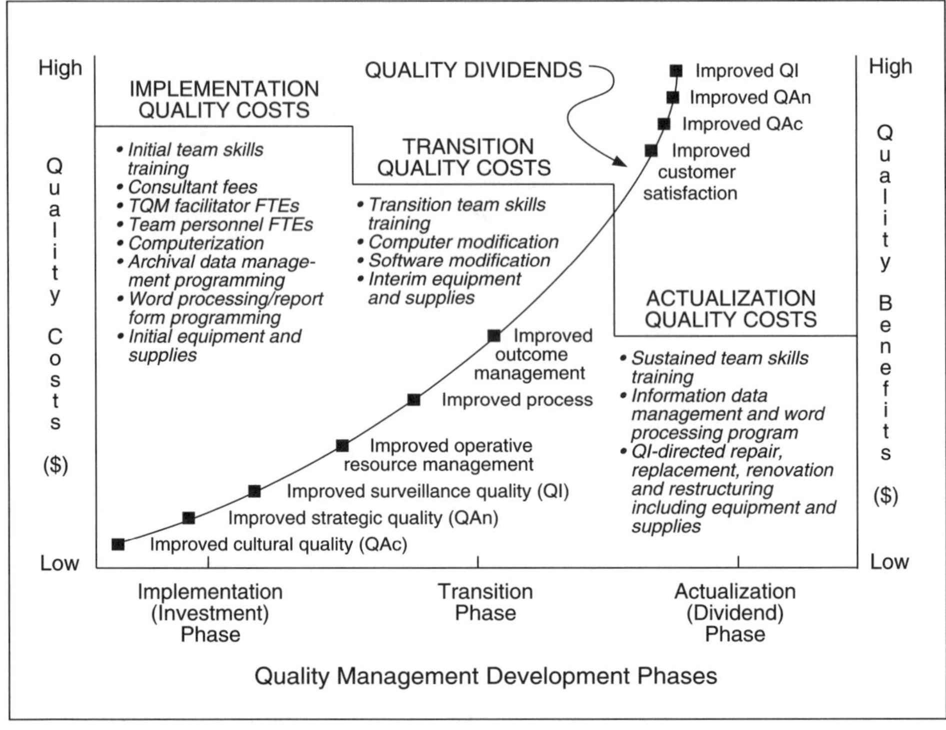

Figure 14.2 Laboratory investments expected during quality management development

As illustrated, low conformance to design specifications results in excessive costs for rejected (scrapped) products or wasted services. This loss is due to inexactness of production—failure to meet production standards or standards of practice. Consequently, integral pieces of the end product may not fit together or function, during trial testing or actual use. One laboratory example is the fictitious chemistry multianalyzer of Chapter 9 that is kept running continuously but at a significant expense of wasted batch runs, wasted specimens and reagents, and wasted employee time. The most excessive waste of resources or services occurs with the lowest—or least effective—quality control (QC), QI, QAn, and QAc administrative expenditure.

Most nonhealthcare industries report costs of poor quality ranging from 20% to 40%. However, comparable figures are not readily available from the healthcare industry. One overall estimate of the cost in clinical laboratory expenditures is 3% of the total laboratory expenditures.[20] One major approach to dealing with runaway healthcare costs is to deal with ineffective, wasteful processes. In the laboratory, this would include improving on malselected tests and products, repeated tests, nonutilized tests, wasted products, and excessive use of quality control and quality assessment.

At the other end of the graphic spectrum of Figure 14.1, the reward for high conformance to design specifications is producing the most satisfactory product or service. At the same time, there is minimal waste of resources or services. However this achievement goes hand in hand with the highest quality management cost: administrative costs of QC, QI, QAn, and QAc increase as conformance to predetermined standards increases.

Toward the middle ground, the graph illustrates an important break-even point at the juncture where wasted resource costs and quality management costs are mutually optimal. This point also defines the level of conformance at which the cost of wasted resources or rejected products equals or counter balances the cost of quality management. Also at this point, total production cost reaches its nadir while overall profit attains its zenith.[d]

Another way to illustrate the cost-benefit microeconomics of quality management is in relation to the developmental phases of implementation and actualization (Refer to Chapter 13). Figure 14.2 illustrates examples of quality management costs matched against their developmental phasing, represented by the stair-stepped line that extends from the graph's upper left to lower right and is matched against the relative high-low scale of quality costs along the left-handed ordinate. In the first phase are the implementation costs. These are the front-loaded expenses of people (ie, talent and time); technical, clerical, and computer equipment; software programming; and supplies—the funds required to begin from scratch. The implementation period is an *investment phase* because so many resources are committed up front. There has to be a speculative assumption that, in the future, there will be less quality management and production costs and proportionately greater quality dividends. People are the most expensive resource—estimated at 75% to 80% of total expenses.[33]

Next, we can anticipate transitional costs that will be incurred as the organization shifts from the implementation to the actualization phase. The laboratorian should plan for some additional training and equipment expenditures, particularly preparatory training to facilitate the transition from centralized management to participative management. Also, there will be some cost of making the transition from archival to informative computer equipment and software.

Finally, Figure 14.2 illustrates the sustaining costs of the actualization phase. The organization cannot rest on its laurels; it must continue to sustain and improve all quality management operations. Maintaining and upgrading require continued expenditure of key resources but still should be less resource-intensive than the implementation phase.

During this phase, QI surveillance will begin to identify operational aspects that require repair, replacement, renovation, or restructuring. These actions will add to the cost of improved quality in the actualization phase. Initially, these costs will be greater because QI usually unmasks major problems that are

[d] The graph in Figure 14.1 portrays profit as the difference between customer cost and total cost of production.

Table III

Estimated Personnel Costs for Implementing Laboratory Quality Management

ESTIMATED MANAGEMENT RESOURCES	ESTIMATED LABORATORY SIZE AND RESOURCE REQUIREMENTS		
	SMALL	MEDIUM	LARGE
Number of technical sections	1-5	5-10	15-25
Number of FTEs per section	1-6	5-10	15-20
Total technical FTEs	1-30	25-100	225-500
Number of administrative sections	0-1	1-3	2-3
Number of FTEs per section	1-2	2-5	5-10
Total administrative FTEs	0-2	2-15	10-30
Total number of given sections	1-6	6-13	17-38
Total number of FTEs	1-32	27-115	235-530
Number of quality management (QM) staff per given section	0-0.5	0.5-1	1
Total number of QM FTEs	0.5-3	3-13	17-28
QM to Non-QM FTE ratio	0.5-0.09	0.11-0.11	0.07-0.05
TQM-CQI consultant-facilitator hours			
Implementation phase	3-5	5-10	10-20
Actualization Phase	0-1	1-5	5-10

These figures include anatomic (AP) and clinical (CP) pathology service- and department-level staff positions

Small-sized laboratory:
- scope of care: limited services
- services and sections: includes a combined AP and CP department-level administrative office, urinalysis, hematology, coagulation, chemistry, blood bank, microbiology, serology, and histology

Medium-sized laboratory:
- scope of care: all standard procedures (not a full extent or reference laboratory)
- services and sections: includes an AP and/or CP service-level administrative office(s) with a separate department-level administrative section

Large-sized laboratory:
- scope of care: comprehensive, full extent procedures (could be a reference laboratory)
- services and sections, including:
  - Separate department-level administrative office
  - Separate CP service-level administrative office, computer support, supply, reception desk, phlebotomy, shipping and receiving, emergency request (stat) laboratory, urinalysis hematopathology, routine chemistry, special chemistry, toxicology and therapeutic drug monitoring, forensic drug analysis, donor center, transfusion service, reference immuno-hematology, bacteriology, mycobacteriology, mycology, virology, serology, diagnostic immunology, and clinical pathology reports and records
  - Separate AP service level administrative office, surgical pathology, autopsy pathology, histology, electron microscopy, diagnostic molecular biology, and anatomic reports and records

relatively expensive to solve. However, once those institutional problems are out of the way and more strategic (ie, QAn) and cultural (ie, QAc) improvements are under way, the costs of stabilized improvement should subside. Then, the actualization phase becomes a *dividend phase*.

In Figure 14.2, the curved line that begins from the graph origin and moves gradually upward to the right represents the anticipated benefit dividends earned as results of all of the quality management investments; these benefits are matched against the relative high-low scale of quality benefits along the right-handed ordinate. The progression of events and the slope of that line depend on how effective and efficient a laboratory's TQM and CQI system turns out to be.

Table III demonstrates an estimation of personnel implementation costs based on the author's personal experience. This cost estimate is intended as a template against which an individual laboratory's quality management costs can be more specifically gauged. Three laboratory sizes are listed to illustrate different economies of scale. For example, the number of FTEs devoted to quality coordination depends on the laboratory size and whether or not various responsibilities are combined or separate. Thus, larger organizations have a more manageable threshold of personnel "critical mass" with more staffing depth to handle various tasks as long as there is reasonable productivity.

As shown in the table, the estimated ratio of quality management (QM) personnel to non-QM staff can range from 0.5:1 (a 50% QM staff requirement) for the smallest, limited scope-of-care laboratory compared to 0.1:1 and 0.05:1 for the medium, expanded-scope laboratory and the largest, comprehensive-scope laboratory respectively. For the small-sized operation, the quality management responsibilities are estimated as requiring the time of a one-half FTE to coordinate quality for a given operational section (ie, the entire small laboratory or one of the small sections). A large-sized laboratory requires a full FTE per section.

It is apparent from the differences in the staffing ratio (ie, percent staffing requirement) that medium- to large-sized laboratories have more staffing depth to absorb the quality management tasks than do the smaller laboratories. For example, if the individual holding down a quality coordinator job leaves, it is easier for the large laboratory to absorb the work until a new coordinator is hired.

Regarding business volume and profit, the larger laboratory also is more apt to have a greater financial margin to afford quality management costs. This might well be true overall. However, the larger the operation, the larger the capital expenses for computerization, automation, and other information management needs. Table III estimates the comparative extent of personal computer work centers needed for the large laboratory. Main frame computer support will be sizably larger—and more expensive to procure, staff, and maintain.

Moran describes how instrument centralization, automation, and computerization are a key to working smarter toward greater profitability.

These improvements in instrumentation are commonly predicated on there being an increased number of tests ordered each year, along with greater demand for decreased turnaround time. The answer is to automate at higher cost. In a 1990 survey, Moran published the following statistics[34]:

	Number of tests		
	< 200,000	200-500,000	> 500,000
Costs	180 beds	295 beds	516 beds
Cost/test	$ 11	$ 11	$ 10
Cost/admisson	$167	$ 212	$ 289
Cost/patient day	$ 30	$ 31	$ 35

The interpretation of this data is that the combination of automation and larger-sized facilities does not always equate to a savings in healthcare costs. Higher quality can cost more for the patient—if costs are not controlled.

In comparison to the hardware, the software programs needed to support quality management need not be so overwhelming in cost. $300 to $500 statistical and analytical software packages are quite sufficient to run the quality management system for a $30 million laboratory business.

In Table III, note that the estimated cost of quality management consultants, coordinators, and facilitators is another potential drain on the operating margin. However, as expensive as they might be, outside experts can be very helpful in analyzing a laboratory's need for establishing a TQM and CQI system. Their unbiased assistance can prove very valuable in pointing out the least expensive and most effective approaches. The larger the laboratory, the more consultant contact hours are necessary to effectively reach all the staff for assessing and teaching basic TQM and CQI skills. This expense can be minimized by the consultant teaching internal facilitator teams. These internal teams can then carry on the laboratory-wide training for both the initial team skill training and the continued assessment and training needed to sustain the organization.

The end analysis is that larger is not necessarily easier or cheaper. In fact, as the laboratory scope of care and support activities grow in size and complexity, quality management is likely to be more expensive. In any case, a judicious expenditure of laboratory resources for quality management must be offset by a significant savings earned in improved quality of the resource, process, and outcome management for *all* laboratory operations. Thus, once committed to quality improvement, stay committed; the money and other resources being invested must be allowed time to reach fruition.

How does a laboratory meet requirements to invest more assets in quality management while the same rules and regulations are draining more assets away from the laboratory? One excellent review by Sharp on managing a "post-TEFRA" (and, now, "post-RVS") laboratory points out that the modern laboratory has moved into a PPS environment where a major objective is to provide all services at costs that are less than the prospectively set reimbursement fee. The PPS has altered the reimbursement formula—changing the formerly stable-cost-volume-profit relationships and making the laboratory a cost center.[35]

Before the PPS, the patient was the principle paying customer because the patient paid or the government subsidized the patient's payment without questioning the cost. With the PPS, the primary, paying customer has become the insurer. Thus the largest post-PPS healthcare customer has become the federal and state governments that subsidize (insure) patients who are either Medicare or Medicaid recipients.

Sharp compares the post-PPS laboratorian with the railroad managers of the 1960s. Railroad men thought they were only in the travel—not transportation—business. Thus, they set their sights on too narrow a definition of their niche in the marketplace. Consequently, they lost out to the truckers and airlines when the railroad travel business declined but the demand for transportation of goods increased. Likewise, the laboratorian cannot change the post-PPS regulatory rules that are repositioning the laboratory in its own marketplace—or justify an overvalued product. Instead the laboratorian must make some sage business considerations that include the following.[35]

- Evaluate the laboratory's cost structure: what are the internal and external financial strengths and weaknesses?
- Institute strategic planning, including marketing tactics: where are the current internal marketing strengths and weaknesses and external opportunities and threats?
- Target DRG categories to improve cost-effectiveness: how can we provide the highest quality DRG-defined services more efficiently?
- Increase test volume: how can we increase the number of customers or identify more customer needs—therefore, increasing our workload volume without loss of endproduct quality?
- Increase productivity: how can our employees process a given workload more efficiently without loss of endproduct quality?
- Decrease total operating/production costs: what activities and services can we perform more cost-effectively or are outmoded and can be reduced, replaced, or deleted without loss of endproduct quality?

The last of these options, "Decrease total operating/production costs," is the most common administrative threat to quality management—and the laboratorian's nightmare. Various articles describing laboratory survival in the post-PPS era include other surgical tactics such as "pruning information flow to the core"—just another reminder that we must practice TQM and CQI with patience and prudence.[31]

So, how do we increase quality management investment while cutting operational costs? This is the quintessential managerial paradox. Right away quality management is on the budget hit list and some compromise must be made to salvage a viable—though perhaps less than optimal—

quality management system. To cope with this paradox, we must go back to one of the primary managerial precepts mentioned under QI indicator selection. The inventory of important aspects of care and the directory of specified, indexed, and focused indicators must be systematically chosen and prioritized. We must base this prioritization on an informed understanding of local quality management costs and management assets available. Conservation of quality management resources through disciplined prioritization is of paramount importance.

So, do we buy into the quality management precepts of TQM and CQI or not? The federal government and the JCAHO and other accreditation organizations say we must pay that price. The most popular theorists and practitioners, such as Philip (*Quality is Free*) Crosby and W. (*The Fourteen Points of Quality*) Deming, say we should buy in. The early practitioners, such as W. A. (*Statistical Quality Control*) Shewhart, proved over the past 6 decades that we need to buy in. And we have had ample positive reinforcement from the examples of Japanese industrial quality management.

Referring back to the Shewhart model for quality management cost in Figure 14.1, there is one other way to meet costs of quality improvement in today's practice of CQI: *improve on Shewhart's break-even point!* Move the juncture of the cost of poor quality and waste and the cost of quality management down and to the right of the graph toward <u>lower</u> quality management costs and <u>higher</u> conformance to design specifications. This strategy calls for an organization-wide commitment to TQM and CQI aimed at improvement of quality management activities for <u>all</u> resources, processes, and outcomes. The winning results would be:

- Improved patient care outcome (and other customer outcomes) with increased customer satisfaction
- Increased selection of laboratory services by all internal and external customers with increased productivity and business volume
- Increased cost-benefits from quality management investment.

All of this is possible for essentially the same quality management dollar—and, eventually, even less once the initial investment has been made.

EVIDENCE OF QUALITY MANAGEMENT COST-EFFECTIVENESS

"How much will the practice of quality management save my laboratory in terms of non-costed operational benefits and costed financial savings?" The second question addresses the cost-benefits of quality management. The answer lies in what the literature reports as quality management success stories.

We can assess the benefits of quality improvement in terms of non-costed as well as costed data. *Non-costed* improvement benefits are anecdotal in nature and represent most quality improvement reports to date. Published reports fall into the general categories of customer satisfaction outcome, patient care outcome, and process management; operative resource management; and organizational management. These accounts represent a mixture of laboratory and nonlaboratory experience—suggesting that there is a need for more laboratories to publish their lessons learned from practicing TQM and CQI.

Regarding outcome management—particularly customer satisfaction in the form of patient care outcome—there have been anecdotal reports of decreased customer complaints as well as more directed surveys of customer satisfaction. One hospital-level survey of 1,500 adult respondents revealed 58% satisfaction based specifically on quality improvement.[37] A Hospital Corporation of America survey of patient satisfaction analysis revealed that patients responded positively to services received and were willing to return and recommend the hospital system to others. Furthermore, these high marks of patient satisfaction compared favorably with hospital profitability.[38] As a laboratory-specific example, the Maine Medical Center laboratory reported the effect of a customer-focused TQM program on improving interdepartmental relations—this report being aimed at a different group of customers.[39]

There is some evidence that high levels of healthcare spending do not automatically produce higher quality care. A study of one million New Jersey acute care hospital patients compared the difference between costs of care given and resultant mortality rates. Hospital services such as neurosurgery, orthopedic, and cardiovascular demonstrated less operational expenditures than the average, and the care resulted in lower mortality rates. Other medical and surgical services showed opposite results. The assumption from this data is that higher quality can be less expensive *if* proper quality management is employed.[40]

Using utilization review as another example, a medical staff halved their cesarean-section rate through collaborative physician review of resource-consumption data using TQM methods. They received clinically valid data relevant to their practices to improve the quality and value of health care. As a spin-off, there was a cooperative changing of practice patterns, and the physicians healed themselves. These successful results from the practice of TQM caused the hospital administration to refrain from the use of economic credentialing—which is antithetical to modern quality management precepts.[41]

The University of Colorado Medical Center laboratory has reported decreasing the newborn baby morbidity from heel sticks using TQM methods. This improvement project was a result of an interdepartmental initiative involving both laboratory and nursing staffs.[42]

Regarding process management, there are much longer lists of improvements associated with the use of systematic quality management. These reports include the experiences of all sizes of laboratories in both urban and rural settings.

- Improved testing automation and communications resulted in increased stat test capability associated with decreased costs of throughput, length of stay, clinical practice, and quality management.[33]
- Improved interdepartmental teamwork resulted in a decreased percentage of stats requested, decreased turnaround times (TAT), and improved urine analysis specimen handling.[43]
- The staff "felt" that their quality was already good before implementing TQM and CQI; on the other hand, "perhaps it was sheer luck." With improved interdepartmental quality management approaches they improved blood count TAT, routine urine analysis processing, patient identification, new test kit development, and laboratory result error reporting.[44]
- Use of TQM and CQI resulted in reduced errors in laboratory test reporting by using TQM-CQI techniques.[45]
- Decreasing the number of repeat tests and decreasing the number of unnecessary mailings resulted in cost savings.[46]
- Cost-benefits resulted from improving TATs, Pap specimen collection, therapeutic dosage monitoring specimen collection, blood culture contamination rates, promptness of delivery of orders/requests to the laboratory, specimen mislabeling, and patient identification.[47,48]
- QI surveillance resulted in improving the labaratory's performance of proficiency testing inspections, incident reports, error reporting, specimen labeling, and patient satisfaction with phlebotomy.[47,48]

Regarding operative resource management, the Hospital Corporation of America has demonstrated the effectiveness of using the QI process as a means of containing costs, not just for finding a new market niche.[38] Godfrey reported that the cost-benefits in financial returns are 5 to 1 or more. This financial improvement stemmed mostly from the discovery of how to decrease the number of required FTEs by streamlining 10% to 80% of the work required for a given process.[46]

Regarding organizational management, there have been precious few published reports. However, there have been isolated, anecdotal accounts of improved employee morale and improved leadership—However, there has been no maesurement of their impact on decision making.[36]

Costed improvement benefits are much more objective but, compared to non-costed benefits, represent a minority of quality improvement reports. However, those that have been published are impressive. Unfortunately, even fewer reports relate directly to the laboratory.

An excellent nonlaboratory example of costed benefits is a recent, very comprehensive quality improvement project at the University of Michigan Medical Center (UMMC).[36] In 1990, the UMMC launched into an institution-wide two-phased TQM and CQI project. During the initial phase, they saved

$260,000 by improving basic operational processes; most savings were from reduction of staff. After the longer, more full-scope phase, they calculated their incremental costs and benefits over the next year as follows:

Benefits costed	$17.8M
Implementation costs	4.0M
Net cost benefit	13.8M (345%).

The UMMC carefully recorded each separate quality improvement project and analyzed the data for cost-benefit. Quality management implementation costs included training, training time, cultural assessment, facilitator salaries, new equipment, consultants, project time, and library support.

A 345% return on a $4 million quality management investment should be impressive enough evidence of the cost-effectiveness of good quality management.[36,46] A $13.8 million cost-benefit might not be significantly sizable compared to the UMMC total annual budget of a large academic healthcare center. However, the percentage of return on the $4 investment is still very satisfactory. The non-costed benefits from the UMMC project add up to significant value in terms of improved customer satisfaction. In the surgical department alone, they documented decreased delay in the admission and discharge process, decreased admission waiting time, 10% increase in operating room (OR) use, 10% decrease of misscheduled cases, 25% decrease of OR cancellations, 33% increase of surgical cases, and 50% decrease of extended length of stay.[36]

SURVIVAL OF QUALITY MANAGEMENT

"Will quality management remain viable in this era of increasing socio-economic constraints?" The third question addresses the future of quality management. Will it survive into the next decade, century, or millennium? Besides the usual skeptics, there are some prophets of failure who are becoming increasingly vocal. For example, the following comments came from a podium at a 1993 ASCP/CAP national meeting workshop on quality improvement:

- "We have to drop our focus on TQM. We haven't been able to do it for over 50 years. The Japanese are dropping it. And Baldridge Award winners are failing."
- "P-D-C-A: Is that the way we do things in the laboratory? We laboratorians don't have time to plan; so, why start with planning? We need to be more intuitive and move ahead without planning. We should start with the Acting step. Thus, A-P-D-C should be the preferable improvement cycle sequence."[f]

[f] The motto for this managerial approach might be "Ready-Fire-Aim."

In addition, there have been red flags in the literature as to whether TQM and CQI are on the way out.[49] It is the author's opinion that there will always be shifting focus and changing paradigms, but we must stay the basic course. Quality management is always simple in theory—but it is seldom easy in practice.

One way to analyze the degree of acceptance of TQM and CQI is to look at the success of the JCAHO's *Agenda for Change*. It is not the only accrediting organization in the country, and various healthcare organizations successfully gain accreditation or licensure from agents other than the Joint Commission. However, it is a leading contender in the accreditation process and is establishing strong precedents through the development of its standards. The Joint Commission's *Agenda* has been most successful because of the TQM and CQI elements that it has embraced since 1987. There is no question that the JCAHO encourages the practice of modern quality management principles.

What do other healthcare leaders say about quality management? In 1990, Ernst and Young performed an international research project that included 240 leading healthcare organizations in the United States, Japan, Canada, and Germany. Among other things, the study revealed that:

- 20% of the U.S. organizations indicated that quality was a primary assessment criterion for senior managers; by 1993, 51% of those same organizations would be using that criterion.
- 31% of the U.S. organizations indicated the importance of customer satisfaction as a primary criterion for strategic planning; by 1993, 72% would be using that criterion.
- 84% of the U.S. organizations indicated that less than 25% of their personnel were involved in quality management teams; by 1993, 41% of the organizations would have 26% to 74% of their personnel involved.

Many questions remain to be answered by this study. How would the organizations define quality? How would they define customer? How would their teams be managed? Who would provide the trained leadership? Where would they find the time with already full schedules? How would leadership function in a cross-cultural environment? Although as many questions were raised by this study as were answered, the responses were reasonably positive. This is especially true considering the inherent, traditional barriers to quality management that exist in healthcare organizations in this country.[21]

Other surveys have asked hospital chief executive officers (CEOs) if they have implemented TQM and CQI. In one survey, 66% of 250 CEOs had implemented TQM.[41]

Another way of ascertaining involvement in quality management is by asking for written quality management plans. Many model plans are available through various healthcare associations.[50,51] According to Jahn, a

1992 *Medical Laboratory Observer* (*MLO*) survey of a member panel at supervisory level or above revealed that QA plans were "pervasive," 91% of 635 respondents having a written QA plan.[47,48] Bachner also reported on a 1990 CAP *Q-Probes* survey that revealed 99% of 550 laboratory respondents had a written QA plan.[52] The next step for all of these organizations would be to make the transition from QA to QI.

The *MLO* survey also revealed that 50% of the 635 respondents already had organization-wide TQM and CQI in place—while 46% were planning to start TQM and CQI in the next two years. Ironically, the stated awareness of the JCAHO requirement for an institution-wide QI plan by 1994 was only at the 33% level. General opinions concerning the effectiveness of the reactive QA approach ranged from 23% for "very favorable" to 67% for "only somewhat" effective. Opinions concerning the effectiveness of the more proactive quality management approach of TQM and CQI ranged from 30% favorable to 49% unsure. One memorable comment was that, "Practice has not yet caught up with theory; we haven't completed the implementation phase yet."[48]

Barriers to Quality Management Success

The *MLO* survey further revealed several potential barriers to the success of TQM and CQI in the current socio-economic environment. About 10% of the 635 respondents described systematic quality management's expense as the single greatest problem with time, paperwork, and personnel requirements as subsidiary drawbacks. Other problems included lack of medical staff collaboration, limited pathologist involvement, continued monitoring without remedial action, coercion (ie, no opportunity to buy in), and limited studies of customer needs and satisfaction.

Godfrey describes bottlenecks that are barriers to effective TQM and CQI processes.[46] These include the following insufficiencies.

- Leadership: remember there has to be a leader. Particular problems that plague laboratory-level leader effect on TQM and CQI include insufficient board or governing body involvement, disruptive turnover of committed medical staff (ie, MD leadership involvement is very important), and disruptive merging and restructuring. In the case of frequent executive turnover, the key internal customer (the employee) should argue with success!
- Communication: There is excessive verbiage—mission statements and plans being good examples. The transmission of information (compared to data) of which there is an abundance in the healthcare environment—is inherently inadequate. Important uses of communication include elevating staff awareness, pointing out successes, continuing education, collaborating, and sharing, delegating, or empowering responsibilities.

- **Structure:** traditional lines of control and communication are important in a healthcare organization. In the course of practicing TQM in a CQI environment, "break it" very carefully—and only after careful participative study and preparation. But, in the end, eventually reroute the lines of control and communication to include the employee and the customer in the decision making process.
- QI: The QI program should be an information analysis process. QI tends to measure customer satisfaction (mostly retroactively), quality of care (mostly concurrently), and internal efficiency and effectiveness (fairly recently). However, there often is inadequate evaluation and follow-up of recommendations.
- QAn: Strategic planning is often not an institutional strength. As a result, there is often no clear, shared mission or vision. Goals and objectives tend to be the useful many but not the vital few. Organizational research and development are not inherently natural and need to be learned.
- QAc: Team skill training is easier to begin than to institutionalize. The laboratory needs full time, in-house facilitators. They cannot be a specialist group with their own nest to feather (ie, preaching QAc for QAc's sake). Paying lip service to training is not enough; there must be a leadership agenda and leader personal involvement in cascade team skills training.
- TQM: Assesment drives the TQM programs, remembering that measuring can produce instant improvement (ie, the Hawthorne effect). But TQM is not just a QI measuring program; it is more than just managing ongoing improvements. TQM should also include systematic oversight of the management of strategic improvement (ie, QAn) and cultural improvement (ie, QAc).

Bench Marks of Quality Management Success

Again, the *MLO* survey offers some excellent bench marks of TQM and CQI success.[47,48] For example, 81% of the respondents reported "quality management coordinator" or facilitator as new job titles, requiring up to three FTEs per laboratory. Fifty-four percent of the respondents saw this as a new job opportunity.

Bachner's *Q-probes* report cites bench mark benefits from practicing quality management.[52] Responding laboratories reported on quality management as very important to managing patient outcome (49%), as a general management tool (45%), and in risk management (41%).

The *Q-Probes* survey identified universal indicators for both anatomic pathology (AP) and clinical pathology (CP) laboratories. In CP, they included routine test result TAT, notification of critical values, errors in reporting of results, stat test result TAT, and frequency of specimen unacceptability. In AP, they included specimen adequacy, correlation of frozen versus permanent section diagnoses, correlation of fine needle biopsy with final diagnoses, and correlation of external consultation with internal diagnoses. Valuable results from practicing TQM and CQI included process redesign, staff counseling, education, and continued monitoring.

Perhaps as convincing an argument for the future of TQM and CQI is written in the words of an executive officer of JCAHO, a medical center laboratory medical director, and a community hospital laboratory manager. All three independently vouch for the practical value of systematic laboratory management and predict its sustained importance not just in the 21st century but for all time.[53]

SUMMARY

There are some key points to keep in mind regarding the cost-effectiveness of systematic quality management. First, the customer-supplier relationship must be the central focus, not the so-called "bottom line"—not profit.

- Healthcare providers supply services to patient customers; patients supply providers with health problems to solve.
- Hospital services, such as the laboratory, supply the healthcare provider customers (and their patients) with information and products; providers (and their patients) supply the laboratory with material to be studied.

So, who is truly the customer and who is the supplier?[56]

Second, there must be some strategy to operating a healthcare laboratory. That strategy must focus on *all* customers' needs; we cannot provide laboratory products and services for the convenience of the laboratory staff. Yet, we must realize the employee as an internal customer.

Third, we must be ready to improve laboratory support of clinical care. At the same time, we must remain cognizant of the need to control the costs of health care. By practicing TQM in a CQI environment, we must be ready to control costs while maintaining reasonable profitability.[3,4,22,53]

Fourth, just as any manufacturing industry can demand improved quality of its raw materials, healthcare providers should be able to demand improved quality of their patients' lifestyle and environmental surroundings. This is true if health care's desired endproduct is truly an improved state of health across the nation.

Fifth, we must expertly and assiduously practice disciplined prioritization. We must balance our quality management effort with our quality management assets. Important aspects of care and their QI indicators must be specific and sensitive.[55] Considering the quality profile described in this text, publishing an entire profile is absolutely impractical, ineffective, and inefficient. Prioritize. We have to be practical to be cost-effective.

Sixth, remembering all 14 of Deming's points of quality management is a praiseworthy achievement; they are at least worth reading. However, if there is any lesson to take away from Deming's list, it would be that we must have committed leadership. This implies that—even in a TQM and CQI environment that is rich in empowerment—there has to be a leader.

Finally, keep in mind the suggestion of Tom Peters: try to practice modern quality management as one would expect Mozart to have performed a piece of music. Being technically flawless was easy for Mozart's competitors, but Mozart played with a soul.[56]

REFERENCES

1. Westgard JO, Barry PL. Beyond quality assurance: committing to quality improvement. Lab Med, April 1969;20:241-247.
2. Shewhart WA. Economic Control of Quality of a Manufactured Product. New York, NY: D Van Nostrand, 1931.
3. Walton M. The Deming Management Method. New York, NY: Putnam Pub Group, 1986.
4. Juran JW. Juran on Leadership for Quality: An Executive Handbook. New York, NY: The Free Press, 1989.
5. Crosby PB. Quality Is Free. New York, NY: McGraw-Hill Book Co., 1979.
6. Shector EAS. Managing for World-Class Quality. Milwaukee, WI: ASQC Press, 1992.
7. Wollschlager LJ. The Quality Promise. Milwaukee, WI: ASQC Press, 1991 .
8. Cesarone D. Improving performance through balancing cost, quality, and value. First Annual Invitational Forum for Liaison Network Organizations. Rosemont, IL: JCAHO, Westin Hotel, June 9-10 1993.
9. Daigh RD. Financial implications of a quality improvement process. Topics Health Care Finance, 1991;17:24-52.
10. Harrington IH. Poor Quality Crisis. Milwaukee, WI: ASQC Press, 1987.
11. Rakich JS, Longest BB, Darr K. Managing Health Service Organizations. Baltimore, MD: Health Professions Press, 1992.
12. Coleman FC. The legislative history of Medicare, Parts I and II. Pathologist, 1981; 35:97-100,156-8.
13. *Corleto v. Shore Memorial Hospital,* 138 N.J. Super. 302, 311 350 A.2d 534, 538 (1975).
14. Roberts JS, Coale JG, Redman RR. A history of the Joint Commission on Accreditation of Hospitals. JAMA, 1987;258:936-40.
15. Lab groups assess implementation of CLIA. Med Lab Observer, 1989;21:17-18.

16. Fried RA. Crisis in health care. Quality Prog, 1992;25(4):67-69.
17. 1992 health-care spending results are in. CLMA Management Briefs, 1993;15:2.
18. Fein R. Prescription for change. Mod Maturity, 1992;35(4): 23-35.
19. $1.7 Trillion: health-care tab in the year 2000. CLMA Management Briefs, 1992;14:5.
20. Barnett RN. Analytical goals in clinical chemistry: the pathologist's viewpoint. Pathologist, June 1977;31:319-22.
21. Anderson CA. Curing what ails U.S. health care. Quality Prog, 1992;25:35-38.
22. Lawrence DM, Early JF. Strategic leadership for quality in health care. Quality Prog, 1992;25:45-48.
23. Wagner L. Healthcare tab to hit $1.7 trillion by 2000. Mod Healthcare,1992;22:4
24. Steinmetz G. Number of uninsured stirs much confusion to health-care debate. Wall Street J, 1993;74(166):A1,A6.
25. Bissell, MG, and CLMA National Affairs Committee. wClinical Laboratory Management Association White Paper. Ensuring Universal Access to Quality Laboratory Services. Malvern, PA: Clinical Laboratory Management Association, Clin Man Rev, 1994;8:185-197.
26. Pear R. 1988 standards for medical labs go unenforced by administration. CLMA Management Briefs, 1991;13:1-3.
27. Kamowski DB, Nadzam D. Overview of the indicator monitoring system. First Annual Invitational Forum for Liaison Network Organizations. Rosemont, IL: JCAHO, Westin Hotel, June 9-10 1993.
28. Eskildson L, Yates GR: Improving health care's suppliers. Qual Prog, 1992;25:107-108.
29. Clinical indicators require drastic cultural changes. Hosp Peer Rev, May 1989:53-5.
30. Getzen TE. What is value? The discounted cash flow approach. Clin Lab Man Rev, 1992;6:237-240.
31. Fantus J. The 10% solution to lab profitability. Med Lab Observer, 1990;22:33-38.
32. Harris DH, Chaney FB. Human Factors in Quality Assurance. New York, NY: John Wiley and Sons, 1969.
33. Korpman RA. Predictions for healthcare informatics. ASCP Colorado Springs III Conference: Blueprint for the Future of Pathology and Laboratory Medicine. Colorado Springs, Co: American Society of Clinical Pathiologists, February 14-16, 1992.
34. Moran EJ. Automation: the key to lab profitability. Hospitals, 1990;64:74-6.
35. Sharp JW. Directing the post-TEFRA laboratory. Pathologist, 1985;39:15-18.

36. Creps LB, Coffey RJ, Warner PA, McClatchy KD. Integrating total quality management and quality assurance at the University of Michigan Medical Center. Qual Rev Bull, 1992;18:250-8.
37. Quality watch. Hospitals, 1990;64:20.
38. Koska MT. High-quality care and hospital profits: is there a link? Hospitals, 1990;64:62,64.
39. Corriveau B. Customer service in the clinical laboratory. Clin Lab Man Rev, 1993;7:49.
40. High costs and quality don't always go together. CLMA Management Briefs, 1989;11:8
41. Johnsson J. TQM: best antidote for MD practice problems. Hospitals, 1992;64:64
42. Romfh PC, Sepulveda-Pacheco AM, DeAndrea A, Young B. Babies provide focus for quality improvement team. Clin Lab Man Rev, 1993;7:145-156.
43. Kinkus CA, McMann NW. A sweeping QA program for a large hospital lab. Med Lab Observer, 1990;22:31-5.
44. Franklin S. Seeking (and finding) painless QA in a tiny lab. Med Lab Observer, 1990;22:37-40.
45. Banning J, Brown J, Hooper L, Hamilton J, Burnett J, Burnett L. Reduction of errors in laboratory test reports using continuous quality improvement (CQI) techniques. Clin Lab Man Rev, 1993;7: 424-436.
46. Godfrey AB, Berwick DM, Roessner J. Can quality management really work in health care? Qual Prog, 1992;25:23-27.
47. Jahn M. Readers' strategies for quality improvement. Part I. Making the grade on the long road to QI. Med Lab Observer, 1992;24: 20-25.
48. Jahn M. Readers' strategies for quality improvement. Part II. How straight is the road to QI. Part II. Med Lab Observer, 1992;24:26-29.
49. TQM: on the way out. CLMA Management Briefs, 1993;15:2.
50. Longo DR, Ciccone KR, Lord JT: Integrated Quality Assessment: A Model for Concurrent Review. Chicago, IL: American Hospital Publishing, Inc, 1989.
51. Spath PL (ed). Innovations in Health Care Quality Measurement. Chicago, IL: American Hospital Publishing, Inc, 1989.
52. Bachner P. Study: Labs' QA commitment solid. CAP Today, 1992;6:10,12,14.
53. Clark GB, Schyve PM, Lephoff RB, Reuss DT. Will quality management paradigms of the 1990s survive into the next century? Clin Lab Man Rev, 1994;8:426-434.
54. Drucker PE. Management: Tasks, Responsibilities, Policies. New York, NY: Harper and Row, 1985.
55. Burke M. Clinical quality initiatives: the search for meaningful—and accurate—measures. Hospitals, 1992;66:26-32,34.
56. Peters T. TQM and music that stirs the soul. CAP Today, 1992;6:94

APPENDIX A
Quality Improvement Feeder Report: General Narrative

Quality Improvement Feeder Report (General)

1. Section and reporting period identification:

Section / Service:____________________________ Submitted: Month_______Year_______

Reporting Period____________________________ thru ____________________________

POSTLABORATORY OUTCOME WORK FLOW SEGMENT

2. Customer satisfaction:

Satisfaction Indicator: state customer code # if appropriate	Threshold	Observation
a. # –		
b. # –		
c. # –		
d. # –		

Evaluation:

Action/Action Person:

Assessment:

3. Patient care outcome:

Outcome Indicator: state Patient Code # if appropriate	Clinical Threshold	Observation
a. # –		
b. # –		
c. # –		
d. # –		

Evaluation:

Action/Action Person:

Assessment:

4. Laboratory safety / environment / security outcome:

Safety Indicator	Threshold	Observation
a.		
b.		
c.		
d.		

Evaluation:

Action/Action Person:

Assessment

Dept of path, Any Hospital
Form 197 (Aug 95)

Quality Improvement (Page 1)
(Previous editions are obsolete)

POSTLABORATORY PROCESS WORK FLOW SEGMENT

5. Laboratory product utilization:

Utilization Indicator: state Provider Code # if appropriate	Clinical Threshold	Observation
a. # –		
b. # –		
c. # –		
d. # –		

Evaluation:

Action/Action Person:
Assessment:

6. Laboratory product turnaround time / backlog
(use Anatomical Pathology report form, if applicable):

Throughput Indicator	Threshold TAT / Backlog	Observation TAT	Observation Backlog
a.	/		
b.	/		
c.	/		
d.	/		

Potential Shift Opportunity? Yes___ No___ If so, attach analysis per shift.
Evaluation:

Action/Action Person:
Assessment

7. Laboratory product distribution:

Distribution Indicator	Threshold	Observation
a.		
b.		
c.		
d.		

Potential Shift Opportunity? Yes___ No___ If so, attach analysis per shift.
Evaluation:

Action/Action Person:
Assessment:

Dept of Path, Any Hospital
Form 197 (Aug 95)

Quality improvement (Page 2)
(Previous editions are obsolete)

INTRALABORATORY PROCESS WORK FLOW SEGMENT

8. Verification of postdeterminative product finalization / postdeterminative specimen handling and integrity:

	Finalization Indicator	Threshold	Observation
a.	____________	________	________________
b.	____________	________	________________
c.	____________	________	________________
d.	____________	________	________________

Potential Shift Opportunity? Yes___ No___ If so, attach analysis per shift.

Evaluation:

Action/Action Person:

Assessment:

---

9. Reference laboratory studies:

	Ref Lab Indicator	Threshold	Observation
a.	____________	________	________________
b.	____________	________	________________
c.	____________	________	________________
d.	____________	________	________________

Evaluation:

Action/Action Person:

Assessment:

---

10. Analytical quality:

	Quality Indicator	Threshold	Observation
a.	____________	________	________________
b.	____________	________	________________
c.	____________	________	________________
d.	____________	________	________________

Potential Shift Opportunity? Yes___ No___ If so, attach analysis per shift.

Evaluation:

Action/Action Person:

Assessment:

Dept of Path, Any Hospital — Quality improvement (Page 3)
Form 197 (Aug 95) — (Previous editions are obsolete)

11. Diagnostic quality / peer review (use Anatomical Pathology report form):

	Quality Indicator: state Provider Code # if appropriate	Technical / Clinical Threshold	Observation
a.	# –		
b.	# –		
c.	# –		
d.	# –		

Potential Shift Opportunity? Yes___ No___ If so, attach analysis per shift.
Evaluation:

Action/Action Person:
Assessment:

12. Predeterminative specimen processing / integrity flow:

	Processing Indicator	Threshold	Observation
a.			
b.			
c.			
d.			

Potential Shift Opportunity? Yes___ No___ If so, attach analysis per shift.
Evaluation:

Action/Action Person:
Assessment:

PRELABORATORY PROCESS WORK FLOW SEGMENT

13. Validation of prelaboratory specimen integrity flow / specimen transportation / specimen preservation / specimen collection / patient preparation:

	Quality Indicator (index specimen/origin)	Threshold	Total Rcvd/Inval	Invalid	% Other
a.	#				
b.	#				
c.	#				
d.	#				

Potential Shift Opportunity?: Yes___ No___ If so, attach analysis per shift.
Evaluation:

Action/Action Person:
Assessment:

Dept of Path, Any Hospital
Form 197 (Aug 95)

Quality improvement (Page 4)
(Previous editions are obsolete)

14. Selection of laboratory test / product / consultation:

	Selection Indicator: state Provider Code # if appropriate	Clinical Threshold	Observation
a.	# –		
b.	# –		
c.	# –		
d.	# –		

Potential Shift Opportunity: Yes___ No___ If so, attach analysis per shift.
Evaluation:

Action/Action Person:
Assessment:

OPERATIVE RESOURCE WORK FLOW SEGMENT

15. Workload management:

	(in raw units)				Current Raw Count:
		Index Procedure Data			
Workload Indicator (index procedures)	Threshold (quota)	Previous Period	Last Period	This Period	Weighted Work Load Ratio
a.					
b.					
c.					
d.					
Total (in CAP units)					

Potential Shift Opportunity? Yes___ No___ If so, attach analysis per shift.
Evaluation:

Action/Action Person:
Assessment:

16. Personnel strength:

Personnel Indicator	# FTE Auth	# FTE On Hand	Net Gain-Loss Now	# of Current Hiring Actions	Threshold % Vacancy	Current% Vacancy	Net Gain-Loss Next Period
Pathologists			±				±
Supervisors			±				±
Technologists			±				±
Clerical			±				±
Total			±				±

Potential Shift Opportunity? Yes___ No___ If so, attach analysis per shift.
Evaluation:

Action/Action Person:
Assessment:

Dept of Path, Any Hospital
Form 197 (Aug 95)

Quality improvement (Page 5)
(Previous editions are obsolete)

17. Productivity measurement:

	Threshold (range)	Previous Period	Last Period	This Period	Trend or Pattern
PQ_p	______–_____	________	______	______	______________
PQ_w	______–_____	________	______	______	______________
PQ_{w1}	______–______	________	______	______	______________

Potential Shift Opportunity: Yes___ No___ If so, attach analysis per shift.
Evaluation:

Action/Action Person:
Assessment:

18. Personnel utilization:

Indicators:	% Avail	Hours: Paid Overtime	Hours: Comp Time	Hours: Nonspec Duty	#16 Hr Double Shifts	Other
Threshold:	________	________	________	________	__|______	________
a. Technologists	________	________	________	________	________	________
b. Clerical	________	________	________	________	________	________
c. Other	________	________	________	________	________	________

Potential Shift Opportunity? Yes___ No___ If so, attach analysis per shift.
Evaluation:

Action/Action Person:
Assessment:

19. Continuing medical education, and training, and professional competence:

	Education/Training/ Competence Indicator	Threshold	Observation
a.	____________________	____________	______________________________
b.	____________________	____________	______________________________
c.	____________________	____________	______________________________
d.	____________________	____________	______________________________

Potential Shift Opportunity? Yes___ No___ If so, attach analysis per shift.
Evaluation:

Action/Action Person:
Assessment:

20. Procedural methods review:

	Review Indicator	Milestone Date	Threshold	Observation
a.				
b.				
c.				
d.				

Evaluation:

Action/Action Person:
Assessment:

21. Computer support (specify total unscheduled downtime in hours/days):

	Support Indicator	Threshold	Observation
a.			
b.			
c.			
d.			

Evaluation:

Action/Action Person:
Assessment

22. Equipment procurement and maintenance (capital/noncapital expense items):

	Equipment Indicator	Threshold (delay)	Observation
a.			
b.			
c.			
d.			

Evaluation:

Action/Action Person:
Assessment:

23. Supply procurement and storage (nonexpendable/expendable expense items):

	Supply Indicator	Threshold (delay)	Observation
a.			
b.			
c.			

Evaluation:

Action/Action Person:
Assessment:

Dept of Path, Any Hospital
Form 197 (Aug 95)

Quality improvement (Page 7)
(Previous editions are obsolete)

24. Facility / working environment / maintenance / repair / renovation / space utilization (capital/noncapital expense items):

	Facility Indicator	Threshold (delay)	Observation
a.	____________	________	________________
b.	____________	________	________________
c.	____________	________	
d.	____________	________	________________

Evaluation:

Action/Action Person:
Assessment:

25. Budget management:

Budget Indicator	Non Allocated	Allocated (contracts)	AIDS	CME	Total
a. % FY Completed (Threshold)	______	______	____	____	____
b. Total $ Budgeted	______	______	____	____	____
c. $ Obligated by Contract	______	______	____	____	____
d. Total Nonobligated Expenditures (b-c)	______	______	____	____	____
e. Total Expend (c+d)	______	______	____	____	____
f. % Budget Balance Expended (e divided by bx100)	______	______	____	____	____
g. Projected $ Needed	______	______	____	____	____

Evaluation:

Action/Action Person:
Assessment:

INTERNAL QUALITY IMPROVEMENT WORK FLOW SEGMENT

26. Internal organizational quality surveillance:

	Internal QI Indicator	Threshold	Observation
a.	____________	________	________________
b.	____________	________	________________
c.	____________	________	________________
d.	____________	________	________________

Evaluation:

Action/Action Person:
Assessment:

Dept of Path, Any Hospital
Form 197 (Aug 95)

Quality improvement (Page 8)
(Previous editions are obsolete)

EXTERNAL QUALITY IMPROVEMENT WORK FLOW SEGMENT

27. Inspections (eg, FDA/JCAHO/CAP/AABB/interim self-inspections):

Inspection Indicator (deficiency/finding)	Threshold	Observation
a. ______	______	______
b. ______	______	______
c. ______	______	______
d. ______	______	______

Evaluation:

Action/Action Person:
Assessment:

28. Proficiency testing surveys:

Survey Indicator: state Survey # and deficiency	Threshold	Observation
a. # –	______	______
b. # –	______	______
c. # –	______	______
d. # –	______	______

Evaluation:

Action/Action Person:
Assessment:

29. Incident reports and complaints:

Incidental Indicator (event/complaint)	Threshold	Observation
a. ______	______	______
b. ______	______	______
c. ______	______	______
d. ______	______	______

Evaluation:

Action/Action Person:
Assessment:

Dept of Path, Any Hospital
Form 197 (Aug 95)

Quality improvement (Page 9)
(Previous editions are obsolete)

QUALITY ANTICIPATION WORK FLOW SEGMENT

30. Organizational research, development, and implementation
(review of reporting period's milestones for strategic planning):

	Planning Indicator	Tasking Milestone (date)	Milestone Threshold	Observation
a.	____________	________	________	____________
b.	____________	________	________	____________
c.	____________	________	________	____________
d.	____________	________	________	____________

Evaluation:

Action/Action Person:
Assessment:

QUALITY ACTUALIZATION WORK FLOW SEGMENT

31. Organization effectiveness:

Actualization Indicator	Threshold	Observations
a. Team assessment:		
Morale	____________	____________
Skills	____________	____________
b. Team skill training (TST):		
Medical staff	____________	____________
Supervisory staff	____________	____________
Technical staff	____________	____________
Resident staff	____________	____________
Clerical staff	____________	____________
Other	____________	____________
c. Team maintenance:		
Continued TST	____________	____________
Personnel actions	____________	____________
Personnel incentives	____________	____________
d. Team effectiveness:		
Leadership commitment	____________	____________
Decision making	____________	____________

Evaluation:

Action/Action Person:
Assessment:

Dept of Path, Any Hospital
Form 197 (Aug 95)

Quality improvement (Page 10)
(Previous editions are obsolete)

32. Laboratory structure / policy / SOP / method / or other changes for improvement:

	Action / change / improvement	Assessment
a.		
b.		
c.		
d.		
e.		

33. Additional comments:

34. Signature block:

QI Technologist	Section Supervisor	Section Manager	Medical Director

35. Feeder report routind recommendation list (copies furnished):

a.
b.
c.
d.

Dept of Path, Any Hospital
Form 197 (Aug 95)

Quality improvement (Page 11)
(Previous editions are obsolete)

APPENDIX B
Quality Improvement Feeder Report: Anatomical Pathology Narrative

Quality Improvement Feeder Report (Anatomical Pathology)

1. Section and reporting period identification:

Section / Service:______________________ Submitted: Month_______Year_______

Reporting Period______________________ thru ______________________

2. Surgical pathology turnaround:

Indicators	Threshold		Observations	
a. Total Surgicals	TBD	Cases	_______	Cases
b. Research Surgicals	TBD	Cases	_______	Cases
c. Rush Surgicals	TBD	Cases	_______	Cases
Average TAT	<1	Day	_______	Hours
≤ 1 Day TAT	_______	Cases		
	<100	% of rushes	_______	%
> 1 Day TAT	>0	Cases	_______	Cases
	>0	% of rushes	_______	%
Not Signed Out	>0	Cases	_______	Cases
	>0	% of rushes	_______	%
d. Routine Surgicals	TBD	Cases	_______	Cases
Average TAT	<2	Days	_______	Days
≤ 2 Days TAT			_______	Cases
e. Special Surgicals	TBD	Cases	_______	Cases
Average TAT	<5	Days	_______	Days
≤ 5 Days TAT			_______	Cases
	<100	% of specials	_______	%
f. Delayed Surgicals				
> 5 Days TAT	>0	Cases	_______	Cases
	>0	% of nonrushes	_______	%
Not Signed Out	>0	Cases	_______	Cases
	>0	% of nonrushes	_______	%

Evaluation:

Action:
Action Person:
Assessment:

TBD = to be determined by local laboratory

Dept of Path, Any Hospital
Form 197A (Aug 95)

Quality improvement (Page 1
(Previous editions are obsolete)

3. Surgical pathology peer review:

Indicators	Threshold	Observation	
a. Total number of cases diagnosed		______	Cases
% of cases to be reviewed/targeted	TBD% .	______	10-100
Target cases reviewed		______	Cases
	TBD%	______	% of total
Nontargeted cases reviewed		______	Cases
		______	% of total

b. Provider #	Discrepancy Observed	Evaluation
1) # ______	______	______
2) # ______	______	______
3) # ______	______	______

Action:
1)
2)
3)

Action Person:
Assessment:

4. Bone marrow turnaround:

Indicators	Threshold		Observation	
a. Total Bone Marrows.	TBD	Cases	______	Cases
b. Rush Bone Marrows	TBD	Cases	______	Cases
Average TAT	< 1	Days	______	Days
≤ 1 Day TAT			______	Cases
	<100	% of rushes	______	%
> 1 Day TAT	>0	Cases	______	Cases
	>0	% of rushes	______	%
Not Signed Out	>0	Cases	______	Cases
	>0	% of rushes	______	%
c. Routine Bone Marrow	TBD	Cases	______	Cases
Average TAT	< 2	Days	______	Days
≤ 2 Days TAT	______	Cases		
	<100	% of routines	______	%
d. Special Bone Marrow	TBD	Cases	______	Cases
Average TAT	< 5	Days	______	Days
< 5 Days TAT			______	Cases
	<100	% of specials	______	%
e. Delayed Bone Marrows			______	Cases
< 5 Days TAT	>0	Cases	______	Cases
	>0	% of rushes	______	%
Not Signed Out	>0	Cases	______	Cases
	>0	% of nonrushes	______	%

Evaluation
Action:
Action Person:
Assessment:

Dept of Path, Any Hospital
Form 197A (Aug 95)

Quality improvement (Page 2
(Previous editions are obsolete)

5. Bone marrow peer review:

Indicators	Threshold	Observations	
a. Total number of cases diagnosed		______	Cases
% of cases to be reviewed/targeted	TBD%	______	% Total
Target cases reviewed		______	Cases
	TBD%	______	%
Nontargeted cases reviewed		______	Cases
		______	% Total

b. Provider #	Discrepancy Observed	Evaluation
1) # ______	______	______
2) # ______	______	______
3) # ______	______	______

Action:
Action Person:
Assessment:

6. Cytopathology turnaround:

Indicators	Threshold (Med/Gyn)		Observation (Med/Gyn)	
a. Total Cytologies	TBD	Cases	______	Cases
Subtotals	(TBD/TBD)	Cases	(/)	Cases
b. Rush Cytologies	TBD/TBD	Cases	___/___	Cases
Average TAT	< 24	Hours	___/___	Hours
≤ 24 Hours TAT			___/___	Cases
	<100	%	___/___	%
> 24 Hours TAT	>0	Cases	___/___	Cases
Not Signed Out	>0 / >0	Cases	___/___	Cases
	>0	Cases	___/___	%
c. Routine Cytologies	TBD/TBD	Cases	___/___	Cases
Average TAT	< 3	Days	___/___	Days
≤ 3 Days TAT			___/___	Cases
	<95	Cases	___/___	%
3-5 Days			___/___	Cases
	>5	Cases.	___/___	%
5 Days TAT	>0	Cases	___/___	Cases
(Delayed)	>0	%	___/___	%
Backlog	>0	Cases	___/___	Cases
	>0	Days	___/___	Days

Evaluation:

Action:

Action Person
Assessment:

Dept of Path, Any Hospital
Form 197A (Aug 95)

Quality improvement (Page 3
(Previous editions are obsolete)

7. Cytopathology peer review:

	Indicators	Threshold (Med/Gyn)		Observation (Med/Gyn)	
a.	Total number reviewed	(TBD/TBD)	Cases	___/___	Cases
	% Positives reviewed	(TBD/TBD)	%	___/___	%
	% Negatives reviewed	(TBD/TBD)	%	___/___	%

b.	Provider #	Discrepancy Observed	Evaluation
	1) # ________	________	________
	1) # ________	________	________
	1) # ________	________	________

Action:

Action Person:
Assessment:

8. Autopsy pathology turnaround:

	Indicators	Threshold		Observations	
a.	Total Number	TBD	Cases	______	Cases
	Pediatric Cases			______	Cases
b.	Hospital Rate	TBD	%	______	%
c.	Preliminary Reports			______	Cases
	Average TAT	≤ 2	Days	______	Days
	≤ 2 Days TAT			______	Cases
		< 100	%	______	%
	> 2 Days TAT			______	Cases
		< 0	%	______	%
d.	Completed Reports			______	Cases
	Average TAT	≤30	Days	______	Days
	≤ 30 Days TAT			______	Cases
		< 100	%	______	%
e.	Delayed Reports				
	> 30 Days TAT	≤30	Cases	______	Cases
		< 5	%	______	%
f.	Autopsy Processing Backlog				
	Total Backlog	>0	Cases	______	Cases
	Initial Draft				
	> 10 Days	<0	Cases	______	Cases
	Final Draft				
	> 25 Days	<0	Cases	______	Cases

Dept of Path, Any Hospital
Form 197A (Aug 95)

Quality improvement (Page 4
(Previous editions are obsolete)

Sign Out

> 30 Days	<0	Cases	______	Cases
Autopsy Slides				
Average TAT	>5	Days	______	Days
Backlog	>0	Cases	______	Cases

Evaluation:

Action:

Action Person:
Assessment:

---

9. Autopsy pathology peer review:

b.	Provider #	Discrepancy Observed	Evaluation
1)	#______	______	______
2)	#______	______	______
3)	#______	______	______

Action
Action Person:
Assessment:

---

10. Additional Comments:

---

11. Signature block:

______	______	______	______
QI Technologist	Section Supervisor	Section Manager	Medical Director

---

Dept of Path, Any Hospital
Form 197A (Aug 95)

Quality improvement (Page 5)
(Previous editions are obsolete)

APPENDIX C
Quality Profile: Chemistry Section

APPENDIX C
Quality Profile: Q1 Report Dec 95
Section: Chemistry

Indicator Grouping/ Specific Indicator: Threshold (Periodicity)	QI Data Observations (Date trend started) J A S O N D
POSTLABORATORY OUTCOME WORK FLOW SEGMENT	
Customer Satisfaction: any positive or negative report; sentinel event!! (Monthly) a. Overall review	Section nominated by Med Dept for Hosp 1996 Quality Management Award; lab's establishing Lab-Nursing Teams was leading factor
b. Thoracic surgery study: TBD	Protocol being coordinated with Thoracic Surgery Service (Nov 95)
Patient Care Outcome: no threat to health status; sentinel event!! (Monthly) a. Overall review	0 = no adverse outcome Last incident in Dec 94 . . . . Patient Code # 0 0 0 0 0 0
b. Pediatric lead level (Quarterly)	– – 0 – – 0 Chart review study began in Mar 95 after incident – = no report scheduled 0 = no adverse outcome
Employee Safety Outcome: no potential or actual hazard; sentinel event! (Monthly) a. Biological	Biohazard labels dc'd IAW CDC universal precautions; NOW technologists' concern over control of HIV specimens has been raised at the management–employee relations level; dept–level task force confirms that contagion is under control
b. Fire	No OFI identified x 12 mo
c. Electrical	No OFI identified x 12 mo
d. Chem/Carcinogen	No OFI identified x 12 mo
e. Radionuclide	No OFI identified x 12 mo
f. Waste Disposal	No OFI identified x 12 mo
g. Enviromental	No OFI identified x 12 mo

! = sentinel event TBD = to be determined

Evaluation of QI Data, TQM System, CQI Process	Action and Action Person: (Date Initiated)	Assessment of Overall Improvement
Continuous quality improvement over the last year has been recognized	Continue the good work!! ACTION: Section team	Continuous improvement cited
Coordination in process	To be ready for QI review by Mar 96 ACTION: Med Dir	Improvement of QI process is ongoing
On target x 12 mo; general survey has not detected any OFI over an inordinate amount of time; but a focused study has been in progress	Change periodicity of evaluation to quarterly ACTION: Supervisor	Improvement of QI process is in progress
On target x 3 qtrs; baseline established	1. Review this study to ensure that it is adequately sensitive 2. Select a new study topic for Jan 96 ACTION: Supervisor	Improvement of the QI process is in progress
Contagion is in control. There is need for greater training and worker awareness of the philosophy and intent of universal precautions	Enhance biohazard training program by Jan 96; coordinate with section volunteers and hosp infection control service ACTION: Laboratory Safety Officer	Biohazard training needs improvement: A more complete assessment is to be made in Feb 96
These four indicators have been on target x 12 mo; there has been no improvement over an inordinate amount of time	Select a focused study for each of the six safety indicators to be scheduled over the next six months. ACTION: Supervisor	Ineffective response to general survey; Sensitivity of QI process needs improvement

Chemistry Quality Profile: Dec 95

Indicator Grouping/ Specific Indicator: Threshold (Periodicity)	QI Data Observations (Date trend started) J A S O N D
POSTLABORATORY PROCESS WORK FLOW SEGMENT	
Laboratory Report Utilization: in keeping with joint laboratory and clinical standards!! (Quarterly) a. Liver profile	– = not scheduled 0 = no provider identified . . . . Provider Code # . . . . – – 73 – – 0
Throughput of Index Procedures: (Quarterly) a. Multichannel analyzer "X" TAT: >3 hours averaged	See Analytical Quality, Personnel, and Equipment groupings; selection of new analyzer began in Jan 95 due to QC problems; there are 6 FTE vacancies 2.5 – – 2.0 – – h h = averaged hours
b. Stat test TAT: > 60 min averaged	– 50 – – 45 – m No OFI identified x 12 mo m = averaged minutes
Report Distribution: no misdirected reports; sentinel event!! (Quarterly)	0 = no OFI identified – = no report required – 0 – – 0 – Survey began in Jul 1995
INTRALABORATORY PROCESS WORK FLOW SEGMENT	
Postdeterminative Product Finalization and Specimen Handling: no loss of product or specimen integrity! (Quarterly)	No OFI identified x 3 qtrs
Reference Laboratory Studies: no adverse effect on patient outcome! (Quarterly)	– – 0 – – 0 General survey began Feb 95 – = not scheduled 0 = no OFI identified
a. α feto protein TAT: >4 days from primary lab submission to return receipt by primary lab	8 3 3 4 3 3 d This study began in Jul 1995 Last clinical complaint Jul 1995 d = averaged days

TAT = turnaround time OFI = opportunity for improvement

Evaluation of QI Data, TQM System, CQI Process	Action and Action Person: (Date Initiated)	Assessment of Overall Improvement
On target; no repeats or new occurrences since September	Coordinate a new study topic for Jun 96 ACTION: Section Medical Supervisor Director	Improvement of the QI process is in process
1. On target for at least 6 mo in spite of QC problems and 6 staff vacancies 2. Threshold of 3 hr is too long–too insensitive; can be improved if clinically important	1. Maintain QC vigilance 2. Negotiate reduction of threshold with clinical staff 3. Resolve staffing and equipment problems ACTION: Supervisor	Improvement of TAT is in progress BUT good TAT is masking QC, equipment, staffing, and QAn/QAc improvement needs
On target x 12 mo; but no significant improvement over an inordinate period	Select a more focused study on ER TAT for Jan 96 ACTION: Supervisor	Improvement was stalled but now is in progress
On target x 6 mo; this seems unrealistic; QI process must lack sensitivity	Select a focused study for Feb 96 ACTION: Supervisor	Improvement of the QI process is in progress
On target x 9 mo; there has been no improvement over an inordinate amount of time	Select a focused study for Mar 1996 ACTION: Supervisor	Improvement was stalled but now is in progress
On target for at least 6 mo; a good baseline for this general survey	Continue with quarterly periodicity ACTION: Supervisor	Effective QI process
6 month baseline is established after initial ref lab TAT of 8 d; problem appears to be resolved	1. Change periodicity to quarterly 2. Consider a new study topic ACTION: Supervisor	Improvement of the QI process is in progress

Chemistry Quality Profile: Dec 95

Indicator Grouping/ Specific Indicator: Threshold (Periodicity)	QI Data Observations (Date trend started) J A S O N D
Analytical Quality: no major discrepancies!! (Monthly) a. Multichannel Analyzer X	Service contract is not available for Analyzer X Selection of new analyzer began in Jan 92! • = no problems cited x = major QC problems

	J	A	S	O	N	D
Acid Phos	x	•	•	•	•	x
BUN	•	x	x	•	x	•
CO2	•	•	•	•	x	•
Glucose	x	•	•	•	•	x
Na/K	x	•	x	•	•	•
ALT (SEPT)	x	•	•	•	•	x
b. Analyzer A and B disparity in alk phos test results; analyzer A is in routine chem; analyzer B is n ICU stat lab: no major disparity!	–	–	–	–	x	x

ICU = intensive care unit	This disparity in alk phos tests was first noted in Nov 95 through a clinical incident report – = no study in progress x = disparity reported
Diagnostic Quality (Peer Review): no major discrepancies! (– – – – – –)	Not appliable; no semiquantitative or qualitative interpretive analysis performed
Predeterminative Specimen Processing: no loss of specimen integrity! (Monthly)	No OFI identified x 7 mo

PRELABORATORY PROCESS WORK FLOW SEGMENT

Validation: > 1% invalidation rate ¥ (Monthly)	This data represents only daytime shift performance of specimen collection

	J	A	S	O	N	D	
a. Ward 22 staff	3	2	3	3	4	5	%
b. Ward 49 staff	2	3	2	3	2	1	%
c. Ward 71 staff	3	2	3	2	3	2	%
d. Ward 73 staff	2	3	2	3	2	3	%
e. Lab staff	1	2	2	1	1	2	%

* adjusted from 5% in July	QI note: Ward 22 is not performing well in other section QI reports

TAT = turnaround time OFI = opportunity for improvement FTE = full time equivalent

Evaluation of QI Data, TQM System, CQI Process	Action and Action Person: (Date Initiated)	Assessment of Overall Improvement
Constant imprecision due to aging instrument; patient studies remain in constant control maintenance, recalibration, and repeat runs; on-site visits to observe best replacement candidate have been scheduled	1. Maintain QC and patient result assurance 2. Replace the instrument immediately or obtain loaned/leased instrument of defer to reference lab NLT 1 Feb 96 ACTION: Supervisor (Jan 95)	Ineffective procurement process; instrument selection is excessively prolonged: EXPEDITE procurement of new analyzer!
Disparity between two different methods in Stat Lab and General Chemistry Lab causing confusion in clinical diagnosis and therapy; results are currently under control	1. Standardize the alk phos methods 2. Coordinate with medical maintenance and suppliers 3. Of necessary obtain new analyzer ACTION: Supervisor (Nov 92)	Improvement is in progress; improved control is only temporary until disparity is resolved
---------	---------	---------
On target x 7 mo; there needs to be a more sensitive QI approach	Initiate a focused indicator in Feb 96 ACTION: Supervisor	Improvement of the QI process is in progress

Overall, slightly increased; demographics (patient name, number) are still main problem Ward 22 is performing poorly in other lab sections No data on evening/night ward shifts	1. Maintain vigilance at specimen receipt window, especially Ward 22 2. Continue teaching on the wards 3. Focus study on each of the three shifts for ward shifts 4. Reduce periodicity from monthly to quarterly ACTION: Supervisor	Improvement of validation and QI processes is in progress

QI Note: There is a need for improvement of validation at the accession point with establishment of a new indicator grouping for patient preparation

Chemistry CQI Profile: Dec 92

Indicator Grouping/ Specific Indicator: Threshold (Periodicity)	QI Data Observations (Date trend started) J	A	S	O	N	D	
Chemistry Test Selection: in keeping with joint laboratory and clinical standards!! (Quarterly)	– = not scheduled 0 = no provider identified Survey started in Jul 92						
a. Serum calcium	. . . Provider Code # . . .						
	–	–	0	–	–	0	
OPERATIVE RESOURCE MANAGEMENT WORK FLOW							
Workload Management:							
a. Productivity quotients: within established limits!! (Monthly)	m = minutes/work hour						
1. PQp (paid): 40 to 45 min/hr	56	52	51	49	46	41	m
2. PQwl (workloaded): 50 to 55 min/hr	112	104	104	98	92	71	m
Personnel Management (Monthly)							
a. Work force:							
1. Vacancy rate: Technologists: >10% vacancy	55	50	45	38	31	21	%
	6 FTE vacancies in Dec 95						
b. Utilization:	s = 16 hour shifts						
1. 16 hour shifts: none!!	18	15	17	14	12	11	s
2. Overtime: > 429 hours	532	496	497	477	419	407	h
	h = hours						
c. Availability:							
1. % availability: < 80%	84	78	85	90	83	85	%
Continuing Education < 3 hour/mo!! (Monthly)	3	3	3	3	3	3	h
	h = hours						

	Evaluation of QI Data, TQM System, CQI Process	Action and Action Person: (Date Initiated)	Assessment of Overall Improvement
	On target x 6 mo; baseline established	Continue for one more quarter; THEN Select a new focused study for Mar 96 ACTION: Supervisor	Improvement of the QI process is in progress
	1. PQp is improving with a successful hiring program 2. PQwl is consistently excessive; but, this stress indicator is improving; the PQ ratio is 1.7 in Dec	Continue to pursue hiring to fill remaining vacancies ACTION: Supervisor	Improvement of the hiring process is in progress
	Six staff vacancies! BUT trend is steadily decreasing as positions are being filled	Fill 6 positions ACTION: Supervisor	Improvement of hiring process is in progress
	Excessive but decreasing!	Continue innovative staffing ACTION: Supervisor	Improving
	On target and decreasing	Continue innovative staffing ACTION: Supervisor	Improving
	On target; superb motivation!!!	Keep up with personnel actions and incentive awards ACTION: Supervisor	Effective total QI process
	Consistently on target x 6 mo; improvement of performance noted	Select a focused study for April 96 ACTION: Supervisor	Improvement of the QI process is in progress

Chemistry Quality Profile: Dec 95

Indicator Grouping/ Specific Indicator: Threshold (Periodicity)	QI Data Observations (Date trend started) J A S O N D
Methods & Procedures Review: must be on time!! (Annually per Monthly Schedule)	Monthly review schedule is up–to–date
Computer Management: a. Unscheduled down time: > 24 hours (Monthly)	No OFI identified x 6 mo
Equipment: resolution of any opportunity must be complete within one quarter!! (Quarterly)	1. Multichannel anAlyzer X is under constant QC scrutiny 2. Analyzers A (routine chemistry) and B (ICU) show disparate results
Supply: no potential for laboratory service limitations!! (Quarterly) a. Overdue supplies: none > 14 d	0 = no supplies overdue None overdue since Jun 95 – 0 – – 0 –
Facility: no potential for equipment failure, biological spoilage or personnel stress!! (Quarterly)	No OFI identified x 2 qtrs
Budget: meet planned expenditure within ± 5% of the monthly target (Monthly)	+3 +4 +3 +4 +10 +9 % Fiscal year (FY) starts in Oct; contracts are front-loaded in the first months of the FY
ORGANIZATIONAL RESOURCE MANAGEMENT WORK FLOW SEGMENT	
Internal Quality Improvement (QI) a. Assessment: there must be evidence of continuous improvement over a reasonable amount of time!! (Quarterly)	Continuous improvement is documented, overall; section has received the 1992 hospital QI award indicating effective QI assessment, overall HOWEVER, see Analytical Quality and Equipment Management grouping for data on instrument replacement problem

Evaluation of QI Data, TQM System, CQI Process	Action and Action Person: (Date Initiated)	Assessment of Overall Improvement
Consistently on target	Finalize review of new annual schedule for Mar 96 ACTION: Supervisor	Improvement of this review process is in progress
On target x 6 mo; general baseline has been established	Establish a focused study for Feb 96 ACTION: Supervisor	Improvement of the QI process is in progress
Replacement of Analyzer X is prolonged; on–site visits are scheduled in Jan 96; eval of Analyzers A and B is in progress	1. Replace multichannel Analyzer X 2. Resolve Analyzer A or B disparity immediately ACTION: Supervisor	Improvement needed; too prolonged decision making re Analyzer X
No report scheduled; next report due Feb 96; on target x 2 qtrs; general survey is too insesitive	Select a focused study for Mar 96 ACTION: Supervisor	Improvement of the QI process is in progress
On target x 2 qtrs; no OFI identified for six months	Select a focused study for Apr 96 ACTION: Supervisor	Improvement of the QI process is in progress
Overexpenditure due to front–loaded contracts; this has been anticipated but it skews the data	Investigate use of an alternative accounting system ACTION: Lab Manager	Budget system is being improved
On target in most operational areas BUT there is a problem in the process of assessing instrument replacement; this QI step needs improvement within a reasonable period	1. Begin a focused study of the instrument selection process for Jan 96 ACTION: Dept Lab Manager 2. React more readily to periods of nonimprovement by fine tuning the QI assessment process ACTION: Supervisor	Overall, very effective internal QI process EXCEPT FOR assessment of equipment selection process effective-ness and related QI process sensitivity

Chemistry Section Quality Profile: Dec 95

Indicator Grouping/ Specific Indicator: Threshold (Periodicity)	QI Data Observations (Date trend started) J A S O N D
b. Communication: there must be adequate sharing of lessons learned!! (Monthly)	No OFI identified x 8 mo Data reveals at least 1 hour of QI inservice training per month x 8 mo
External Quality Improvement (QI) (Monthly) a. Proficiency surveys: all results must be ≤ 2 SID* or found "Acceptable"!! 1) HCG (RIA)	* SDI = Standard Deviation Interval (Index) – = no survey scheduled 0 = no deficiencies – – 0 – – 2.2
2) Glucose (Multichannel Analyzer X)	– – 2.8 – – 2.6
b. JCAHO/CAP/ other inspection: no unresolved findings!	No unresolved findings from any previous inspections
c. Incident reports and complaints: every report is a sentinel event!!	Liver profile report cited as inaccurate by physician on Ward 17 (Male Medicine)
Quality Anticipation (QAn) (Quarterly) a. Organizational research: all milestones will be attained!!	3/3 = 3 of 3 milestones attained – = report not scheduled – – 1/3 – – 1/2 Interpretation: only 1/3 attained in Sep and 1/2 in Dec resulted in usable data due to faulty survey designs
b. Development: all milestones will be attained!!	– 0 – – 0 – 0 = no milestones missed; all attained
c. Implementation: all milestones will be attained!!	3/3 – – 2/2 – –

Evaluation of QI Data, TQM System, CQI Process	Action and Action Person: (Date Initiated)	Assessment of Overall Improvement
On target x 8 mo; there has been no improvement over an inordinate amount of time	Select a focused indicator study for Mar 96 ACTION: Supervisor	Improvement of the QI process is in progress
Bead washing error in Dec; no trend	1. Investigate the analytical process 2. Audit QC data for any trend of repeated HCG (RIA) inaccuracies for the next 3 mo 3. Assess remedial actions in Mar 96 ACTION: Supervisor	Improvement of the analytical process is in progress
Daily QC acceptable with repeated maintenance and repeat runs; aging multichannel Analyzer X is being replaced	1. Watch QC carefully 2. Replace the problematic analyzer ACTION: Supervisor	Internal and external QI processes for equip mgmt need improvement
QI Note: per CLIA 88, section supervisor is to survey entire scope of procedures to identify need for internal proficiency testing		
On target	None needed	Effective QI process
Calculation transcription error; no trend	Investigate the transcription process ACTION: Supervisor	Assessment of improvement is to be determined
All research surveys are reported as completed on time, BUT effectiveness of research approach has been spotty	1. Establish focused studies and analyze effectiveness of all projects 2. Proceed to development phase with successful projects 3. Report in Jan 96 ACTION: Supervisor	Internal QI and QAn research processes need improvement
No report scheduled; above comment raises concern over focus of this indicator	Report due in Feb 96 comment on project effectiveness ACTION: Supervisor	TBD
No report scheduled; consider improving the focus of this indicator	Report due in Jan 96 comment on project effectiveness ACTION: Supervisor	TBD

Chemistry Quality Profile: Dec 95

Indicator Grouping/ Specific Indicator: Threshold (Periodicity)	QI Data Observations (Date trend started) J A S O N D
Quality Actualization (QAc) (Monthly) a. Team building: 1. Morale: no adverse effect on team effectiveness!!	Morale is excellent based on the review of Nov team survey and supporting indicators; this has been a consistent observation for 12 mo
2. Skills training (TST): no skills lacking that adversely affect team effectiveness!!	Skills training schedule is on time; at least one hour per month; all work shifts have been consistent for 12 months
b. Team maintenance: 1. Continuing TST	As noted above
2. Personnel actions: none overdue!!	0= no action overdue 0 0 0 0 0 0 None overdue x 12 mo
3. Personnel incentives: none overdue!!	0 0 0 0 0 0 None overdue x 12 mo
c. Team effectiveness 1. Decision making: no problem too hard or unresolved >3 months!!	Most OFI have been adequately addressed by the section team; if too hard, they have been correctly submitted to the appropriate higher echelon or lateral dept; HOWEVER, there has been: 1) insufficient attention paid to the replacement of the multichannel Analyzer X and 2) prolonged response to indicator inactivity
2. Leadership Commitment: TBD	

Evaluation of QI Data, TQM System, CQI Process	Action and Action Person: (Date Initiated)	Assessment of Overall Improvement
On target x 12 mo; there has been no improvment over an inordinate amount of time	Select a focused study for Feb 96 ACTION: Supervisor	Improvement of the QI process has been stalled but now is in progress
On target x 12 mo; there has been no improvement over an inordinate amount of time	Select a focused study for Mar 96 ACTION: Supervisor	Improvement of the QI process now is in progress
As noted above	As noted above	As noted above
On target x 12 mo; there has been no improvement over an inordinate period	Select a focused study for Apr 96 ACTION: Supervisor	Improvement of the QI process is in progress
On target x 12 mo; there has been no improvement over an inordinate period	Select a focused study for May 96 ACTION: Supervisor	Improvement of the QI process is in progress
Generally on target EXCEPT FOR 1) delayed decision to replace analyzer x and 2) poor reaction to prolonged indicator inactivity in several key management areas	1) Start focused study on decision making for instrument replacement for Jan 96 2) React more readily to indicator inactivity ACTION: Medical Director	Improvement of the overall QI process and decision making process has been stalled but now is in progress

QI Note: Begin reporting on “Leadership Commitment” as a new QAc indicator grouping for Jan 96

APPENDIX D
Quality Profile: Hematology Section

APPENDIX D
Quality Profile: QI Report Dec 95
Section: Hematology

Indicator Grouping/ Specific Indicator: Threshold (Periodicity)	QI Data Observations (Date trend started) J A S O N D
POSTLABORATORY OUTCOME WORK FLOW SEGMENT	
Customer Satisfaction: any positive or negative report; sentinel event!! (Monthly)	0 0 0 0 0 0 0 = no reports received
Patient Care Outcome: no threat to life or limb; sentinel event!! (Monthly)	. . . . Patient Code # . . . . – – 0 0 0 0 0 = no OFI identified – = not implemented
Employee Safety Outcome: no potential or actual hazard; sentinel event! (Monthly)	OFI = opportunity for improvement
a. Biological	No OFI identified x 12 mo
b. Fire	No OFI identified x 12 mo
c. Electrical	No OFI identified x 12 mo
d. Chem/Carcinogen	No OFI identified x 12 mo
e. Radionuclide	Not applicable
f. Waste Disposal	No OFI identified x 12 mo
g. Environmental	Summer temperatures were excessively high causing intermittent employee heat stress and instrument malfunction (Jul 95)
POSTLABORATORY PROCESS WORK FLOW SEGMENT	
Laboratory Report Utilization: in keeping with laboratory and clinical standards (Monthly)	0 = no OFI identified
a. Platelet counts	. . . . Patient Code # 0 0 0 0 0 0
b. Manual differential count	0 0 0 0 0 0 Study began in May 95

! = sentinel event QM = quality management

Evaluation of QI Data, TQM System, CQI Process	Action and Action Person: (Date Initiated)	Assessment of Overall Improvement
No positive or adverse spot reports received in the last six months	Select focused indicators for bone marrow and cytogenetics TAT for Feb 96 ACTION: Supervisor	Improvement of the QI process is ongoing
On target; 4 month general baseline established based on general survey and incident reports	Select a focused indicator for Mar 96 ACTION: Supervisor	Improvement of the QI process is ongoing
Five of these indicators have been "on target" x 12 mo; there has been no improvement over an inordinate amount of time	Prioritize these five safety indicators; select a focused study for one of the highest priority ACTION: Supervisor	Ineffective TQM system; the QI process needs improvement
-------	-------	
"On target" x 12 mo	See above action	
Inadequate summer ventilation noted since Jul 1994; see facility grouping	Contract for facility renovation ACTION: Lab Manager (Aug 94)	Ineffective facility engineer response; improve QM interface
QI Note: The resolution of this problem has been inordinately delayed, requiring the Lab Dept Med Dir to coordinate with hospital admin and facility engineers		

On target x 6 mos: baseline established with no healthcare provider cited for inappropriate utilization of platelet counts	Change periodicity of indicator review from Monthly to Quarterly ACTION: Medical Director	Improvement of the QI process is ongoing; BUT it is likely that more focused studies will be needed soon
On target x 8 mo; baseline established	None needed—yet	

Hematology Quality Profile: Dec 95

Indicator Grouping/ Specific Indicator: Threshold (Periodicity)	QI Data Observations (Date trend started) J	A	S	O	N	D	
Turnaround Time (TAT) of Index Procedures (Monthly)							
a. Routine CBC: >4 hours avg TAT	3	4	4	4	4	5	h
b. Coagulation: > 4 hours avg TAT	3	4	4	4	4	5	h
c. Urinalysis: > 4 hours avg TAT avg = average	3	4	4	4	4	5	h
d. Routine bone marrow Dx: < 95% within 2 days TAT	80 Dx = diagnosis	80	85	85	89	89	%
e. Special bone marrow Dx: < 95% within 5 days TAT	90	90	92	92	94	95	%
Report Distribution: no misdirected reports; sentinel event! (Monthly)	No OFI identified x 8 mo						
INTRALABORATORY PROCESS WORK FLOW SEGMENT							
Postdeterminative Product Finalization and Specimen Handling: no loss of product or specimen integrity (Quarterly)	No OFI identified x 3 qtr qtr = quarter(s)						
Reference Laboratory Studies: no adverse effect on patient outcome! (Monthly) a. Cytogenetics avg TAT: > 10 days	NR = no data reported 27	NR	NR	NR	NR	30	d
b. Backlog: none!!	20 c = total cases	32	29	31	21	28	c

Evaluation of QI Data, TQM System, CQI Process	Action and Action Person: (Date Initiated)	Assessment of Overall Improvement
Baseline shows borderline adequacy with excess in Dec which reflects growing technologist staff shortage	1. Fill 6 staff technologist positions 2. Continue innovative staffing and/or blood drawing schedule 3. Investigate adequacy of urine preservation re TAT ACTION: Supervisor	Improvement of the TAT process is needed; this section is marginally effective: Staffing problem raises question of QM interface with Personnel Office
Borderline adequate TAT		
Borderline adequate TAT: adequacy of preservative must be considered		
Routine TAT is 6% in excess; both TATs show improving trend due to innovative staff scheduling; secretarial shortage remains the major cause	1. Fill secretarial vacancy 2. Reorganize the work flow ACTION: Department Administrative Supervisor	Improvement needed: Secretarial vacancy also requires Personnel Office interface
On target for just about the maximum allotted time (6 to 9 months inactivity)	Select a focused indicator study for Jan 96 ACTION: Supervisor	Improvement of the QI process is ongoing
On target x 9 mo	Select a focused indicator study for Feb 96 ACTION: Supervisor	Improvement of the QI process is ongoing
Excessive TAT; reporting by section is consistent	1. Improve on the reporting for this indicator 2. Negotiate with reference lab; if necessary find another ref lab ACTION: Medical Director	Improvement of the QI process and ref lab consultation process is needed
Consistently excessive		

Hematology CQI Profile: Dec 92

Indicator Grouping/ Specific Indicator: Threshold (Periodicity)	QI Data Observations (Date trend started) J A S O N D
Analytical Quality: no major discrepancies! (Monthly)	No OFI identified x 4 mos
Diagnostic Quality (Peer Review): no major discrepancies! (Monthly)	. . . . . Provider Code # — . . . . . 0 0 0 0 0 0 (Example: bone marrows, cytospins, or other diagnostic or interpretive clinical microscopy)
Predeterminative Specimen Processing: no loss of specimen integrity (Monthly)	No OFI identified x 10 mo
PRELABORATORY PROCESS WORK FLOW SEGMENT	
Validation: > 10% invalidation rate (Monthly) a. Ward 22 staff	7 20 9 21 11 26 %
Laboratory Product Selection: in keeping with laboratory and clinical standards (Monthly)	. . . . . Provider Code # — . . . . . – – 0 0 0 0 0 = no discrepancies – = not implemented
OPERATIVE RESOURCE MANAGEMENT WORK FLOW SEGMENT	
Workload Management: a. Productivity quotients: within established limits (Monthly) 1. PQp (paid): 35 to 40 min/hr	m = minutes/work hour 37 36 42 46 51 60

	Evaluation of QI Data, TQM System, CQI Process	Action and Action Person: (Date Initiated)	Assessment of Overall Improvement
	On target, establishing a baseline	Continue baseline ACTION: Supervisor	Improvement of QI is in progress
	On target x 6 mos; baseline established	1. Review quarterly 2. Select a focused indicator for Feb 96 ACTION: Supervisor	Improvement of the QI process is in progress
	"On target" x 10 mo; this is an inordinately long period of indicator inactivity	Select a focused indicator for Jan 96 ACTION: Supervisor	Improvement of the QI process is ongoing
	Excessively high invalidation rate on Ward 22; information on individual shifts is not available	1. Educate; try new methods on Ward 22 2. Review QI data from each of the 3 work shifts ACTION: Supervisor	Ineffective QI process to date; BUT the approach is improving
	On target x 4 mos; baseline being established; no provider cited for inappropriate selection	None needed	Improvement of the selection process is in progress
	PQp is excessive and increasing	1. Continue innovative staff management 2. Select workload to be sent to ref lab ACTION: Supervisor 3. Improve QM interface with Personnel Office to fill vacancies ACTION: Admin Sup	Effective dept QI process BUT ineffective extra dept/hospital QI process: the lab needs Personnel Office assistance

Hematology Quality Profile: Dec 95

Indicator Grouping/ Specific Indicator: Threshold (Periodicity)	QI Data Observations (Date trend started) J A S O N D
Personnel Management (Monthly) a. Work force: 1. Vacancy rate: Technologists: > 10% vacancy	FTE = full time equivalent 6 FTE vacancies in Dec 25 22 22 30 31 31 %
Secretaries: > 10% vacancy	1 FTE vacancy in Dec 15 15 10 10 5 5 %
b. Utilization: 1. 16 Hour shifts: none!!	(Technologists only) 9 23 19 16 22 31 s
2. Overtime: > 400 hours	(Technologists only) 391 402 323 469 557 661 h
c. Availability: 1. % availability: < 80%	(Technologists only) 83 82 82 80 84 81 %
Continuing Education < 3 hour/mo (Monthly)	No OFI identified x 5 mo; all personnel/shifts trnd
Methods & Procedures Review: must be on time! (Annually per Monthly Schedule)	Monthly review schedule is up-to-date
Computer Management: a. Unscheduled downtime: > 24 hours (Monthly)	0 0 0 72 48 48 h System hard drive crashed in Oct with repeat crises
Equipment: repair must be complete within one quarter (Quarterly)	No OFI identified x 3 qtrs
Supply: no potential for laboratory service limitations (Quarterly)	No OFI identified x 2 qtrs
Facility: no potential for equipment failure, biological spoilage, or personnel stress (Quarterly)	Heat stress and equipment failure due to poor temp control; see note under Employee Safety (Jul 95)

Evaluation of QI Data, TQM System, CQI Process	Action and Action Person: (Date Initiated)	Assessment of Overall Improvement
Very serious shortage of technologists and increasing	1. Fill 6 positions 2. Obtain pay raise to attract new employees and stop attrition ACTION: Admin Supervisor	Ineffective hiring process: Personnel Office must give support
Excessive shortage; but improving	Fill 1 position ACTION: Admin Supervisor	Improving staffing situation IF!! trend continues
Very serious stress factor; increasing	(see above re hiring for vacancies)	Utilization data reflect a need to improve the technologist staffing process
Very serious stress factor; increasing		
On target; superb motivation	None needed	Effective (No improvement needed)
On target x 5 mo; baseline in progress	None needed	Effective
Consistently on target—mostly due to supervisor's personal efforts	Make this as much of a team effort as possible ACTION: Supervisor	The team approach (QAc) needs improvement
Recent downtime is adding to stress at the bench; began in Oct when hard drive malfunctioned	Coordinate repair/replacement of hard drive with Compute Operations ACTION: Lab Manager	Needs improvement: An adverse trend is developing
On target	Consider reducing the threshold level starting Jan 96 ACTION: Supervisor	Improvement of the QI process is ongoing
On target x 2 qtrs	None needed	Effective
Recurrent problem; coordination in process	Continue coordinative effort with facility engineers ACTION: Lab Manager (Jul 95)	QM interface needs improvement; requires hosp admin and engineer assistance

Hematology Quality Profile: Dec 95

Indicator Grouping/ Specific Indicator: Threshold (Periodicity)	QI Data Observations (Date trend started) J A S O N D	
Budget: meet planned expenditure within ± 5% of the monthly target (Monthly)	0 0 0 0 +9 +11 % Fiscal year starts in Oct	
ORGANIZATIONAL RESOURCE MANAGEMENT WORK FLOW SEGMENT		
Internal Quality Improvement (QI) a. QI process there must be evidence of continuous improvement! (Monthly)	Continuous improvement is documented with several opportunities being investigated	
b. Communication: there must be adequate sharing of lessons learned (Monthly)	No OFI identified x 9 mo At least 1 hour of QI in-service training per month has been accomplished	
External QI: (Monthly) a. Proficiency Surveys: all results must be within 2 SDI* or "Acceptable"!!	*SDI = Standard Deviation Interval (Index) Results from three surveys were returned; all were 100% correct during the reporting period	
b. JCAHO/CAP/other inspection: no unresolved findings!	No unresolved findings	
c. Incident reports and complaints: every report is a sentinel event!!	No adverse reports received x 8 mo	
Quality Anticipation (QAn) (Quarterly) a. Organizational research: all milestones will be attained!!	– 0 – – 0 – 0 = no milestone missed	
b. Development: all milestones will be attained!!	– – 0 – – 0	

Evaluation of QI Data, TQM System, CQI Process	Action and Action Person: (Date Initiated)	Assessment of Overall Improvement
Threshold has been exceeded x 2 mo due to front-loaded contacts	Select an alternative accounting system ACTION: Lab Manager	The budget can be improved
On target x 6 mo	Find new improvement processes as alternatives to the JCAHO ten-step process ACTION: Lab Manager	Improvement of the QI process is ongoing
On target x 9 mo	Select a focused indicator for Mar 96 ACTION: Supervisor	Improvement of the QI process is ongoing
All on target	None needed	Effective
On target	None needed	Effective
On target x 8 mo	None needed	Effective
No report scheduled	None needed	Effective
On target x 6 mo; all pilot projects are in progress; excellent performance in spite of staff shortage	Select a focused indicator for Mar 96 ACTION: Supervisor	Improvement of the QI process is ongoing

Hematology Quality Profile: Dec 95

Indicator Grouping/ Specific Indicator: Threshold (Periodicity)	QI Data Observations (Date trend started) J A S O N D	
c. Final implementation: all milestones will be attained!!	0 – – 0 – –	
Quality Actualization (QAc) (Monthly) a. Team building 1. Morale: no adverse impact on team effectiveness!!	No opportunity cited; productivity and other indicators suggest growing work stress	
2. Skills training (TST): no skills lacking that adversely affect team effectiveness!!	No opportunity cited; consistent x 12 mo	
b. Team maintenance 1.Continuing TST	As noted above	
2. Personnel actions: none overdue!!	No OFI identified x 7 mo	
3. Personnel incentives: none overdue!!	No OFI Identified x 10 mo	
c. Team effectiveness 1. Decision making: no problem too hard or resolved > 3 mo	Most opportunities have been adequately addressed at the section level EXCEPT!! resolving the excessive summer temperature, in-house TAT, and ref lab performance problems; Several QI indicators have gone for too long without improvement of the QI process, itself	
2. Leadership commitment: adequate QM resources must be onhand	There were several complaints of QM resource shortage during the reporting period due to staff vacancies	

Evaluation of QI Data, TQM System, CQI Process	Action and Action Person: (Date Initiated)	Assessment of Overall Improvement
No report scheduled	None needed	Effective to date
Could be perceived as being "on target" HOWEVER Method of data collection/evaluation needs to be more proactive	1. Survey all employees, all shifts 2. Emphasize team building 3. Select a focused indicator for Jan 96 ACTION: Supervisor	Questionably effective: The QI process needs improvement
On target under the present QI definition for an inordinately long time; the indicator needs to be redefined	1. Use survey to ascertain employee concern and needs 2. Evaluate team building schedule 3. Select a focused study for Feb 96 ACTION: Supervisor	Questionably effective TST: Improve on QI process
——————	——————	——————
"On target" x 7 mo; this is too long a perod of indicator inactivity	Select a focused indicator for Mar 96 ACTION: Supervisor	Improvement of the QI process is ongoing
"On target" x 10 mo this is too long a perod of indicator inactivity	1. Develop new incentive awards to recognize those personnel who show motivation under work stress 2. Select a focused indicator for Apr 96 ACTION: Supervisor	Improvement of the QI process is ongoing
Delay is noted in resolving several process-level opportunities for improvement of performance	1. Review section/service/dept-level decision making process regarding temp, TAT, staffing and ref lab OFI (internally and externally) 2. Select focused indicators covering facility engineer, medical maintenance, staffing, and ref lab coordination for Feb 96 ACTION: Medical Director	The decision making process is flawed: needs improvement of specific areas of the QM interface both internally and externally
Data are too general; there is need for more precise description of section leadership needs	Form a section team consensus of leader commitment: Jan 96 ACTION: Medical Director	Improvement of the QI process is ongoing

APPENDIX E
Quality Profile: Microbiology Section

APPENDIX E
Quality Profile: QI Report Dec 95
Section: Microbiology

Indicator Grouping/ Specific Indicator: Threshold (Periodicity)	QI Data Observations (Date trend started) J A S O N D
POSTLABORATORY OUTCOME WORK FLOW SEGMENT	
Customer Satisfaction: any positive or negative report; sentinel event!! (Monthly)	0 0 0 0 0 0 0 = no opportunity
a. Medical patient survey (Quarterly)	This new QI study protocol is being coordinated with the Dept of Medicine
Patient Care Outcome: no threat to life or limb; sentinel event!! (Monthly)	0 = no opportunity . . . . .Patient Code # . . . . . 0 0 0 0 0 0 Last incident in May 95
Employee Safety Outcome: no potential or actual hazard; sentinel event! (Monthly) a. Biological	1. Two techs in the Mtb lab have shown positive PPD skin conversion in the last month; hood and ventilation system have been found to be inadequate Mtb = tuberculosis
	2. Hospital-wide plan is underway to discontinue use of biohazard labels on specimens: Lab techs do not trust the new universal precautions and want to continue use of the biohazard labels
b. Fire	No OFI identified x 12 mo
c. Electrical	No OFI identified x 12 mo
d. Chem/Carcinogen	No OFI identified x 12 mo
e. Radionuclide	No OFI identified x 12 mo
f. Waste Disposal	No OFI identified x 12 mo
g. Environmental	See temperature control problem under "Facility"

! = sentinel event

Evaluation of QI Data, TQM System, CQI Process	Action and Action Person: (Date Initiated)	Assessment of Overall Improvement
No positive or adverse spot reports in the last six months	Evaluate the general customer feedback process ACTION: Supervisor	Effective action and QI process for a general survey
Coordination is in process; protocol is due Feb 96	Focused indicator to be ready by Feb 96 ACTION: Medical Director	Improvement of the QI process is in progress
On target x 7 mo	Select a focused study for Mar 96 ACTION: Supervisor	Improvement of the QI process is in progress
Hospital safety ventilation system needs renovation: hood alarms that are in place do not work; alarm system used as QC "Failsafe" malfunctioned	1. Close Mtb Lab and use reference lab until the problem is resolved 2. Coordinate major engineering project for major renovation of Mtb lab ACTION: Lab Manager	Effective QI process BUT ineffective QC!!
Laboratory personnel are intensely anxious over this issue and are ready to go through union procedures if not satisfied	1. Follow universal precautions 2. Educate the personnel re universal precautions per CLIA and OSHA ACTION: Supervisor	Impending ineffective organiz-ation performance IF personnel do no understand precautions
Five indicators have been "on target" for an inordinately long time; the QI process is poorly designed for these five indicators	Prioritize all five of these indicators and select a focused study for most important one for Jan 96 ACTION: Supervisor	Improvement of the QI process is in progress
Temperature control problem	See "Facility" indicator grouping	Improvement is needed at the facility engineer QM interface

Microbiology QualityProfile: Dec 95

Indicator Grouping/ Specific Indicator: Threshold (Periodicity)	QI Data Observations (Date trend started) J A S O N D	
POSTLABORATORY PROCESS WORK FLOW SEGMENT		
Laboratory Product Utilization: in keeping with laboratory and clinical standards (Monthly)	Provider Code # 0 0 0 0 0 0 Last incident in June 95 0 = no opportunity	
Turnaround Time (TAT) of Index Procedures (Monthly) a. Stat Gram stain for surgery: > 30 min avg TAT	m = minutes avg = averaged 46 41 44 47 50 40 m	
b. Stat Gram stain for other: > 60 min avg TAT	68 70 68 71 68 62 m	
c. Stat AFB stain: > 120 min avg TAT	146 128 129 135 131 134 m	
d. Stat antigen assays: > 120 min avg TAT	71 75 70 73 102 113m	
Report Distribution: no misdirected reports; sentinel event!! (Monthly)	Ward 22 complained of nonreceipt of five Gram stain reports from 7 thru 11 Dec 95	
INTRALABORATORY PROCESS WORK FLOW SEGMENT		
Postdeterminative Product Finalization and Specimen Handling: no loss of product or specimen integrity! (Monthly)	No OFI identified x 12 mo	
Reference Laboratory Studies: no adverse effect on patient outcome! (Monthly)	No OFI identified x 6 mo	
Analytical Quality: no major discrepancies! (Monthly)	No OFI identified x 7 mo	

OFI = opportunity for improvement

Evaluation of QI Data, TQM System, CQI Process	Action and Action Person: (Date Initiated)	Assessment of Overall Improvement
No incident reports since June 95 (x 6 mo)	Select a focused study for Mar 96 ACTION: Medical Director	Improvement of the QI process is in progress
1. All TATs are marginally excessive consistent with 6 staff vacancies 2. The transportation process requires investigation 3. Thresholds could be too low; if they are reasonable, TAT might be reflecting staff shortage or underutilization of tests.	1. Evaluate transportation process 2. Evaluate the thresholds 3. If thresholds are reasonable, evaluate lab staff shortage versus med staff utilization of tests 4. Or modify TAT threshold levels ACTION: Supervisor	Improvement of the QI process is in progress
On target but TAT is increasing; there's been one tech vacancy in this unit since Nov 95	Consider restaffing the unit or sending workload to a ref lab ACTION: Supervisor	Improvement of the TAT process is in progress–so far
There was a problem in distributing Gram stain reports to Ward 22; the cause is unknown; computer was functioning okay	Finish investigative evaluation of distribution of Gram stain reports to Ward 22 for Jan 93 ACTION: Supervisor	Process of Gram stain reporting to Ward 22 needs improvement
On target x 12 mo; this is an too long a period of indicator inactivity	1. Begin a quarterly review 2. Select a focused study for Jan 96 ACTION: Supervisor	Improvement of an unduly delayed QI process is in progress
On target x 6 mo	Select a focused study for Feb 96 ACTION: Supervisor	Improvement of the QI process is in progress
On target x 7 mo	Select a focused study for Mar 96 ACTION: Supervisor	Improvement of the QI process is in progress

Microbiology Quality Profile: Dec 95

Indicator Grouping/ Specific Indicator: Threshold (Periodicity)	QI Data Observations (Date trend started) J A S O N D
Diagnostic Quality (Peer Review): no major discrepancies! (Monthly)	. . . . . Provider Code #. . . . . 0 0 0 0 0 0 0 = no discrepancies
Predeterminative Specimen Processing: no loss of specimen integrity (Monthly)	No OFI identified x 3 mo
PRELABORATORY PROCESS WORK FLOW SEGMENT	
Validation: > 2% invalidation rate (Monthly)	No OFI identified x 5 mo
Laboratory Product Selection: in keeping with laboratory and clinical standards (Monthly)	. . . . . Provider Code #. . . . . 0 0 0 0 0 0 0 = no discrepancies
OPERATIVE RESOURCE MANAGEMENT WORK FLOW SEGMENT	
Workload Management: a. Productivity quotients: within established limits (Monthly) 1. PQp (paid): 30 to 35 min/hr	m = minutes/work hour 34 37 41 40 33 30 m
2. PQwl (specified): 40 to 45 min/hr	62 65 75 70 58 56 m
Personnel Management (Monthly) a. Work force: 1. Vacancy rate: Technologists: > 10% vacancy	FTE = full time equivalent 6 FTE vacancies in Dec 95 25 23 23 21 21 21 %
b. Utilization 1. 16 Hour shifts: none!	0 0 0 0 0 0 s
2. Overtime: > 500 hours	624 649 642 591 573 526 h

QM = quality management

Evaluation of QI Data, TQM System, CQI Process	Action and Action Person: (Date Initiated)	Assessment of Overall Improvement
On target for at least 6 mo	Select a focused study on bronchoalveolar lavage interpretations ACTION: Supervisor	Improvement of the QI process is in progress
On target x 3 mo; baseline being established	None needed	Improvement of the process is in progress
On target; but Ward 22 is performing poorly in other sections	None needed per current sectional data; but review Ward 22 as a specific indicator for Jan 96 ACTION: Supervisor	Improvement of the QI process is in progress
On target x 6 mos; a baseline has been established	1. Change periodicity to quarterly 2. Select a focused indicator for Apr 96 ACTION: Medical Director	Improvement of the QI process is in progress
PQp was excessive from Aug thru Oct as a result of staff shortage; PQp is now on target	1. Fill six vacancies ACTION: Admn Sup 2. Continue innovative staffing ACTION: Supervisor	Improvement of the staffing process is in progress
PQwl is very high, reflecting significant staff shortage; however, trend is toward improvement		
Excessive vacancy rate; the staffing level has plateaued x 3 mo	1. Fill six vacancies 2. Improve QM interface between Lab and Personnel Office ACTION: Admin Supervisor	Ineffective extra-dept QI process: Lab needs support of Personnel Office
On target	None needed	Effective
Excessive; indicates stress; appears to be plateaued	See above staffing requirement	Effective but expensive

Microbiology QualityProfile: Dec 95

Indicator Grouping/ Specific Indicator: Threshold (Periodicity)	QI Data Observations (Date trend started) J A S O N D
c. Availability: 1. % availability: < 80%	81 86 84 87 84 81 %
Continuing Education < 3 hour/mo (Monthly)	No OFI identified x 12 mo in the face of short staff
Methods & Procedures Review: must be on time! (Annually per Monthly Schedule)	Monthly review schedule has been up-to-date x 12 mo in the face of staff shortages
Computer Management: a. Unscheduled downtime: > 24 hours (Monthly)	3 3 2 30 0 50 h
Equipment: repair must be complete within one quarter (Quarterly)	
a. Microscan	Needs installation of computer interface (Apr 95)
b. BacTec	Needs rewiring (Jul 94)
c. Parasitology Hood	Needs new filters (Sep 95)
Supply: no potential for laboratory service limitations (Quarterly)	No OFI identified x 2 qtrs
Facility: no potential for equipment failure, biological spoilage or personnel stress (Monthly)	Poor temperature control in Mycology and Virology labs; seasonal problem compounded by proximity of Mtb autoclave (Aug 95)

Evaluation of QI Data, TQM System, CQI Process	Action and Action Person: (Date Initiated)	Assessment of Overall Improvement
Consistently on target but slowly decreasing; new incentives are needed	Outstanding motivation needs to be recognized ACTION: Supervisor	Effective BUT watch for deterioration
On target x 12 mo; this is too long!!	Select focused study ACTION: Supervisor	Improve the QI process
Consistently on target x 12 mo; this indicator has been inactive for too long!	Select a focused study for Feb 96 ACTION: Supervisor	Improvement of the QI process is in progress
Inordinate amount of down time affecting second shift and weekend staff; pattern is random, over all, but could be slowly increasing	1. Continue liaison with Computer Operations 2. Review and upgrade backup plan ACTION: Lab Manager	Improvement is in progress: Watch QM interface with Comp Operations
QI Note: This opportunity to improve Medical Maintenance support will be raised to the hospital administration by the Department Medical Director		
Inoperable without interface; poor response by Med Maint	Continue liaison with Med Maint ACTION: Lab Manager (Apr 95)	Overall ineffective QI process; protracted Med Maint response is due to their being understaffed: Need hosp admin support
Resolved after 1 1/2 years	None needed; issue closed (Jul 94)	
Inoperable without filters; poor response by Med Maint	Continue liaison with Med Maint ACTION: Lab Manager (Sep 95)	
On target x 2 qtrs	None needed	The QI process is ongoing
Recurrent problem; seasonal; in view of the ventilation/hood problem, this needs to be addressed with a major renovation study encompassing all environmental control factors	Coordinate major renovation study with engineers ACTION: Lab Manager (Aug 91)	Ineffective action and QI process: Need support of facility engineers and admin funding

Microbiology QualityProfile: Dec 95

Indicator Grouping/ Specific Indicator: Threshold (Periodicity)	QI Data Observations (Date trend started) J A S O N D
Budget: meet planned expenditure within ± 5% of the monthly target (Monthly)	-1 -2 0 0 5 +10 % Fiscal year starts in Oct
ORGANIZATIONAL RESOURCE MANAGEMENT WORK FLOW SEGMENT	
Internal Quality Improvement (QI) a. Assessment: there must be evidence of continuous improvement! (Monthly)	Continuous improvement is documented with several opportunities being pursued; however, appropriate assessment has been delayed in several instances
b. Communication: there must be adequate sharing of lessons learned! (Monthly)	No OFI identified x 9 mo At least 1 hour of QI in-service training per month has been provided
External QI (Monthly) a. Proficiency surveys: all results must be < 2 SDI or found "Acceptable"!!	SDI = Standard Deviation Interval (Index) Results of two surveys returned in this reporting period: both 100% correct. All surveys have been correct for last 12 months
b. JCAHO/CAP/other inspection: no unresolved findings!	No unresolved findings
c. Incident reports and complaints: every report is a sentinel event!!	No incident reports or complaints received x 12 mo
Quality Anticipation (QAn) Quarterly a. Organizational research: all milestones will be attained! (Quarterly)	0 – – 0 – – 0 = no milestone missed

Evaluation of QI Data, TQM System, CQI Process	Action and Action Person: (Date Initiated)	Assessment of Overall Improvement
Overexpended due to increased workload and new instrument costs along with the usual frontloaded contracts at the beginning of fiscal year	1. May need a "plus-up" 2. Identify an alternative accounting system to avoid front loading ACTION: Lab Manager	Effective; the excess expenditure has been anticipated: Improvement is in progress
The assessment step has inadequately increased employee safety, report distribution, & personnel, equipment, and facility mgmt	Monitor the continued assessment of the safety, report distribution, staffing, equipment, facility issues ACTION: Supervisor	Improvement of the QI process is in progress
On target x 9 mo; this is too long a period of indicator inactivity	Select a focused study for Apr 96 ACTION: Supervisor	
QI Note: The QM team is to identify an alternative QI evaluation process for use in adjunct to the JCAHO ten-step process; there is a need to improve lab QI response to OFIs of varying complexity		
The external PT program has been on target x 12 mo; there is a need to review internal PT per CLIA 88	1. Review the selection of external PT surveys for completeness 2. Per CLIA 88, ascertain the need for internal PT ACTION: Supervisor	Effective; improvement of the QI process is ongoing
On target since last inspection	None needed	Effective
On target x 12 mo; this general survey approach is not effective	Select a focused study directed at a key customer ACTION: Supervisor	Ineffective: QI process needs improvement
No report scheduled; two research surveys are in progress	None needed	Effective QAn process

Microbiology QualityProfile: Dec 95

Indicator Grouping/ Specific Indicator: Threshold (Periodicity)	QI Data Observations (Date trend started) J A S O N D
b. Developmental: all milestones will be attained! (Quarterly)	– 0 – – 0 –
c. Final implementation: all milestones will be attained! (Quarterly)	– – 0 – – 0
Quality Actualization (QAc) (Monthly) a. Team building 1. Morale: no adverse impact on team effectiveness	Morale is decreased in the Mtb lab unit based on a Nov team survey and review of supporting indicators; these problems are linked to a recent contagion incident See Employee Safety Outcome
2. Skills training (TST): no skills lacking that adversely affect team effectiveness	TST schedule is as planned all shifts are involved; has been consistent x 12 mo
b. Team maintenance 1. Continuing TST	As noted above
2. Personnel actions: none overdue!	0 0 0 0 0 0 Same trend since Mar 95 0 = none missed
3. Personnel incentives: none overdue!	0 0 0 0 0 0 Same trend since Mar 95
c. Team effectiveness 1. Decision making: no problem too hard or unresolved > 3 mo	Most opportunities have been adequately addressed by the section team; if too hard, they have been submitted to the correct echelon or lateral department EXCEPT!! for resolving facility temperature and equipment maintenance problems!!

Evaluation of QI Data, TQM System, CQI Process	Action and Action Person: (Date Initiated)	Assessment of Overall Improvement
No report scheduled; two pilot projects are in progress	None needed	Effective
On target x 6 mo; two newly implemented activities are in progress	Establish 6 month QI baselines for the two new activities using focused studies ACTION: Supervisor	Effective
Morale decreased; employees are very concerned over loss of infection control due to malfunctioning hood	Increase team bldg in the Mtb unit; assure the employees that the lab is back in control ACTION: Supervisor	Team morale needs improvement; the QI process is intact
On target x 12 mo; this is too long a period of indicator inactivity	Select a focused study of the effectiveness of the TST program for Jan 96 ACTION: Supervisor	Improvement of the QI process is in progress
--------	--------	--------
On target x 10 mo	Select a focused study to improve personnel management for Feb 96 ACTION: Supervisor	Improvement of the QAc process is ongoing
On target x 8 mo	Select a focused study to improve personnel management for Mar 96 ACTION: Supervisor	Improvement of the QAc process is ongoing
Overall on target EXCEPT for stated issues	Select a focused study to measure effectiveness of the coordination of facility renovation and equipment maintenance at lab QM interface levels for Jan 96 ACTION: Medical Director	Ineffective action and QI and QAc processes

QI Note: 1. Initiate monitoring "Leadership Commitment" as a new indicator topic as of Jan 96
2. Evaluate changing the periodicity of reporting for this entire QAc grouping to a quarterly schedule—except for the Team Effectiveness indicators

APPENDIX F
Quality Profile: Transfusion Service

APPENDIX F
Quality Profile: QI Report Dec 95
Section: Transfusion Service

Indicator Grouping/ Specific Indicator: Threshold (Periodicity)	QI Data Observations (Date trend started) J A S O N D
POSTLABORATORY OUTCOME WORK FLOW SEGMENT	
Customer Satisfaction: any positive or negative report; sentinel event!! (Monthly)	1a. Due to clinical staff complaints, hospital has formed an administrative Task Force to assist the Trans Service in filling staff vacancies (Dec 95)
	1b. Patient had a hemolytic reaction on Ward 22; See Patient Care Outcome/Utilization Indicators
Patient Care Outcome: no threat to life or limb; sentinel event!! (Monthly) a. Hemolytic transfusion reaction none!!	0 = adverse outcome . . . . . . .Patient Code # . . . . 0 0 0 0 0 53* * = Nonfatal hemolytic transfusion reaction (Patient #53) on Ward 22 (Med) during the 12 to 8 shift: nurse mistakenly mixed the identify of 2 brothers on the same ward
Employee Safety Outcome: no potential or actual hazard; sentinel event! (Monthly) a. Biological	Recent concern of technologists over HIV has unmasked their perception that there is need for improved control (Nov 95)
b. Fire	No OFI identified x 12 mo
c. Electrical	No OFI identified x 12 mo
d. Chem/Carcinogen	No OFI identified x 12 mo
e. Radionuclide	Not applicable
f. Waste Disposal	No OFI identified x 12 mo
g. Environmental	The staff complained of heat in Room A03 (platelet storage) in Dec; usually is a problem in the summer

! = sentinel event OT = overtime HTF = hospital task force

Evaluation of QI Data, TQM System, CQI Process	Action and Action Person: (Date Initiated)	Assessment of Overall Improvement
Evidence over several months has shown that QI/QAn/QAc programs, QM interface, and QF process are ineffective	Coordinate with the Hospital Task Force (HTF) ACTION: Section Medical Director	Ineffective TZM system, QM interface, and QI process: Section needs improved intra- and extra-departmental support
Hospital assistance is being provided to perform QI functions thru the Task Force	Design focused stdy of blood util on Ward 22 for Jan 96 ACTION: Task Force	
Reaction was non-fatal; serious problem with Ward 22 staff, especially the 12-8 (night) shift, who are not receiving training in patient identification and transfusion techniques; tng may require OT expenditure	1. Coordinate with C, Nursg and C, Med regarding training & supervisory responsibilities 2. Study use of "floating" staff 3. Study pt identification process ACTION: Medical Director	Ineffective QI process: Needs improved response at HTF level to a known operative-level training requirement
There is need for increased training and improving staff awareness of universal precaution rationale	Enhance biohazard training program by Jan 96 ACTION: Hospital Infection Control (Nov 95)	There is effective contagion control BUT infect control training needs to be improved
These 4 indicators have been on target x 12 mo; there has been no improvement over an inordinate amount of time	1.Exclude any immediate problems ACTION: Dept Lab Safety Officer 2.Establish focused studies over the next year ACTION: Acting Supervisor	Improvement has been stalled due to staffing problems; prioritize QI carefully until section is rebuilt
QI Note: There is evidence of an ineffective TQM system, QM interface, and QI process; see notes under Blood Product Utilization, Postderminative Finalization, and Facility indicator groupings		

Transfusion Service Quality Profile: Dec 95

Indicator Grouping/ Specific Indicator: Threshold (Periodicity)	QI Data Observations (Date trend started) J A S O N D
POSTLABORATORY PROCESS WORK FLOW SEGMENT	
Blood Component Utilization: in keeping with joint laboratory and clinical standards! (Monthly) a. Packed red blood cell utilization: threshold on file	0 = no provider identified . . . . . Provider Code # . . . . . 0 0 0 0 0 46* * = on-the-spot report re "nurse #46" and a transfusion reaction on Ward 22 during the 12 to 8 shift
b. Frozen blood utilization: threshold on file	0 0 0 0 0 0 % Baseline started in July
c. Fresh frozen plasma (FFP) utilization: threshold TBD	Clinical indicators, for study of FFP in coordination with Med Dept
Throughput of Index Procedures: (Monthly) a. Type and crossmatch TAT: > 4 hours average TAT	h = averaged hours 3 3 3.5 4 4.5 5 h
b. Type and crossmatch backlog: none>4 hours TAT per day	0 0 0 0 32 64 c c = averaged backlogged cases per day per mo
Report/Component Distribution: no misdirected reports or products; sentinel event!! (Quarterly)	No OFI identified x 12 mo

TAT = turnaround time FTE = full time employment

Evaluation of QI Data, TQM System, CQI Process	Action and Action Person: (Date Initiated)	Assessment of Overall Improvement
The OFI at hand is related to the transfusion reaction on Ward 22; nurse "#46" on 12 to 8 shift is cited as responsible	1. Appraise training needs for all Ward 22 shifts ACTION: Chief Nurse 2. Schedule refresher training for all Ward 22 shifts per appraised needs 3. Investigate all systemic causes ACTION: Medical Director	Ineffective QI process: Needs improved follow-up on training requirement, especially for 4 to 12 and 12 to 8 ward shifts
On target x 6 mo	None needed, yet	QI process is effective to date
QI Note: Improvement of this important aspect of care (IAC) is not as critical as it is for other operational activities such as Staffing and Analytical QC: therefore, postpone this indicator for now.		
1. There is excessive TAT and backlog with progressive deterioration associated with severe staff shortage, loss of supervisor, and increasing signs of employee stress 2. Dec backlog represents need for 1 Additional FTE	1. Basic human resource problems have to be solved 2. Innovative staffing and motivation approaches are needed 3. Begin use of reference lab ACTION: Acting Supervisor	Ineffective QC, QI, QAn and QAc processes are worsening: Needs improvement of severely critical systemic problems
On target x 12 mo; no improvement over an inordinate amount of time	Select a focused study for Jan 96 ACTION: Acting Supervisor	Improvement decisions were stalled but now are in progress

Transfusion Service Quality Profile: Dec 95

Indicator Grouping/ Specific Indicator: Threshold (Periodicity)	QI Data Observations (Date trend started) J A S O N D
INTRALABORATORY PROCESS WORK FLOW SEGMENT	
Postdeterminative Report/Component Finalization and Specimen Handling: no loss of product or specimen integrity!! (Quarterly) a. Special study: * platelet storage ambient temperature: < 20 to > 24°C (°C = degrees Centigrade)! *Ordered by medical director after an on-the-spot report on 21 December Jul–Nov temps are archival monthly averages; Dec temp is months high!	25 25 24 23 23 27° C x = averaged/look-back 1. 27°C was Dec high temp 2. Staff complaints over xs temperature in the platelet storage Room A03 began in mid Dec 95 3. A new frozen blood freezer was moved into Rm A03 on 15 Dec without attention to the additional heat produced. The freezer was removed on 21 Dec 4. Lab discarded 5 platelet units (10%) after 21 Dec report of 27°C temp 5. Ambient temp has been in control since 21 Dec
Reference Laboratory Studies: no adverse impact on patient outcome! (Quarterly)	No OFI identified x 3 qtrs
Analytical Quality: no major discrepancies!! (Monthly)	0 0 1 1 2 4 These occurrences represent mistakes in interpretation of crossmatch and other antibody-antigen reactions at the bench by more than one individual One incident report in Dec involved a case of inaccurate temperature recording for the blood reefer (refrigerator)
Diagnostic Quality: (Peer Review): no major discrepancies! (– – – – – –)	No documented peer control or assessment is being performed
Predeterminative Specimen Processing: no loss of specimen integrity! (Monthly)	No OFI identified x 4 mo

Evaluation of QI Data, TQM System, CQI Process	Action and Action Person: (Date Initiated)	Assessment of Overall Improvement
1. Temp QC is off target!! Bimodal pattern 2. Seasonal problem abated but not resolved: inadequate response by QI team 3. Dramatic increase in the last month without adequate response by QI team 4. There is no recording alarm system for the ambient platelet temperature 5. There might be a need for a lock box on wall thermostat	1. Install temp recorder/alarm 2. Investigate need for thermostat lock 3. Consider use of storage incubator vs another room 4. Hold inservice tng on QC and QI re platelet storage 5. Coordinate with Fac Engineers to resolve summer temp problem 6. Report temp as a maximum, not as an average ACTION: Acting Supervisor	Ineffective QC and QI processes!! Improvement of QC and QI processes is needed immediately QI Note: conduct an investigative evaluation of QC and TQM programs immediately
On target x 3 qtrs; no improvement over an inordinate amount of time	Select a focused indicator for Mar 96 ACTION: Acting Supervisor	Improvement was stalled but now is in progress
1. Increasing incidence of major discrepancies over the last 4 mo; not limited to any one person 2. Supervisor resigned in Nov; acting Supervisor is in place 3. Critical staff shortage persists	1. Increase overview of bench QC 2. Consider automation of hi vol procedures ACTION: Acting Supervisor 1. Fill staff vacancies; place priority on supervisor job 2. Determine interim processing options: ie,curtailment and referral! ACTION: Medical Director	Ineffective QC and QI processes! Resolving personnel shortage requires support of Hosp Admin, Personnel Office, and Task Force Inffective QI process to date
--------	QI Note: It is the opinion of the departmental quality management team that peer control and assessment must be implemented	
On target; baseline being established	None needed	Effective QI process to date

Transfusion Service Quality Profile: Dec 95

Indicator Grouping/ Specific Indicator: Threshold (Periodicity)	J	A	S	O	N	D	
	QI Data Observations (Date trend started)						
PRELABORATORY PROCESS WORK FLOW SEGMENT							
Validation: > 0% invalidation rate; ie, (no cases invalidated)!! (Monthly)	Because this is a sentinel event, invalidation is reported on a case-by-case basis						
a. Ward 22 staff	0	0	3	3	3	4	c
b. Ward 49 staff	0	0	1	0	0	0	c
c. Ward 71 staff	0	0	0	0	1	0	c
d. Ward 73 staff	0	0	0	1	0	0	c
e. Lab staff	0	0	0	0	0	0	c
	c = number of separate cases invalidated. These cases represent various examples of improper specimen collection rejected by the lab						
Blood Product/Procedure Selection: in keeping with joint laboratory and clinical standards! (Monthly)	0 = no provider identified; – – = not implemented						
	. . . . Provider Code #						
a. Packed red blood cells	– –	– –	– –	0	0	0	
b. Fresh frozen plasma (FFP): the standards are to be determined	Blood utilization committee (BUC) requests the lab establish this indicator to focus on the Thoracic Surgery Service practice of selecting FFP based on findings reported in BUC committee minutes						
OPERATIVE RESOURCE MANAGEMENT WORK FLOW SEGMENT							
Workload Management:							
a. Productivity quotients: within established limits (Monthly)	m = minutes/workhour						
1. PQp (paid): 30 to 38 min/hr	39	45	49	52	56	61	m
2. PQwl (workloaded): 46 to 51 min/hr	50	59	64	69	72	83	m

CAP = College of American Pathologists

Evaluation of QI Data, TQM System, CQI Process	Action and Action Person: (Date Initiated)	Assessment of Overall Improvement
Ward 22 has a severe problem with unabated occurrence of validation discrepancies in spite of 3 inservice training sessions; problems are restricted to night (12-8) shift; are temp "floater" staff involved? Ward staff shortage persists. Training problem was noted in Sep 94 CAP interim inspection. See related notes under patient Outcome and External Inspection indicator groupings	1. Maintain vigilance at specimen receipt window 2. Teach on the ward intensively 3. Schedule meeting with MD and RN directors regarding processing training and supervisory improvements ACTION: Section Medical Director	Ineffective QC and QI processes; specimen collection is out of control on Ward 22! Since an 1994 interim CAP survey deficiency, no effect of external QI on QC: Needs extensive improvement at interdept QM interface
On target x 3 mo; baseline is being established	Continue baseline ACTION: Blood Bank Manager (if there is one) or Medical Director	Effective QI process
BUC has identified a need for improvement of FFP selection by the Thoracic Surgery Service (TSS): joint selection standards need to be established	Coordinate with C, TSS, to establish improved clinical indications for requesting FFP; to begin monitoring in Mar 96 ACTION: Medical Director	Improvement of the FFP selection process is in progress
PQP is excessive and increasing suggesting severe employee stress situation	Pursue the hiring for vacant staff positions ACTION: Department Administrative Supervisor (if there is one) or Dept Lab Manager	Ineffective hospital QI process: This section needs hospital admin and Personnel Office support
PQwl is consistently excessive; a steadily worsening trend		

Transfusion Service Quality Profile: Dec 95

Indicator Grouping/ Specific Indicator: Threshold (Periodicity)	QI Data Observations (Date trend started) J A S O N D
Personnel Management (Monthly)	
a. Work Force:	– = no vacancy to report
1. Vacancy rate:	– – – – 100 100%
Supervisor: no vacancy allowed; sentinel event!	1 FTE vacancy since Nov 95
Technologists: > 10% vacancy	21 31 38 45 50 55 % 6 FTE vacancies in Dec 95
b. Utilization	s = 16 hour shifts
1. 16 hour shifts: none!!	6 8 9 10 11 12 s
2. Overtime (OT) > 126 hours	h = hours 419 450 477 532 655 702 h 30% of OT in Dec was performed by cross trained personnel
c. Availability:	
1. % availability (technologists): < 80%	90 85 84 83 79 78 %
Continuing education < 3 hour/mo! (Monthly)	Reflects hrs of immunohematology inservice training
a. Trans Svc staff	1 1 0 1 0 0 h
b. Ward 22 staff	Ward 22 evening and night shifts have not been involved in routine or special inservice training re transfusion technique (see External QI notes)
Methods & Procedures Review: must be on time!! (Annually per Monthly Schedule)	SOPs have not been reviewed per schedule for 6 mo

Evaluation of QI Data, TQM System, CQI Process	Action and Action Person: (Date Initiated)	Assessment of Overall Improvement
Supervisor position vacated in Nov 95	1. Fill 7 positions with priority on supervisor position 2. Request class action pay raise ACTION: Admin Supervisor 1. Determine interim staffing options 2. Send routine abo and prenatals to reference lab 3. Increase technical automation ACTION: Acting Supervisor 1. Transfer cross trnd staff from other sections ACTION: Dept Lab Manager	Ineffective QI process: Obtain emergency assistance from Hospital Admin and Personnel Office to relieve staff vacancy problem
There are six vacancies and the trend is increasing alarmingly		
Excessive and increasing	Implement more innovative staffing providing more crosstrained staff from other sections ACTION: Acting Sup with Dept Lab Manager	Ineffective QI process: Requires Hosp Admin and Personnel Office assistance
Excessive; has become increasingly severe		
Off target!!; TREND: technologist availability is steadily decreasing.	1. Fill vacancies 2. Increase incentives ACTION: Acting Supervisor	Has been effective BUT!! this QI parameter began deteriorating in Nov
Off target on regular schedule! Are nondaytime personnel being trained??	Maintain the CME goal of 3 hours/mo ACTION: Acting Supervisor	Ineffective CME and QI processes: Improvement needed
Education and training program is not servicing nondaytime shifts on wards	Coordinate with Chief of Nursing and Medicine to facilitate Ed/tng Program ACTION: Medical Director	Ineffective followup of CAP requirements for improvement!
Off target because of staff shortage	Resume review schedule, using cross-sectional support ACTION: Acting Supervisor	Improvement of the review process is in progress

Transfusion Service Quality Profile: Dec 95

Indicator Grouping/ Specific Indicator: Threshold (Periodicity)	QI Data Observations (Date trend started) J A S O N D	
Computer Management: a. Unscheduled downtime: > 24 hours (Monthly)	No OFI identified x 2 mo	
Equipment: repair must be complete within one quarter!! (Quarterly)	0 – – 0 – – 0 = no OFI identified – = no report scheduled	
Supply: no potential for laboratory service limitations!! (Quarterly) a. Overdue supplies: none > 14 d	0 = no supplies overdue – – 0 – – 0 None overdue since Apr 95	
Facility: no potential for equipment failure, biological spoilage, or personnel stress!! (Quarterly)	– x – – – x * x = an adverse incident – = no OFI identified * Staff complaint of excess heat in platelet storage room (A03) occurs in Dec, routinely in the summer months, eg, Aug	
Budget: meet planned expenditure within ± 5% of the monthly target (Monthly)	+4 +5 +3 +2 +9 +11 % Fiscal year starts in Oct; a front-loaded budget is in use; data do not include wage expenditures	
ORGANIZATIONAL RESOURCE MANAGEMENT WORK FLOW SEGMENT		
Internal Quality Improvement (QI) (Monthly) a. Assessment: there must be evidence of continuous improvement!!	There is lack of effective assessment in several key management areas as shown by their respective indicators	
b. Communication: there must be adequate sharing of lessons learned: > 1 hr training per month!!	Communicating QI lessons learned is greatly limited by staff shortage and lack of time for nonworkloaded activities; there has been < 1 hr of QI inservice training per month for the last 3 months	

Evaluation of QI Data, TQM System, CQI Process	Action and Action Person: (Date Initiated)	Assessment of Overall Improvement
On target x 2 mo; baseline is being established	None needed	Improvement of the QI process is in progress
No report scheduled; next report due Jan 96	----------	----------
On target x 2 qtrs	Select a focused study ASAP ACTION: Acting Supervisor	Improvement of QI process is in prog
Note: Lab product storage (eg, rbc, platelets, cryo) could be reported here as a "supply" indicator		
Room A03 (Plat Storage Room) has seasonal ventilation or air balance problem; See Postdeterminative Finalization notes re platelet storage problem	Schedule engineer study to assess cause and feasibility of resolution of hi ambient summer temp ACTION: Acting Supervisor (Dec 95)	Ineffective QI process: Needs improvement of QM interface
Overexpenditure at start of fiscal year causes a skewing of the budget data; and there is a need to capture wage data	Seek an alternative accounting system to even out contract expenditures and capture wage data ACTION: Lab Manager	Improvement of the budget process is in progress
Both indicators support the need for improving the assessment and communication steps of the QI process. This is particularly evident under the customer satisfaction, patient care, postdeterminative product handling, TAT, analytical quality, workload management, and staffing indicator groupings	1. Improve staffing 2. Start team rebuilding (QAc) 3. Begin quality planning (QAn) 4. Bolster training of QI improvement program process ACTION: Medical Director	Ineffective internal QI process: Improving staffing requires hosp admin assistance!! Improving section team integrity requires department facilitation

Transfusion Service Quality Profile: Dec 95

Indicator Grouping/ Specific Indicator: Threshold (Periodicity)	QI Data Observations (Date trend started) J A S O N D
External QI (Monthly)	SDI = Standard Deviation Interval (Interval)
a. Proficiency surveys: all results must be > 2 SDI or found "Acceptable"!!	– = no survey reported 0 = no deficiencies UA = "Unacceptable"
1. Antibody screen profile	– – UA – – UA
b. JCAHO/CAP/other inspection: no unresolved deficiencies!!	1. Ineffective training of evening (4-12) and night (12-8) nursing shifts 2. The training problem re evening and night nursing shifts cited in 1994 CAP interim survey is still unresolved
c. Incident reports and complaints: every report is a sentinel event!!	0 0 1 2 2 3 Adverse complaints re xs TAT in Sep, Oct, Nov, and Dec. One report in Dec concerned the hemolytic transfusion reaction on Ward 22
Quality Anticipation (QAn) (Quarterly)	
a. Organizational research: all milestones will be attained!!	No new survey projects have been scheduled x 6 mo
b. Development: all milestones will be attained!!	No new projects scheduled x 6 mo
c. Implementation: all milestones will be attained!!	– – 2/3 – – 0/1 – = no report scheduled 2/3 = 2 of 3 milestones attained

CAP = College of American Pathologists XS = excess

Evaluation of QI Data, TQM System, CQI Process	Action and Action Person: (Date Initiated)	Assessment of Overall Improvement
This recent trend of inaccuracy appears related to staff shortage and workload stress; poses as a problem in view of CLIA '88 requirements: lab could be closed! See Analytical Quality Grouping data	1. Correct the staffing problem 2. Review this report with the technical staff 3. Send portion of workload to reference lab immediately ACTION: Acting Supervisor	Ineffective TQM system; QI, QAn, and QAc programs all need improvement: Assessment is pending on follow-up of remedial actions
1. Ward 22 training is ineffective; the need to enhance ward staff tng is critical; 2. Followup on CAP inspection, including interim survey, has been ineffective	1. Upgrade the plans for education and training on Ward 22 2. Review the process of inspection follow-up ACTION: Department Chairman (Dec 95)	Ineffective follow-up of external QI findings: Entire external QI process needs improvement
Hemolytic reaction due to mistaken patient identify on Ward 22; see data under Customer Satisfaction, Patient Outcome, and Invalidation groupings	Same as mentioned under Customer Satisfaction, Patient Care Outcome, and Invalidation groupings	Ineffective external QI process requires improvement at the interdepartmental Qual Impvmt/Risk Mgmt level!
This phase of the QAn program has been neglected	Reprioritize and reschedule QAn as part of QAc team building effort ACTION: Medical Director Staff vacancy must be solved to bring QAn back on track or dept must provide ancillary support ACTION: Admin Supervisor	Ineffective QAn and QI processes: Vacancy problem must be solved to realize effective infrastructural programs such as strategic planning
This phase of the QAn program has been neglected		
Increasing failure to meet milestones without QI follow-up due to supervisor and staff shortage		

QI Note: The implementation project missed December was designed to enhance Ward 22 staff training in transfusion techniques, including nondaytime staff; this was a critical milestone, as evidenced by the hemolytic reaction on Ward 22.

JCAHO = Joint Commission on Accreditation of Healthcare Organizations

Transfusion Service Quality Profile: Dec 95

Indicator Grouping/ Specific Indicator: Threshold (Periodicity)	QI Data Observations (Date trend started) J A S O N D
Quality Actualization (QA) (Monthly) a. Team building: 1. Morale no adverse impact on team effectiveness!!	1. Morale is poor based on anecdotal evidence, causing documented ineffectiveness; two more resignations have been threatened 2. There are obvious signs of staff "burn out" as evidenced by several supporting indicators 3. Main cause of morale problems is staff shortage and excessive workload
2. Skills training (TST): no skills lacking that adversely affect team effectiveness: < 1 hour/qtr for TST!!	1. Lab staff needs special attention to improve morale and effectiveness 2. Ward 22 evening & night shifts need educ/tng in team skills building (plus instruction in transfusion technique)
b. Team maintenance: 1. Continuing TST	As noted above
2. Personnel actions: none overdue!!	0 0 0 0 1* 1 0 = none overdue * = resolved late
3. Personnel incentives: none overdue!!	0 0 0 0 0 0 No new incentives have been initiated in 6 mo
c. Team effectiveness 1. Decision making: no problem too hard or unresolved > 3 months!!	All three infrastructural programs (QI/QAn/QAc) are crippled; the platelet storage problem is a good example of disabled quality management and poor organizational team decision making

!! = sentinel event

Evaluation of QI Data, TQM System, CQI Process	Action and Action Person: (Date Initiated)	Assessment of Overall Improvement
Staff shortage and the resultant overburdening workload are crippling team morale and effectiveness; there is no objective data derived from direct employee input	1. Determine reasons why techs have been leaving (other than staff shortage); run a survey of current staff; review exit surveys 2. Resolve workload-staffing burdens ACTION: Medical Director	Ineffective QAc and QI processes: Staffing action requires highest level assistance
1. Time for team bldg in Trans Service must be made available by innovative staffing and scheduling in lab and ward 2. Improved coordination is needed between interdepartmental leadership re Ward 22 training	1. Increase tm bldg in Trans Service 2. Coordinate with Chiefs of Nursing and Med re trng in tm bldg and trans technique on Ward 22 ACTION: Medical Director	Ineffective QAc and QI processes in Trans Svc and Ward 22
--------	--------	--------
One promotion action overdue this month; trend developing	Meet personnel needs on time ACTION: Admin Supervisor	Ineffective QAc and QI processes
No new incentives provided for 6 mo when they have been especially needed	Institute new incentives by Jan 96 ACTION: Lab Manager	QAc and QI processes need improvement
Team decision making is currently grossly ineffective due to staff shortage and excessive workload	1. Coordinate with the HTF and fill all vacancies 2. Rebuild the team 3. Reprioritize all organizational activities 4. Hire a TQM consultant ACTION: Medical Director	Seriously ineffective QI, QAn, & QAc processes: Several problems are "too hard" for this section to improve
QI NOTE: Begin monitoring "Leadership Commitment" as a new, ongoing monthly QAc indicator grouping for Jan 96; target departmental, service, and section level leadership involvement in support of the QI, QAn, and QAc programs		

APPENDIX G
Quality Profile: Histopathology Section

APPENDIX G
Quality Profile: QI Report Dec 95
Section: Histopathology

Indicator Grouping/ Specific Indicator: Threshold (Periodicity)	QI Data Observations (Date trend started) J A S O N D	
POSTLABORATORY OUTCOME WORK FLOW SEGMENT		
Customer Satisfaction: any positive or negative report; sentinel event!! (Monthly)	Department has been targeted by a Hospital Quality Management Task Force to resolve a protracted surgical TAT problem as reflected by the Histopathology Quality Profile	
a. Major customer survey (Quarterly)	The new QI protocol is being coordinated with the Chief of Dermatology Service	
Patient Care Outcome: no threat to life or limb; sentinel event!! (Monthly)	. . . . . . .Patient Code # . . . . – – 0 0 0 53* 0 = no problem – = not implemented	
Employee Safety Outcome: no potential or actual hazard; sentinel event! (Monthly)	OFI = opportunity for improvement	
a. Biological	No OFI identified x 12 mo	
b. Fire	Number of fire alarms not adequate per fire marshal inspection (Aug 94)	
c. Electrical	No OFI identified x 6 mo	
d. Chem/Carcinogen	Excessive fumes due to poor ventilation over grossing table per on-site CAP inspection (May 93)	
e. Radionuclide	Not applicable	
f. Waste Disposal	No OFI identified x 5 mo	
g. Environmental	See Chemical Carcinogen indicator above, and Facilitygrouping under operative resources management	

! = sentinel event TAT = turnaround time

Evaluation of QI Data, TQM System, CQI Process	Action and Action Person: (Date Initiated)	Assessment of Overall Improvement
Continuous problem with surgical diagnosis TAT noted over the last 9 mo—not resolved by the AP Service	Anatomic (AP) Svc is working with Hosp Task Force to resolve the problem ACTION: AP Service Medical Director	Improvement of TAT process has been delayed but now is in progress
Coordination in process	Have first study completed for review by Mar 96 ACTION: AP Medical Director	Improvement of the QI process is in progress
On target; a 4 month general baseline has been established following a general survey of past incident reports	Select a more specific indicator for Jan 96 ACTION: Supervisor	Improvement of the QI process is in progress
On target x 12 mo	Select a more specific indicator for Feb 93 ACTION: Supervisor	Improvement of the QI process is in progress
Additional alarms need to be installed by facility engineer See notes re CAP inspection finding re ventilation of dangerous fumes	Install the fire alarms immediately! ACTION: Lab Manager (Sep 94)	No improvement x 3 mo: Need facility engineer support
On target x 6 mo	None needed; but we have waited 6 mo	Effective to date
Protected problem due to inability to obtain facility engineer priority	Coordination with engineers must be effected for renovation (June 93) ACTION: Lab Manager with Sec Medical Director	Ineffective QI process: Improvement needs hosp admin support
-------	-------	-------
On target x 5 mo	None needed	Effective
Inadequate ventilation of gross specimen inspection area	See Chemical /Carcinogen indicator	See Chemical / Carcinogen indicator

CAP = College of American Pathologists

Histopathology Quality Profile: Dec 95

Indicator Grouping/ Specific Indicator: Threshold (Periodicity)	QI Data Observations (Date trend started) J A S O N D
POSTLABORATORY PROCESS WORK FLOW SEGMENT	
Anatomic Diagnosis Utilization: in keeping with laboratory and clinical standards (Monthly)	0 = no discrepancies – – = not implemented
a. Frozen section	. . . . . Provider Code # . . . . . -- -- 85 0 0 0
b. Rush surgicals	Joint laboratory clinical standards being determined with Surg Dept
Turnaround Time (TAT) of Index Procedures (Monthly)	% = averaged percent
a. Routine surgical Dx: < 95% within 2 days TAT	46 9 20 58 4 9 % TAT became excessive in Apr 95
b. Special surgical Dx: < 95% within 5 days TAT	46 83 62 34 88 86 % TAT became excessive in Apr 95
Report Distribution: no misdirected reports! (Monthly)	0 0 0 0 0 0 Baseline began in Jul 93 0 = no deficiencies
INTRALABORATORY PROCESS WORK FLOW SEGMENT	
Postdeterminative Product Finalization and Specimen Handling: no loss of product or specimen integrity! (Quarterly)	No OFI identified x 7 mo
Reference Laboratory Studies: no adverse effect on patient outcome! (Monthly)	d = averaged days – – = not implemented
a. Tissue Dx consultation (Lab ABC) TAT: none > 5 days (averaged)	-- -- 4 4 5 4 d
Backlog: no cases backlogged > 5 days old	-- -- 0 0 0 0 c c = total cases

Evaluation of QI Data, TQM System, CQI Process	Action and Action Person: (Date Initiated)	Assessment of Overall Improvement
On target x 4 mo; no repeat by #85 noted; establishment of a new baseline is in progress See Lab Product Selection Grouping	None needed x 4 mo	Effective: Improvement of the utilization process is in progress
To be determined (TBD) by Feb 96	TBD ACTION: Medical Director	QI process is ongoing
TAT for both indicators is excessive x 9 mo; there is some improvement of special surgical TAT; but, both TAT are beyond CAP requirements due to technologist and secretary vacancies; improvement of special Dx TAT has been at the great express of the routine Dx TAT	1. Send routine cases to ref lab 2. Resolve technol/secretary hiring actions 3. Review section's authorized staff strength—it might be too low!! 4. Automate AP LIS hospital-wide ACTION: AP Service Lab Manager	Ineffective QI process: Improvement of chronic staffing problem requires aid of Hosp Task Force and Pers Office
On target x 6 mo; baseline has been established for this general survey	Select a specific indicator for May 96 ACTION: Supervisor	Improvement of the QI process is in progress

Evaluation of QI Data, TQM System, CQI Process	Action and Action Person: (Date Initiated)	Assessment of Overall Improvement
On target x 7 mo	Select a focused indicator for Mar 96 ACTION: Supervisor	Improvement of the QI process is in progress
On target x 4 mo	None needed	Effective reference laboratory performance and QI process
On target x 4 mo		

LIS = Laboratory Information System

Histopathology Quality Profile: Dec 95

Indicator Grouping/ Specific Indicator: Threshold (Periodicity)	QI Data Observations (Date trend started) J	A	S	O	N	D	
b. Estrogen receptor assays (Lab XYZ)	d = averaged days						
TAT: none > 4 days (averaged)	--	--	--	5.0	5.0	5.3	d
Backlog: no cases backlogged > 4 days old	--	--	--	4	6	9	c
	c = total cases						
Analytical Quality: no major discrepancies! (———)	No analytical procedures are performed in this section						
Diagnostic Quality per Peer Review: no threat to life or lime (monthly)	0 = no discrepancies						
a. Total number of discrepancies (including false negative review)	1	2	0	2	0	1	
	No major discrepancies x 10 mo						
	. . . . .Pathologist Code #						
1. Froz-Perm discrepancies	83	–	–	23	–	90	
	– = no code cited						
2. Cyto-Perm discrepancies	–	17	–	–	–	–	
3. Perm-QI discrepancies	–	84	–	80	–	–	
Predeterminative Specimen Processing: no loss of specimen integrity (Monthly)	0 = no opportunity – – = not implemented						
a. Tissue specimen lost	7	5	4	5	0	0	
b. Block lost	0	0	0	0	0	0	
c. Block containing foreign tissue	0	0	0	0	0	0	
d. Block poorly oriented	--	--	--	--	5	3	
e. Floater on slide	0	0	0	0	2	0	
f. Solution changes too infrequent	--	--	--	--	--	1	
g. Solution too hot	--	--	--	--	--	1	

Evaluation of QI Data, TQM System, CQI Process	Action and Action Person: (Date Initiated)	Assessment of Overall Improvement
Marginally excessive TAT x 3 mo	1. Keep up the pressure on Lab XYZ to meet TAT requirement 2. Identify other reference lab options immediately ACTION: Laboratory Manager	Improvement of ref lab TAT is needed immediately
Increasing backlog x 3 mo		
QI Note: Flow cytometry or molecular biological analytical procedures would fit here if performed in the AP lab in support of classical tissue diagnosis		
No discrepancies injurious to life or limb x 10 mo; no repeats or patterns	1. Review all subject cases with individual staff members 2. Reconsider the reporting of minor discrepancies in this profile; is it helpful or not? Or should only major discrepancies be reported? A policy is needed for Jan 96 ACTION: Section Medical Director	The peer review process is intact and ongoing Improvement of the QI process is in progress
No further review needed; case #90 involved only a minor discrepancy; no repeats or patterns		
On target x 2 mo; new Med Dir arrived in Jul; improved supervision is noted; 6 FTE vacancies still present a serious problem	1. Resolve recurrent problems 2. Fill vacancies 3. Maintain vigilance 4. Monitor QC daily and establish new baselines where needed ACTION: Section Supervisor	Effective intradept QI process; BUT Ineffective hospital QI process: Technologist and secretary shortages are an institutional problem requiring hospital Personnel Office and Admin support
On target x 6 mo		
On target x 6 mo		
Recurrent problem; minimal documentation		
On target x 1 mo		
Recurrent flaw, but not documented		
Recurrent flaw, but not documented		

Histopathology Quality Profile: Dec 95

Indicator Grouping/ Specific Indicator: Threshold (Periodicity)	QI Data Observations (Date trend started) J A S O N D	
h. Section poorly stained	0 0 0 0 0 1	
i. Section fragmented and chattered	0 2 0 0 0 0	
j. Section too thick	0 4 0 0 0 0	
k. Slide mislabeled	2 0 3 3 1 3	
PRELABORATORY PROCESS WORK FLOW SEGMENT		
Validation: > 2% invalidation rate (Quarterly)	0.5 -- -- 0.7 -- -- No OFI identified x 3 qtrs	
Anatomic Consultation Selection: in keeping with laboratory and clinical standards (Monthly)	. . . . .Provider Code # . . . . . 0 0 0 0 0 0 0 = no OFI identified This general survey began in Apr 95	
a. Frozen section (FS) selection	0 0 0 0 0 24 #24 requested FS on tissue from a routine, uncomplicated tonsillectomy	
OPERATIVE RESOURCE MANAGEMENT WORK FLOW SEGMENT		
Workload Management: (Monthly) a. Productivity quotients: within established limits	m = calculated workloaded minutes per paid hour	
a. PQp (paid): 40 to 45 min/hr	45 60 59 43 47 45 m	
b. PQwl (Specified) 50 to 55 min/hr	87 97 93 106 81 85 m m = workloaded minutes per specified hour	

Evaluation of QI Data, TQM System, CQI Process	Action and Action Person: (Date Initiated)	Assessment of Overall Improvement
1 case poorly stained in this period	(see above)	(see above)
On target x 4 mo		
On target x 4 mo		
Recurrent: workload stress or negligence ??? How many techs involved? Is this a system/process problem, an individual employee problem, or a supervisory problem?	Investigate the cause of this trend ACTION: Supervisor	Ineffective technical and QI process over a 6 mo trend: technical & investigative methods need improvement
QI Note: All the above processing problems reflect inadequate staffing, training, supervision, QAn and/or QAc; histotechnology Med Dir is to evaluate the cause and offer recommendations at next month's QI meeting		
On target x 3 qtr for this general survey	Design a study of the adequacy of clinical info for Derm surg path cases by Mar 96 ACTION: Medical Director	Improvement of the QI process is in progress
1. On target x 9 mo; no OFI identified for too long a period 2. Provider #24 requested a FS on tissue not meeting lab-clin standards for FS selection	1. Discontinue general survey 2. Sharpen focus on selection of FS by ENT surg service; is there a process problem? Establish a joint study. ACTION: HP Med Dir 1. Interview #24 ACTION: ENT Med Dir	Improvement of the selection process is in progres at the operative and organizational levels
Both PQ indicators are consistently excessive, indicating a serious level of workrelated stress and decreased work force production effectiveness; Review comments regarding personnel management and utilization	See comments below regarding the need to fill staff vacancies	Effective personnel management thru the intradept QI process; Ineffective personnel hiring thru the extra dept QI process

HP = histopathology section

Histopathology Quality Profile: Dec 95

Indicator Grouping/ Specific Indicator: Threshold (Periodicity)	QI Data Observations (Date trend started) J A S O N D
Personnel Management (Monthly)	FTE = full time equivalent
a. Work Force: 1. Vacancy rate: Technologists: > 10% vacancy	6 FTE vacancies in Dec 95 68 25 50 38 38 38 % New Med Dir arrived in Jul
Secretaries: > 10% vacancy	5 5 10 10 15 15 % 3 FTE vacancies in Dec 92
b. Utilization 1. 16 hour shifts: none	s = total 16 hr shifts 0 0 0 0 0 0 s Techs and secretaries work one daytime shift only
2. Overtime (OT) Technologists: > 256 hours	h = total OT hours 37 83 87 97 93 49 h
Secretaries: > 80 hours	0 0 0 0 0 0 h
c. Availability 1. % availability: < 80%	85 79 79 74 70 83 %
Continuing Education :< 3 hour/mo (Monthly)	No OFI identified x 2 mo Indicator begun in Nov 93
Methods & Procedures Review: must be on time! (annually per monthly schedule)	6/6 4/6 7/6 7/6 6/6 6/6 6/6 = # reviewed/# scheduled
Computer Management a. Unscheduled downtime: > 24 hours (Monthly)	No computerized database system is in place for this anatomic pathology activity (Jan 94)
Equipment: repair must be complete within one quarter (Quarterly)	– 0 – – 0 – 0 = no limitations

Evaluation of QI Data, TQM System, CQI Process	Action and Action Person: (Date Initiated)	Assessment of Overall Improvement
6 positions vacant; very serious shortage; increasing trend; is affecting TAT (see supporting indicator grouping for TAT)	1. Fill 6 positions 2. Obtain pay raise 3. Send workload to a ref lab 4. Consider using more automation and split shifts ACTION: Department Administrative Supervisor	Overall effective intradept QI process; BUT!! Extradept QI process is ineffective: Personnel Office must provide improved support; improve the QI process at the QM interface
3 positions vacant; significant shortage affecting TAT	Fill 3 positions ACTION: Admin Sup	
More than one shift or split shift scheduling could expedite the work	Utilize multiple or split shifting scheduling ACTION: Supervisor	
Good support for a one shift schedule	Develop more innovative staffing using multiple shifts ACTION: Supervisor	
Secretaries are not working overtime or in split shifts		
On target in Dec; motivation is better this month BUT! for how long? Are incentives adequate?	Investigate adequacy of incentive program ACTION: Supervisor	Improvement of the QAc program is in progress
On target; baseline is being established	None needed	Improvement in progress
On target; excellent persistence in the face of staff shortage	None needed	Effective review and QI processes
The need for automated data base processing has been recognized for two yr; the QM interface between the lab and the hosp admin/comp ops has been ineffective	Select and obtain an AP Lab Information System ACTION: Lab Manager with support of AP Service Medical Director (Dec 95)	Ineffective QI process: Need Hosp Admin and Computer Operations support
No report scheduled; on target x 2 qtrs; no OFI identified for at least 6 mo	Select a focused study for Apr 96 ACTION: Supervisor	Improvement of the QI process is in progress

Histopathology Quality Profile: Dec 95

Indicator Grouping/ Specific Indicator: Threshold (Periodicity)	QI Data Observations (Date trend started) J A S O N D
Supply: no potential for laboratory service limitations (Quarterly)	0 – – 0 – – 0 = no limitations
Facility: no potential for equipment failure, biological spoilage, or personnel stress! (Quarterly)	Personnel heat stress and equipment failure due to poor seasonal temp control (July 95)
Budget: meet planned expenditure with ± 5% the monthly target (Monthly)	-- -- -- NR NR -5 % – – – = not implemented NR = not reported
ORGANIZATIONAL RESOURCE MANAGEMENT WORK FLOW SEGMENT	
Internal Quality Improvement (QI) (Monthly) a. Assessment: there must be evidence of continuous improvement!	Several problematic indicator groupings have not displayed significant continuous improvement over reasonable periods of time; this suggests inadequate assessment of the QI process
b. Communication: there must be adequate sharing of lessons learned! (Monthly)	Review of QI planning/CME schedules show no followup sharing of QI lessons learned x 2 mo
External QI: (Monthly) a. Proficiency surveys: all diagnoses must be correct per peer review survey!	Results of one survey were returned for this reporting period: all diagnoses 100% correct for the last 6 mo
b. JCAHO/CAP/Other inspection: no unresolved findings! 1. CAP inspection	Insufficient ventilation over grossing table: excessive formaldehyde fumes noted on occupational health measurement and on-site CAP inspection (May 93) See Employee Safety grouping (chemical hazard) note
2. Fire marshal inspection	Fire alarms not adequately accessible (Aug 95)

Evaluation of QI Data, TQM System, CQI Process	Action and Action Person: (Date Initiated)	Assessment of Overall Improvement
No report scheduled; on target x 2 qtrs; no OFI identified for at least 6 mo	Select a focused study for May 96 ACTION: Supervisor	Improvement of the QI process is in progress
Recurrent seasonal problem; coordination in process	Continue coordinative effort with engineers ACTION: Lab Manager (Jul 95)	Ineffective QM interface Improve the engineering support
Initially section was not reporting; now on target in Dec 92	Establish a 6 mo baseline ACTION: Supervisor	Improvement of the QI process is in progress

1. Assessment at the section and higher levels needs improvement 2. The section needs team building to be more effective in assessment skills	1. Coordinate with Hosp Qual Task Force 2. Revitalize the team building program ACTION: Section Medical Director	Ineffective QI and QAc processes: Section needs dept and hosp level assistance
QI CME schedule reflects NO sessions devoted to sharing of QI lessons learned	Schedule planning/educ sessions for QI follow-up ACTION: Sec Medical Director	Improvement of the QI process is in progress
On target x 6 mo	None needed	Effective
Poor followup of CAP phase II deficiency; need coordination with facility engineers; next CAP inspection scheduled for Mar 96	1. Coordinate with facility engineer and hosp admin ACTION: AP Lab Mgr (May 93) 1. Study failed CAP inspection followup process ACTION: Sec Medical Director	Ineffective QI process and QM interface: Improve facility engineer support needed
Additional alarms need to be installed by facility engineer	Coordinate installation of alarms ACTION: Lab Manager (Aug 92)	Ineffective QM interface with engineers

Histopathology Quality Profile: Dec 95

Indicator Grouping/ Specific Indicator: Threshold (Periodicity)	QI Data Observations (Date trend started) J A S O N D
c. Incident reports and complaints: every report is a sentinel event!!	4 3 3 2 4 2 Recurrent complaints of prolonged report TAT since April 92
Quality Anticipation (QAn)	Missed research projects are simply not being done
a. Organizational research: all milestones will be attained!! (Monthly)	2/3 – – 0/2 – – 2/3 = 2 or 3 milestones attained
b. Development: all milestones will be attained! (Monthly)	– 1/1 – – 3/3 – Current projects include improved Med/Derm/Surg department interfacing
c. Implementation: all milestones will be attained! (Monthly)	– – 0/0 – – 0/0 No projects scheduled for this quarter
Quality Actualization (QAc) (Monthly) a. Team building: 1. Morale: no adverse affect on team effectiveness	No surveys of personnel were accomplished in the last month; anecdotal comments are that morale is "good;" no formal complaints have been received for 10 months since the inception of this QI indicator
2. Skill training (TST): no skills lacking that adversely impact on team effectiveness	Team building and training are not on schedule; several operative managemetn, QI, QAn, and QAc indicators suggest growing stress among staff
b. Team maintenance 1. Continuing TST	As noted above
2. Personnel actions: none overdue!	0 0 0 0 0 0 0 = non overdue The last overdue action occurred in May

Evaluation of QI Data, TQM System, CQI Process	Action and Action Person: (Date Initiated)	Assessment of Overall Improvement
Recurrent complaints of prolonged TAT of diagnostic reports from general surgery and urology; trend is diminishing	Solve Routine and Special Diagnostic report TAT problem with Hosp Qual Mgmt Task Force ACTION: Medical Director	Improvement of TAT and QI processes is in progress
No report scheduled; valuable surveys are not being done due to staff shortage (there is no "catching up" of missed research opportunities)	Follow-up on designing of new QAn survey for Mar 96 ACTION: Supervisor with dept support	Improvement of the QAn process is in progress
No report scheduled; projects are on track with Med, Derm, and Surg depts	Follow-up with full implementation with dept support ACTION: Supervisor	No assessment for this period
Off target x 2 qtrs; no new projects scheduled due to staff shortage	Capitalize on current developmental projects ACTION: Supervisor	Ineffective QAn process: Improve on development follow-up
No opportunities cited; HOWEVER< other QI indicators suggest growing workload stress & threatened morale	Survey all section employees ACTION: Supervisor with support of Section Medical Director	Ineffective QI process: Improve on a more active measurement of morale
Off target due to staff shortage; the QAc TST process is crucial for an effective TQM/CQI system	Reestablish an effective QAc team skills training schedule ACTION: Medical Director	Ineffective QI and QAc processes: Improve the leadership commitment Revitalize!!
--------	--------	--------
On target x 8 mo	Select a focused study for Feb 96 ACTION: Supervisor	Improvement of the QI process is in progress

Histopathology Quality Profile: Dec 95

Indicator Grouping/ Specific Indicator: Threshold (Periodicity)	QI Data Observations (Date trend started) J A S O N D
3. Personnel incentives: None overdue!	0 0 0 0 0 0 Last deficiency in providing a personnel incentive award was noted in Feb 95
c. Team effectiveness 1. Decision making: no problem too hard or unresolved > 3 mo	Several opportunities have NOT been adequately addressed by the section teams; when too hard to be resolved at the section level, problems have not been submitted to the appropriate supporting echelon
2. Leadership commitment: there must be evidence of leader involvement in and support of all quality management activities	As of this reporting period, this is a new indicator grouping. The format and collection methods are being determined. The first data will be reported in Jan 96. Supporting QAc indicators suggest a need for revitalized leader commitment

	Evaluation of QI Data, TQM System, CQI Process	Action and Action Person: (Date Initiated)	Assessment of Overall Improvement
	On target x 10 mo; this is too long a period of indicator inactivity	Update incentive program to reward outstanding staff motivation ACTION: Supervisor	Improvement of the QAc program is in progress
	Overall, off target as evidenced by customer Dissatisfaction!! Need to take better advantage of opportunities to improve surg TAT, coordination with facility engineers, overall technical supervision, staff hiring and utilization, inspection followup, QI, QAn, and QAc	Form an AP Service task force to determine needs of this section to reestablish appropriate skills and tools for effective decision making ACTION: AP Service Medical Director	Ineffective QAc process: Need to improve basic team actualization skills to enhance team decision making
	To be determined in Jan 96	Implement and report this indicator by Jan 93 ACTION: Section Medical Director	Improvement of the QAc process is in progress

Index

Numbers in **boldface** refer to pages on which figures appear.

B

C

D

E

F

G

H

I

J

K

L

P

Q

S

Z